W9-CAX-582

Production Planning and Inventory Control

Production Planning and Inventory Control

Dennis W. McLeavey
Seetharama L. Narasimhan
University of Rhode Island

Allyn and Bacon, Inc.
Boston London Sydney Toronto

Library of Congress Cataloging in Publication Data

McLeavey, Dennis W.
Production planning and inventory control.

Includes bibliographies and index.
1. Production planning. 2. Inventory control.
I. Narasimhan, Seetharama L., 1936– . II. Title.
TS176.M374 1985 658.5 84-2829
ISBN 0-205-08147-9

Printed in the United States of America

10 9 8 7 6 5 4 3 2 1 89 88 87 86 85 84

contents

foreword

I am extremely pleased to contribute this foreword to *Production Planning and Inventory Control* by Dennis McLeavey and Seetharama Narasimhan. This book incorporates state-of-the-art material on production, inventory, and distribution management. In today's competitive environment, with high-cost money, these disciplines are taking an increasingly important role in the manufacturing and service sectors.

I had the opportunity to review this work while it was being prepared and tested. The book unifies several important topics in forecasting, inventories, distribution, material requirements planning, capacity planning, master production scheduling, production activity planning/control, and project management. The authors clearly explain many difficult concepts with several examples and illustrations. From my experience as a manufacturing executive and as the chief executive and operating officer of Uniroyal Incorporated, I think that many practitioners and executives in materials management and production planning will find this book useful in bringing many important concepts into sharp focus and applying them to real-world problems.

The material treated in this book strikes an appropriate balance between theory and application. From my teaching experience as an executive-in-residence at the University of Rhode Island, I believe that educators and students will find this book an important source of up-to-date material on production and inventory management. In summary, the book is timely, comprehensive, and an important source for both practitioners and academics.

David Beretta

preface

This book provides a unified treatment of production planning and control. The body of professional knowledge presented in the book most closely reflects the interests of the American Production and Inventory Control Society (APICS), including master planning, inventory planning and control, material requirements planning, shop floor control, and master production scheduling. In most cases, we treat these topics in more depth than is necessary for the APICS certification exams.

We are somewhat concerned about the dichotomy between practitioners with simple solutions and academics with sophisticated solutions. We neither bow before experience nor melt before formulas; we agree with Mark Twain, who said, "It is difference of opinion that makes horse races." Another of Twain's sayings summarizes our position on experience: "We should be careful to get out of an experience only the wisdom that is in it—and stop there; lest we be like the cat that sits down on a hot stove lid. She will never sit down on a hot stove lid again—and that is well; but also she will never sit down on a cold one any more."

Several features distinguish this text, the most distinctive of which is the heavy use of worked examples at the points where we introduce concepts. Also, extensive tables and figures illustrate difficult concepts. Precise definitions and descriptions make the book satisfying for study purposes, and all materials have been classroom tested. Given a choice between mathematical wizardry and clarity of presentation, we have tried to choose simple, intuitive explanations. We have not hesitated to present difficult concepts, but we have tried to make them easy to understand. We present mathematics where necessary but view it as a servant to our main interests of production control.

This book comes out at an important time, when production control and materials management are becoming recognized as activities that contribute heavily to economic growth. In a recent *Washington Post* article, Yoshi Tsurumi claims that U.S. managers are often "technically illiterate" and out of touch [1]. Tsurumi compared the top three executives of 24 leading Japanese manufacturers with the top three executives of 20 leading American competitors in such fields as computers, steel, and automobiles.

Two-thirds of the Japanese executives had science or engineering degrees, compared with only one-third of the American executives. Furthermore, none of the Japanese executives without technical training had risen through legal or financial ranks. Tsurami claims that the whole preparation of American executives tends to make them aloof from the factory floor and from the human beings who are involved in the day-to-day task of making products.

We hope that our book can contribute to an increased preparation of American business students for the realities of economic life. Although production management and production planning and control have not been viewed as glamorous subjects in U.S. business schools, production is at the heart of our economy.

REFERENCE

1. Yoshi Tsurumi, "U.S. Managers Often 'Technically Illiterate' and Out of Touch," *Washington Post*, Sunday, July 31, 1983. Reprinted in *Pacific Basin Quarterly*, No. 10 (Summer/Fall 1983), p. 15.

acknowledgments

Several people have helped us in the formation of our ideas and the preparation of this book. Specifically, we want to thank Edward W. Davis, University of Virginia; James T. Clark, IBM; Albert B. Bishop, Ohio State University; George Johnson, Rochester Institute of Technology; Vincent Pellegrino, IBM; John F. Muth, Indiana University; Gene Groff, Georgia State University; and several reviewers who criticized various stages of the manuscript.

We benefited greatly from informal reviews of specific chapters by Professors Paul Mangiameli and Russell C. Koza, University of Rhode Island; David Beretta, Executive-in-Residence, University of Rhode Island; R. G. Brown, Materials Management Systems; Ray Lankford, Plossl and Lankford; Howard Coleman; and Norman Dyer, MCA Associates.

The American Production and Inventory Control Society (APICS) has been very helpful to us in many ways. George Johnson answered several of our questions through his Dear APICS service. Both the Mystic Seaport and the Providence chapters of APICS provided ideas along the way and gave us a forum for testing the book in certification exam preparation minicourses. APICS officers from these two chapters also helped us form an APICS student chapter at the University of Rhode Island (URI).

We thank our families for their support. We probably could have finished this book two years sooner, but our families are more important than books.

Finally, we thank Charlotte Manni and Deborah Cotoia for their excellent typing of several versions of this manuscript. They handled mathematical symbols without flinching and in so doing provided an excellent example for the readers of this book.

chapter one

Introduction

Production and inventory control involves the planning, execution, and control of production rates and inventory levels to achieve customer satisfaction at minimum cost. For progressive companies, good production and inventory control can be a competitive weapon.

In this text, we will study the problems of managing the flow of materials from the purchase of raw materials to the distribution of the finished product or service. Although the "people" problems involved in this creation of value are equally important, we will focus attention on the technical questions of forecasting, inventory control, output planning, and scheduling.

A simple example should help introduce some of the concerns of this text. On average, how much cash do you carry in your wallet—$5, $10, $50, $100? Believe it or not, by carrying money, you have addressed a production control problem. First, you must have forecast your usage for a planning horizon of perhaps a week. Second, you decided how much cash to withdraw from the bank. If you forecast $100 in cash spending next week but withdrew only $50 in cash, you must be planning two trips to the bank. Why not carry more in your wallet? Presumably, you are concerned about theft and, perhaps, impulse buying. Why not carry less? The less money you carry, the more trips to the bank are required. Even in this simple example, you have faced trade-offs in your choice of order quantity at the bank.

The issue of trade-offs is central to production and inventory control. Any production or transformation system exhibits the following seven conflicting measures of performance:

1. *Volume:* How much is produced or how many customers are served in a year? Larger quantities are often associated with higher productivity.
2. *Variety:* How many different types of products are produced by the company?

3. *Quality:* What percentage of products shipped or services rendered meet design specifications? Are the specifications for a superior product or for an acceptable one?
4. *Timeliness:* Are the products or services available when the customer requires them?
5. *Place:* Are the products or services available where the customer requires them?
6. *Satisfaction:* Are the participants in the production or transformation process satisfied and fulfilled in their work?
7. *Cost:* Have the products or services been created at minimum or acceptable cost?

Some companies minimize cost at the expense of quality, whereas others "build up to quality, not down to price." Some focus on only a few products and get rid of the "cats and dogs." Others seek to be the "color house of the industry."

Such trade-offs lead to the characterization of a transformation process, because a focus on some of the measures of performance dictates the nature of the appropriate transformation process. For example, fast-food operations (high volume, low variety) require that the restaurant staff know their repetitive duties and not be asked to make decisions.

Types of Transformation Processes and Layouts

Transformation processes can be characterized on several dimensions. Most characterizations seek to yield insights into appropriate managerial responses. For example, the owner of a small business facing tremendous sales growth would do well to recognize that high-volume production demands a *product layout*. Product layouts permit high volume because people and/or machines are arranged in work stations along a line (e.g., an automobile assembly line, a cafeteria). By contrast, many small businesses begin with a *process layout*, whereby people and/or machines with similar capabilities are arranged together in a work center (e.g., an X-ray room at a hospital).

For services, we employ a variation of Chase's classification system [1]. Chase suggests that managers should consider the degree of customer contact with the service system. He defines extent of contact as the ratio of the time the customer spends in the service system relative to the time it takes to serve the customer. A restaurant would be a high-contact service; the home office of a bank would be a low-contact service. High-contact and low-contact services must be treated differently. For example, Chase suggests that customers in high-contact systems must be accommodated in the production schedule, whereas low-contact system customers are concerned mainly with completion dates.

TABLE 1.1 Service Classification Scheme

	High Contact	*Low Contact*
Uncertain service specifications	Health center, barber shop	Auto repair, clothing repair
Certain service specifications	Movie theatre, train	Maintenance, baggage handling

Our own classification system simply adds a product specification dimension, similar to Timms and Pohlen's [6, p. 23] product specification dimension for manufacturing. If a system's service specifications can be established with a reasonable certainty that they will meet customer needs and desires without responding very differently to individual customers, then that system has *certain* service specifications. The simple, two-dimensional system in table 1.1 illustrates this concept.

Such a classification system helps isolate control problems and their possible solutions. For example, a restaurant would normally have high contact and uncertain specifications. To become efficient with high volume, fast-food restaurants have created certainty of service specifications by reducing both the variety of choice for the customer and the discretion needed by the employee.

For manufacturing businesses, a similar classification scheme can highlight the types of production control problems likely to arise. The scheme shown in table 1.2 can be elaborated to include the process industry (oil and chemicals) at the extreme of high volume/certain specifications and the unit manufacturing industry (submarines and houses) at the extreme of low volume/uncertain specifications. Repetitive or mass production was present in China between 800 and 500 B.C. Hua Jue-ming [2] describes the mass production of iron castings near Wenxian in Henan. Individual molds were stacked one on top of another, sharing a single gate, or point of entry, for the molten metal. This technique economized on both metal and fuel. In the early part of the twentieth century, Henry Ford applied mass production concepts to automobile manufacturing by installing a conveyorized assembly line at the River Rouge plant on the outskirts of Detroit.

The job shop is a solution for low sales volume and uncertain product specifications. Uncertain specifications occur when customer needs and desires cannot be determined without dealing directly with the individual

Table 1.2 Manufacturing Classification Scheme

	Low Sales Volume	*High Sales Volume*
Uncertain product specifications	Job shop or flow shop production to order (e.g., molded rubber parts)	Hybrid shop production to stock and assembly to order (e.g., machine tools)
Certain product specifications	Batch or intermittent production to stock (e.g., textiles)	Repetitive or mass production to stock (e.g., automobiles)

customer. Parts manufacture by machine shops usually takes place in a job shop environment; general-purpose machinery is arranged by type, and each order takes a unique path through the plant. A community hospital certainly is an example of a job shop: Where does someone with a broken arm go? What path does a pregnant woman take through the hospital?

For a manufacturing example of a job shop, consider the manufacture of molded rubber parts for the automobile industry. Parts such as distributors and windshield wiper blades are made by molding rubber around metal inserts. Typically, the customer (another manufacturer) supplies the inserts to the job shop, which performs the molding operations specifically to the customer's order. The molding press used depends on the quantity and size of the parts to be molded. Indeed, the customer owns the mold in most cases. The press used depends on the size of the mold. Clearly, each order seeks its own way through the job shop, even though it proceeds through the three main operations (1) mixing the rubber and cutting it into sheets; (2) cooking it in the molds; and (3) finishing and packing.

In such a job shop, forecasting holds little interest for management; instead, the shop works from a backlog of orders. Thus, scheduling becomes the key issue: Can we get the order to the customer on time?

Closely allied to the job shop is the flow shop, in which orders flow along the same path through the plant but each order has a unique processing time at each work station. The manufacture of precision instruments for hospitals might be done along such a flow line. In flow shops, scheduling still represents the main challenge. In a way, the scheduling problem is somewhat simpler, because orders flow through a standardized route of work centers.

Any arrangement other than an assembly line can be termed a job shop, but we prefer to make further distinctions. In the aforementioned job and flow shops, all production quantities were determined by customer order. When product specifications are known, we have batch manufacturing. Batch manufacturing shops could also be called flow shops and even job shops; the distinguishing issue is the question of batch sizes. Normally, batch manufacturing might be represented by a flow line of production to stock. Furniture manufacturing and soft-drink bottling are examples of flow line production to stock, with line changeovers. In such operations, batch size or length of production runs becomes the main production control question.

Returning to the cases of high volume sales, we have assembly lines for production to stock and hybrid lines for production to order. In assembly line manufacturing, our primary interest is in line balancing and the elimination of bottlenecks.

The hybrid shop is an attempt to guarantee the efficiencies of assembly line production to stock while maintaining the flexibility of the job shop to meet customer orders. Highest level assemblies are produced to stock and are then assembled to customer order. Furniture and machine tool manufacturing are examples of hybrid shop environments. Forecasting highest level assembly usage becomes important in such operations; beyond that, the problems of both batch size determination and job shop scheduling arise.

There are some parallels between the service system classification and the manufacturing classification just developed. The problems of low contact/certain specifications are similar to those of assembly lines. Similarly, cases of high contact/uncertain specifications yield job shop problems—as, for example, in a hospital. An example of batch manufacturing in the service area is seen in the determination of the number of train cars to schedule at various times of the day.

The Open Systems Approach

In examining production control systems for various transformation processes and layouts, it is important to take a systems approach. An open system is a highly complex network of interdependent relationships with a considerable capacity for adaptation to change. Using a biological analogy, Katz and Kahn [3] give nine characteristics of open systems. Within the Katz and Kahn framework, there are nine production control implications:

1. *Importation of energy.* Open systems import energy from their environment. Humans breathe oxygen. A business uses raw materials and human labor.
2. *Throughput.* Open systems transform the energy available to them. The body converts starch and sugar into heat and action. A business creates a product or service.
3. *Output.* Open systems export some product into the environment. A business provides a product or service to a customer.
4. *Systems as cycles of events.* The pattern of activities of the energy exchange has a cyclic character. The sale of a product provides funds for purchasing more raw materials and for wages.
5. *Negative entropy.* Considered a universal law of nature, entropy is the movement of organisms toward disorganization or death; however, the open system can acquire negative entropy by importing more energy than it expends (i.e., creating a buffer). Many of us carry our negative entropy around our waists. A business builds up inventories.
6. *Information input, negative feedback, and the coding process.* Information comes to the open system from its environment. High costs, for example, provide negative feedback to the organization.

Coding refers to the selective perception of information. For example, some people are incapable of accepting criticism and hence block out negative feedback.

7. *The steady state.* A steady state refers to the balance between energy inflow and product export. The analogy of the human body suggests that organisms tend toward steady state, with some ups and downs. Systems attempt to cope with external forces by acquiring control over them. For example, no business wants to be at the mercy of a single supplier. Thus, the open system may grow, but steady state is seen as the organization's attempt to preserve its character.
8. *Differentiation.* Businesses move toward multiplication and elaboration of roles, with greater functional specialization. Computer specialists, inventory specialists, and the like, abound in the modern company.
9. *Equifinality.* Open systems can reach the same final state from differing initial conditions and by a variety of paths.

These nine characteristics of open systems yield insights that are useful in appraising production control systems. We are not concerned with precise formulation of an open systems theory of production control, but we use these nine characteristics as a pragmatic set of questions/hypotheses about our system.

As an example, consider two classic cases in production control: Blitz and Chaircraft [4]. We are staunch proponents of the case method of teaching production control, but we oppose the usual practice of giving the student a set of two or three questions on which to base the analysis. Unfortunately, knowing the questions already solves half the problem. In reality, skill in asking the right questions is at least as important as the ability to analyze data for answering a question. The open systems characteristics can provide the student or analyst with a powerful base from which to generate good questions.

In the Blitz case, for example, a small but growing job shop produces electrical circuit boards to order for electronics manufacturing companies. At the time of the case, the company is experiencing rapid growth in sales. The case is very detailed and cannot be discussed adequately in a brief paragraph, but application of our open systems questions will take us quickly to the nub of the case. Blitz is not in *steady state,* as evidenced by the rapid rise in sales. *Negative feedback* centers on missed due dates. Mixing of small and large orders causes interference, which can be alleviated by *differentiation.* A line layout may be more appropriate for large orders at Blitz. The question of whether or not Blitz is in steady state thus leads quickly to one important dimension of analysis in the Blitz case.

Chaircraft, another popular case, also responds to the pressure of open systems thinking. Chaircraft is a large furniture manufacturer that has recently moved out of steady state and has improved its sales organization enough to produce a 10% to 20% sales growth rate. *Negative feedback* on costs is seen as the cause of a profit decline. Examination of costs reveals that production fluctuation costs in the rough mill and the parts machining area are high. Dry kiln capacity poses a bottleneck problem. *Energy imported* cannot be easily matched to finished item requirements, because there is a fixed capacity on the rate of import of lumber through the kilns. The company did not keep any finished goods inventory (no *negative entropy* here) but, rather, assembled to customer order. One fundamental question in the case is where to seek *negative entropy* in order to reduce production fluctuations. The key to the case is to level production through finished parts and to use a finished parts inventory to separate the early stages of manufacture from frame assembly. Information input questions lead us to consider faster mechanisms of getting customer order information back to the early stages of manufacture. *Differentiation* questions are also important to the case. Feeding the wrong lumber through kilns causes eventual shortages in frame parts assembly. If only one type of lumber and one type of chair were produced, this problem would vanish. Thus, questions of product design arise. Over time, various chairs become naturally differentiated from one another. To what extent can we thwart this differentiation process by the use of common parts?

In both the Blitz and the Chaircraft cases, then, our open systems questions lead us to the real issues in the case. We recommend using this base when you face either a case or a real production control problem. In fact, we have yet to encounter a production control situation that completely defies the power of this approach.

Production Control Topics

When we begin to analyze production control systems, as in the Blitz and Chaircraft cases, we are invariably led to certain prototypical production control topics: what to produce, how much is needed, how much we have, what it takes to produce it, when it is needed, whether we have the capacity. Production control can be defined as the attempt to answer these questions within operations policy guidelines.

This text follows the logical flow of these questions, subject to pedagogical constraints. We begin with forecasting, because we think it is important to know how much is needed before we decide how much to produce. Occasionally, however, we need to understand the details of one topic before we can examine another topic, even though the questions may flow naturally in reverse order. For example, a statement of what is to be produced item by item and week by week for the next three months (the master schedule) logically precedes a plan to supply raw materials and parts for the items (material requirements planning). From a teaching and learning point of view, however, a prior understanding of material requirements planning enriches the study of master scheduling by allowing the student to appreciate the ramifications of a schedule on the timing of capacity needs.

The text can be outlined according to the natural production control topics and the questions that arise regarding the delivery of goods and services. The chapters are classified by the major questions of interest:

1. *What should be produced, how much, when, and where?* Chapters 2 and 3, on forecasting, attempt to answer these questions. The related performance measures are volume, variety, timeliness, and place.

2. *How much do we have, and how much more do we need?* Chapters 4, 5, 6, and 8 address these questions. For items that exhibit independent demand, such as retail items, chapters 4 and 5 show the traditional methods of producing/ordering when inventories are depleted to certain levels. Chapter 8 is the analogous chapter for derived demand situations, in which parts and subassembly requirements are dictated by end item assembly requirements. Chapter 6 considers the same questions with the imposition of cost constraints across all items in the inventory. The performance measures most directly related to these chapters are volume, variety, and cost.

3. *Where should we hold the items?* Chapter 7 examines the trade-offs that revolve around place utility. Of all chapters, this one addresses the most complex issues, because place utility involves all end items across all locations.

4. *How much can we produce?* Chapters 9 through 11 provide three levels of answers to capacity questions:

Time Span	*Type of Planning*
Yearly	Aggregate output planning
Quarterly	Capacity planning
Monthly	Master production scheduling

In aggregate output planning over an eighteen-month horizon, overall production rates are analyzed in terms of man-hours needed to produce all products together. Capacity planning examines capacity needs for product lines or groups. Master production scheduling considers the exact requirements of producing specific items during specific weeks. The related performance measures in these chapters are timeliness and cost.

5. *When should we produce?* Chapters 12 through 15 form a unit to answer this question under a variety of transformation types. These range from repetitive production to intermittent production to unit production. In a rushed attempt to meet due dates, slippage occurs in quality or lead times. In one sense, chapters 12 through 15 could be called lead time chapters, since they deal with how items can be scheduled so as to yield

acceptable lead times. The related performance measures in these chapters are timeliness and cost.

Text Objective

In this text, we seek to push the reader far beyond the elementary concepts presented in most introductory operations management texts. Yet we do not seek to provide the advanced technical coverage found in texts that emphasize operations research in production planning and control. Thus, this text is a bridge between the simple introductory approach and the advanced mathematical approach to the subject.

As a consequence of this approach, the text does not attempt to be all-encompassing; rather, it presents representative concepts and the flavor of each area. After reading the text, however, you should be able to digest any article or text in the field, except those that require more pure mathematics than you may have.

Summary

This chapter has viewed production and service transformation systems from various angles. The purpose of taking these different views has been to develop insights for managerial decision making.

To make decisions, we must first know what our measures of "goodness" are, since decisions are unimportant unless their outcomes have value. Transformation systems are valued according to several criteria: volume, variety, quality, timeliness, place, satisfaction, and cost.

Some tension exists among these measures of performance. Variety, for example, can come at the expense of volume and volume at the expense of quality. To respond to the demands of customization in manufacturing or services, organizations need to maintain flexibility by arranging their transformation process in a process layout, with equipment arranged by function. Volume requirements can be met more easily, however, with an assembly line layout, with work stations arranged by product.

Facing production control decisions in ongoing, ever-changing environments, production control managers need to keep life in perspective. Applying open systems theory to their situations can yield questions and insights that are useful in decision making. For example, recognition that unexpected sales growth is pushing the system out of steady state might raise the following questions about the transformation process:

1. What should be produced, how much, when, and where?
2. How much do we have, and how much more do we need?

3. Where should we hold the items?
4. How much can we produce?
5. When should we produce? How are we to schedule?

PROBLEMS

1. In your business or university, what transformation measures are viewed as most important? What trade-offs have been made?
2. Classify your business or university using the manufacturing or service system scheme suggested in this chapter.
3. Apply open systems concepts to your business or university. What questions arise? What is the appropriate response for your organization?
4. What type of service system is a Midas Muffler repair shop? What does such a repair shop need to do well in order to stay in business (i.e., what is its *primary task*). What is the *distinctive competence* of Midas Mufflers (i.e., what do they do well?). Do brake systems and mufflers present similar or dissimilar operating problems for Midas?
5. What do the New York Yankees do well at Yankee stadium (their distinctive competence)? What do they need to do well to stay in business (their primary task)? What about the Toronto Blue Jays? Classify baseball teams by type of service system.
6. Read the Hua article [2] on mass production of iron castings in ancient China? What line layout might the Chinese have used? How would you classify their production system?
7. MacDonald's added breakfast to their product line. Is this consistent with what they do well for lunch? What must be done well to succeed in the fast-food business?
8. Apply the open systems framework to your life. Do you normally operate at the margin, or do you meet deadlines with time to spare? Is there any room for negative entropy in your life?
9. Discuss the similarities and the differences in the marketing of high-contact versus low-contact services.
10. Discuss the similarities and the differences in the marketing of *services* with certain versus uncertain product specifications.
11. Discuss the similarities and the differences in the marketing of high sales volume versus low sales volume manufactured goods.

12. Discuss the similarities and the differences in the marketing of *products* with certain product specifications versus those with uncertain specifications.

13. Data base management systems are a type of computer software designed to allow flexibility for various computer applications. These systems involve overhead costs. Do such systems represent a line or a job shop approach to information requirements? Read some material on data base management systems, and discuss the trade-offs involved in adopting the data base approach. (Kroenke [5] gives a good description of data base management systems).

14. Deregulation has allowed banks to pay higher interest rates on savings accounts. In the past, savings and loan institutions and some banks lobbied against such deregulation. What threw the banking and savings and loan institutions out of steady state? What is your judgment on the future course of health and action for these institutions? In production terms, answer these questions in terms of raw materials and products.

15. Insurance companies have faced serious changes in their way of doing business. Consumer interest in term insurance (as opposed to whole life insurance) has increased. To what do you attribute this? What has been the industry's response? What future do you see for the insurance industry? Is the industry in steady state?

16. Try to classify each of the following types of organizations:
    a. Data-processing department
    b. Consulting practice
    c. Medical clinic
    d. Dental practice
    e. Cafeteria
    f. Grocery store
    g. Welding shop
    h. City civic center

17. Some people do not take criticism well. Discuss this statement in light of open systems theory. Have you had any C's in your course work? How did you interpret the C? How can a C help your future success?

18. What inventory control problems are faced by your local chain grocery store? What about your local corner grocery store?

19. Electric Boat, a division of General Dynamics, produces submarines. How important is good forecasting to Electric Boat? How important is good scheduling? What about inventory control?

20. A. T. Cross produces a variety of pens and pencils. How important is good forecasting to A. T. Cross? How important is good scheduling? What about inventory control?

REFERENCES AND BIBLIOGRAPHY

1. R. B. Chase, "Where Does the Customer Fit in a Service Operation?" *Harvard Business Review,* Vol. 56, No. 6 (November-December 1978), pp. 137–142.
2. Jue-ming Hua, "The Mass Production of Iron Castings in Ancient China," *Scientific American* (January 1983), pp. 121–128.
3. D. Katz and R. L. Kahn, *The Social Psychology of Organizations* (New York: John Wiley & Sons, 1967).
4. P. Marshall et al., *Operations Management: Text and Cases* (Homewood, Ill.: Richard D. Irwin, 1975).
5. David M. Kroenke, *Business Computer Systems: An Introduction* (Santa Cruz, Calif.: Mitchell Publishing Company, 1981).
6. H. L. Timms and M. F. Pohlen, *The Production Function in Business,* 3d ed. (Homewood, Ill.: Richard D. Irwin, 1975).

appendix 1A

Production Planning: Past, Present and Potential

Cary M. Root, CPIM
American Logistics Group

Production planning is the crucial interface between a business's strategic plan, marketing plan, financial plan, and master production schedule. It impacts major allocation decisions for corporate resources such as material, facilities, money, and people. And yet, it is one of the most under utilized and misunderstood functions in a company.

The purpose of this article is to increase awareness of the production planning process and to suggest improvements which can improve the bottom-line in any manufacturing business. After a brief introduction, the article reviews *the past*—the original literature published on the subject, the limitations of applying that literature to the real-world, and one important topic that was glossed-over. Next, the article looks at *the present*—the inadequacy of current production planning processes, and what can be done to improve them. Finally, the article examines *the potential* of production planning—what can be done to achieve the still untapped reservoir of capabilities and benefits that exists in today's manufacturing businesses.

Many of the frequently recorded problems in manufacturing can be traced to one cause—operating in a reactionary or fire-fighting mode. Many companies used and some continue to use shortage lists to focus on "hot jobs" which needed expediting. This method seldom worked. While the "hot jobs" were being herded through the plant, the other ones were being neglected. Before long, all of them were "hot jobs." To solve this we invented "super hot jobs."

Then managers began using time phasing techniques such as MRP for more than just order launching. As a priority planning tool, it allowed them to grab hold of the reigns, and break the vicious expediting circle.

From *Inventories and Production*, May/June 1983, 3(3), pp. 6–10. Reprinted by permission.

The often heard but seldom listened to moral is true: You can't control what you don't plan.

The same is true of the production planning role. Do you recognize any of these symptoms?

—The production work force is increased to take care of an unexpected business surge, then an unexpected downturn causes excess idle time.
—Customer service complains that production isn't making a sufficient amount of the "right" products, and wants increased inventories to prevent lost sales.
—Finance complains that the high inventory levels are too costly, and must be reduced.
—Purchasing is frustrated because of numerous production scheduling changes which cause them to constantly reschedule vendor shipments.
—Marketing does not understand why manufacturing is not producing items in closer alignment with the sales forecast.
—Production control complains that it cannot get efficient runs from the product mix and quantities that production planning sets for it. They are forced to make machine set-ups or changeovers that are unnecessary, time consuming, and costly.
—Production planning is frustrated because manufacturing is constantly deviating from the plan.

These symptoms are caused by inadequate production planning. The cause, not the symptoms, must be addressed for an adequate cure. How do you cure them? Plan, Plan, Plan!

Regardless of the type of product, and whether the manufacturing environment is make-to-stock, make-to-order, or both, the basic concepts are the same. The three fundamental steps to sound planning are: Identify where you are now, figure out where you want to be, and then determine how you are going to get there. Granted, when you are knee-deep in alligators it's easy to know where you want to be—away from the alligators! This natural reflex, however, is exactly what causes a company to get into a reactionary mode. Production planning means looking beyond this week's scheduling headaches, and figuring out how to get permanently away from the alligators *and* into a better inventory position *and* improve customer service. All at the same time. It's easy to say and hard to do, but well worth the effort.

The Past

In 1963 the first edition of the *APICS Dictionary* defined production planning as "The function of setting the limits or levels of manufacturing operations in the future." Do not confuse it with production scheduling. They are very different. Production planning is an overall top management control function. Production scheduling involves the development of more detailed information *from the production plan.*

The basic data needed to plan production are:

—Desired total inventory units at the end of the planning period
—Actual total starting inventory units
—Total sales forecast for the planning horizon
—Number of periods in months or weeks for the planning horizon

The *Production and Inventory Control Handbook* provides a formula to compute a monthly or weekly production rate which achieves level production throughout the planning horizon.

$$\text{Level rate} = \frac{\text{ending inventory} - \text{starting inventory} + \text{forecast}}{\text{number of periods}}$$

As an example, consider the development of a level production rate for ashtrays where:

Ending inventory (month 12) = 500,000 units
Starting inventory (month 1) = 300,000 units
Forecast (12 months) = 1,000,000 units
Number of periods = 12 months

Substituting into the above formula:

$$\begin{aligned}\text{Level rate} &= \frac{\text{ending inventory} - \text{starting inventory} + \text{forecast}}{\text{number of periods}} \\ &= \frac{500{,}000 - 300{,}000 + 1{,}000{,}000}{12} \\ &= 100{,}000 \text{ ashtrays/month}\end{aligned}$$

Manufacturing needs to produce 100,000 ashtrays every month for the next year. This kind of level production rate may not be practical because of seasonality in the customers' buying patterns, the desire to build inventory prior to plant shutdown, or a host of other real-world considerations. Accordingly, production rates are typically calculated on a period by period basis. Setting the number of periods in the level rate formula to 1, the production rate for any one period can be computed as:

$$\text{Rate (any period)} = \text{ending inventory} - \text{starting inventory} + \text{forecast}$$

As an example, let's calculate the production rate in October given the following information:

Product Family: Ashtrays

	AUG.	SEPT.	OCT.
Forecast	80,000	90,000	100,000
Production	85,000	90,000	?
Month Ending Inventory	375,000	375,000	400,000

Rate (October) = ending inventory (October) − starting inventory (October) + forecast (October)

Since the *starting* inventory position in October is the same as the *ending* inventory position a month earlier in September,

Rate (October) = 400,000 − 375,000 + 100,000 = 125,000 ashtrays

This calculation has to be done for every month, and therefore involves extra work. It does, however, provide more practical, realistic production rates and can be well worth the effort.

Although the literature abounds with simple formulas like the ones just presented, it glosses over some of the more important, practical aspects of production planning. The policies and procedures needed to initiate production planning in a company are one such aspect. Here are four steps needed to start a formal production planning function:

1. *Identify product family groups.* Each should consist of products that go through similar manufacturing operations or facilities. The purpose is to make for a smooth transition from item to item when the production plan is relayed to production scheduling.
2. *Select a common unit of measure for planning.* Most often, number of items is used. Other possibilities are standard units or production hours. Do not use dollars.
3. *Choose a suitable time period.* The most commonly used is a month. Sometimes a week is selected.
4. *Determine an adequate planning horizon.* The bare minimum should be the cumulative lead time of the end-item with the longest lead time and its components in each family group. The maximum is only limited by the availability of forecast information and the span of the business strategy. A workable horizon is somewhere between these two extremes. Additional factors to consider are the product's seasonality, financial planning requirements, and other resource capacity needs.

The Present

Today, production planning is used in the majority of manufacturing businesses. In many, however, it is still an informal and incomplete process. In his book *Production and Inventory Management in the Computer Age*, Ollie Wight said "Whether they explicitly recognize it or not, most companies establish some kind of production plans." They do, but that is not enough. In order to survive in today's business world, companies need to contain total costs and improve customer service, and also to increase productivity, profitability, and asset utilization. A formal production planning system is required to do this effectively.

There are many formal production planning systems in use today. But what separates a good one from a mediocre one? A good production planning function must possess each of these twelve characteristics:

1. Effectively interface with the corporate business strategy. Examples of this type of information are aggregate inventory objectives, customer service goals, union agreements relative to workforce stability, and overall resource availability concerns or constraints.
2. Effectively interface with the corporate financial plan. Since the production plan determines how much labor and material are to be purchased, the cash flow impact must be evaluated and traded-off against other financial alternatives.
3. Effectively interface with the marketing plan. In addition to the sales forecasts which are a basic data requirement, marketing should provide insights on planned promotions (where the effect on sales has not been worked into the forecast), and specific customer service objectives which must be translated into inventory considerations.
4. Have good formal communication among all functions having input to the production plan. The formal communication process should take the form of a regularly scheduled monthly or weekly meeting. The vice presidents of marketing, finance, manufacturing, engineering, and even corporate planning should attend. The chief operating officer should chair the meeting and ensure that everyone gets involved. At the meeting, various alternative plans are presented and discussed. The results must be a consensus of what the new production plan will be. Once all departments are truly involved in the production planning process and they do not feel the plan is being "shoved down their throats," the informal communication among departments will also begin to improve.
5. Include performance measurements. It is imperative to monitor the degree of execution of the production plans, as well as how well each sub-plan achieves its objectives. Performance mea-

surements should be tied to personnel evaluations. Some of the criteria which may be worthwhile monitoring are inventory objectives, customer service targets, and actual vs. planned production.

6. Be realistic. A recently developed production plan called for a 25% increase in the work force over a six month period. Personnel said there was no way to hire and train that many people in time so the production plan had to be revised. Don't lie to the production plan. If unachievable information is put into the planning process, unachievable plans will come out.
7. Include tolerance limits for every critical aspect of the plan. For instance, "inventory should not be allowed to build more than x% from one month to the next, or more than y% per year. Otherwise, a special meeting must be held and certain review procedures followed." Tolerance limits can also be set for production rate changes, inventory decreases, and even sales forecast changes from one month to the next. There are no universal criteria that all companies can follow. Rather, each company must determine its own critical variables in the production plan and then set up tolerance limits for them.
8. Include capacity limits for all critical resources. If there are overall machine or process limitations, the production plan should not exceed them. This is rough-cut capacity planning, not detailed machine loading taking into account the sequencing of jobs. It is higher level capacity planning done at the level of the production plan.
9. Contain time fences. These are necessary to avoid major disruptions and inefficiencies on the factory floor. One example is a point in the production plan (e.g. the second month out) before which no mix changes are permitted. Another time fence should be set up for the production quantities in the plan (e.g. the fourth month out).
10. Include tolerance limits around the time fences. Because some amount of change within the time fences may be unavoidable, it is usually a good idea to set tolerance limits around them. For example, no quantity changes that are 2% over or 5% under the plan are permitted within the first four months.
11. Use timely information. As obvious as this may seem, it is amazing how many companies use information that is a month old "because the month-end close wasn't complete when the production plan was developed." It can be difficult changing procedures and deadlines that have been in place for years, but if it means getting more timely information into the planning process, do it.
12. Be able to reconcile a sales month with a production month. They are used for different purposes and generally are not the same. They may start and end on different days of the month, and may

even have a different number of days within them. If the production planning process does not compensate for this difference, erroneous results occur. As an example: the June sales forecast (June 1 through June 30) is for 80,000 ashtrays but production control uses the June production month which is May 15 through June 15 to schedule the factory. The beginning inventory is 370,000 on May 25 and the desired ending inventory is 375,000 on June 23. If the June production rate is calculated as:

Rate (June) = 375,000 − 370,000 + 80,000 = 85,000 ashtrays

a serious mistake is made. If the company is experiencing increasing sales due to seasonality or market expansion, then the sales forecast from May 15 through June 15 will be lower than for June 1 through June 30. Therefore, when the June sales forecast is aligned with the production month, as it should be, the real production rate will be for less than 85,000 ashtrays.

The production plan *must* be developed from information that covers the same time intervals.

These twelve characteristics of good production planning can make the difference between a mediocre function that retards a company's growth, and a good one that supports and enhances corporate strategic, financial, manufacturing and marketing objectives.

The Potential

The full potential of the production planning function has eluded recognition. It is an untapped reservoir of capabilities offering innumerable benefits.

First, a common misconception must be overcome to achieve this potential. "Production planning doesn't really make sense in a make-to-order environment, right?" Wrong. "And what about service parts or assemble-to-order operations?" Production planning works and should be applied in both of these situations. This is fortunate because many companies can't be "neatly" categorized as just one of the above. In fact, some specific end products can't even be categorized as one or the other. Production plans need to cover *all* significant demands on a company.

Second, production planning is a computationally intense process. Technological advances in the data processing industry with the resulting decline in the price/performance ratio of computers has provided the necessary tools to efficiently manage data. It is not uncommon to find production planners who spend 85% to 95% of their time number crunching. Since this is what computers do best, an automated system can free up most of the planners' time and allow them to develop better plans instead of just a plan that works.

Interactive processing is an important adjunct to computerization. It allows the production planner to sit at a terminal and "converse" with the computer to develop good plans. The planner's intelligence and the computer's incredibly fast computational ability are an unbeatable combination which opens up the full potential of production planning in three areas:

1. Use of more detailed information and logic in the planning process
2. Sensitivity analysis
3. Decision support.

1. *Ability to use more detailed information and logic in the planning process.* Where possible, this means using a level of detail comparable to that in the master production schedule. In many industries, finished goods (or end items) can be used for the calculation of production rates instead of aggregated product families. The results can still be summarized and reported by product family, but the extra level of detail makes for a better plan. How much detail should be used? As much as makes sense. Some scheduling information is useless in production planning and should not be used. For example, job sequencing and machine set-ups occur daily or even hourly. The smallest time increment that production planning recognizes is a month or a week. Any level of detail smaller than this is aggregated into a month or a week anyway and "washed-out." A general rule of thumb is use as much detail as possible that still retains its meaning and usefulness in monthly or weekly time buckets.

Another consideration is the product structure used in the bill of material. In many industries where highly modular bills are used, there might be hundreds-of-thousands or even millions of unique end-items. It would hardly make sense to include each one in the production planning calculations.

One of the World's major tire companies used to develop its production plans using only the beginning and ending inventory, the sales forecast, and the total capacity of each tire shop. By installing an interactive computer system, it is now also able to incorporate all of the following details in its production planning:

—Rubber curing rates
—Mold availability
—Use of "common molds" to make different tires
—Inventory replenishment criticality
—Inventory surplus priority numbers
—Inventory deficit priority numbers

Curing rates, mold availability, and common molds are detailed manufacturing considerations which enable production planning to develop plans that are more acceptable to, and usable by production scheduling.

Inventory criticality and priority numbers are detailed marketing considerations. Inventory replenishment criticality involves comparing the actual inventory level with a minimum level required to meet an acceptable level of customer service on an item-by-item basis. The farther below the required level that an item falls, the more likely it will be produced sooner than other items.

Inventory surplus and deficit priority numbers are assigned to each item by marketing. The former shows which items to plan producing first when a sufficient amount of inventory exists on all items. Sufficient here means both meeting anticipated sales and an acceptable level of customer service. The latter shows which items to plan first when plant capacity won't permit producing enough inventory to meet sales or service.

Through the use of more detailed information in the planning process, other operations of the company like manufacturing and marketing are more realistically considered, with the result being better company-wide production plans.

2. The next area of potential is *sensitivity analysis*. Since the production plan is based on projections of the future, it is bound to be wrong 100% of the time. Sometimes high, sometimes low, but always wrong. It is therefore very useful to analyze each plan in terms of how sensitive its results are to potential errors in the sales forecast. A computer can quickly and easily modify the forecast and report at what points inventory, service, and other parameters become critical.

3. The final area of potential is decision support. The use of an interactive, computer based system to evaluate "what-if" questions, is perhaps the most powerful, yet untapped aspect of production planning. For instance, how is the plan impacted if:

—Equipment is purchased which increases departmental capacity?
—Additional overtime is authorized?
—A labor strike occurs?
—Customer service standards are modified?
—An across-the-board inventory reduction program is attempted?

These and other important questions can be analyzed by using production planning as a decision support system.

Summary and Conclusion

Many problems in a company result from inadequate production planning. A company's first step is to recognize the importance of doing it. The second is to formalize the process. Important policies and procedures needed to start from scratch are:

1. Identify product family groups
2. Select a common unit of measure
3. Choose a suitable time period
4. Determine a reasonable planning horizon

Next, to improve the function make sure that it:

1. Effectively interfaces with the corporate business strategy, the corporate financial plan and the marketing plan
2. Has good formal and informal communication with all functions having input to the plan
3. Includes performance measurements
4. Is realistic
5. Includes tolerance limits
6. Includes capacity limits for all critical resources
7. Contains time fences
8. Includes tolerance limits around the time fences
9. Uses timely information
10. Is able to reconcile sales and production months

In order to achieve its full potential, production planning needs to cover *all* significant demands on a company. Additional potential can be realized through the use of interactive computer processing in three ways:

1. Using more detail in the planning process
2. Evaluating the impact of, and compensating for, forecast error
3. Being more prepared for future uncertainties through decision support "what-if" analysis.

This article has presented the characteristics of a good production planning function, and what can be done to develop its full potential. The benefits of doing so are higher productivity, lower inventory, and higher customer service—all at the same time.

FOR FURTHER READING

1. Bailey, Peter and Farmer, David, *Managing Materials in Industry:* Grower Press, 1972.
2. Baumback, Clifford M., *APICS Dictionary of Inventory Control Terms and Production Control Terms.* 1st Edition, Washington, D.C.: American Production and Inventory Control Society, 1963.

3. Bedworth, David D., *Industrial Systems:* Ronald Press Company, 1973.
4. Buffa, Elwood Spencer and Taubert, William H., *Production-Inventory Systems; Planning and Control:* Richard D. Irwin, Inc., 1972.
5. Greene, James H., *Production and Inventory Handbook:* McGraw-Hill, Inc., 1970, pp. 9–1 to 9–28.
6. Kretz, Larry J. and Bryant, Arthur S., *Production Planning—An Old Solution to a New Problem*. APICS Proceedings of 21st Annual Conference, Hollywood, Florida, October 24–27, 1978, pp. 652–664.
7. Ling, Richard C., "*Production Planning—An Executive Process,*" Richard C. Ling Report, Number 2, February 1980.
8. Moore, Franklin, *Production Management:* Richard D. Irwin, Inc., 1973.
9. Pollack, Morris, "Production Planning: The Fundamentals for Preparing a Production Plan," APICS Annual Conference, 1972.
10. Silver, E. A., "Medium Range Aggregate Production Planning: State of the Art," *Production and Inventory Management*—1st quarter, 1972.
11. Udaloy, John, "Solving Manufacturing Problems, Inventory and Production Management Opportunities," APICS Annual Conference, 1973.
12. Wagner, G. R., "Mind Support Systems," *IPC Interface—Manufacturing and Engineering, International Computer Programs, Inc*., Spring 1982, pp. 19–22.
13. Wight, Oliver W., *Production and Inventory Management in the Computer Age:* Cahners Publishing Company, Inc., 1974, pp. 60–61.

chapter two

Forecasting

Introduction

This chapter will provide an appreciation of the value of forecasting, an understanding of some of the major techniques, and insight into the selection of an appropriate technique for a given situation. This knowledge is necessary for designing a successful materials flow system.

Forecasts are simply statements about the future. Good forecasts can be quite valuable; it would be worth a great deal, for example, to receive tomorrow's Wall Street Journal today. Not all forecasts are useful, however. For example, some people have used AFC super bowl victories to predict a poor year for the Dow Jones stock averages and NFC victories to predict a good year. This is nonsense, of course. It is clear that we must distinguish between forecasts per se and *good* forecasts.

Forecasting is the art of specifying meaningful information about the future. Long-run planning decisions require consideration of many factors: general economic conditions, industry trends, probable competitor actions, overall political climate, and so on. *Extrinsic forecasts* are formulated on external associations—for example, between sales of appliances and disposable personal income or between house sales and mortgage availability. For financial planning, companies need extrinsic forecasts of the year's aggregate sales by product line. These aggregate forecasts are of little use in production planning, however, in which we must plan production quantities of every item in the product line. In some companies with as few as five major product lines, there may be 10,000 individual items to be forecast. Such *item forecasting* requires routine projections of past data. This chapter presents sophisticated methods of projecting data—methods analogous to the old pencil and ruler trick. Such projection forecasts are usually termed *intrinsic forecasts*. Hence, this chapter is about item or intrinsic forecasting.

Item forecasts are required only for end items. Demand for car doors in an automobile assembly plant, for example, can be derived simply by doubling or "exploding" the end item forecast for two-door cars.

FORECASTING PERIOD

Forecasts are often classified according to time period and use. In general, short-term (up to one year) forecasts guide current operations. Medium-term (one to three years) and long-term (over five years) forecasts support decisions on plant location and capacity. The item forecasts discussed in this chapter are aimed at the ordering or production lead time, normally a matter of weeks or months. Typically, we want to know the average demand during lead time for inventory control purposes.

FORECAST ACCURACY

Forecasts are never perfect. Since we are basically dealing with methods that project from past data, our forecasts will be less reliable the further into the future we predict. Causal or explanatory models generally will give the greatest accuracy, especially in predicting turning points, but they do so at a great cost in computation time and data storage. For a product group or family, we can probably get reasonably good forecasts by using explanatory models. A product group forecast will also be more accurate than a single-item forecast, since it is easier to forecast a group of items than a single item.

To appreciate fully the greater accuracy of product group forecasts, we will take a closer look. Suppose that we have ten items in a group or family. All items have the same standard deviation ($\sigma = 2{,}000$) but different means (μ_i, $i = 1, \ldots, 10$). The group mean is $\Sigma_{i=1}^{10} \mu_i$. Although the demands for individual items in a family might be interdependent, assume for simplicity that they are independent. Then the standard deviation of the group demand would be $\sqrt{10}\,\sigma$, since the variance of the sum is the sum of the variances. For our example, suppose that $\mu_i = 40{,}000$ and $\Sigma_{i=1}^{10} \mu_i = 400{,}000$. Now examine the coefficient of variation, which is the ratio of a variable's standard deviation to its mean. For the first item, the coefficient of variation is $2{,}000/40{,}000 = 0.05$. The coefficient of variation for the family is $(\sqrt{10} * 2{,}000)/400{,}000 = 0.016$.

FORECASTING APPROACHES

Forecasting approaches vary with the number of items to be forecast and the dollar importance of the decisions. Decisions regarding plant capacity and plant location can be made with long-term, aggregate forecasts, and we would probably be willing to expend a substantial amount of money and computer time to gain accuracy. Economic order quantity (EOQ) decisions for low-value items are based on short-term, individual item forecasts for which we don't want to spend much money.

Econometric models, Box-Jenkins methods, and market surveys are expensive but relatively accurate at the aggregate level. When the consequences of the decision are costly, these approaches can be justified.

TABLE 2.1 Forecasting Model Selection According to Problem Type

	Few Time Series, Costly Decisions	*Thousands of Series, Routine Decisions*
Large amount of past data available	Box-Jenkins [1] Econometrics [17]	Exponential smoothing [13] Moving averages
Little past data available	Delphi method [4] Market surveys [4]	Bayes methods [11]

However, a typical forecasting problem in a production-inventory system includes thousands of individual items. For such problems, the exponential smoothing methods presented in this chapter have a distinct advantage in computational ease, data storage requirements, and cost. Table 2.1 summarizes the relationship of approaches to problem types.

For production planning purposes, what we consider a "good" forecasting system has the following characteristics:

1. Accuracy
2. Low computer time requirements
3. Low computer storage requirements
4. Low dollar cost of software purchase or development
5. On-line capabilities
6. Ability to link into an existing data base management system.

COMPONENTS OF DEMAND

For systematic analysis of historical data, analysts often use time series analysis. Typically, the production-inventory analyst views demand as composed of a base or central tendency, a trend, seasonal variation, cyclical (business cycle) variation, and random variation (noise).

Common Time Series Forecasting Models

The most common and relatively easiest methods for developing a forecast from past data are simple moving averages, weighted moving averages, exponential smoothing, and regression analysis. The calculations in all these methods can be done with a desk calculator or microcomputer.

SIMPLE MOVING AVERAGE

A moving average is obtained by averaging the demand data from several of the most recent periods. When the demand data do not have rapid growth or seasonal characteristics, the technique can be useful in removing random fluctuations for forecasting. As n (the number of observations to be included in the moving average) increases, the model tends to smooth or dampen out noise. As n grows larger, however, more data are included, and the model becomes less responsive to changes in sales patterns. A simple n-period moving average is defined as follows:

$$\text{Moving average } (MA) = \frac{\text{sum of old demand for last } n \text{ periods}}{\text{number of periods used in the model}}$$

$$= \frac{\sum_{j=1}^{n} D_{t-j+1}}{n} \tag{2.1}$$

$$= \frac{D_t + D_{t-1} + D_{t-2} + \ldots + D_{t-n+1}}{n}$$

where t is the index of the current period, j is a general index, and D_j is the demand during period j.

The average moves over time. After each period has elapsed, the demand for the oldest period is removed and the demand for the newest period is added to the next calculation:

$$MA_t = MA_{t-1} + \frac{D_t - D_{t-n}}{n} \tag{2.2}$$

Example 2.1

Table 2.2 presents twelve-month demand data for exhaust pipes. Forecasts using three-month and six-month moving averages are also exhibited.

TABLE 2.2 Three- and Six-Month Moving Averages Used as Forecasts

Month	*Demand* (D_t)	*Three-Month Moving Average Forecast** (f_t)	*Three-Month Moving Average* (MA_t)	*Six-Month Moving Average Forecast* (f_t)	*Six-Month Moving Average* (MA_t)
January	450	—	—	—	—
February	440	—	—	—	—
March	460	—	450	—	—
April	510	450	470	—	—
May	520	470	497	—	—
June	495	497	508	—	479
July	475	508	497	479	483
August	560	497	510	483	503
September	510	510	515	503	512
October	520	515	530	512	513
November	540	530	523	513	517
December	550	523	537	517	526

Note: The average at time t becomes a forecast for time $t+1$.

* Using f_t as the forecast for period t, f_t is set equal to the most recently calculated moving average, $f_t = ma_{t-1}$.

The actual demand is quite variable. However, the three-month moving average is much more stable, because the demand for any one month receives only one-third weight. The larger the value of n, the greater the dampening effect.

For the three-month moving average in table 2.2,

$$MA_4 = MA_3 + \frac{D_4 - D_{4-3}}{3}$$

$$= 450 + \frac{510 - 450}{3}$$

$$= 470$$

WEIGHTED MOVING AVERAGE

The moving average gives equal weight to each observation of past demand used in the average. Sometimes the forecaster wishes to use a moving average but does not want all n periods weighted equally. A weighted moving average allows any desired weights to be placed on old demand. An n-period weighted moving average is defined as follows:

$$\text{Weighted moving average } (WMA) = \sum_{t=1}^{n} C_t D_t \qquad (2.3)$$

where

$$0 \leqslant C_t \leqslant 1$$

that is, C_t is a fraction used as a weight for period t, and

$$\sum_{t=1}^{n} C_t = 1$$

In general, more weight is given to the most recent demand and hence the weighted moving average model discounts the value of past information. Thus, the forecast tends to be more responsive to genuine changes in demand.

Example 2.2

If n is three periods, we can assign the following weights for the data in table 2.2: $C_1 = 0.25$, $C_2 = 0.25$, and $C_3 = 0.50$. Thus the weight of 0.50 applies to the most recent observation. We then obtain

$$WMA = (450 * 0.25) + (440 * 0.25) + (460 * 0.50)$$

$$= 452.5$$

TABLE 2.3 Forecast Comparisons Using Moving Average and Weighted Moving Average

Month	*Demand* (D_t)	*Three-Month Moving Average Forecast* (f_t)	*Three-Month Moving Average* (MA_t)	*Three-Month Weighted Moving Average Forecast* (f_t)	*Three-Month Weighted Moving Average (0.25, 0.25, 0.50), Most Recent* (MA_t)
January	450	—	—	—	—
February	440	—	—	—	—
March	460	—	450	—	453
April	510	450	470	453	480
May	520	570	497	480	503
June	495	497	508	503	505
July	475	508	497	505	491
August	560	497	510	491	523
September	510	510	515	523	514
October	520	515	530	514	528
November	540	530	523	528	528
December	550	523	537	528	540

A comparison of three-month moving average and weighted moving average forecasts is given in table 2.3.

SIMPLE EXPONENTIAL SMOOTHING

We begin with a very simple demand process $D_t = \mu + \varepsilon_t$ where ε_t is normally distributed, with mean zero. We would like a model capable of forecasting this process, even when we have an occasional shift in μ, the central tendency. With no shifts, this formula reflects random error around a stable central tendency.

Simple exponential smoothing is a special type of averaging technique that is suitable for forecasting this process. Indeed, Muth [12] showed that the exponential forecast is optimal for such a demand process.

The equation for simple exponential smoothing uses only two pieces of information: (1) actual demand for the most recent period and (2) the most recent forecast. At the end of each period, a new forecast is made. Thus,

$$\text{New exponential average} = \text{old exponential average} + \text{fraction (current demand} - \text{forecast)}$$

Using the exponential average in one period as a forecast for the next period, we have a process for revising the average upward or downward, depending on forecast error. Current demand minus forecast gives forecast error. Demand that is higher than forecast causes us to revise the average upward, and demand that is lower than forecast causes a downward revision.

Simple exponential smoothing has the following equation:

$$F_t = F_{t-1} + \alpha(D_t - F_{t-1})$$

where F_t is the exponential average at time t, D_t is the actual demand in period t, and α is a smoothing constant between zero and one. If we use F_{t-1} as a forecast for D_t, then the error term e_t would be

$$e_t = D_t - F_{t-1}$$

For example, suppose that demand is 100 and that the old average was 90. Using the old average as a forecast, the error term would be 100 − 90 = 10. Hence, we would revise the average upward a little. If the smoothing factor is 0.2, the new average will be 92, determined as follows:

$$F_t = F_{t-1} + \alpha(D_t - F_{t-1})$$

$$= 90 + 0.2(100 - 90) = 92$$

Slightly rearranging the equation, we obtain the usual form:

$$F_t = \alpha D_t + (1 - \alpha)F_{t-1} \tag{2.4}$$

$$= 0.2(100) + 0.8(90) = 92$$

Because the simple exponential average will not always be our forecast, we must emphasize the general nature of our revision process. Letting f_t be the forecast of period t sales, we have

$$f_t = F_{t-1}$$

TABLE 2.4 Simple Exponential Smoothing Forecast

Month	*Actual Demand* (D_t)	*Forecast* (f_t)	*Old Average* (F_{t-1})	*New Average* (F_t)	*Weights*[a]
March	460	480	480.00	476.00	0.027
April	510	476	476.00	482.80	0.034
May	520	483	482.80	490.24	0.042
June	495	490	490.24	491.19	0.052
July	475	491	491.19	487.95	0.066
August	560	488	487.95	502.36	0.082
September	510	502	502.36	503.89	0.102
October	520	504	503.89	507.11	0.128
November	540	507	507.11	513.69	0.160
December	550	514	513.69	520.95	0.200

[a] At the end of December, F_{DEC} implicitly applies these weights to the sales from March through December. To see this, calculate $F_{DEC} = 0.2(550) + 0.16(540) + 0.128(520) + \ldots + 0.027(460)$.

and

$$F_t = \alpha D_t + (1 - \alpha)f_t$$

From equation (2.4), we can see that F_t implicitly captures all past data, even though we use only D_t and F_{t-1} in the calculation at period t. Consider the sequence of forecasts where t = December, and use the data from table 2.4:

$$F_{t-1} = \alpha D_{t-1} + (1 - \alpha)F_{t-2} = 0.2(540) + 0.8(507)$$

$$F_t = \alpha D_t + (1 - \alpha)F_{t-1} = 0.2(550) + 0.8(514)$$

or

$$F_t = \alpha D_t + (1 - \alpha)[\alpha D_{t-1} + (1 - \alpha)F_{t-2}]$$

$$= 0.2(550) + 0.8[0.2(540) + 0.8(507)]$$

or

$$F_t = \alpha D_t + (1 - \alpha)\alpha D_{t-1} + (1 - \alpha)^2 F_{t-2}$$

$$= 0.2(550) + 0.16(540) + 0.64(507)$$

In general,

$$F_t = \alpha \sum_{k=0}^{t-1} (1 - \alpha)^k D_{t-k} + (1 - \alpha)^t F_0 \qquad (2.5)$$

where F_0 is the initial estimate of μ. For t sufficiently large, $(1 - \alpha)^t$ would approach zero, since α is a fraction. Hence, the initial forecast gets washed out.

Example 2.3

A firm uses simple exponential smoothing, with $\alpha = 0.2$ to forecast demand. The forecast for the month of March was 500 units, whereas the actual demand turned out to be 460 units.

1. Forecast the demand for the month of April.
2. Assume that the actual demand for the month of April turned out to be 480 units. Forecast the demand for the month of May. Continue forecasting for the rest of the year, assuming the subsequent demand as displayed in table 2.4.
3. Assume that the current average is used as a forecast for the next month.

Solution:

$$f_{\text{APRIL}} = F_t = F_{t-1} + \alpha(D_t - F_{t-1})$$
$$= 500 + 0.2 * (460 - 500) = 492 \text{ units}$$
$$f_{\text{MAY}} = 492 + 0.2\,(480 - 492) = 489.6$$

SELECTION OF THE SMOOTHING CONSTANT

Higher values of the smoothing constant give higher responsiveness to both random fluctuations and shifts in the underlying process. A stable central tendency with large random fluctuation requires a low smoothing constant. A high smoothing constant is more appropriate for small random fluctuations around a somewhat unstable central tendency.

A higher value of the smoothing constant corresponds to fewer months in a moving average. The average age of the data used in a forecasting system can be calculated as $\bar{k} = 0 * C_t + 1 * C_{t-1} + 2 * C_{t-2} + \ldots + n * C_{t-n}$, where C_t is the weight assigned to the data from period t. Brown [2, p. 107] has shown that the average age of the data in a moving average is $(n - 1)/2$. In an exponentially smoothed average, he finds an average age of $(1 - \alpha)/\alpha$. Hence, choosing smoothing constants to give the same average age of the data would produce $\alpha = 2/(n + 1)$ or $n = (2 - \alpha)/\alpha$.

As a general rule, the smoothing constant for a constant model should be between 0.01 and 0.3. How do we decide on a value for each of the one thousand items to be forecast? First, graphs of sample items are absolutely indispensable. Second, we use trial and error. If we have four years of available data, we might use the first three years as an analysis sample and the last year as a holdout or "trial future" sample. We try various values of α on the analysis sample and choose the one that minimizes a measure, such as sum of squared error. We then forecast the trial future period by period to check out how our system will respond to fresh data.

WINTERS TREND MODEL

Peter Winters [16] developed a very popular model for handling both trends and seasons. For explanatory purposes, we will demonstrate his trend calculations first and then add his seasonal factors in the next section. Winters used the Holt trend model, which begins with the usual trend estimation:

$$T_t = \beta(F_t - F_{t-1}) + (1 - \beta)T_{t-1} \tag{2.6}$$

where β is a fraction, T_t is the trend estimate at time t, and F_t is the exponential average at time t. Updating the exponential average requires that we recognize that a forecast now involves the exponential average plus a trend:

$$f_t = F_{t-1} + T_{t-1} \tag{2.7}$$

With this in mind, we can recall our general version of simple exponential smoothing:

$$F_t = \alpha D_t + (1 - \alpha)f_t$$

Substitution for f_t gives

$$F_t = \alpha D_t + (1 - \alpha)(F_{t-1} + T_{t-1}) \tag{2.8}$$

Thus, we see that the trend factor becomes part of the old average to be smoothed. This means that F_t no longer behaves as a simple exponentially smoothed average.

Therefore, as a first step, we find F_t using equation (2.8). The second step involves the computation of T_t given by equation (2.6). Finally, we find the trend-adjusted forecast using equation (2.7).

The forecast made at the end of the period t for period $t + 1$ would be

$$f_{t+1} = F_t + T_t$$

Example 2.4

For the data in Example 2.1, calculate forecasts with $\alpha = 0.2$, $\beta = 0.2$, $T_0 = 9$, and $F_0 = 480$ (see table 2.5, and begin March):

$$\mathrm{F}_1 = 0.2(460) + 0.8(480 + 9) = 483.2$$

$$\mathrm{T}_1 = 0.2(483.2 - 480) + 0.8(9) = 7.84$$

SEASONALLY ADJUSTED EXPONENTIAL SMOOTHING

Seasonal demand patterns are characteristic of many demand series, reflecting the Christmas season, the summer doldrums, and the like. It is possible that the seasonal effect could be additive; for example, regardless of the weekly sales rate for the rest of the year, Christmas season sales could be 200 units per week higher. The seasonal effect can also be multiplicative—such as a Christmas weekly sales rate that is double the prevailing weekly rate for the rest of the year.

We can then consider a seasonal demand generation process:

$$D_t = \mu * \delta_t + \varepsilon_t$$

TABLE 2.5 Winter's Trend Model

Month	*Demand* (D_t)	*Simple Exponential Average*[a]	*Winter's Exponential Average* (F_t)	*Trend* (T_t)	*Winter's Forecast* (f_t)
			480.00	9.00	
March	460	476.00	483.20	7.84	489.00
April	510	482.80	494.83	8.60	491.04
May	520	490.24	506.74	9.26	503.43
June	495	491.19	511.80	8.42	516.00
July	475	487.95	511.18	6.61	520.22
August	560	502.36	526.23	8.30	517.79
September	510	503.89	529.62	7.32	534.53
October	520	507.11	533.55	6.64	536.94
November	540	513.69	540.16	6.63	540.20
December	550	520.95	547.43	6.76	546.79
January	555	527.76	554.35	6.79	554.19
February	569	536.01	562.72	7.11	561.15

Note: $\alpha = 0.2$; $\beta = 0.2$; $T_0 = 9$; $F_0 = 480$.

[a] Given for comparison purposes. Note how the simple exponential average lags the upward trend.

where μ is the permanent or base sales level and δ_t is a seasonal factor. For example, $\delta_2 = 1.2$ indicates that demand in period 2 is 20% higher than the base level for the year.

Since the simple exponential smoothing average estimates μ, we could estimate δ_t by an index, $I_t = D_t/F_t$. If the simple exponential average is 200 and sales for period 1 were 230, we would calculate I_1 as 1.15. Then next year, with a simple exponential average of 250, we would estimate period 1 sales at $I_1 * F_{t-1} = 1.15 * 250 = 288$.

The seasonal factors allow us to convert back and forth between period sales and the exponential average. If period 1 sales came in at 300, we could deseasonalize these to $300/1.15 = 261$ and use this deseasonalized figure to update the exponential average. Surely the old average of 250 is too low if actual sales were 300 and our seasonalized forecast was 288. The model then becomes

$$F_t = \alpha \frac{D_t}{I_{t-m}} + (1 - \alpha)F_{t-1}$$

$$F_t = 0.2\left(\frac{300}{1.15}\right) + (0.8)250 = 252 \qquad (2.9)$$

$$= 0.2\,(261) + 0.8\,(250) = 252$$

where I_{t-m} is the index calculated $m = 12$ months ago for monthly forecasts or $m = 52$ weeks ago for weekly forecasts. Once we have a new exponential average, we can update the seasonal factor. Winters used

$$I_t = \gamma \frac{D_t}{F_t} + (1 - \gamma)I_{t-m} \tag{2.10}$$

where γ is a smoothing constant, preferably set at $\gamma \leqslant 0.05$. Finally, the forecast made at the end of period t for period $t + 1$ becomes

$$f_{t+1} = F_t * I_{t+1-m} \tag{2.11}$$

Further, the full-blown Winters model includes the trend method in the previous section. In that case, F_t includes a smoothed trend factor. The revised equations would be

$$F_t = \alpha \frac{D_t}{I_{t-m}} + (1 - \alpha)(F_{t-1} + T_{t-1}) \tag{2.12}$$

$$T_t = \beta(F_t - F_{t-1}) + (1 - \beta)T_{t-1} \tag{2.13}$$

$$I_t = \gamma \frac{D_t}{F_t} + (1 - \gamma)I_{t-m} \tag{2.14}$$

$$f_{t+1} = (F_t + T_t) * I_{t+1-m} \tag{2.15}$$

For simplicity in presentation, we will use only seasonal components in the following example and will ignore trend calculations. The sample computation in table 2.6 indicates how initial indices can be calculated from two years of past monthly data. Calculate the average demand for each

TABLE 2.6 Sample Seasonal Index Computation

	Demand			
Month	*1983*	*1984*	*Average Demand*[a]	*Seasonal Index* (I_t)
January	80	100	90	0.957
February	75	85	80	0.851
March	80	90	85	0.904
April	90	110	100	1.064
May	115	131	123	1.309
June	110	120	115	1.223
July	100	110	105	1.117
August	90	110	100	1.064
September	85	95	90	0.957
October	75	85	80	0.851
November	75	85	80	0.851
December	80	80	80	0.851

[a] Average monthly demand: 1128/12 = 94.

month, and then average these to get average monthly demand. Then divide each month's average by average monthly demand to get initial seasonal factors.

Table 2.7 indicates the forecast computations as we move into the year 1985 with our initial seasonal factors. Set $\alpha = 0.1$, $\gamma = 0.05$ and $F_{DEC} = 94$, the average monthly demand. Then the forecast for January would be

$$f_{JAN} = F_{DEC} * I_{JAN-12} = 94 * 0.957 = 90$$

Using equations (2.9) and (2.10) to update the exponential average and the indices, and using table 2.7 for the demand, we have

$$F_{JAN} = \alpha\left(\frac{D_{JAN}}{I_{JAN-12}}\right) + (1 - \alpha)\, F_{DEC}$$

$$= 0.1\left(\frac{95}{.957}\right) + 0.9 * 94 = 94.5$$

$$I_{JAN} = \gamma\left(\frac{D_{JAN}}{F_{JAN}}\right) + (1 - \gamma)\, I_{JAN-12}$$

$$= 0.05\left(\frac{95}{94.5}\right) + 0.95 * 0.957 = 0.96$$

and

$$f_{FEB} = F_{JAN} * I_{FEB-12} = 94.5 * 0.851 = 80.4$$

TABLE 2.7 Computation of Seasonalized Forecasts

Month	*Demand* (D_t) *1985*	*Deseasonalized Demand* (D_t/I_{t-12})	*Average* (F_t) $F_0 = 94$	*Forecast* (f_t)	*Old Seasonal Factor* (I_{t-12})	*New Seasonal Factor* (I_t)
January	95	99.27	94.50	89.96	0.957	0.959
February	75	88.13	93.86	80.42	0.851	0.848
March	90	99.56	94.43	84.85	0.904	etc.
April	105	98.68	94.86	100.47	1.064	.
May	120	91.67	94.54	124.17	1.309	.
June	117	95.67	94.65	115.62	1.223	.
July	102	91.32	94.32	105.72	1.117	.
August	98	92.11	94.10	100.36	1.064	.
September	95	99.27	94.62	90.05	0.957	.
October	75	88.13	93.97	80.52	0.851	.
November	85	99.88	94.56	79.97	0.851	.
December	75	88.13	93.91	80.47	0.851	.

Note: $\alpha = 0.1$; $\delta = 0.05$; $F_{DEC} = 94$; $f_t = F_{t-1} * I_{t-12}$.

Having studied the Winters linear trend and his seasonal factors, we can now combine them in one model, usually referred to simply as the Winters model.

THE COMPLETE WINTERS MODEL

Given the following data:

	1982	*1983*	*1984*
Quarter 1	146	192	272
Quarter 2	96	127	155
Quarter 3	59	79	98
Quarter 4	133	186	219

we will develop forecasts for 1985 using the complete Winters model, with $\alpha = 0.2$, $\beta = 0.1$ and $\delta = 0.05$.

As developed earlier, the complete model has four main formulas:

$$F_t = \alpha\left(\frac{D_t}{I_{t-m}}\right) + (1 - \alpha)(F_{t-1} + T_{t-1}) \tag{2.12}$$

$$T_t = \beta(F_t - F_{t-1}) + (1 - \beta)T_{t-1} \tag{2.13}$$

and

$$I_t = \delta\left(\frac{D_t}{F_t}\right) + (1 - \delta)I_{t-m} \tag{2.14}$$

$$f_{t+1} = (F_t + T_t) * I_{t+1-m} \tag{2.15}$$

To begin, we see that

$$F_1 = 0.2\left(\frac{146}{?}\right) + 0.8(? + ?)$$

involves the unknown values of F_0, T_0, and I_{-3}. What can we do? We need initial values for the intercept and the slope of a trend line (see figure 2.1).

There are two ways to get these initial estimates. We could regress demand against time, or we could make simple rough estimates. To develop rough estimates, we again use the difference in average sales ($\overline{D}$) between the two years:

$$\overline{D}_{1982} = 108.5$$

$$\overline{D}_{1983} = 146.0$$

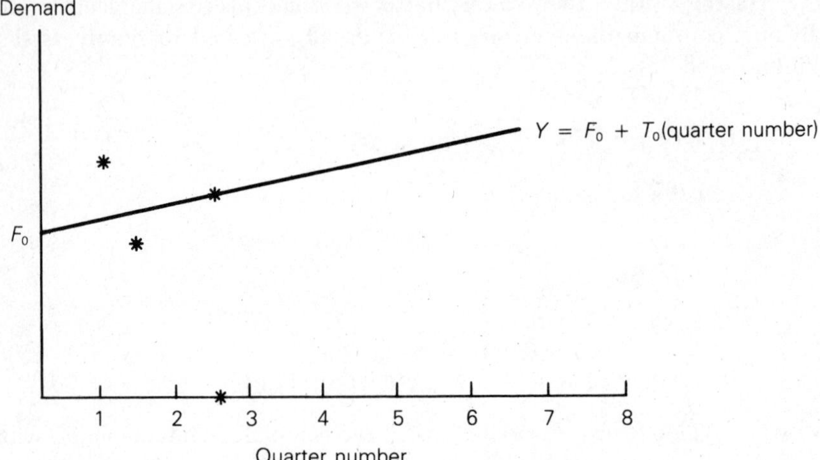

* 2.5 = balance point for year. In the case of monthly data, 6.5 is the balance point for the year with six months above and six months below the balance point.

FIGURE 2.1 Simple line fit to demand

Hence, the yearly upward trend is 37.5. On a quarterly basis, the trend would be 9.38 = 37.5/4.

We know, then, that

$$D_t = F_0 + 9.38(\text{quarter number})$$

Further, we know that the average for 1982 sales sits right at the midpoint of the year:

$$108.5 = F_0 + 9.38(2.5) \text{ (2 discrete quarters below and 2 above 2.5)}$$

or

$$F_0 = 85.05$$

In general,

$$F_0 = \overline{D} - T_0(2.5) \quad \text{for quarterly data}$$

and

$$F_0 = \overline{D} - T_0(6.5) \quad \text{for monthly data.}$$

Using our rough equations, we can now fill in our trend line estimates of sales:

Trend Line Sales Estimates

	1982	*1983*
Q1	94.43	131.95
Q2	103.81	141.33
Q3	113.19	150.71
Q4	122.57	160.09

For example:

1982Q1: 94.43 = 85.05 + 9.38

1983Q2: 103.81 = 85.05 + 2(9.38)

From these trend line estimates, we can develop initial seasonal indices.

$$\text{Index} = \frac{\text{demand}}{\text{trend line estimate}}$$

Seasonal Index Estimates

	1982	*1983*	*Average*	
Q1	1.55	1.46	1.51	= (1.55 + 1.46)/2
Q2	0.92	0.90	0.91	
Q3	0.52	0.52	0.52	
Q4	1.09	1.16	1.13	
			4.07	

For example:

1982Q1: 1.55 = 146/94.43

1983Q2: 0.92 = 96/103.81

These indices add up to 4.07, however, where we would expect them to add to 4. To correct them, we multiply through by 4/4.07:

Average	*Initial Index*		I_{t-4}
1.51 * (4/4.07)	= 1.48	= I_{-3}	$I_{1-4} = I_{-3}$
0.91 * (4/4.07)	= 0.89	= I_{-2}	$I_{2-4} = I_{-2}$
0.52 * (4/4.07)	= 0.51	= I_{-1}	$I_{3-4} = I_{-1}$
1.13 * (4/4.07)	= 1.11	= I_0	$I_{4-4} = I_0$
4.07 * (4/4.07)	= 4.00		

Now we are ready to proceed with Winters's updating equations:

$$F_1 = 0.2\left(\frac{146}{1.48}\right) + 0.8(85.05 + 9.38) = 95.27$$

$$T_1 = 0.1(95.27 - 85.05) + 0.9(9.38) = 9.46$$

$$f_2 = (95.27 + 9.46) * 0.89 = 93.21$$

$$I_1 = 0.05\left(\frac{146}{95.27}\right) + 0.95(1.48) = 1.48$$

$$F_2 = 0.2\left(\frac{96}{0.89}\right) + 0.8(95.27 + 9.46) = 105.36$$

$$T_2 = 0.1(105.36 - 95.27) + 0.9(9.46) = 9.52$$

$$f_3 = (105.36 + 9.52) * 0.51 = 58.59$$

$$I_2 = 0.05\left(\frac{96}{105.36}\right) + 0.95(0.89) = 0.89$$

Continuing in this fashion, we eventually reach F_{12}, T_{12}, and I_9, I_{10}, I_{11}, and I_{12}. Rather than working this out completely by hand, it would be wise to write a simple program. Such an exercise will seal your understanding.

$$F_{12} = 199.92 \qquad I_9 = 1.49$$

$$T_{12} = 9.48 \qquad I_{10} = 0.90$$

$$I_{11} = 0.52$$

$$I_{12} = 1.11$$

To forecast 1984, we then have

1984Q1: $f_{13} = (199.92 + 9.48) * 1.49 = 312$

1984Q2: $f_{14} = [199.92 + (2 * 9.48)] * 0.90 = 197$

1984Q3: $f_{15} = [199.92 + (3 * 9.48)] * 0.52 = 119$

1984Q4: $f_{16} = [199.92 + (4 * 9.48)] * 1.11 = 264$

In terms of the actual application of the Winters model, McClain [9] gives us some cause for concern. First, he demonstrates that disturbances picked up in the seasonal factors are long-lived, since these factors are smoothed only once per season. Accordingly, McClain recommends using only very small values of the smoothing constant γ and feels that even zero would be reasonable. Second, he indicates that the choice of α and β must be made very carefully. If values of β are too large relative to α, oscillatory behavior results. The situation for seasonal factors was not studied, but oscillations occurred in the trend model for $\alpha < 4\beta/(1 + \beta)^2$. Since we normally start with a value of α, it is appropriate to give an equation specifying the largest value of β allowed. To prevent oscillations, we must have

$$\beta \leqslant \left(\frac{2}{\alpha} - 1\right) - \sqrt{\left(\frac{2}{\alpha} - 1\right)^2 - 1}$$

Example 2.5

If we want $\alpha = 0.3$ to create a responsive system, we would need $\beta \leqslant 0.089$ to prevent oscillations. In some applications, we have used $\alpha = 0.2$, $\beta = 0.05$ and $\gamma = 0.01$ to cover several hundred demand series. Dennis McLeavey implemented a successful forecasting system in which he specified β by making an equality out of the foregoing formula. In this system, one needs to choose only α because β is determined by formula from α. This produces automatic attenuation or dampening of the trend factor.

Monitoring the Forecasting System

Any forecasting system needs to be regularly monitored for error magnitude and bias. Reasonable errors are to be expected, but any forecaster dreads bias. In this section, we will discuss techniques for monitoring forecasts.

Example 2.6

One company had the misfortune to use a computerized forecasting system that continually provided examples of bias and unreasonably large errors. Although it was installed by a well-known consulting firm, the forecasting system was too naive to be practical. To forecast demand for the next week, the procedure began by finding the second highest quarter's sales out of the previous four quarters. Sales for that quarter were then divided by thirteen to put them on a weekly basis, and this figure was used as a forecast. In times of recession however, the system looked back at the good times of the year before and badly overestimated demand. This positive bias showed up in overproduction in the factories. After some time, when the recession would near its end, the company would adjust to bad times. You can guess the result when the economy would start expanding again—an example of negative bias.

MEAN ABSOLUTE DEVIATION

The simplicity of calculation of the mean absolute deviation has made it the most popular technique for monitoring forecast error. We shall define forecast error as actual demand minus the forecast:

$$e_t = D_t - f_t$$

where D_t is demand in period t and f_t is the forecast made at the end of period $t - 1$ for period t. Then we can define the sum of absolute deviations (SAD) and the mean absolute deviation (MAD)

$$SAD = \sum_{t=1}^{n} |e_t| \qquad MAD = \frac{\sum_{t=1}^{n} |e_t|}{n}$$

For several error probability distributions, including the normal, Brown [2, p. 282] has shown that MAD is proportional to the standard deviation of forecast errors:

$$MAD = 0.8\sigma \quad \text{or} \quad \sigma = 1.25MAD$$

Example 2.7

A firm generates monthly forecasts. For one item, the forecast is 100,000 units, with a MAD of 5,000 units. What would be the 66% prediction interval for next month's demand?

$$x = \mu \pm \sigma = 100{,}000 \pm 1.25 * 5000\text{(appropriate relationship)}$$

$$= 100{,}000 \pm 6250$$

Note: $x = \mu \pm 1\sigma = \mu \pm 1.25\text{MAD}$

TRACKING SIGNAL

Positive bias should lead to forecasts consistently above the mark and negative bias to forecasts consistently below it. A tracking signal can be created to monitor bias continually. Because a good forecasting system should have equally balancing positive and negative errors, the cumulative or running sum of forecast errors (RSFE) should be close to zero:

$$RSFE = \sum_{t=1}^{n} e_t \approx 0$$

where $e_t = D_t - f_t$. If the forecasts are consistently too high, we would get a large negative RSFE. A common tracking signal, S, tells us something about the relative size of RSFE.

$$S = \frac{RAFE}{MAD} = \frac{\sum e_t/n}{\sum |e_t|/n}$$

where $RAFE$ is the running average forecast error. If positive and negative errors are canceling out, S will be close to zero. If large negative errors occur consistently, S will approach negative unity. We then have $-1 \leqslant S \leqslant 1$.

ADAPTIVE RESPONSE SYSTEMS

Trigg and Leach [14] at Eastman Kodak developed a method of adjusting the responsiveness of the system in the face of bias or large values of S: Simply set α equal to the absolute value of the tracking signal, $\alpha = |S|$. Thus, $|S|$ gets large whenever the forecasts are consistently out of line—precisely when we would like to make our system more responsive by raising α.

Although we could use the RAFE and MAD as given, computational convenience and the exponential smoothing spirit suggest that we should use exponential averages:

$$MAD_t = h|e_t| + (1 - h)MAD_{t-1}$$

$$RAFE_t = h(e_t) + (1 - h)RAFE_{t-1}$$

$$S_t = RAFE_t/MAD_t$$

where h is a smoothing constant, often set at $h = 0.05$.

Other adaptive response systems have been proposed, some of which were studied by Whybark [15]. The fundamental principle appears in the Trigg and Leach [14] model. In the forecasting system developed by McLeavey and mentioned in Example 2.5, the trend-smoothing constant β is determined by formula from α and hence automatically adjusts to changes in α. With an upper limit on α of 0.3, this system worked extremely well in practice.

Example 2.8

The actual demand for an item is not behaving as forecasted. Using $h = 0.05$, $RAFE_0 = 0$ and $MAD_0 = 0$, calculate the tracking signal (see table 2.8).

$$RAFE_1 = 0.05(105 - 100) + 0.95 * (0) = 0.25$$

$$MAD_1 = 0.05|105 - 100| + 0.95|0| = 0.25$$

TABLE 2.8 Computation of Tracking Signal

Month	*Actual*	*Forecast*	*RAFE*	*MAD*	S
January	105	100	0.25	0.25	1.00
February	96	100	0.04	0.44	0.09
March	102	100	0.14	0.52	0.27
April	97	100	−0.02	0.64	−0.03
May	121	101	0.98	1.61	0.61
June	118	102	1.73	2.33	0.74
July	119	103	2.44	3.01	0.81
August	123	104	3.27	3.81	0.86
September	121	105	3.91	4.42	0.88

SELECTING AN APPROPRIATE FORECASTING MODEL

In this chapter we have progressed from the simple exponential smoothing model to the Winters model and to adaptive response systems. Brown [2] and Montgomery and Johnson [11] give us an even greater variety of models from which to choose. Brown [3], Makridakis and Wheelwright [7], Makridakis et al. [8] and McLeavey et al. [10] can bring you up to date on the latest issues and debates on forecast model selection. How do we go about choosing a forecasting system to handle thousands of items on a routine basis? Although experience will help to answer this question, we will give you at least a starting point in the form of a series of steps:

1. Graph the data for a random sampling of about thirty items at daily, weekly, or monthly intervals, depending on the company's needs.
2. If the data exhibit trends and/or seasons, you are probably safe in working with the Winters model. Groff [5] has shown that this model does about as well as most others for a variety of data series. If the data are intermittent (i.e., demand does not occur every period), exponential smoothing will not work very well, and you are probably better off fitting a probability distribution to the data as in our next chapter. Also, Holt et al. [6] and Brown [2] provide excellent chapters on forecasting with probability distributions.
3. Experiment with smoothing factors according to the procedures outlined earlier for the selection of smoothing constants.
4. Initialize the system with the chosen set of smoothing factors. If you are to forecast next month's demand, you need to bring the system all the way up to last month.
5. Update the system period by period.

Summary and Conclusions

This chapter has introduced some practical methods for making routine forecasts for thousands of items. The underlying thread in the chapter has been the question of responsiveness. We want our system to respond to underlying changes but not to random fluctuations.

In one chapter we can take you only so far, however. For those interested in more advanced work, Montgomery and Johnson [11] will do an excellent job of taking you the next mile.

This chapter has developed two fundamental concepts: measuring forecast error and exponential averaging. Exponential averaging assigns declining weights to past observations. In the Winters model, the averaging process is applied to the permanent component or base level, to the trend, and to seasonal indices. After mean absolute deviation and standard deviation have been developed as error measures, the exponential averaging process can be used to calculate the mean absolute deviation.

PROBLEMS

Each of the following problems uses one of the data series in table 2.9. Visualize a company with hundreds of such series, one for each color, style, size, and so on, of each product. Problems 1 through 7 are based on quarterly data.

1. For data series A, calculate a simple exponential average. Try $\alpha = 0.1$ and $\alpha = 0.3$, $F_0 = 300$. What is the forecast for quarter 1 of 1985?
2. For series B1, calculate a simple exponential average. Try $\alpha = 0.1$ and $\alpha = 0.3$, $F_0 = 300$. Which is the better α? What is the forecast for quarter 1 of 1985?
3. For series B2, calculate a simple exponential average. Try $\alpha = 0.1$ and $\alpha = 0.3$, $F_0 = 300$. Which is the better α? What is the forecast for quarter 1 of 1985?
4. For series C, calculate a simple exponential average with $\alpha = 0.2$ and $F_0 = 300$. What is the forecast for quarter 1 of 1985?
5. For series C, calculate a Winters trend average with $\alpha = 0.2$, $\beta = 0.05$, $F_0 = 300$, $T_0 = 0$. What is the forecast for quarter 1 of 1985?
6. For series D, calculate a Winters seasonal exponential average with $\alpha = 0.2$, $\gamma = 0.05$, and $F_0 = 300$. What is the forecast for quarter 1 of 1985?

TABLE 2.9 Data for Problems

Type of Series	Year	Q1			Q2			Q3			Q4		
		Jan.	*Feb.*	*Mar.*	*Apr.*	*May*	*June*	*Jul.*	*Aug.*	*Sep.*	*Oct.*	*Nov.*	*Dec.*
A. Constant	1984	97	93	110	98	104	103	99	108	106	94	109	95
B1. Impulse	1984	97	93	110	138	104	103	99	108	106	94	109	95
B2. Step	1983	97	93	110	98	130	133	129	138	136	124	139	125
	1984	122	127	125	126	139	127	134	128	134	136	132	121
C. Trend	1983	97	96	116	107	116	118	117	129	130	121	139	128
	1984	128	136	137	141	157	148	158	155	164	169	168	160
D. Constant with seasons	1982	145	121	121	88	73	52	50	75	95	103	142	143
	1983	138	126	105	86	76	49	52	69	94	117	133	137
	1984	164	139	117	82	64	53	53	65	95	99	139	141
E. Trend with seasons	1982	146	125	128	96	81	59	59	90	117	133	181	192
	1983	192	177	151	127	110	74	79	109	148	186	218	240
	1984	272	237	202	155	123	97	98	130	182	219	272	299
F. Intermittent	1983	85	54	98	90	0	0	92	0	99	0	78	0
	1984	78	0	55	75	87	0	73	0	0	0	0	53
G. Real company data	1982	212	254	291	236	194	229	255	239	303	231	207	219
	1983	201	246	268	176	178	256	199	192	261	161	142	163
	1984	172	143	219	128	157	132	128	170	219	134	108	208
H. Real company data	1982	162	205	265	158	145	171	145	165	251	186	193	183
	1983	192	200	245	149	185	174	159	175	252	172	166	166
	1984	165	199	233	164	158	182	182	139	231	165	173	181

Note: All figures in thousands of units.

7. For series E, calculate a Winters linear trend and ratio seasonals average. Use $\alpha = 0.2$, $\beta = 0.05$, $\gamma = 0.05$. What is the forecast for quarter 1 of 1985?

For the 1983 data series B2, our forecasting system generated the following forecasts:

	J	F	M	A	M	J	J	A	S	O	N	D
Forecast	100	100	100	100	102	104	106	108	110	112	114	116
Actual	97	93	110	98	130	133	129	138	136	124	139	125

8. For each month, calculate the running average of forecast error, the mean absolute deviation, and the tracking signal. Use $h = 0.05$. How would an adaptive response help the situation? (Assume $RAFE_0 = 1$ and $MAD_0 = 5$.)
9. Recommend a procedure to handle data series F.
10. Which model would you use for series G? Approximately what parameter values would you judge to be reasonable?
11. Which model would you use for series H? Approximately what parameter values would you judge to be reasonable?
12. What smoothing factor (α) is equivalent to six months in a moving average process? Is that a relatively high or low α?
13. What number of months would be equivalent to a α of 0.1? How responsive would such a moving average be?
14. We are presently in December and we've been using simple exponential smoothing ($\alpha = 0.3$) for the last twelve months. Hence, we have applied a weight of 0.3 to December sales and 0.21 to November sales in calculating December's exponential average. What weight did we apply to September's and October's sales?
15. Economists differentiate between demand and quantity demanded. In this chapter, we have not preserved that distinction. On the other hand, we have consistently spoken of demand rather than sales. We do this because sales figures do not adequately capture demand. What about lost sales due to stockouts? How would you recommend handling the following:
    a. Sales returns
    b. Orders for future delivery
    c. Keypunch errors in sales figures
    d. Special promotions.

The remaining questions should be solved with the help of a computer.

16. For demand series E, generate monthly forecasts for 1985. Justify your choice of α, β, and γ.

17. For demand series F, generate monthly forecasts for 1985. How meaningful are these forecasts? Can you suggest any sensible way to handle such data? What might cause such lumpiness?

18. For demand series H, choose a model and generate monthly forecasts for 1985. Now generate quarterly forecasts for 1985. Of which forecasts are you more confident?

19. Using a random number generator, generate a monthly demand series with the characteristics

$$D_t = 500 + 10t \pm e_t$$

where e_t is normally distributed with mean 500 + 10t and variance 100. Generate six years of data. Now, using the first five years to develop your forecasting system, attempt to forecast year 6, using (a) Winters trend model with seasons, and (b) Winters trend model without seasons. Which model gives you the best results?

20. Using a random number generator, generate a monthly demand series with the characteristics

$$D_t = 500 + 10_t \pm e_t \qquad t \leq 24$$
$$D_t = 2000 + 3t \pm e_t \qquad t > 24$$

where e_t is normally distributed with mean 500 ± 10t (2000 + 3t for $t > 24$) and variance 100. Generate six years of data. Now try to forecast year 6, using Winters trend model with seasons and using the trend model only.

21. In problem 20, how good is 1.25MAD as an estimate of the standard deviation of forecast error?

REFERENCES AND BIBLIOGRAPHY

1. G. E. P. Box and G. M. Jenkins, *Time Series Analysis: Forecasting and Control*, rev. ed. (San Francisco: Holden-Day, 1976).
2. R. G. Brown, *Smoothing, Forecasting and Prediction of Discrete Time Series* (Englewood Cliffs, N.J.: Prentice-Hall, 1963).
3. R. G. Brown, "The Balance of Effort in Forecasting," *Journal of Forecasting*, Vol. 1, No. 1 (January–March 1982), pp. 49–53.
4. P. E. Green and D. S. Tull, *Research for Marketing Decisions*, 4th ed. (Englewood Cliffs, N.J.: Prentice-Hall, 1978).

5. G. K. Groff, "Empirical Comparison of Models for Short Range Forecasting," *Management Science,* Vol. 20, No. 1 (September 1973), pp. 22–31.
6. C. C. Holt et al., *Planning Production, Inventories and Work Force* (Englewood Cliffs, N.J.: Prentice-Hall, 1960).
7. S. Makridakis and S. C. Wheelwright, *Forecasting Methods and Applications* (New York: John Wiley & Sons, 1978).
8. S. Makridakis et al., "The Accuracy of Extrapolation Methods," *Journal of Forecasting,* Vol. 1, No. 2 (April–June 1982), pp. 111–153.
9. J. O. McClain, "Dynamics of Exponential Smoothing with Trend and Seasonal Terms," *Management Science,* Vol. 20, No. 9 (May 1974), pp. 1300–1304.
10. D. W. McLeavey, et al., "An Empirical Evaluation of Individual Item Forecasting Models", *Decision Sciences,* Vol. 12, No. 4, (1981), pp. 708–714.
11. D. C. Montgomery and L. A. Johnson, *Forecasting and Time Series Analysis* (New York: McGraw-Hill, 1976).
12. J. F. Muth, "Optimal Properties of Exponentially Weighted Forecasts," *Journal of the American Statistical Association,* Vol. 55, No. 290 (1960), pp. 299–306.
13. C. C. Pegels, "Exponential Forecasting: Some New Variations," *Management Science,* Vol. 15, No. 5 (January 1969), pp. 311–315.
14. D. W. Trigg and A. G. Leach, "Exponential Smoothing with an Adaptive Response Rate," *Operational Research Quarterly,* Vol. 18, No. 1 (1967), pp. 53–59.
15. D. C. Whybark, "A Comparison of Adaptive Forecasting Techniques," *Logistics and Transportation Review,* Vol. 8, No. 3 (1972), pp. 13–26.
16. P. R. Winters, "Forecasting Sales by Exponentially Weighted Moving Averages," *Management Science,* Vol. 6, No. 3 (1960) pp. 324–342.
17. R. J. Wonnacott and T. H. Wonnacott, *Econometrics* (New York: John Wiley & Sons, 1970).

appendix 2A

Double Exponential Smoothing and Trend-Adjusted Exponential Smoothing

Two other forecasting models are quite popular, perhaps because of the robustness of trend-based models. McLeavey et al. [1], for example, found that double exponential smoothing performed well on a variety of demand patterns for forecasts one period ahead and twelve periods ahead. Double exponential smoothing and trend-adjusted exponential smoothing are alternative ways of incorporating trends into exponential smoothing. These two approaches can be shown to be exactly equivalent to Winters trend model (the Holt model) if the proper parameter values are chosen for each model. We present the double exponential smoothing and the trend-adjusted models here only because they have been so popular in the literature. The Winters model is as good.

Double Exponential Smoothing

Simple exponential smoothing does not cope very well with a trend. If we were to take equation 2.5 for simple exponential smoothing and to note that $E(S_t) = \mu + \delta t$, we could derive the expected value of the simple exponentially smoothed average. We would discover that we have undershot the mark:

Taking expectations

$$E(F_t) = \alpha \sum_{k=0}^{t-1} (1 - \alpha)^k E(D_{t-k}) + (1 - \alpha)^t F_0$$

and substituting for $E(D_{t-k})$

$$E(F_t) = \alpha \sum_{k=0}^{t-1} (1 - \alpha)^k [\mu + \delta (t - k)] + (1 - \alpha)^t F_0$$

As $t \to \infty$, we obtain

$$E(F_t) = [\mu + \delta t]\alpha \sum_{k=0}^{\infty} (1 - \alpha)^k - \delta\alpha \sum_{k=0}^{\infty} k(1 - \alpha)^k$$

$$E(F_t) = \mu + \delta t - \frac{1 - \alpha}{\alpha}\delta$$

$$E(F_t) = E(D_t) - \frac{1 - \alpha}{\alpha}\delta$$

Figure 2A.1 portrays the situation. At this juncture, we are helpless in estimating $E(D_t)$, since all we have are the figures F_t, D_t, and $(1 - \alpha)/\alpha$. What we need is an estimate of $[(1 - \alpha)/\alpha]\ \delta$, the vertical distance between $E(D_t)$, and our present position F_t.

Double or second-order exponential smoothing uses a trick to estimate $E(D_t)$. We can treat the F_t as a data series to be exponentially smoothed. The second-order smoothed average, $F_t^{(2)}$, will bear the same relationship to F_t as F_t bears to D_t. Specifically,

$$F_t^{(2)} = \alpha F_t + (1 - \alpha)F_{t-1}^{(2)}$$

$$E(F_t^{(2)}) = E(F_t) - \frac{(1 - \alpha)}{\alpha}\delta \quad \text{(cf. equation 2.6).}$$

and

$$E(\text{forecast of single average}) = E(\text{single average}) - \frac{(1 - \alpha)}{\alpha}\delta.$$

Now we are prepared to estimate $E(D_t)$. From equation 2.6, F_t can be expected to undershoot the mark by $[(1 - \alpha)/\alpha]\ \delta$. An estimate of $E(D_t)$ would be $F_t + [(1 - \alpha)/\alpha]\ \delta$. We have just seen, however, that $F_t^{(2)}$ can be expected to undershoot F_t by the same distance $[(1 - \alpha)/\alpha]\ \delta$. Using $F_t - F_t^{(2)}$ to estimate $[(1 - \alpha)/\alpha]\ \delta$, our estimate of $E(D_t)$ will be $F_t + F_t - F_t^{(2)} = 2F_t - F_t^{(2)}$. To forecast D_{t+j}—that is, to generate a j-period-ahead forecast, we could use $E(D_t)$ + slope * j. Since the height over the base gives us the slope, we take $F_t - F_t^{(2)}$ over $(1 - \alpha)/\alpha$ as the slope in figure 2A.1. At the end of period t, we would forecast demand in period $t + 1$ as

$$f_{t+1} = 2F_t - F_t^{(2)} + \frac{\alpha}{(1 - \alpha)}(F_t - F_t^{(2)}) * 1$$

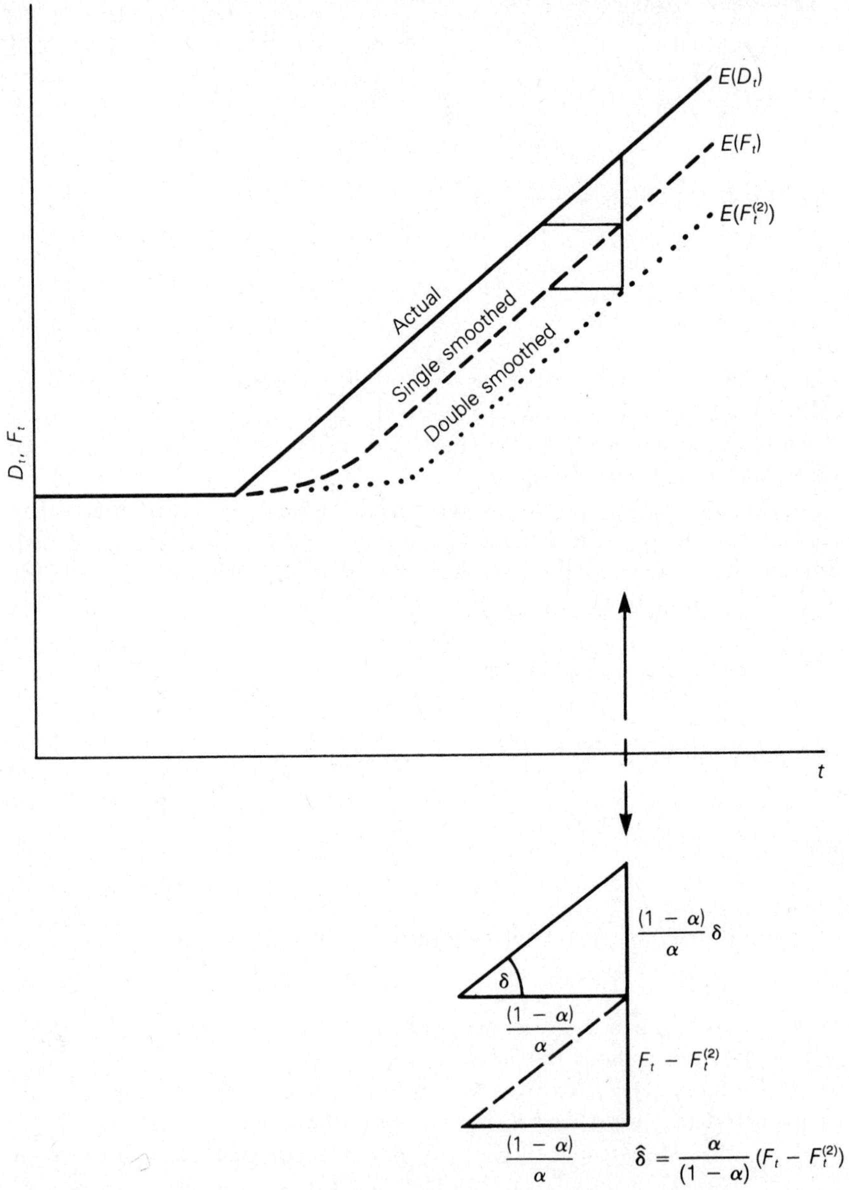

$E(D_t)$

$E(F_t)$

$E(F_t^{(2)})$

Actual

Single smoothed

Double smoothed

D_t, F_t

t

$\frac{(1-\alpha)}{\alpha}\delta$

δ

$\frac{(1-\alpha)}{\alpha}$

$F_t - F_t^{(2)}$

$\frac{(1-\alpha)}{\alpha}$

$$\hat{\delta} = \frac{\alpha}{(1-\alpha)}(F_t - F_t^{(2)})$$

FIGURE 2A.1 The response of simple exponential smoothing to a trend

TABLE 2A.1 Double Exponentially Smoothed Forecast

Month	*Demand* (D_t)	*Average* (F_t) $F_0 = 480$	*Average* $F_t^{(2)}$	*Forecast* f_t
March	460	476	479.2	472
April	510	482.8	479.9	472
May	520	490.2	482	486.4
June	495	491.2	483.8	500.5
July	475	488	484.6	500.5
August	560	502.4	488.2	492.3
September	510	503.9	491.3	520.2
October	520	507.1	494.5	519.7
November	540	513.7	498.3	522.9
December	550	521	502.8	533
January				543.8

Example 2A.1

Develop a double smoothed forecast for the firm in example 2.3, using $\alpha = 0.2$, $F_0 = 480$, and $F_0^{(2)} = 480$ (see table 2A.1).

$$F_1^{(2)} = 0.2 * 476 + 0.8 * 480 = 479.2$$

$$f_2 = 2 * 476 - 479.2 + \frac{0.2}{0.8}(476 - 479.2) = 472$$

$$F_2 = 0.2\,(510) + 0.8\,(476) = 482.8$$

$$F_2^{(2)} = 0.2(482.8) + 0.8(479.2) = 479.9$$

Trend-Adjusted Exponential Smoothing

An equivalent method of handling the same trend process relies on a direct estimate of the slope δ. The demand process, $E(D_t)$, will again be estimated by $F_t + [(1 - \alpha)/\alpha]\,\delta$. To estimate δ, we simply smooth the differences between succeeding exponentially smoothed averages:

$$T_t = \beta(F_t - F_{t-1}) + (1 - \beta)T_{t-1}$$

with $T_0 = 0$. This procedure is justified by the observation that $E(F_t) - E(F_{t-1}) = E(D_t) - E(D_{t-1})$ from equation 2.6, but that $E(D_t) - E(D_{t-1}) = \delta$. Hence, T_t estimates δ, and we can use $F_t + [(1 - \alpha/\alpha]\,T_t$ to estimate $E(D_t)$.

Our forecast for period $t + 1$ would be

$$f_{t+1} = F_t + \frac{(1 - \alpha)}{\alpha}T_t + T_t = F_t + \frac{1}{\alpha}T_t$$

TABLE 2A.2 Trend-adjusted Exponentially Weighted Forecast

Month	*Demand* (D_t)	*Average* (F_t) $F_0 = 480$	*Trend* (T_t)	*Forecast* (f_t)
March	460	476	−0.8	
April	510	482.8	0.72	472
May	520	490.2	2.04	486.4
June	495	491.2	1.83	500.4
July	475	488	0.82	500.4
August	560	502.4	3.54	492.1
September	510	503.9	3.13	520.1
October	520	507.1	3.14	519.6
November	540	513.7	3.83	522.8
December	550	521	4.60	532.9
January				544

Example 2A.2

Develop a trend-adjusted exponential forecast for the firm in example 2.3. Assume $T_0 = 0$, $F_0 = 480$, and $\alpha = 0.2$, $\beta = 0.2$ (see table 2A.2).

$$T_1 = 0.2\,(475 - 480) + 0.8(0) = -0.8$$

$$f_2 = 476 + \frac{1}{0.2}(-0.8) = 472$$

REFERENCE

1. D. W. McLeavey et al., "An Empirical Evaluation of Individual Item Forecasting Models," *Decision Sciences*, Vol. 12, No. 4 (1981), pp. 708–714.

appendix 2B

Forecasting by Extrapolation: Conclusions from Twenty-Five Years of Research

J. Scott Armstrong
Wharton School, University of Pennsylvania

Have advances in extrapolation methods helped to make better short-range forecasts now than in 1960? I am defining extrapolation as methods that rely solely on historical data from the series to be forecast. No other information is used. This class of methods is widely used in forecasting, especially for inventory control, process control, and in situations where other relevant data are not available.

This paper describes a forecasting procedure that was used in 1960. Then it presents evidence from research published over the last quarter of a century.

Short-Range Forecasting in 1960

As an industrial engineer at Eastman Kodak in the early 1960s, I examined the short-range forecasting system for color print orders from customers.

Acknowledgments: Partial support for this paper was provided by the Dept. of Decision Sciences, College of Business Administration, U. of Hawaii. Helpful comments were provided by R. G. Brown, R. Carbone, C. Chatfield, K. Cogger, M. Haight, E. Gardner, S. Gillis, R. Fildes, A. Koehler, J. Ledolter, E. Lusk, E. Mahmoud, S. Makridakis, D. McLeavey, M. May, J. B. O'Brien, and others. It is safe to say that not all of these reviewers are in complete agreement with all of the viewpoints presented here.

These forecasts were needed to schedule part-time workers and to control inventories. The procedure that had been used for many years prior to 1960 had the following characteristics:

- Weekly historical data on each type of order were collected on the basis of billing records. In general, these data were thought to be accurate. Outliers were adjusted or removed.
- Graphs were prepared for the more important items.
- The forecasts were then prepared judgmentally by a man who had been doing this job for many years.

Existing literature implied that better forecasts could be obtained by using objective methods. Accordingly, I developed and tested a model that used exponential smoothing of deseasonalized data. The deseasonalizing also included adjustments for trading days and holidays. Search procedures were then used to find the most appropriate smoothing factors for the average and the additive trend. The procedures were based primarily on Brown [1959] and Shiskin [1958].

Historical comparisons showed that the exponential smoothing model was superior to the judgmental method for almost all items. Side-by-side comparisons over the next six months provided additional evidence on the superiority of the exponential smoothing model.

Progress Since 1960

Many sophisticated approaches to extrapolation methods have been developed since 1960. Sophistication has come in two forms: sophisticated methods are used to select the appropriate type of model (e.g., Box-Jenkins procedures), and complex models are used to analyze historical data.

This sophistication calls for a better understanding of mathematics. It has also led to an increase in jargon. (For example, the term "univariate time series methods" is often used instead of "extrapolation.") Sophisticated approaches frequently lead to more complex forecasting models which are difficult to understand. Forecasters tell me that few of the people in their organization understand these sophisticated methods.

Numerous theoretical papers have made claims for the superiority of the more sophisticated methods. Often, these methods are shown to provide a better fit to historical data.

Are these more sophisticated methods better? One can examine this question using many criteria. On the *cost* side, more sophisticated methods are generally more difficult to understand, and they cost more to develop, maintain, and operate. On the *benefit* side, more sophisticated methods may be expected to produce more accurate forecasts and to provide a better assessment of uncertainty. (Other criteria are also important, but in this paper I am considering only forecasting.)

An assessment of the relative accuracy of sophisticated versus simple methods is provided in Table 2B.1. This table lists all the published studies that I could find (although I would not claim that the list is exhaustive). In addition to a library search, I relied heavily on experts in the field to identify relevant studies. Only empirical studies that provided forecast comparisons were included. My ratings of sophistication were subjective and others might have different opinions. The simple end of the continuum includes "no change" or "constant trend" models. Exponential smoothing was regarded as more sophisticated than moving averages, despite the fact that exponential smoothing is less expensive. Added sophistication is provided by methods where the parameters change as new observations are received, or by methods that use more terms or more complex relationships to time. Box-Jenkins procedures provide a sophisticated approach to selecting and estimating the proper model.

Table 2B.1 shows that the scientific evaluation of extrapolation methods is comparatively recent. None of the 38 studies were published prior to 1960. Six studies were published in the 1960s, and 24 were published in the 1970s. This indicates a rapid growth rate in evaluation research on extrapolation methods.

More important, Table 2B.1 provides little evidence to suggest that sophistication beyond the methods available in the 1960s has had any payoff. Relatively simple methods seem to offer comparable accuracy; 21 studies concluded that there were negligible differences, and for the 17 studies showing differences, 11 favored sophistication, and six favored simplicity. However, of the 11 cases favoring sophistication, three have since been challenged, and three cases were based on the superiority of exponential smoothing (available prior to 1960). We are left with five comparisons favoring sophistication and six favoring simplicity.

In general, the findings on sophisticated methods are puzzling, and it is unlikely that they could have been anticipated in 1960. Many of the sophisticated methods made good sense. For example, it seemed reasonable to expect that models in which the parameters are automatically revised as new information comes in should be more accurate. Results of the studies offer little support to this viewpoint: Four studies favor the use of adaptive parameters, two show no difference, and three suggest that adaptive parameters are less accurate. Furthermore, Gardner's [1983] reevaluation of Chow's [1965] data yielded different conclusions, and Ekern's [1981] reanalysis of data from the Whybark [1973] and Dennis [1978] studies challenged their conclusions, so three of the positive findings did not hold up. The box score for models with adaptive parameters does not look good so far. A simulation study by Kahl and Ledolter [1983] suggested that adaptive methods help if, in fact, the parameters do vary. Otherwise,

TABLE 2B.1 The Accuracy of Sophisticated Versus Simple Methods for Forecasting

Study	*Major Comparisons*	*Results*
Winters (1960)	exponential smoothing vs. moving averages	+
Frank (1969)	" " " " "	+
Elton & Gruber (1972)	" " " " "	+
Chow (1965)	adaptive vs. constant parameters	+
Whybark (1972)	" " " "	+
Smith (1974)	" " " "	+
Dennis (1978)	" " " "	+
Brown and Rozeff (1978)	Box-Jenkins vs. simple trend	+
Newbold & Granger (1974)	Box-Jenkins vs. exponential smoothing	+
Reid (1975)	" " " "	+
Dalrymple (1978)	Box-Jenkins vs. regression	+
Kirby (1966)	exponential smoothing vs. moving averages	0
Adam (1973)	" " " "	0
Raine (1971)	adaptive vs. constant parameters	0
Dancer & Gray (1977)	" " " "	0
Chatfield & Prothero (1973)	Box-Jenkins vs. no-change	0
Albrecht et al. (1977)	" " "	0
Bates Granger (1969)	Box-Jenkins vs. exponential smoothing	0
Groff (1973)	" " " "	0
Geurts & Ibrahim (1975)	" " " "	0
Mabert (1976)	" " " "	0
Chatfield (1978)	" " " "	0
Kenny & Durbin (1982)	" " " "	0

Torfin & Hoffman (1968)	6 models of varying complexity	0
Markland (1970)	4 " " " "	0
Johnson & Schmitt (1974)	10 " " " "	0
Carey (1978)	21 " " " "	0
Hagerman & Ruland (1979)	3 " " " "	0
Makridakis & Hibon (1979)	22 " " " "	0
Ruland (1980)	8 " " " "	0
Makridakis et al. (1982)	21 " " " "	0
Armstrong (1975)	complex curve vs. rule of thumb	0
Mabert (1978)	adaptive vs. constant parameters	
Gardner & Dannenbring (1980)	adaptive vs. constant parameters	–
McLeavey, Lee & Adam (1981)	" " " "	–
Ledolter & Abraham (1981)	simple vs. complex models	–
Coggin & Hunter (1982–3)	" " " "	–
Brandon, Jarrett & Khumawala (1983)	Box-Jenkins vs. 8 simple models	–

For "results" a "+" means sophisticated methods were more accurate, a "0" means negligible difference, and a "–" means simple methods were more accurate.

adaptive methods react unfavorably to random noise and lead to greater errors. But Kahl and Ledolter questioned whether it is possible to identify situations where the parameters do change in the real world. It does suggest that manual intervention might help when other evidence clearly indicates that a change has occurred (e.g., the new tax laws might affect the relationships).

Highly complex models may reduce accuracy. While these complex models provide better fits to historical data, this superiority does not hold for forecasting. The danger is especially serious when limited historical data are available. Ledolter and Abraham [1981] show that unnecessary parameters in the estimation model will increase the mean square forecast error by $1/n$ (where n is the number of historical observations).

Of particular interest in the evaluations listed in Table 2B.1 are the large scale empirical studies by Makridakis and Hibon [1979], which examined forecasts for 111 time series, and Makridakis et al. [1982], which examined forecasts for 1001 time series (the latter study being known as the M-Competition). In general, these studies did not offer much support for sophisticated methods. Both studies were subjected to much re-examination, especially the M-Competition (see Armstrong and Lusk [1983]). McLaughlin [1983], one of the commentators in the M-Competition, reanalyzed forecasts from 15 of the methods, and found that a naive model based on the assumption that the next period would be the same as the last (using seasonally adjusted data) was superior to more sophisticated extrapolations for nine of 15 comparisons.

Some have suggested that sophisticated methods will prove more accurate if *properly used* by experts (e.g., see Chatfield [1978, p. 266]). Is it important to match the sophistication of the method with the expertise of the user? Evidence to date suggests, surprisingly, that this concern is not an important one, given that the user has achieved a certain (seemingly modest) level of expertise. For example, the M-Competition results were largely supportive of Makridakis and Hibon [1979] even though the M-Competition was designed to have outstanding experts for each method. Automatic procedures produced accuracy from sophisticated methods equivalent to that produced when these methods were used by experts [Hill and Fildes 1984]; this suggests that there is little need for experts. Also, a study by Carbone, Andersen, Corriveau and Corson [1983] found that students with a modest amount of instruction were able to do as well as experts when using Box-Jenkins and other methods. In an extension of the preceding study, however, Carbone and Gorr [1984] found that nine hours of classroom instruction were not sufficient to bring the accuracy of novices up to that obtained by experts.

Some have suggested, based on *ex post* interpretations of the M-Competition, that sophistication might be relevant in certain situations. I would have found this argument more convincing had their hypotheses on "which methods would be better in what situations" been stated *prior* to the M-Competition.

My conclusions about the value of simple methods for forecasting in business and economics reminds me of the history of extrapolation methods for demographic forecasting. Dorn [1950] and Hajnal [1955], in their reviews of the evidence, both suggested that the more thought demographers put into their extrapolations, the more complex their methods became, but the poorer their accuracy.

Alternatives to Sophistication

Although the development of sophisticated methods has yielded little gain to date some areas do seem worthy of further research. It may be possible to clearly identify which methods will be better in given situations. To do this, I suggest experimental studies comparing specific methods, rather than the M-Competition, where models that utilized a variety of methods were contrasted. For example, one might study whether the attenuation (or dampening) of trend factors would produce better forecasts in situations involving large changes. Also, one could examine whether the attenuation of seasonal factors improves accuracy in situations with large but difficult to measure seasonal factors.

Lawrence [1983] concluded that people can do as well as computers and sophisticated methods in extrapolating trends. These results were obtained even though the people had no information other than the historical data on the series being forecasted. In other words, the extrapolation by person was based on the same information as the extrapolation by computer. More recent results by Lawrence, Edmundson, and O'Connor [1984] support Lawrence's original findings. However, Carbone and Gorr [1984] found that objective extrapolations were more accurate than subjective ("eyeball") extrapolations. These studies suggest that further research is needed on when and how to use judgment for extrapolation.

Still another area of promise is the strategy of combining forecasts from different extrapolation methods. Newbold and Granger [1974], in a study of 80 monthly time series, showed that the best forecast can, usually, be improved by combining it with a forecast from another extrapolation method. Morris [1977], in a forecast of the sunspot cycle, reduced the error by 50% when combining forecasts from two different extrapolation models; however, the weights on each forecast were selected after the fact, so the gain is suspect. Additional evidence is provided in Table 2B.2, which summarizes all studies that I could find that made an estimate of the magnitude of error reduction that resulted from combining forecasts. The Bates and Granger and the Ogburn results are based on my reanalysis of their results.

TABLE 2B.2 Percentage Reduction in Error by Combining Extrapolation Forecasts (vs. Average Error of Component Forecasts)

			Entries Are the Percentage Error Reductions When the Number of Methods Combined Was:			
Study	*Data*	*Criteria**	2	3	4	5
Armstrong [1978, p. 167]	International Photographic Market	MAPE	17	37	—	—
Bates & Granger [1969]	International Air Travel	RMSE	12	—	—	—
Ogburn [1946]	Air Travel Market	MAPE	—	—	—	64
Reinmuth & Geurts [1979]	Salt Lake Retail Sales	Theil's U2	80	92	—	—
Bunn [1979]	Tourists to Hawaii	RMSE	60	—	—	—

*MAPE = Mean Absolute Percentage Error; RMSE = Root Mean Square Error

The combinations produced significant gains in comparison with the typical (average) forecast error of the methods used, but the sample sizes for these studies were small.

More impressive evidence on the value of combined forecasts was presented by Makridakis and Winkler [1983] using data from the 1001 series in the M-Competition data. If one does not know which of a set of extrapolation forecasts is most accurate (this being the typical case), then combining forecasts produces dramatic gains. Although the extent of the gains diminished with each additional method in their study, substantial benefits were made even for the fourth or fifth methods.

The question of how many forecasts to combine is, of course, a cost/benefit issue. Even if you know which is the best extrapolation method (an unusual situation), the strategy of combining forecasts is likely to help, especially if a number of methods are combined.

Given that we know little about the best way to weight the components of a combined forecast, I suggest starting with the cheapest method, and then invest in successively more expensive methods. Use methods that are as different as possible, and simply weight each forecast equally. (However, recent results by Winkler and Makridakis [1983], suggest that weighting may yield small gains in some situations.)

Conspicuous by its absence is research on the best way to assess uncertainty in these forecasts. Williams and Goodman [1971] and Newbold and Granger [1974] did find that the confidence intervals developed by simulating the use of the extrapolation to "forecast" over a historical period provided good estimates of uncertainty. Other than that, much uncertainty exists about how to best estimate uncertainty.

Conclusions

Since 1960, significant effort has been devoted to the development of sophisticated methods for forecasting by extrapolation. Shortly after this, research began to evaluate these new methods. Research on the evaluation of extrapolation methods has been growing rapidly and evidence is now available from more than 40 studies.

For further research on extrapolation, experimental designs should be used to assess hypotheses on each component in specific situations (e.g., what is the value of attenuating the trend where large changes are forecasted?), the assessment of the most effective way to use experts, the use of combined forecasts, and the best way to assess uncertainty.

In addition to using empirical and simulated data, researchers can test hypotheses using previously published research. Only recently has the number of studies become large enough to allow for this type of research. *Quantitative* reviews of this research would be especially valuable, as demonstrated in the experiment by Cooper and Rosenthal [1980].

For the practitioner, the implications are clear: Relatively simple methods, like those described by Brown [1959], Shiskin [1958], and Winters [1960], are adequate. The analyst should make adjustments for outliers, trading days, and seasonality, then using a relatively simple method such as exponential smoothing to estimate trend and seasonal factors. Simple methods provide equivalent accuracy at a lower cost and they are easier to understand. Remember the advice of William of Occam, who said "one should not introduce complexities unless absolutely necessary." (Despite the fact that William died of the Black Death in 1349, "Occam's Razor" is good advice.) Finally, combine the forecasts from two or more simple methods and use equal weights.

REFERENCES

Adam, Everett, Jr. 1973, "Individual Item Forecasting Model Evaluation," *Decision Sciences*, Vol. 4, No. 4, pp. 458–470.

Albrecht, W. S.; Lookabill, L. L.; and McKeown, J. C. 1977, "The Time Series Properties of Annual Earnings," *Journal of Accounting Research*, Vol. 15, No. 2, pp. 226–244.

Armstrong, J. Scott 1975, "Monetary Incentives in Mail Surveys," *Public Opinion Quarterly*, Vol. 39 (Spring), pp. 111–116.

Armstrong, J. Scott 1978, *Long-Range Forecasting: From Crystal Ball to Computer*, John Wiley, New York.

Armstrong, J. Scott and Lusk, Edward J. 1983, "The Accuracy of Alternative Extrapolation Models: Analysis of a Forecasting Competition Through Open Peer Review," *Journal of Forecasting*, Vol. 2, No. 3, pp. 259–262, with commentary and replies on pages 263–311.

Bates, J. M. and Granger, C. W. J. 1969, "The Combination of Forecasts," *Operational Research Quarterly,* Vol. 20, No. 4, pp. 451–468.

Box, George E. and Jenkins, G. M. 1970, *Time Series Analysis: Forecasting and Control.* Holden-Day, San Francisco.

Brandon, C. H.; Jarrett, J. E.; and Khumawala, S. B. 1983, "Revising Forecasts of Accounting Earnings: A Comparison with the Box-Jenkins Method," *Management Science,* Vol. 29, No. 2, pp. 256–263.

Brown, L. D. and Rozeff, M. S. 1978, "The Superiority of Analyst Forecasts as Measures of Expectations: Evidence from Earnings," *Journal of Finance,* Vol. 33, No. 1, pp. 1–16.

Brown, Robert G. 1959, *Statistical Forecasting for Inventory Control.* McGraw-Hill, New York.

Bunn, Derek W. 1979, "The Synthesis of Predictive Models in Marketing Research," *Journal of Marketing Research,* Vol. 16 (May), pp. 280–283.

Carbone, Robert; Andersen, A.; Corriveau, J.; and Corson, P. P. 1983, "Comparing for Different Time Series Methods the Value of Technical Expertise, Individualized Analysis and Judgmental Adjustment," *Management Science,* Vol. 29 (May), pp. 559–566.

Carbone, Robert A. and Gorr, Wilpen L. 1984, "The Relative Accuracy of Judgmental Forecasting of Time Series," *Journal of Forecasting* (in press).

Carey, K. J. 1978, "The Accuracy of Estimates of Earnings from Naive Models," *Journal of Economics and Business,* Vol. 30, No. 3, pp. 182–193.

Chatfield, C. 1978, "The Holt-Winters Forecasting Procedure," *Applied Statistics (C),* Vol. 27, No. 3, pp. 264–279.

Chatfield, C. and Prothero, D. L. 1973, "Box-Jenkins Seasonal Forecasting: Problems in a Case Study," *Journal of the Royal Statistical Society: Series A,* Vol. 136, Part 3, pp. 295–352.

Chow, W. M. 1965, "Adaptive Control of the Exponential Smoothing Constant," *Journal of Industrial Engineering,* Vol. 16, No. 5, pp. 314–317.

Coggin, T. Daniel and Hunter, John E. 1982–3, "Analysts EPS Forecasts Nearer Actual than Statistical Models," *Journal of Business Forecasting,* Vol. 1 (Winter), pp. 20–23.

Cooper, Harris M. and Rosenthal, Robert 1980, "Statistical Versus Traditional Procedures for Summarizing Research Findings," *Psychological Bulletin,* Vol. 87, No. 3, pp. 442–449.

Dalrymple, Douglas J. 1978, "Using Box-Jenkins in Sales Forecasting," *Journal of Business Research,* Vol. 6, No. 2, pp. 133–145.

Dancer, Robert and Gray, Clifford 1977, "An Empirical Evaluation of Constant and Adaptive Computer Forecasting Models for Inventory Control," *Decision Sciences,* Vol. 8, No. 1, pp. 228–238.

Dennis, J. D. 1978, "A Performance Test of a Run-Based Adaptive Exponential Forecasting Technique," *Production and Inventory Management,* Vol. 19, No. 2, pp. 43–46.

Dorn, Harold F. 1950, "Pitfalls in Population Forecasts and Projections," *Journal of the American Statistical Association,* Vol. 45, No. 251, pp. 311–334.

Ekern, Steinar 1981, "Adaptive Exponential Smoothing Revisited," *Journal of the Operational Research Society,* Vol. 32, No. 9, pp. 775–782.

Elton, Edwin J. and Gruber, Martin J. 1972, "Earnings Estimates and the Accuracy of Expectational Data," *Management Science,* Vol. 18, No. 8, pp. B409–B424.

Frank, Werner 1969, "A Study of the Predictive Significance of Two Income Measures," *Journal of Accounting Research,* Vol. 7, No. 1, pp. 123–136.

Gardner, Everette S., Jr. 1983, "Evolutionary Operation of the Exponential Smoothing Parameter: Revisited," *Omega,* Vol. 11, No. 6, pp. 621–623.

Gardner, Everette S., Jr. and Dannenbring, David G. 1980, "Forecasting with Exponential Smoothing: Some Guidelines for Model Selection," *Decision Sciences,* Vol. 11, No. 2, pp. 370–383.

Geurts, Michael D. and Ibrahim, I. B. 1975, "Comparing the Box-Jenkins Approach with the Exponentially Smoothed Forecasting Model Application to Hawaii Tourists," *Journal of Marketing Research,* Vol. 12 (May), pp. 182–188.

Groff, Gene K. 1973, "Empirical Comparison of Models for Short Range Forecasting," *Management Science,* Vol. 20, No. 1, pp. 22–31.

Hagerman, R. L. and Ruland, W. 1979, "The Accuracy of Management Forecasts and Forecasts of Single Alternative Models," *Journal of Economics and Business,* Vol. 31, No. 3, pp. 172–179.

Hajnal, John 1955, "The Prospects for Population Forecasts," *Journal of the American Statistical Association,* Vol. 50, No. 270, pp. 309–327.

Hill, Gareth and Fildes, Robert 1984, "The Accuracy of Extrapolation Methods: An Automatic Box-Jenkins Package (SIFT)," *Journal of Forecasting* (in press).

Johnson, T. E. and Schmitt, T. G. 1974, "Effectiveness of Earnings per Share Forecasts," *Financial Management,* Vol. 3 (Summer), pp. 64–72.

Kahl, Douglas R. and Ledolter, Johannes 1983, "A Recursive Kalman Filter Forecasting Approach," *Management Science,* Vol. 29, No. 11, pp. 1325–1333.

Kenny, Peter B. and Durbin, James 1982, "Local Trend Estimation and Seasonal Adjustment of Economic and Social Time Series," (with discussion), *Journal of the Royal Statistical Society: Series A,* Vol. 145 (1982), Part 1, 1–41.

Kirby, Robert M. 1966, "A Comparison of Short and Medium Range Statistical Forecasting Methods," *Management Science,* Vol. 13, No. 4, pp. B202–B210.

Lawrence, M. J. 1983, "An Exploration of Some Practical Issues in the Use of Quantitative Forecasting Models," *Journal of Forecasting,* Vol. 2, No. 2, pp. 169–179.

Lawrence, M. J., Edmundson, R. H., and O'Connor, M. J. 1984, "An Examination of the Accuracy of Judgmental Extrapolation," *Journal of Forecasting* (in press).

Ledolter, Johannes and Abraham, Bovas 1981, "Parsimony and its Importance in Time Series Forecasting," *Technometrics,* Vol. 23, No. 4, pp. 411–414.

Mabert, Vincent A. 1976, "Statistical versus Sales Force-Executive Opinion Short Range Forecasts: A Time Series Case Study," *Decision Sciences,* Vol. 7, No. 2, pp. 310–318.

Mabert, Vincent A. 1978, "Forecast Modification Based Upon Residual Analysis: A Case Study on Check Volume Estimation, *Decision Sciences,* Vol. 9, No. 2, pp. 285–296.

Makridakis, Spyros; Andersen, A.; Carbone, R.; Fildes, R.; Hibon, M.; Lewandowski, R.; Newton, J.; Parzen, E.; and Winkler, R. 1982, "The Accuracy of Extrapolation (Time Series) Methods: Results of a Forecasting Competition," *Journal of Forecasting,* Vol. 1, No. 2, pp. 111–153.

Makridakis, Spyros and Hibon, Michele 1979, "Accuracy of Forecasting: An Empirical Investigation," *Journal of the Royal Statistical Society Series A,* (with discussion), Vol. 142, Part 2, pp. 97–145.

Makridakis, Spyros and Winkler, Robert L. 1983, "Averages of Forecasts: Some Empirical Results," *Management Science,* Vol. 29, No. 9, pp. 987–996.

Markland, Robert E. 1970, "A Comparative Study of Demand Forecasting Techniques for Military Helicopter Spare Parts," *Naval Research Logistics Quarterly,* 17, No. 1, pp. 103–119.

McLeavey, Dennis W.; Lee, T. S.; and Adam, E. E. 1981, "An Empirical Evaluation of Individual Item Forecasting Models," *Decision Sciences,* Vol. 12, No. 4, pp. 708–714.

Morris, M. J. 1977, "Forecasting the Sunspot Cycle," *Journal of the Royal Statistical Society Series A,* Vol. 140, Part 4, pp. 437–468.

Newbold, Paul and Granger, C. W. J. 1974, "Experience with Forecasting Univariate Time Series and the Combination of Forecasts," *Journal of the Royal Statistical Society Series A,* Vol. 137, Part 2, pp. 131–165.

Ogburn, William F. 1934, "Studies in Prediction and Distortion of Reality," *Social Forces,* Vol. 13, No. 2, pp. 224–229.

Raine, Jesse E. 1971, "Self-Adaptive Forecasting Reconsidered," *Decision Sciences,* Vol. 2, No. 2, pp. 181–191.

Reid, David J. 1975, "A Review of Short Term Projection Techniques," in H. A. Gordon (ed.), *Practical Aspects of Forecasting.* Operational Research Society, London.

Reinmuth, James E. and Geurts, Michael D. 1979, "A Multideterministic Approach to Forecasting," in S. Makridakis and S. C. Wheelwright (eds.), *Forecasting,* North Holland, New York.

Ruland, W. 1980, "On the Choice of Simple Extrapolative Model Forecasts of Annual Earnings," *Financial Management,* Vol. 9 (Summer), No. 2, pp. 30–37.

Shiskin, Julius 1958, "Decomposition of Economic Time Series," *Science,* Vol. 128, No. 3338, pp. 1539–1546.

Smith, David E. 1974, "Adaptive Response for Exponential Smoothing: Comparative System Analysis," *Operational Research Quarterly,* Vol. 25, No. 2, pp. 421–435.

Torfin, Gary P. and Hoffman, T. R. 1968, "Simulation Tests of Some Forecasting Techniques," *Production and Inventory Management,* Vol. 9, No. 2, pp. 72–78.

Whybark, D. Clay 1973, "A Comparison of Adaptive Forecasting Techniques," *Logistics and Transportation Review,* Vol. 8, No. 3, pp. 13–26.

Williams, W. H. and Goodman, M. L. 1971, "A Simple Method for the Construction of Empirical Confidence Limits for Economic Forecasts," *Journal of the American Statistical Association,* Vol. 66, No. 336, pp. 752–754.

Winkler, Robert L. and Makridakis, Spyros 1983, "The Combination of Forecasts," *Journal of the Royal Statistical Society Series A,* Vol. 146, Part 2, pp. 150–157.

Winters, Peter R. 1960, "Forecasting Sales by Exponentially Weighted Moving Averages," *Management Science,* Vol. 6, No. 3, pp. 324–342.

chapter three

Multi-Item Forecasting

Chapter 2 presented many techniques for generating individual item forecasts. These techniques can also be used to forecast the demand for a group or family of items. For example, an apparel line may consist of several sizes and colors, or an automotive line may have several choices of an option, such as four-, six-, and eight-cylinder engines. As another example, a specific item may be stocked in several distribution locations, which are known as stock keeping units (SKU). In many of these situations, forecasts of individual item demands are neither economically feasible nor desirable, as will be discussed in the chapter on the master production schedule. We also know that we can generate a more accurate forecast for a group of items than for individual items in the group. Therefore, in many instances, we will resort to forecasting a group, family, or line of items as a whole. Once the total forecast for the entire line is generated, we can generate forecasts for every item in the line. Similarly, the total requirements forecast of a specific item in many distribution locations can be allocated to individual locations.

An accurate forecast of demand for an item at each specific location can improve customer service while keeping inventory and transportation costs in line. A better demand forecast for every item can definitely improve production planning, as exhibited in figure 3.1. In general forecasts of families of products assist manufacturing in committing a base plan or a rate of manufacture. Then a detailed forecast of each item is planned for the master production schedule.

Item-level forecasts are the major inputs to the material requirements planning (MRP) systems via master production schedules. Therefore, these forecasts are important for overall planning in many instances [6]. A later chapter will focus on the importance of keeping the number of end items as low as possible on the master production schedule, using a technique known as modularization to accomplish this goal. Several other special situations exist in the industry, however. For example, many seasonal items such as wood stoves, fans, and other consumer goods are carried only during a particular season. Many of these seasonal items also reach a peak during

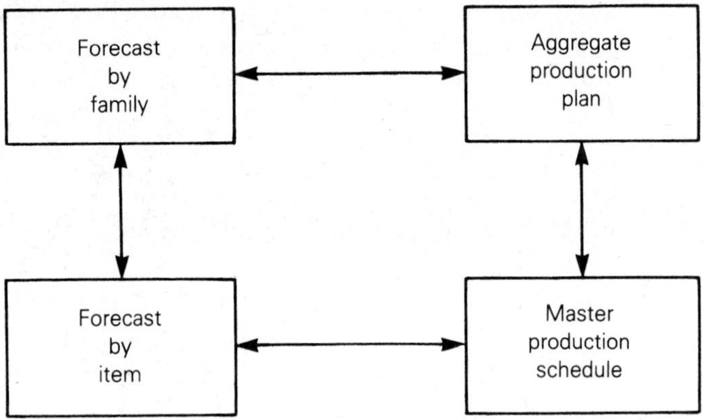

FIGURE 3.1 Demand management

the season before the demand slows down. The timing of the peak may vary, but the total demand for the season may be forecast most accurately using regression analysis or other forecasting techniques. Such situations require what is known as multi-item or multidimensional forecasting, whereby forecasts can be generated simultaneously for each item in the group. The first step of such forecasting involves estimating the probability distribution of demand for each item in the group (line or family) or SKU. The second step is to apply one of the models described in this chapter to forecast the demand for an individual item belonging to a group. To utilize these models, we should have a forecast for the group of items as a whole, which can be accomplished by using one of the models described in chapter 2.

Vector Smoothing Method for an Item

Brown [1] illustrates the use of smoothing techniques to find current estimates of the probability distribution of demands. The item demands are grouped into several intervals, and the probability of an item demand falling in an interval is estimated initially with the existing demand data. As new demands become available, the probability values are updated using smoothing techniques. The procedure is known as the vector smoothing method:

$$P_{k,t+1} = \alpha q_{kt} + (1 - \alpha)P_{kt}$$

where $P_{k,t+1}$ represents the updated probability distribution of an item in the interval k for the period $t + 1$, α is the smoothing constant, and q_{kt} is the actual distribution of demand during period t. The vector smoothing technique requires that the time series being forecast be relatively stable or that the demand be slowly shifting as a function of time.

Example 3.1

The following table exhibits the class intervals and the frequency distribution of demand for the past seven weeks. Assuming that the actual demand during the thirty-seventh day was twenty-one, find the updated probabilities, using $\alpha = .20$:

K	*Interval*	*Frequency*	$P_{k,37}$
1	0–9	11	0.306
2	10–19	17	0.472
3	20–29	5	0.139
4	30–40	3	0.083

Solution: Since the actual demand during the thirty-seventh day was twenty-one, it falls in the third interval. Therefore, $q_{3,37} = 1$, and all other values in the q vector become zeros. Since the value of $P_{k,37}$ is given in the table, we can update the probabilities using the preceding formula. The current estimates of the probability distribution of demand are as follows:

$$P_{k,38} = \alpha q_{k,37} + (1 - \alpha)P_{k,37}$$

$$= (0.2)\begin{bmatrix}0\\0\\1\\0\end{bmatrix} + (1 - 0.2)\begin{bmatrix}0.306\\0.472\\0.139\\0.083\end{bmatrix}$$

$$= \begin{bmatrix}0\\0\\0.2\\0\end{bmatrix} + \begin{bmatrix}0.245\\0.378\\0.111\\0.066\end{bmatrix} = \begin{bmatrix}0.245\\0.378\\0.311\\0.066\end{bmatrix}$$

Hence, the expected value of the demand for the thirty-eighth day is seventeen, which is obtained by adding the products of medians and their associated probabilities.

Vector Smoothing Method for Multiple Items

The smoothing technique can also be extended to forecast demand for individual items making up a group of products [7]. The group may represent, for example, different models of bicycles, engines, or hoists. To generate forecasts for individual items, we should have an updated forecast for the total group.

Suppose, for example, that we have K items belonging to a group. Let P_{kt} represent the probability that a demand will occur for item k at time t. The basic law of probabilities requires that individual probabilities of all K items in the group sum to one; that is,

$$\sum_{k=1}^{K} P_{kt} = 1 \qquad \text{for all time periods } t$$

Furthermore, all probabilities in the previous period are assumed to be known. This is true since we can either calculate the probabilities from the actual demands in the past or estimate them from market research activities in the case of a new product. As the cumulative demands D_{kT} for the item k are known at time T, to start the system, we can compute an estimate for P_{kt} for item k in the group:

$$P_{kt} = \frac{D_{kT}}{D_T} = \frac{D_{kT}}{\Sigma D_{kT}}$$

where D_T represents the sum of all item demands in the group up to time T. Now the probability mix for the item k can be updated using smoothing formulas discussed in chapter 2:

$$P_{kt} = \alpha q_{k,t-1} + (1 - \alpha)P_{k,t-1}, \quad \text{where } q_{k,t-1} = \frac{D_{k,t-1}}{D_{t-1}}$$

Here, $D_{k,t-1}$ and D_{t-1} represent the demand for item k and the total demand for the group, during period $t-1$. Using these most recent probability mixes, we can generate forecasts for individual items:

$$F_{kt} = P_{kt} * F_t$$

where F_{kt} represents the forecast for item k at time t given the total forecast F_t of the group at time t. Notice that the sum of all item forecasts in the group is always equal to the forecast for the group. The only remaining question is what value we should assign to the smoothing constant. The value of α can change over time, and its magnitude depends on the amount of trend in the total demand. The following rule of thumb is suggested:

$$\alpha = \min\left(\frac{D_t}{D}, 0.20\right)$$

where D_t represents the group's total demand during period t and D is the total demand for all items in the group last year. Both are known quantities. As is true with all simple exponential smoothing models, the vector smoothing should be used only when the demand is fairly constant or is slowly changing over time.

Example 3.2

Table 3.1 presents six months of data for three different types of exhaust pipes belonging to a group even though the firm forecasts demand only as a group. The November group forecast is twenty-three units.

1. Based on the past demands, generate forecasts for individual exhaust pipes for the month of November.
2. If the actual sales for individual items during November were ten, five, and twelve, whereas the group's forecast was thirty for December, generate individual item forecasts for December.

The total group demand during the previous year was 360 units.

Solution: Based on the six-month demand data, we can compute the probability of selling each item in November. If past demand is not known, we would have to estimate it from experience:

$$P_{1,\text{NOV}} = \frac{78}{204} = 0.38$$

$$P_{2,\text{NOV}} = \frac{39}{204} = 0.19$$

$$P_{3,\text{NOV}} = \frac{87}{204} = 0.43$$

Since the group forecast for November is twenty-three, we can compute item forecasts for November using the probability mix (rounded to the nearest digit):

TABLE 3.1 Vector Smoothing Forecast

	Item 1		*Item 2*		*Item 3*		*Group Total*	
Month	*Demand*	*Fore-cast*	*Demand*	*Fore-cast*	*Demand*	*Fore-cast*	*Demand*	*Fore-cast*
May	7		4		8			
June	17		5		25			
July	20		8		15			
August	16		8		17			
September	14		7		16			
October	4		7		6			
Totals	78		39		87			
November	10	8.7	5	4.4	12	9.9	27	23
December		11.4		5.7		12.9		30

$$F_{1,\text{NOV}} = (0.38)(23) = 8.7$$

$$F_{2,\text{NOV}} = (0.19)(23) = 4.4$$

$$F_{3,\text{NOV}} = (0.43)(23) = 9.9$$

Once the actual demand for November is known, we can update the probability mix as follows. The values of α and q_{kt} are computed as

$$\alpha = \min\left(\frac{27}{360}, 0.20\right)$$

$$= 0.075$$

and

$$q_{1,\text{NOV}} = \frac{10}{27} = 0.37$$

$$q_{2,\text{NOV}} = \frac{5}{27} = 0.19$$

$$q_{3,\text{NOV}} = \frac{12}{27} = 0.44$$

Therefore,

$$P_{1,\text{DEC}} = (0.075)(0.37) + (0.925)(0.38) = 0.38$$

$$P_{2,\text{DEC}} = (0.075)(0.19) + (0.925)(0.19) = 0.19$$

$$P_{3,\text{DEC}} = (0.075)(0.44) + (0.925)(0.43) = 0.43$$

The group forecast for December is thirty. We can generate an item forecast (rounded to the nearest digit) as follows:

$$F_{1,\text{DEC}} = (0.38)(30) = 11.4$$

$$F_{2,\text{DEC}} = (0.19)(30) = 5.7$$

$$F_{3,\text{DEC}} = (0.43)(30) = 12.9$$

When the actual December demand for these items becomes known, we can similarly generate forecasts for January and so on.

The vector smoothing method can also be extended to forecast demand for each SKU item used in various distribution locations [6]. In this case, we have K different locations instead of several items in the group. We define P_{kt} as the probability of demand for location k at time t for the SKU instead of for an item. The following example illustrates this concept.

Example 3.3

The following data refer to SKU items in three different locations. The total group forecast for April is 11,500 units. Find April item forecasts.

$P_{11,\text{MAR}} = 0.2$ $\alpha = 0.2$ $D_{11,\text{MAR}} = 2010$ $q_{1,\text{NOV}} = 0.22$

$P_{21,\text{MAR}} = 0.5$ $D_{21,\text{MAR}} = 4090$ $q_{2,\text{NOV}} = 0.44$

$P_{31,\text{MAR}} = 0.3$ $D_{31,\text{MAR}} = 3100$ $q_{3,\text{NOV}} = 0.34$

Solution: Suppose that the probabilities were recomputed for April, using the same formula given in the previous section, as

$$P_{11,\text{APR}} = (0.2)\,(0.22) + (0.8)\,(0.20) = 0.20$$

$$P_{21,\text{APR}} = (0.2)\,(0.44) + (0.8)\,(0.50) = 0.49$$

$$P_{31,\text{APR}} = (0.2)\,(0.34) + (0.8)\,(0.30) = 0.31$$

The forecasts for April, rounded to the nearest integer, would be

$$F_{11,\text{APR}} = (0.21)(11500) = 2415$$

$$F_{21,\text{APR}} = (0.49)(11500) = 5635$$

$$F_{31,\text{APR}} = (0.30)(11500) = 3450$$

Using these forecasts, planners are able to see how many units of the item should be stocked in each location.

The Blending Method

The blending method, developed by Cohen [2], can be used to forecast demands for end items belonging to a group or SKUs of an item located at several distribution points. With this method, a forecast for the entire group is blended with the average demand for each item. Let F be the forecast for the group at time t and let σ be the corresponding standard error of the forecast. In addition, let $\overline{D}_k$ be the average demand for item k and let S_k be the standard error associated with the average demand $\overline{D}_k$. According to basic statistics, the sum of all item averages in the group is equal to the group average $\overline{D}$. Therefore,

$$\overline{D} = \sum \overline{D}_k$$

Assuming that the demand for an item in the group is independent of other items in the group, we can also define the variance of the group average $\overline{D}$ as

$$S_{\overline{D}}^2 = \sum_{k=1}^{K} S_k^2$$

Using the past data, we can now find the forecast F_k for item k:

$$F_k = \overline{D}_k + w_k (F - \overline{D})$$

where the weighing (smoothing) factor is defined as

$$w_k = \frac{S_k^2}{(S_{\overline{D}}^2 + \sigma^2)}$$

The item forecast formula consists of two components. The first component represents the average item demand, whereas the second component makes an adjustment to the average. The adjustment is done by multiplying the difference between the group forecast and the demand by a weighing factor w_k that is specific for the item k.

Example 3.4

Using the data given in example 3.2, find the forecasts for all items by blending methods for the month of November. The variance σ^2 associated with the group forecast $F = 23$ is given as 260.

Solution: Mean and sample standard deviation of each item are calculated as follows for the data given in table 3.1:

Item	*Mean*	*Sample Variance*	*Sample S.D.*
1	13.0	38.4	6.20
2	6.5	2.7	1.64
3	14.5	46.7	6.83

The mean and variance of group demand are

$$D = \overline{D}_1 + \overline{D}_2 + \overline{D}_3$$

$$= 13 + 6.5 + 14.5 = 34$$

$$S_{\overline{D}}^2 = S_1^2 + S_2^2 + S_3^2$$

$$= 38.4 + 2.7 + 46.7 = 87.8$$

The weights for all individual items are

$$w_1 = \frac{S_1^2}{S_{\bar{D}}^2 + \sigma^2} = \frac{38.4}{87.8 + 260} = 0.110$$

Similarly,

$$w_2 = \frac{2.7}{87.8 + 260} = 0.008$$

$$w_3 = \frac{46.7}{87.8 + 260} = 0.134$$

and the November forecasts rounded to the nearest integer are

$$\begin{aligned} F_{1,\text{NOV}} &= \bar{D}_1 + w_1 (F - \bar{D}) \\ &= 13 + (0.110)(23 - 34) \\ &= 12 \end{aligned}$$

Similarly,

$$F_{2,\text{NOV}} = 6.5 + (0.008)(23 - 34) = 6$$

$$F_{3,\text{NOV}} = 14.5 + (0.134)(23 - 34) = 13$$

This example illustrates the use of the blending method for forecasting several items in a group. In a similar fashion, we can solve problems involving multiple stocking locations.

Percentage Done Estimating Method

The percentage done method illustrated by Hartung [3] and by Hertz and Schaffer [5] provides forecasts of the total season's demand for an individual item belonging to a product line or group. It centers on bringing the seasonality factor into the multi-item forecasting problem. This is particularly important in the retailing markets, where an item may be carried only during the season. Examples of such items include wood stoves, fans, clothing, and a variety of consumer goods. Many manufacturers of clothing, for example, also own a chain of retail stores. Therefore, it is very important to take all factors into consideration when determining how much of a particular item or of items in a group will be needed in stock during a season at each location and to devise a proper production planning and inventory control strategy.

In estimating the percentage done, the items are grouped into homogeneous lines. A line is a group of more or less similar merchandise, such as men's shirts or children's shoes. Although a line is usually carried year after year, additions and deletions of items to each line are encountered during consecutive seasons. A season is a portion of the year consisting of several periods. As goods are sold, we need to know how much inventory of what item needs to be replenished—in short, how much more of what item we need to manufacture.

The percentage done method assumes that at any given time of the season in every year, the same percentage of the total season's demand for an item is encountered. The method involves dividing the updated sales by the corresponding percentage to forecast the total demand for the season. From a knowledge of the inventory on hand and total sales to date, we can compute the remainder of the quantity to be produced for the current season. We can also extend this analysis to cover the same item stocked in several locations. The procedure consists of the following steps:

Step 1: Using prior year demand data, find the percentage of cumulative sales of the *group* of items for each time period.

Step 2: Using the current year cumulative demands for each *item* in the group and the corresponding percentage done estimates for the group in the previous year, generate item forecasts for this season's total demand.

Step 3: Calculate the quantity of each item in the group that needs to be produced.

Example 3.5

The cumulative sales and percentage done estimates of the previous year for three items are as follows:

Cumulative Sales to Week t

Item (k)	WEEK 1	WEEK 2	WEEK 3	WEEK 4	WEEK 5	WEEK 6
1	7	24	44	60	74	78
2	4	9	17	25	32	39
3	8	33	48	65	81	87
Totals	19	66	109	150	187	204
P_t	9.3	32.4	53.4	73.5	91.7	100

The demands for the items during week 1 were 15, 10, and 18, respectively. The inventories of the items at the start of season were 100, 50, and 120. Based on the results of the first week of demand, how many more of each item should the management expect to produce for this season?

Solution: The demands during week 1 for all items were

$$D_{11} = 15$$

$$D_{21} = 10$$

$$D_{31} = 18$$

Since we know that the percentage done estimate for the group for that period is 9.3%, the total season forecast can be calculated as follows:

$$F_1 = \frac{15}{0.093} = 161$$

$$F_2 = \frac{10}{0.093} = 108$$

$$F_3 = \frac{18}{0.093} = 194$$

From our knowledge of the total season's forecast F_k and the current cumulative production P_k, we can compute the remainder quantity of items R_k expected to be produced for the season:

$$R_1 = F_1 - P_1$$

$$= 161 - 100 = 61$$

$$R_2 = 107 - 50 = 57$$

$$R_3 = 194 - 120 = 74$$

Suppose that at the end of the second period of this season, week 2, we know the cumulative demand for all items to be

$$D_{12} = 55$$

$$D_{22} = 29$$

$$D_{32} = 65$$

We can update the estimates for total seasonal demand and future production requirements using (the percentage done estimate for period two) $P_2 =$ 0.324:

$$F_1 = \frac{55}{0.324} = 170$$

$$F_2 = \frac{29}{0.324} = 90$$

$$F_3 = \frac{65}{0.324} = 201$$

and the remainder of the quantity expected to be produced for the season is updated as:

$$R_1 = 170 - 100 = 70$$

$$R_2 = 90 - 50 = 40$$

$$R_3 = 201 - 120 = 81$$

Similarly, we can update our estimates during every period for planning production needs of all items.

Percentage of Aggregate Demands Method

The percentage of aggregate demands method was originally developed by Hausman and Sides [4] for forecasting demands of style goods. They dealt with a group of items sold through a catalog during a season consisting of many weeks. Many seasonal items have a slow pickup of demand at the beginning of the season and then reach a peak, after which the demand slows down. This pattern is typical of toys, perfumes, and many other items.

The first step in the method involves consolidating the weeks into intervals consisting of approximately equal total demands. For example, figure 3.2a exhibits the demand curve for the group during the previous season. We divide the total area into several segments, resulting in unequal interval lengths, as shown in figure 3.2b. We will update the forecasts periodically at these intervals for all items in the group. In this method, the season total forecast F for the group must be available.

Step 1: Let D_{kT} represent the cumulative demand for item k at time T, and let D_T be the cumulative demand for the group. The percentage of sales at time $t = T$ for item k is

$$P_{kT} = \frac{D_{kT}}{D_T} = \frac{D_{kT}}{\Sigma D_{kT}}$$

Step 2: The item forecast F_k for the season is given by

$$F_k = P_{kT} * F$$

We see that two variables affect the item forecast for the season. The group forecast F for the season is assumed to be known. It could change as the

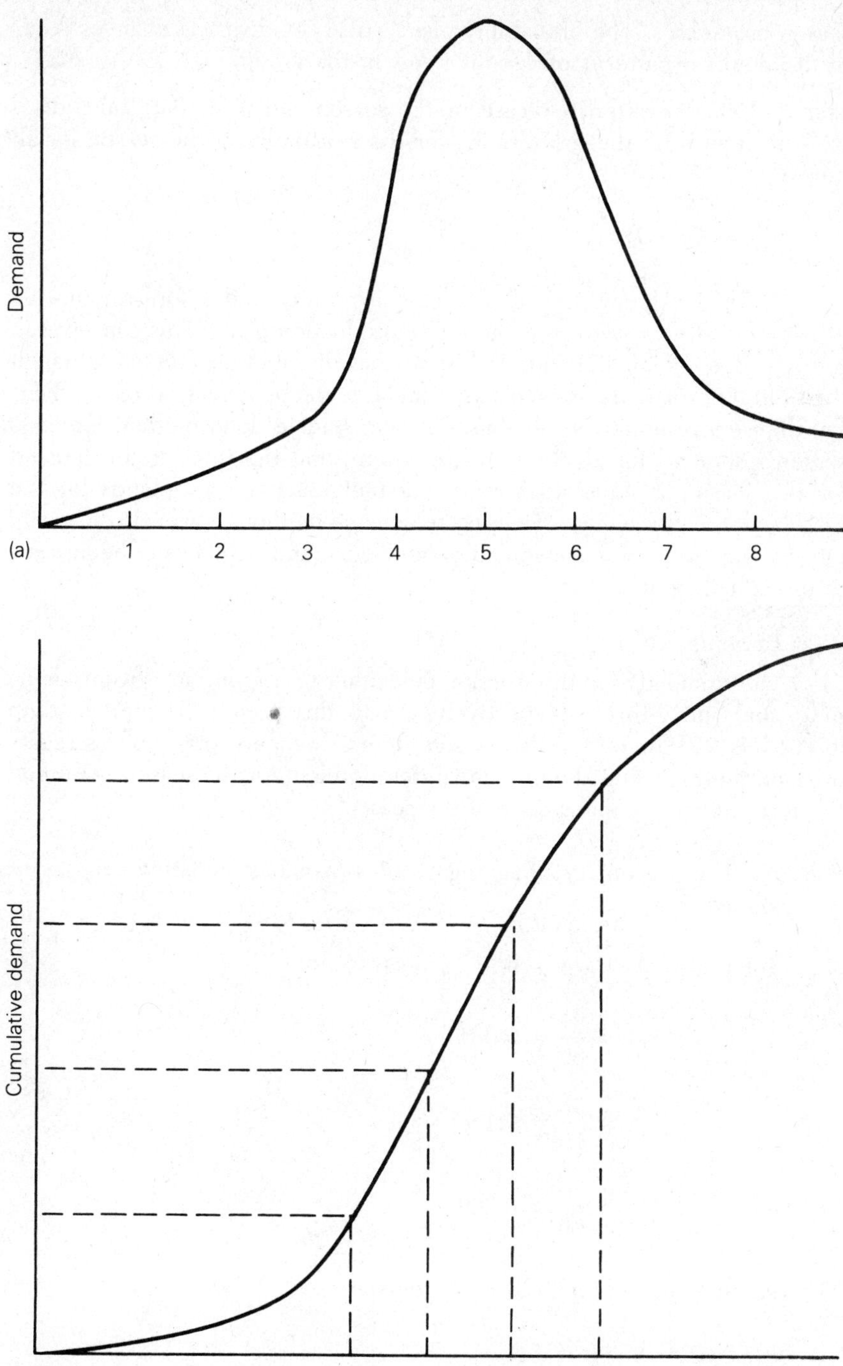

FIGURE 3.2 (a) Real time periods (b) periods for percentage of aggregate demand method

season progresses. The probability mix P_{kT} also could vary as changes occur in the demand patterns of various items in the group.

Step 3: Using the item forecast for the season and up-to-date sales data, we can determine the forecast R_{kT} for the remainder of the season for all items:

$$R_{kT} = F_k - D_{kT}$$

From our knowledge of available inventory and a forecast for the remainder of the season, we can devise production plans. This concept can be extended for an item located at several distribution points. Although the solution procedure appears to be similar to the percentage done method, the difference should be obvious. The percentage done method forecasts season's demand for all items in the group, and the total group demand for the season is equal to the sum of individual item demands for the season. In the percentage of aggregate demand method, however, the group forecast for the season is assumed to be known, and we allocate the forecast to individual items.

Example 3.6

The demands for three items belonging to a group are twenty-four, nine, and thirty-three, respectively, up to this period. The total group forecast is 204 items for the season. Using the percentage of aggregate demand method, find the individual item forecast for the season. Also find the forecast for the remainder of the season.

Solution: The percentage of aggregate sales (demand) to date for the items is calculated first:

$$\text{Total sales } D_T = 24 + 9 + 33 = 66$$

$$P_{1,1} = \frac{24}{66} = 0.364$$

$$P_{2,1} = \frac{9}{66} = 0.136$$

$$P_{3,1} = \frac{33}{66} = 0.500$$

The season forecasts for individual items are

$$F_1 = (204)(0.364) = 74$$

$$F_2 = (204)(0.136) = 28$$

$$F_3 = (204)(0.500) = 102$$

The forecasts for the remainder of the season are

$$R_1 = 74 - 24 = 50$$

$$R_2 = 28 - 9 = 19$$

$$R_3 = 102 - 33 = 69$$

As mentioned earlier, it is important to keep in mind that the total forecast may vary as the season passes, and the percentage aggregate sales may vary as actual sales data are compiled. They are updated periodically according to the periods displayed in figure 3.2.

Summary

In this chapter, we discussed several models for forecasting demand for multiple items belonging to a family or for a single item stocked at several locations. The vector smoothing method provides the updated probabilities of items for every period. These probabilities are then used to prorate individual item forecasts. The blending method gives the weights for every item in the family. Using these weights in an exponential smoothing model, we can generate individual item forecasts. The percentage done method deals specifically with a family of items whose demand is restricted to a season. Finally, the percentage of aggregate demand method is used for seasonal demand items with a peak. It is also possible to forecast a family of items stocked in several locations. Cohen [2] extends the blending method to solve what are known as multiclassified problems. Commercial packages incorporating some of these techniques are available in the marketplace. Finally, we emphasize that better forecasts help to consolidate items being transported to a warehouse and hence reduce the total cost of production and logistics.

PROBLEMS

1. The following are the actual demand data for the Knit Picker; group the data into approximately six class intervals: 127, 139, 135, 148, 162, 137, 171, 150, 120, 149, 140, 155, 157, 156, 91, 142, 120, 173, 142, 149, 128, 149, 120, 169, 145, 156, 185, 151, 184, 130
2. Calculate the probability distribution of demand for the Knit Picker. Given that the actual demand during the thirty-first week was 165, find the updated probabilities for the distribution of demand using the following values for α: 0.1, 0.2, and 0.3.

3. The following are the class intervals and the corresponding frequency distributions of demand for Kailees:

K	*Interval*	*Frequency*
1	0–19	15
2	20–39	20
3	40–59	15
4	60–79	10
5	80–100	5

Find the probability distribution for the demand for Kailees. Given that 65 Kailees were sold during the most recent period, provide the updated probabilities for various intervals of demand.

4. The following is the distribution of the cookie boxes sold by the scoutmaster for the past seventy days:

Number of Cookie Boxes	*Frequency*
0–14	4
15–29	20
30–44	24
45–59	11
60–74	6
75–89	5

Find the probability distribution for the sales of cookie boxes. Given that fifty-one cookie boxes were sold during the most recent period, find the updated probabilities for various sales ranges.

5. A radio manufacturer who has decided to enter the market with a new product has sought the opinion of the new product manager. His answers for the past thirty days are as follows: 3, 4, 5, 2, 3, 4, 3, 5, 4, 3, 4, 3, 3, 2, 5, 4, 2, 3, 3, 4, 3, 5, 4, 3, 3, 2, 4, 3, 4, 5. Find the probability distribution for the number of models contemplated. Based on the given information, what are the updated probabilities for the next period?

6. The following table exhibits the actual demand data for the past five months:

Month	*Item 1*	*Item 2*	*Item 3*
1	100	70	80
2	110	80	75
3	125	60	95
4	105	70	90
5	95	65	98

a. Using vector smoothing method, generate current values of probabilities of demand for individual items.
b. If the actual sales for the sixth month were 100, 70, and 95 for items 1, 2, and 3, respectively, generate current estimates of item forecasts for the seventh month using the vector smoothing method—given the group forecast for the seventh month as 300.

7. Using the sales data given in problem 6, provide an item forecast for the seventh month using the blending method. The variance associated with the group forecast is given as 350.

8. The following table gives sales data for the Piedmont Fertilizer Company for a line of products during the past year:

Item	*Mar*	*Apr*	*May*	*Jun*	*Jul*	*Aug*
PX1	10	15	13	16	21	8
PX2	8	10	13	16	19	10
PX3	17	22	18	26	30	20

The demand for these products during March and April and the inventories at the start of the season are as follows:

Item	*Mar*	*Apr*	*Inventory*
PX1	11	17	50
PX2	10	13	50
PX3	20	23	70

Based on first week's sales data, provide item forecasts for the remainder of the season, using the percentage done estimating method.

9. In problem 8, how many more of each product in the line should Piedmont expect to produce this season?
a. Based on March sales data only.
b. Based on March and April sales data.

10. Donald King caters hamburgers at the beach. The total forecast for this season is 5800. To date, the demand for single, double, and triple hamburgers has been 300, 800, and 400. Using the percentage of aggregate demand method, find the individual hamburger forecast for the season. For the remainder of this season, how much should Donald King expect to sell?

11. The following are the sales data for four different items belonging to a group. The firm forecasts demand only as a group. August forecast is 760 units.

Month	*Item 1*	*Item 2*	*Item 3*	*Item 4*
Jan	260	94	125	197
Feb	251	90	129	188
Mar	235	100	126	186
Apr	287	99	137	185
May	304	98	140	173
Jun	290	96	135	188
Jul	315	97	142	193

Based on past sales data, generate a forecast for individual items for the month of August.

12. If the actual sales in August were 310, 105, 125, and 205, respectively, for the four items listed in problem 11, and if the September group forecast is 800, generate individual item forecasts for September.

13. Using the sales data given in problem 11, generate an item forecast for August by the blending method. The variance associated with the group forecast is 525.

14. The following are the weekly sales for a family of items during a season last year:

Item	*Week 1*	*Week 2*	*Week 3*	*Week 4*	*Week 5*	*Week 6*	*Week 7*
1	400	500	600	600	500	400	300
2	100	100	200	200	200	100	50
3	250	300	300	300	200	100	100

If the demands for these items during the first week of this season were 450, 100, and 275, respectively, and the inventories at the start of the season were 2000, 500, and 1100, based on the first week's sales data generate item forecasts for the remainder of the season. How many more of each item should the firm expect to produce this season?

15. If the demands for the items in problem 14 during the second week of the season are 450, 100, and 250, respectively, how would your estimates vary?

16. The demands for the items in problem 14 during the third week of the season are 600, 250, and 350, respectively. What are your new estimates of sales for the remainder of this season?

17. The demands for three items belonging to a group are 260, 94, and 125 up to this period. Total group forecast for the season is 2580. Using the percentage of aggregate demand method, find the individual item forecast for the season. Also find the forecasts for the remainder of the season.

18. The demands for the three items in problem 17 to date were found to be 700, 250, and 390. The total group forecast for the season remains the same. Using the percentage of aggregate demand method, find the individual item forecast for the season.

19. With the information given in problem 18, find the forecast for the remainder of the season.

20. The following table exhibits the sales data for XYZ manufacturing company for a line of products during the past year:

Periods

ITEM	1	2	3	4
1	11	14	18	10
2	26	31	32	30
3	5	6	8	7

If the demand for these products during the first period at the start of the season was twenty, thirty, and six, respectively, provide item forecasts for the remainder of the season using the percentage done estimating method.

REFERENCES AND BIBLIOGRAPHY

1. R. G. Brown, *Smoothing, Forecasting and Prediction of Discrete Time Series* (Englewood Cliffs, N.J.: Prentice-Hall, 1962).
2. G. D. Cohen, "Bayesian Adjustment of Sales Forecasts in Multi Item Inventory Control Systems," *Journal of Industrial Engineering,* Vol. 17, No. 9 (1966), pp. 474–479.
3. P. Hartung, "A Simple Style Goods Inventory Model," *Management Science,* Vol. 19, No. 2 (August 1973), pp. 1452–1458.
4. W. P. Hausman and R. S. G. Sides, "Mail Order Demands for Style Goods: Theory and Data Analysis," *Management Science,* Vol. 20, No. 2 (October 1973), pp. 191–202.
5. D. B. Hertz and K. H. Schaffir, "A Forecasting Model for Management of Seasonal Style Goods Inventories," *Operations Research,* Vol. 8, No. 2 (1960), pp. 45–52.
6. R. C. Link, "Richard C. Link Report," Winston-Salem, N.C., January 1983.
7. N. T. Thomopoulos, *Applied Forecasting Methods*. (Englewood Cliffs, N.J.: Prentice-Hall, 1980).

appendix 3A

Forecasting Information Systems: The Data Base Module

Conway Lee Lackman

Forecasts are frequently as useful as the data base upon which they are built. The value of forecasts basically depends on two requisites: accuracy and timeliness. These standards for performance are clearly stated in the job description of most forecasters. Forecast outcomes generally stated in the form of data must be based on timely, reliable and accurate data.

Standards for Forecasting Data

Accuracy depends on the availability and coverage of the data and the competence of the compiling source of data. Timeliness depends upon the form the data is stated in and its accessibility. For example, we might rate two of the several data sources to be treated in this article on the following criteria:

Source	*Coverage*	*Availability*	*Accuracy*	*Timeliness*
1. Survey of Current Business	Excellent—all major U.S. Economic Aggregates	Excellent—available hard copy from U.S. Commerce Department or on Interactive NBER Data base	Good—except corporate profits	Good—every month covering previous month
2. Country Business Patterns	Fair—income data occasionally missing	Fair—hard copy from U.S. Commerce Dept.	Fair—income & housing data often 10% in error	Fair—available every year on a selected basis for the previous year

From the *Journal of Systems Management*, January 1981. Reprinted by permission.

Forecasters require data from external source one for macro-economic forecasting. Data from source two is used for regional sales forecasting in particular to identify independent variables used in the forecast.

In turn, we can rate two internal data sources to be discussed on the same criteria:

Source	*Coverage*	*Availability*	*Accuracy*	*Timeliness*
1. Customer Invoices	Company sales data (units and revenue)	Good—enters data base distributed company wide	Good—accuracy check by market research dept.	Fair—late in the month orders often can't be included
2. Vendor invoices and payroll vouchers	Product costs	Good—enters data base during production run	Fair—error due to absence of latest price and averaging to get standard costs	Good—standard cost system with fast turn-around time

Forecasters require data from internal source one for the company sales forecast. Data from source two is matched with source one in order to produce a company profit forecast (i.e. forecasted sales (revenues) less forecasted costs = forecasted profits).

In considering data sources such as in this article, the forecaster should evaluate the required data in terms of the standards required for the forecasting project. Tradeoffs will often have to be made in the selection of data sources among the aforementioned four criteria in light of the standards of the forecasting project. For example, if the lead time for the project is lengthy, timeliness may be traded off for more coverage and accuracy in an effort to satisfy the accuracy standard of the forecasting project. With this in mind, let us review the major data sources for forecasting.

External Data

GOVERNMENT SOURCES

Government data, as pointed out earlier, is a useful resource in forecasting. The U.S. Federal government is the most pertinent data source for macroeconomic (and international) forecasting. The Department of Commerce supplies two major macroeconomic data series: The Survey of Current Business (SCB) and Business Cycle Development (BCD). The SCB provides a quarterly and in some cases monthly time series on all important aggregate economic indicators including GNP, Personal Consumption by major sector (i.e., durables), Gross Private Domestic Investment by sector (i.e., business investment) imports, exports, and government spending by source in current

TABLE 3A.1 Time Series on Selected Industries

BASIC MATERIALS

t	*Steel (mil. net tons)*	*Aluminum (mil. lbs.)*	*Crude Petroleum (000 bls./day)*	*Paper (000 Short Tons)*
1966	134.1	—	—	—
1967	127.2	8,946	8,811	46,899
1968	131.5	9,963	9,095	51,245
1969	141.3	10,822	9,235	54,058
1970	131.5	10,109	9,631	52,471
1975	128.0	10,400	9,700	53,000
1980 Est.	133.0	11,400	9,940	55,000*

PRODUCER GOODS

			Construction		*Transport*	
t	*Electronic Computers (mil. $) (val. of shipments)*	*Machine Tools (mil. $) (val. of shipments)*	*New Const. in place (bil. $)*	*Housing† Starts (units)*	*Autos (mil. units)*	*Trucks & Buses (mil. units)*
1967	3,771	2,841	76.2	1,322	7.4	1.54
1968	4,163	2,817	84.7	1,546	8.8	1.86
1969	5,097	2,801	90.9	1,500	8.2	1.92
1970	4,842	2,540	91.3	1,467	6.6	1.69
1975	5,084	1,942	106.0	2,040	8.5	1.98
1980 Est.	5,592	2,517	117.0	2,105	9.0	2.05

	Consumer Goods		Trade & Service (mil. $)				
t	*Household (mil. $) Appliances (val. of shipments)*	*Meat Packing (mil. $) (val. of shipments)*	*Total Retail*	*Dept. Store*	*Hardware*	*Apparel*	*Medical Total (bil. $)*
1967	5,328	15,576	313,400	27,704	2,894	—	50.8
1968	5,955	16,285	339,300	33,323	3,200	11,930	56.6
1969	6,161	18,087	351,600	36,378	3,284	12,370	63.7
1970	6,114	19,172	364,600	38,449	3,224	12,395	70.9
1975	6,497	20,332	390,500	41,909	3,417	12,908	78.9
1980 Est.	6,948	21,541	421,700	46,100	3,588	13,620	88.0

* "Economy at Midyear and 1980 Projections". *U.S. Individual Outlook*. U.S. Commerce Department, Bureau of Domestic Commerce, Washington, D.C.

† Mobile Homes excluded.

and constant dollars. SCB provides also a full series of financial and monetary data (i.e., money supply, interest rates) and a series of price indexes as well as a series on industrial production by standard industrial classification (SIC). SIC divides industries by generic category. SIC 01 is food and beverages. SCB is nearly all inclusive data source for development of macroeconomic and industry forecasting models.

The BCD is the major source of data on business cycles. BCD illustrates cyclical movements of major economic aggregates over extended as well as near term time periods. Most importantly, BCD is a unique source of anticipations data (i.e., what industry and consumers expect economic indicators to be in the next quarter). Examples of such series are first anticipations of businessmen on their expected expenditures for new plant and equipment. These series are referred to as Diffusion Indexes. These series are used extensively as will be shown later in certain forecasting models such as business investment forecasts.

Commerce also issues the *U.S. Industrial Outlook,* which provides annual series on production sales and value added by SIC as shown on Table 3A.1. *The Census of Transportation* provides truck, rail, and water shipments by originating SIC which is useful in the transportation forecasting.

The Bureau of Census (BOC) supplies several aggregate economic series necessary for macroeconomic and industry forecasting. *The Census of Population & Housing* provides annual series on U.S. population-total and by age group—and a series on housing—residential and commercial. These data are especially important as will be seen in forecasting consumer durables and telephone services. The BOC also published long time series on such data, the *Historical Statistics of the U.S., 1787*—as shown on Table 3A.2. BOC also provides such data on a regional basis in *County Business Patterns* which depicts these series for both counties and Standard Metropolitan Statistical Areas (SMSA). Another BOC source useful in industry forecasting is the *Census of Business,* which records wholesale and retail sales by SIC.

The Department of Labor, Bureau of Labor Statistics (BLS) is the major source of monthly and quarterly series on employment, unemployment, wages, cost of living, and consumer and wholesale prices indexes. BLS data is helpful in developing the real sector (production, wages, unemployment) of macro econometric forecasting models.

The Federal Reserve Board is the major source of monthly and quarterly financial and monetary series. Money supply series by varying definitions (i.e., M_1, M_2, M_3) are uniquely available in the *Federal Reserve Bulletin* (FRB). The FRB includes interest rate series on most monetary instruments, e.g., short and long term government securities and U.S. Flow of Funds as well as private sector financial data, including uses and sources of corporate funds.

A secondary government data source is the state and local level. The Commerce and Labor Departments, county planning commissions and mu-

TABLE 3A.2 Size of the U.S. Labor Force Compared to the Total U.S. Population

Year	*Population (in millions)*	*Labor Force (in millions) (includes the military)*	*Percent of Population*
1790	3.9		
1800	5.3		
1810	7.2		
1820	9.6	2.9	30.2
1830	12.9	3.9	30.2
1840	17.0	5.4	31.7
1850	23.2	7.7	33.1
1860	31.4	10.5	33.4
1870	39.8	12.9	32.4
1880	50.2	17.4	34.6
1890	62.9	23.3	37.2
1900	76.0	29.0	38.2
1910	92.0	37.4	40.8
1920	105.7	42.4	40.0
1930	122.8	48.8	37.4
1940	131.7	56.2	42.5
1950	150.7	63.9	42.3
1970	188.5	75.4	40.0
1980 Est.	213.2	90.2	42.3

Source: Historical Statistics of the U.S. U.S. Bureau of the Census, Washington, D.C.

nicipal Chambers of Commerce collect demographic data (such as population, dwelling units, personal income, manufacturers value added) which is the basis for regional forecasting (See Table 3A.3).

PRIVATE SOURCES

The two major private data sources are industry trade associations and private consultants. The trade association data is usually free but is restricted to what the industry wishes to show. The consultant's data base costs about $1000 to $1500 per year but is often more comprehensive and is usually available on an interactive computer system which will access data in the format required in fractions of the time that such data is obtainable from trade association hard copy data.

Trade association data is usually confined to industries, rather than economic aggregates. The National Automobile Manufacturer's Association (NAMA) is typical, reporting unit production of autos and trucks on a monthly basis as shown on Table 3A.5. Data from NAMA is a useful base for auto forecasting at the industry level. Table 3A.4 lists some major trade association data sources by industry.

Private consultants provide on line interactive data bases (for a $1,000–$2,000 per year fee) and hard copy data on economic aggregates, as well as regional (see Table 3A.3), industries (see Table 3A.6) and occasionally

TABLE 3A.3 Demographic Data in Two Regions

	(1) Arlington Heights, Ill.					*(2) West Los Angeles, Cal.*				
Time	*1970*	*1974*	*1975*	*1976*	*1977*	*1970*	*1974*	*1975*	*1976*	*1977*
(1) Population + 16	25,000	41,000	47,000	54,000	109,000	31,676	35,602	38,000	45,000	94,000
(2) Dwelling Units (Occupied)	8,500	13,900	16,000	23,000	50,000	8,300	13,000	15,000	21,000	43,000
(3) Median Income ($)	10,800	12,300	13,500	16,000	19,500	9,246	9,600	11,000	12,500	15,000
(4) Retail Sales ($ 000)	40,000	61,524	70,000	77,000	130,000	24,000	38,600	50,000	61,000	120,000
(5) Average Home Value ($)	14,500	25,700	28,000	41,000		14,000	22,700	27,000	31,000	44,000
(6) Housing Starts	31,000	42,000	45,000	61,000	85,000	28,000	35,000	38,000	48,000	59,000
(7) Mfg. V.A.	2.2	5.05	5.3	6.8	10.3	2.0	5.5	5.8	7.9	12.0

Sources: (1) Cook County Planning Commission and (2) Los Angeles County Planning Commission.

TABLE 3A.4 Sources of Industry Data

Industry	*Trade Association*
Steel	American Iron & Steel Institute
Appliances	Association of Home Appliances Manufacturers
Men's Clothing	Menswear Retailers of America

company data. Data Resources, Inc. (DRI), the supplier of Table 3A.6, and Chase Econometrics, Inc., are leading nonspecialized suppliers of data on U.S. and European economies and industries. More specialized suppliers of data such as Market Research Corporation of America (MRCA) and A.C. Nielsen (ACN) supply disaggregated industry and company data, i.e., by market segment and product type. Their stress is also more regional. MRCA provides data and forecasts by brand in leading consumer goods product markets. ACN provides sales analysis of products moving in retail channels by brand for almost any specified region in the U.S.

Other private data sources include labor organizations (e.g., AFL-CIO), currently publishing data on prices, wages, and employment, and private firms which are generally the data suppliers of those firms. Prominent suppliers of financial data include Moody's, Standard and Poor's (S & P), and Dun and Bradstreet (D & B). The S & P tapes contain series on sales, earnings, profits and return on equity and may be purchased at rates comparable to the cost of an economic data base. D & B provides sales and financial data by SIC by firm belonging to a given SIC. Table 3A.7 illustrates the D & B report grouping the firms in SIC 2085 Distilled & Blended Liquors. The D & B supplementary report contains unit and dollar sales for SIC 2085 and for each firm listed on Table 3A.7. The same type of information is available from D & B for most of the other SIC's which compose U.S. industry.

Internal Data

Company sales forecasts have the highest priority among corporate forecasts. Such forecasts rely greatly on the internal data of the company. As discussed earlier, the company sales data base should provide historical sales revenue and units for the total company (and for specific products where needed for product forecasts). The frequency of such data should be at least monthly in order to obtain monthly or quarterly short run forecasts. These data can be aggregated to annual frequency for purposes of producing a long run company sales forecasts. A cost data base composed of monthly standard costs was shown earlier to be indispensable in making profit forecasts, a general requirement of corporate plans.

A data base composed of company product prices is often useful for company sales forecasts, where company prices are an explanatory variable with regard to demand.

TABLE 3A.5 Monthly U.S. Motor Vehicle Production

	Passenger Cars						
	1964	*1965*	*1966*	*1967*	*1968*	*1969*	*1970*
Jan.	745,835	828,142	816,558	670,122	808,811	846,167	601,676
Feb.	675,581	770,643	767,063	519,978	715,422	711,925	550,583
Mar.	723,811	963,101	911,603	683,214	796,411	761,134	628,460
Apr.	786,824	862,442	809,985	657,241	791,186	710,278	661,007
May	726,007	837,701	795,166	750,504	915,071	712,932	719,155
June	777,595	899,676	821,486	763,940	816,557	786,429	807,514
July	587,292	740,576	461,665	390,849	604,790	427,438	449,659
Aug.	190,159	314,828	147,610	285,758	196,072	375,405	287,959
Sept.	573,420	492,110	647,559	572,723	679,707	754,700	478,365
Oct.	411,501	849,386	834,613	641,884	934,982	850,190	390,014
Nov.	680,835	913,146	833,964	685,716	873,779	675,612	372,674
Dec.	866,632	863,476	757,440	790,730	715,832	612,182	603,062
Total	7,745,492	9,335,227	8,604,712	7,412,659	8,848,620	8,224,392	6,550,128

	Trucks and Buses						
	1964	*1965*	*1966*	*1967*	*1968*	*1969*	*1970*
Jan.	140,149	146,342	159,432	153,689	162,709	178,702	154,638
Feb.	132,064	132,226	156,013	141,787	152,440	163,000	142,564
Mar.	144,338	173,877	173,958	153,586	171,220	176,931	154,777
Apr.	154,991	161,084	161,274	138,782	169,360	165,097	146,741
May	142,700	155,139	168,733	159,071	198,224	148,313	171,191
June	157,928	172,037	178,055	155,897	183,679	170,183	191,145
July	123,914	126,086	135,738	98,697	144,609	148,065	137,714
Aug.	98,816	115,212	69,267	103,242	107,443	123,980	149,529
Sept.	118,392	146,659	128,771	107,383	165,003	164,552	136,929
Oct.	80,251	155,912	156,024	108,504	195,100	198,544	109,908
Nov.	121,040	156,870	156,900	139,952	173,189	179,197	93,871
Dec.	147,785	161,159	147,382	150,487	148,814	164,955	144,814
Total	1,562,368	1,802,603	1,791,587	1,611,077	1,971,790	1,981,519	1,733,821

	Total Motor Vehicles						
	1964	*1965*	*1966*	*1967*	*1968*	*1969*	*1970*
Jan.	885,984	974,484	975,990	823,811	971,520	1,024,869	738,314
Feb.	807,645	902,869	923,076	661,765	867,862	874,925	693,147
Mar.	868,149	1,136,978	1,085,561	836,800	967,631	938,065	783,237
Apr.	941,815	1,023,526	971,259	796,023	960,546	875,375	867,746
May	868,707	992,840	963,939	909,575	1,113,295	861,245	890,346
June	935,523	1,071,713	999,541	919,837	1,000,236	956,612	998,655
July	711,206	866,662	597,403	489,546	749,399	575,503	587,371
Aug.	288,975	430,040	216,877	389,000	303,515	499,385	437,481
Sept.	691,812	638,769	776,330	680,106	8[illegible],710	919,252	615,291
Oct.	491,752	1,005,298	990,637	750,388	1,130,082	1,048,734	499,921
Nov.	801,875	1,070,016	990,864	825,668	1,046,968	854,809	466,541
Dec.	1,014,417	1,024,635	904,822	941,217	864,646	777,137	747,871
Total	9,307,860	11,137,830	10,396,299	9,023,736	10,820,410	10,205,911	8,283,949

TABLE 3A.6 Summary of Industry Employment

	65	66	67	68	69	70	71
Food	1757	1777	1787	1782	1791	1782	1754
Textile	926	964	959	994	1003	978	962
Apparel	1354	1402	1398	1406	1409	1372	1362
Lumber	607	615	597	600	607	573	580
Furniture	431	462	455	472	484	460	459
Paper	639	667	679	691	711	707	688
Chemical	908	961	1001	1030	1060	1051	1015
Petroleum	183	184	183	187	182	191	190
Rubber	471	511	516	561	598	580	582
Leather	353	364	351	355	343	322	308
Stone, Clay & Glass	628	644	629	635	657	639	629
Iron & Steel	657	652	635	636	644	629	580
Fabricated Metals	1269	1351	1363	1390	1440	1380	1332
Non-Electrical Machinery	1736	1910	1970	1966	2033	1977	1791
Electrical Machinery	1659	1909	1959	1975	2020	1923	1788
Motor Vehicles & Parts	843	861	815	874	914	809	877
Instruments	389	431	451	462	477	459	432

Source: Data Resources, Inc.

Competitor Data

In many cases, competitors' sales and prices are required to make competitor market share and/or a company sales forecast. For example, for a firm to know its competitors market share, a data base of competitors sales is essential. In many cases, such as forecasting in the oligopoly market setting, competitors' prices and sales are major explanatory variables in a company sales forecast. In these situations, the firm needs a competitor data base which includes their historical sales and prices.

Forecasting Methods and Data Bases

A deficient data base can only exploit any shortenings of a given forecasting method and most methods have some shortcomings. Proper operation and maintenance of an accurate and timely data system gives the forecaster an instrument with which to control and minimize the shortcomings of various forecasting methods. As the range of basic forecasting methods are applied to business problems it is hoped that the reader will remember the mutual dependence of any forecast method on an accompanying reliable data base.

TABLE 3A.7 Businesses by Product Classification

PUSARCH WINE CO
4500 2ND AVE SIC 5095
BROOKLYN N Y 11232 2084

GOLD SEAL VINEYARDS INC
20 E 46TH ST SIC 2084
NEW YORK N Y 10017

WILE JULIUS SONS & CO
320 PARK AVE SIC 5095
NEW YORK N Y 10022 2084

PETERS WINE CELLARS INC
6355 PLAINFIELD PIKE SIC 2084
CINCINNATI OHIO 45236

RICHARDS WINE CELLAR
112-20 POCOHONTAS ST SIC 2084
PETERSBURG VA 23803 5095

AMERICAN WINE GROWERS
5417 E MARGINAL WAY S SIC 2084
SEATTLE WASH 98124

2085 DISTILLED RECTIFIED, & BLENDED LIQUORS

GUILD WINE CO
FILBERT & MYRTLE AVES SIC 5095
LODI CAL 95240 2085 2084

SCHEPIAN DISTRIBUTION CO
2254 E 49TH ST SIC 5095
LOS ANGELES CAL 90058 2085

HEUBLEIN INC
330 NEW PARK AVE SIC 2085
HARTFORD CONN 06101 2035

FEDERAL DISTILLERS INC
15 MONSIGNOR OBRIEN SIC 5095
CAMBRIDGE MASS 02141 2085

MOHAWK LIQUEUR CORP
1965 PORTER ST SIC 2085
DETROIT MICH 48216

WALKER HIRAM & SONS INC
8325 JEFFERSON E SIC 2085
DETROIT MICH 48214

SOUTHERN COMFORT CORP
1220 N PRICE RD SIC 2085
ST LOUIS MO 63132

MC CORMICK DISTILLING
1 1/4 MILES SE SIC 2085
WESTON MO 64098

COINTREAU LTD
110 W FRANKLIN SIC 2085
PENNINGTON N J 08534

LAIRD & CO
SCOREYVILLE-LAIRD RD SIC 2085
SCOREYVILLE N J 07724 2084

CANANDAIGUA INDUSTRIES
116 W BUFFALO ST SIC 2085
CANANDAIGUA N Y 14424

AUSTIN NICHOLS & CO
55-30 58TH ST SIC 5095
MASPETH N Y 11378 2085

AMERICAN DISTILLING CO
150 E 42ND ST SIC 2085
NEW YORK N Y 10017

ALA COCA-COLA BOTTLING
420 NOELE ST
ANNISTON ALA 36200

COCA-COLA BOTTLING CO
310 NO ST ANDREWS
OCTMAN ALA 36300

COCA-COLA BOTTLING CO
200 N ROYAL ST
MOBILE ALA 36601

PHOENIX COCA-COLA BTLNG
225 E EUCKEYE RD
PHOENIX ARIZ 85034

COCA-COLA BOTTLING CO
1334 S CENTRAL AVE
LOS ANGELES CAL 90051

SEVEN-UP BOTTLING CO LA
5101 S ALAMEDA ST
LOS ANGELES CAL 90053

SEVEN-UP BTLG SAN EPNCAC
5101-15 S ALAMEDA
LOS ANGELES CAL 90058

LYCAS-PAGAUS INC
2545 16TH ST
SAN FRANCISCO CAL 41916

PEPSI-COLA BOTTLING CO
19700 S FIGUEROA ST
TORRANCE CAL 90510

DENVER COCA-COLA BOTTLING
3825 YORK ST
DENVER COLO 80205

BARTON DISTILLING CO
200 S MICHIGAN AVE SIC 2085
CHICAGO ILL 60604

BEAM JAPES & DISTILLING
65 E SOUTH WATER ST SIC 2085
CHICAGO ILL 60601

CONSOLIDATED DISTILLED
3215-3261 S KEDZIE SIC 5095
CHICAGO ILL 60623 2084 2085

WATERFILL & FRAZIER
120 S LA SALLE ST SIC 2085
CHICAGO ILL 60503

GRAIN PROCESSING CORP
1600 OREGON ST SIC 2085
NUSCATINE IOWA 52761 2834 2818

DOUBLE SPGS DISTILLERS
SIC 2085
BARDSTOWN KY 40004

HEAVEN HILL DISTILLERIES
2 1/2 MI SE 51 HWY 49 SIC 2085
BARSTOWN KY 40004

SAMUELS T W DISTILLERY
PKY 245 SIC 2085
DEATSVILLE KY 40016

BROWN-FURMAN DISTILLERS
1908 HOWARD ST SIC 2085
LOUISVILLE KY 40210

CANADA DRY CORP
100 PARK AVE SIC 2086
NEW YORK N Y 10017 5095 2085

DISTILLERS CO
620 FIFTH AVE SIC 2085
NEW YORK N Y 10020

NATL DISTILLERS CHEMICAL
99 PARK AVE SIC 2085
NEW YORK N Y 10016 3432 2816 2911
2392 5095

SCHENLEY INDUST INC
1290 AVE OF AMERICS SIC 2085
NEW YORK N Y 10019 2445 5095

SEAGRAM JOSEPH E & SONS
375 PARK AVE SIC 2085
NEW YORK N Y 10022 6516

STANDARD BRANDS INC
625 MADISON AVE SIC 2099
NEW YORK N Y 10022 2085 2096 2082
2048 2852

21 BRANDS INC
23 W 52ND ST SIC 5095
NEW YORK N Y 10019 2085

BROWNS J T & SONS CO
CAREW TOWER SIC 2085
CINCINNATI OHIO 45202

CONTINENTAL DISTILLING
1429 WALNUT ST SIC 2085
PHILADELPHIA PA 19107 2445

ASSOC COCA-COLA BOTTLING
320 ORANGE AVE
DAYTONA BEACH FLA 32014

CANADA DRY BOTTLING CO
711 MARGARET ST
JACKSONVILLE FLA 32203

FLORIDA COCA-COLA BOTTLING
2334 MARKET ST
JACKSONVILLE FLA 32206

COCA-COLA BTLG CO MIAMI
301 N W 29TH ST
MIAMI FLA 33137

WOMETCO ENTERPRISES INC
306-316 N MIAMI AVE
MIAMI FLA 33101

HYGEIA COCA-COLA BOTTLING
1625 N PALAFOA ST
PENSACOLA FLA 32501

HIGCOA GROCERY CO
SOUTH MAIN ST
QUINCY FLA 32351

TAMPA COCA-COLA BOTTLING
13TH ST & YORK
TAMPA FLA 33601

ATLANTA COCA-COLA BOTTLING
864 SPRING ST N E
ATLANTA GA 30378

Source: *Dun & Bradstreet Million Dollar Directory*, 1974.

chapter four

Basic Inventory Systems

Inventory control is a critical aspect of successful management. With high prime interest rates, companies cannot afford to have any money tied up in excess inventories. The objectives of good customer service and efficient production must be met at minimum inventory levels. This is true despite the fact that inflation causes finished goods inventories to increase in value. Putting inventory on the shelf ties up money, and to minimize the amount tied up, the company must match the timing of demand and supply so that the inventory goes on the shelf just in time for the customer to require it.

In this chapter, we will develop several systems for handling inventory trade-offs under varying conditions. All the models presented have been implemented in various companies. We will discuss how the models work and when they are applicable. It is important to realize that there is no all-purpose, automatic inventory control system; all systems need the intervention and monitoring of intelligent users.

Functions and Types of Inventories

Inventory is a stock of physical goods held at a specific location at a specific time. Each distinct item in the inventory at a location is termed a stock keeping unit (SKU) and each SKU has a number of units in stock. Each location is a stock point. The local supermarket, for example, is a stock point with a huge inventory of food. Dairy Farms 2% milk in half-gallon containers is an SKU with a specific number of units in stock.

Why do companies keep inventories? Inventories exist because demand and supply cannot be matched for physical and economic reasons. We go to the supermarket to buy a half-gallon container of milk. How could the store supply it without inventorying milk? Our demand obviously cannot be matched to the cow's supply in time, place, or form.

TRANSACTION STOCKS

Transaction stocks are those necessary to support the transformation, movement, and sales operations of the firm. Active *work-in-process stocks*—materials currently being worked on or moving between work centers—constitute a large part of transaction stocks, as do *pipeline inventories.* Pipeline or *transportation inventories* are inventories in transit. The size of the pipeline inventory is as much a function of the length of the pipeline as of the rate of sales at the retail stock point. Figure 4.1 compares two pipeline systems to show that a longer pipeline requires a larger inventory to match the same sales rate.

Transaction stocks cannot be reduced, because they support the sales rate directly. There are no frills in transaction stocks.

ORGANIZATION STOCKS

Organization stocks represent investment opportunities to achieve operating efficiencies. *Fluctuation* or *safety stock* is an organization stock designed to buffer against uncertainty. Average daily sales of twenty containers of milk, for example, can be met by a transaction stock of twenty units. Sales above twenty would have to be supported by a buffer stock held to avoid stockouts when sales are higher than expected.

Anticipation inventory or *leveling inventory* may be an attractive investment if it is cheaper to hold stock than to alter short-term production capacity. Seasonal peaks in demand may be met by building inventories earlier during periods of slack demand and excess capacity.

Lot size or *cycle inventories* are held to achieve some payoff from setting up equipment. Having set up equipment, manufacturing people

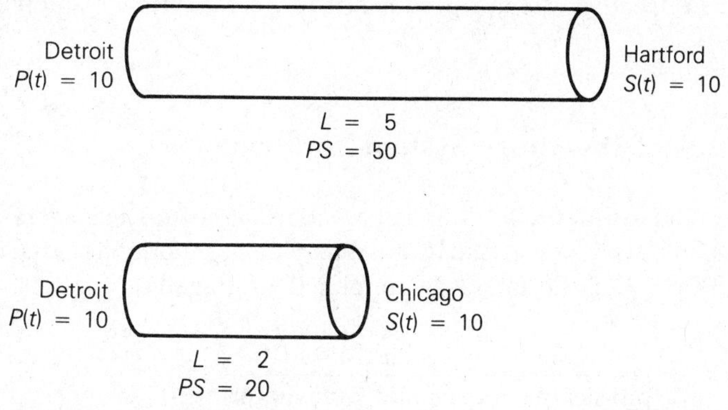

FIGURE 4.1 Pipeline inventories

Key: $P(t)$ = daily production rate; $S(t)$ = daily sales rate; L = lead time in days; PS = pipeline stock.

invariably want a long production run to avoid repeating the setup for the same item in the near future. Going to the bank to cash a check, for example, involves travel time and down time from other activities. For that reason, most of us carry a lot size or cycle stock in our wallets to avoid going to the bank every time we want to make a purchase.

The last two types of organization stocks are more specialized investment opportunities. *Scheduling stocks* are work-in-process stocks held between operations to allow schedulers a choice of jobs to place on the productive resource. In this way, high resource utilization can be achieved. *Speculative stocks* are those held in anticipation of price increases.

EXCESS STOCK

Excess stock has no purpose. Unlike transaction and organization stock, it owes its existence to oversight rather than to necessity or to operating efficiency.

LEVELS OF INVENTORY

Within the framework of transaction, organization, and excess stock, inventory may occur at various levels or echelons within the company. An *echelon*, *level*, or *stage* is a stock point that is under control of the company. Raw materials, work in process, high-level components, and finished products belong to different echelons. *Raw materials* are raw in the sense that the company has not done any work on them. *Work-in-process* inventories are manufacturing inventories that are undergoing processing or are in line at *work centers*—centers with similar man/machine capabilities. *High-level components* are parts and assemblies that are ready to be assembled into the finished product. These are often stored ready to be assembled when needed. *Finished goods* are products that are ready to be shipped to the customer.

Measures of Inventory System Performance

Return on investment (ROI) is very important to top managers who are accountable for company profitability. Where do inventories fit in the company scheme? Consider the following simplified ROI analysis:

$$\text{ROI} = \frac{\text{sales} - \text{cost of good sold}}{\text{physical} + \text{receivables} + \text{inventory}}$$

Inventories represent 25% of the assets of many companies. Of all the elements in the ROI formula, inventory offers the most promise for most managers and consultants. A decrease in the inventory investment can lead to a fast improvement in ROI.

Considering the inventory system on its own, however, one finds that the performance measures reflect the interests of the inventory system participants. Marketing creates a customer service measure: a certain number of orders should be shipped complete from stock or a certain percentage of units demanded should be shipped without backorder. Stockouts mean poor service, and an unacceptable stockout record probably means termination for the responsible inventory manager.

Financial managers think in terms of cost—the less inventory the better. Probably because they do not like borrowing money at high interest rates, financial people fear the holding costs of inventory. Since these costs are relatively easy to quantify, many financial people have undue influence on inventory systems. They erroneously assume that all inventory is excess stock or that the only inventory should be transaction stock. Of course, financial managers who are enlightened by a course in production control understand that organization stocks must be analyzed as an investment.

In addition to holding costs, financial people also think in terms of inventory turns. Inventory turnover is the ratio of the cost of sales in a period to the cost of average inventory on hand. For example, suppose that the cost of sales last month was $100,000, with a beginning inventory of $40,000 and an ending inventory of $60,000 for an average of $50,000. This equates to two turns per period. Although it is interesting, the inventory turns measure varies so greatly by type of business that we recommend it be viewed judiciously if not hostilely.

Manufacturing people are also involved in inventory decisions. Hurt by excessive setups and down time, is it any wonder that they become frustrated by short production runs when they are asked to produce the same item again this week after a very short run two weeks ago? Unfortunately, most companies keep poor records of setup costs and do not factor them into inventory investment targets as well as they might. This is partly because of the difficulty in providing reasonable setup cost estimates. The lower status of the manufacturing people relative to the financial and marketing people in some companies also contributes to a relative lack of attention to setup costs.

Inventory planning and control requires trade-offs between the three major system objectives: customer service, inventory investment, and production efficiency. Explicit or implicit costs associated with these objectives always exist, regardless of whether or not they can be measured accurately.

Holding or *carrying costs* are costs relevant to the inventory decision of when and how much to order. They represent future cash flows that will be changed by decisions to hold more or less inventory. Insurance, obsolescence, deterioration, property taxes, and the cost of capital can add up to 40% of the cost of the item in today's economy. Clearly, holding costs are relevant to the decision to order one more unit. (In this text, we use the terms holding and carrying costs interchangeably.) If a company faces out-of-pocket costs of $10 per unit to put an item on the shelf and if it must borrow money at 25%, then the cost to carry that extra item is

$2.50 plus the cost of insurance, obsolescence, deterioration, and tax. The company would be willing to pay up to $2.50 to retrieve $10. If there were an opportunity to earn 30% on an investment elsewhere in the company, management would be willing to pay up to $3 to retrieve $10. The key concept is one of out-of-pocket costs. If stock already exists at an earlier stage in manufacture, the holding cost at a later stage is the incremental investment of ordering the items through to the next stage, often called the *echelon holding cost.*

Setup costs or *ordering costs* that vary with the frequency of ordering must be considered in inventory decisions. Clerical costs of order preparation and order receiving must be carefully examined to insure that only marginal clerical costs are counted as ordering costs. Labor costs involved in setting up equipment make up setup costs. *Profits forgone* because of down time, which are often neglected, must be included when equipment is being operated at capacity. In the retail and distribution arena, the term *ordering cost* is used; the term *setup cost* generally refers to the sum of setup and ordering cost in a manufacturing environment.

Stockout costs are almost impossible to measure. A stockout occurs when a customer demands an item for which there is no inventory to meet the demand. The stockout may become a lost sale or a backorder. If it becomes a lost sale, revenue is lost. If it becomes a backorder, extra clerical costs and expediting costs occur. Both cases cause loss of customer goodwill.

Of the various measures of inventory system performance, holding costs have received the greatest attention. For example, a popular inventory control system categorizes inventory by dollar volume with the implicit objective of isolating those SKUs that tie up the most dollars. Since it appears in so many companies, we will begin our study of inventory control methods with the holding cost–oriented ABC system.

Inventory Distribution by Value: The ABC System

Not all customers and not all SKUs are equally important. The company president's golfing buddy should receive top priority, as should SKUs tying up an exorbitant proportion of dollars. The ABC system of inventory planning recognizes that 20% of the SKUs will account for 80% of the dollar value of the inventory. Consider the following case of five SKUs:

SKU	*Annual Demand*	*Cost*	*Dollar Volume*
1	5,000	$2	$ 10,000
2	1,000	$2	$ 2,000
3	10,000	$8	$ 80,000
4	5,000	$1	$ 5,000
5	1,500	$2	$ 3,000
			$100,000

Ranking these by dollar volume, we have

Label	*SKU*	*Dollar Volume*	*% SKUs*	*% Total Dollar Volume*
A	3	$80,000	20%	80%
B	1	$10,000	20%	10%
B	4	$ 5,000	20%	5%
C	5	$ 3,000	20%	3%
C	2	$ 2,000	20%	2%

Usually, the ABC system picks 15% to 20% of the items, representing 80% of dollar value, to be A items. Here SKU 3 would be an A item. Next, about 30% to 40% of the items form a B category, accounting for 15% of the total. Here, SKU 1 and SKU 4 would become B items. The rest are C items. This pattern has been replicated over and over in many companies: A = 20% SKUs/80% value, B = 40% SKUs/15% value, and C = 40% SKUs/5% value.

For purposes of forecasting, inventory control, and scheduling, smart managers keep their eyes on A items personally. No automatic forecasting system or automatic inventory control system will handle these items without their continuing intervention.

Inventory Systems

With a knowledge of the inventory costs involved and the selective perception suggested by the ABC system, we are now ready to study inventory systems designed to handle cost trade-offs. As we might expect, different systems are appropriate for different item categories. The fundamental decisions of inventory management are (1) when to order and (2) how much to order. To answer these questions, we must trade off costs, we must know what is likely to be sold, and we must know how much we have now. Sales forecasting, inventory record keeping, and inventory decision rules form the basis of most inventory control systems.

In this chapter, we will confine our attention to the when and how much questions with very simple systems. Although the most elementary models are not encountered in practice, an understanding of them allows us to work with the more complex models. Inventory systems under certainty take demand as fixed at a specified rate. Once we understand these systems, we can modify them to account for uncertainty.

THE BASIC ORDER POINT/ORDER QUANTITY SYSTEM

Suppose that annual demand for an item is $D = 10{,}000$ units. Throughout this chapter, we will assume a five-day work week with two weeks' vacation in July, giving us a 250-day year. The demand rate would

TABLE 4.1 Setup Costs for Trial Lot Sizes

Order Quantity (Q)	*Number of Orders*	*Annual Setup Cost ($)*
10,000	1	500
1,000	10	5,000
1	10,000	5,000,000

then be $d = 10{,}000/250 = 40$ per day. (We will forgo the use of Greek symbols for rates.) Further, annual per unit holding costs (h) are 40% of the cost of the item. The item's cost, $c = \$10$, gives $h = 0.4 * \$10 = \$4$. Setup costs are $S = \$500$. When and how much should the company produce? Table 4.1 displays three *order quantities* or *lot sizes*. (We use the term order quantity and production quantity somewhat interchangeably.) Immediately, we rule out ordering one unit at a time, since the $5,000,000 annual setup cost is prohibitive. With annual demand $D = 10{,}000$ and an order quantity $Q = 1{,}000$, we see that there would be $10{,}000/1{,}000 = 10$ orders in a year; that is, $D/Q = 10$. The annual setup cost is simply the number of orders times the setup cost per order, or $(D/Q) * S$. For $Q = 1{,}000$, we have annual setup cost of $(10{,}000/1{,}000) * \$500$. Annual setup costs increase as Q decreases, as can be seen in figure 4.2. Marginal analysis reveals that annual setup costs A are decreasing with Q at the rate of $-DS/Q^2$, since $dA/dQ = -DS/Q^2$. Raising Q from 1,000 to 2,000 saves $2,500, but raising it from 4,000 to 5,000 saves only $250.

At the same time that annual setup costs decrease with increases in Q, annual holding costs increase. With an order size of $Q = 1{,}000$, average inventory would be $Q/2 = 500$. This can be seen in figure 4.3. Over the first 100 days of the year, we move through four cycles, from 1,000 units in inventory to zero units, losing $d = 40$ units per day from inventory. Inventory declines linearly between $A = 1{,}000$ and $B = 0$. For such a

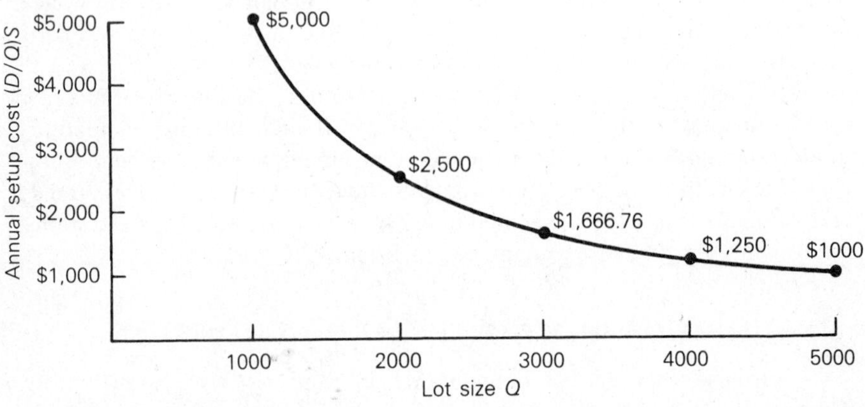

FIGURE 4.2 Annual setup cost as a function of lot size

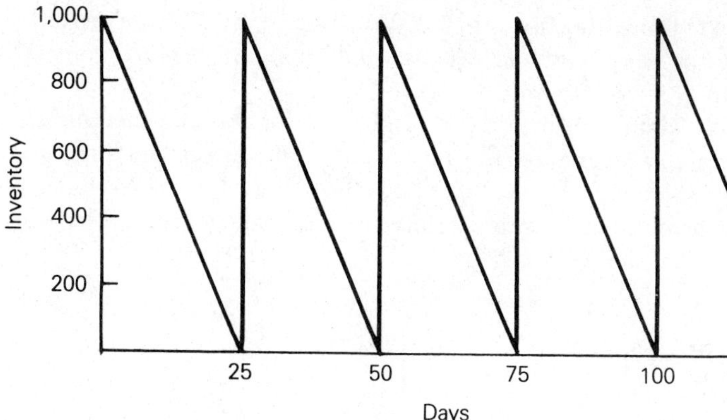

FIGURE 4.3 Inventory cycles

linear function, the average falls at the midpoint or geometric balance point of $(A + B)/2$. Since $A = Q$ and $B = 0$, average inventory is $Q/2$. This model thus depends heavily on the assumption of a constant sales rate producing a linear decline in the inventory position. In such a case, the annual holding costs are $(Q/2)h$. In our case, $h = 0.40 * \$10 = \$4$, giving an annual holding cost line of $\$4Q/2 = \$2Q$. This is pictured in figure 4.4.

Using marginal analysis, the annual holding costs H are increasing with Q at the rate of $2, since

$$\frac{dH}{dQ} = \frac{d\left(\frac{Q}{2} * h\right)}{dQ} = \frac{h}{2} = \frac{4}{2} = 2.$$

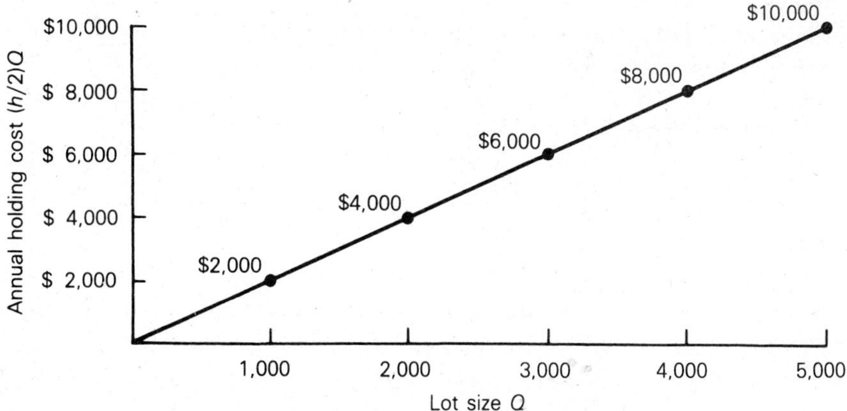

FIGURE 4.4 Annual holding cost as a function of lot size

Raising Q from 1,000 units to 2,000 increases annual holding costs by $2,000, exactly the same cost increase as would occur in moving from $Q = 4{,}000$ units to $Q = 5{,}000$ units.

We should be willing to raise Q so long as the incremental savings in setup cost overcome the incremental increase in holding cost. Annual setup cost changes by $-DS/Q^2$, which is equivalent to a savings of DS/Q^2. Equating the savings with the incremental holding cost, we have $DS/Q^2 = h/2$. Solving for Q, we have

$$Q^* = \sqrt{\frac{2DS}{h}}$$

where Q^* is the famous economic order quantity (EOQ) formula of 1915 vintage. Applied to our example, the optimal order quantity is

$$Q^* = \sqrt{\frac{2 * 10{,}000 * 500}{4}} = 1581$$

At the EOQ of 1581, the incremental setup cost of $2 per unit is exactly balanced with the incremental holding cost of $2 per unit; that is, $DS/Q^2 = h/2$. Peculiar to the cost functions in this model, annual setup costs happen to equal annual holding costs at the optimal Q; that is, $DS/Q = (Q/2)h$. Equating incremental costs equates annual costs in this case, but you should not accept this as a general principle for other cost functions.

Although the EOQ model has assumed a constant demand rate, the model itself is rather robust. Changes in annual demand or in the ratio of setup to holding costs do not cause severe changes in Q. Similarly, small changes in Q do not cause large changes in total relevant costs. To see this, consider the inventory cost equation $TRC(Q) = (Q/2)\,h + (D/Q)\,S$. We consider only costs that are relevant to the inventory decision, using the symbol $TRC(Q)$ to mean total relevant costs dependent on Q. Figure 4.5 combines the holding costs of figure 4.4 and the setup costs of figure 4.2 into a total relevant cost figure.

At the optimal $Q = 1581$, total relevant costs are

$$TRC = \frac{1581}{2} * 4 + \frac{10{,}000}{1581} * 500 = \$3{,}162 + \$3{,}162 = \$6{,}324$$

Doubling demand from 10,000 to 20,000 will not double Q but will raise it to 2,236, or $\sqrt{2}$ times the old EOQ. Inserting doubled demand in the EOQ formula, we obtain the new EOQ:

$$EOQ = \sqrt{\frac{2(2D)S}{h}} = \sqrt{2}\sqrt{\frac{2DS}{h}}.$$

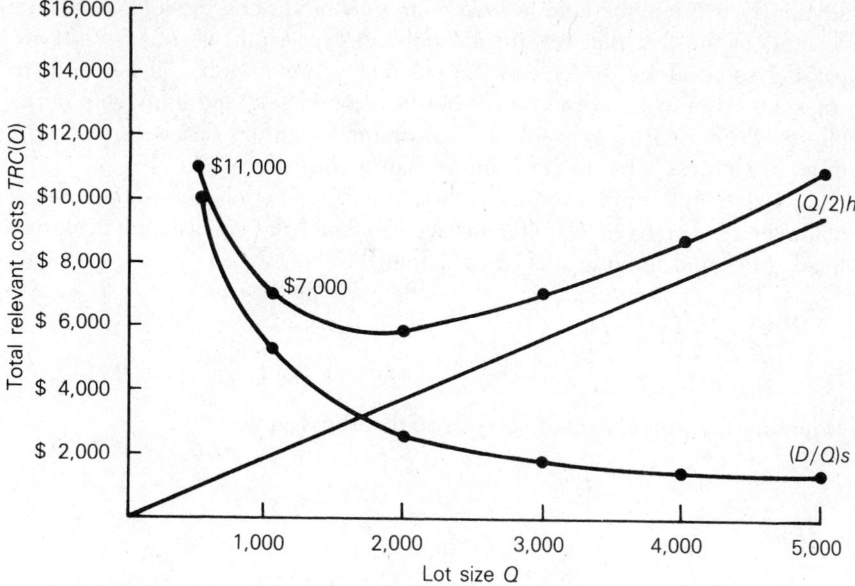

FIGURE 4.5 Total relevant costs

Similarly, total relevant costs are not very sensitive to small deviations from EOQ. At $Q = 1{,}000$, $TRC(Q) = \$7{,}000$; at $Q = 2{,}000$, $TRC(Q) = \$6{,}500$. Neither figure is far from $TRC(Q) = \$6{,}324$ for the EOQ.

In the scenario so far, we have been showing the next order arriving at precisely the time the first lot is used up. EOQ has answered the question of *how much* to order. Now we need to figure out *when* to order. We shall define lead time as the time between placing or releasing the order and receiving it. Assume that the lead time in our example is five days ($L = 5$). Because demand is certain, five days of supply will cover lead time demand. If we set a reorder point (ROP) at $Ld = 5 * 40 = 200$ units to cover lead time demand, then we will order $Q^* = 1581$ units when inventory on hand reaches 200 units.

PRODUCTION RATE MODEL

The basic EOQ/ROP model has assumed that the entire lot quantity is delivered at the end of the fixed lead time. In some manufacturing situations, however, the end of the lead time may signal the receipt of the first items of the production run. At a production rate of 100 units per day, it would take $Q/p = 1{,}000/100 = 10$ days to produce a lot size of 1,000 units. During that time, $(Q/p)d = 10 * 40 = 400$ units would be lost to sales. Effectively, this reduces the annual holding costs, because we never hold 1,000 units in stock but only a maximum of 600 units, $Q - (Q/p)d$. Consequently, we may be able to save money by increasing the lot size to take account of the fact that we are not holding every unit we receive but are passing some along directly to the customer. For example, if I set out to stack a cord of wood at the rate of one cord per week, and if my wife burns one-tenth of a cord per week, my maximum inventory will be nine-tenths of a cord unless I try to stack more than a cord per week.

Using logic similar to that in the basic EOQ model, we see that annual holding costs $1/2[Q - (Q/p)d]h$ are calculated on half the maximum inventory level. Marginal holding costs would then be

$$\frac{dH}{dQ} = \frac{h}{2}\left(1 - \frac{d}{p}\right)$$

Equating incremental holding costs and setup savings,

$$\frac{DS}{Q^2} = \frac{h}{2}\left(1 - \frac{d}{p}\right)$$

we can derive an economic production quantity (EPQ):

$$EPQ = \sqrt{\frac{2DS}{h(1 - d/p)}}.$$

With the costs in our example,

$$EPQ = \sqrt{\frac{2 * 10{,}000 * 500}{4 * (1 - 40/100)}} = 2{,}041$$

Figure 4.6 displays the solution, and table 4.2 gives a comparison of EOQ and EPQ. As we suspected, the EPQ gives a larger Q than the EOQ because the entire EPQ is never held in inventory. The maximum inventory is $Q(1 - d/p) = 2{,}041 * 0.6 = 1{,}225$.

QUANTITY DISCOUNTS

In the simple EOQ model, we counted only setup and ordering costs as relevant. If there are volume or quantity discounts for purchasing larger quantities, the purchase price is also a relevant cost. The total relevant cost formula in this case should be

$$TRC(Q) = \text{annual holding} + \text{annual ordering} + \text{annual purchase}$$

$$TRC(Q) = \left(\frac{Q}{2}\right)h + \left(\frac{D}{Q}\right)S + Dp$$

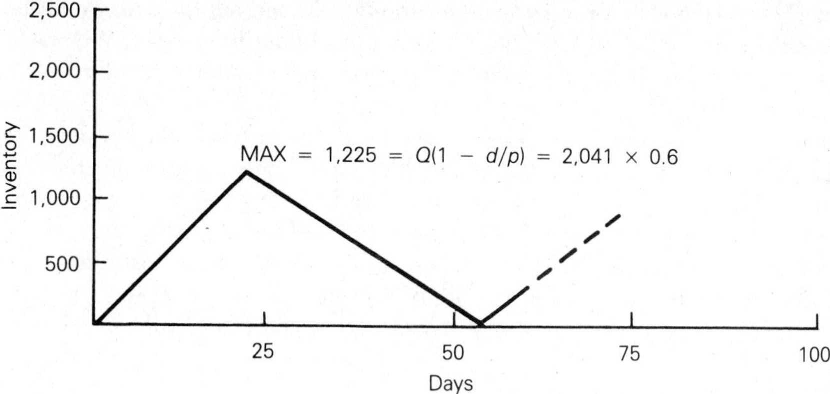

FIGURE 4.6 Production rate model

For example, quantities under 1,000 may cost \$12, those over 1,000 but under 4,000 may cost \$10, and those from 4,000 up may cost \$8. What, then, should be our order quantity? From our earlier work, we know that the EOQ at a price of \$10 is 1,581. Should we take that quantity or should we go for the price break? Let's compare TRCs, noting that 1,581 falls in the \$10 quantity range:

$$TRC(1{,}581) = \frac{1{,}581}{2} * 4 + \frac{10{,}000}{1{,}581} * 500 + 10{,}000 * 10$$

$$= 3{,}162 + 3{,}162 + 100{,}000 = \$106{,}324$$

$$TRC(4{,}000) = \frac{4{,}000}{2} * 3.2 + \frac{10{,}000}{4{,}000} * 500 + 10{,}000 * 8$$

$$= 6{,}400 + 1{,}250 + 80{,}000 = \$87{,}650$$

There is no comparison! We should definitely go for the price break, but should we go for a quantity higher than the price break? What is the EOQ at a price of \$8?

$$Q^* = \sqrt{\frac{2 * 10{,}000 * 500}{0.4 * 8}} = 1767.76$$

TABLE 4.2 Comparison of EOQ and EPQ

	EOQ	*EPQ*
Q	1,581	2,041
D/Q	6.325	4.9
Annual setup cost	\$3,162.5	\$2,450
Annual holding cost	\$3,162.5	\$2,450
TRC	\$6,324	\$4,900

At $Q^* = 1{,}768$, holding costs would be \$2,829 and setup costs would be about the same, *but the purchase discount would not be granted.* We would be stuck with a purchase price of \$10 per unit for annual total relevant costs of \$105,658. If we cannot achieve the EOQ point at the \$8 price, our best bet is to go up to the price break quantity of 4,000 units. We have no desire to go any higher, since that would only increase our holding costs, which are already too high compared to setup costs. Going to the price break reduces annual purchase price and annual setup cost at the expense of an increase in holding costs. If this results in a net cost reduction, then we will move to the price break quantity.

This suggests a procedure for handling quantity discount problems:

Step 1: Solve for EOQ at each price:

$$Q^*(p) = \sqrt{\frac{2DS}{h(p)}}$$

where $h(p)$ is a function of purchase price, such as $h(p) = 0.4p$, and $Q^*(p)$ shows Q as a function of p.

Step 2: If $Q^*(p)$ falls outside the quantity range for which the price can be obtained, throw it away.

Step 3: Select the price break quantities—those quantities that give us the next lowest price. In this example, there is a price break quantity at 1,000 units and another one at 4,000.

Step 4: Compare all remaining EOQs and all price break quantities in $TRC(Q) = (Q/2)h + (D/Q)S + Dp$ and choose the Q giving the smallest $TRC(Q)$.

This procedure can be visualized in figure 4.7, where the $TRC(Q)$ curves include purchase price. Table 4.3 gives intermediate calculations for figure 4.7. The three EOQs at the different prices are $Q^*_{12} = 1{,}443$, $Q^*_{10} = 1{,}581$, and $Q^*_8 = 1{,}768$. Q^*_{12} and Q^*_8 do not match with their price ranges. We cannot order Q^*_{12} and select the price break quantities of 1,000 and 4,000 units. $Q = 1{,}000$ at a price of \$10 is uninteresting because we've already seen that the optimal Q at a price of \$10 is $Q^*_{10} = 1{,}581$. At the upper end, $Q = 4{,}000$ is interesting because that quantity can get us a price break. Comparing the candidates $Q^*_{10} = 1{,}581$ and $Q = 4{,}000$, we choose $Q = 4{,}000$ with $TRC(4{,}000) = \$87{,}650$, considerably lower than $TRC(1{,}581) = \$106{,}324$.

In the quantity discount case, lower annual purchase costs can offset increased annual holding costs. Is it better to be at the optimal point (EOQ) on a higher per unit cost curve or to be at a nonoptimal point on a lower per unit cost curve?

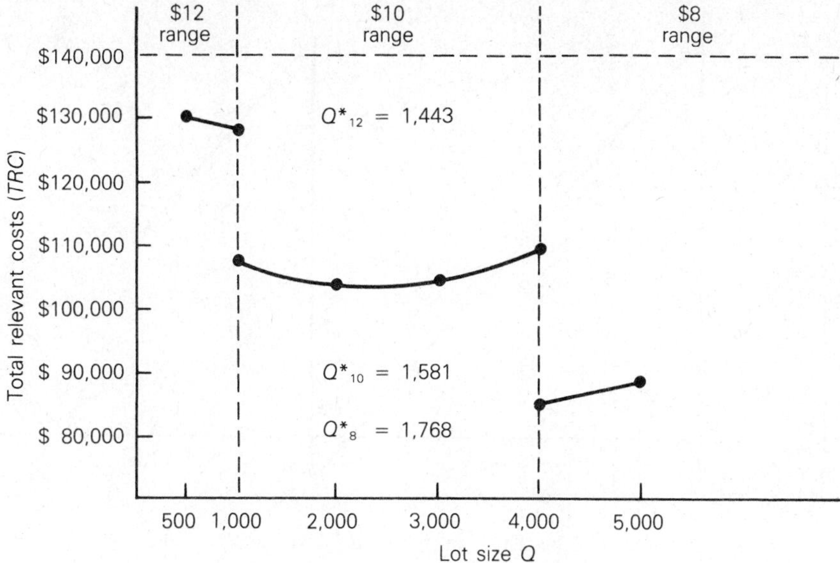

FIGURE 4.7 Total relevant costs for quantity discount model

Table 4.3 Total Relevant Costs

Q	*Per Unit* *($12)*	*Purchase Price* *($10)*	*($8)*
500	$131,200	OR[a]	OR
1,000	OR	$107,000	OR
2,000	OR	$106,500	OR
3,000	OR	$107,665	OR
4,000	OR	OR	$87,650
5,000	OR	OR	$89,000

[a] OR = outside range (i.e., price and quantity do not match).

EOQ WITH SHORTAGES

Earlier in this chapter, we mentioned that backorders come at the cost of extra clerical work, additional expediting, and customer dissatisfaction. If these are priced at $\$\pi$ per unit per year, how many backorders should be allowed per cycle (see figure 4.8)?

In one sense, backorders are simply negative inventory. If we order in lot sizes of Q and allow B backorders per cycle, then the average backorders would be $B/2$, just as the average inventory would be $M/2 = (Q - B)/2$. On each cycle, the maximum inventory is $M = Q - B$, because the new lot is immediately depleted by the backorder from the previous cycle.

The total relevant cost curve must now reflect backorder costs as well

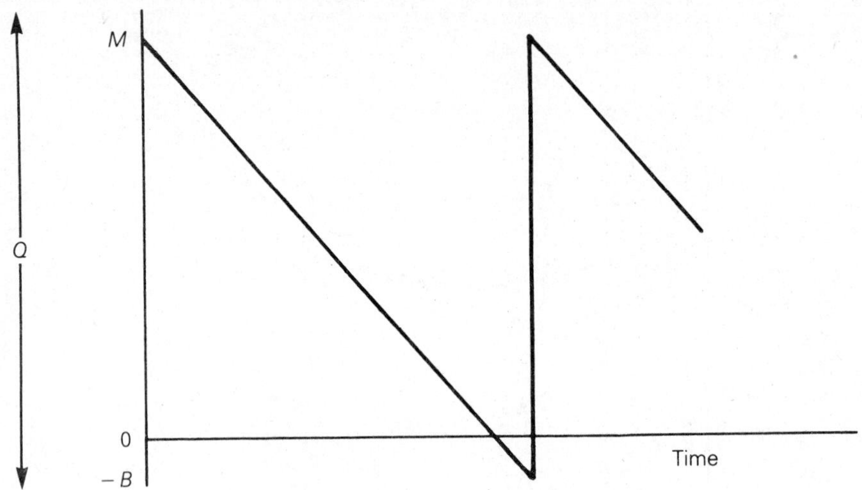

FIGURE 4.8 EOQ cycles with backorders

For example: $M = 90$, $Q = 100$, $B = 10$; $Q = M + B$.

as setup and holding costs. In addition, we now have two decisions: how much to order and how many backorders to allow.

$$TRC(Q,B) = \frac{(Q - B)}{2} * h * \frac{(Q - B)}{Q} \quad \text{(annual holding cost)}$$

$$+ \frac{B}{2} * \pi * \frac{B}{Q} \quad \text{(annual backorder cost)}$$

$$+ \frac{D}{Q} * S \quad \text{(annual setup cost)}$$

Here, $(Q - B)/Q$ represents the time on each cycle when positive inventory exists, and B/Q gives the time when negative inventory exists. For example, a maximum in inventory of $M = Q - B = 100 - 10 = 90$ and a demand rate of one unit per day would have each cycle lasting 100 days, 90 of which have a positive inventory situation. Since the holding cost is on a per unit per year basis, we must apply that cost only to times of positive inventory.

Similarly, B/Q is the fraction of the year with a backorder position. For example, an annual demand of 1000, a Q of 100, and B of 10 would give ten cycles in a year, with only 10% of each cycle spent in a backorder position. Restating the total relevant cost curve, differentiating, and setting the partial derivatives to zero, we can solve the optimal values of Q and B:

$$TRC(Q,B) = \frac{(Q - B)^2 h}{2Q} + \frac{B^2 \pi}{2Q} + \frac{DS}{Q}$$

$$= \frac{(Q^2 - 2QB + B^2)h}{2Q} + \frac{B^2 \pi}{2Q} + \frac{DS}{Q}$$

$$= \frac{Qh}{2} - Bh + \frac{B^2 h}{2Q} + \frac{B^2 \pi}{2Q} + \frac{DS}{Q}$$

$$\frac{\partial TRC(Q,B)}{\partial B} = -h + \frac{2Bh}{2Q} + \frac{2B\pi}{2Q} = 0$$

$$\frac{B}{Q}(h + \pi) = h$$

$$B = Q\left(\frac{h}{h + \pi}\right)$$

$$\frac{\partial TRC(Q,B)}{\partial Q} = \frac{h}{2} - \frac{B^2 h}{2Q^2} - \frac{B^2 \pi}{2Q^2} - \frac{DS}{Q^2} = 0$$

Multiplying through by $2Q^2$, we have

$$Q^2 h - B^2(h + \pi) - 2DS = 0$$

and substituting for B, we have

$$Q^2 h - Q^2 \frac{h^2}{(h + \pi)^2}(h + \pi) - 2DS = 0.$$

Simplifying further, we obtain

$$Q^2 h - Q^2 h \left(\frac{h}{h + \pi}\right) - 2DS = 0$$

$$Q^2 h \left(1 - \frac{h}{h + \pi}\right) = 2DS$$

$$Q^2 = \frac{2DS}{h}\left(\frac{h + \pi}{\pi}\right)$$

$$Q = \sqrt{\frac{2DS}{h}}\sqrt{\frac{h + \pi}{\pi}}$$

Example 4.1

Suppose that $D = 10{,}000$, $S = 500$, $h = 10$, and $\Pi = 40$. Solve for Q, B, and M.

Solution: We obtain

$$Q^* = \sqrt{\frac{2(10000)500}{10}}\sqrt{\frac{10 + 40}{40}}$$

$$= 1000 * 1.118 = 1118$$

$$B^* = 1118\left(\frac{10}{10 + 40}\right) = 223.6$$

$$M = 1118 - 224 = 894.$$

PERIODIC INVENTORY SYSTEMS

In the EOQ model with shortages, we began to think more about time—how much time was spent in a positive inventory position versus a backorder position. Nevertheless, our model was based on a continuous monitoring of inventory. Implicitly, we assumed that we would place an order to arrive just as our backorder position reached its optimal value.

In reality, however, many firms order periodically without a continuous tracking of inventory positions. With the EOQ-based models developed so far, it is relatively easy to convert to such a periodic system.

Ordering Q units at a time, there will be D/Q cycles in a year, but the time between orders will be Q/D. For example, $Q/D = 1000/12000$ would have us order every month. Letting T be the time between orders and using our EOQ model with shortages,

$$T = \frac{Q}{D} = \frac{\sqrt{\frac{2DS}{h}}\sqrt{\frac{h + \pi}{\pi}}}{D}$$

$$T^* = \sqrt{\frac{2S}{hD}}\sqrt{\frac{h + \pi}{\pi}}$$

Example 4.2

Suppose that $D = 10{,}000$, $S = 500$, $h = 10$, and $\pi = 40$. Solve for the optimal time between orders.

Solution: We obtain

$$T^* = \sqrt{\frac{2 * 500}{10 * 10{,}000}}\sqrt{\frac{10 + 40}{40}} = 0.1 * 1.118 = 0.1118$$

Then $Q^* = T * D = 0.1118 * 10{,}000 = 1{,}118$. On a 250-day working year, 0.1118 * 250 ≈ 28, so we should order 1,118 units every twenty-eight days.

Summary

Holding cost, setup cost, and stockout cost trade-offs have been the focus of this chapter. Because these trade-offs arise in the management of organization stocks rather than transaction stocks, they are essentially investment decisions: Should we invest in inventories to avoid excessive setups and downtime or to buffer against uncertain demand?

The amount of money to be invested in inventories depends on the dollar volume of sales. Hence, the ABC classification by dollar volume underlies the rest of the work in the chapter. If we can cheaply obtain reduced setup costs and increased protection against the uncertainties of demand for a particular product, we do not need to be overly concerned about inventory investment control.

Inventory control questions for items requiring significant inventory investment led to the question of how much to order and how often. Starting with the basic economic order quantity (EOQ) model, we traded off holding versus setup costs. We assumed instantaneous resupply, no quantity discounts, no shortages, and steady, deterministic demand.

Because the basic EOQ model was so restrictive, we relaxed the assumptions one by one. Examination of resupply time led to the model of usage during production. Quantity discounts created discontinuities in the relevant cost function and required an algorithm rather than a simple equation. Finally, by allowing shortages or backorders, we created a mirror image problem: How large should the maximum inventory be and how large should the maximum backorder position be?

Throughout our work with deterministic models, we have maintained an interest in the sensitivity of our decisions to changes in demand, setup costs, and holding costs. In addition, implicit or imputed costs arise. For example, specifying the number of cycles in a year provides information about the ratio of setup to holding costs.

In the next chapter, the deterministic demand assumption will be relaxed, and demand uncertainty will be handled by safety stocks.

PROBLEMS

1. A manufacturer carries stock of an item with an annual demand of 30,000 units. Although the inventory manager cannot estimate setup cost or holding cost precisely, she feels that the ratio of the two is

somewhere between 100 to 1 and 150 to 1; that is, $S/h = 100$ to $S/h = 150$. Calculate EOQ on both conditions.

2. How sensitive is the optimal Q to the S/h ratio? If S/h doubles or triples, what happens to Q^*?

3. How sensitive is Q to annual demand? If annual demand doubles or triples, what happens to Q^*?

4. Rather than expressing its order quantity in units, the Posifax Company uses dollars: $EOQ = \$500 = 250 * \$2$, where \$2 is the unit cost of the product. Further, the holding cost is $r * C$, where r is 40%. Recalling that $EOQ = \sqrt{2DS/rC}$, develop an EOQ formula for EOQ in dollars: $EOQ_{\$} = Q * C = ?$

5. With annual demand of 30,000 units, an S/h ratio of 100 to 1, and a lead time of ten days, what reorder point should the Marco Company use? Marco is open for business 250 days per year, and sales are assumed to occur at a constant rate. What would happen if the lead time sometimes went up to fifteen days?

6. A machine produces the product at a rate of 2,000 units per day. The annual demand of 200,000 occurs at a constant rate over the 250 business days in the year. Inventory carrying costs are 30% annually, and the unit variable production cost is \$25. The setup cost is \$500. What is the economic production quantity?

7. Two students must wash and dry dishes at a summer camp. There are exactly 100 dishes to be washed. The washer works at a rate of four dishes per minute. The dryer follows at a rate of three dishes per minute. What is the maximum number of dishes washed and waiting to be dried?

8. A company faces an annual demand of 10,000 units. Setup costs are \$200 per order, and the company orders in lot sizes of 1,000 units. What must be the company's holding cost per unit per year?

9. A company faces an annual demand of 10,000 units and a holding cost per unit per year of \$5. If the company insists that its lot size of 500 units is the correct one, what must be its setup cost per order?

10. A company annually orders one million pounds of a certain raw material for use in its own curing process. With annual holding costs estimated at 35% of the purchase price of \$50 per 100-pound bag, the purchasing manager wants to decide on an order size. Marginal paperwork costs are \$10 per order. For orders of 500 bags or more, the purchase price falls to \$45 per bag; for orders of 1000 bags or more, the price is \$40 per bag. What is the optimal order size?

11. An item has annual usage of 1000 units. The ordering cost is \$5, and the purchase price is \$3 each. With a carrying cost percentage of 25% and quantity discounts of 5% when 150 units or more are bought and 10% when 300 units or more are bought, what is the optimal order quantity?

12. Inventory costs for an important class of items are found to consist of a per unit storage cost, C_s, based on the maximum inventory level, and a regular holding cost, C_h, expressed as a percentage of the average dollar value of inventory. Develop a formula for EOQ under these conditions.

13. A company faces an annual demand of 1000 units for a particular product, setup costs of \$200 per setup, annual per unit holding costs of 25% of the product's value of \$12, and backorder penalties of \$10 per unit per year. What is the optimal order quantity?

14. A company orders in lot sizes of 2000 units. The holding cost per unit per year is \$8, and the backorder penalty per unit per year is \$15. What should be the maximum inventory held, and what should be the maximum backorder position?

15. With an annual demand of 200 units, setup costs of \$250, and holding costs of \$8 per unit per year, what is the optimal time between orders? Use a 250-day working year and specify the time in days.

16. With an annual demand of 2000 units, setup costs of \$250, holding costs of \$8 per unit per year, and backorder penalty costs of \$24 per unit per year, what is the optimal time between orders? Use a 250-day working year and specify the time in days.

17. In the shortage model, we saw that

$$B^* = Q\left(\frac{h}{h + \pi}\right)$$

Now show that

$$B^* = \sqrt{\frac{2DS}{\pi}}\sqrt{\frac{h}{h + \pi}}$$

18. In the shortage model, we saw that

$$B^* = Q\left(\frac{h}{h + \pi}\right)$$

Develop a similar type of formula relating M^* to Q and then show that

$$M^* = \sqrt{\frac{2DS\pi}{h(h + \pi)}}$$

19. In the standard EOQ model, we saw that

$$Q^* = \sqrt{\frac{2DS}{h}}$$

Now express $TRC(Q^*)$ in terms of D, S, and h only.

20. Modify the usage during production model to allow shortages.

appendix 4A

Inventory Carrying Cost May Be Less Than You've Been Told

by Philip Rhodes, CPIM

"Our inventory carrying costs are 30 percent or more of inventory value." Production people have been getting this message for years. These figures are used to justify shorter production runs and smaller purchase quantities. It is not unusual, however, for the actual cost of carrying finished goods or in-process material to be *less than one half as large as this 30 percent figure*. A similar miscalculation is often made, although to a lesser extent, for purchased materials. *This misconception stems from not looking at inventory by segment and not properly considering the manufacturing cost structure*. Production people often intuitively understand the fallacies which are the subject of this article, but cannot always communicate them effectively to the financial function and top management. The four fallacies discussed below are intended to help close this communications gap.

Fallacy #1

In calculating the inventory carrying cost (an interest rate "i" times inventory value), the fully absorbed or standard cost of material is generally used as the inventory value. For many *capital intensive manufacturers*, however, a very substantial portion of this cost represents allocations of fixed overhead—costs which are incurred regardless of production.

The inventory value used in calculating the cost of carrying inventory should include only *direct variable costs of production* (e.g. raw material, direct labor) and *volume sensitive indirect costs* (e.g. utilities used directly in the process, materials handling). *The inventory values used in calculating the carrying cost should exclude all fixed cost.* When the fixed cost, for example, is 50 percent of the standard cost, a reduction in inventory of $1.00 provides a cash-in-flow of $.50 *not* $1.00 as is usually assumed when calculating the inventory carrying cost.

Fallacy #2

In developing i, the inventory carrying cost percentage, recognition is not generally given to the increasing replacement cost of the inventory. In fact, inventory itself may represent an investment which is appreciating in value. Typically, for example, 20 percent is used as the opportunity cost of the capital tied-up in inventory.

If, however, the company has in the past realized a 20 percent return on its capital investments and the cost of replacing the inventory goes up seven percent per year, the difference between 20 percent and seven percent *not* the full 20 percent should be used in determining i. In other words, *the return on the inventory investment offsets to a significant extent the investment opportunity lost by tying-up the company's capital in inventory.*

Fallacies #1 and #2 can, in combination, cause a very substantial overstatement of inventory carrying cost. In the example below [table 4A.1] the *effective* carrying cost is 14 percent. As typically calculated it is 30 percent.

TABLE 4A.1 The Effective Carrying Cost

	As Typically Calculated	*As Discussed Above*
Carrying Cost "i":		
Opportunity Cost	20%	13%
Obsolescence, Damage, Shrinkage	5%	5%
Warehousing and Other General Overhead	5%	10%[a]
Total	30%	28%
Inventory "value"	$1.00	$.50
Calculated cost of carrying the inventory (i times inventory value)	$.30	$.14
Effective carrying cost % for the $1.00 in inventory (at fully absorbed cost)	30%	14%

[a] "Warehousing and Other General Overhead" is shown as 5% in the first column and twice that in the second column. This is because these same costs are being allocated in the second column over a variable cost inventory value only half as large as the fully absorbed cost in the first column.

As will be discussed below, obsolescence, damage, shrinkage and warehousing cost percentages are also often overstated.

Fallacy #3

Typically the carrying cost percentage includes a figure of five percent more to account for losses due to obsolescence, damage and shrinkage. The danger of obsolescence, however, relates primarily to how well inventories are balanced rather than to the total level of inventory.

In general, as a *percentage*, obsolescence is very low for items with low inventory (expressed in periods of supply) but, as the number of periods of supply of an item increases, the danger of obsolescence rises exponentially. The obsolescence factor should be excluded from the value of i when establishing order quantities. Across the board reductions in lot size have little impact on this factor. *Instead, maximums expressed on a periods of supply basis should be carefully established, item-by-item, for all inventory items* and engineering change procedures carefully controlled.

The use of a straight percentage is also inappropriate in figuring damage and shrinkage costs. These costs are more closely related to total production than to the level of inventory. It is only as a warehouse reaches capacity with the resulting use of various overflow areas, including outside warehousing, that the inventory level influences these costs.

As storage space becomes tight, materials may be moved several times before being issued to production or shipped. Also as space becomes tight, aisles are narrowed and other inappropriate or unsecured storage space comes into use. At this point losses related to inventory levels can become very substantial.

Fallacy #3 is essentially the fallacy of using average rather than incremental costs in decision making.

Fallacy #4

A related fallacy, as it also leads to the understatement of optimal lot sizes, is the use of production setup costs which are unrealistically low when calculating EOQs. *In many production processes yields and quality both may increase significantly after the process (run) has "settled down."*

In hand-assembly operations there can be a similar "learning curve" effect. Cost systems rarely measure this well known phenomenon. The costs of generating "shop packets," issuing materials and controlling orders in the shop can also be significant. If these various costs are measured and included as part of the setup cost for purposes of calculating optimal OQs, the EOQ will, in some cases, become substantially larger.

Conclusion

As the four fallacies discussed in this brief article demonstrate, formal analyses are rarely as straightforward as they appear. To be the master rather than slave of even "simple" mathematical models, such as those used to estimate the inventory carrying cost and EOQ, it is essential to understand the numerous hidden assumptions behind the calculations.

This article is *not* intended to suggest manufacturers should not be concerned about their inventory levels. To the contrary, *it is absolutely essential that order quantities be carefully controlled.* We all know cases of companies with a four year supply of an item because "the job was running good." Also common are instances in which production, in excess of authorized, has resulted in serious shortages of a raw material with a long purchasing leadtime. Excessive lot sizes contribute to broken setups and large WIP inventories which in turn lead to additional materials handling, damage and lost parts.

As this article illustrates, inadequate quantitative analysis can lead to incorrect conclusions. Production people are often very savvy about the complex interrelationships among *real* costs. Their knowledge, not the simplified formulas found in textbooks, should be the starting point for establishing "optimal" lot sizes.

To use quantitative methods effectively in any area of operations requires objectivity, considerable training and experience.

chapter five

Inventory Systems under Risk

Once we begin to move closer to reality, we must recognize that demand is never certain but that it occurs with some probability. Inventory models that consider risk or probability attempt to manage the chance of stockout by trading off holding costs, setup costs, and stockout costs.

In this chapter, we begin with a single-period trade-off between forgone profit, if not enough inventory is held, and loss on excess inventory sold at salvage. This simple trade-off focuses attention on stockout risk (the probability of stocking out), a concept underlying the entire chapter. Specifically, profit and cost if available lead us to an implied optimal stockout risk. If forgone profit and cost figures are unavailable, then at least their ratio can be imputed from the stockout risk the decision maker is willing to accept.

Before embarking on our journey into more difficult EOQ terrain, we need to recognize that many practitioners disparage EOQ models, sometimes with justification and sometimes without. Nevertheless, EOQ keeps coming back. Why?

There are cases in which EOQ should not be applied. (An entire later chapter is devoted to material requirements planning (MRP) for such cases.) Nevertheless, EOQ's staying power results from some simple characteristics of forecasting systems and inventory trade-offs. First, forecasting systems yield normally distributed error terms. If the error terms are not normally distributed, a good forecasting expert will be able to produce more accurate forecasts by incorporating another term to remove more explained variance from the forecasts. Second, end item or finished goods inventories embody cost trade-offs, whether or not they are explicitly recognized. The very act of specifying a lot size—any lot size—says something about managers' risk aversion and their concept of the relative magnitude of setup versus holding costs.

Throughout this chapter, we will constantly examine acceptable stockout risks. We can impute a stockout penalty for a stockout risk, just as we can derive an acceptable stockout risk if we are given a stockout penalty cost. This, then, will be a chapter on trade-offs, beginning with the most ubiquitous of all inventory problems—the trade-off of holding too little or too much inventory for a specified season or time period.

Single-Period Model

In New York City several years ago, an enterprising graduate student made \$10,000 one December selling Christmas trees. He purchased the trees at \$4 per tree and sold them at \$9. Although \$10,000 was enough to pay for a year's expenses at the university, the student was greedy. The next year, he expanded his business and managed to lose \$20,000. (After Christmas, a tree may be worth \$1—for firewood.)

Such single-period problems may be the most common inventory problem faced by businesses. Newspapers, milk, clothing, and many other consumer goods have a specified shelf life, after which they lose much of their value.

Assume that the graduate student's location in the city will generate for him an average demand of 2,000 trees ($\bar{x}$ = 2,000). The standard deviation of quantity demanded is 100 trees. Assuming that demand is normally distributed, there is a 0.50 probability that demand could be larger than 2,000 trees and a 0.16 probability that demand could be larger than 2,000 plus one standard deviation—that is, 2,000 + 100 = 2,100 trees. For a z value of 1.0, the area in the upper tail of the unit normal curve is 0.1587 (see appendix 5A at the end of this chapter).

k or z value	*SOR*
1.0	0.1587

What stockout risk should the student be willing to take? Good business majors would surely reply: "That depends on the rewards." The larger the per unit profit on a tree, the less willing the student should be to accept stockout risk; conversely, the larger the per unit loss on trees remaining unsold after Christmas, the more willing he should be to accept stockout risk so as to avoid being stuck with too many trees. Marketing majors might be tempted to create a Christmas tree tradition for Easter, but we prefer a more conservative solution to the problem.

We shall try to answer the question of how much risk the student should take. Let S = sales price, C = cost, and V = salvage value, so that the example here yields S = \$9, C = \$4, and V = \$1. Relying again on marginal analysis, the marginal profit (MP) on a tree is $S - C = \$5$ and the marginal loss (ML) is $C - V = \$3$. To order Q rather than $Q - 1$ trees, the expected profit on the marginal tree must be greater than or equal to the expected loss. Let p be the probability of selling the marginal tree. Then our profit criterion can be manipulated into a decision rule:

$$\begin{aligned} \text{expected profit} &\geqslant \text{expected loss} \\ p(MP) &\geqslant (1 - p)ML \\ p(MP) &\geqslant ML - p(ML) \\ p(MP + ML) &\geqslant ML \\ p &\geqslant \frac{ML}{MP + ML} \end{aligned}$$

Applying this rule to our example, we derive a minimum acceptable probability of selling the Qth tree:

$$p \geqslant \frac{3}{5 + 3} = \frac{3}{8} = 0.375$$

Therefore, the graduate student should buy the Qth tree provided that he has a 0.375 or better chance of selling it. Equivalently, the probability that quantity demanded will equal or exceed Q must be 0.375. Stockout risk (SOR), however, is precisely the probability that quantity demanded will exceed supply. Hence, our enterprising student is willing to accept SOR = 0.375. If we were to raise the marginal profit on a tree to \$6, he should be less willing to accept a higher stockout risk and, using $p \geqslant ML/(MP + ML)$, he would lower p to 0.33.

The rest is mechanical. The graduate student had enough foresight to save his production control text. Checking out appendix 5A for an upper tail area of 0.375, he finds a z value of 0.32. He should then order the mean plus 0.32 standard deviations worth of trees—that is, $\bar{x} + zs_x = 2000 + 0.32(100) = 2032$. (Note that we are using the normal distribution rather than the t because $n \geqslant 30$). In capsule form, the single period model has

$$SOR \geqslant ML/(MP + ML)$$

$$Q = \bar{x} + z_{SOR}\, s_x$$

$$MP \uparrow \text{ implies } SOR \downarrow$$

$$ML \uparrow \text{ implies } SOR \uparrow$$

Percent Order Service Safety Stock and the Multiperiod Case

Returning to our EOQ/ROP multiperiod model, we need to take account of stockout risk in a similar fashion. Usually, an item forecast is fed to the inventory system as an estimate of $\bar{x}_L$, the mean demand during lead time. Most forecasting systems also provide an estimate of the mean absolute deviation of lead time demand (MAD_L). Although the standard deviation is the preferred measure, habit has enthroned MAD, even though its ease of calculation is no longer important thanks to modern computers.

For the normal distribution, MAD is approximately 0.8σ. Because the sample mean absolute deviation is an unbiased estimate of the mean absolute deviation, just as the sample standard deviation is an unbiased estimate of the standard deviation, we can equivalently take MAD $= 0.8s$ or $s = 1.25$ MAD, where we adopt the sloppy but conventional notation that MAD stands for either the population or the sample mean absolute deviation.

Our multiperiod EOQ/ROP system can now be captured by the illustration in figure 5.1. Here, we assume that $\bar{x}_L = 200$, $MAD_L = 32$, $L =$ 5 days, $D = 10{,}000$, $S = 1{,}500$, and $h = 30$, using $Q^* = \sqrt{2DS/h}$, Q^*

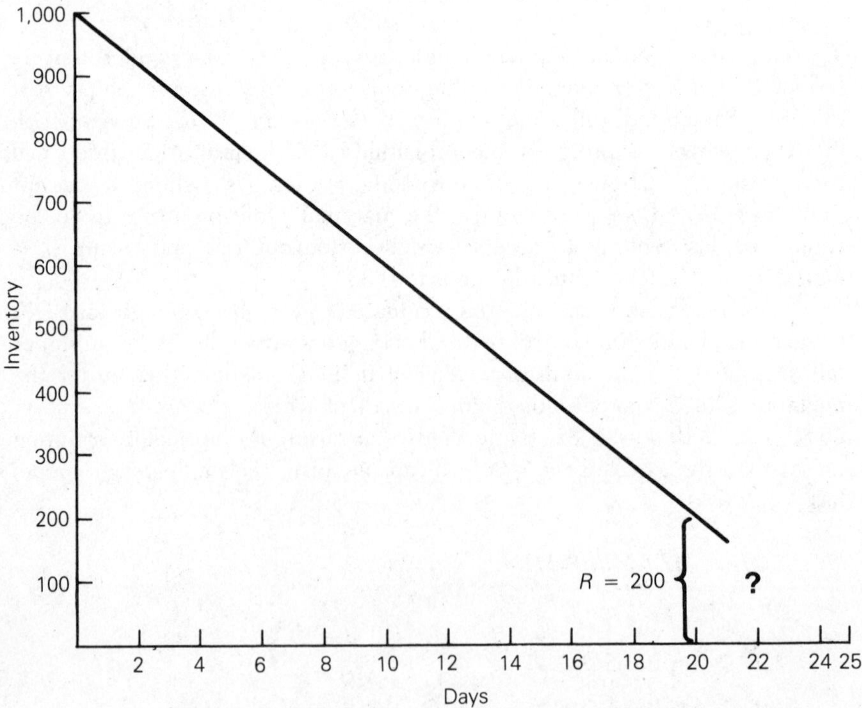

FIGURE 5.1 One cycle of EOQ/ROP with risk

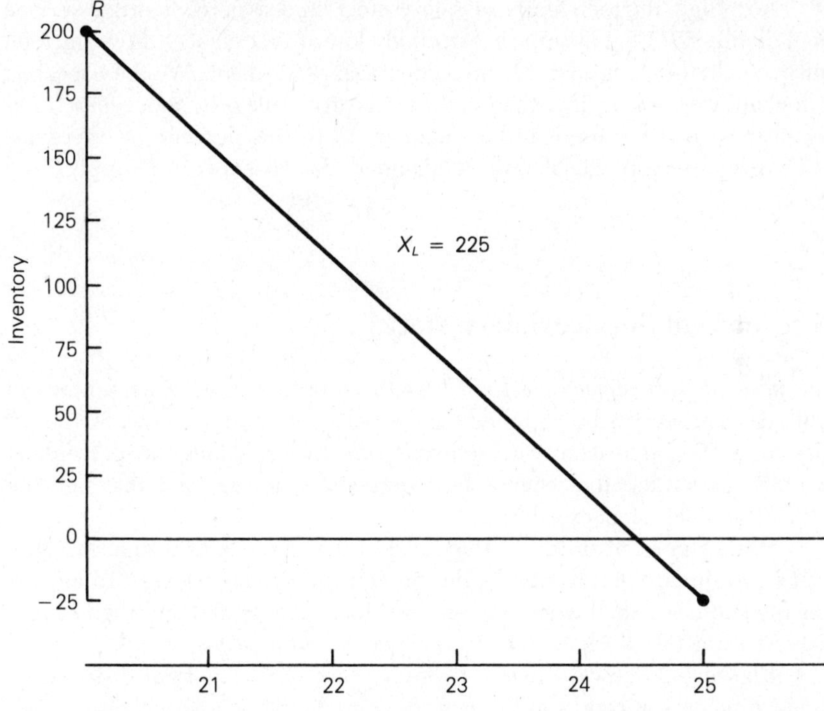

FIGURE 5.2 One cycle of ROP with risk

= 1,000 for this example. Also, there are ten cycles, because $D/Q^* = 10{,}000/1{,}000 = 10$. Figure 5.1 shows only one cycle (see also figure 5.2).

For the moment, suppose that the inventory manager is willing to accept a 0.375 probability of stockout on any cycle. What, then, should be the reorder point? Defining *percent order service* as the probability of satisfying all demand on a cycle, we have

$$OSL = 1 - OSOR$$

where *OSOR*, *order stockout risk*, is the probability that lead time demand will exceed lead time supply and *OSL*, the *percent order service level*, is the probability that lead time demand can be satisfied by the reorder quantity—the lead time supply. In our example, $OSL = 1 - 0.375 = 0.625$. In a manner identical to the order quantity calculation in the Christmas tree model, we calculate the reorder quantity. With $\bar{x}_L = 200$, $s_L = 1.25\ MAD_L = 1.25(32) = 40$, and $z_{0.375} = 0.32$, the desired lead time supply or reorder quantity is

$$R = \bar{x}_L + z_{SOR}\, s_x$$

$$R = 200 + 0.32(40) = 213 \text{ units}$$

Although thirteen units of safety stock and a percent order service level of only 62.5% may appear extremely low at first glance, these thirteen units actually buy considerable protection against stockout. We are expecting a stockout position in less than eight of twenty cycles, or about four times per year with the present order quantity. With this percent order service level, what percentage of units demanded do we expect to supply from stock?

Percent Unit Service Safety Stock

The *percent unit service level* answers the question of what percentage of units demanded can be supplied from stock. Sometimes known as the *fill rate*, it is the opposite of the *stockout rate* that specifies the percentage of units demanded that cannot be supplied from stock and that become either lost sales or backorders.

With a percent order service level of 0.625 and a lead time MAD of thirty-two units, what would be the percent unit service level? To answer this question, we shall work through the stockout rate first and then simply convert from the stockout rate to the percent unit service level.

Figure 5.3 shows R as the reorder point on the normal distribution of lead time demand and k as the reorder point on the unit normal distribution of lead time demand. The familiar standardization gives $R = (d_L - \bar{d}_L)/\sigma_L$. For the special case of R, $k = (R - \bar{d}_L)/\sigma_L$.

Fortunately, tables exist to give us the expected number of stockouts on the unit normal distribution. These tables are calculated from

$$E(Z - k)^+ = \int_0^k 0 f(z)\,dz + \int_k^\infty (z - k) f(z)\,dz$$

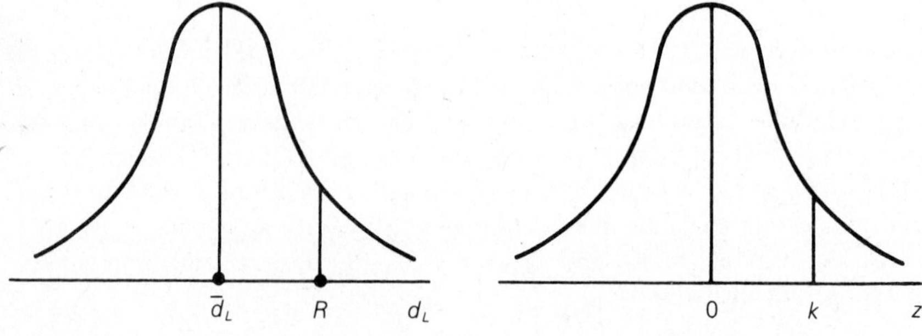

FIGURE 5.3 Stockouts on the normal versus unit normal

which is the standardized equivalent of

$$E(X - R)^+ = \int_0^R 0f(x)\,dx + \int_R^\infty (x - R)f(x)\,dx$$

For demand less than the reorder point, the stockout quantity is zero; for demand greater than the reorder point, the stockout quantity is demand minus the reorder point. Appendix 5A provides a table for the partial expectation, $E(Z - k)^+$ or $g(k)$.

In our example, we determined the reorder point using 0.32 standard deviations of safety stock to provide a 62.5% order service level. The expected number of stockouts per cycle on the unit normal curve would be

$$E(Z - k)^+ = g(k) = g(0.32) = 0.26$$

Conversion back to the normal distribution of lead time demand stems from observing the standardization relationships:

$$z - k = \left(\frac{x - \bar{x}_L}{\sigma}\right) - \left(\frac{R - \bar{x}_L}{\sigma}\right) = \frac{x - R}{\sigma}$$

so that

$$x - R = \sigma(z - k)$$

and

$$E(X - R)^+ = \sigma * E(Z - k)^+ = \sigma g(k)$$

In our case, $\sigma = 1.25\ MAD = 1.25(32) = 40$, and $g(k) = 0.26$. Hence, $E(X - R) = 40(0.26) = 10.4$. On every cycle, the expected number of stockouts is 10.4. On average, each cycle faces $Q = 1000$ units of demand, so that the unit stockout rate (USOR) would be $USOR = 10.4/1000 = 0.0104$. The associated percent unit service level (USL) is 0.9896.

Suppose that the inventory manager indicates that he really had meant a 99% unit service level. How would we calculate the appropriate safety stock directly?

$$USOR = \frac{E(X - R)^+}{Q}$$

(e.g., $10/1000 = 0.01$), but $E(X - R)^+ = \sigma g(k)$, where σ is the standard deviation of lead time demand, giving

$$\text{USOR} = \frac{\sigma g(k)}{Q}$$

or

$$g(k) = \frac{Q * USOR}{\sigma} = \frac{Q(1 - USL)}{\sigma}$$

and the unit service level can be expressed as 1-USOR, i.e.

$$USL = 1 - \frac{g(k)\sigma}{Q}$$

In our example, $g(k) = (1000 * 0.01)/40 = 0.25$. Finding the k in the table corresponding to $g(k) = 0.25$, we get $k = 0.35$. Hence, 0.35 standard deviations of safety stock ($SS = 0.35 * 40 = 14$ units) gives a 99% unit service level.

The following steps are necessary for calculating σ-based safety stock from a unit service objective:

1. Specify USL; $USL = 0.99$.
2. Calculate $USOR = 1 - USL$; $USOR = 0.01$.
3. Calculate $g(k) = (Q/\sigma)USOR$; $g(k) = (1000/40)0.01 = 0.25$.
4. Find the safety factor k giving $g(k) = 0.25$; $k = 0.35$.
5. Set safety stock at k standard deviations; $SS = k\sigma = 0.35(40) = 14$.
6. Set the recorder point to cover lead time demand plus safety stock; $R = \bar{x}_L + SS = 200 + 14 = 214$.*

Backorder or Lost Sale Costs

As most inventory managers will do, ours has specified a 99% service level without explicitly considering stockout costs. Because we already have holding cost estimates, we can now derive the *implicit* or *imputed* stockout costs that the inventory manager used intuitively. Our analysis will distinguish between the backorder and the lost sales case. The analysis is important in its own right, because it will allow us to specify safety stocks when we are provided with stockout cost estimates but no desired service levels.

BACKORDER CASE

In the *backorder* case, we note that raising the reorder point by one unit will cost us $h(Q/D) = \$3$ per cycle. This is so because we will hold the unit for almost the entire cycle, regardless of whether or not it is used to satisfy demand. If we do not add the unit to the reorder point, we suffer a backorder penalty of $\$\pi$ per unit (expediting costs, extra paperwork, ill will) with probability SOR. Balancing these marginal costs gives

---

* The reorder points for the order and unit service levels are shown in the Exhibit on page 717.

Per cycle marginal cost of adding 1 unit to R
= per cycle marginal cost of *not* adding 1 unit to R

$$h(Q/D) = OSOR(\pi)$$

$$OSOR = \frac{hQ}{\pi D} \quad \text{or} \quad \pi = \frac{hQ}{OSOR * D}$$

In our case, we must determine π, the *imputed* backorder cost given the inventory manager's 99% unit service level. Recall that we calculated a safety stock of fourteen units for a 99% USL. Such a safety stock yields a 36.3% order service level (OSL). This is so because $z\sigma = z(40) = 14$ gives a z value of 0.35. With $h = \$30$ per unit per year, $Q = 1{,}000$, $D = 10{,}000$, and $OSOR = 0.363$, we estimate the backorder cost to be \$8.26 per unit:

$$\pi = \frac{30(1{,}000)}{0.363(10{,}000)} = \$8.26$$

Our inventory manager has second thoughts, however; \$8.26 sounds too low! He or she really thinks the backorder penalty is more in the area of \$15 per unit.

Undaunted, the inventory analyst checks this out in terms of implied OSOR, USOR, and safety stock:

$$OSOR = \frac{hQ}{\pi D} = \frac{30(1{,}000)}{15(10{,}000)} = 0.2$$

$$SS = z_{0.2}\sigma = 0.84(40) \simeq 34$$

$$USOR = \frac{\sigma g(k)}{Q} = \frac{40g(0.84)}{1{,}000} = \frac{40(0.112)}{1{,}000} = 0.004$$

$$USL = 1 - 0.004 = 0.996$$

In the backorder case, stockout costs of \$15 per unit lead to a 99.6% unit service level. But what about the lost sales case? Why would that be any different?

LOST SALES CASE

In the lost sales case, the stockout cost π^1 includes forgone revenue in addition to customer ill will. Marginal analysis also yields slightly different results because of the impact of lost sales on inventory levels. Adding one unit to R costs $h(Q/D)$ in holding. If we do not add the unit, the penalty in the event of stockout includes π^1 and some wasted holding $h(Q/D)$. To see this, suppose that $D = 20$ and $Q = 10$. A stockout on the first cycle implies that eleven units of demand have occurred, while ten units have been supplied. To start the next cycle, the full supply of $Q = 10$ units is on hand. (Compare this to the backorder case, where the backorder would deplete the beginning inventory down to nine units.) With $D = 20$, only nine units of demand remain for the second cycle. Hence, one *extra* unit of inventory will be held through the second cycle.

Marginal cost of adding

1 unit to reorder point $h(Q/D)$

= marginal cost of *not* adding

1 unit to reorder point OSOR * [πth (Q/D)]

$$h(Q/D) = SOR * [\pi^1 + h(Q/D)]$$

$$OSOR = \frac{h(Q/D)}{\pi^1 + h(Q/D)}$$

$$OSOR = \frac{hQ}{hQ + \pi^1 D}$$

Assuming a lost sale penalty of \$15 per unit, we would have

$$OSOR = \frac{30(1{,}000)}{30(1{,}000) + 15(10{,}000)} = 0.167$$

An OSOR of 0.167 calls for z value of about 0.97 and, consequently, about thirty-nine units of safety stock $(SS) = 0.97 * 40)$. Converting to percent unit service level can be done readily:

$$USL = 1 - \frac{g(k)\sigma}{Q}$$

$$= 1 - \frac{g(0.97)(40)}{1{,}000}$$

$$= 1 - \frac{0.088(40)}{1{,}000} = 0.996$$

Comparing the backorder and lost sales case for the same stockout penalty, the lost sales case uses slightly more safety stock.

Joint Determination of *Q* and *R*

Had Q been 500 rather than 1,000 units, more safety stock would be needed to cover the increased number of cycles in the year. Returning to the backorder case, recall that the safety stock was fourteen units, with ten cycles per year. Now, with $D/Q = 10{,}000/500 = 20$ cycles per year, we must search for a k to yield $g(k) = 0.125$, because, by formula,

$$g(k) = \frac{Q(USOR)}{\sigma} = \frac{500(0.01)}{40} = 0.125 \qquad \begin{aligned} SS &= k\sigma \\ SS &= 0.78 * 40 = 31.2 \end{aligned}$$

Looking for k in the appendix, we find $k = 0.78$. The corresponding safety stock is about thirty-one units. Since $\bar{x}_L = 200$, the reorder point for $Q = 500$ is 232. The interrelationships between Q and R can be visualized by this simple comparison between two order sizes. The larger order size:

Q	SS	R	D/Q	$Q/2$
500	32	232	20	250
1,000	14	214	10	500

yields lower safety stock and fewer setups but higher cycle inventory. The smaller order size yields just the reverse. Thus, to determine Q and R, we must examine them together.

Because the stockout penalty is assessed on the number of units stocked out, the expected stockout cost per cycle is $\sigma g(k) * \pi$. In the previous example, the expected number of units stocked out per cycle was $\sigma g(k) = 40 * 0.125 = 5$ units. With a penalty cost of \$8 per unit stocked out, the expected stockout cost per cycle was 5 * \$8 = \$40.

By analogy to setup cost, we can modify the EOQ formula to include the expected stockout cost per cycle. Adding what we already know about the determination of the reorder point for the backorder case, we have a set of formulas to determine Q and R jointly:

$$Q^* = \sqrt{\frac{2D[S + \pi\sigma_L g(k)]}{h}}$$

$$g(k) = \frac{Q^*\ USOR}{\sigma_L}$$

$$OSOR = \frac{hQ}{\pi D}$$

$$R = \bar{x}_L + k * \sigma_L$$

We shall try it and improvise as we go, again using the same example with $S = 1{,}500$ and $USL = 99\%$ versus $USL = 95\%$. First, for $USL = 99\%$:

Step 1: Calculate Q^*, ignoring stockouts.

$$Q^* = \sqrt{\frac{2 * 10{,}000 * 1{,}500}{30}} = 1{,}000$$

Step 2: Calculate $g(k)$ for $Q^* = 1{,}000$.

$$g(k) = \frac{1{,}000 * 0.01}{40} = 0.25$$

$$k = 0.35$$

Step 3: From appendix 5A, determine $OSOR = 36.3\%$, with $z = k = 0.35$.

Step 4: Calculate $\pi = (hQ)/(OSOR * D) = (30 * 1{,}000)/(0.363 * 10{,}000) = 8.26$.

$$Q^* = \sqrt{\frac{2 * 10{,}000 * (1{,}500 + 8.26 * 40 * 0.28)}{30}}$$

$$Q^* = 1{,}027$$

Step 5: Calculate $g(k)$ for the new $Q^* = 1{,}027$.

$$g(k) = \frac{1{,}027 * 0.01}{40} = 0.257$$

$$k \simeq 0.33$$

Step 6: Repeat steps 4 and 5 until two successive values of Q (or k) are the same. We must settle, then, on $Q = 1{,}028$, $k = 0.33$, and $R = 200 + 0.33 * 40 = 213$.

Now, for $USL = 95\%$:

Step 1: Calculate Q^*, ignoring stockouts.

$$Q^* = \sqrt{\frac{2 * 10{,}000 * 1{,}500}{30}} = 1{,}000$$

Step 2: Calculate $g(k)$ for $Q^* = 1{,}000$.

$$g(k) = \frac{1{,}000 * 0.05}{40} = 1.25$$

$$k = -1.19$$

(Read down the far right-hand column of Appendix 5A until you reach 1.25.)

Step 3: Calculate $OSOR = 1 - 0.117 = 0.883$, with $z = k = -1.19$.

Step 4: Calculate $Q^* = 1{,}055$, with $\pi = 3.40$. $\left(\text{from } \pi = \dfrac{h * Q}{OSOR * D}\right)$

Step 5: Calculate $g(k)$ for $Q^* = 1{,}055$:

$$g(k) = \frac{Q * USOR}{\sigma}$$

$$g(k) = \frac{1{,}055 * 0.05}{40} = 1.32$$

$$k \simeq -1.27$$

Step 6: We must settle here on $Q = 1{,}057$, $k = 1.32$, and $R = 200 - 1.32 * 40 = 147.2$.

To follow the sequence further, consider the case where the desired service level cannot be specified but the backorder cost is estimated at $15 per unit. In that case, we must do some extra calculations to find the USOR;

Step 1: Calculate Q^*, ignoring stockouts:

$$Q^* = 1{,}000$$

Step 2: Calculate $g(k)$ for $Q^* = 1{,}000$:

$$OSOR = \frac{hQ}{\pi D} = \frac{30 * 1{,}000}{15 * 10{,}000} = 0.2$$

$$z_{0.2} = 0.84$$

$$k = z_{0.2} = 0.84$$

$$g(k) = g(0.84) = 0.112$$

$$USOR = \frac{g(k) * \sigma}{Q^*} = \frac{0.112 * 40}{1{,}000} = 0.00448$$

$$USL = 0.995$$

Step 3: Calculate Q^* for $g(k) = 0.112$

$$Q^* = \sqrt{\frac{2 * 10{,}000 * (1{,}500 + 15 * 40 * 0.112)}{30}}$$

$$Q^* = 1{,}022$$

Step 4: Calculate $g(k)$ for $Q^* = 1{,}022$:

$$g(k) = \frac{Q^*\ USOR}{\sigma} = \frac{1{,}022 * 0.0048}{40} = 0.114$$

Step 5: Repeat steps 3 and 4 until Q or k repeats:

$$Q^* \simeq 1{,}023$$
$$k \simeq 0.14$$

Remember that the expected stockout cost per cycle acts analogously to the setup cost: The higher the expected stockout cost per cycle, the larger the EOQ; and the higher the setup cost, the larger the EOQ.

Lead Time Adjustments

To this point, our entire analysis has been based on $\bar{x}_L$ and s_L, the mean and standard deviation of lead time demand. Most forecasting systems in use today yield monthly forecasts. Since the lead time may not be in months, some conversion is necessary. When lead time is variable, this conversion can be cumbersome. Many suggest simply forecasting demand during lead time as a data series, rather than combining separate estimates of lead time and demand per unit time. In many companies, lead time demand is not recorded. For that reason, we should take a close look at lead time adjustments.

Suppose that our lead time is two weeks and our forecast is for a four-week month. Obviously, the forecast for lead time demand would be simply half the four-week forecast—but what about MAD for lead time demand? To answer this question, we must resort to some elementary statistics. If two random variables are identically and independently distributed, then the variance of the sum is the sum of the variances:

$$\text{var}(X_1 + X_2) = \text{var}(X_1) + \text{var}(X_2)$$
$$\text{S.D.}(X_1 + X_2) = \sqrt{\text{var}(X_1) + \text{var}(X_2)}$$

where S.D. is the standard deviation.
Intuitively, this bit of statistics reveals that the standard deviation of a sum is less than the sum of the standard deviations. Suppose that the standard deviation of X_1 is 100 and the standard deviation of X_2 is 100. The standard deviation of $X_1 + X_2$ would be $\sqrt{100^2 + 100^2} \simeq 141$—only 40% more than the variance of one of the variables taken alone. If we have several variables, all with the same standard deviation, we can simplify the situation:

$$\text{var}(X_1 + X_2 + \ldots + X_n) = n\ \text{var}(X_1)$$
$$\text{S.D.}(X_1 + X_2 + \ldots + X_n) = \sqrt{n} * \text{S.D.}(X_1)$$

In our example, $\text{S.D.}(X_1 + X_2) = \sqrt{2} * \text{S.D.}(X_1)$.

Applying these concepts to lead time demand, we first need to calculate the ratio of lead time to forecast interval:

$$k = \frac{\text{lead time}}{\text{forecast interval}} = \frac{2 \text{ weeks}}{4 \text{ weeks}} = \frac{1}{2}$$

Then calculate $\bar{x}_L = k * \bar{x}_f$, where $\bar{x}_f$ is the four-month forecast. If s_f = 1.25MAD is the standard deviation of forecast error, then we have $s_L = \sqrt{k}\, s_f$, where s_L is the standard deviation of lead time forecast error. We can summarize lead time conversion in four formulas:

$$k = \frac{\text{lead time}}{\text{forecast interval}} \qquad \left(\text{e.g., } k = \frac{1}{2}\right)$$

$$\bar{x}_L = k * \bar{x}_f \qquad \left(\text{e.g., } 500 = \frac{1}{2}(1{,}000)\right)$$

$$s_L = \sqrt{k} * s_f \qquad \left(\text{e.g., } 70.7 = \sqrt{\frac{1}{2}}(100)\right)$$

$$MAD_L = \sqrt{k} * MAD_f \qquad \left(\text{e.g., } 56.6 = \sqrt{\frac{1}{2}}\,(80)\right)$$

Continuing our example with $k = 1/2$, suppose that $\bar{x}_f = 1{,}000$ and $MAD_f = 80$. Then $s_f = 1.25 * 80 = 100$, $s_L = 70.7$, and $\bar{x}_L = 1/2 * 1{,}000 = 500$.

Lead Time Variability

Lead time variability must also be accounted for. Although the preferred approach is to measure actual demand during each lead time and then to forecast lead time demand with its associated standard deviation, most forecasting and inventory control systems are not designed to do this. Another approach is to *manage* the lead time so that lead time can be ignored in safety stock calculations. An approach of last resort is to measure lead time variability and to merge it with demand variability.

If we assume that lead times are normally distributed with mean $\overline{LT}$ and standard deviation σ_{LT}, it is possible to derive an estimate of the standard deviation of demand during uncertain lead time. Brown [1, p. 376] showed that variance of lead time demand equals variance of lead time demand given average lead time plus variance of lead time demand given average demand:

$$\sigma^2_{LTD} = \overline{LT}\,\sigma^2_f + \bar{x}^2_f\,\sigma^2_{LT}$$

where f refers to the forecast interval.

The variance of lead time demand given average lead time is the variance stemming from demand variability. To derive $\overline{LT}\,\sigma^2_f$ we proceed using the variance rule: variance (sum) = sum (variances), where sum = $d_1 + d_2 + \ldots + d_L$.

The variance of lead time demand given average demand is the variance stemming from lead time variability. To derive $\bar{x}^2_f\,\sigma^2_{LT}$, we must use the relation $\text{var}(kX) = k^2\,\text{var}(X)$; that is, the variance of the product of a constant times a variable is a product of the square of the constant times the variance of the variable.

Brown [3, pp. 148–151] claims that MAD is no longer appropriate to the real world of computers. He also advises steering clear of mathematical models of the standard deviation over randomly varying lead times. Since Brown originally developed both of these ideas, we must assume that he has seen the error of his youthful ways. Nevertheless, MAD persists and, short of simulation, an estimate of the variance of lead time demand during uncertain lead times cannot easily be avoided given current forecasting and data collection practices.

Time-Varying Demand

In a later chapter, we will recommend the use of a minimum cost per period algorithm to determine order quantities for highly fluctuating demand rates. For the typical seasonal sales pattern, however, the EOQ approach developed in this chapter should be satisfactory. At this point, we might merely consider the reorder point under time-varying demand:

$$R = x_L + SS$$

When the forecasts indicate a trough in demand, the reorder point will decline, only to increase when the forecasts pick up again. The reorder point constantly adjusts to the projected activity level.

Anticipated Price Increases

As we examine real-world variations on the models in this chapter, we must face the reality of inflation. For items that we sell, inflation has little effect on our models, since it is always better to satisfy customer demand by holding inventory for as little time as possible. For items that we purchase, anticipated price increases can entice us to purchase early.

Again, marginal analysis yields a simple decision rule, suggested by McClain and Thomas [4]. If the price of an item is about to increase by $\$X$ permanently, what should the order quantity be? Ordering Q units, we will hold the last unit ordered for Q/D years for a marginal holding cost of $h(Q/D)$. Other savings will result from postponing one setup, but we will ignore these as they are small. Equating the marginal benefits and costs $X = [h(p)Q]/D$ and solving for Q^* (the optimal Q), we find

$$Q^* = X\frac{D}{h(p)}$$

For example, a \$5 anticipated increase from \$25 to \$30, with 30% holding costs and an annual demand of 1,000 units, would give an optimal order quantity

$$Q^* = \frac{5 * 1{,}000}{0.3 * 25} = 667$$

Inventory Control Systems

Various inventory control systems may be encountered in practice. Here we present some of these systems as variations of the models given in this chapter.

1. *Periodic system:* Every T years (e.g., 0.2 years), we order an amount to bring us up to a target level S. Hence, Q is variable, as shown in figure 5.4. If we add one unit to S, we will hold an item for a fraction T of the year at a cost of h per year. The holding cost for that unit is then hT. This will be worth the money, provided that hT is not greater than the expected stockout cost $SOR(\pi)$. The decision rule then becomes: Determine S so that $hT = SOR(\pi)$, or

$$SOR = \frac{hT}{\pi}$$

$$S = \bar{x}_p + z_{SOR} * \sigma_p$$

where σ_p is the standard deviation of demand over the planning interval $T + L$.

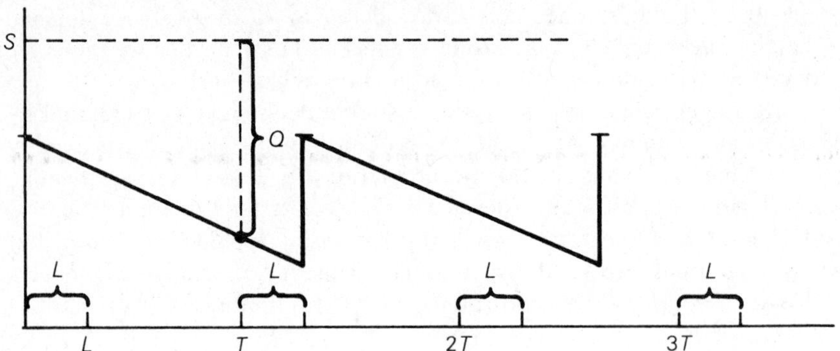

FIGURE 5.4 Cycles in a periodic inventory system

Because $T = Q/D$, we can easily determine the optimal T from the EOQ formula:

$$Q^* = \sqrt{\frac{2DS}{h}}$$

$$T^* = Q^*/D = \sqrt{\frac{2S}{hD}}$$

We can then calculate S and Q:

$$S = \bar{x}_p + z_s\sigma_p$$

where x_p is the mean usage during the planning interval $T + L$. Similarly, σ_p is the standard deviation of planning interval demand. $Q = S - I$, where I is the current on hand plus on order.

The periodic system had more appeal in precomputer days, because it does not require continuous inventory records. The long planning interval, with its associated demand variation, causes more safety stock to be held than in the similar (Q, R) system. Of course, joint determination of S and T can also be considered.

2. (Q, Q) is a two-bin policy. When inventory falls to the reorder point Q, an order is placed for Q units. This system makes stores clerks happy, because no fancy record keeping is needed. They merely open the second bin and place an order.

3. (S, s) is the most robust policy and is optimal under the greatest number of conditions. When inventory falls to s, an order is placed up to the level S; that is, the order is the difference between current inventory and S. If demand occurs one unit at a time, then a (Q, R) policy would be

identical. Otherwise, current inventory may be less than R when the order is placed, and the (Q, R) system would order Q, whereas the (S, s) system would order S minus current on hand and on order (I).

4. $(S, S\text{-}1)$ is a base stock policy. When inventory falls below S, an order is placed up to S. Known in industry as the sell-one/buy-one policy, this procedure is used for low-demand items. We will see it again in the chapter on multilocation inventories.

Summary

In this chapter, we dealt with a company facing demand uncertainty. The models of the preceding chapter were extended and modified to cope with this uncertainty. Using marginal analysis, we found that we could derive safety stock rules. Just as the preceding chapter examined the setup versus holding cost trade-off, this chapter balanced stockout costs against the costs of holding safety stock. In addition to demand uncertainty, a company can also face lead time uncertainty. Safety stock should cover lead time demand. Hence, forecasts must be converted to a lead time base, and the variance of lead time forecasts then becomes the basis for safety stock calculations.

Imputed or implicit costs appeared throughout this chapter. The act of specifying a desired or acceptable service level reveals information about the relative magnitude of the costs involved.

Finally, the uncertain real world offers the challenge of time-varying demand and price increases. Generally, a good forecasting system will project seasonal demand rates so that we can adjust inventory levels over the year. With inflation, anticipated price increases can also cause us to change our order quantity.

Since the end-of-chapter problems will require a fair amount of student effort, we present here a summary approach for tackling the problems. The main equations are

$$Q = \sqrt{\frac{2D[S + \pi\sigma g(k)]}{h}}$$

$$R = \mu_L + k\sigma_L$$

$$OSOR = \frac{hQ}{\pi D}$$

$$USOR = \frac{\sigma g(k)}{Q}$$

The following points should be kept in mind:

TABLE 5.1 Classification of Safety Stock Calculation Methods

	Order Service Level	*Unit Service Level*
Stockout cost known; optimal service level derived	$OSOR = \frac{hQ}{\pi D}$	$OSOR = \frac{hQ}{\pi D}$ implies a k value $USOR = \frac{g(k) * \sigma}{Q}$
Stockout cost imputed; desired service level specified	$\pi = \frac{hQ}{OSOR * D}$	$g(k) = \frac{Q * USOR}{\sigma}$ implies a k value and consequent $OSOR$

1. k depends on the desired demand coverage.
2. Lead time demand is the basis of the system.
3. Lead time may vary over the year.
4. Price increases would automatically change the holding costs and thus must be considered.

Classifying the problem as shown in table 5.1 will aid in developing a solution.

We encourage the student to embellish the scheme as necessary to help in the solution of the chapter problems. For any further work of this type, Brown [2] can serve as a comprehensive reference to the appropriate use of order points and order quantities.

PROBLEMS

For all problems, assume the company is open for business 5 days a week for 50 weeks a year.

1. Seasonal demand for air conditioners at the Koolair store is normally distributed, with mean equal to 100 units and standard deviation equal to 20. The retail price per unit is $275 and the cost to the store is $170. For ordering once to cover seasonal demand, the store manager needs an optimal number of air conditioners to order. In the past, the manager has sold off units at a 50% discount once the peak heat spell is over. How many units should the manager order?

2. A perishable item is ordered only once each demand period. Acquisition cost is $3, selling price is $5, and salvage value is $1.50. What is the optimal order quantity?

Demand	*Probability*
100	0.1
110	0.2
120	0.2
130	0.3
140	0.1
150	0.1

3. Find the optimal reorder point for the following item, using percent order safety stock. Mean weekly demand is 400 units, with a standard deviation of 100 units. Setup costs are $50 per order, and inventory carrying costs are $1.30 per unit per year. The desired order service level is 95% and the lead time is one week.

4. The monthly demand for an item was recorded as follows:

1	*2*	*3*	*4*	*5*	*6*	*7*	*8*	*9*	*10*	*11*	*12*
335	295	275	305	304	338	290	305	285	275	295	311

   Calculate the mean absolute deviation and the standard deviation of forecast error if the forecast is 300 per month. What safety stock would be required if orders are received monthly and if two stockout occurrences in twelve months are acceptable.

5. A company orders in lot sizes of 100 units while facing annual demand of 2,000. Holding costs are $10 per unit per year, and the desired order service level is 95%. What is the implicit stockout cost assuming the backorder case?

6. A company orders in lot sizes of 100 units while facing annual demand of 3,000. Holding costs are $8 per unit per year, and the desired order service level is 98%. What is the implicit stockout cost assuming the lost sales case?

7. A forecasting system yields weekly forecasts. The current forecast is 100 units for the next week, and the weekly MAD is 20. Lead time is one week. Annual demand is 8,000 units, and the company uses an order quantity of 500 units. To provide 99% unit service, what safety stock should be kept?

8. A forecasting system yields weekly forecasts. The current forecast is 100 units per week, and the weekly MAD is 40. Lead time is one week. To provide 99% unit service, the company holds a safety stock of about 45 units. Annual demand is 9,000 units, and the company uses an order quantity of 500 units. To preserve the same service level, what order size would allow the company to carry no safety stock? How many inventory cycles would occur in a year?

9. A company decides to order in larger lot sizes to avoid carrying safety stock. Specifically, the company increases its order quantity from 500 units to 600 units. At the same time, a safety stock of 30 units is completely eliminated. Which order quantity yields lower annual holding costs.

10. Annual demand for an item is 1,000 units. Unit price is $1.50, and the annual holding cost is 35% per year. Backorder costs are $3 per unit, and setup costs are $15 per lot. Lead time is eight days and the standard deviation of lead time demand is eight units. What are the joint optimal Q and R levels?

11. Annual demand for an item is 1,000 units. Unit price is $5, and the annual holding cost is 35% per year. Backorder costs are impossible to estimate, although management desires a 98% unit service level. Setup costs are $10 per lot. Lead time is eight days, and the standard deviation of lead time demand is eight units. What are the joint optimal Q and R levels? What are the *implicit* backorder costs?

12. For a particular item, management desires s 98% unit service level. Weekly demand averages 1,000 units, with a standard deviation of 100 units. Setup costs are $200, and holding costs are $10 per unit per year. Lead time is five working days on average, with a standard deviation of one day. Determine the joint optimal Q and R levels. Point out any possible weakness in this application of inventory control models.

13. Orders for an item are received one week after they are placed, and the ordering cost is $10. Demand during this lead time is normally distributed, with a mean of nine units and a standard deviation of two units. Holding costs are $1.50 per unit per week, and the stockout cost is $10 per unit of unsatisfied demand. All unsatisfied demand is lost. What are the joint optimal Q and R levels?

14. Find the optimal reorder point for the following item, using percent order safety stock. Mean yearly demand is 20,000 units, with a standard deviation of 1,000 units. Setup costs are $50 per order, and inventory carrying costs are $1.30 per unit per year. The desired order service level is 95%, and the lead time is two weeks.

15. A forecasting system yields weekly forecasts. The current forecast is 100 units per week, and the weekly MAD is 20. Lead time is approximately normally distributed, with a mean of five working days and a standard deviation of two working days. Annual demand is 9,000 units, and the company uses an order quantity of 1,000 units. To provide 98% unit service, what safety stock should be kept? Assume the backorder case.

16. Reliable rumor has it that our petroleum-based raw material will undergo a 20% price increase next month. We are currently placing an order for 1,000 units at $20 per unit. Given an annual demand of 10,000 units and a holding cost percentage of 35%, should we revise our order quantity? If so, what should it be?

17. A forecasting system yields weekly forecasts. The current forecast is 100 units for the next week, and the weekly MAD is 20. Lead time is approximately normally distributed, with a mean of five working days and a standard deviation of three working days. Annual demand is 8,000 units, and the company uses an order quantity of 1,000 units. To provide 98% unit service, what safety stock should be kept?

18. A forecasting system yields weekly forecasts. The current forecast is 100 units for the next week, and the weekly MAD is 20. Lead time is approximately normally distributed, with a mean of sixteen working days and a standard deviation of three working days. Annual demand is 8,000 units, and the company uses an order quantity of 1,000 units. To provide 98% unit service, what safety stock should be kept?

19. For a 5% order stockout risk, what is the implied cost of a backorder for the following item? Using a combined (Q, R) model, the company faces annual sales of 500 units. The inventory holding charge is $25 per unit per year. Setup cost is $20, and the standard deviation of lead time demand is 25 units.

20. For a certain item, weekly demand is forecast at 120 units, with a standard deviation of 20 units. The inventory carrying charge is 25% of the unit value of $20. Setup costs are $25. With a lead time of eight days, determine the appropriate reorder point to maintain a 90% order service level. Now assume that the per unit backorder cost is $3. Determine the appropriate order quantity and order point using a joint optimal (Q, R) policy.

REFERENCES AND BIBLIOGRAPHY

1. R. G. Brown, *Smoothing, Forecasting and Prediction of Discrete Time Series*, (Englewood Cliffs, N.J.: Prentice-Hall, 1963).
2. R. G. Brown, *Decision Rules for Inventory Management* (New York: Holt, Rinehart and Winston, 1967).
3. R. G. Brown, *Materials Management Systems* (New York: John Wiley & Sons, 1977).
4. J. O. McClain and L. J. Thomas, *Operations Management* (Englewood Clliffs, N.J.: Prentice-Hall, 1980).

appendix 5A

Table of the Unit Normal Distribution

Number of Standard Deviations of Safety Stock (k or z)	*Stockout Risk (SOR)*	*Expected Stockouts [g(k) or g(z)]*[a]	*Expected Stockouts [g(−k) or g(−z)]*[a]
0.00	0.5000000	0.3989423	0.3989423
0.01	0.4960106	0.3939622	0.4039622
0.02	0.4920216	0.3890221	0.4090221
0.03	0.4880335	0.3841218	0.4141218
0.04	0.4840465	0.3792614	0.4192614
0.05	0.4800611	0.3744409	0.4244409
0.06	0.4760777	0.3696602	0.4296602
0.07	0.4720968	0.3649193	0.4349193
0.08	0.4681186	0.3602182	0.4402182
0.09	0.4641435	0.3555569	0.4455569
0.10	0.4601721	0.3509353	0.4509353
0.11	0.4562046	0.3463535	0.4563535
0.12	0.4522415	0.3418112	0.4618112
0.13	0.4482832	0.3373086	0.4673086
0.14	0.4443300	0.3328455	0.4728455
0.15	0.4403823	0.3284220	0.4784220
0.16	0.4364405	0.3240379	0.4840379
0.17	0.4325051	0.3196931	0.4896931
0.18	0.4285763	0.3153877	0.4953877
0.19	0.4246546	0.3111216	0.5011216
0.20	0.4207403	0.3068946	0.5068946
0.21	0.4168339	0.3027068	0.5127068
0.22	0.4129356	0.2985579	0.5185579
0.23	0.4090459	0.2944480	0.5244480
0.24	0.4051652	0.2903770	0.5303770
0.25	0.4012937	0.2863447	0.5363447
0.26	0.3974319	0.2823511	0.5423511
0.27	0.3935802	0.2783960	0.5483960
0.28	0.3897388	0.2744794	0.5544794
0.29	0.3859082	0.2706012	0.5606012
0.30	0.3820886	0.2667612	0.5667612
0.31	0.3782805	0.2629594	0.5729594
0.32	0.3744842	0.2591956	0.5791956

Number of Standard Deviations of Safety Stock (k or z)	*Stockout Risk (SOR)*	*Expected Stockouts [g(k) or g(z)]*[a]	*Expected Stockouts [g(−k) or g(−z)]*[a]
0.33	0.3707000	0.2554697	0.5854697
0.34	0.3669283	0.2517815	0.5917815
0.35	0.3631694	0.2481310	0.5981310
0.36	0.3594236	0.2445181	0.6045181
0.37	0.3556913	0.2409425	0.6109425
0.38	0.3519728	0.2374042	0.6174042
0.39	0.3482683	0.2339030	0.6239030
0.40	0.3445783	0.2304388	0.6304388
0.41	0.3409030	0.2270114	0.6370114
0.42	0.3372428	0.2236207	0.6436207
0.43	0.3335979	0.2202665	0.6502665
0.44	0.3299686	0.2169487	0.6569487
0.45	0.3263552	0.2136671	0.6636671
0.46	0.3227581	0.2104215	0.6704215
0.47	0.3191775	0.2072119	0.6772119
0.48	0.3156137	0.2040379	0.6840379
0.49	0.3120670	0.2008996	0.6908996
0.50	0.3085375	0.1977966	0.6977966
0.51	0.3050257	0.1947288	0.7047288
0.52	0.3015318	0.1916960	0.7116960
0.53	0.2980559	0.1886981	0.7186981
0.54	0.2945985	0.1857348	0.7257348
0.55	0.2911597	0.1828060	0.7328060
0.56	0.2877397	0.1799116	0.7399116
0.57	0.2843388	0.1770512	0.7470512
0.58	0.2809573	0.1742247	0.7542247
0.59	0.2775953	0.1714320	0.7614320
0.60	0.2742531	0.1686728	0.7686728
0.61	0.2709309	0.1659469	0.7759469
0.62	0.2676288	0.1632541	0.7832541
0.63	0.2643472	0.1605942	0.7905942
0.64	0.2610862	0.1579671	0.7979671
0.65	0.2578460	0.1553724	0.8053724
0.66	0.2546269	0.1528101	0.8128101
0.67	0.2514288	0.1502798	0.8202798
0.68	0.2482522	0.1477814	0.8277814
0.69	0.2450970	0.1453147	0.8353147
0.70	0.2419636	0.1428794	0.8428794
0.71	0.2388520	0.1404754	0.8504754
0.72	0.2357624	0.1381023	0.8581023
0.73	0.2326950	0.1357600	0.8657600
0.74	0.2296499	0.1334483	0.8734483
0.75	0.2266273	0.1311670	0.8811670
0.76	0.2236272	0.1289157	0.8889157

Number of Standard Deviations of Safety Stock (k or z)	*Stockout Risk (SOR)*	*Expected Stockouts* [g(*k*) *or* g(*z*)][a]	*Expected Stockouts* [g(−*k*) *or* g(−*z*)][a]
0.77	0.2206499	0.1266943	0.8966943
0.78	0.2176954	0.1245026	0.9045026
0.79	0.2147638	0.1223404	0.9123404
0.80	0.2118553	0.1202073	0.9202073
0.81	0.2089700	0.1181032	0.9281032
0.82	0.2061080	0.1160278	0.9360278
0.83	0.2032693	0.1139809	0.9439809
0.84	0.2004541	0.1119623	0.9519623
0.85	0.1976625	0.1099718	0.9599718
0.86	0.1948945	0.1080090	0.9680090
0.87	0.1921502	0.1060738	0.9760738
0.88	0.1894296	0.1041659	0.9841659
0.89	0.1867329	0.1022851	0.9922851
0.90	0.1840601	0.1004312	1.0004312
0.91	0.1814112	0.0986038	1.0086038
0.92	0.1787864	0.0968028	1.0168028
0.93	0.1761855	0.0950280	1.0250280
0.94	0.1736088	0.0932791	1.0332791
0.95	0.1710561	0.0915557	1.0415557
0.96	0.1685276	0.0898578	1.0498578
0.97	0.1660232	0.0881851	1.0581851
0.98	0.1635431	0.0865373	1.0665373
0.99	0.1610871	0.0849142	1.0749142
1.00	0.1586553	0.0833155	1.0833155
1.01	0.1562477	0.0817410	1.0917410
1.02	0.1538642	0.0801904	1.1001904
1.03	0.1515050	0.0786636	1.1086636
1.04	0.1491700	0.0771602	1.1171602
1.05	0.1468591	0.0756801	1.1256801
1.06	0.1445723	0.0742230	1.1342230
1.07	0.1423097	0.0727886	1.1427886
1.08	0.1400711	0.0713767	1.1513767
1.09	0.1378566	0.0699871	1.1599871
1.10	0.1356661	0.0686195	1.1686195
1.11	0.1334996	0.0672736	1.1772736
1.12	0.1313569	0.0659494	1.1859494
1.13	0.1292382	0.0646464	1.1946464
.14	0.1271432	0.0633645	1.2033645
1.15	0.1250720	0.0621035	1.2121035
1.16	0.1230245	0.0608630	1.2208630
.17	0.1210005	0.0596429	1.2296429
18	0.1190002	0.0584429	1.2384429
19	0.1170233	0.0572628	1.2472628
.20	0.1150697	0.0561024	1.2561024
.21	0.1131395	0.0549613	1.2649613

Number of Standard Deviations of Safety Stock (k or z)	*Stockout Risk (SOR)*	*Expected Stockouts* [g(*k*) or g(*z*)][a]	*Expected Stockouts* [g(−*k*) or g(−*z*)][a]
1.22	0.1112325	0.0538395	1.2738395
1.23	0.1093486	0.0527366	1.2827366
1.24	0.1074878	0.0516525	1.2916525
1.25	0.1056498	0.0505868	1.3005868
1.26	0.1038347	0.0495394	1.3095394
1.27	0.1020424	0.0485100	1.3185100
1.28	0.1002726	0.0474985	1.3274985
1.29	0.0985254	0.0465045	1.3365045
1.30	0.0968006	0.0455279	1.3455279
1.31	0.0950980	0.0445684	1.3545684
1.32	0.0934176	0.0436258	1.3636258
1.33	0.0917592	0.0427000	1.3727000
1.34	0.0901227	0.0417906	1.3817906
1.35	0.0885081	0.0408975	1.3908975
1.36	0.0869150	0.0400204	1.4000204
1.37	0.0853435	0.0391591	1.4091591
1.38	0.0837934	0.0383134	1.4183134
1.39	0.0822645	0.0374832	1.4274832
1.40	0.0807567	0.0366681	1.4366681
1.41	0.0792699	0.0358680	1.4458680
1.42	0.0778039	0.0350826	1.4550826
1.43	0.0763586	0.0343118	1.4643118
1.44	0.0749337	0.0335554	1.4735554
1.45	0.0735293	0.0328131	1.4828131
1.46	0.0721451	0.0320847	1.4920847
1.47	0.0707809	0.0313701	1.5013701
1.48	0.0694367	0.0306690	1.5106690
1.49	0.0681122	0.0299813	1.5199813
1.50	0.0668072	0.0293067	1.5293067
1.51	0.0655217	0.0286451	1.5386451
1.52	0.0642555	0.0279963	1.5479963
1.53	0.0630084	0.0273600	1.5573600
1.54	0.0617802	0.0267360	1.5667360
1.55	0.0605708	0.0261243	1.5761243
1.56	0.0593800	0.0255246	1.5855246
1.57	0.0582076	0.0249367	1.5949367
1.58	0.0570534	0.0243604	1.6043604
1.59	0.0559174	0.0237955	1.6137955
1.60	0.0547993	0.0232420	1.6232420
1.61	0.0536989	0.0226995	1.6326995
1.62	0.0526161	0.0221679	1.6421679
1.63	0.0515507	0.0216471	1.6516471
1.64	0.0505026	0.0211369	1.6611369
1.65	0.0494715	0.0206370	1.6706370
1.66	0.0484572	0.0201474	1.6801474

Number of Standard Deviations of Safety Stock (k or z)	*Stockout Risk (SOR)*	*Expected Stockouts [g(k) or g(z)]*[a]	*Expected Stockouts [g(−k) or g(−z)]*[a]
1.67	0.0474597	0.0196678	1.6896678
1.68	0.0464786	0.0191982	1.6991982
1.69	0.0455140	0.0187382	1.7087382
1.70	0.0445654	0.0182878	1.7182878
1.71	0.0436329	0.0178469	1.7278469
1.72	0.0427162	0.0174151	1.7374151
1.73	0.0418151	0.0169925	1.7469925
1.74	0.0409295	0.0165788	1.7565788
1.75	0.0400591	0.0161739	1.7661739
1.76	0.0392039	0.0157776	1.7757776
1.77	0.0383635	0.0153897	1.7853897
1.78	0.0375379	0.0150103	1.7950103
1.79	0.0367269	0.0146389	1.8046389
1.80	0.0359303	0.0142757	1.8142757
1.81	0.0351478	0.0139203	1.8239203
1.82	0.0343794	0.0135727	1.8335727
1.83	0.0336249	0.0132327	1.8432327
1.84	0.0328841	0.0129001	1.8529001
1.85	0.0321567	0.0125750	1.8625750
1.86	0.0314427	0.0122570	1.8722570
1.87	0.0307418	0.0119461	1.8819461
1.88	0.0300540	0.0116421	1.8916421
1.89	0.0293789	0.0113449	1.9013449
1.90	0.0287165	0.0110545	1.9110545
1.91	0.0280665	0.0107706	1.9207706
1.92	0.0274289	0.0104931	1.9304931
1.93	0.0268034	0.0102220	1.9402220
1.94	0.0261898	0.0099570	1.9499570
1.95	0.0255880	0.0096981	1.9596981
1.96	0.0249978	0.0094452	1.9694452
1.97	0.0244191	0.0091981	1.9791981
1.98	0.0238517	0.0089568	1.9889568
1.99	0.0232954	0.0087211	1.9987211
2.00	0.0227501	0.0084908	2.0084908
2.01	0.0222155	0.0082660	2.0182660
2.02	0.0216916	0.0080465	2.0280465
2.03	0.0211782	0.0078322	2.0378322
2.04	0.0206751	0.0076229	2.0476229
2.05	0.0201821	0.0074186	2.0574186
2.06	0.0196992	0.0072192	2.0672192
2.07	0.0192261	0.0070246	2.0770246
2.08	0.0187627	0.0068347	2.0868347
2.09	0.0183088	0.0066493	2.0966493
2.10	0.0178644	0.0064684	2.1064684
2.11	0.0174291	0.0062920	2.1162920

Number of Standard Deviations of Safety Stock (k or z)	*Stockout Risk (SOR)*	*Expected Stockouts [g(k) or g(z)]*[a]	*Expected Stockouts [g(−k) or g(−z)]*[a]
2.12	0.0170030	0.0061198	2.1261198
2.13	0.0165857	0.0059519	2.1359519
2.14	0.0161773	0.0057881	2.1457881
2.15	0.0157776	0.0056283	2.1556283
2.16	0.0153863	0.0054725	2.1654725
2.17	0.0150034	0.0053205	2.1753205
2.18	0.0146287	0.0051724	2.1851724
2.19	0.0142621	0.0050279	2.1950279
2.20	0.0139034	0.0048871	2.2048871
2.21	0.0135525	0.0047498	2.2147498
2.22	0.0132093	0.0046160	2.2246160
2.23	0.0128737	0.0044856	2.2344856
2.24	0.0125454	0.0043585	2.2443585
2.25	0.0122244	0.0042347	2.2542347
2.26	0.0119106	0.0041140	2.2641140
2.27	0.0116038	0.0039964	2.2739964
2.28	0.0113038	0.0038819	2.2838819
2.29	0.0110106	0.0037703	2.2937703
2.30	0.0107241	0.0036617	2.3036617
2.31	0.0104441	0.0035558	2.3135558
2.32	0.0101704	0.0034527	2.3234527
2.33	0.0099031	0.0033524	2.3333524
2.34	0.0096419	0.0032546	2.3432546
2.35	0.0093867	0.0031595	2.3531595
2.36	0.0091375	0.0030669	2.3630669
2.37	0.0088940	0.0029767	2.3729767
2.38	0.0086563	0.0028890	2.3828890
2.39	0.0084242	0.0028036	2.3928036
2.40	0.0081975	0.0027205	2.4027205
2.41	0.0079763	0.0026396	2.4126396
2.42	0.0077603	0.0025609	2.4225609
2.43	0.0075494	0.0024844	2.4324844
2.44	0.0073436	0.0024099	2.4424099
2.45	0.0071428	0.0023375	2.4523375
2.46	0.0069469	0.0022670	2.4622670
2.47	0.0067557	0.0021985	2.4721985
2.48	0.0065691	0.0021319	2.4821319
2.49	0.0063872	0.0020671	2.4920671
2.50	0.0062097	0.0020041	2.5020041
2.51	0.0060366	0.0019429	2.5119429
2.52	0.0058678	0.0018833	2.5218833
2.53	0.0057031	0.0018255	2.5318255
2.54	0.0055426	0.0017693	2.5417693
2.55	0.0053862	0.0017146	2.5517146
2.56	0.0052336	0.0016615	2.5616615

Number of Standard Deviations of Safety Stock (*k or z*)	Stockout Risk (*SOR*)	Expected Stockouts [g(*k*) or g(*z*)][a]	Expected Stockouts [g(−*k*) or g(−*z*)][a]
2.57	0.0050850	0.0016099	2.5716099
2.58	0.0049400	0.0015598	2.5815598
2.59	0.0047988	0.0015111	2.5915111
2.60	0.0046612	0.0014638	2.6014638
2.61	0.0045271	0.0014178	2.6114178
2.62	0.0043965	0.0013732	2.6213732
2.63	0.0042693	0.0013299	2.6313299
2.64	0.0041453	0.0012878	2.6412878
2.65	0.0040246	0.0012470	2.6512470
2.66	0.0039071	0.0012073	2.6612073
2.67	0.0037926	0.0011688	2.6711688
2.68	0.0036812	0.0011314	2.6811314
2.69	0.0035726	0.0010952	2.6910952
2.70	0.0034670	0.0010600	2.7010600
2.71	0.0033642	0.0010258	2.7110258
2.72	0.0032641	0.0009927	2.7209927
2.73	0.0031668	0.0009605	2.7309605
2.74	0.0030720	0.0009293	2.7409293
2.75	0.0029798	0.0008991	2.7508991
2.76	0.0028901	0.0008697	2.7608697
2.77	0.0028029	0.0008412	2.7708412
2.78	0.0027180	0.0008136	2.7808136
2.79	0.0026355	0.0007869	2.7907869
2.80	0.0025552	0.0007609	2.8007609
2.81	0.0024771	0.0007358	2.8107358
2.82	0.0024012	0.0007114	2.8207114
2.83	0.0023275	0.0006877	2.8306877
2.84	0.0022557	0.0006648	2.8406648
2.85	0.0021860	0.0006426	2.8506426
2.86	0.0021183	0.0006211	2.8606211
2.87	0.0020524	0.0006002	2.8706002
2.88	0.0019884	0.0005800	2.8805800
2.89	0.0019263	0.0005604	2.8905604
2.90	0.0018659	0.0005415	2.9005415
2.91	0.0018072	0.0005231	2.9105231
2.92	0.0017502	0.0005053	2.9205053
2.93	0.0016949	0.0004881	2.9304881
2.94	0.0016411	0.0004714	2.9404714
2.95	0.0015889	0.0004553	2.9504553
2.96	0.0015383	0.0004396	2.9604396
2.97	0.0014891	0.0004245	2.9704245
2.98	0.0014413	0.0004099	2.9804099
2.99	0.0013950	0.0003957	2.9903957
3.00	0.0013500	0.0003819	3.0003819
3.01	0.0013063	0.0003687	3.0103687

Number of Standard Deviations of Safety Stock (k or z)	*Stockout Risk (SOR)*	*Expected Stockouts [g(k) or g(z)]*[a]	*Expected Stockouts [g(−k) or g(−z)]*[a]
3.02	0.0012639	0.0003558	3.0203558
3.03	0.0012228	0.0003434	3.0303434
3.04	0.0011830	0.0003314	3.0403314
3.05	0.0011443	0.0003197	3.0503197
3.06	0.0011068	0.0003085	3.0603085
3.07	0.0010704	0.0002976	3.0702976
3.08	0.0010351	0.0002871	3.0802871
3.09	0.0010009	0.0002769	3.0902769
3.10	0.0009677	0.0002670	3.1002670
3.11	0.0009355	0.0002575	3.1102575
3.12	0.0009043	0.0002483	3.1202483
3.13	0.0008741	0.0002394	3.1302394
3.14	0.0008448	0.0002308	3.1402308
3.15	0.0008164	0.0002225	3.1502225
3.16	0.0007889	0.0002145	3.1602145
3.17	0.0007623	0.0002068	3.1702068
3.18	0.0007364	0.0001993	3.1801993
3.19	0.0007114	0.0001920	3.1901920
3.20	0.0006872	0.0001850	3.2001850
3.21	0.0006637	0.0001783	3.2101783
3.22	0.0006410	0.0001718	3.2201718
3.23	0.0006190	0.0001655	3.2301655
3.24	0.0005977	0.0001594	3.2401594
3.25	0.0005771	0.0001535	3.2501535
3.26	0.0005571	0.0001478	3.2601478
3.27	0.0005378	0.0001424	3.2701424
3.28	0.0005191	0.0001371	3.2801371
3.29	0.0005010	0.0001320	3.2901320
3.30	0.0004835	0.0001271	3.3001271
3.31	0.0004665	0.0001223	3.3101223
3.32	0.0004501	0.0001177	3.3201177
3.33	0.0004343	0.0001133	3.3301133
3.34	0.0004189	0.0001091	3.3401091
3.35	0.0004041	0.0001050	3.3501050
3.36	0.0003898	0.0001010	3.3601010
3.37	0.0003759	0.0000972	3.3700972
3.38	0.0003625	0.0000935	3.3800935
3.39	0.0003495	0.0000899	3.3900899
3.40	0.0003370	0.0000865	3.4000865
3.41	0.0003249	0.0000832	3.4100832
3.42	0.0003132	0.0000800	3.4200800
3.43	0.0003018	0.0000769	3.4300769
3.44	0.0002909	0.0000740	3.4400740
3.45	0.0002803	0.0000711	3.4500711
3.46	0.0002701	0.0000684	3.4600684

Number of Standard Deviations of Safety Stock (k or z)	*Stockout Risk (SOR)*	*Expected Stockouts [g(k) or g(z)]*[a]	*Expected Stockouts [g(−k) or g(−z)]*[a]
3.47	0.0002603	0.0000657	3.4700657
3.48	0.0002508	0.0000632	3.4800632
3.49	0.0002416	0.0000607	3.4900607
3.50	0.0002327	0.0000583	3.5000583
3.51	0.0002241	0.0000560	3.5100560
3.52	0.0002158	0.0000538	3.5200538
3.53	0.0002078	0.0000517	3.5300517
3.54	0.0002001	0.0000497	3.5400497
3.55	0.0001927	0.0000477	3.5500477
3.56	0.0001855	0.0000458	3.5600458
3.57	0.0001785	0.0000440	3.5700440
3.58	0.0001718	0.0000423	3.5800423
3.59	0.0001654	0.0000406	3.5900406
3.60	0.0001591	0.0000390	3.6000390
3.61	0.0001531	0.0000374	3.6100374
3.62	0.0001473	0.0000359	3.6200359
3.63	0.0001417	0.0000345	3.6300345
3.64	0.0001364	0.0000331	3.6400331
3.65	0.0001312	0.0000318	3.6500318
3.66	0.0001261	0.0000305	3.6600305
3.67	0.0001213	0.0000292	3.6700292
3.68	0.0001166	0.0000280	3.6800280
3.69	0.0001122	0.0000269	3.6900269
3.70	0.0001078	0.0000258	3.7000258
3.71	0.0001037	0.0000248	3.7100248
3.72	0.0000996	0.0000237	3.7200237
3.73	0.0000958	0.0000228	3.7300228
3.74	0.0000920	0.0000218	3.7400218
3.75	0.0000884	0.0000209	3.7500209
3.76	0.0000850	0.0000201	3.7600201
3.77	0.0000816	0.0000192	3.7700192
3.78	0.0000784	0.0000184	3.7800184
3.79	0.0000753	0.0000177	3.7900177
3.80	0.0000724	0.0000169	3.8000169
3.81	0.0000695	0.0000162	3.8100162
3.82	0.0000667	0.0000155	3.8200155
3.83	0.0000641	0.0000149	3.8300149
3.84	0.0000615	0.0000143	3.8400143
3.85	0.0000591	0.0000137	3.8500137
3.86	0.0000567	0.0000131	3.8600131
3.87	0.0000544	0.0000125	3.8700125
3.88	0.0000522	0.0000120	3.8800120
3.89	0.0000501	0.0000115	3.8900115
3.90	0.0000481	0.0000110	3.9000110
3.91	0.0000462	0.0000105	3.9100105

Number of Standard Deviations of Safety Stock (k or z)	*Stockout Risk (SOR)*	*Expected Stockouts [g(k) or g(z)]*[a]	*Expected Stockouts [g(−k) or g(−z)]*[a]
3.92	0.0000443	0.0000101	3.9200101
3.93	0.0000425	0.0000097	3.9300097
3.94	0.0000408	0.0000092	3.9400092
3.95	0.0000391	0.0000088	3.9500088
3.96	0.0000375	0.0000085	3.9600085
3.97	0.0000360	0.0000081	3.9700081
3.98	0.0000345	0.0000077	3.9800077
3.99	0.0000331	0.0000074	3.9900074

[a] If k is negative, the stockout risk is one minus the tabled number.

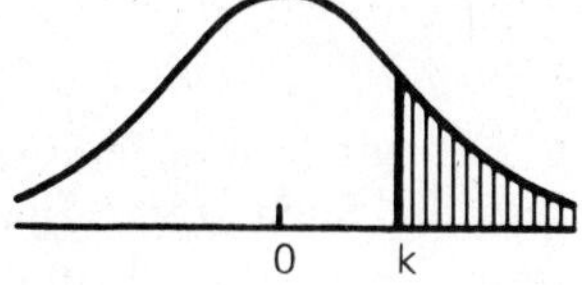

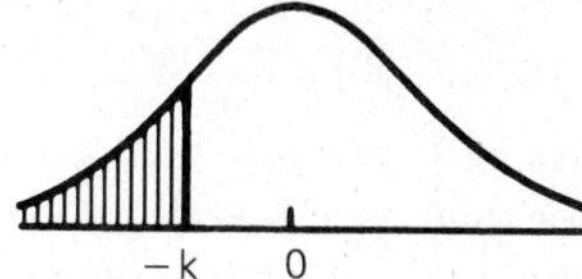

Shaded area is the tabled number.

chapter six

Aggregate Inventory Management

In this chapter, we will develop techniques for managing all inventory items together rather than each inventory item separately. Such aggregation into larger EOQs means heavier inventory investment but reduced setup expense. Increased safety stock means better customer service but, again, a heavier total inventory investment. For an overall investment target, we must determine what the optimal order quantities are.

Even with only two inventory items, aggregate inventory management problems appear. Suppose, for example, that the first item has an EOQ of 1,000 units but the second item has an EOQ of 500 units. Further, suppose that the firm has an inventory investment target of $500. If each item were valued at $1 per unit, the average inventory investment would be $750, missing the investment target by $250.

This chapter will explore such issues and problems and will present techniques for dealing with them.

LIMIT

The lot-size inventory management interpolation technique (LIMIT) was developed to aid practitioners in handling aggregate inventory trade-offs between holding and setup costs. Because the notation of Plossl and Wight [4] has become standard in seminars on LIMIT, we shall use it here. Our derivation of the appropriate formulas, however, is much simpler than theirs.

We shall take D as annual demand, S as setup cost, I as the inventory carrying percentage, and c as the per unit value of the item. The subscript i, when used, refers to the ith inventory item.

Suppose that we have a trial lot size Q_T, calculated from our best estimates of holding and setup costs—$D = 10{,}000$, $S = \$125$, $I = 0.25$, and $c = \$10$:

$$Q_T = \sqrt{\frac{2DS}{Ic}} = \sqrt{\frac{2 * 10{,}000 * 125}{0.25 * 10}} = 1{,}000$$

That lot size depends specifically on I and yields $D/Q = 10$ setups in the year. If we were limited to fewer setups in the year—such as five—then our *limit order quantity* would have to be increased to 2,000 units. The very action of limiting the number of setups to five implies a disbelief in our original ratio of holding to setup costs. Given a Q of 2,000 units and the same setup cost, the implied holding percentage would be 6.25%:

$$Q_L = \sqrt{\frac{2 * 10{,}000 * 125}{0.0625 * 10}} = 2{,}000$$

Letting I_L be the limit carrying percentage and I_T the trial percentage, we can show the relationship between the trial and the limit lot size. The relationship is a function of the trial and limit carrying percentages:

$$Q_L = \sqrt{\frac{2DS}{I_L c}}$$

$$Q_T = \sqrt{\frac{2DS}{I_T c}}$$

$$\frac{Q_L}{Q_T} = \frac{\sqrt{2DS}}{\sqrt{I_L c}} * \frac{\sqrt{I_T c}}{\sqrt{2DS}} = \frac{\sqrt{I_T}}{\sqrt{I_L}}$$

$$Q_L = Q_T \sqrt{I_T/I_L} = M * Q_T$$

with $M = \sqrt{I_T/I_L}$

In our example,

$$Q_L = 1{,}000 * \sqrt{0.25/0.0625} = 2{,}000$$

and $M = 2$.

If we could always know the limit carrying percentage, we could stop now and use the foregoing formula to adjust lot sizes. Generally, however, we know only the trial carrying cost and the limit on the annual setup hours. From the annual setup hours limit, we must adjust our trial lot sizes. We shall proceed by defining H_L as the limit on total setup hours across all SKUs. Also, H_T represents total setup hours across all SKUs, based on the trial lot sizes. Letting h_i be the hours required per setup for item i and recognizing that $Q_L = M * Q_T$, we have

$$\frac{H_T}{H_L} = \frac{\Sigma\left(\frac{D_i h_i}{Q_{Ti}}\right)}{\Sigma\left(\frac{D_i h_i}{Q_{Ti} * M}\right)} = \frac{\Sigma\left(\frac{D_i h_i}{Q_{Ti}}\right)}{\frac{1}{M}\Sigma\left(\frac{D_i h_i}{Q_{Ti}}\right)} = M$$

That is,

$$\frac{H_T}{H_L} = M$$

But $M = \sqrt{I_T/I_L}$ and so $(H_T/H_L)^2 = I_T/I_L$.

This gives us two fundamental formulas for LIMIT applications:

$$I_L = I_T\left(\frac{H_L}{H_T}\right)^2$$

$$M = \frac{H_T}{H_L} = \sqrt{\frac{I_T}{I_L}}$$

Suppose that our present setup hours total 49 and our limit is 35. How can we adjust our order quantities to accommodate this limit? We have $H_T = 49$ and $H_L = 35$, which gives us $M = H_T/H_L = 49/35 = 1.4$. In Example 6.1, we will use the same numbers and will also show how they might arise. If we raise our order quantities by 1.4, we should reduce our annual setup hours by 1.4. Is this plausible? Remember that annual setup hours on an individual item would be D/Q times hours per setup. Increasing our order size to $1.4Q$ would give annual setup hours of $D/(1.4Q)$ times hours per setup.

Suppose that $D = 10{,}000$, $Q = 845$, and there are two hours per setup. Then $D/Q * h = (10{,}000/845) * 2 = 23.67$ total trial setup hours. Now, raising the order quantity by 1.4 would give $[10{,}000/(1.4 * 845)] * 2 = 23.67/1.4 = 16.9$ hours. The trial setup hours are 1.4 times the revised setup hours ($23.67 = 1.4 * 16.9$).

Example 6.1

The two items in our inventory have been managed in a "seat of the pants" fashion for several years. The following table shows the current situation:

Item	*Annual Usage*	*Setup Hours per Order*	*Unit Cost of Item*	*Present Order Quantity*	*Yearly Setup Hours*
A	10,000	2	10	769	13 * 2 = 26
B	5,000	3	15	1,667	3 * 3 = 9
Total					35

Current setup costs are $62.50 per hour. Now some bright, young inventory analyst has criticized our present order quantities. The inventory manager insists that we cannot afford more than 35 setup hours per year for these items (and has indicated that the inventory analyst should get lost). How can this situation be handled using LIMIT? First, we shall specify $H_L =$ 35 hours. Further, our best estimate of the carrying cost percentage is 35%. Calculating trial lot sizes as a starting point, we obtain the following:

Item	*Cost per Setup*	*Trial Q*	*Approximate Yearly Setup Hours*
A	$125.00	845	24
B	$187.50	598	25
Total			49

$$M = \frac{H_T}{H_L} = \frac{49}{35} = 1.4$$

This leads us directly to the LIMIT order quantities:

Item	*LIMIT Quantity*	*Approximate Yearly Setup Hours*
A	1.4 * 845 = 1,183	10,000/1,183 * 2 = 17
B	1.4 * 598 = 837	5,000/837 * 3 = 18
Total		35

$$Q_L = M * Q_T = 1.4 * Q_T$$

Now we are in a position to examine the merits of our gyrations. Recall that the present order quantities had no particular merit. The trial order quantities gave a good setup versus carrying cost trade-off but a faulty setup to carrying cost ratio. The LIMIT quantity should give a good trade-off, based on the carrying to setup ratio implied by a limit on the setup hours. Table 6.1 summarizes these trade-offs. To develop this table, we note that the true carrying percentage is 17.9%; that is,

$$I_L = I_T\left(\frac{H_L}{H_T}\right)^2 = 0.35\left(\frac{35}{49}\right)^2 = 0.179$$

TABLE 6.1 LIMIT Lot Size Trade-offs at a 17.9% Holding Rate

	Lot Size	*Annual Holding Cost ($)*	*Annual Setup Cost ($)*	*Total Relevant Costs ($)*
Q_P–A	769	688	1,625	2,313
Q_P–B	1,667	2,238	563	2,801
Total		2,926	2,188	5,114
Q_T–A	845	756	1,479	2,235
Q_T–B	598	803	1,568	2,370
Total		1,559	3,047	4,605
Q_L–A	1,183	1,059	1,057	2,116
Q_L–B	837	1,124	1,120	2,244
Total		2,183	2,177	4,360

Based on this implied carrying cost percentage of 17.9%, we next compare the total costs implied by the present, the trial, and the LIMIT order quantities.

Table 6.1 reveals that our LIMIT lot sizes yield the lowest total relevant costs possible within a limit of thirty-five hours annual setup. Approximately seventeen setup hours on item A and eighteen hours on item B make more sense than twenty-six on A and only nine on B. It is not hard to see that we could have obtained the LIMIT order quantities if we had used a carrying cost percentage of 17.9% rather than 35% in the EOQ formula. However, we did not know that the correct percentage was 17.9 until we calculated M.

Exchange Curves

The LIMIT example demonstrated that the optimal lot size depends on the holding percentage. At a holding rate of 35%, the trial lot sizes were optimal. Then, limiting annual setups to thirty-five hours, we had a holding rate of 17.9%, and the LIMIT lot sizes became optimal. Figure 6.1 provides a rough sketch of the situation. The exchange curve sketched in the figure shows the optimal exchange between setup and holding costs. The present situation, represented by Q_P, involves higher holding costs than necessary for the given level of aggregate setup cost.

Out of curiosity, you should wonder what the *optimal* annual setup costs would be for the annual holding costs represented by Q_P. That point is shown in figure 6.1 as Q_R. To rephrase the question: Given a willingness to invest $2,926 in holding costs, what order quantities would give the lowest setup costs? To solve this problem, we shall move to a more powerful form of analysis that will allow us to handle general exchange curves.

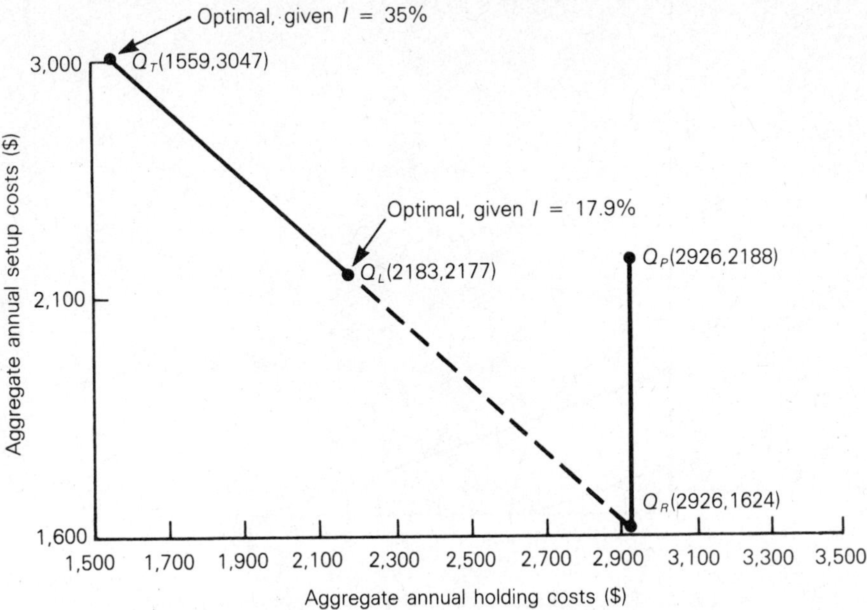

FIGURE 6.1 Holding/setup exchange curve (17.9% holding percentage)

Lagrange Multipliers

For a modest investment of time and effort, you can learn one of the most useful analytical techniques in business and economics. The use of Lagrange multipliers allows us to maximize profits or minimize costs subject to constraints. We shall use only basic calculus to establish the plausibility of the technique.

Suppose that we have a profit function we are trying to maximize subject to some constraints: Maximize $f(x, y) = x + 3y$ subject to $g(x, y) = x^2 + y^2 - 10 = 0$. We normally would see the constraint in the form $x^2 + y^2 = 10$, the equation of a circle. As in linear programming, we can draw the objective function in two dimensions by specifying arbitrary profits and then solving for x and y. For example, the two isoprofit lines shown in figure 6.2 come from $x + 3y = 9$ and $x + 3y = 3$. From the graph in figure 6.2, it is apparent that maximum profit occurs at the point of tangency of the profit line and the constraint line. But how do we solve for that point?

First, examine the profit line: $\pi = x + 3y$. Rewriting this in terms of y as a function of x would give us $y = (\pi/3) - (1/3)x$. The slope of the profit line is thus $-1/3$. By calculus, $dy/dx = y_x = -1/3$.

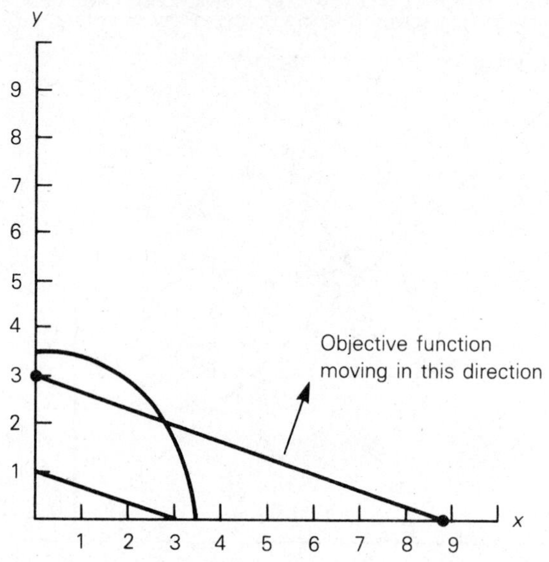

FIGURE 6.2 Lagrangian geometry in two dimensions

What about the slope of the constraint circle? Given $g(x, y) = x^2 + y^2 - 10 = 0$, we can solve for y in terms of x:

$$y^2 = 10 - x^2$$

$$y = \sqrt{10 - x^2}$$

and differentiating, we obtain

$$y_x = \frac{1}{2}(10 - x^2)^{-1/2} * (-2x)$$

$$= \frac{-x}{\sqrt{10 - x^2}}$$

$$= \frac{-x}{y}$$

Equating the slope of the profit line and the constraint line gives

$$-\frac{1}{3} = -\frac{x}{y}$$

or $y = 3x$. But $y^2 = 10 - x^2$ and so

$$(3x)^2 = 10 - x^2$$
$$9x^2 = 10 - x^2$$
$$x = 1$$

With $x = 1$, we have $y^2 = 10 - 1 = 9$, and $y = 3$. Our conclusion, then, is that profits are maximized at $(x, y) = (1, 3)$ with profits of $x + 3y = 10$.

As a shortcut, we might note that the profit function and the constraint equation can be differentiated easily using a rule from calculus: where

$$f(x, y) = 0, \qquad y_x = -\frac{f_x}{f_y}$$

In our case, we have

$$\pi = x + 3y$$

or

$$f(x, y) = x + 3y - \pi = 0$$

and

$$y_x = -\frac{f_x}{f_y} = -\frac{1}{3}$$

Similarly,

$$g(x, y) = x^2 + y^2 - 10 = 0$$

gives

$$y_x = -\frac{g_x}{g_y} = -\frac{2x}{2y} = -\frac{x}{y}$$

As before, we now equate the slopes, $-1/3 = -x/y$.

The Lagrange multiplier technique utilizes the principle of equating the slopes of the profit and constraint equations. Given a profit function $f(x, y)$ and a constraint function $g(x, y)$, the technique calls for the creation of a Lagrangian function $f(x, y) + \lambda g(x, y)$. When we equate the derivatives with respect to x, y, and λ to zero, we reproduce the slope condition at the same time that we satisfy the constraint equation:

$$L(x, y, \lambda) = f(x, y) + \lambda g(x, y) \text{ (the Lagrangian function)}$$

$$L_x = f_x + \lambda g_x = 0$$

$$\text{implies } \lambda = -\frac{f_x}{g_x} \tag{6.1}$$

$$L_y = f_y + \lambda g_f = 0$$

$$\text{implies } \lambda = \frac{f_y}{g_y} \tag{6.2}$$

$$L_\lambda = g(x, y) = 0 \tag{6.3}$$

Equating 6.1 and 6.2 gives the slope condition:

$$-\frac{f_x}{g_x} = -\frac{f_y}{g_y} \quad \text{or} \quad -\frac{f_x}{f_y} = -\frac{g_x}{g_y} = y_x$$

and equation 6.3 provides satisfaction of the constraint. We shall apply the technique to our example: Maximize $f(x, y) = x + 3y$ subject to $g(x, y) = x^2 + y^2 - 10$. Form the Lagrangian function

$$L(x, y, \lambda) = x + 3y - \lambda(x^2 + y^2 - 10)$$

and differentiate with respect to x, y, and λ:

$$L_x = 1 - 2\lambda x = 0 \tag{6.4}$$

$$L_y = 3 - 2\lambda y = 0 \tag{6.5}$$

$$L_\lambda = x^2 + y^2 - 10 = 0 \tag{6.6}$$

Solve for λ:

$$\lambda = \frac{1}{2x} \tag{6.7}$$

$$\lambda = \frac{3}{2y} \tag{6.8}$$

Equation 6.7 and 6.8 gives

$$\frac{1}{2x} = \frac{3}{2y} \tag{6.9}$$

$$y = 3x$$

Solving for y in equation 6.6 gives

$$y = \sqrt{10 - x^2} \tag{6.10}$$

and equating this with 6.9 allows us to solve for x:

$$y = 3x = \sqrt{10 - x^2}$$

$$9x^2 = 10 - x^2$$

$$x = 1$$

Hence, $y = 3$. The solution to our maximization problem is then $x = 1$ and $y = 3$, giving the profit $f(1, 3) = 1 + 3 = 4$.

Applying this method to our original pursuit of Q_R, we can specify the minimization problem and then form the Lagrangian function. The problem is to minimize:

$$\frac{D_1}{Q_1}(S_1) + \frac{D_2}{Q_2}(S_2) = \frac{10{,}000}{Q_1}(125) + \frac{5{,}000}{Q_2}(187.50)$$

subject to an inventory investment constraint

$$\frac{Q_1}{2}(Ic_1) + \frac{Q_2}{2}(Ic_2) = 2{,}926 = \frac{Q_1}{2} * 0.179 * 10 + \frac{Q_2}{2} * 0.179 * 15$$

Forming the Langrangian function, we obtain

$$L = \frac{D_1S_1}{Q_1} + \frac{D_2S_2}{Q_2} + \lambda\left[\frac{Q_1}{2}(Ic_1) + \frac{Q_2}{2}(Ic_2) - 2{,}926\right]$$

$$\frac{\partial L}{\partial Q_1} = -\frac{D_1S_1}{Q_1^2} + \frac{\lambda Ic_1}{2} = 0 \tag{6.11}$$

$$\frac{\partial L}{\partial Q_2} = -\frac{D_2S_2}{Q_2^2} + \frac{\lambda Ic_2}{2} = 0 \tag{6.12}$$

$$\frac{\partial L}{\partial \lambda} = \frac{Q_1}{2}(Ic_1) + \frac{Q_2}{2}(Ic_2) = 2{,}926 \tag{6.13}$$

$$Q_1 = \sqrt{\frac{2D_1S_1}{\lambda Ic_1}} = \frac{1}{\sqrt{\lambda}} * EOQ_1$$

$$Q_2 = \sqrt{\frac{2D_2S_2}{\lambda Ic_2}} = \frac{1}{\sqrt{\lambda}} * EOQ_2$$

where

$$EOQ_1 = \sqrt{\frac{2 * 10{,}000 * 125}{0.179 * 10}} = 1{,}181.8$$

$$EOQ_2 = \sqrt{\frac{2 * 5{,}000 * 187.50}{0.179 * 15}} = 835.7$$

Substituting Q_1 and Q_2 into the constraint equation, we can solve for λ:

$$\frac{1}{\sqrt{\lambda}}\left[\frac{EOQ_1}{2}(Ic_1) + \frac{EOQ_2}{2}(Ic_2)\right] = 2{,}926$$

$$\frac{1}{\sqrt{\lambda}}(2{,}180) = 2{,}926$$

$$\frac{1}{\sqrt{\lambda}} = \frac{2{,}926}{2{,}180} = 1.342$$

$$\lambda = 0.555$$

Finally,

$$Q_1 = \frac{1}{\sqrt{\lambda}} * EOQ_1$$

$$= 1.342 * 1{,}181.8 = 1{,}586$$

$$Q_2 = \frac{1}{\sqrt{\lambda}} * EOQ_2$$

$$= 1.342 * 835.7 = 1{,}122$$

$$(Q_1/2)h_1 + (Q_2/2)h_2 = (1{,}586/2) * 10 * 0.179 + (1{,}122/2) * 15 * 0.179$$

$$= 2{,}926$$

With holding costs of \$2,926, the setup costs are

$$\frac{D_1}{Q_1}(S_1) + \frac{D_2}{Q_2}(S_2) = \frac{10{,}000}{1{,}586} * 125 + \frac{5{,}000}{1{,}122} * 187.50 = 1{,}624$$

These costs should be compared with the present annual setup costs of \$2,188.

Unknown Costs

If the per unit holding percentage is unknown, the Lagrange multiplier takes on an interesting interpretation. In such a case, we can minimize the annual setup costs subject to a constraint on the average value of the inventory; that is, minimize $(D_1/Q_1) * S_1 + (D_2/Q_2) * S_2$ subject to $(Q_1/2)c_1 + (Q_2/2)c_2 = Y$. Lagrangian analysis would give:

$$Q_1 = \sqrt{\frac{2D_1S_1}{\lambda c_1}}$$

$$Q_2 = \sqrt{\frac{2D_2S_2}{\lambda c_2}}$$

but then the Lagrange multiplier is simply the unknown holding cost percentage.

Table 6.2 shows a comparison of the company's present order quantities with those generated by constraining the holding investment. For the same investment, the setup costs are about \$500 lower when the lot sizes are adjusted to get away from the relatively high number of setups for item A.

Holding/Service Exchange

So far we have analyzed the holding setup exchange. Let us now look at the holding service exchange. Safety stocks are based on a number of standard deviations of lead time demand. The higher the number of standard

TABLE 6.2 Comparison of Present Quantities and Investment Constrained Quantities at a 17.9% Holding Rate

	Lot Size	*Annual Holding Cost (\$)*	*Annual Setup Cost (\$)*	*Total Relevant Costs (\$)*	*Annual Demand*	*Cost per Setup (\$)*	*Unit Cost (\$)*
Q_P–A	769	688	1,625	2,313	10,000	125.0	10
Q_P–B	1,667	2,238	563	2,801	5,000	187.5	15
Total		2,926	2,188	5,114			
Q_R–A	1,586	1,420	788	2,208	10,000	125.0	10
Q_R–B	1,122	1,506	836	2,342	5,000	187.5	15
Total		2,926	1,624	4,550			

deviations, the higher will be the service level and the corresponding holding cost. Correcting and expanding an example from McClain and Thomas [2], we will analyze the service level versus holding cost trade-off.

We will begin by reviewing some of our findings from single-item inventory control before moving to the aggregate level. Consider item X from the following two-item table:

Item	*Annual Demand*	*Cost per Unit*	*Holding Cost per Unit per Year*	*Cost per Setup*	*Backorder Cost*	*Standard Deviation of Lead Time Demand*
X	10,000	$5	$1	$50	$10	50
Y	1,000	$5	$1	$50	$10	5

$$Q^* = \sqrt{\frac{2 * 10{,}000 * 50}{1}} = 1{,}000$$

Recall now that marginal analysis in the backorder case calls for adding another unit to safety stock, so long as (the number of cycles times the probability of a backorder without the marginal unit) times (the per unit backorder penalty) is greater than or equal to the cost of holding the marginal unit for a year:

$$\frac{D}{Q} * OSOR * \pi \geq h$$

Solving for the optimal OSOR, we have

$$OSOR^* = \frac{hQ}{\pi D}$$

In this example,

$$OSOR^* = \frac{1 * 1{,}000}{10 * 10{,}000} = 0.01$$

For simplicity, we will not jointly determine Q and R. For OSOR = 0.01, k would be 2.32. Hence, the appropriate safety stock would be $2.32\sigma_L$ = 2.32 * 50 = 116 units of safety stock.

Similar calculations for item Y would yield $OSOR$ = 0.1 and 1.28 * 5 = 6.4 units of safety stock. Now, adding items X and Y together, we would have 122.4 units of safety stock, or holding costs of $122.40 at $1 per unit.

Unit Stockout Objective

Suppose that we are now asked to limit ourselves to \$100 in holding costs on safety stock. What should the safety stocks be? If we use Lagrangian analysis in the unit stockout objective case, we find

$$OSOR_i = \lambda\left(\frac{h_i Q_i}{\pi_i D_i}\right)$$

and

$$k_1\sigma_1 h_1 + k_2\sigma_2 h_2 = 100$$

For our example, we shall try different λ values. By trial and error, we can adjust the safety stock investment until it approximates our target. With $\lambda = 1.5$:

$$OSOR_1 = 1.5(0.01) = 0.015$$

$$OSOR_2 = 1.5(0.1) = 0.15$$

$$k_1 = 2.17 \quad \text{(from appendix 5A)}$$

$$k_2 = 1.04$$

$$2.17(50) + 1.04(5) = 113.7$$

With $\lambda = 2$:

$$OSOR_1 = 2(0.01) = 0.02$$

$$OSOR_2 = 2(0.1) = 0.2$$

$$k_1 = 2.06$$

$$k_2 = 0.84$$

$$2.06(50) + 0.84(5) = 107.2$$

With $\lambda = 2.5$:

$$OSOR_1 = 2.5(0.01) = 0.025$$

$$OSOR_2 = 2.5(0.1) = 0.25$$

$$k_1 = 1.96$$

$$k_2 = 0.68$$

$$1.96(50) + 0.68(5) = 101.4$$

Since this gives us a value close to $100 worth of safety stock, we will stop with the suggestion that further search could give us an exact value. Nevertheless, the procedure we've used gives us a new breakdown of safety stock. Previously, we employed 116 units of item X safety stock and 6.4 units of item Y safety stock. With our investment constraint at $100, we employ 98 units of X safety stock and 3.4 units of Y safety stock.

The key to the unit stockout situation, the Lagrange multiplier adjusts the ratio of holding cost to stockout penalty. Rewriting the stockout probability relationship as a function of Q_i/D_i gives

$$OSOR_i = \frac{\lambda h_i}{\pi_i} * \left(\frac{Q_i}{D_i}\right) \quad \text{rather than} \quad \lambda\left(\frac{h_i Q_i}{\pi_i D_i}\right)$$

We started with a ratio $h_i/\pi_i = 1/10 = 0.1$, but that ratio gave us total holding costs of $122.40, which are too high. To reduce the holding costs, we need a larger ratio of holding cost to stockout penalty. Our revised ratio of $\lambda(h_i/\pi_i) = 2.5(0.1) = 0.25$ forces us to hold less inventory.

The formal statement of this problem with a unit stockout objective would be as follows: Minimize $\Sigma(D_i/Q_i)\sigma_i g(k_i)\pi_i$ subject to: $\Sigma\ k_i\sigma_i h_i = I = 100$; that is, minimize (the number of cycles) times (the expected number of stockouts per cycle) times (the per unit backorder penalty), subject to a constraint on the aggregate safety stock holding.

We do not present the Lagrangian calculations here, because they involve differentiating an integral. The interested reader is referred to Peterson and Silver [3] for a discussion of special results for differentiating the normal integral or the normal loss integral. The result of the Langrangian analysis is the relationship:

$$OSOR_i = \lambda\left(\frac{h_i Q_i}{\pi_i D_i}\right)$$

UNKNOWN COSTS

As an appealing benefit of the Lagrangian approach, cost specification loses its importance. Suppose that management is willing to specify a constraint on total safety stock investment, $\Sigma\ k_i\sigma_i c_i = \$500$. Suppose also that the order quantities, Q_i, have been previously determined. We can find the optimal safety stock without knowing either the holding costs or the stockout penalties, because management's specification of safety stock investment implies a ratio of holding cost to stockout penalty. In our example, the ratio is 0.25, as we shall see:

$$OSOR_i = \lambda\left(\frac{Q_i}{D_i}\right) = 0.25\left(\frac{Q_i}{D_i}\right)$$

Here, rather than having $\lambda(h_i/\pi_i)$ as the holding cost to stockout penalty ratio with known h_i and π_i, we simply have λ as the ratio. We then try values of λ until we find one that gives a total safety stock holding investment of \$500. A value of $\lambda = 0.25$ comes close:

$$OSOR_1 = 0.25\left(\frac{Q_i}{D_i}\right) = 0.25\left(\frac{1{,}000}{100}\right) = 0.025$$

$$OSOR_2 = 0.25\left(\frac{Q_2}{D_2}\right) = 0.25\left(\frac{100}{100}\right) = 0.25$$

$$k_1 = 1.96$$

$$k_2 = 0.68$$

$$k_1\sigma_1 h_1 + k_2\sigma_2 h_2 = 1.96(50)(5) + 0.68(5)(5) = 507$$

Note that the formulation with unknown costs gives one ratio of holding to stockout costs for all items in the inventory.

Stockout Situation Objective

Stockout situations and units stocked out are not the same. Each stockout situation can lead to several units being stocked out. In the order service level, we look at the probability of having a stockout position or situation on a cycle. The expected number of units stocked out per cycle goes into our calculation of unit service level.

Recall that our original unconstrained solution involved $2.32\sigma_1$ units of item X safety stock and $1.28\sigma_2$ units of item Y safety stock. This gave us $2.32(50) + 1.28(5) = 122.4$ units of safety stock, for a holding cost of \$122.40. The question now is whether we can have fewer stockout situations for the same holding cost.

With the data from our problem,

Item	D	Q	h	π	σ_L	K	*OSOR*
X	10,000	1,000	1	10	50	2.32	0.01
Y	100	100	1	10	5	1.28	0.10

the original solution would give:

$$\frac{D_1}{Q_1}OSOR_1 + \frac{D_2}{Q_2}OSOR_2 = \frac{10{,}000}{1{,}000}(0.01) + \frac{100}{100}(0.1)$$

$$= 0.10 + 0.10 = 0.2 \text{ stockout situation}$$

The safety stock holding cost would be

$$k_1\sigma_1 h_1 + k_2\sigma_2 h_2 = 2.32(50) + 1.28(5) = 122.4$$

It would not be too surprising to get fewer stockout situations with a situation-oriented objective function: Minimize $(D_1/Q_1) * OSOR(k_1) + (D_2/Q_2) * OSOR(k_2)$ subject to $k_1\sigma_1 v_1 + k_2\sigma_2 v_2 = Y$, where v_1 is the item cost per unit.

Forming the Lagrangian in our example gives

$$L(k_1, k_2, \lambda) = \frac{D_1}{Q_1} * OSOR(k_1) + \frac{D_2}{Q_2} * OSOR(k_2)$$

$$+ \lambda(k_1\sigma_1 v_1 + k_2\sigma_2 v_2 - Y).$$

Setting the first partial derivatives to zero gives

$$\frac{\partial L}{\partial k_1} = -\frac{D_1}{Q_1} f(k_1) + \lambda\sigma_1 v_1 = 0$$

$$\frac{\partial L}{\partial k_2} = -\frac{D_2}{Q_2} f(k_2) + \lambda\sigma_2 v_2 = 0$$

$$\frac{\partial L}{\partial \lambda} = k_1\sigma_1 v_1 + k_2\sigma_2 v_2 - Y = 0$$

Note that $f(k)$ is the density function for the unit normal distribution, as in figure 6.3. Intuitively, as k increases, the area $OSOR(k)$ decreases at the rate $f(k)$. For a proof, see Peterson and Silver [3]. Solving for k, we find

$$f(k_i) = \lambda\frac{Q_i}{D_i}\sigma_i v_i$$

and $k_1\sigma_1 v_1 + k_2\sigma_2 v_2 = Y$.

Noting that

$$f(k) = \frac{1}{\sqrt{2\pi}} \exp(-k^2/2)$$

we can solve to find

$$k = \sqrt{2 \ln\left(\frac{D}{\lambda\sqrt{2\pi}Qv\sigma}\right)}$$

In our example, $\lambda = 1/745$ gives $k_1 = 2.23$ and $k_2 = 2.23$. Check it out.

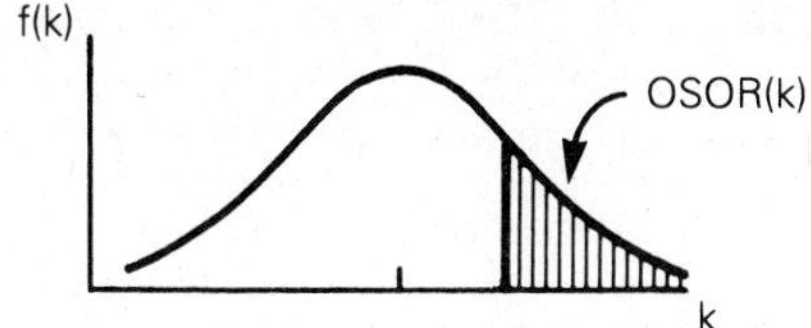

$$k_1 = \sqrt{2 \ln \left(\frac{745(10{,}000)}{\sqrt{2(3.1416)}(1{,}000)(5)(50)} \right)}$$

Substituting these values of k_1 and k_2 into the objective function, we can determine the expected number of stockout situations in a year:

$$\frac{D_1}{Q_1}(OSOR_1) + \frac{D_2}{Q_2}(OSOR_2) = \frac{10{,}000}{1{,}000}(0.0129) + \frac{100}{100}(0.0129) = 0.14$$

By comparison, the previous solution gave 0.2 expected stockout situations per year.

What does λ mean? At the optimal, we know now that

$$L(k_1, k_2, \lambda) = \frac{D_1}{Q_1}OSOR_i + \frac{D_2}{Q_2}OSOR_2 + \lambda(k_1\sigma_1 v_1 + k_2\sigma_2 v_2 - Y)$$

$$= 10(0.0129) + 1(0.0129) + \lambda(612 - Y)$$

Differentiating with respect to Y, we have $dL/dY = -\lambda$. Note that $L(k_1k_2\lambda)$ is the expected number of stockout situations if Y is \$612. Then λ represents the reduction in expected stockouts per \$1 increase in Y.

If the decision were whether or not to invest \$1 more in safety stock, marginal analysis would require that the cost to carry an extra dollar of safety stock equal the reduction in expected stockout situations times the cost per stockout situation:

$$r = \lambda B \quad \text{or} \quad \lambda = r/B$$

where r is the carrying percentage and B is the cost per stockout situation.

To obtain a value for λ, we use the method of successive approximations:

1. Guess a value of λ.
2. Solve for k_1, k_2. If the value under the square root is negative, return to 1. Let

$$X_i = \frac{D_i}{\sqrt{2\pi}\, Q_i v_i \sigma_i}$$

Then calculate

$$k_i = \sqrt{2 \ln (X_i/\lambda)}$$

3. Solve for implied inventory investment.
4. Calculate the ratio of desired inventory investment to the investment generated in step 3 and call that ratio INRAT. Clearly, a ratio greater than unity means that we need to revise the k values upward or, correspondingly, the λ value. Multiply the k values by INRAT.
5. Solve for λ. We know that

$$k_1 = \sqrt{2 \ln (x_1/\lambda)}$$

Solving now for λ, we would find

$$\lambda = \frac{X_1}{\exp(k_1^2/2)}$$

6. Return to step 2 and repeat the process until two successive iterations yield approximately the same λ value.

Let's go through the steps with our example.

1. Guess $\lambda = 1/100$.
2. $X_1 = 10{,}000/[2.51(1{,}000)(5)(50)] = 0.0159$; $X_2 = 100/[2.51(100)(5)(5)] = 0.0159$; $k_1 = \sqrt{2 \ln[100(0.0159)]} = 0.963$; $k_2 = \sqrt{2 \ln[100(0.0159)]} = 0.963$.
3. Inventory investment $= k_1\sigma_1 v_1 + k_2\sigma_2 v_2 = 0.963(50)(5) + 0.963(5)(5) = 264.83$.
4. Desired inventory investment is \$612. Then new k values are $(612/264.55) * 0.963 = 2.23$.
5. Because $X_1 = X_2 = 0.0159$, no further adjustments need be made and

$$\lambda = \frac{0.0159}{\exp(2.23^2/2)} = 0.00132$$

When $X = X_1 = X_2$, then $k = k_1 = k_2$, and $k = \sqrt{2 \ln (x/\lambda)}$. Problem 12 at the end of this chapter provides an example where $X_1 \neq X_2$.

TABLE 6.3 Comparison of Safety Stock Policies

	Unit Objective		*Situation Objective*	
	Unlimited Holding Cost Budget	*\$100 Budget on Holding Cost*	*\$122.40 Budget on Holding Cost*	*\$100 Budget on Holding Cost*
k_1 value	2.32	1.96	2.23	1.82
k_2 value	1.28	0.68	2.23	1.82
Expected number of stockout situations	0.2	0.5	0.14	0.15
Holding costs	\$122.40	\$101.40	\$122.40	\$100.10
Expected stockout costs	\$ 19.63	\$ 54.64	\$ 22.67	\$ 68.53
Inventory investment	\$612.00	\$507.00	\$612.00	\$500.50

Comparison of the Safety Stock Policies

Retracing our steps, we have now worked with three different sets of safety stock values for three different objectives. To gain some perspective, we now compare these policies on the measures of dollar investment, expected stockout situations, and expected stockout costs. Table 6.3 presents only solutions; we ask that you make the intermediate calculations to assure yourself that you know what is going on.

So far, we have considered only the trade-off of holding cost or investment versus service level. In an earlier chapter, we stressed the interaction between safety stock and order quantities in the (Q, R) model. Recall that larger Qs mean fewer exposures to stockout and hence allow lower safety stock in the reorder point calculation (R = expected lead time demand plus safety stock).

What we need is a formulation to cover both trade-offs: investment versus service and investment versus setup. With a unit stockout objective, we would have the following problem: Minimize

$$\sum \frac{D_i}{Q_i} \sigma_i g(k_i)$$

subject to

$$\sum \frac{Q_i}{2} v_i + \sum k_i \sigma_i v_i = Y$$

We could solve this problem by the Lagrangian method coupled with the method of successive approximations. Gardner and Dannenbring [1] do this, and you should be able to understand their article after studying this chapter.

Summary

This chapter has examined aggregate inventory trade-offs. The LIMIT technique provides an algebraic way of adjusting lot sizes in order to meet an overall constraint on setup hours. Using the LIMIT technique, we soon discovered that an overall constraint on setup hours implies a carrying cost percentage, and so we saw yet another example of imputed or implicit costs.

In analyzing the holding cost to setup cost trade-off subject to overall budget constraints, we found that the Lagrange multiplier technique can handle the same problems as LIMIT. Not only can this powerful technique handle other holding/setup questions, but it also allows us to analyze holding cost versus inventory investment constraints. Returning to our study of unit- and situation-oriented service objectives, we employed Lagrange multipliers to develop optimal safety stocks within budget constraints.

In the various trade-offs made, the Lagrange multiplier always seemed to have a meaning. In a model minimizing annual setup hours, the Lagrange multiplier was the holding cost percentage. In meeting a unit stockout objective, the multiplier appeared as the ratio of per unit holding cost to per unit stockout penalty. Finally, the multiplier showed up as the ratio of the holding cost percentage to the cost per stockout situation in a model designed to meet a stockout situation objective.

From basic inventory models to aggregate inventory models, we have constantly discovered implicit or imputed costs. In this chapter on aggregate inventories, budget statements about setup hours or inventory investment were viewed as statements about cost ratios.

The next chapter changes the pace. Not only will we be concerned about aggregate inventories, but we will also consider where to locate inventories—whether it is better to hold inventory centrally or to duplicate inventories across the country. Because the problems of multilocation inventories are so complex, we no longer find conclusive results or formulas. The next chapter will discuss the controversy about the best approach.

PROBLEMS

1. Suppose that D = 5,000, S = \$150, c = \$15, and we require five setups in the year. What is the implied annual holding cost percentage per unit per year?

2. Suppose that D = 5,000, S = \$150, c = \$15, and I = 10%. Now we are asked to revise I to 35%. What multiplier M should be used in revising the original Q? What will the new Q be? Check this against the EOQ formula, with I = 0.35. What is the ratio of the number of

setups under the original to the number of setups under the revised carrying percentage?

3. Two inventory items have been managed in a "seat of the pants" fashion for several years. The following table shows the current situation:

Item	*Annual Usage*	*Setup Hours per Order*	*Unit Cost*	*Present Quantity*	*Setup Cost*
A	8,000	2	\$16	1,000	\$75/hour
B	2,000	4	\$ 8	1,000	\$75/hour

For trial purposes, assume $I = 0.35$ and calculate lot sizes. Within the constraint of twenty-four hours of setup per year, revise the lot sizes. What is the implied carrying percentage? Does the initial carrying percentage guess make any difference?

4. Solve the following problem using the Lagrange multiplier method: Maximize $f(x, y) = 3x + 2y$ subject to $x^2 + y^2 = 20$.

5. Solve the following problem using the Lagrange multiplier method: Minimize $f(x, y) = 1/x + 4/y$ subject to $x + 1.4y = 10$.

6. Using the Lagrange multiplier technique, we go through the same steps for finding a maximum or a minimum. How do we know which we have? An analogy to the second derivative test could be used, but a pragmatic approach suggests that we simply graph the objective function. In problem 4, did we get a maximum? In problem 5, did we get a minimum?

7. Solve the following problem using the Lagrange multiplier method: Minimize $f(x, y) = 1{,}250{,}000/x + 937{,}500/y$ subject to $0.895x + 1.345y = 2926$.

Problems 8 through 14 use the following data:

Item	*Annual Demand*	*Cost per Unit*	*Holding Cost per Unit per Year*	*Cost per Setup*	*Backorder Cost*	*Standard Deviation of Lead Time Demand*
A	8,000	10	\$1	\$500	\$20	40
B	8,000	20	\$2	\$300	\$20	30

8. What are the optimal stockout probabilities for the two items? Assume the backorder case. What safety stocks should be set for the two items based on single item inventory control methods?

9. With a unit stockout objective and a constraint of \$200 worth of holding costs on safety stock, calculate the revised safety stocks.

10. With the same two items, A and B, determine whether a different allocation of safety stocks will minimize stockout situations subject to an inventory holding constraint of $200. What would the allocation be?

11. Develop a table similar to table 6.3 to specify expected stockout situations and expected stockout costs, with k values of $k_A = 2.12$ and $k_B = 2.07$.

12. Develop a table similar to table 6.3 to compare expected stockout situations and expected stockout costs for the unit and situation objectives. Use the $200 holding cost budget constraint.

13. Write a computer program to find optimal λ values in the unit stockout objective case. Use the method of successive approximations.

15. For items X and Y we allow backorders. Further, we require that safety stock investment costs per year be limited to $200 for these two items. The MAD on X is 100 and on Y is 50. Holding and stockout costs are unknown. Item X has annual demand of 1,000 and an order quantity of 100. Item Y has annual demand of 2,000 and an order quantity of 500. What safety stock should be held? What is the implied ratio of holding to stockout cost?

16. Two inventory items have the following data:

Item	*Annual Usage*	*Cost per Setup*	*Value per Unit*
A	10,000	$125.00	$10
B	5,000	$187.50	$15

What carrying cost percentage makes the order quantities $Q_A = 1{,}586$ and $Q_B = 1{,}122$ optimal?

17. Two inventory items have the following data:

Item	*Annual Usage*	*Order Quantity*	*Value per Unit*	*Standard Deviation of Lead Time Demand*
A	10,000	10,000	5	40
B	100	100	5	5

The inventory investment budget is $200. Find the optimal amounts of safety stock for each item, beginning with a Lagrange multiplier of 1/100.

18. Examine table 6.3. For a $100 budget on holding costs, why does the unit objective employ k values of 1.96 and 0.68 while the situation objective employs equal values of 1.82? What are the order stockout risks for these k values?

19. Suppose that we decide to minimize average inventory investment subject to a constraint on total setup hours. Is that sensible? What would be the appropriate order quantities? How would you interpret the Lagrange multiplier?

20. Two items in inventory have the following data:

Item	*Annual Usage*	*Cost per Setup*	*Value per Unit*
A	10,000	$125.00	$10
B	5,000	$187.50	$15

At a holding cost percentage of 17.9%, we found the optimal *Q*s to be $Q_A = 1{,}586$ and $Q_B = 1{,}122$. Our budget constraint of $2926 was exactly satisfied, and the Lagrange multiplier was 0.555. What would be the decrease in annual setup costs for $1 increase in the holding cost budget?

REFERENCES AND BIBLIOGRAPHY

1. E. S. Gardner and D. D. Dannenbring, "Using Optimal Policy Surfaces to Analyze Aggregate Inventory Trade-offs," *Management Science*, Vol. 25, No. 8 (August 1979), pp. 709–720.
2. J. O. McClain and L. J. Thomas, *Operations Management* (Englewood Cliffs, N.J.: Prentice-Hall, 1980), pp. 389–392.
3. R. Peterson and E. A. Silver, *Decision Systems for Inventory Management and Production Planning* (New York: John Wiley & sons, 1979).
4. G. W. Plossl and O. W. Wight, *Production and Inventory Control* (Englewood Cliffs, N.J.: Prentice-Hall, 1967).

appendix 6A

Using Optimal Policy Surfaces to Analyze Aggregate Inventory Tradeoffs

Everette S. Gardner, Jr.
University of North Carolina at Chapel Hill
David G. Dannenbring
Columbia University

1. Introduction

In the authors' opinion, a serious gap exists between theory and practice in inventory management. One reason is that the marginal ordering, holding, and shortage costs typically assumed in the theory are difficult, if not impossible, to measure in practice [1], [4], [7], [9], [13], [21], [22], [24], [27], [29]. For example, in Ziegler's survey [29], he concludes that all the suggested approaches to determining ordering costs in the accounting literature result in average rather than marginal costs. The holding cost in practice is mostly composed of the cost of capital, which is a highly subjective measure [1], [14], [16], [21], [29]. The use of shortage costs in inventory models has not been adopted by most practitioners [1], [3], [4], [13], [21], [22], [29] since there is no basis for their measurement in accounting methodology [29].

Another problem in practice is that inventory theory has traditionally emphasized single-item models which provide insufficient insights for the management of multi-item inventories. Most practitioners are primarily concerned instead with aggregate inventory control [1], [2], [18], [21], [27]

Reprinted by permission of Everette S. Gardner, Jr., & David G. Dannenbring, Using Optimal Policy Surfaces to Analyze Aggregate Inventory Tradeoffs, *Management Science*, **25**(8), August 1979, pp. 709–720.

to meet specific aggregate objectives or constraints for customer service, workload, and investment.

This paper presents an approach to decision making in inventory systems that avoids cost measurement problems and incorporates aggregate objectives and constraints. While traditional theory is based on the objective of cost minimization we propose that inventory decisions be conceived as policy tradeoffs on a three-dimensional response surface, the "optimal policy surface." The axes of the surface are measured in aggregate terms: the percentage of inventory shortages as a measure of customer service; the workload in terms of the number of annual stock replenishment orders; and total investment (the sum of cycle and safety stocks). The surface is optimal in the sense that the number of shortages at any point on the surface is minimal for the corresponding combination of workload and investment values. Aggregate inventory decisions are defined as the selection of some combination of the three variables. We show that decisions resulting in combinations of variables that do not lie on the surface cannot be optimal, regardless of the underlying cost structure of the firm.

A similar theoretical construct for the case of deterministic demand, the "optimal policy curve," was originally developed by Starr and Miller [24]. We review their ideas in the next section, and then generalize to the stochastic case. Model formulations and solution algorithms are presented, with computational results for four inventories drawn from a large military distribution system. The results show that the concept of the optimal policy surface can be a useful practical tool for inventory decisions.

2. The Optimal Policy Curve

When demand is deterministic, there is an underlying set of optimal relationships in any inventory between aggregate cycle stock investment and workload. This set of relationships may be called an "optimal policy curve." An example is shown in figure 6A.1, which was derived with Lagrangian multipliers [24], and gives the minimum cycle stock investment for a specified workload or vice versa. Points located below the curve are infeasible combinations of investment and workload, while points above the curve are nonoptimal. For example, a management decision to operate at point *A* in figure 6A.1 represents an investment of $350,000 and a workload of 5,000 annual orders. But at point *B*, workload can be reduced to 3,000 for the same investment. An alternative is to move to point *C*, where the workload is still 5,000 but investment has been reduced to $225,000.

The optimal policy curve is a powerful concept, since it shows exactly how workload and investment may be exchanged for each other. "The executive, with his intimate knowledge of the circumstances of the company, can often quickly converge on the optimal point on the curve for the

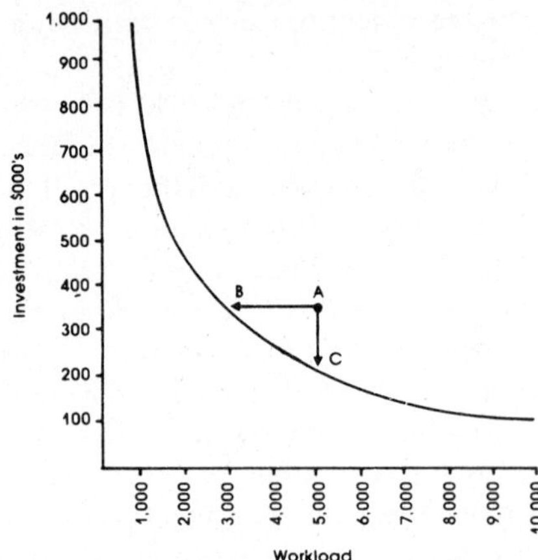

FIGURE 6A.1 The optimal policy curve for deterministic demand

company without having had to convert his knowledge into the form of carrying and ordering costs—something which can often be done only badly if at all." [24]. There is considerable evidence that the concept of the optimal policy curve has been successful in practice. A simplified computational procedure to derive the optimal policy curve, the "Limit" technique, was developed by Plossl and Wight [21] for the American Production and Inventory Control Society, and the procedure is part of the body of knowledge required to gain certified practitioner status in that organization. Another method of deriving the optimal policy curve was developed by Prichard and Eagle [22]. Other variations of deterministic inventory models which link several items with investment constraints may be found in [11] and [12].

3. The Optimal Policy Surface

With stochastic demand, management decisions are much more complex. Cycle and safety stock investment decisions are interdependent for each line item. Interactions also exist between items, since some aggregate mix of cycle and safety stock investment must be selected and allocated across the items stocked. To treat these complexities, the optimal policy concept must be extended to three dimensions, as illustrated in Figure 6A.2, which was constructed from a sample of 500 line items in a military distribution system. The vertical axis measures customer service in terms of the percentage of annual customer requisitions which are backordered (short). Depending on management objectives, various other measures could be used for the vertical axis, such as the percentage of sales dollars short or the number of shortage occurrences. The investment axis in figure 6A.2 is stated as the sum of aggregate cycle and safety stocks, while workload is the number of annual stock replenishment orders.

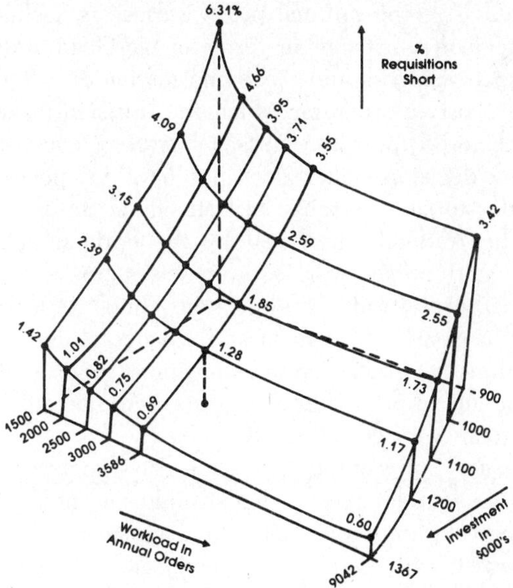

FIGURE 6A.2 The optimal policy surface for stochastic demand

Figure 6A.2 is an optimal policy surface, since it gives the minimal or optimal level of requisitions short for the range of workload and investment shown. For any one of the three variables, the surface also shows the range of optimal combinations of the other two. If management chooses to operate with an aggregate investment of $900,000, the surface shows that requisitions short will vary from 6.13% to 3.42%, depending on the workload decision. If a workload of 3,000 annual orders is selected, requisitions short will vary from 0.75% to 3.71%, depending on the investment decision.

The optimal policy surface provides a sound theoretical basis for aggregate inventory decisions in this sense: any optimal decision must result in a point located on the optimal policy surface. Any point located below the surface is infeasible, and any decision that results in a point located above the surface can be improved by moving back to the surface.

To illustrate, current management policy for the inventory sample in figure 6A.2 results in the following combination of variables: workload = 3,586, investment = $1,367,000, and requisitions short = 0.89%. For the same workload and investment coordinates, a modest reduction in requisitions short could be made to a level of 0.69%. However, the workload could be cut to less than 2,300 annual orders (a reduction of 35%) and retain current levels of requisitions short and investment. If the investment budget is tight, another choice is to cut investment by about 8.5% to $1,250,000 without changing the other two variables. Other points on the surface would yield simultaneous improvement in all three variables over current policy.

Since customer service objectives depend on a host of complex policy issues in practice [22], the optimal policy surface is useful in quantifying exactly what the firm must pay in terms of workload and investment to meet these objectives. Although cost information is not incorporated in figure 6A.2, any cost information which the decision-maker is willing to use can be considered after the surface has been constructed. The key point is that the decision-maker does not have to specify marginal cost estimates in order to see the range of tradeoffs in the inventory.

Most of the tradeoffs displayed by the optimal policy surface are straightforward. With a fixed workload, increases in investment simply add safety stock and thereby reduce requisitions short. At a fixed investment level, increases in workload result in an exchange of cycle stock for safety stock, again leading to a reduction in requisitions short. It should be noted that these comments apply to the aggregate behavior only; the effects on individual items can vary considerably.

Most of the axis limits of the surface are also straightforward. At infinite (unconstrained) investment levels, there would be enough safety stock so that the percentage of requisitions short would approach zero for any workload constraint. As investment levels are reduced, safety stock would eventually disappear, so that for a given workload the lowest feasible investment level would be the same as that for the deterministic optimal policy curve. At this limit, requisitions short would, of course, be very large. For a specific investment level there is a similar lower limit on workload, without safety stock, equivalent to that found with the optimal policy curve.

It should be recognized that if budget restrictions are particularly severe, it would be necessary to consider the possibility that the aggregate safety stock level is negative. The model formulated here does not treat this possibility although suitable modifications could accomplish this consideration.

The effects of increases in workload are more complex. The right-hand edge of the surface is the limit of effective constraint on aggregate workload, since a solution with an unconstrained workload will always provide fewer expected requisitions short than would be the case for workload equality constraints larger than the edge. The reason that this limit exists has to do with the two ways in which workload impacts on requisitions short. With a fixed investment constraint, increases in workload are equivalent to increases in the number of exposures to risk of stockout. On the other hand, the increased workload leads to a change in the mix of cycle and safety stock, the reduced need for cycle stock being channeled into increased safety stock.

Thus, as workload increases, the increase in exposure risk tends to increase expected requisitions short while the change in investment mix works in the opposite direction. The net effect is favorable for low to moderate workload levels, but eventually the effect of exposure risk overwhelms the protection afforded by the increased safety stock. Thus we can refer to the right-hand edge of the surface as the edge of optimality since any further increase in workload would only serve to increase requisitions short. It is certainly feasible to choose workload levels beyond the edge, but never optimal.

In the next section, we show how to derive the edge with a Lagrangian model which minimizes the number of shortages subject only to an investment constraint. Since workload is unconstrained, the optimal workloads found by the model serve to define the edge of optimality. Points to the left of the edge can be derived by enriching the same model with a workload constraint. Although details are given only for the requisitions short objective function, extensions to other common objective functions can be made by following the same computational scheme [9].

4. Locating the Edge of Optimality

To locate any single point on the edge of optimality, the objective function is:

$$\text{Min } Z = \sum_i \frac{D_i}{Q_i} \int_{Ri}^{\infty} \left(\frac{X_i - R_i}{m_i} \right) f(x)dx \tag{1}$$

subject to the investment constraint

$$\sum_i \left(\frac{Q_i}{2} + S_i \right) = I \tag{2}$$

where

Z = expected annual number of customer requisitions backordered or short,

D_i = annual sales in dollars for item i,

Q_i = order quantity in dollars for item i,

R_i = reorder point in dollars (sum of safety stock plus leadtime demand stock) for item i,

X_i = leadtime demand in dollars for item i,

m_i = customer requisition size in dollars for item i,

$f(x)$ = probability density function for leadtime demand,

S_i = safety stock in dollars, for item i, and

I = investment constraint in dollars.

The assumptions in this formulation are that the length of the leadtime is constant, and that the customer requisition sizes for each line item are constants and are independent of the level of demand. For this example, we shall also assume that leadtime demand is normally distributed, although the solution procedure applies to other distributions as well.

The next step is to form the Lagrangian function, L:

$$L = \sum_i \frac{D_i}{Q_i} \int_{Ri}^{\infty} \frac{(X_i - R_i)}{m_i} f(x)dx + \lambda_I \left[\sum_i \left(\frac{Q_i}{2} + S_i \right) - I \right], \tag{3}$$

where λ_I = the Lagrangian multiplier.

Differentiating with respect to Q_i, S_i, and λ_I, we obtain the first order conditions:

$$\frac{\partial L}{\partial Q_i} = \frac{-D_i}{Q_i^2 m_i} \int_{R_i}^{\infty} (X_i - R_i) f(x)dx + \frac{\lambda_I}{2} = 0, \tag{4}$$

$$\frac{\partial L}{\partial S_i} = \frac{-D_i}{Q_i m_i} \int_{R_i}^{\infty} f(x)dx + \lambda_I = 0, \text{ and} \tag{5}$$

$$\frac{\partial L}{\partial \lambda_I} = \sum_i \left(\frac{Q_i}{2} + S_i \right) - I = 0. \tag{6}$$

Since all model functions are convex, we know that any solution to the first order conditions will be an optimal solution. Unfortunately, there is no direct solution for any of the variables in the problem. The approach followed here is essentially the method of successive approximations which iteratively searches for the simultaneously optimal values of λ_I and the Q_i and S_i for each line item.

Other formulations of stochastic models linking several items with average investment constraints have been proposed by Daeschner [5], Gerson and Brown [10] and Schrady and Choe [23]. To find the optimal solution to these Lagrangian models, the authors proposed either trial and error search [5], [10] or conversion of the problem to a sequence of unconstrained optimization problems using the SUMT technique [23]. Unfortunately, these procedures prove to be tedious and expensive in large applications [9], [23] and become even more difficult when the present model is enriched with a workload constraint, as shown in the next section. Hadley and Whitin [12] have also emphasized the computational difficulties associated with constrained stochastic inventory models.

The method of successive approximations (see [25] for a discussion) can be used to converge rapidly on the optimal value of λ_I which, in turn, can be used to derive the optimal Q_i and S_i values for each line item in the inventory.

Before describing the search algorithm, some simplifying notation is introduced. Let

$$P_i = \int_{R_i}^{\infty} f(x)dx, \tag{7}$$

$$E_i = \int_{R_i}^{\infty} (X_i - R_i) f(x)dx, \tag{8}$$

$$F_i = D_i / m_i. \tag{9}$$

P_i is the probability of a stockout during one order cycle. E_i is the partial expectation of demand or the expected number of dollars short per order cycle. F_i is the annual frequency of demand for each line item.

Although not derived here, simple algebra provides the equations used in the search:

$$\lambda_I = \sum_i F_i P_i / 2\left(I - \sum_i S_i\right), \tag{10}$$

$$Q_i = \sqrt{2F_i E_i / \lambda_I}, \tag{11}$$

$$P_i = \lambda_I Q_i / F_i. \tag{12}$$

A summary of the steps in the search algorithm using equations (10)–(12) is shown in figure 6A.3. We begin with an initial assumption of zero safety stock for each line item, which allows us to use (10) to derive an initial λ_I, which, in turn, determines the initial Q_i's using (11). Equation (12) is next used to calculate appropriate stockout probabilities, P_i, which then determine

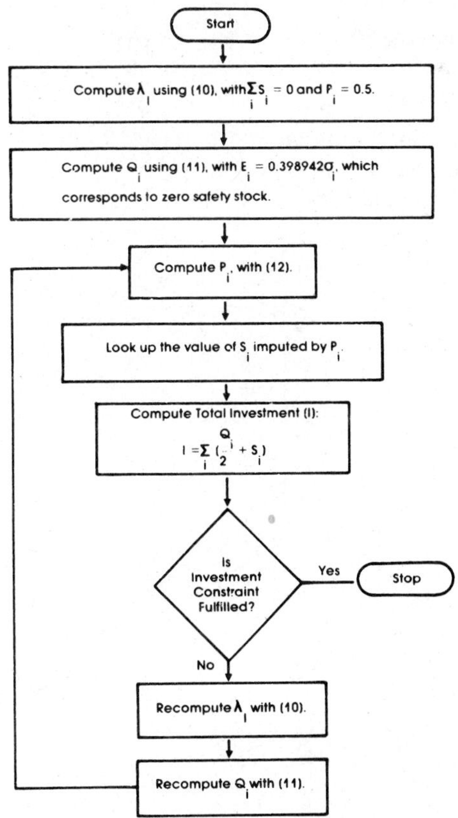

FIGURE 6A.3 The investment-constrained search algorithm

specific safety stock levels, S_i. This process is repeated until the investment constraint is fulfilled, iteratively updating λ_I, Q_i, P_i, and S_i.

The search algorithm summarized in figure 6A.3 has been run more than 100 times on data sets ranging in size from 500 to more than 40,000 line items. In every case, the model converged to within 1% of the investment constraint in twelve iterations or less. CPU time in Fortran, Level H, on the IBM 370/155 has been modest, averaging only 0.36 seconds per iteration per 1,000 line items. An example of the way the search algorithm behaves is given in figure 6A.4. The data used were the same as those used to derive the optimal policy surface in figure 6A.2. The model assumed an investment constraint of $1,367,000 and converged to the minimum requisitions short value of 0.60% in 9 iterations. (This point corresponds to the point at the lower right corner of figure 6A.2.) The curved path followed by the model is representative of all the data sets tested. To complete the edge of optimality, the model was run four more times with the investment levels shown in figure 6A.2.

5. Locating Interior Points on the Optimal Policy Surface

To locate any interior point on the surface, (to the left of the edge of optimality), a workload constraint is added to (1) and (2):

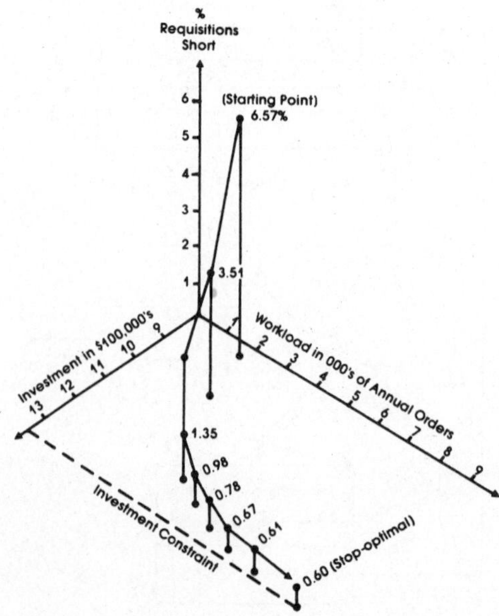

FIGURE 6A.4 Convergence of the investment-constrained search

$$\sum_i \frac{D_i}{Q_i} = W \tag{13}$$

where W = workload constraint in number of annual orders.

The Lagrangian function becomes:

$$L = \sum_i \frac{D_i}{Q_i m_i} \int_{R_i}^{\infty} (X_i - R_i) f(x) dx$$
$$+ \lambda_W \left(\sum_i \frac{D_i}{Q_i} = W \right) + \lambda_I \left[\sum_i \left(\frac{Q_i}{2} + S_i \right) - I \right].$$

Solution of this model leads to identical equations for λ_I and P_i as derived for the simpler model, equations (10) and (12), respectively. To these are added the optimal condition λ_W,

$$\lambda_W = \frac{1}{W} \left[\frac{\lambda_I \sum_i Q_i}{2} - \sum_i \frac{F_i E_i}{Q_i} \right] \tag{15}$$

and a modified optimal equation for Q_i, which incorporates the effects of both the investment and workload constraints,

$$Q_i = \sqrt{2(F_i E_i + \lambda_W D_i)/\lambda_i}. \tag{16}$$

The search strategy employed for this model is similar to the previous case and is outlined in figure 6A.5. As before, it is assumed initially that no safety stock is maintained for any of the items. This permits, using (10), direct calculation of an initial approximation for λ_I. Note, however, that the equations for λ_W and Q_i are interdependent, preventing their use in the initialization phase. Rearranging equation (12), however, we can derive an equation for Q_i which does not require an estimate of λ_W:

$$Q_i = F_i P_i / \lambda_I = 0.5 F_i / \lambda_I \tag{17}$$

The Q_i's based on (17) can then be used to provide an initial estimate of λ_W from (15). Thereafter the search progresses by iteratively updating values for Q_i, P_i (and correspondingly S_i), λ_I, and λ_w, using equations (16), (12), (10), and (15), until both the workload and investment constraints are fulfilled.

The model with both constraints has also been run on more than 100 data sets, and has always converged to a point within 1% of both constraints within 30 iterations. CPU time has averaged about 0.41 seconds per 1,000 line items. An example of the way the search behaves is given in figure

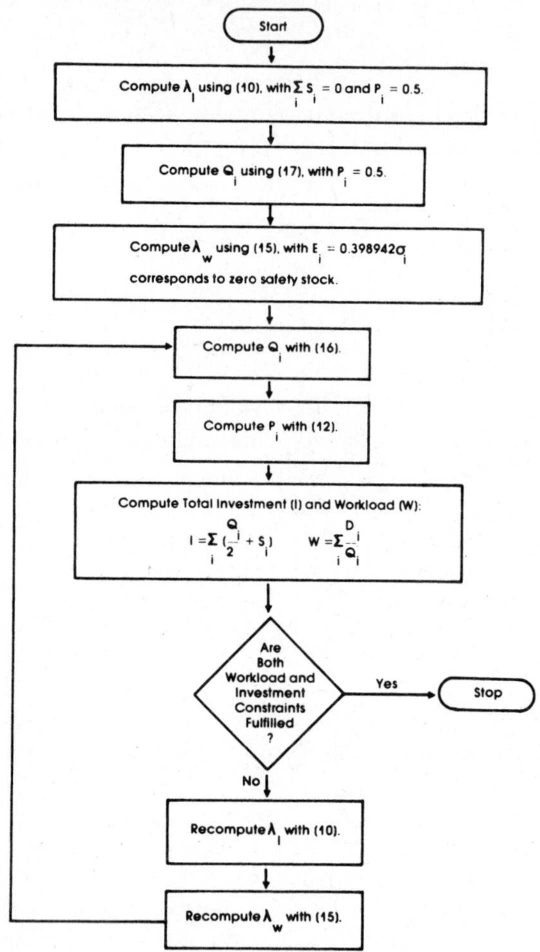

FIGURE 6A.5 The workload- and investment-constrained search algorithm

6A.6, with a workload constraint of 3,586 orders and an investment constraint of \$1,367,000 (refer to those coordinates in figure 6A.2). After seven iterations, the model reached a requisitions short level of 0.98%. Between that point and the optimum of 0.69%, the model required an additional 23 iterations (which were not plotted individually).

There are some interesting analogies between the order quantity and safety stock expressions in (16) and (12) and those that would be derived using a well-known classical model with a cost-based objective function. To illustrate, let C_0 be the marginal ordering cost, C_h be the annual inventory carrying cost expressed as a percentage of dollar value, and C_s be the shortage or penalty cost per customer requisition short or backordered.

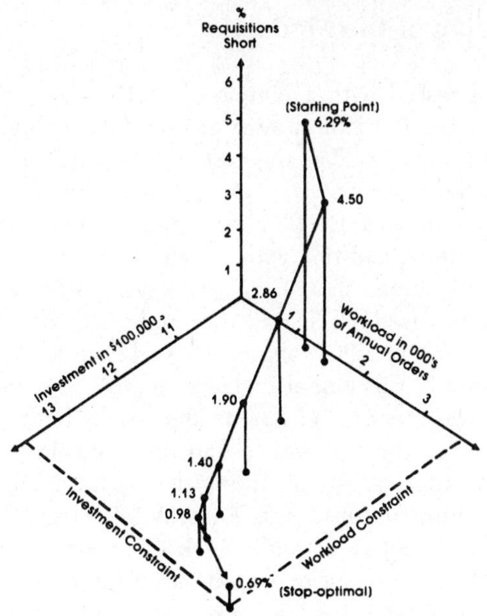

FIGURE 6A.6 Convergence of the workload- and investment-constrained search

Then the total annual costs for the ith line item are:

$$TC_i = \frac{C_0 D_i}{Q_i} + \frac{C_h Q_i}{2} + C_h S_i + \frac{C_s D_i}{m_i Q_i} \int_{R_i}^{\infty} (X_i - R_i) f(x) dx. \tag{18}$$

Solution of this model using classical optimization techniques requires that

$$Q_i = \sqrt{2[F_i E_i + (C_0/C_s) D_i]/(C_h/C_s)} \tag{19}$$

and

$$P_i = (C_h/C_s) Q_i / F_i. \tag{20}$$

A simple comparison of (19) and (20) with (16) and (12) shows that they are equivalent provided that

$$C_0/C_s = \lambda_W, \tag{21}$$

$$C_h/C_s = \lambda_I. \tag{22}$$

Therefore, one way in which the constrained models can be interpreted is that the Lagrangian multipliers act as surrogates for the marginal cost information.

6. An Application of the Models

The models were tested with a sample of 78,180 line items representing the complete inventories at four of thirty stock points in a military distribution system. The line items used in the test represent about 20% of the line items stocked in the system. Order quantities in the system are currently computed with a standard EOQ model. Safety stocks are computed independently of order quantities with a Lagrangian model that minimizes the number of requisitions short for a given safety stock budget. Trial and error procedures are used to: (1) find the single Lagrangian multiplier that allocates safety stock, (2) adjust aggregate workload at each stock point to constraints imposed by personnel budgets, and (3) adjust the sum of cycle and safety stock investment to constraints imposed by budget considerations.

The first step in the test was to find the point on the optimal policy surface (the value of requisitions short) that corresponds to the current workload and investment constraints for each inventory. These results are compared to current policy in table 6A.1. In every case, current policy could be improved by moving to a position on the optimal policy surface. The results shown in table 6A.1 are expected values, computed with the assumptions and approximations discussed above in the sections on model development. Since these assumptions and approximations are identical to those used in the current inventory system, the results are strictly comparable. In practice the actual requisitions short achieved using the current policies is normally somewhat higher than that predicted by the model. This difference in predicted and actual performance is due to a number of factors, including the exercise of local control by stock point managers and the existence of line items currently in an out-of-stock status or which have relatively poor current stock positions. Further exploration of the surface showed that workload cuts averaging 25% could be made at each stock point without changing current investment or requisitions short. Some reductions in investment could also be made for the existing workload and requisitions short.

There appear to be two related reasons for these potential improvements. First, the optimal policy surface is built up from simultaneous solutions for

TABLE 6A.1 Comparison of Current Policy to the Optimal Policy Surface

		Expected Value of Req·.sitions Short		
Stock Point	*Line Items Stocked*	*Current Policy*	*Optimal Policy*	*Current Minus Optimal*
1	12,262	6.72%	0.78%	5.94%
2	5,309	8.49	2.35	6.14
3	43,882	1.55	0.45	1.10
4	16,997	3.28	0.88	2.40

order quantities and safety stocks for each line item. In current policy, these two elements are computed independently of each other. Since standard deviations of leadtime demand in the system are relatively large, we rely on Groff and Muth's conclusion [20] that simultaneous solutions should give better results. Second, the surface gives a better aggregate mix of cycle and safety stock investment than current policy. In current policy, the aggregate mix is roughly 40% cycle stock and 60% safety stock. These percentages are reversed for the corresponding workload and investment coordinates on the optimal policy surface.

7. Conclusions

Given the difficulties in measuring the traditional inventory costs and the strategic advantages of exploring aggregate inventory tradeoffs, we propose that inventory model-builders bypass the use of marginal costs and work directly with those aggregate variables that can be measured—the number of inventory shortages, workload, and investment. Since the response surface that shows the relationships among these variables is optimal, we can state that management decisions should result in points located on the surface. This statement is true, regardless of the particular cost structure of any firm, and provides a sound theoretical basis for decision-making. If objective cost information is available, it can be considered after the surface is constructed. The computational results presented show that the models used to derive the optimal policy surface are efficient, and could make improvements in one inventory system.

REFERENCES

1. Brown, R. G., *Decision Rules For Inventory Management*, Holt, New York, 1967.
2. ———, *Materials Management Systems—A Modular Library*, Wiley, New York, 1977.
3. Buchan, J. and Koenigsberg, E., *Scientific Inventory Management*, Prentice-Hall, Englewood Cliffs, N.J., 1963.
4. Churchman, C. W., *Prediction and Optimal Decision—Philosophical Issues of A Science of Values*, Prentice-Hall, Englewood Cliffs, N.J., 1961.
5. Daeschner, W. E., *Models For Multi-Item Inventory Systems Under Constraints*, Unpublished Ph.D. Dissertation, Naval Postgraduate School, 1975.
6. Everett, H., "Generalized Lagrange Multiplier Method for Solving Problems of Optimum Allocation of Resources," *Operations Res.*, Vol. 1, No. 3 (May–June, 1963).
7. Eagle, R. H., *Optimal Inventory Decisions Under Constraints*, Unpublished Ph.D. Dissertation, University of North Carolina, 1968.

8. Fetter, R. B. and Dalleck, W. C., *Decision Models For Inventory Management*, Irwin, Homewood, Ill., 1961.
9. Gardner, E. S., *Aggregate Inventory Models: Theory and Applications*, Unpublished Ph.D. Dissertation, University of North Carolina, 1978.
10. Gerson, G. and Brown, R. G., "Decision Rules for Equal Shortage Policies," *Naval Res. Logist. Quart.*, Vol. 17, No. 3 (September, 1970).
11. Groff, G. K. and Muth, J. F., *Operations Management: Analysis For Decisions*, Irwin, Homewood, Ill., 1972.
12. Hadley, G. and Whitin, T. M., *Analysis of Inventory Systems*, Prentice-Hall, Englewood Cliffs, N.J., 1963.
13. Hansmann, F., *Operations Research In Production and Inventory Control*, Wiley, New York, 1962.
14. Johnson, R. W., *Financial Management*, Allyn and Bacon, Boston, Mass., 1971.
15. Jones, C. H., "The Manager's Use of Simulation Models," *1970 APICS Conference Proceedings*, American Production and Inventory Control Society, Washington, D.C.
16. Lambert, D. M., "*The Development of An Inventory Costing Methodology*," National Council of Physical Distribution Management, Chicago, Ill., 1975.
17. Magee, J. F., and Boodman, D. M., *Production Planning and Inventory Control*, 2nd ed., McGraw-Hill, New York, 1967.
18. Mather and Plossl, Inc., *News Note* #19, Atlanta, Georgia (May, 1978).
19. Mayer, R. R., "The Interrelationship Between Lot Sizes and Safety Stock in Inventory Control," *Indust. Engr*. Vol. 16, No. 4 (July–August, 1965).
20. Parker, L. L., "Economical Reorder Quantities and Reorder Points With Uncertain Demand," *Naval Res. Logist. Quart*., Vol. 11, No. 4 (December 1964).
21. Plossl, G. W. and Wight, O. W., *Production and Inventory Control*, Prentice-Hall, Englewood Cliffs, N.J., 1967.
22. Prichard, J. W. and Eagle, R. H., *Modern Inventory Management*, Wiley, New York, 1965.
23. Schrady, D. A. and Choe, V. E., "Models for Multi-Item Continuous Review Inventory Policies Subject to Constraints," *Naval Res. Logist. Quart.* Vol. 8, No. 4 (December, 1971).
24. Starr, M. K. and Miller, D. W., *Inventory Control: Theory and Practice*, Prentice-Hall, Englewood Cliffs, N.J., 1962.
25. Wagner, H. M., *Principles of Operations Research*, Prentice-Hall, Englewood Cliffs, N.J., 1969.
26. Whitin, T. M., *The Theory of Inventory Management*, Princeton Univ. Press, Princeton, N.J., 1953.
27. Wight, O. W., *Production and Inventory Management In The Computer Age*, Cahners, Boston, Mass., 1974.
28. Wilde, D. and Beightler, C., *Foundations of Optimization*, Prentice-Hall, Englewood Cliffs, N.J., 1967.
29. Ziegler, R. E., *Criteria for Measurement of the Cost Parameters of an Economic Order Quantity Inventory Model*, Unpublished Ph.D. Dissertation, University of North Carolina, 1973.

chapter seven

Distribution Inventory Management

This chapter will deal with inventory control issues arising from the reality that customers are not conveniently located next to the factory. Often, inventory must be stored in several locations, as shown in figure 7.1.

We are concerned here with place utility. A customer wants to buy a portable television, for example, from a local store. Because shipment is not instantaneous, the local store will hold an inventory of televisions. When the local store needs resupply, the store wants immediate delivery from a company in its vicinity. Otherwise, delivery might take too long for the customer to wait. How often have you been told that your order will take two weeks because the store is out of stock and the factory is three thousand miles away, on the opposite coast—or in Taiwan or Stuttgart?

Immediate supply can be guaranteed from three thousand miles away if the company is willing to pay expediting costs. If a company supplies high-dollar-value, small items, such as medical sutures, orchids, and printed circuit boards, expediting may be appropriate. Normally, a company that is able to supply items quickly has a marketing advantage. Such rapid response can be achieved either through information and transportation or by holding inventories close to the customers at the time the customers want the items.

Referring to figure 7.1, the factory warehouse provides inventory storage at the production site. The regional distribution centers may be located in the Northeast, the Southeast, and so on, to serve customers in the various regions of the country. About five or six can cover the United States within twelve hours of 90% of the population. Finally, the local service center is closest to the customer. A service center in each metropolitan area might distribute supplies to retail outlets. In this scheme, the company owns the factory, the factory warehouse, the regional distribution center, and the local service center.

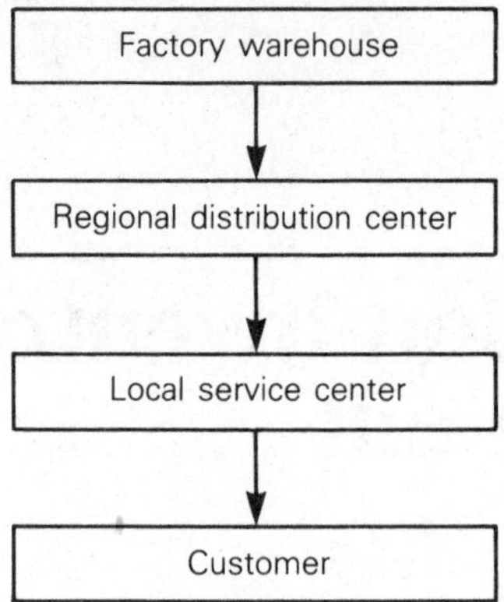

FIGURE 7.1 Multilocation inventories

Our objective in this chapter is to explain the trade-offs involved in holding inventories at various locations, so that the reader can appraise the advantages and disadvantages of such systems as distribution requirements planning (DRP). The weaknesses of single-item, single-location inventory control methods should be apparent when they are applied in the multilocation setting. The main issues are (1) where to have warehouses and what to stock and (2) how to replace stocks, given the answer to the first issue.

Multilocation System Definitions

Various multilocation systems can be classified using electronics and forestry analogies (see figure 7.2). *Arborescent systems* have branches spreading apart, with the products flowing to different branches. *Coalescent systems* have materials coming together into one end item. *Series systems* have locations feeding each other in a direct path.

Several cycles or lead times make up the lead time separating the customer from the original raw materials. A firm with short lead times can respond more quickly to customer desires. The *procurement* cycle is the lead time necessary for the plant to obtain raw materials from its suppliers. The *replenishment* lead time is the time it takes to replenish stock at the distribution center—from the time necessary to place an order with the factory through the time of receiving the order. Scheduling, production, and shipment time make up the factory's portion of replenishment lead time, unless the factory is buffered by finished goods stock. Finally, the *order* cycle is the time taken between the distribution center or the service center and the retail outlet.

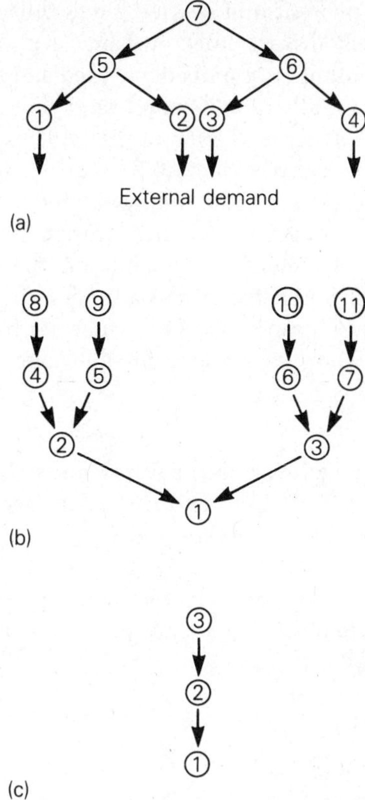

FIGURE 7.2 Multilocation systems: (a) arborescent distribution system (arrows point in direction of flow to customer); (b) coalescent assembly system; (c) series system

Lead Time	*Starting Event*	*Ending Event*
(a) Procurement	Factory order or vendor	Receive raw materials
(b) Production	Generate work order	Receive finished goods at factory
(c) Distribution or replenishment	Generate distribution order	Receive finished goods at warehouse
(d) Order	Generate order	Receive finished goods at next echelon

Measures of multilocation inventory system performance parallel those we found in single-location inventory problems:

1. *Fill rate*, or percent unit service, gives the average fraction of unit demand satisfied from stock on hand (e.g., 90%).
2. *Fills* are the number of units demanded and satisfied per unit time; that is, fills = (fills rate)(demand rate). For example, given a 90% fill rate and a demand rate of 20 units per week, we have an average of 18 fills per week ($0.9 \times 20 = 18$).
3. *Expected backorders* is the time-weighted average number of backorders outstanding at a stocking location. Including times of zero backorders, this measure depends on the fill rate—that is, the probability of *no* backorders at a random point in time. Expected backorders per year = (% time when no backorders possible) (0) + (% time when backorders possible)(average backorders).

Example 7.1

Suppose that annual demand is 1,000 units ($D = 1{,}000$), the order quantity is 100 units ($Q = 100$), and the maximum backorder position is 10 units ($B = 10$). What is the expected number of backorders?

Solution: On any cycle, the average backorder position is $B/2 = 5$. The percentage of time when backorders are possible is $B/Q = 10/100 = 0.1$. Hence, the expected backorders per year is

$$\frac{B}{Q} * \frac{B}{2} = \frac{10}{100} * \frac{10}{2} = 0.5.$$

4. *Expected delay* is the average time necessary to satisfy a unit of demand. The unit may be supplied instantaneously, or there may be some wait for expediting. Expected number of units backordered = (expected delay)(demand rate). This relationship comes from simple pipeline flow theory, in which the expected number of customers in the system equals the arrival rate times the expected waiting time. For example, if two customers per minute arrive at a carwash and if each customer's car takes six minutes to move through the waiting line and be washed, then there will be an average of $2 * 6 = 12$ customers in the system either waiting or being washed. Similarly, if the expected number of backorders in an inventory system is twelve and two units are demanded per day, the average time to supply each unit must be six days.

Example 7.2

Suppose that annual demand is 1,000 units ($D = 1{,}000$), the order quantity is 100 units ($Q = 100$), and the maximum backorder position is 50 units ($B = 50$). What is the expected delay or the average time to satisfy a unit of demand?

Solution: On a 250 working day year, the demand rate is $d = 1{,}000/250 = 4$ units per day.

$$\frac{\text{Expected backorders}}{\text{Demand Rate}} = \frac{(B/Q)(B/2)}{d} = \frac{B^2}{2dQ}$$

$$= \frac{(50/100)(50/2)}{4} = \frac{2500}{800}$$

$$= 3.125 \text{ days}$$

5. *Inventory holding cost* is the cost of holding inventory, including insurance, obsolescence, deterioration, property taxes, and the cost of capital. Inventory holding cost may also be a management policy variable.
6. *Setup costs* and *ordering costs* are the costs of preparing or receiving an order. In the factory, these are the costs of setting up the equipment. Elsewhere, they are the clerical costs of order processing and receiving (including inspection).
7. *Stockout costs* are the costs of lost sales or backorders. In the lost sales case, revenues are forgone. With backorders, *expediting*, *transshipment* from an alternative supplier, or *substitution* of a similar item in stock all create costs in addition to the costs of *delay*. Stockout costs may not be observed in any operational way.
8. *System stability* costs are costs associated with overreaction to changes in demand rates. These costs are also usually nebulous.
9. Several of the measures can be found in Brown [2].

Echelon Inventory and Echelon Holding Costs

For analytical purposes, *echelon inventory* at a stocking point includes all inventory that either is at that stocking point or has passed through that stocking point. Defined by Clark and Scarf [3] in 1960, this concept was picked up by Orlicky [7, p. 54], who argued that "for a low-level inventory item, the quantity that exists under its *own identity*, as well as any quantities existing as (*consumed*) components of parent items, parents of parent items, etc., must be accounted for.

The *echelon holding cost rate* at a given inventory stocking point is the incremental cost of holding a unit of system inventory at that stocking point rather than at an earlier or predecessor point. For example, the echelon holding cost at a service center would be the incremental cost of holding inventory at the service center rather than at the regional warehouse.

Now we have arrived at a key point. From an accounting standpoint, the same total dollar holding cost will be computed whether the inventory analyst uses conventional holding rates applied to conventional inventory or echelon holding cost rates applied to echelon inventory. Economic order quantity calculations will be quite different, though, and may not apply at all to field stocks.

Example 7.3

In a serial system, suppose that there is an average of 100 units of inventory at stage 2 and 80 units at stage 1. Under both the conventional and the echelon system, total holding costs would be $2,200. In table 7.1, the total inventory holding costs are calculated by both methods. Stage 1 is the stage closest to the customer.

Example 7.4

In a serial system, suppose that stage 2 has an annual demand of 2,000 units, a setup cost of $500, and conventional holding costs of $10 per unit per year. Standard EOQs and simple echelon EOQs are shown in table 7.2. The simple echelon EOQ uses the echelon holding rate.

We have found, then, that echelon rates work well from an accounting point of view while they isolate the setup cost versus holding cost trade-off at each stage. The EOQs should not be blindly calculated at stage 1, since the conventional holding rate would cause us to hold too little inventory.

More complicated EOQ formulas have been derived [4] to handle the problem of interaction between lot sizes at various stages in the system. System-myopic heuristics treat two stages at a time. For our purposes, however, the main lesson is the impact of echelon holding rates on the geographic distribution of inventory.

Several features of an echelon holding rate system center on a general shift of inventories toward the customer. Comparing echelon systems to conventional systems, we find the following:

1. The same size and frequency of orders will be placed by the stocking point farthest from the customer, because the conventional and the echelon rates will be the same at this level.
2. The same total system inventory will be held. The larger lot sizes at the levels closer to the customer indicate that lots will not stay long at predecessor levels. This is illustrated in figure 7.3. If the lot size at stage 1 is increased, the average inventory at stage 2 will decrease.
3. Inventories will be shifted toward the retail level.

Industrial Dynamics

When production is separated from demand by several echelons, each with its own ordering rules and cycles, oscillations become amplified through

TABLE 7.1 Equivalence of Echelon and Conventional System Costs

Stage	*Conventional Holding Rate*	*Echelon Holding Rate*	*Average Inventory*	*Average Echelon Inventory*	*Conventional Holding Cost*	*Echelon Holding Cost*
2	\$10	\$10	100	180	10(100) = \$1,000	10(180) = \$1,800
1	\$15	\$ 5	80	80	15(80) = \$1,200	5(80) = \$400
Total					\$2,200	\$2,200

TABLE 7.2 Simple Echelon EOQ versus Conventional EOQ

Stage	*Conventional Holding Rate*	*Echelon Holding Rate*	*Conventional EOQ*	*Simple Echelon EOQ*	*Demand and Setup Data*
2	\$10	\$10	$\sqrt{\frac{2(2000)500}{10}} = 447$	$\sqrt{\frac{2(2000)500}{10}} = 447$	$D_2 = 2{,}000$ $S_2 = \$500$
1	\$15	\$ 5	$\sqrt{\frac{2(2000)100}{15}} = 164$	$\sqrt{\frac{2(2000)100}{5}} = 283$	$D_1 = 2{,}000$ $S_1 = \$100$

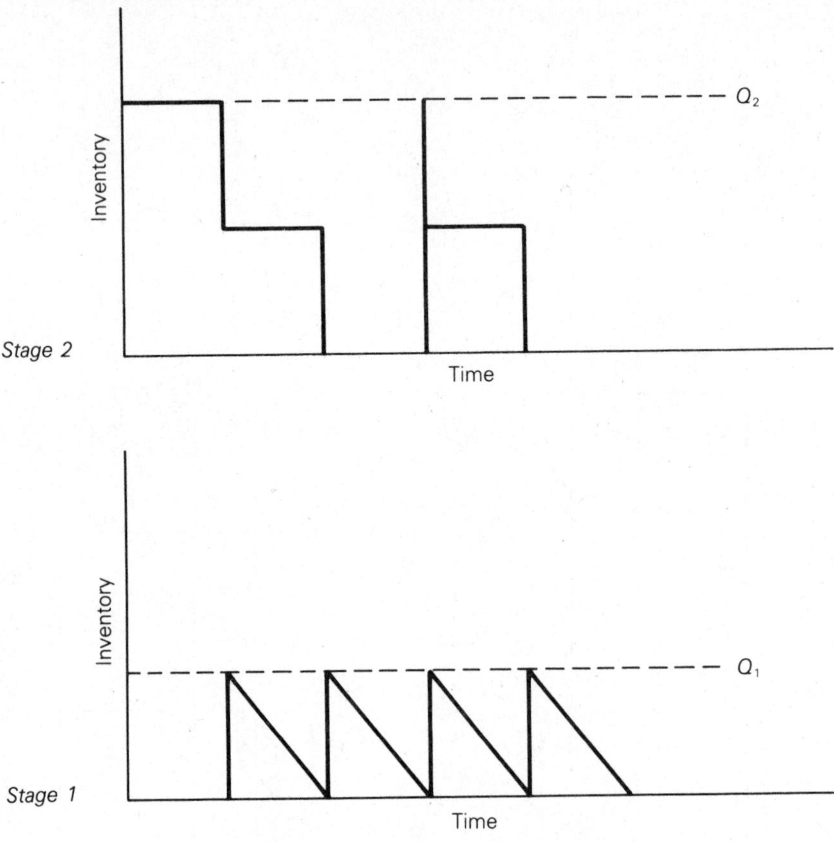

FIGURE 7.3 Inventory in a series system

the system. On an upswing in sales, for example, all service centers are likely to place their orders quickly in batch sizes large enough to contend with the upward trend. During a downswing, their inventories will carry them for a longer time.

As an illustration of the amplification phenomenon, we will consider the simple accelerator effect from retail sales to service center inventories.

Example 7.5

A service center seeks to maintain inventories at double the level of current sales; that is,

$$I_t^* = 2S_t$$

Lead time at the service center is one week.

Consider sales as shown in table 7.3. Using an order decision rule that attempts to restore inventory to the desired level of twice current sales, the increase in sales is magnified in the service center's ending inventories. Table 7.3 shows this amplification.

TABLE 7.3 Inventory Amplification with Order Lead Time

Month	*Beginning Inventory* (B_t)	*Retail Sales* (S_t)	*Desired Inventory* (I_t^*)	*Ending Inventory* (I_t)	*Order Size* (O_t)
0					200
1	400	200	400	200	200
2	400[a]	200	400	200	200
3	400	200	400	200	200
4	400	210	420	190	230
5	390	220	440	170	270
6	400	230	460	170	290
7	440	230	460	170	290
8	460	230	460	230	230
9	520	230	460	290	170
10	520	220	440	300	140
11	470	210	420	260	160
12	400	200	400	200	200
13	360				

[a] Open order for 200 units arrives.

Two root causes for amplification of fluctuations can be distinguished: (1) the ordering policy and (2) lead times. Table 7.4 shows the same sales leading to smaller fluctuations in service center inventories because there is no time lag between ordering and receiving the inventory.

Centralization of Inventories

So far, we have been concerned mainly with order decision rules in the multilocation setting. There is also a question, however, of where to locate safety stocks. This section will examine order decision rules and safety stock

TABLE 7.4 Inventory Amplification without Order Lead Time

Month	*Beginning Inventory* (B_t)	*Retail Sales* (S_t)	*Desired Inventory* (I_t^*)	*Ending Inventory* (I_t)	*Order Size* (O_t)
1	400	200	400	200	200
2	400	200	400	200	200
3	400	200	400	200	200
4	400	210	420	190	230
5	420	220	440	200	240
6	440	230	460	210	250
7	460	230	460	230	230
8	460	230	460	230	230
9	460	230	460	230	230
10	460	220	440	240	200
11	440	210	420	230	190
12	420	200	400	220	180

rules together to demonstrate their combined pressure to centralize inventories. A later section will isolate safety stock considerations in an attempt to allocate stocks through the system.

Consider a single stocking site with a (Q, R) system. Using notation similar to that in earlier chapters, D = annual demand, S = setup cost, h = holding cost per unit per year, σ = standard deviation of lead time demand, k = number of standard deviations of lead time demand used to determine safety stock, SS = safety stock, and TRC = total relevant cost. The relevant annual cost equation would be

$$TRC(Q, R) = \frac{D(S)}{Q} + \frac{Q(h)}{2} + h(SS) \tag{7.1}$$

Noting that $SS = k\sigma$ and letting $Q = \sqrt{2DS/h}$, we can rewrite the relevant cost equation as

$$TRC(Q, R) = \sqrt{2ShD} + hk\sigma \tag{7.2}$$

Compare this to problem 19 in Chapter 4.

If we now had N such stocking points, each with annual demand D_i and standard deviation σ_i, the total *decentralized* relevant cost equation would be

$$TRC = \left(\sqrt{2Sh}\sum_{i=1}^{N}\sqrt{D_i}\right) + \left(hk\sum\sigma_i\right) \tag{7.3}$$

assuming the same h for k for all stocking points.

By comparison, we could centralize these inventories at one location. Ignoring transportation costs, the total relevant costs would be

$$TRC = \sqrt{2Sh}\sqrt{D} + hk\sigma \tag{7.4}$$

where

$$\sqrt{D} = \sqrt{\sum_{i=1}^{N} D_i} \leq \sum_{i=1}^{N}\sqrt{D_i}$$

and

$$\sigma = \sqrt{\sum_{i=1}^{N}\sigma_i^2} \leq \sum_{i=1}^{N}\sigma_i$$

assuming independence between locations.

Example 7.6

Two inventory locations have annual demands and costs as shown.

S	h	D	k	σ	$\sqrt{D}$
100	10	1000	1.64	50	31.62
100	10	2000	1.64	50	44.72
		3000		70.7	54.77

The *decentralized* system is given by equation (7.3):

$$TRC = \sqrt{2(100)10}\,(\sqrt{1{,}000} + \sqrt{2{,}000}) + 10(1.64)(50 + 50)$$

$$= 5{,}054$$

For the *centralized* system, equation (7.4) gives

$$TRC = \sqrt{2(100)10}\,\sqrt{3{,}000} + 10(1.64)70.7$$

$$= 3{,}609$$

The advantages of centralization hinge on two separate effects:

1. The square root of total demand is less than the sum of the square roots of individual location demand.
2. The standard deviation of total lead time demand is less than the sum of the standard deviation of individual location demand.

Safety Stocks

Centralization pressure on both lot size and safety stocks tells only part of the story. The remainder of the story centers on the measure of stockouts. If a stockout incidents measure is used, there is no incentive to maintain backup stock at the distribution center to speedily handle stockout situations at the service center. Only under a time-weighted stockout measure does backup stock make sense—that is, only when it matters how long we are out of stock.

Even with a time-weighted stockout measure, backup stock has only an indirect effect on expected delay at stage 1 or on the fill rate at stage 1. Consider a two-stage system, with stage 1 as the retail outlet and stage 2 as the service center. Recall that the fill rate (F_1) is the fraction of retail unit demand satisfied from stock on hand—that is, without delay. Customer expected delay (T_1) is the average time to fill a unit of demand at the retail level.

Stage 2 ⟶ Stage 1 ⟶

Stage 2	Stage 1
$D_2 = 1{,}000$	$D_1 = 1{,}000$
$B_2 = 20$	$S_1 = 20$
$h_2 = 5$	$h_1 = 5$
$Q_2^* = 200$	$Q_1 = 200$
$d = 4$ per day (250-day year)	$d = 4$ per day
$L_2 = 10$ days	$L_1 = 5$ days

For the moment, consider the time delay at stage 2 only. If there is safety stock at stage 2, the expected time delay would be zero. All orders placed on stage 2 by stage 1 should be met from stock. If stage 2 has negative safety stock however, such as a maximum backorder position of $B_2 = 20$, there will certainly be a delay in filling such orders. The average backlog would be $B_2/2 = 20/2 = 10$.

We have already shown in this chapter that the expected delay can be calculated as (expected backorders/demand rate). Letting T be the expected delay and using the concept of example 7.2, we have

$$T_2 = \frac{B_2^2}{2dQ_2}$$

In our example, the expected delay would be given as

$$\frac{B_2^2}{2dQ_2} = \frac{20^2}{2(4)200} = 0.25 \quad \text{or one-quarter day}$$

At stage 1, the effective stage 1 safety stock (ESS_1) is stage 1 safety stock minus the expected demand during expected stage 2 delay: $ESS_1 = S_1 - dT_2$; for example, $ESS_1 = 20 - 4(0.25) = 19$.

If trade-offs are to be made between reducing the expected backorders at stage 2 and increasing safety stocks at stage 1, what should be done? A unit of stock added to stage 2 would reduce the maximum backorder position to nineteen units and the expected stage 2 delay would be

$$T_2 = \frac{19^2}{2 * 4 * 200} = 0.23$$

Hence, the effective safety stock would be

$$ESS_1 = 20 - 4(0.23) = 19.08 \text{ units}$$

On the other hand, increasing stage 1 safety stock by one unit would increase stage 1 effective safety stock by one unit:

$$ESS_1 = 21 - 4(0.25) = 20$$

These findings are consistent with the material requirements planning (MRP) philosophy that safety stock should be kept at end item levels only, not at intermediate levels. In distribution systems, however, these findings must be balanced against centralization pressures.

Distribution Inventory Systems

Now that we have uncovered some of the principles of the multilocation inventory problem, we are ready to examine some systems in use. Each of these systems solves the problem by ignoring some of its aspects and concentrating on others

LEVEL DECOMPOSITION SYSTEMS

Level decomposition systems set aggregate service level objectives for all items at an echelon. For example, the objective at the main distribution center might be 95% service, interpreted as a 95% fill rate. With n items in the inventory, the problem can be stated as follows:

$$\text{Minimize} \sum_{i=1}^{n} \begin{pmatrix} \text{unit value} \\ \text{on item } i \end{pmatrix} \begin{pmatrix} \text{safety stock} \\ \text{on item } i \end{pmatrix}$$

$$\text{subject to} \sum_{i=1}^{n} \left(\frac{\text{item demand rate}}{\text{aggregate demand rate}} \right) \begin{pmatrix} \text{item} \\ \text{fill rate} \end{pmatrix} \geq 0.95$$

Example 7.7

Two items (A and B) are valued at \$10 and \$15, respectively, with demand rates of three per day and seven per day. With an aggregate service level objective of 0.95, the problem would be: Minimize $10s_1 + 5s_2$ subject to 0.3(fill rate on A) + 0.7(fill rate on B) $\geq$ 0.95. If the fill rate on item A were 0.90, the fill rate on item B would have to be 0.97. With unit service objectives on A and B, we could calculate the safety stocks required for these item fill rates and then evaluate the costs in the objective function.

Although this problem can be solved using the Lagrange multiplier technique, our objective here is to describe the basics of the system, not the mathematics. Level decomposition systems will have some items with high fill rates and some with low, depending on the costs involved. Items with high fill rates at one echelon will wind up with high fill rates at another echelon. Safety stocks will be duplicated. In level decomposition systems, no mechanism allows safety stocks at one echelon to be related to safety stocks at another echelon.

MULTIECHELON SYSTEMS

Multiechelon systems, sometimes called differentiated distribution or item decomposition systems, focus on effective safety stock. Muckstadt and Thomas [6] examine multiechelon methods applied to low-demand-rate items. Because the mathematics of such systems is complex, we present only simple differentiated distribution concepts and encourage the interested reader to pursue the Muckstadt and Thomas [6] article.

Heskett, Glaskowsky, and Ivie [5] mention that dual (differentiated) distribution systems are the outgrowth of ABC inventory policies. The ABC system differentiates items on the basis of such variables as sales volume, unit value, or customer importance. Rather than the standard ABC breakdown by dollar volume, a breakdown by unit volume makes sense for distribution systems. The effect of such a breakdown is shown in table 7.5. With such a breakdown, single-location methods can be used to determine appropriate ordering policies.

DISTRIBUTION REQUIREMENTS PLANNING (DRP) SYSTEMS

Distribution requirements planning (DRP) simply translates material requirements planning (MRP) logic to a distribution system. In what follows, we assume that the reader has at least a rudimentary knowledge of MRP. If you have not studied MRP, please skip ahead to chapter 8 and read the sections on the parts requirement problem, the bill of materials, and the mechanics of MRP.

Consider a system in which a distribution center in North Carolina supplies service centers in Connecticut and California. Lead time from

TABLE 7.5 Differentiated Distribution System

Local Service Level	*Type of Item*	*Where Located*	*Central Service Level*
High	High volume/high price	Locally	Low
High	High volume/low price	Locally[a]	Low
Low	Low volume/high price	Centrally[a]	High
Low	Low volume/low price	Centrally	High

[a] Ideal candidates for these locations.

North Carolina to California is three weeks; to Connecticut, one week. The North Carolina distribution has a one-week replenishment lead time.

Even in this simple example, we will see both the attraction and the oversimplification of the DRP approach. Clearly, the attraction lies in treating the North Carolina demand as dependent or derived demand. Rather than the conventional approach of using past demand at North Carolina to forecast future demand, we use only the derived demand as gross requirements. At the distribution center, then, no safety stock needs to be held against demand variance—only against replenishment lead time variance from the factory. All safety stock against demand uncertainty will be held at the service centers, as in the MRP approach.

Just as practitioners have criticized operations researchers for over-sophistication, practitioners have fallen into an oversimplification trap with DRP. Note in table 7.6 that EOQs have been used at the service centers. Technically, these EOQs should be calculated on echelon holding costs, not on standard holding costs. Except for transportation expense, there is

TABLE 7.6 DRP Example with Lot Sizes

CAL—Service Center	*0*	*1*	*2*	*3*	*4*	*5*	*6*	*7*	*8*	*9*
Forecast		25	25	25	25	25	25	25	25	25
On hand	125	100	75	50	25	0	175	150	125	50
Planned order release				200						
$L = 3$, $Q = 200$										

CONN—Service Center	*0*	*1*	*2*	*3*	*4*	*5*	*6*	*7*	*8*	*9*
Forecast		50	50	50	50	50	50	50	50	50
On hand	110	60	10	160	110	60	10	160	110	60
Planned order release			200				200			
$L = 1$, $Q = 200$										

NC—Distribution Center	*0*	*1*	*2*	*3*	*4*	*5*	*6*	*7*	*8*	*9*
Gross requirements			200	200			200			
On hand	265	265	65	65	65	65	65	65	65	65
Planned order release			200			200				
$L = 1$, $Q = 200$										

NC—Factory	*0*	*1*	*2*	*3*	*4*	*5*	*6*	*7*	*8*	*9*
Gross requirements			200			200				
On hand	300	300	100	100	100	400	400	400	400	400
Planned order release			500							
$L = 3$, $Q = 500$										

Note: Example assumes that service center requirements continue at the forecast level indefinitely.

TABLE 7.7 DRP Example with Lot Sizes at Factory Only

CAL—Service Center	0	1	2	3	4	5	6	7	8	9	10	11	12
Forecast		25	25	25	25	25	25	25	25	25	25	25	25
On hand	125	100	75	50	25	0	0	0	0	0	0	0	0
Planned order release				25	25	25	25	25	25	25	25*	25	25

$L = 3$

* to cover period 13.

CONN—Service Center	0	1	2	3	4	5	6	7	8	9	10	11	12
Forecast		50	50	50	50	50	50	50	50	50	50	50	50
On hand	110	60	10	0	0	0	0	0	0	0	0	0	0
Planned order release			40	50	50	50	50	50	50	50	50	50	

$L = 1$

NC—Distribution Center	0	1	2	3	4	5	6	7	8	9	10	11	12
Gross requirements			40	75	75	75	75	75	75	75	75	75	75
On hand	265	265	225	150	75	0							
Planned order release						75	75	75	75	75	75	75	

$L = 1$

NC—Factory	0	1	2	3	4	5	6	7	8	9	10	11	12
Gross requirements						75	75	75	75	75	75	75	75
On hand	300	300	300	300	300	225	150	75	0	425	350	275	200
Planned order release							500						

$L = 3$, $Q = 500$

then little difference between holding stock at the service center rather than at the distribution center. Hence, on-hand inventory at the distribution center ought to be shipped out as soon as possible to provide extra protection at the service centers.

In table 7.7, we show some improvement by lot sizing at the factory only. At least we have pruned away meaningless lot sizes. Indeed, this version of DRP comes closest to what we think is the best approach to the problem—the "fair shares" approach invented by R. G. Brown in about 1960 in Akron, Ohio (well before DRP ever came on the scene).

FAIR SHARES ALLOCATION SYSTEMS

Examining the same situation with Brown's [1] fair shares allocation procedure, we see the difference between a push system and a pull system. DRP is a pull system; it depends on service center or retail EOQs to "pull" inventory through the system. Fair shares allocation is a push system, pushing inventory from the distribution center to the service center according to factory or distribution center stock levels. Both systems project requirements on the manufacturing location, giving it visibility in specifying when to produce.

Using the same example, we show the fair shares allocation approach in table 7.8. To follow the table, consider the following fair shares allocation steps:

1. Perform lot-for-lot (net requirements by period) explosions from the service centers.
2. The gross requirements resulting at the distribution center or factory are called net shipping requirements. Any desired safety stocks should be added to give a final figure for net shipping requirements.
3. Economic order quantity calculations or other trade-off calculations are made with regard to setups and scheduling at the factory. In our example, we show the factory producing in lot sizes of 500 units.
4. When inventory is available at the distribution center, fair shares are calculated. How many weeks of national (total) net shipping requirements can the distribution center inventory support? A fair share for a warehouse is the net shipping requirements to that warehouse through the time that the source's available stock will cover national net shipping requirements. In table 7.8, the 265 units on hand at the distribution center will support net shipping requirements through week 5. Time-phased net requirements through week 5 for California call for a fair share of 75 units.

In distinguishing between DRP with lot-for-lot explosions and fair shares allocation, it is important to recognize that fair shares allocation separates shipping decisions from requirements explosions. Although a DRP system could be patchworked to mimic fair shares, a typical DRP system would plan on many small shipments to match the lot-for-lot explosions. Rather than parceling out inventory according to planned orders, fair shares allocates on-hand inventory according to up-to-date net requirements.

Underlying this difference between lot-for-lot DRP and fair shares allocation is a different approach to the use of information. A fair shares system waits until the last moment before determining shipment sizes. All available information is utilized. Inventory status at the source and *current* net shipping requirements at each warehouse are considered.

BASE STOCK SYSTEMS

Whether fair shares or DRP techniques are used, low order rates at the service center level are quite common. DRP allows the service center to establish its own ordering rules. In a fair shares system, the service center

TABLE 7.8 Fair Share Example

CAL—Service Center	*0*	*1*	*2*	*3*	*4*	*5*	*6*	*7*	*8*	*9*	*10*	*11*	*12*
Forecast		25	25	25	25	25	25	25	25	25	25	25	25
On hand	125	100	75	50	100	175	150	125	100	75	50	25	0
Time-phased net (cumulative) requirement (monthly)				25	50	75	25	25	25	25	25	25	25
Planned receipt					75	100							

$L = 3$ 75 covers through week 5

CONN—Service Center	*0*	*1*	*2*	*3*	*4*	*5*	*6*	*7*	*8*	*9*	*10*	*11*	*12*
Forecast		50	50	50	50	50	50	50	50	50	50	50	50
On hand	110	60	200	350	300	250	200	150	100	50	0	284	234
Time-phased net (cumulative) requirement (monthly)			40	90	140	190	50	50	50	50	50	50	50
Planned receipt			190	200								334	

$L = 1$ 190 covers through week 5

fair share $= 334 = \frac{50}{75}(500)$

NC—Distribution Center	*0*	*1*	*2*	*3*	*4*	*5*	*6*	*7*	*8*	*9*	*10*	*11*	*12*
Net shipping (cumulative) requirements (monthly)			40	115	190	265	75	75	75	75	75	75	75
On hand	265	0	0	0	0	0	0	0	0	0	0	0	0
Planned shipment		265	300*									500	
Time-phased net requirement						75	75	75	75	75	75	75	75
Planned receipt			300								500		

$L = 1$ 265 covers through week 5

* This planned shipment includes a 200-unit fair share to CONN and a 100 fair share shipment to CAL.

NC—Factory	*0*	*1*	*2*	*3*	*4*	*5*	*6*	*7*	*8*	*9*	*10*	*11*	*12*
Gross requirements						75	75	75	75	75	75	75	75
On hand	300	0	0	0	0	0	0	0	0	0	0	0	0
Planned shipment		300**								500			
Planned order release							500						

$L = 3$, $Q = 500$

** This planned shipment represents 4 weeks of shipping requirements (weeks 5 through 8).

simply passes along demand rate information, facilitating centralized production and distribution decisions. Because low order rates are so pervasive, we need to examine one final system based on decentralized ordering: the base stock system.

The base stock approach, known as the sell-one/buy-one system, can be characterized as an (S, S) order up to policy. At one Sears location, for example, three sofas of a particular style might be kept in stock as a target level S. Should the store sell one, one more is ordered, because the inventory has dropped below the reorder point. With a two-week lead time, a reorder point (S) of three, and an averge order rate of one unit every two weeks, the system might behave as shown in table 7.9.

In about 1957, George Kimball distinguished replenishment orders from base stock orders. Base stock orders modify net demand on the source but preserve information about end consumption. If we sell 100 but reduce stock by 10, the ordinary system orders 90. Base stock system orders would show a replenishment order of 100 and a base stock order of -10, giving a net order of 90. The source can then see that the pipeline is changing, not end consumption.

For such a system, the decision varible S must be determined. With constant lead times, marginal analysis yields a familiar relationship. Let $OSOR(S)$ be the probability of stockout as a function of the target level/reorder point S. Let π be the per unit stockout cost and h be the holding cost per unit per year. Then we have the condition for an optimal solution:

Expected holding cost = expected stockout cost

$$h[1 - OSOR(S)] = \pi[OSOR(S)]$$

$$OSOR(S)\,(\pi + h) = h$$

$$OSOR(S) = \frac{h}{\pi + h}$$

But how can we end this chapter with such a simple, single-location statement? Don't let us get away with it!

First, note that constant lead times don't make much sense in our multiechelon structure, because a great deal depends on whether or not the supplying echelon has the item in stock. We are again faced with the question of expected delay. Second, we had better use echelon holding cost; but use of echelon holding cost will most probably result in an extremely low optimal stockout probability.

TABLE 7.9 Base Stock System

Time (Weeks)	*On Hand (End of Week)*	*Sell*	*Order*	*Order Receipt*
1	3	0		
2	2	1	1	
3	2	0		
4	3	0		1
5	2	1	1	
6	1	1	1	
7	2	0	0	1
8	3	0	0	1

To date, the best work in this area has been done by Muckstadt and Thomas [6] and Brown [2]. At this time, no systematic comparison of the three main systems has been made, but this chapter's objective has been met if the reader now understands the main ideas behind DRP, fair shares, and base stock systems.

Conclusion

This chapter has surveyed multilocation inventory principles and systems. Recognizing that the larger problem encompasses the question of facilities location, we nevertheless have been content to examine questions of how best to allocate stock within a given system.

Can any conclusions be drawn from our study? As mentioned earlier, this field still has no uniformly accepted methods, but this chapter has examined some dimensions of the problem:

1. If we use EOQ concepts, they should be based on echelon holding costs. This approach questions simplistic use of DRP.
2. Because low order rates are so common, base stock concepts coupled with multiechelon methods ought to yield good answers. The mathematics involved in this approach will probably preclude any practical applications unless someone can invent a simple DRP/fair shares–type system employing base stock concepts.
3. Safety stock generally should be kept at the levels closest to the customer, even though pressures for centralization arise from the smaller variance of central demand.

For further research in the field, the reader should refer to Schwarz [8] and Stenger and Cavinato [9].

PROBLEMS

1. Consider two products, A and B, supplied by a factory (stage 2) to a distribution center (stage 1). Costs and demand rates are as follows:

	Stage 2		*Stage 1*		
ITEM	CONVENTIONAL HOLDING COST	SETUP	CONVENTIONAL HOLDING COST	SETUP	DEMAND RATE
A	$10	$500	$15	$25	1000
B	$12	$500	$18	$25	2000

a. What are the appropriate EOQs, using echelon holding rates?
b. What are the average echelon holding costs at the two stages?
c. What assumption about stage 2 demand rates makes your answer to part b questionable?

2. A service center seeks to maintain inventories at three times current sales. Lead time at the service center is one week. Sales are 100 units for the first four weeks and 200 units per week thereafter. With a beginning inventory of 300 units and an open order for 100 units to arrive at the beginning of week 2, create a table showing beginning inventory, sales, desired ending inventory, actual ending inventory, and orders for twelve months.

3. Two inventory locations have annual demands and costs as shown.

S	h	D	k	σ
\$250	\$10	2,000	2.08	60
\$250	\$10	3,000	2.08	60

S = setup cost, h = holding cost per unit per year, D = annual demand, k = safety factor, and σ = standard deviation of lead time demand. Assume that the centralized location would exhibit the same s, h, and σ.

a. What dollar advantage comes from the EOQ effect on centralized inventory?
b. What dollar advantage comes from the standard deviation effect on centralized inventory?
c. What is the total dollar advantage of centralization versus decentralization?

4. In a two-stage system with a distribution center supplying a service center, the expected delay at the distribution center is one-half day. The demand rate at the service center is 20 units per day, the service center safety stock is 30 units, and the service center EOQ is 150 units.

a. What is the service center effective safety stock?
b. What is the expected delay at the service center?

5. Suppose that we have a factory supplying a distribution center. At the factory, annual demand for an item is 10,000 units, holding costs are \$10 per unit per year, and the cost per setup is \$750. How would you allocate 80 units of safety stock between the two locations?

Problems 6 through 11 use the following data: A factory in Chicago serves warehouses in Nashville and St. Louis. Normal lead time from the factory to either warehouse is one week. The Nashville warehouse faces demand of 40 units per week, and the St. Louis warehouse faces demand of 30 units per week, with order quantities of 200 units at each warehouse and on-hand quantities of 60 units and 40 units, respectively.

The EOQ at the factory is 500 units, the replenishment lead time is one week, and there are 100 units on hand. For each problem, develop tables for all three locations in the format shown in table 7.10.

6. Develop the DRP factory shipment schedule for the next nine weeks.
7. Develop the fair shares factory shipment schedule for the next nine weeks.
8. Suppose that the warehouses use an order point system with safety stocks of ten units. The reorder point (ROP) for each warehouse would be

$$ROP_{\text{Nashville}} = 40 + 10 = 50$$

$$ROP_{\text{St. Louis}} = 30 + 10 = 40.$$

   Develop the order point factory shipment schedule for the next nine weeks.
9. Revise the DRP factory shipment schedule to include the ten units of safety stock at each warehouse.
10. Revise the fair share system to include the ten units of safety stock at each warehouse.
11. Ignoring safety stocks, develop the DRP factory shipment schedule, permitting lot sizing at the factory only.
12. The number of bin trips (N) to put away stock in the field can be represented by annual demand divided by order quantity (D/Q). Show that $N = \sqrt{(Dh)/(2S)}$, where h is the holding cost per unit per year and S is the setup cost.

TABLE 7.10 Table Format for Problems 6 through 11

Nashville	*0*	*1*	*2*	*3*	*4*	*5*	*6*	*7*	*8*	*9*
Gross requirements		40	40	40	40	40	40	40	40	40
On hand	60									
Planned order release										

St. Louis	*0*	*1*	*2*	*3*	*4*	*5*	*6*	*7*	*8*	*9*
Gross requirements		30	30	30	30	30	30	30	30	30
On hand	40									
Planned order release										

Chicago	*0*	*1*	*2*	*3*	*4*	*5*	*6*	*7*	*8*	*9*
Gross requirements										
On hand	100									
Planned order release										

13. Compare bin trips for a DRP system and a fair shares system. Assume that a factory supplies four warehouses such that annual demand is divided equally among the four. Further, each warehouse faces an ordering or acquisition cost of A, where A is considerably smaller than the factory setup cost S. What is the ratio of annual bin trips under fair shares to annual bin trips under DRP?

14. Suppose that annual demand is 6,000 units, the order quantity is 500 units, and the maximum backorder position is 60 units. What is the expected number of backorders?

15. Suppose that annual demand is 600 units, the order quantity is 500 units, and the maximum backorder position is 60 units. What is the expected delay or the average time to satisfy a unit of demand?

16. A service center seeks to maintain inventories at exactly the three-month moving average of sales. Consider sales as shown, a current moving average of 200 units, and a beginning inventory of 400 units.

	1	2	3	4	5	6	7	8	9	10	11	12
Monthly sales	200	200	200	210	220	230	230	230	230	220	210	200

With a service center lead time of one week, develop a table to show beginning inventory, desired inventory, ending inventory, and order sizes. Ordering decisions are made at the end of each month according to the current sales information and that of the previous two months. Compare your results to table 7.3 in the chapter. Can you draw any conclusions?

17. For two warehouses with equal demand, $D_1 = D_2$, national demand is $D = D_1 + D_2$. Show that the square root of national demand is less than or equal to the sum of the square roots of warehouse demand.

18. We saw that $ESS_1 = S_1 - \lambda T_2$ represented effective stage 1 safety stock. Also,

$$T_2 = \frac{B_2^2}{2\lambda Q_2}$$

where B_2 is the maximum backorder position at stage 2, λ is the demand rate, Q_2 is the stage 2 order quantity, and T_2 is the expected stage 2 delay. What are the partial derivatives of ESS_1 with respect to S_1, B_2, λ, and Q_2? Provide some justification for your results.

19. Using the simple backorder model from chapter 4, we found that the expected delay at stage 2 was represented by

$$T_2 = \frac{B_2^2}{2\lambda Q_2}$$

where B_2 is the maximum backorder position at stage 2, λ is the demand rate, and Q_2 is the stage 2 order quantity. What are the partial derivatives of T_2 with respect to B_2, λ, and Q_2^2? Provide some justification for your results.

20. The manager of a furniture department at Sofa's scoffs at quantitative approaches to management. Nevertheless, she always seems to maintain about three units of a certain style couch on hand. If one is sold, she replaces it. With three on hand, she is adamant that she has very little chance of stocking out. Because the couches have a wholesale value of $500 each ($1,000 retail) and because Sofa's has investment opportunities at 12% annual return, the holding cost per couch appears to be $65 per year (including storage and the like). What, then, is the per unit stockout cost that exists only in the manager's intuition? As far as we can determine, "little chance" means 10% order stockout risk to the manager.

REFERENCES AND BIBLIOGRAPHY

1. R. G. Brown, *Materials Management Systems* (New York: Wiley-Interscience, 1977).
2. R. G. Brown, *Advanced Service Parts Inventory Control*, 2nd ed. (Norwich, Vt.: Materials Management Systems, Inc., 1982).
3. A. J. Clark and H. Scarf, "Optimal Policies for a Multi-echelon Inventory Problem," *Management Science*, Vol. 6, No. 4 (July 1960), pp. 475–490.
4. S. C. Graves and L. B. Schwarz, "Single Cycle Continuous Review Policies for Arborescent Production/Inventory Systems," *Management Science*, Vol. 23, No. 5 (January 1977), pp. 529–540.
5. J. L. Heskett, N. A. Glaskowsky, and R. M. Ivie, *Business Logistics*, 2nd ed. (New York: Ronald Press, 1973).
6. J. A. Muckstadt and L. J. Thomas, "Are Multi-Echelon Inventory Methods Worth Implementing in Systems with Low-Demand-Rate Hems?" *Management Science*, Vol. 26, No. 5 (May 1980), pp. 483–494.
7. J. Orlicky, *Material Requirements Planning* (New York: McGraw-Hill, 1975).
8. L. B. Schwarz, "Physical Distribution: The Analysis of Inventory and Location," *AIIE Transactions* (June 1981), pp. 138–150.
9. A. Stenger and J. Cavinato, "Adapting MRP to the Outbound Side—Distribution Requirements Planning," *Production and Inventory Management Journal* (4th quarter 1979), pp. 1–14.

appendix 7A

The New Push for DRP

Robert Goodell Brown

Large corporations that produce mechanical equipment, or service parts, or consumer goods, often distribute their products through regional field warehouses or distribution centers. Many merchant wholesalers operate chains of warehouses to distribute products obtained from independent vendors to the retail outlets.

In this article we shall assume that you have several warehouses, and that you have a resonable basis for deciding the range of products to be stocked in each one. We will also leave unchallenged the modes of transportation used to bring replenishment stocks into those warehouses.

Let's go even further. Let's assume you know how to forecast demand on each SKU (stock-keeping unit, a product in a particular location) and that you have economical and competitive procedures for setting the necessary and sufficient levels of safety stock for the customer service.

Our primary focus will be on the systems and procedures used to replenish the stocks of the products carried in each of your warehouses.

There are three systems to be compared: (a) an order-point, order quantity system, (b) a Distribution Requirements Planning (DRP) system, and (c) a "push" system.

Order-Point, Order-Quantity

It is still quite common to find that stocks of items carried in each warehouse are replenished when the available stock (on hand plus due in) falls to an order point. The order point is calculated as a forecast of requirements for that SKU over some replenishment lead time, plus an appropriate safety

---

From *Inventories and Production*, July/August 1981, pp. 25–27. Reprinted by permission.

stock. The amount of stock ordered from the source, whether a corporate factory or an outside vendor, can be computed as some sort of "economical" order quantity. This can be visualized in figure 7A.1.

This system was widely publicized by IBM's Wholesale IMPACT programs in the 1960s. Many companies found that the logic built into that system did improve the reliability of forecasts, that the safety stocks did give better customer service with lower investment, and the replenishment lot quantities did improve the balance of the cost of acquisition against the cost of holding stocks. However IMPACT, and other order-point, order-quantity, systems are parochial. They look at the needs of the replenishment system only from the point of view of a single warehouse at a time, as for an independent merchant wholesaler with only one location.

In recent years progress has been made in improving the techniques of forecasting, and there are better decision rules for computing safety stocks. We shall assume that you have profited by those developments.

An order-point, order-quantity replenishment system suffers from a grave defect, even when properly designed, implemented, and managed.

Such a system reacts to demand, without anticipating it. A new re-

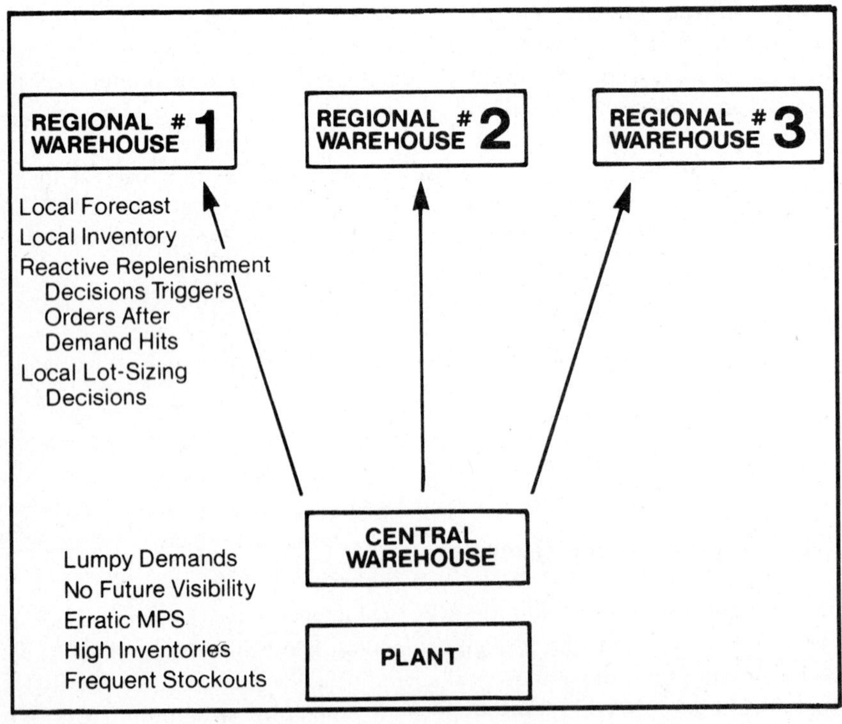

FIGURE 7A.1 Order-point replenishment

plenishment order is generated after the available stock has fallen below the order point. That means that the source never really does have the total planned lead time to get more stock delivered. It should have been ordered a few days ago. Allowance can be made for that delay by increasing the planning lead time used in computing order points.

But that also means that the source receives "lumpy" demand from all the warehouses it supplies. Sometimes several different warehouses order the same product at about the same time, and clean out the stock at the source. The next warehouse that needs the same product is faced with a backorder. Backorders tend to increase the replenishment lead time. Therefore, to maintain service, the warehouse increases its order point again.

Any source will try to do a good job of planning. But when the demand is "lumpy", it is hard to forecast. The source will increase its stock of finished products to try to maintain some desired fill rate. That means there will be times when all warehouses have plenty, and the source carries stock for which there is no current demand. When there is a rush of coincidental orders, some warehouses are going to have to wait until the source can get more.

Distribution Requirements Planning

The people who brought you MRP have looked at this problem and have come up with DRP as a method of improving the situation. The concepts are an extension, and a simplification, of Materials Requirements Planning.

Instead of generating an order for more stock after the available stock has reached order point, each warehouse develops the equivalent of a master schedule as shown in figure 7A.2. It shows well into the future the probable timing of each replenishment order. The gross requirements are generated by the current forecast and safety stock objectives. The gross available stock is a time-phased statement of what is on hand and what is due in. The net requirements are the difference between the gross requirements and the gross available stock. The master schedule is simply a series of standard (economical?) order quantities timed to cover the net requirements.

What makes DRP so simple is that there can't be any problem with the accuracy of the bill of materials. A case of product 1234 in the Phoenix warehouse takes precisely one case of product 1234 at the source. The only problem is having a reasonable value for the planned transit time from the source to Phoenix to offset those requirements.

Under a DRP system, the source no longer has to forecast lumpy requirements. It will have a schedule of time-phased shipping requirements with which to plan production. With better visibility of those requirements,

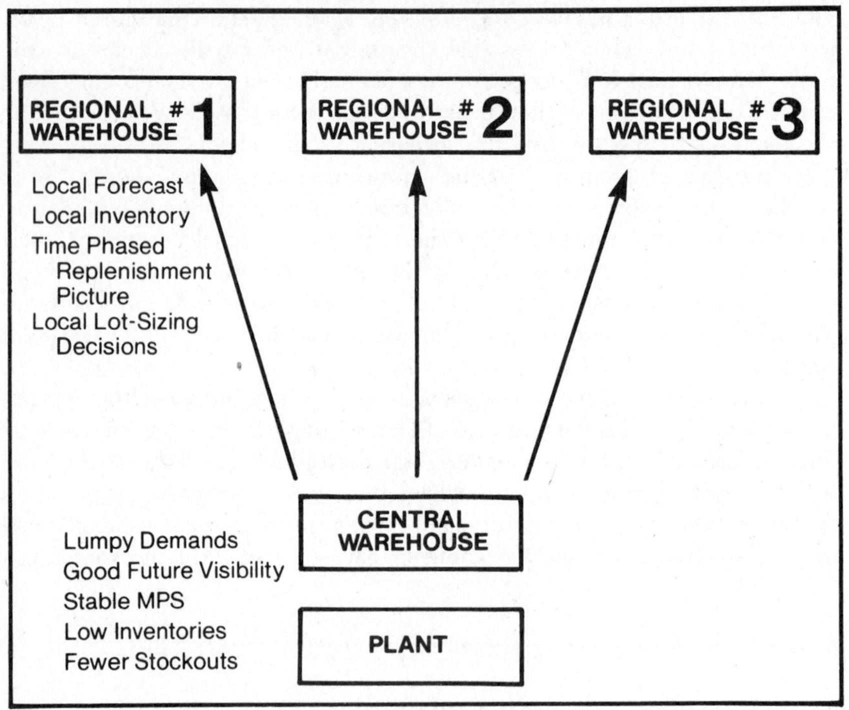

FIGURE 7A.2 Distribution requirement planning

the source can plan its manufacturing to have stock when needed (with much less stock to buffer the inevitable uncertainty in precise timing) and not carry stock during periods that no warehouse will need any.

Because the source can be expected to have stock when required (barring strikes, quality problems, machine breakdowns and the like), the effective lead time for the warehouse is shorter and more dependable. Thus the warehouses can reduce their safety stock and still give the same service to customers.

Implementation in a company that already uses MRP is absurdly simple. Create one more step in the process routing called "transport to warehouse". Establish the master schedule by SKU at the warehouse level instead of at the part-number level for the factory.

"Push" Distribution

The DRP scheme still considers an environment in which the replenishment lot sizes are computed by (or for) each warehouse. Since the warehouse is typically restocked in some finite number of truck-load shipments a year, there is a real question whether there is any cost to acquire one more line of a product. The costs are much more likely to depend on the frequency of truckloads, rather than on the frequency of replenishing a single product.

There is also a question about the relevance of the cost to hold stock. In an integrated corporation that distributes the products it makes, shifting inventory from the factory to a warehouse does not change corporate inventory balances at all.

The "economical" order quantity formula was derived to balance the expenses incurred with each acquisition against the capital invested in working stock. Both elements are in question in an integrated corporation. But never mind. One can cobble up values for the necessary factors and apply the formula blindly.

"Push" distribution as shown in figure 7A.3 is another alternative, that also requires central planning and control, just like DRP. There is one essential difference.

Under "push" distribution, the net requirements—not time-phased replenishment orders—are exploded back to give the source net shipping

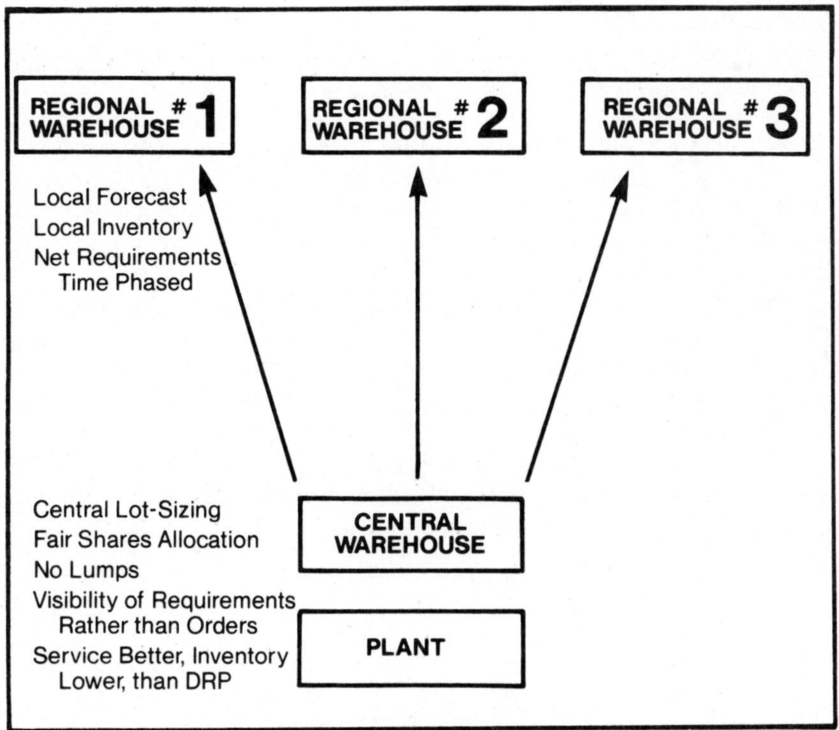

FIGURE 7A.3 Push distribution

requirements. There is a considerable difference between the accumulated net shipping requirements and the forecast of national sales. The most obvious difference is the timing of seasonal peaks in demand. Products to be sold in April in Minnesota will need to be available for shipment probably sometime in February or March.

A more subtle difference is the balance of stock among locations. If Atlanta has too much and Seattle has too little, the total stock in the system may look sufficient to cover the forecast for the next six weeks. Nonsense! Seattle needs some now, and the excess in Atlanta is irrelevant.

Under a "push" system, lot-sizing is done at the source where there really are set-up costs, and there really is a difference in total corporate investment depending on the quantity manufactured at one time.

Shipments to the warehouses are governed as to priority by the latest ship date—the time when there are net shipping requirements for that SKU. The timing of replenishment shipments is based on the forecast, the safety stock, and the lead time, just as in an order-point system, or a DRP system.

But the quantity shipped under a push system is a fair share of what is available in the total system. If there is enough stock to bring the available stock at all warehouses above their individual order points, then the fair share is a quantity that will bring the available stock to the same time supply beyond order point. (It may be advisable to limit the maximum order for space available or age of stock.)

If the total stock can't bring available stock up to order point everywhere, then a fair share will cover the lead-time stock at all locations, plus the same fraction of the safety stock. When stock is low, it isn't possible to give the desired service. If every warehouse has the same fraction of intended stock the total system will give better service than with any other way of allocating stocks.

The DRP and push systems both use a central planning system to give the source time-phased visibility of real field requirements. Both systems use net requirements which take account of local forecasts, safety stocks, and available stock, offset by the relevant replenishment lead time from the source.

The essential difference is that DRP tends to do lot sizing at the warehouse level and explode those orders. A push system does the lot-sizing at the source and distributes fair shares of what is available.

Comparison

Both the DRP and push systems will give much better service to customers, on stocked items, with less inventory than an order-point system. They both give the source visibility of future requirements so that it is economical to provide the right quantity at the right time, without shortages and without excessive stock levels.

The DRP system will entail an investment in working stock at the field level because of the lot-sized orders. That is in addition to the working stock the source has to plan to carry because of the economics of manufacturing.

The push system does not have any field working stock. The stock that results from manufacturing economics is distributed in fair shares among all the warehouses.

The push system also has one other advantage over DRP. Because the quantities to be shipped are computed at the time when a warehouse needs replenishment, they will exactly match the quantity available to be shipped. If the source has had difficulties and doesn't have all the stock it planned, the stock that is available is distributed equitably. If there happens to be more stock than is required (for example, stabilization stock built to anticipate a seasonal peak or a promotion) the push system allows one to use the cubic space available in field warehouses to store it.

The added degree of flexibility assures good service with even lower levels of inventory investment.

appendix 7B

Letters to the Editor

We (Andre Martin and Darryl Landvater) read with interest the recent article by Robert Goodell Brown titled "The New Push for DRP" (*Inventories & Production,* Volume 1, No. 3). We believe the article has created some misconceptions in the minds of your readers, and left some important things unsaid.

We are asking you to publish our explanation. We feel you owe this to your readers, and that the dialogue will generate a good deal of interest on the part of the readers.

Our comments are the following:

In his recent article, "The New Push for DRP", Robert Goodell Brown has created some misconceptions concerning the use of DRP. The misconception is the impression that DRP and a push system using fair shares are two different methods for scheduling a distribution environment. In fact, they are *not different*. Fair Shares Allocation is one way to calculate the lot sizes for shipment to the distribution centers, and there are others. DRP can use any number of calculations to represent the lot sizes which are shipped to the distribution centers.

It is up to each company to decide how they want to make their shipments to their distribution centers, and then use a lot sizing calculation which represents this. Some companies ship a number of weeks of supply to the distribution centers. In such a situation, they use a lot sizing calculation which creates planned orders covering the specified number of weeks of supply. Other companies consider pallet size, storage, and frequency of shipping schedules to determine the quantities to ship to their distribution centers. If a company ships product to their distribution centers using fair shares allocations, then they should use a lot sizing calculation which represents this.

The implication in the article, however, is that using a different lot

From *Inventories and Production,* November/December 1981, pp. 3–4. Reprinted by permission.

size calculation means the scheduling system is not DRP. This cannot be the case any more than using a particular order quantity calculation, like lot-for-lot for example, means that a company is not using MRP.

DRP, like MRP, is a fundamental scheduling system. It simply represents what is going on in the real world. If you ship a number of weeks of supply to the distribution centers, DRP simply represents that. If you allocate a supply order using a particular calculation (like Fair Shares Allocation), DRP represents that as well. There is no magic in DRP. It's not done with mirrors. DRP is a simple, powerful scheduling system that represents reality.

In his article, Bob also failed to make one important thing clear. It is the fact that you must represent what you plan to do in the system. If you choose to use Fair Shares Allocation, or any other lot sizing calculation for that matter, the planned orders must represent this quantity. In his explanation of Fair Shares Allocation, Bob explains that the net requirements from the different distribution centers are shown as requirements at the central supply facility. He also explains that these requirements are then used to calculate fair shares for each of the distribution centers. These shares are the planned order quantities—the quantities to be shipped to the different distribution centers.

He does not state that the planned order quantities *must* be represented in the system. This oversight is unfortunate since readers may be inclined to leave the net requirements as simply that, net requirements. If this is done, the actual shipments to the distribution centers will not be represented in the system. Consequently, the system is no longer a simulation of reality, and therefore cannot be used for other types of planning, like transportation planning and simulation

The analagous situation in MRP would be, for example, where lot-for-lot ordering is used for an item with requirements of 100/week. However, out in the factory, a lot size of 1,000 will actually be produced and this quantity will last for 10 weeks. If the planned orders are left at quantities of 100 in each week, capacity requirements planning will not tell the truth. The capacity planning report will show capacity requirements for a small number of hours each week. In reality, a large number of hours are needed in the first week, and then no hours are required for the next ten weeks.

In a distribution system, this same type of planning is done for transportation. Railcars, trucks, tankers, etc. are all planned using the projected weight and cube to be transported from the central supply facility to the distribution centers. Without this type of planning, effective use is not made of both the available weight and cube. With this type of planning, transportation planners have been able to save significant amounts of money for their companies. This is especially important with the rise in transportation costs.

In addition, this information is necessary for other types of planning in addition to transportation planning. It is especially useful in simulating different distribution networks. For example, a planner can reconfigure the distribution network in the computer, run DRP, and look at the effects in terms of transportation costs. The beauty of DRP is that it is an accurate and detailed simulation of what is projected to happen in the future. As such, there are virtually an unlimited number of different ways to extract and present the information for use by managers and planners.

To summarize, DRP is a simple but powerful scheduling system for a distribution operation. It is a representation of reality. If you ship a certain number of weeks of supply to the distribution centers, make sure the system shows this. If you use Fair Share Allocation to calculate the quantity to be shipped, make sure the system shows this. However, *above all,* represent what is actually happening in the system. If you don't, the system is no longer a simulation of reality, and therefore it will not be effective for planning.

Andre Martin
Darryl Landvater
Oliver Wight Video Productions, Inc.
Williston, Vermont

I fully intended to distinguish between what is commonly called DRP and what I call Fair Shares. There is a fundamental difference, which Martin and Landvater make clear in their letter. DRP uses planned orders. What I have called Fair Shares does not have any orders in the system at all until it is time to ship. I made the distinction between planning orders in advance, which requires extra working stock in the system—by any technique of calculation, and calculating a Fair Share quantity at the last moment on the basis of latest information. It is important that that information takes account of current stock status and requirements, and most importantly, what is available now to ship. The results can, as I pointed out, be rounded to practical handling quantities.

The distinction is that planning in advance, which they seem to say is unavoidable, requires extra working stock. Calculating fair shares does work, and does require less inventory in the system. It is not simply an alternative way of computing planned orders.

Robert G. Brown
President
R. G. Brown Materials Management Systems, Inc.
Norwich, VT

appendix 7C

DRP—A Profitable New Corporate Planning Tool

André Martin

Corporations can no longer afford to treat physical distribution (PD) like an orphan that nobody wants. For too long PD's position in the corporate hierarchy has been an area of conflict rather than harmony. As a result, many firms waste valuable time and money trying to find a suitable parent for the PD function.

The scenario usually looks like this: marketing runs PD and controls inventory. Usually, in such instances, customer service is good but inventories are too high. Yet manufacturing does not gain the benefits it needs from using the inventory as a buffer to smooth production. Why? Because marketing is always catching manufacturing off balance by asking for products on short notice to keep inventories balanced and customer service at a high level.

In response to this problem, management decides to shift the PD function from marketing to manufacturing. This immediately results in better inventory management and coordination with production scheduling, but inevitably, customer service begins to deteriorate.

After another short period of finger pointing, backbiting and bickering, management gets involved again, but this time settles on a third option. It creates a separate physical distribution department. Unfortunately, this arrangement satisfies neither marketing nor manufacturing and lasts only until the pressure mounts and the reshuffling begins again. Re-organizing to solve this type of problem is like re-arranging the deck chairs on the *Titanic*—it doesn't address the fundamental weakness.

In its quest to find a solution, management usually tries a number of

From *Canadian Transportation & Distribution Management,* November 1980, pp. 51–66. Reprinted by permission.

other options, including the hiring of consultants or the implementation of highly publicized concepts like management information systems, short interval scheduling, centralization, decentralization, etc. But these steps also miss the point.

The answer lies in solving what is known as the fundamental manufacturing equation, which asks: What do we need? What do we have? What do we need to make or obtain? What does it take to make it? The solution that is described in this article addresses this equation, and proves that it does work.

The solution is Distribution Resource Planning (DRP)—a computerized system that allows companies to completely and accurately manage distribution and manufacturing jointly. Remarkable results have been achieved with DRP. In fact, a company which was one of the first to pioneer DRP has experienced the following benefits over a four-year period:

- Total inventory turnover improved by 62%.
- Service levels improved from the mid-80s to the mid-90s(%).
- Distribution costs were slashed by 15%.
- Product write-offs due to obsolescence were reduced by 80%.
- Manufacturing productivity increased by 27%.
- Purchased-cost savings exceeded 5% of total purchases in four consecutive years.

The current rate of annual savings in this company is actually six times greater than the sum originally invested to implement the entire system. Before describing how DRP can achieve such results, however, it's first necessary to backtrack a little and look at four critical distribution problems.

Problem 1: Lumpy Demand

A serious distribution problem in many companies is that the systems they are using assume that the demand on their central supply facility will be smooth. These systems assume that if 120,000 units of a product are needed over the course of a year, that means 10,000 would be needed each month and, 2,500 would be needed each week. The trouble is that an average is just that. Over the course of a year it might work out to be reasonably close, but dramatic variations from that average can and will occur—and create havoc in distribution and manufacturing.

These variations can be quite large at times, and there are a number of reasons for this. Probably the most important is the different ordering patterns from a firm's various distribution centers. For example, several weeks may go by with few or possibly none of them ordering a product. Then three or four distribution centers may all order at the same time. The quantity on hand at the central facility is based on an average usage quantity. However, this quantity cannot possibly handle several distribution centers all ordering the same product at the same time. Those situations make averages seem like meaningless numbers.

There are also other reasons for lumpy demand of this type, including: (a) different customer ordering patterns; (b) differences in the transportation lead time between the central supply facility and the distribution centers; (c) the fact that the distribution centers order from the central supply facility in quantities which are larger than their immediate needs. Therefore, each can contribute to the deviation between what a distribution center actually orders and the average demand used for planning.

Problem 2: Order Points

The problem with order points is that they don't tell the truth about what is needed and when it's needed. Let's look at an example of a company that has several distribution centers, a central distribution supply facility, and two manufacturing levels (figure 7C.1).

In the situation pictured in figure 7C.1, the Chicago distribution center has 225 units on hand, which is below the re-order point of 345. The re-order point was calculated by taking the demand over the lead time (115/wk × 2 wks) plus one week of safety stock (115). Because the Chicago distribution center is below the re-order point, this triggers an order for this product from the central supply facility. The order for 900 is the normal order quantity for shipping this product to Chicago.

The New York distribution center is also below the order point. The order point for this facility was calculated in the same way as the order point for Chicago. Like Chicago, an order is created for 1000, in this case for shipment from the central supply facility to the New York distribution center.

The problem surfaces when these two orders arrive at the central supply facility. According to the order point system, there is no problem at the central supply facility; the on-hand balance is 1500 and the order point is 1150. However, when the two orders arrive in the same week from Chicago (for 900) and New York (for 1000), there is not enough on hand (1500) to satisfy the orders. As a result, the central supply facility goes on backorder, and the distribution centers only get part of what they need.

Because the central supply facility is out of stock, an order is immediately triggered to produce more product. This order has a three-week lead time. If this weren't enough, in the next week Montreal will be below the order point of 141 (164 − 47 week = 117) and will order 500 from the central supply facility. The central supply facility is out of stock and will not have this item for another two weeks. Then it will take two more weeks to get the product to Montreal. By that time, Montreal will be out and will have

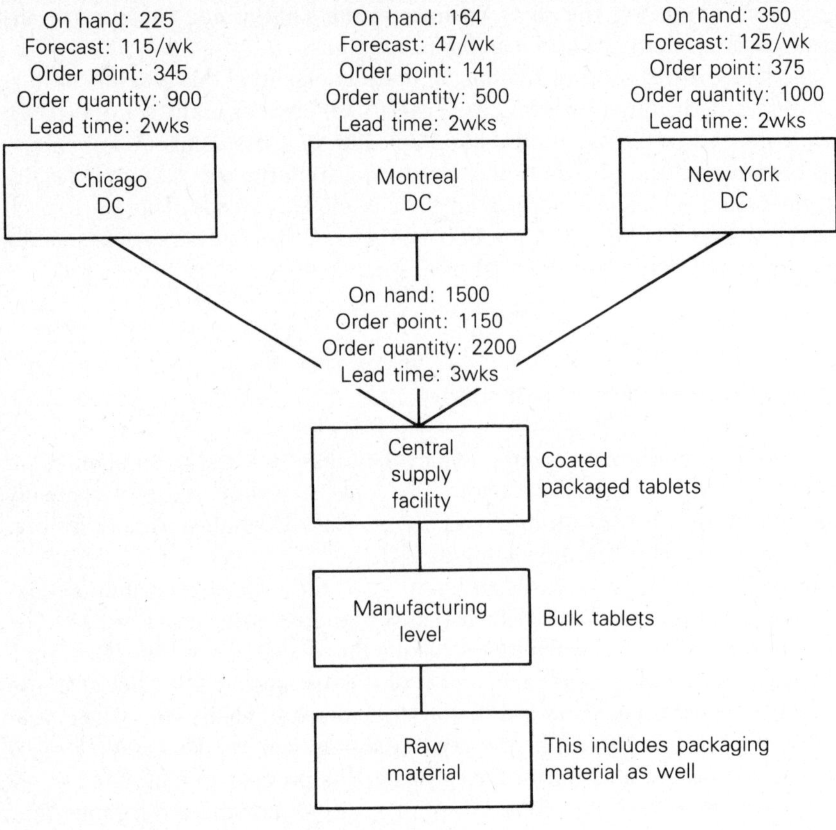

FIGURE 7C.1

been on backorder for almost two weeks. To summarize the points of this example:

(1) At the beginning of the week everything looked good based on the order point system.

(2) At the end of the first week, the central supply facility was wiped out, and smaller than normal shipments had to be made to the distribution centers. That adds up to extra costs in transporting the product.

(3) At the end of the second week, Montreal ordered from the central supply facility but there was no stock to satisfy the order.

(4) In the fifth week, the Montreal distribution center goes on backorder. However, if the company had chosen to use premium freight, it would be possible to keep Montreal off backorder.

You will note that the order point system gave no warning of what was about to happen. The company was forced to ship less than normal order quantities, and was faced with either using normal transportation and going on backorder, or using premium freight to stay off backorder. Not a very impressive record for a system which is supposed to show what is needed and when.

Problem 3: Where Does Inventory Come From?

The problem with most distribution systems is that they assume inventory will be available in the central supply facility. Based on that assumption, a firm then goes about determining how best to allocate and distribute that inventory to the different distribution centers. The fact is that inventory is not always available in the central supply facility. In fact, shortages are one of the most serious problems in managing a distribution network.

PD books seldom put the proper perspective on how inventories are made available to the distribution centers. These books cover the subject superficially; they concentrate on inventory re-ordering procedures, EOQ's, safety stock calculations, fixed order intervals, fair share calculations, etc. They leave the impression that inventory at a central supply facility is there for the asking.

And more recent volumes also fail to attack this fundamental problem. Instead, they take even more sophisticated approaches to stepping around the problem. They talk about inventory in motion, complementary inventory items such as skates in the winter and baseball equipment in the summer in order to lower storage and carrying costs. But they sidestep the issue of how the inventory is made available to distribution.

It's sad, but really not surprising. Oliver Wight described it well when he said: "When people don't understand a fundamental problem, their solutions will be over-sophisticated and overly complex". *The fundamental problem here is how to get a system that is integrated with manufacturing. One that will not only distribute the product in the best way, but will also make sure that the product is available for distribution.*

Distribution Resource Planning is the way to integrate distribution and manufacturing. The two disciplines are welded together into a single system for producing and distributing the product. Product availability is planned from the top of the product structure to the bottom. The same planning method is used to make the product available in the distribution centers, at the central supply facility, at the manufacturing levels, and finally at the raw material level. Planning a product that will be moved through three distribution centers is done in the same way that a manufactured or purchased part is planned for use in three different parent assemblies. There is no gap where the system stops and assumes that something will somehow be made available.

But DRP is not limited to companies with their own manufacturing facility. Some companies purchase all the products they distribute rather than manufacture them. Such companies can use DRP to develop a close working relationship with their vendors. They are still integrating distribution and manufacturing—it's just that the manufacturing is owned by someone else.

Problem 4: Planning and Maintaining Priorities

One problem with conventional inventory management systems is that they are not able to cope with change. When something changes, people in distribution and manufacturing need to know what effects that change will have on material, capacity, warehousing, freight, etc. And they need to know about these effects far enough in advance to do something about them. For example, take the situation where sales exceed the forecast. An order point system does not identify what the effects of that change are. People are not warned of what will have to be done to handle the increased sales. The first time they become aware of the change is when they have to re-order sooner than they would have had to otherwise, or when they run out of the product.

The ability to see what and when a product is needed is called priority planning. It not only refers to getting the right information, but also keeping it up-to-date as conditions change. In addition to sales that exceed forecast, as mentioned above, there are any number of other reasons for change, including:

(1) Sales that are different than what was forecast. The only sure thing about a forecast is that it will always be wrong. Sometimes forecasts are only off by a little and other times they are off significantly.

(2) Machines that break down and reliable manufacturing processes that suddenly stop working.

(3) Absenteeism and sickness causing production delays. In addition, people don't always want to work overtime on Saturdays or for extended periods of time.

(4) Scrap and rejects. Most firms aim for zero defects in quality control, but few are able to achieve anything close to it.

(5) Late vendor deliveries. We have trouble delivering on time, why should we assume that our vendors are any different?

These and many other factors make planning priorities extremely critical to a company's success in executing the plan. The most powerful aspect of DRP is it's ability to predict problems before they occur. *The further in advance you can see a problem developing, the better your chances of being able to solve it.*

Knowing what you need and when on a continuing, up-to-date basis allows you to develop good schedules for distribution, manufacturing, and purchasing. This is where many firms have dropped the ball in the past—

why marketing, physical distribution, manufacturing, and purchasing could never really work as an efficient, cohesive team.

DRP Offers the Solution

DRP is predicated on the fact that all inventory levels are linked and must be scheduled at the same time. It does not assume that inventory at the central supply facility is there for the asking. DRP is a priority planning technique that continually scheduled and reschedules all inventory levels and keeps priorities up-to-date.

To illustrate this, let's take the order point example used earlier in this article and recalculate the needs using the DRP approach. This was the situation where both Chicago and New York were below the order points and were both ordering from the central supply facility. Montreal was low on stock and would order the next week. Figure 7C.2 shows the results using DRP. Notice that with DRP, we have two planned shipments to Chicago and New York that are overdue. The order point never showed that. Notice also that the safety stock in the DRP display is the forecast quantity for one week. This is the same as the quantity used in the order point example.

In Montreal, you will note that a planned order is due for release during week one. The master scheduler is getting urgent messages to add to the master schedule to cover the difference between the distribution demands in the past due, week one and the on-hand balance. The order point did not give us any indication of trouble until the end of week one when the central supply facility was out of stock.

In fact, DRP would have been giving us warnings of trouble many weeks before. It would have projected the shortage at the central supply facility and warned the master schedule of the problem. To illustrate this, let's go back four weeks and look at the DRP displays (figure 7C.3).

You can see that even four weeks earlier, DRP was planning for the distribution demands. A master schedule order to manufacture is due for release in week one so that there will be enough to cover the distribution demands four weeks later. The order point didn't even identify the problem until it was on top of planners four weeks later. By then there was no time to fix it. Figure 7C.4 compares the information from the order point system with the information from DRP for this example.

DRP, however, is much more than an inventory ordering technique that tells the truth about what is really needed and when. It has evolved with time and has now become a total distribution/manufacturing system that plans and controls all of a company's operating activities (figure 7C.5).

DRP was born in manufacturing. It is the natural extension of Manufacturing Resource Planning (MRP II) into the world of marketing and

Montreal distribution center

On-hand balance -164
Safety stock -47
Lead time -2 wks
Order quantity -500

	Past	Week							
	Due	1	2	3	4	5	6	7	8
Forecast		47	47	47	47	47	47	47	47
In transit									
Projected on-hand	164	117	70	523	476	429	382	335	288
Plnd. shpmts.-Rcpt. date				500					
Plnd. shpmts.-Ship date		500							

Chicago distribution center

On-hand balance -225
Safety stock -115
Lead time 2 wks
Order quantity -900

	Past	Week							
	Due	1	2	3	4	5	6	7	8
Forecast		115	115	115	115	115	115	115	115
In transit									
Projected on-hand	225	110	895	780	665	550	435	320	205
Plnd. shpmts.-Rcpt. date			900						
Plnd. shpmts.-Ship date	900								

New York distribution center

On-hand balance -350
Safety stock -125
Lead time -2 wks
Order quantity -1000

	Past	Week							
	Due	1	2	3	4	5	6	7	8
Forecast		125	125	125	125	125	125	125	125
In transit									
Projected on-hand	350	225	1100	975	850	725	600	475	350
Plnd. shpmts.-Rcpt. date			1000						
Plnd. shpmts.-Ship date	1000								

Central supply facility

On-hand balance -1500
Safety stock -287
Lead time -3 wks
Order quantity -2200

	Past	Week							
	Due	1	2	3	4	5	6	7	8
Distribution demands	1900	500	0	0	0	0	0	0	0
Scheduled receipts									
Projected on-hand	-400	-900	-900	-900	-900	-900	-900	-900	-900
Master schedule-Rcpt.									
Master schedule-Start									

FIGURE 7C.2

Montreal distribution center

On-hand balance -352
Safety stock -47
Lead time -2 wks
Order quantity -500

	Past	Week							
	Due	1	2	3	4	5	6	7	8
Forecast		47	47	47	47	47	47	47	47
In transit									
Projected on-hand	352	305	258	211	164	117	70	523	476
Plnd. shpmts.-Rcpt. date								500	
Pind. shpmts.-Ship date						500			

Chicago distribution center

On-hand balance -685
Safety stock -115
Lead time -2 wks
Order quantity -900

	Past	Week							
	Due	1	2	3	4	5	6	7	8
Forecast		115	115	115	115	115	115	115	115
In transit									
Projected on-hand	685	570	455	340	225	1010	895	780	665
Plnd. shpmts.-Rcpt. date						900			
Plnd. shpmts.-Ship date				900					

New York distribution center

On-hand balance -850
Safety stock -125
Lead time -2 wks
Order quantity -1000

	Past	Week							
	Due	1	2	3	4	5	6	7	8
Forecast	125	125	125	125	125	125	125	125	125
In-transit									
Projected on-hand	850	725	600	475	350	225	1100	975	850
Plnd. shpmts.-Rept. date							1000		
Plnd. shpmts.-Ship date					1000				

Central supply facility

On-hand balance -1500
Safety stock -287
Lead time -3 wks
Order quantity -2200

	Past	Week							
	Due	1	2	3	4	5	6	7	8
Distribution demands	0	0	0	900	1000	500	0	0	0
Scheduled receipts									
Projected on-hand	1500	1500	1500	600	1800	1300	1300	1300	1300
Master schedule-Rcpt.					2200				
Master schedule-Start		2200							

FIGURE 7C.3

Results of DRP versus the order point

LOCATION	ORDER POINT	DRP
CHICAGO	Below order point, order from central	Planned order overdue for release from central
NEW YORK	Below order point, order from central	Planned order overdue for release from central.
MONTREAL	Beginning of Week: Above order point, no action needed. End of Week: Below order point order from central.	Planned order due for release from central that week.
CENTRAL SUPPLY	Beginning of Week: Above order point, no problem apparent. End of Week: Below order point, out of stock, not enough stock to satisfy Chicago and New York. The Next Week: Still out of stock and not able to satisfy Montreal. Montreal goes on backorder.	Four Weeks Earlier: Projects a shortage four weeks in the future. Master schedule order scheduled to cover the shortage. Master schedule order due for release in normal lead time. Planned shipments are made, no backorders.

FIGURE 7C.4 Results of DRP versus the order point

physical distribution. Manufacturing Resource Planning is, without question, the most significant development in manufacturing management of the last decade. DRP will be as significant to the management of physical distribution in the 80s.

Distribution Planning and Scheduling

Not only does DRP manage inventories and provide a powerful vehicle in integrating physical distribution with manufacturing through production

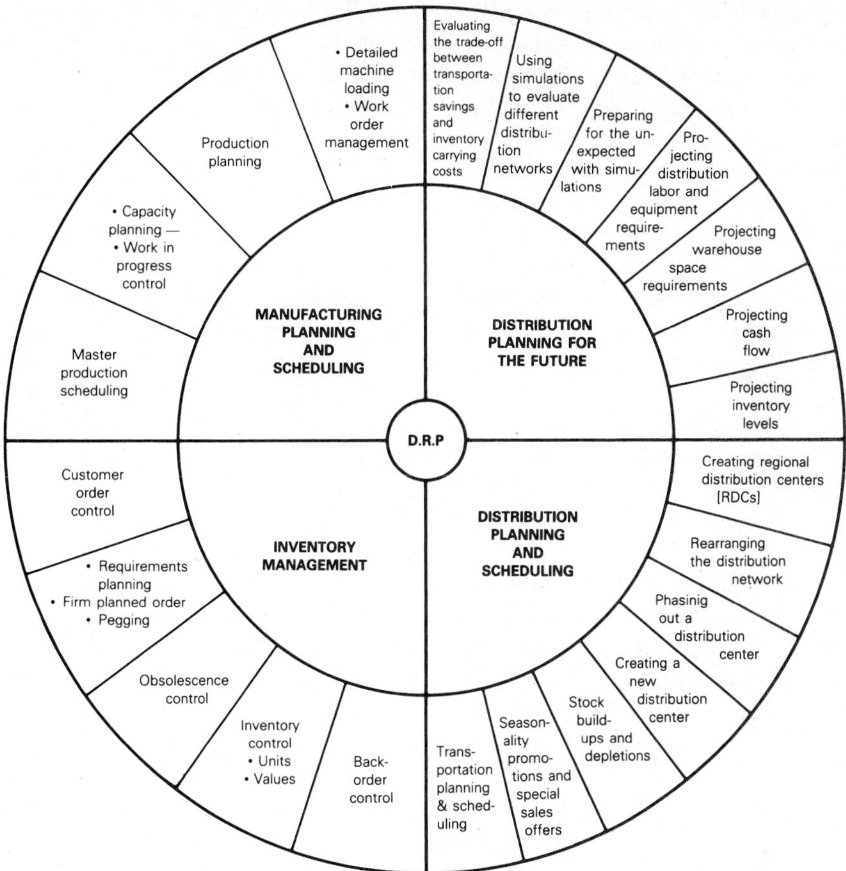

FIGURE 7C.5

planning and master production scheduling, it also opens up new horizons for PD in a manner that was not possible before.

Through accurate time phasing into the future, DRP becomes an easy and valuable tool for planning transportation requirements from supply facilities to distribution centers. This information can be used to maximize the utilization of whatever mode of transportation you are using. Data can be made available by destination point, by week, giving the total weight and cube to be shipped. It can also be used to negotiate freight rates, change modes of transportation or to evaluate the economics of adding to or creating your own fleet.

DRP also considers a set shipping schedule from the supply source to destination points. It handles set shipping schedules in stride while maintaining visibility over the true needs for product. This aspect of DRP is valuable to companies that are confronted with heavy traffic movements and must operate under stringent shipping schedules. For example, it helps to deal with special situations like the following:

• Seasonality, promotion, and special sales offers: these factors are a way of life in many companies and a good deal of money can be made or lost depending on whether they are handled well. They all have one thing in common: there is a period of time when the items are selling at a rate which is greater than the rate at which they can be manufactured. That means some manufacturing will have to be started in advance of the peak selling season, and that those items will have to be stocked. The objective is to use the stock build-up before the peak selling season, plus the manufacturing capacity, to meet the peak sales demand. *And* to do it without creating and carrying unnecessary inventory. *And* to do it without causing unnecessary manufacturing inefficiencies. Because DRP is fully integrated with manufacturing, it provides the vehicle to effectively plan and control these events.

• Stock build-ups and depletions using temporary storage: there are a number of instances where inventory must be built up and depleted, and cannot be stored at the central supply facility, including: plant shutdowns due to renovations or vacation, installation of new equipment, upcoming union contracts, etc. In these cases, most firms use some kind of temporary outside storage to hold their inventory build-up, and then they deplete it. As a result, the plant will be closed and products cannot be made. This means that planning this inventory build-up and depletion has to be done right. If the wrong—or insufficient—inventory is stockpiled, customer service can be dealt a serious blow, and a great deal of money can be lost.

This example is really quite similar to the one provided for inventory build-up to handle seasonality, promotions, and special sales offers. The difference is that, here, an outside storage area must be used to handle the inventory build-up. Using an outside storage area is not always restricted to the situations mentioned earlier. In some cases, the size of the inventory build-up for seasonality, promotions, or a special sales offer may require an outside storage area.

Using DRP, the only thing that must be done is to establish the new storage area (the stockpile) in the system. It is not possible to begin stockpiling the inventory within DRP until the stocking location exists within the system. A number must be created for each item that will be stored in the stockpile. These item numbers must then be linked to the central supply facility.

As illustrated in figure 7C.6, all the distribution centers and the stockpile will be drawing from the central supply facility. Once the distribution network has been set up this way, inventory build-up in the stockpile can begin. Production planning and master scheduling is used to see the distribution demands, evaluate the manufacturing and purchasing capacity, and develop production plans and master production schedules which will

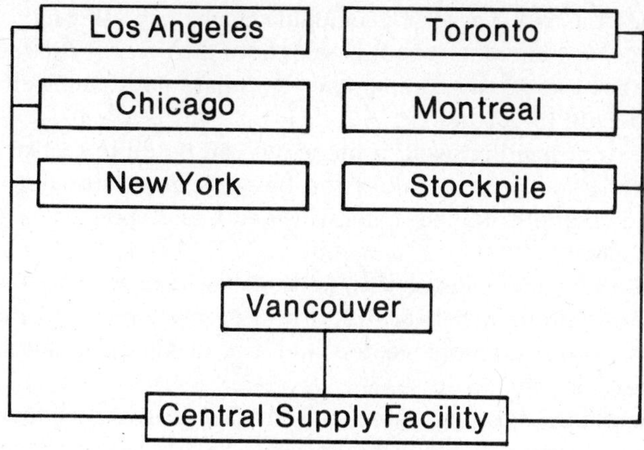

FIGURE 7C.6

provide enough product to satisfy both the day-to-day needs of the distribution network and also to begin stockpiling inventory.

• Creating or phasing out of a distribution center: there are a number of reasons for creating a new distribution center. Business expansion is probably the major reason. When a new distribution center is created, a number must be created for each of the items to be stocked there. In addition, DRP needs the planning information like lead time, order quantity, safety stock, etc. for each of these items, as well as a bill of material or table entry showing the supply facility for the item.

Generally, when a new distribution center is created, it affects the demand at one or more of the existing centers. This is not *always* true, however. Going into a new market or opening a distribution center in a new country might not affect the others. When other distribution centers are affected, it may also be necessary to re-evaluate the order quantities and safety stocks. Since the demand on the center has changed, these numbers may have to be updated.

The advantage of this method is that all distribution planners have to do is create a new distribution center in DRP and change the forecasts. The logic of DRP and master scheduling take care of the rest. Demands from the new center and the reduced demands from the affected centers will be posted to the master production schedule. The master scheduler can evaluate this and see if the master production schedule is sufficient to cope with the opening of the new distribution center. If not, the master production schedule may be changed, the date for shipping this product from the new center may be changed, or firm planned orders could be used to ship enough of the products to the new center to supply the customers until more of the product is available.

There are also situations where distribution centers are phased out.

Many times this is because of geographic changes in sales mix, like losing several large customers, or a shift in sales from the east coast to the midwest. Other reasons are strictly competitive. If you are not doing well in an area you may decide to get out.

If it is not handled well, a phase-out can be quite costly. If it is not planned well, you may be out of the business in an area but yet have a lot of stock in that distribution center which must be disposed of or transported to another facility.

• Re-arranging the distribution network: there are a number of situations where the distribution network is to be re-arranged. These include consolidating several distribution centers into one, dividing a facility into several new acquisitions, etc.

Each of these situations can be solved using DRP and the tools explained earlier. These changes to the distribution network, regardless of how complex they may appear, are just combinations of creating new distribution centers and phasing out existing ones.

• Creating regional distribution centers: sometimes, it makes sense to create regional distribution centers. These are large facilities that service satellite distribution centers in the nearby geographic area. The primary reasons for creating regional distribution centers include: faster customer service, better freight rates, lower warehousing costs, and lower inventories.

It is very simple to handle regional distribution centers through DRP. All that has to be done is to show a distribution center as being supplied from a regional center as opposed to being supplied from the central supply facility. This approach is illustrated in figure 7C.7.

This example does not represent a complete distribution network. It is just a sample from a much larger network. As DRP is predicated on the fact that all inventory levels are linked and must be scheduled, all that needs to be done with DRP in this given environment is to tell the system the new relationship that will exist among the various levels of inventories comprising the network. DRP is not limited in any way by the different types of distribution networks that may exist.

Planning the future in physical distribution has never been an easy task. Yet this activity is crucial and contributes immensely to the planning of other key corporate functions. Marketing and physical distribution are the two most dynamic functions in a manufacturing company because both

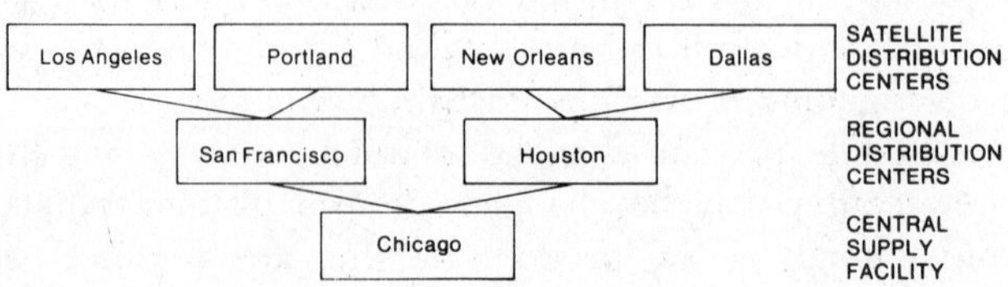

FIGURE 7C.7

are the closest to the marketplace. That is where the action is in the real world and, unless marketing and physical distribution are able to forecast as accurately as they possibly can, chances are that most of the efforts exerted by the other functions are going to fail.

In most companies, marketing and physical distribution drive manufacturing (in particular). And even if manufacturing has an MRP system to manage its operation, it will simply be unable to achieve substantial benefits unless it is fully integrated with marketing and physical distribution through DRP. Listed below are some key examples:

- Projecting sales and inventory levels in the distribution system.
- Projecting cash flow requirements.
- Projecting warehouse space requirements.
- Projecting distribution labor and equipment requirements.

Good short-range business and production planning cannot be done effectively and will suffer substantially unless these key activities are properly planned and managed.

Poor planning in these areas normally results in poor customer service performance, higher distribution costs, greater risk of product obsolescence and misuse of available manufacturing capacities which inevitably contributes to increasing productions costs.

Until DRP came along, most systems used by marketing and physical distribution were developed to meet the needs of these functions. They then passed along their information to manufacturing and finance. In addition, all distribution systems in current use have embodied in their logic some type of order point or one of its derivatives.

Is it any wonder why none of them operate satisfactorily? Is it any wonder why MRP first saw birth in manufacturing? The only way you can cope with a dynamic environment is to develop systems that give you a fighting chance of keeping up. MRP was the answer that manufacturing was looking for. Order points were shelved in manufacturing when MRP came along. Now order points must meet the same fate in PD if we are to fully realize the total potential that an integrated distribution/manufacturing system can offer.

DRP has been proven in practice to be the best tool to project the future. DRP already projects inventory levels. This aspect is inherent in its planning logic; it thrives on this information in order to determine what is needed and when. Quantifying those inventory projections and displaying them in a format that is suitable to your needs is quite simple and straightforward with DRP.

Once inventories are projected, the resulting planned orders from the distribution centers can be used to project labor and equipment requirements for the supply and receiving locations. Bills of labor can be developed stating how much labor and equipment is required to load a van or railcar. These bills can then be used with the planned orders from distribution to calculate labor and equipment needs.

The same approach can be used to develop warehouse space requirements. The sum of the projected inventory levels for all products for a given location can be added up, using a computer. This information, multiplied by a space utilization factor, will result in projections of space requirements. Using DRP to perform these calculations will yield far better results than any software optimizing models in use today. The reason is that DRP simulates what is going to happen in a distribution network and tells it like it is.

chapter eight

The Planning of Material Requirements

This chapter will examine the parts requirement problem. An end product may contain several subassemblies and parts. Each subassembly and each part takes a certain amount of production lead time. The subassemblies and parts also require raw materials that have delivery lead times. The parts requirement problem, then, is to determine the size and timing of parts and subassembly production and raw material orders.

Several researchers and practitioners worked on this problem in the 1950s and 1960s. As early as 1954, in the very first issue of *Management Science*, Andrew Vaszonyi [5] described the problem and presented a matrix algebra approach to its solution. In those days, the problem was also known as the explosion and netting problem in the planning of material requirements. In the late 1960s, Joseph Orlicky [3] at IBM began to popularize the list processing solution known as material requirements planning (MRP). His work culminated in the outstanding book *Material Requirements Planning*, published in 1975.

It is important to distinguish between the parts requirement problem and the MRP solution. MRP has strengths and weaknesses that make it extremely attractive, but it is not the only answer. Further refinements of MRP and profitable applications require an understanding of the advantages and drawbacks of the MRP approach.

The Parts Requirement Problem

Suppose that we have an end product A, composed of subassemblies that are made up, in turn, of parts and raw materials. We will imagine that our product A is a tricycle. The product structure, or bill of materials (BOM), for the tricycle might be pictured as a product tree. Figure 8.1 is a product

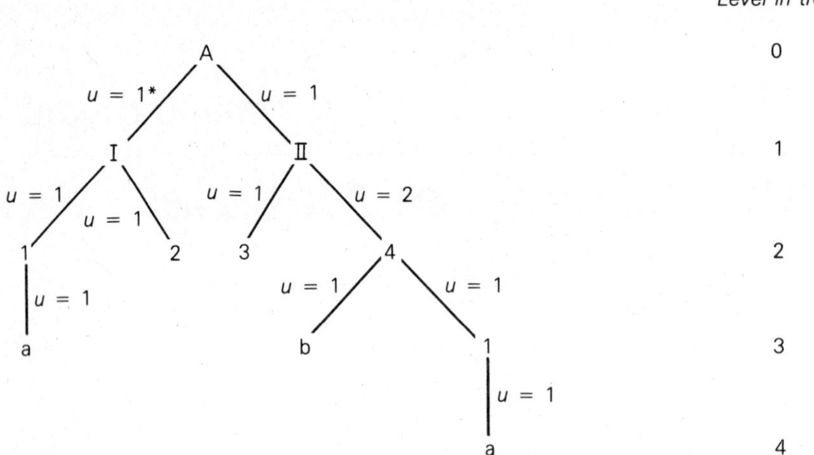

*u is usage; u = 1 indicates that one unit of I, for example, goes into one unit of A.

FIGURE 8.1 Product tree structure

tree structure showing what goes into an end item A. Figure 8.2 shows the product tree for our tricycle. Such a bill of materials could also be drawn up for a bicycle, which would contain a frame, two wheel assemblies, a brake assembly, a seat, and a set of handlebars. In a later chapter, questions of options—such as five-speed or ten-speed—will arise; for now, however, we'll look only at simple end products with fixed sets of subassemblies and parts.

The product structure or bill of materials can be described in several ways. The infamous Professor J. R. Gozinto formulated the *gozinto* matrix representation (see figure 8.3). (Despite popular misconception, J.R. was not related to another famous management scientist, H. L. Gantt.) The indented bill of materials, developed by I. N. (Buckey) Dent, concisely summarizes the same information (see figure 8.4).

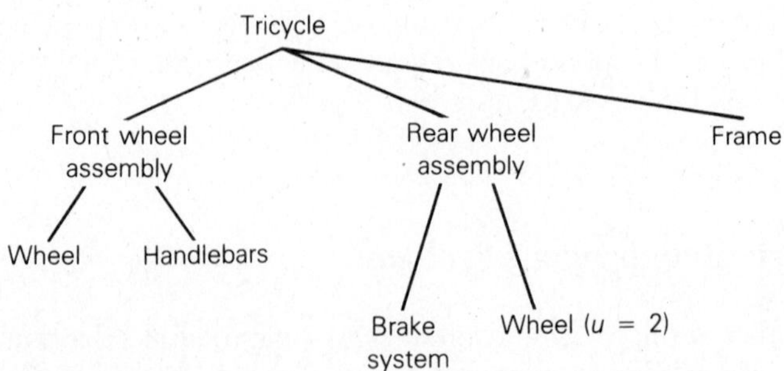

FIGURE 8.2 Tricycle product tree

	A	I	II	1	2	3	4	a	b
A									into
I	1								
II	1								
1		1							
2		1					1		
3			1						
4			2						
a				1					
b							1		
goes									

FIGURE 8.3 Gozinto table (rows go into columns)

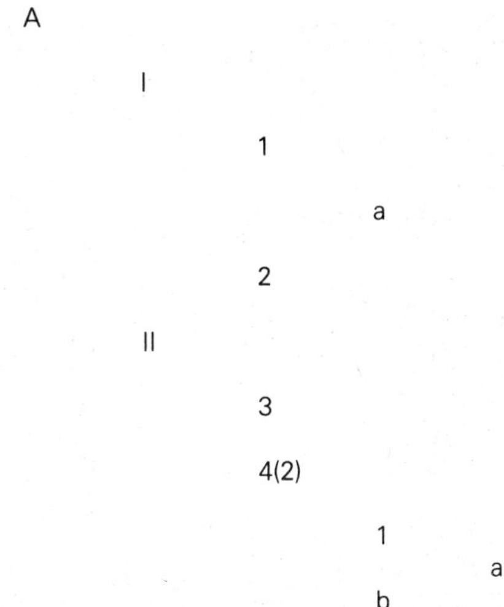

FIGURE 8.4 Indented bill of materials

Current inventory balances of parts, subassemblies, and end items are given in our inventory records, as follows:

	Item	*On-Hand Inventory (OH)*	*Lead Time in Weeks (L)*
End item	A	0	1
Subassembly	I	40	1
Subassembly	II	15	2
Part	1	10	3
Part	2	20	4
Part	3	15	1
Part	4	30	2
Raw material	a	10	3
Raw material	b	10	3

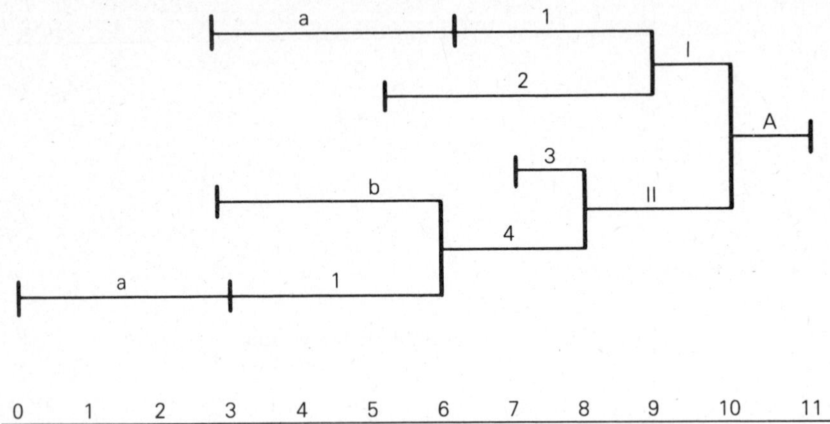

FIGURE 8.5 Time-phased product tree structure

Figure 8.5 shows the product tree structure on a time-phased basis. The longest, or critical, path is A–II–4–1–a, with a cumulative lead time of eleven weeks.

The Mechanics of MRP

Suppose that we must produce twenty units of product A six weeks from now. Noting that only ten units of raw material a appear as an on-hand balance, how many more units of material a do we need to ensure its availability for production in end item A? As a quick reaction, we might guess that we need an extra ten units. On second thought, however, we notice that subassembly I shows a balance of forty units (already containing material a), and subassembly II shows a balance of fifteen units. Further, we already have sufficient on-hand quantities of parts 3 and 4 to produce the five additional units of subassembly II needed. Hence, fifteen units of end item A can be produced without ordering up any additional material a. The purchasing department would have cursed if we had followed our first hunch, and rightly so.

To keep track of inventory interactions from the end item to the raw material level, we can construct a set of tables based on the product tree structure. MRP computer programs, available from many vendors, perform calculations similar to those we will do with this set of tables.

Note from figure 8.5 that end item A requires a one-week lead time. This includes time to assemble the two subassemblies I and II into the end item A. Later, we will examine other elements of lead time, but it is important now to recognize that subassemblies I and II must be completed and ready to be assembled when work begins on end item A. Suppose that the master production schedule (MPS) calls for production of twenty units of A by week 7 and 100 units of A by week 9. Because A has a one-week assembly time, this means that the order to produce 20 units of A is released at the beginning of week 6. Hence, subassemblies I and II must be ready at the beginning of week 6. With a one-week lead time, end item A should be completed by the beginning of week 7. Table 8.1 displays the master production schedule and shows the basic MRP logic.

MRP logic uses the following relationships:

$$\text{Net requirements} = \text{total requirements} - \text{available inventory}$$

$$= \begin{bmatrix} \text{gross requirements} \\ + \\ \text{allocations} \end{bmatrix} - \begin{bmatrix} \text{on hand} \\ + \\ \text{scheduled receipts} \end{bmatrix}$$

Planned order release is the time that the order is released so that the units will be ready to meet the requirements.

In our example, gross requirements are for twenty units in week 7. No inventory has been allocated—that is, dedicated to an order. No previous orders have been issued for which we are expecting receipt; that is, there are no scheduled receipts.

Since on-hand inventories are zero, net requirements are simply equal to the gross requirements of twenty units in week 7. Backing off by one week for lead time, the planned order release occurs in week 6.

The master production schedule can reflect an economic order quantity decision at the end item level. Suppose that the master production schedule were based on a (Q, R) system, with $Q = 90$, $R = 30$, demand rate $d = 15$, and lead time $L = 2$ weeks. Table 8.2 demonstrates the nature of the reorder point in a (Q, R) system; the reorder point triggers an order release.

In this case, the order will cover six weeks' worth of gross requirements. Gross requirements will arbitrarily be considered to occur at the middle of the week, but planned orders will be released at the beginning of the week. On-hand inventories show inventory status at the end of the week and here reflect the loss of fifteen units per week. The planned order

TABLE 8.1 MPS for End Item A

	Week Numbers									
	0	*1*	*2*	*3*	*4*	*5*	*6*	*7*	*8*	*9*
Gross requirements (GR)								20		100
On hand at end of period (OH)	0	0	0	0	0	0	0			
Planned order release (POR)							20		100	

$L = 1$

TABLE 8.2 Time-phased Order Point

	0	*1*	*2*	*3*	*4*	*5*	*6*	*7*	*8*	*9*	*10*	*11*	*12*
GR		15	15	15	15	15	15	15	15	15	15	15	15
OH	45	30	15	0	75	60	45	30	15	0	75	60	45
POR			90						90				

Note: Inventory projected negative in week 4. Place order to avoid negative.
$Q = 90$, $R = 30$, $L = 2$ weeks.
Reorder point is never really used, but rather MRP logic takes over.

release schedule for the end item can be considered a master production schedule. An order for ninety units is released at the beginning of week 2, after the ending inventory of week 1 hits the reorder point of thirty units. The order takes two weeks to process and thus arrives at the beginning of week 4, ready to be used to satisfy gross requirements in week 4. At this stage, it is useful to record our conventions for time-phasing requirements:

1. Gross requirements (GR) will occur at the middle of a period.
2. On-hand inventory (OH) will be measured at the end of a period.
3. Planned order releases (POR) will occur at the beginning of a period.

As a warm-up before tackling our MRP problem, consider a situation in which gross requirements are 70 units in week 2. On-hand inventories are 100 units, of which 50 have been allocated. A previous order has been made for 10 units, which are expected to arrive at the beginning of week 1. The normal lead time is one week. What would the MRP table look like? (AC is allocated inventory, and SR is scheduled receipt.) We would have:

	Week 0	*Week 1*	*Week 2*
GR			70
AC	50	50	
OH	100	100	
SR		10	
POR		(10)	

$$\text{Net requirements} = [GR + AC] - [OH + SR]$$
$$= [70 + 50] - [100 + 10] = 10$$

By time phasing the net requirements, an order for 10 units is released at the beginning of week 1.

Now that table 8.1 and table 8.2 are understood, we are prepared to carry our original example all the way back from end item A to raw materials. As the MPS, table 8.1 gives the planned order releases for 20 units of A

TABLE 8.3 MRP Table for Subassembly I

	0	1	2	3	4	5	6	7	8	9
GR							20		100	
OH	40	40	40	40	40	40	20	20		
POR								80[a]		

[a] Subassembly I has a one-week lead time

in the sixth week and 100 units of A in the eighth week. To produce 20 units of A in the sixth week, we need 20 units of subassembly I and 20 units of subassembly II. These subassemblies must be ready at the beginning of week 6 so that they can be assembled into end item A during week 6. Table 8.3 displays the netting process for subassembly I. All calculations are based on the information given in figure 8.1 and repeated in table 8.4.

Proceeding in this fashion, we would move to subassembly II and then to parts 1, 2, 3, and 4. Part 1 causes some difficulty because it goes into subassembly I and also into part 4, as shown in table 8.4. If we draw up a table for part 1 as it goes into subassembly I, we will then need to repeat ourselves when we prepare a table for part 4. A more convenient way to handle this is to assign lowest level codes—a code for the lowest level in the tree at which an item occurs. Part 1 occurs at level 2 and also at level 3. Hence, its lowest level code will be 3. To avoid any double counting in creating tables, we need only draw up the tables in order of the items' lowest level codes. Table 8.4 gives the lowest level codes for the items given in figure 8.1. According to these lowest level codes, we can safely draw up tables in the sequence A, I, II, 2, 3, 4, 1, b, a. Table 8.5 shows the entire set of inventory interactions implied by the master schedule of 20 units of A in week 6 and 100 units of A in week 8. The following "rules of the road" should be kept in mind:

TABLE 8.4 Problem Information Summary

	Lowest Level Codes (LLC)		*Inventory Records*	
Indented BOM	*Item*	*Code*	*OH*	*L*
A				
I				
1	A	0	0	1
a	I	1	40	1
2	II	1	15	2
II	1	3	10	3
3	2	2	20	4
4(2)	3	2	15	1
1	4	2	30	2
a	a	4	10	3
b	b	3	10	3

1. Planned order releases at a higher level become gross requirements at a lower level.
2. Usage rates must be noted (e.g., each unit of subassembly II requires two units of part 4).

MRP Concepts and Advantages

Several concepts can now be defined and explained against the background of the foregoing example. What are the inputs and outputs of an MRP system? Where is MRP applicable? Where does MRP fit in the overall production control environment? What are the advantages of the MRP approach?

MRP applies primarily to production systems exhibiting *parent–component* relationships. The component item goes into the parent item. Manufacture of assembled products is an obvious example. If the end items can be stated in a master production schedule, an MRP system can be applied fruitfully.

The master production schedule (MPS) specifies the quantities of end items to be produced by time period several months into the future. End items may be finished products or the highest level assemblies from which these products can be built. The *planning horizon* for the MPS must be at least as long as the cumulative lead time for purchasing and manufacturing. In our example, the critical path through the product structure was A-II-4-1-a, with a total lead time of eleven weeks. Hence, we must plan at least eleven weeks into the future to ensure that we have time to produce or order the requirements along this path.

Whereas MRP is applicable to parent–component production systems, traditional order-point techniques fail to accommodate parent–component relationships. Forecasting and order-point systems treat each component separately; but there is no need to forecast individual part requirements if we have a schedule of end item production. Alfred Sloan [4] recognized this as early as 1921, when analysts at General Motors made a "purely technical calculation" of the quantity of materials required to support the level of production necessary to yield a given number of cars. Each car has five wheels, so we need not make independent forecasts of the number of car wheels required. We may want to forecast automobile sales, however, representing *independent*, or external, demand. Once we have determined the production levels needed to support the sales forecasts, the *dependent*, or derived, requirements of wheels can be obtained by multiplication.

In forecasting, separate treatment of individual items wastes valuable information; however, having separate order points for individual items causes excessive holding costs while increasing risks of stockout. Instead, parent–component items should be matched so that planned orders for the parent become gross requirements for the component.

TABLE 8.5 MRP Tables for the Entire Product Tree

A	*0*	*1*	*2*	*3*	*4*	*5*	*6*	*7*	*8*	*9*
POR							(20)		(100)	

LLC = 0, *L* = 1
LLC = lowest level code, *L* = lead time.

I	*0*	*1*	*2*	*3*	*4*	*5*	*6*	*7*	*8*	*9*
GR							(20)		100	
OH	40	40	40	40	40	40	20	20	0	0
POR								(80)		

LLC = 1, *L* = 1 (goes into A)

II	*0*	*1*	*2*	*3*	*4*	*5*	*6*	*7*	*8*	*9*
GR							20		(100)	
OH	15	15	15	15	15	15	0	0	0	0
POR					5		(100)			

LLC = 1, *L* = 2 (goes into A)

2	*0*	*1*	*2*	*3*	*4*	*5*	*6*	*7*	*8*	*9*
GR								(80)		
OH	20	20	20	20	20	20	20	0	0	0
POR				60						

LLC = 2, *L* = 4 (goes into I)

3	*0*	*1*	*2*	*3*	*4*	*5*	*6*	*7*	*8*	*9*
GR					5		(100)			
OH	15	15	15	15	10	10	0	0	0	0
POR						90				

LLC = 2, *L* = 1 (goes into II)

4	*0*	*1*	*2*	*3*	*4*	*5*	*6*	*7*	*8*	*9*
GR					10		200			
OH	30	30	30	30	20	20	0	0	0	0
POR					180					

LLC = 2, *L* = 2 (goes into II on a 2 for 1 basis)

1	*0*	*1*	*2*	*3*	*4*	*5*	*6*	*7*	*8*	*9*
GR					180			80		
OH	10	10	10	10	0	0	0	0	0	0
POR		170			80					

LLC = 3, *L* = 3 (goes into I and 4)

b	*0*	*1*	*2*	*3*	*4*	*5*	*6*	*7*	*8*	*9*
GR					180					
OH	10	10	10	10	0	0	0	0	0	0
POR		170								

LLC = 3, *L* = 3 (goes into 4)

TABLE 8.5 MRP Tables for the Entire Product Tree (*Continued*)

a	*0*	*1*	*2*	*3*	*4*	*5*	*6*	*7*	*8*	*9*
GR		170			80					
OH	10	0	0	0	0	0	0	0	0	0
POR		80								
SR[a]		160								

LLC = 4, *L* = 3 (goes into 1)

[a] SR = scheduled receipt; indicates the scheduled date of receipt of an order *already* released (i.e., an open order as opposed to a planned order).

To see the weakness of separate order points, we shall begin by studying the accusation that they cause excessive holding costs. Tables 8.6 and 8.7 show the reaction of order point and MRP to lumpy demand. The order-point system places the order much too early and hence carries inventory wastefully. Lumpy demand is not peculiar to parent–component systems, but it is certainly characteristic of them. Lot sizing at the parent level causes lumpy demand at the component level. Lumpy demand is *discontinuous* (periods of zero demand) and *irregular* (the size of the lumps varies). In an environment of parent–component relationships and associated lumpy demand, the traditional EOQ system yields excessive holding costs.

Although the order-point system causes excessive holding costs, the increased inventory levels do not contribute to increased service levels, because the inventory is held at the wrong time. The service level is the probability that inventory will be available at the time it is required. The complementary probability is the probability of stockout. Low stockout probabilities at the component level can still yield a fairly high stockout probability on all components taken together. If a parent item has, for example, ten components, and if each of these components has a probability of stockout of 0.01, then the probability of having all the items in stock ready for production of the parent item will be only $0.90 = 0.99^{10}$. Hence,

TABLE 8.6 Excessive Holding in an Order-Point System

	0	*1*	*2*	*3*	*4*	*5*	*6*	*7*	*8*	*9*
GR		15	15	0	0	0	15	90	0	0
OH	45	30	15	15	105	105	90	0	0	0
POR			90							

Q = 90, *R* = 30, *L* = 2; units held = 405.

TABLE 8.7 Reasonable Holding in an MRP System

	0	*1*	*2*	*3*	*4*	*5*	*6*	*7*	*8*	*9*
GR		15	15	0	0	0	15	90	0	0
OH	45	30	15	15	15	15	0	0	0	0
POR						90				

L = 2; units held = 135.

parent–component relationships must be managed on a matched basis. It is not good to have the parent and component items forecast and controlled separately; even with excellent control at the individual item level, the probability of being able to produce the parent item with all components present in sufficient quantities is rather low. It is the special ability of MRP to plan for component requirements all the way from the end item level to the raw material level.

The inputs to the MRP system are (1) the master production schedule, (2) the bill of materials, and (3) the inventory status file. The output of the MRP system consists of the timing and the quantity of subassemblies, parts, and raw materials. This output can be used, first, to plan purchasing action and, second, to plan manufacturing action. A planned order release is a signal that we are going to produce a certain amount of a component in a specific time period. Further, the production action items also indicate that we will have needs against capacity. We will see later in the text that an MRP system also enables us to plan our capacity requirements.

Lot Sizing

In our MRP discussion so far, we have used the lot-for-lot inventory lot sizing technique: whatever the net requirement is, we produce exactly that amount. For end item A, this meant that we planned production orders for 20 units in week 6 and 100 units in week 8. Should we combine these into one large order, thereby reducing setup costs? The answer depends heavily on the ratio of holding costs to setup costs.

THE LOT-FOR-LOT TECHNIQUE

To examine holding versus setup cost trade-offs, consider the problem presented in table 8.8, which is an MRP table showing that several orders are released, each one week in advance of the net requirement. In the table, net requirements equal gross requirements minus beginning inventory as it is used up to cover requirements by period. Similarly, ending inventory from the previous week plus any order release due to be completed for the current week minus the gross requirements for the current week gives

TABLE 8.8 MRP Lot Sizing Problem: Lot-for-Lot Technique

	0	*1*	*2*	*3*	*4*	*5*	*6*	*7*	*8*	*9*	*10*
Gross requirements		35	30	40	0	10	40	30	0	30	55
On hand	35	0	0	0	0	0	0	0	0	0	0
Planned order release		30	40	0	10	40	30	0	30	55	0

Holding costs = \$2/unit/week, setup cost = \$200, gross requirements average per week = 27, lead time = 1 week.

current ending inventory. The lot-for-lot (L-4-L) technique yields zero holding costs but seven separate setups, for a total cost of $1,400.

THE EOQ APPROACH

As a first effort at achieving better costs, we might try an economic order quantity system:

$$Q^* = \sqrt{\frac{2dS}{h}} = \sqrt{\frac{2(27)(200)}{2}} = 74$$

Table 8.9 shows the EOQ solution. The EOQ solution requires four setups, totaling $800, plus an inventory holding cost of $790, for total costs of $1,590. The EOQ approach assumes a constant requirements rate. The requirements here are lumpy, however; they occur in some time periods but not in others. Moreover, not only are the requirements discontinuous, but the size of the lumps is irregular, ranging from ten to fifty-five units.

To handle the discrete nature of the problem with lumpy demand, several approaches have been advocated. At one extreme are the EOQ-based procedures, which start from a misapplication, and at the other extreme is a dynamic programming approach that yields optimal solutions.

MINIMUM COST PER PERIOD APPROACH

Because it is effective and can be readily understood, it is useful to start with a compromise technique: the minimum cost per period (MCP) approach. If we combine two periods, the cost per period will be the sum of setup plus holding costs divided by the two periods. For example, combining the net requirements for periods two and three would give a cost per period of $140, calculated as $200 setup cost plus forty units held at $2 per unit, all divided by two periods. Table 8.10 displays the MCP calculations, and table 8.11 shows a solution by the MCP approach.

The MCP solution yields $600 in setup costs plus $310 in holding costs (ignoring required holding cost on beginning inventory), a total cost of $910. This is $490 less than the cost by the L-4-L technique.

TABLE 8.9 MRP Lot Sizing Problem: EOQ Approach

	0	*1*	*2*	*3*	*4*	*5*	*6*	*7*	*8*	*9*	*10*
GR		35	30	40	0	10	40	30	0	30	55
OH	35[a]	0	44	4	4	68	28	72	72	42	61
POR		74			74		74			74	

$L = 1$; holding cost = $(44 + 4 + \ldots + 61) * 2$.

[a] In our holding cost calculations, we exclude the beginning inventory of thirty-five units because we incur the holding costs on these units regardless of any decisions we make. We include only relevant costs.

TABLE 8.10 MCP Calculations

Trial Periods Combined	*Trial Lot Size (Cumulative Net Requirements)*	*Cumulative Cost*	*Cost per Period*[a]
2	30	200	$200.00
2,3	70	280	140.00
2,3,4	70	280	93.33
2,3,4,5[b]	80[b]	340	85.00
2,3,4,5,6	120	660	132.00
(Combine periods 2, 3, 4, and 5 because cost per period is a minimum)			
6	40	200	200.00
6,7	70	260	130.00
6,7,8[b]	70	260	86.67
6,7,8,9	100	440	110.00

[a] Cost per period = cumulative cost divided by number of periods combined.

[b] POR combines these periods and cumulative net requirements.

TABLE 8.11 MRP Lot Sizing Problem: MCP Approach

	0	*1*	*2*	*3*	*4*	*5*	*6*	*7*	*8*	*9*	*10*
GR		35	30	40	0	10	40	30	0	30	55
OH	35	0	50	10	10	0	30	0	0	55	0
POR		80				70			85		

To see the close similarity between MCP and EOQ concepts, we can develop a cost per period formulation yielding the EOQ solution. Suppose that we have $d = 27$, $h = \$2$, and $S = \$200$ (recall that d is weekly demand and h is the weekly holding cost per unit). Then the cost per period (CPP) is a function of Q:

$$CPP(Q) = \frac{Q}{2}h + \frac{S}{(Q/d)}$$

where Q/d specifies the number of periods covered by the lot size (e.g., $Q/d = 81/27$ covers three periods of demand). Differentiating now and setting the derivatives to zero, and solving for Q would give

$$Q^* = \sqrt{\frac{2ds}{h}}.$$

Does this look familiar?

Although the MCP procedure works well, other approaches have also been developed and used, some with more success than others. Because these procedures can be found in practice and because no single procedure has been accepted as best, it is necessary to study several additional approaches.

PERIOD ORDER QUANTITY APPROACH

Weakest among the other approaches is the EOQ-based period order quantity (POQ). Earlier, we found the EOQ to be 74 units, with an average demand of 27 units per week. Annual requirements would be 27 * 52 = 1,404. Annual requirements divided by EOQ would be 19 orders per year (D/Q = 19). The time between orders would thus be 52 weeks divided by 19 orders, or 2.7 weeks between orders. Hence, POQ equals the quantity to cover P^* periods of net requirements, where $P^* = N/(D/EOQ)$, N is the number of periods in a year, and D represents annual requirements. Table 8.12 shows the POQ solution: order three weeks' supply each order; every third time, order two weeks' supply. (In this text, we adopt the convention that POQ covers a certain number of periods of positive requirements. Facing the requirements (0, 0, 0, 20, 0, 20, 20), a three-period POQ would be 60, enough to cover seven actual periods. Hence, fewer setups will occur than EOQ would dictate if there are many periods with zero requirements.)

The total cost for the POQ solution is $980. The POQ approach performs better than the EOQ approach because it adapts to the requirements of a set of periods. In facing periods 2 through 5, the POQ approach would have one order for eighty units. The EOQ approach would have one order of seventy-four units, and hence a remnant of four units would be carried unnecessarily from period 1 through 4 until the shortfall of six units became evident for period 5. The advantage of POQ, then, is that it is dynamic—the order quantity changes in response to the net requirements. As we shall see later, this dynamic quality has advantages and disadvantages.

LEAST UNIT COST APPROACH

Rather than minimizing cost per period, the least unit cost (LUC) approach attempts to minimize cost per unit. Careful examination of the technique reveals its myopic nature. Table 8.13 shows the calculations, and table 8.14 gives the planned order releases and planned inventory status. The cost of the LUC approach is $600 setup plus $390, for a total cost of $990. This total cost can also be calculated as 70 units at $4 per unit plus 80 units at $5 per unit plus 85 units at $3.65 per unit, for a total cost of $990. The myopic nature of the LUC approach stems from the range of costs from $3.65 per unit to $5 per unit. The LUC approach averages $4.21

TABLE 8.12 MRP Lot Sizing Problem: POQ Approach

	0	*1*	*2*	*3*	*4*	*5*	*6*	*7*	*8*	*9*	*10*
GR		35	30	40	0	10	40	30	0	30	55
OH	35		50	10	10	0	60	30	30	0	0
POR		80				100				55	

TABLE 8.13 LUC Calculations

Trial Periods Combined	*Trial Lot Size (Cumulative Net Requirements)*	*Cumulative Cost*	*Cost per Unit*
2	30	200	$6.67
2,3	70	280	4.00
2,3,4	70	No change—hence ignore	
2,3,4,5	80	340	4.25
(Combine periods 2 and 3 at a cost of $4 per unit)			
4,5	10	200	20.00
4,5,6	50	280	5.60
4,5,6,7	80	400	5.00
4,5,6,7,8	80	No change—hence ignore	
4,5,6,7,8,9	110	640	5.82
(Combine periods 4, 5, 6, and 7 at $5 per unit)			
8,9	30	200	6.67
8,9,10	85	310	3.65
(Combine periods 8, 9, and 10 at $3.65 per unit)			

(Keep raising the lot size until cost per unit increases)

TABLE 8.14 MRP Lot Sizing Problem: LUC Approach

	0	*1*	*2*	*3*	*4*	*5*	*6*	*7*	*8*	*9*	*10*
GR		35	30	40	0	10	40	30	0	30	55
OH	35	0	40	0	0	70	30	0		55	0
POR		70			80				85		

per unit for this problem—that is, a total cost of $990 divided by net requirements of 235 units.

PART PERIOD BALANCING APPROACH (LEAST TOTAL COST)

The part period balancing (PPB), or least total cost (LTC), procedure is based rather fallaciously on EOQ. In the EOQ approach, the optimal solution happens to be at the point where setup and holding costs are equal. There is no reason to believe that such a result should hold in the case of lumpy demand. Indeed, our EOQ solution to the problem yielded setup costs of $800 and holding costs of $790—a reasonable balance; yet this balanced solution of $1,590 is far from optimal. Nevertheless, the PPB procedure attempts to balance setup and holding costs through the use of economic part periods. An economic part period (EPP) is the ratio of setup cost to holding cost. In our case, EPP = 200/2 = 100 units. Thus, holding 100 units for one period would cost $200, the exact cost of a setup:

Cost per setup = EPP * (holding cost/unit/period)

However, holding 50 units for two periods would also cost $200 and could be thought of as 100 part periods. Hence, the PPB procedure simply combines requirements until the number of part periods most nearly approximates the EPP. Table 8.15 shows the calculations and table 8.16 shows the results, with total costs of $980.

In the foregoing examples, we have seen several lot sizing rules. The minimum cost per period rule performs well in a variety of cases and is probably the best heuristic rule to follow. It is important to recognize, however, that lot sizes for the parent item become gross requirements for the component items. If the parent item were fairly far out in the schedule and the raw material item were early in the schedule, then we can visualize that lot sizes at the end product level would work themselves all the way back down to subcomponents and to raw materials. Generally, lot sizing is effective at the end product level but becomes less effective as we get down to the raw materials. At the raw material level, there is insufficient horizon, because the master production schedule may extend thirty weeks into the future, whereas the implications for raw materials may extend only ten weeks into the future. Thus, we do not have a long enough planning horizon on the raw material level to do effective lot sizing.

In addition to the horizon problem, we also have the problem that the holding to setup cost trade-offs have been considered for single levels only. It would obviously be much more complicated to examine the trade-

TABLE 8.15 PPB Calculations

Periods Combined	*Trial Lot Size (Cumulative Net Requirements)*	*Part Periods*
2	30	0
2,3	70	40 = 40 × 1
2,3,4	70	40
2,3,4,5	80	70 = 40 × 1 + 10 × 3
2,3,4,5,6	120	230 = 40 × 1 + 10 × 3 + 40 × 4
(Combine periods 2 through 5)		
6	40	0
6,7	70	30
6,7,8	70	30
6,7,8,9	100	120 = 30 × 1 + 30 × 3
(Combine periods 6 through 9)		
10	55	0

TABLE 8.16 MRP Lot Sizing Problem: PPB Approach

	0	*1*	*2*	*3*	*4*	*5*	*6*	*7*	*8*	*9*	*10*
GR		35	30	40	0	10	40	30	0	30	55
OH	35	0	50	10	10	0	60	30	30	0	0
POR		80				100				55	

TABLE 8.17 Use of Lot Sizing Rules

Technique	*Number of Companies*
Fixed period requirements	7
Lot-for-lot	6
Fixed order quantity	5
Economic order quantity	4
Price breaks	3
Part period balancing	2
Planner decided lot sizes	2
Least total cost	1

off of a lot sizing rule at the parent level on the holding costs and setup costs all the way down through the assemblies.

Actual industry practice on lot sizing varies widely, as described in a survey published in 1979, in which Urban Wemmerlov [6] interviewed thirteen MRP users in the mechanical and electronics industries. Time-variant (dynamic) lot sizing techniques such as LTC and PPB were used by very few companies. Wemmerlov concluded that companies avoid these techniques because changes in top levels are transmitted down through lower stages, producing system nervousness—exaggerated response at component levels to small changes at parent levels. At assembly and subassembly stages, the popular lot-for-lot technique helped maintain stability and minimized the amount of material tied up. The three most commonly used techniques were fixed period requirements, lot-for-lot, and fixed order quantity. For fixed period requirements, some companies used an ABC system, with four-week requirements for A items, eight weeks for B, and so on. Table 8.17 displays the results of the Wemmerlov survey.

Uncertainty and Change in MRP Systems

If all would go as planned, we could end this chapter right now. In the real world, however, very little goes as planned. Scheduled receipts do not come in on time; planned order sizes are changed when they are released as actual orders because of capacity constraints; changes in gross requirements dictate changes in lot sizes at subcomponent levels; and the unavailability of raw materials for one subcomponent negates the need for a fellow subcomponent because both must be ready for the parent production. Hence, we may want to change the status of an already existing open order and move its due date backward or forward in time. The uncertainty introduced in MRP systems can be neatly summarized in a chart originally drawn up by Whybark and Williams [7] and displayed here as table 8.18. One could summarize this section by simply stating that Murphy's law applies to MRP

TABLE 8.18 Categories of Uncertainty in MRP Systems

	Sources of Uncertainty	
Types	*Demand*	*Supply*
Timing	Requirements shift from one period to another	Orders not received when scheduled
Quantity	Requirements for more or less than planned	Orders received for more or less than planned

systems; in fact, Murphy's law applies at the end item levels and its corollary applies at the component and raw material level.

The classic way to handle uncertainty is to introduce safety stock. If I need $100 to make a trip, I might add another $50 just for safety. That extra $50 is safety stock. I hope I won't need that safety stock; but if Murphy has anything to say about it, I will. In an MRP system, safety stock is normally included at the end item level; because of the parent–component matching relationships, this automatically introduces safety stock at all levels through the assembly. As an alternative to safety stock, some companies use safety lead time. The next four tables show the different effects of safety stock versus safety lead time. It is important to recognize that safety stock simply means that we do not want to see our inventory dip below a certain level. Thus, in the end item MRP rules, we place a planned order to cover a time period in which we are projecting negative inventories. With safety stock, we place the planned order to cover the time period in which we are projecting inventory below the safety stock level. Safety lead time, on the other hand, indicates that we will place the order a number of periods before it would normally have to be placed.

Tables 8.19 and 8.20 show the difference in the same time-phased order-point (TPOP) system with and without safety stock. In both cases, the order quantity is ninety units and the lead time is two weeks. Without

TABLE 8.19 TPOP without Safety Stock

	0	*1*	*2*	*3*	*4*[a]	*5*	*6*	*7*	*8*	*9*	*10*[a]
GR		15	15	15	15	15	15	15	15	15	15
PR					90						90
OH	45	30	15	0	75	60	45	30	15	0	75
POR			90						90		

PR = planned receipt.

$L = 2,\ Q = 90,\ R = 30$

[a] Projected negative

For a time-phased order point system, MRP logic is applied to a typical order point situation.

TABLE 8.20 TPOP with Safety Stock

	0	*1*	*2*	*3*[a]	*4*	*5*	*6*	*7*	*8*	*9*[a]	*10*
GR		15	15	15	15	15	15	15	15	15	15
PR				90						90	
OH	45	30	15	90	75	60	45	30	15	90	75
POR		90						90			

$SS = 10, L = 2, Q = 90, R = 30 + 10 = 40$

[a] Projected below 10 units.

safety stock, the reorder point is thirty units; this point moves to forty units with ten units of safety stock. In the face of a fifteen-unit weekly demand rate, the safety stock system causes the planned order release to occur one week earlier.

Tables 8.21 and 8.22 contrast the use of safety stock and safety lead time under conditions of time-varying requirements. In table 8.21, a safety stock of twenty units on an average weekly demand of fifteen units corresponds to roughly one and a half weeks of supply. This safety stock actually causes the planned order release to occur two weeks in advance with the requirements pattern shown. A safety lead time of one week shows up in table 8.22 as a planned order release one week early. Note that the due date on the planned order also moves ahead one week.

In his survey of thirteen MRP users, Wemmerlov [6] found much skepticism about the use of safety stock (see table 8.23). Because safety stock causes orders to be placed earlier than absolutely necessary, practitioners

TABLE 8.21 TPOP with Safety Stock and Time-varying Requirements

	0	*1*	*2*	*3*	*4*	*5*	*6*	*7*	*8*	*9*[a]	*10*
GR		15	15	15	15	25	25	10	10	10	10
SR			90								
PR								90			
OH	45	30	105	90	75	50	25	105	95	85	75
POR						90					

$SS = 20, L = 2, Q = 90$

[a] Projected negative without POR.

TABLE 8.22 TPOP with Safety Lead Time (SLT) and Time-varying Demand

	0	*1*	*2*	*3*	*4*	*5*	*6*	*7*	*8*	*9*[a]	*10*
GR		15	15	15	15	25	25	10	10	10	10
SR			90								
PR									90		
OH	45	30	105	90	75	50	25	15	95	85	75
POR							90				

$SLT = 1, L = 2, Q = 90$

[a] Projected negative without POR.

TABLE 8.23 Use of Safety Stock

Location of Safety Stock	*Number of Companies*
End item/finished good level	5
Low level items[a]	5
All levels	3
Total	13

[a] Protection against vendor supply variability.

felt that it distorts the true priorities. No one wants rush orders because of safety stocks!

Net Change versus Regenerative MRP Systems

Conceptually, a *regenerative MRP system* provides the simplest approach to changes. *Regeneration* means running the entire system, exploding from the MPS through to component requirements across the board. A weekly or biweekly processing run can keep requirements updated reasonably well. The longer the time from the previous run, the more unreliable the information is, since changes invalidate some of the requirements.

Net change MRP systems avoid the gradual obsolescence of information by updating inventory records and requirements as transactions occur. Partial explosions of items affected by changes allow the system to be continually accurate and up to date.

In the next few tables, we shall see examples of changes and updates. After getting a feel for net change systems, we can then evaluate the merits of regeneration versus net change.

In the first set of tables, we shall consider the concepts of *cashing requisitions* and *allocating inventory*. In real life, all action takes place now. In MRP terminology, now is called an *action bucket*. When a planned order release appears in period 1, it is sitting in the action bucket, and the appropriate response is to release the order. The order is released to the shop floor with a specified due date and appropriate paperwork. Part of the paperwork is an authorization (requisition) to withdraw the appropriate material for work on the item. One withdraws the material by cashing the requisition. Because the order may wait in line at the work center after being released, an uncashed requisition may exist for some time. During this uncashed time, the component's on-hand inventory is overstated, because some of the inventory is targeted for the order already released. The inventory already targeted for this purpose is called *allocated inventory*.

Tables 8.24 through 8.28 show the entire sequence of allocating inventory and cashing the requisition. Tables 8.24 and 8.25 give the standard parent–component plans with a POR in the action bucket. Table 8.26 shows the identical situation after the order has been released. Now that the order is open, a scheduled receipt becomes associated with it. Table 8.27 shows

TABLE 8.24 Standard Parent Item—Time-varying Requirements

	0	*1*	*2*	*3*	*4*	*5*	*6*	*7*	*8*	*9*	*10*
GR		15	15	15	15	25	25	10	10	10	10
AC[a]											
SR											
PR				90						90	
OH	45	30	15	90	75	50	25	15	5	85	75
POR		90						90			

$L = 2$, $Q = 90$, $SS = 5$

[a] AC represents an allocation—allocated inventory.

TABLE 8.25 Standard Component Item

	0	*1*	*2*	*3*	*4*	*5*	*6*	*7*	*8*	*9*	*10*
GR		90						90			
AC											
SR											
PR											
OH	200	110	110	110	110	110	110	20	20	20	20
POR											

TABLE 8.26 Standard Parent Item after Order Release

	0	*1*	*2*	*3*	*4*	*5*	*6*	*7*	*8*	*9*	*10*
GR		15	15	15	15	25	25	10	10	10	10
AC											
SR				90							
PR										90	
OH	45	30	15	90	75	50	25	15	5	85	75
POR		0						90			

TABLE 8.27 Standard Component Item with Uncashed Requisition

	0	*1*	*2*	*3*	*4*	*5*	*6*	*7*	*8*	*9*	*10*
GR		0						90			
AC	90										
SR											
PR											
OH	200	110	110	110	110	110	110	20	20	20	20
POR											

TABLE 8.28 Standard Component Item with Cashed Requisition

	0	*1*	*2*	*3*	*4*	*5*	*6*	*7*	*8*	*9*	*10*
GR		0						90			
AC	0										
SR											
PR											
OH	110	110	110	110	110	110	110	20	20	20	20
POR											

the corresponding change at the component level before the requisition is cashed. The gross requirements associated with the parent's ninety-unit POR disappear from the action bucket. Rather than deduct the ninety units from on-hand inventory at the component level, the on-hand balance remains the same and the ninety units are shown as allocated. Then, after the requisition is cashed, the on-hand balance and the allocation are both reduced by the ninety units in question.

Tables 8.29, 8.30, and 8.31 display the same allocation and cashing process, but this time with a partial order cancellation. Here the POR of ninety units has been released as seventy units, with twenty units canceled as not needed. In table 8.30, the component's gross requirements (associated with the parent item's ninety-unit POR) disappear. The on-hand balance remains the same, but now seventy units are shown as allocated. Cashing appears simply in table 8.31 as the balancing reduction of on-hand and allocated inventory by the seventy units of material released to the parent item.

Allocations and cashed requisitions arise in net change systems because inventory transactions are triggering the MRP program. Each inventory

TABLE 8.29 Parent Item POR Released with Partial Cancellation

	0	*1*	*2*	*3*	*4*	*5*	*6*	*7*	*8*	*9*	*10*
GR		15	15	15	15	25	25	10	10	10	10
AC											
SR				70							
PR								90			
OH	45	30	15	70	55	30	5	85	75	65	55
POR		0				90					

TABLE 8.30 Component Uncashed Position

	0	*1*	*2*	*3*	*4*	*5*	*6*	*7*	*8*	*9*	*10*
GR		0				90					
AC	70										
SR											
PR											
OH	200	130	130	130	130	40	40	40	40	40	40
POR											

TABLE 8.31 Component Cashed Position

	0	*1*	*2*	*3*	*4*	*5*	*6*	*7*	*8*	*9*	*10*
GR		0				90					
AC	0										
SR											
PR											
OH	130	130	130	130	130	40	40	40	40	40	40
POR											

record must be in balance, with projected gross requirements matched by on-hand inventories, scheduled receipts on open orders, and planned receipts on properly timed PORs. If any transaction throws the record out of balance, the record must be updated immediately with revised PORs. If transaction-triggered revisions also affect a parent or component item, the principle of *interlevel equilibrium* requires that the PORs and gross requirements of the two levels be immediately realigned.

The Wemmerlov [6] survey found that five of the thirteen companies used net change while the other eight used regeneration. Of the eight using regeneration, six restrained much of the printout so that the weekly output showed only exception messages. Net change systems, as Wemmerlov points out, are genuine exception systems; hence, the regeneration users were modifying their systems to look somewhat like net change.

Regeneration users generally were disinterested in net change, because their data-processing times were acceptable and their business was not that dynamic. Regeneration is suitable for a stable environment in which a weekly massive batch processing run is sufficient to provide timely information. In a more volatile environment in which requirements are subject to rapid change, a net change system may be more suitable.

System Nervousness, Firm Planned Orders, and Time Fences

Carlson, Jucker, and Kropp [1] define MRP *system nervousness* as the shifting of scheduled setups. More accurate, updated requirements can be a mixed blessing, because new, optimal schedules may disrupt previous plans. If no setup was scheduled in a particular period, expectations were raised concerning personnel scheduling and machine loading. To schedule a setup afterward is clearly undesirable.

Expanding the Carlson definition a little, we define system nervousness as an exaggerated response at component levels to small changes at parent levels. This response justifies particularly bad responses from personnel when scheduled setups must be shifted.

Forrester [2] studied the related problem of *industrial dynamics*. He found that, in a multiechelon system, small changes in demand at the retail level cause wide fluctuations in inventory levels at the factory. The more echelons there are and the longer the lead times, the wider are fluctuations.

Tables 8.32 through 8.35 show how a small change at the parent item level can cause headaches at the component level. Tables 8.32 and 8.33 display an innocent parent–component relationship. Table 8.34 shows the same pair, except that the parent's gross requirements of forty units in period 3 have been increased to forty-five units. With that change, the

TABLE 8.32 Standard Parent Item before Period 3 GR Revision

	0	*1*	*2*	*3*	*4*	*5*	*6*	*7*	*8*	*9*	*10*
GR		35	30	40	0	10	40	30	0	30	55
AC											
SR											
PR							100				55
OH	115	80	50	10	10	0	60	30	30	0	0
POR						100				55	

Parent L = 1; POQ (covers three periods of positive requirements)

TABLE 8.33 Standard Component before Parent Revision

	0	*1*	*2*	*3*	*4*	*5*	*6*	*7*	*8*	*9*	*10*
GR						100				55	
AC											
SR											
PR						80				55	
OH	20	20	20	20	20	0	0	0	0	0	0
POR			80				55				

Component L = 3; L-4-L

TABLE 8.34 Standard Parent Item after Period 3 GR Revision

	0	*1*	*2*	*3*	*4*	*5*	*6*	*7*	*8*	*9*	*10*
				(40)							
GR		35	30	45	0	10	40	30	0	30	55
AC											
SR											
							(100)				(55)
PR						75				85	
OH	115	80	50	5	5	70	30	0	0	55	0
						(100)				(55)	
POR					75				85		

Parent item period 3 change from GR 40 to 45; L = 1

Circled numbers show PORs and PRs without change for comparison purposes.

TABLE 8.35 Standard Component after Parent Revision

	0	*1*	*2*	*3*	*4*	*5*	*6*	*7*	*8*	*9*	*10*
						(100)				(55)	
GR					75				85		
AC											
SR											
						(80)				(55)	
PR					55				85		
OH	20	20	20	20	0	0	0	0	0	0	0
			(80)				(55)				
POR		55				85					

Component reaction, L = 3

Circled numbers show GRs, PRs, and PORs without change.

POR of 100 units in period 5 is too late, because there is no longer enough projected inventory to cover period 5. The solution is to move the POR ahead to period 4. According to the lot sizing rule, however, three weeks' supply calls for seventy-five units to cover five units of net requirements in period 5, forty in period 6, and thirty in period 7. Table 8.34 shows the parent item's projected position with the new PORs. Table 8.35 presents the troubled picture of a change in setup. This system is nervous. A five-unit change in the parent item's period 3 gross requirements leads to an immediate need for a period 1 POR at the component level. A comparison of tables 8.33 and 8.35 reveals that the time and quantity of both PORs change at the component level.

To avoid this type of nervousness, *time fences* can be established. A fence is the shortest reasonable lead time from raw material to finished product or assembly. Within that time fence, no rescheduling is allowed except under extenuating circumstances. The master schedule must thus be fixed for the period of the time fence.

Without a time fence, we may still be able to save the day by *upward pegging*, which simply means chaining upward from the component to the parent item where it is used. *Full pegging* means chaining all the way back to the master schedule. Tables 8.36 through 8.41 show how to use upward pegging and *firm planned orders* (FPO) to solve shortage problems caused by schedule changes.

TABLE 8.36 Standard Parent from Table 8.34 after Period 7 Revision

	0	*1*	*2*	*3*	*4*	*5*	*6*	*7*	*8*	*9*	*10*
GR		35	30	45	0	10	40	30 70	0	30	55
AC											
SR											
PR						115				85	
OH	115	80	50	5	5	110	70	0	0	55	0
POR					115				85		

L = 1; POQ (covers 3 periods of positive requirements)

TABLE 8.37 Standard Component after Parent Revision

	0	*1*	*2*	*3*	*4*	*5*	*6*	*7*	*8*	*9*	*10*
GR					115				85		
AC											
SR											
PR					95				85		
OH	20	20	20	20	0	0	0	0	0	0	0
POR		95				85					

L = 3

TABLE 8.38 Subcomponent after Parent Revision

	0	1	2	3	4	5	6	7	8	9	10
GR		95				85					
AC											
SR											
PR											
OH	55										
POR											

$L = 1$

Note: the indented bill of materials shows:
Parent
  Component
    Subcomponent

TABLE 8.39 Parent from Table 8.36 with Firm Planned Order

	0	1	2	3	4	5	6	7	8	9	10
GR		35	30	45	0	10	40	70	0	30	55
AC											
SR											
PR						(115) 75	(0) 40			85	
OH	115	80	50	5	5	70	70	0	0	55	0
POR					(115) 75	(0) 40			85		

Firm planned order breaks up POQ in period 4 to relieve pressure on subcomponent.

TABLE 8.40 Standard Component Reaction to Firm Planned Order

	0	1	2	3	4	5	6	7	8	9	10
GR					(115) 75	40			85		
AC											
SR											
PR					55	40			85		
OH	20	20	20	20	0	0	0	0	0	0	0
POR		55	40			85					

$L = 3$

TABLE 8.41 Subcomponent Feeling Much Better

	0	1	2	3	4	5	6	7	8	9	10
GR		55	40			85					
AC											
SR											
PR			40								
OH	55	0	0	0	0	0	0	0	0	0	0
POR		40			85						

$L = 1$

Suppose that the gross requirements of thirty units in period 7 of table 8.34 were increased to seventy units. The result of a chain reaction is shown in tables 8.36 through 8.38.

Suppose, now, that the inventory planner suddenly detects a problem: the subcomponent item that has a procurement lead time of one week is needed right away. Facing a crisis, the planner pegs the subcomponent upward and then finds that the planned order quantity on the parent item covers periods 5, 6, and 7. The solution becomes evident. The parent item planned order can be reduced without causing a problem.

The inventory planner reduces the planned order in question by forty units (the amount of shortage in the subcomponent) and designates it as a firm planned order. The FPO generally involves a special computer command by the planner. The result is indicated in table 8.39 by an arrow under the POR. The additional forty units are ordered in the next planning period or as a part of the next order. The resulting chain reactions are shown in tables 8.40 and 8.41. The planned order is now called "frozen." When the MRP system replans and generates requirements, the frozen orders will not be touched.

The preceding situation illustrates a problem of coverage induced by an increase in the subcomponent requirements. The same type of problem would also arise if some items at the parent level or the component level were scrapped. Suppose that the vendor goofed or that the transportation mode was temporarily crippled. The result would create a chain reaction for which an FPO might be required. As an alternative to reducing the quantity of parent planned orders in the time buckets, it may be possible to reduce the lead time of a component or a subcomponent in some instances. For example, if we can get the component to level 1 in two weeks instead of in the regular three-week lead time, we will not encounter the problem in the subcomponent level 3. A firm planned order can resolve this problem by freezing the scheduled receipt of that particular component. Some of the problems at the end of this chapter will illustrate this concept.

System nervousness goes with the MRP territory. In one way or another, it must be handled. Users who avoid net change systems or dynamic lot sizing rules generally deal with system nervousness by trying to avoid it as much as possible. Carlson et al. [1] proposed quantifying the cost of nervousness and then trading it off against the cost of nonoptimal lot sizes. Many practitioners, however, disparage lot sizing altogether. Because setup costs and holding costs are realities, a cavalier attitude toward lot size rules must be based on the notion that nervousness costs overwhelm lot size costs.

Because setups require both capacity and material, it is not surprising that practitioners try to avoid system nervousness. A change in setup to an earlier time slot requires that the supporting material be ready earlier and that labor and machine capacity be available.

Summary

This chapter has developed the basic principles of material requirements planning and described how to use a simple master production schedule, bill of materials, and inventory status report to explode the requirements for subassemblies, parts, and raw materials.

Because setup costs and holding costs are important, the subject of lot sizing appears in the MRP context. Such lot sizing rules as minimum cost per period and part period balancing were developed.

Finally, this chapter explored some of the responses available in the face of change. Our survey of change-related problems was by no means exhaustive; nevertheless, it should provide a taste of the kinds of problems and solutions that appear after the MRP system begins to operate.

PROBLEMS

1. Given the following BOM, MPS, and inventory status, develop MRP tables for all items. Use the L-4-L technique.

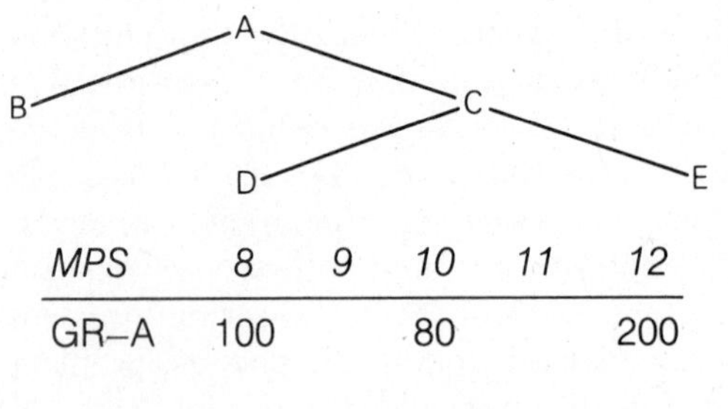

(Usage is one-for-one on all items.)

MPS	*8*	*9*	*10*	*11*	*12*
GR–A	100		80		200

Item	*OH*	*LT*
A	0	1
B	30	2
C	30	1
D	50	2
E	100	3

2. Given the following BOM, MPS, and inventory status, develop MRP tables for all items (ten tables in total).

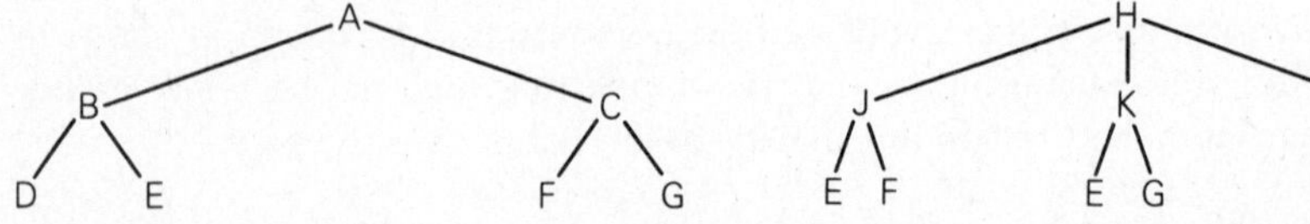

MPS	*8*	*9*	*10*	*11*	*12*
GR–A	100		50		150
GR–H		100		50	

Item	*OH*	*LT*
A	0	1
B	100	2
C	50	2
D	50	1
E	75	2
F	75	2
G	75	1
H	0	1
J	100	2
K	100	2

3. Set up a table using the time-phased order-point system for an independent item, using the following data:

   Weekly demand = 25 units
   Order quantity = 150 units
   Order point = 35 units
   Lead time = 1 week
   Beginning inventory = 50 units

Problems 4 through 7 are based on an item that has the following gross requirements and a beginning inventory of forty units:

	1	*2*	*3*	*4*	*5*	*6*	*7*	*8*	*9*	*10*	*11*	*12*
GR	30		40		30	70	20		10	80		50

Holding cost = $2.50/unit/week
Setup cost = $150
Lead time = 1 week

4. Develop an MCP solution and calculate total relevant costs.
5. Develop a POQ solution and calculate total relevant costs.
6. Develop an LUC solution and calculate total relevant costs.
7. Develop a PPB solution and calculate total relevant costs.
8. An item has a forecasted demand of twenty-five units per week and a beginning inventory of seventy-five units. With a lead time of two weeks, an order quantity of 200 units, and a reorder point of seventy units, develop a TPOP schedule. How much safety stock is being

carried? How much later would the POR occur if the safety stock were dropped?

Problems 9 through 11 are based on the following data: A parent item has projected gross requirements of twenty units per week for ten weeks and a beginning inventory of sixty units. The item has a 2-week lead time and an order quantity of sixty units. The parent item has a component whose lead time is one week and whose on-hand balance is sixty units. The component is scheduled lot-for-lot.

9. Develop a set of tables to describe the parent–component relationship
   a. Before the first order is released.
   b. After the first order is released but before the requisition is cashed.
   c. After the requisition is cashed.
10. Because of capacity problems, the first order was released for thirty units, rather than for sixty units as planned. Develop a set of tables to describe the parent–component relationship
    a. After the order release but before the requisition was cashed.
    b. After the requisition was cashed.
11. The gross requirements for period 4 are canceled; everything else remains as in the original data. Develop the appropriate parent–component tables to show the effect of this change.

Problems 12 through 15 are based on the following data. A parent item faces the following gross requirements.

	1	*2*	*3*	*4*	*5*	*6*	*7*	*8*	*9*	*10*
GR	0	40	30	40	10	70	40	10	30	60

The parent item has a one-week lead time, and the lot-for-lot rule is employed. Beginning inventory is twenty units. The parent item has a component whose lead time is also one week and whose starting inventory position is thirty units. At the component level, production occurs in lot sizes to cover three weeks of net requirements.

12. Develop the parent–component MRP tables to show the original planned positions.
13. At the parent level, gross requirements for period 2 are canceled. Develop the parent–component tables to show the net effect of this cancellation.
14. With the parent level gross requirements canceled for period 2, show how a firm planned order could be used to avoid a change in the timing of setups within the first four weeks.

15. At the component level, there is enough capacity to produce seventy-five units in period 1. Gross requirements at the parent level increase from forty units to fifty units in period 2. What problem arises? What solution would you recommend?

16. It is possible to show that a cost per unit formulation yields the EOQ solution when the demand rate is constant. Letting S be the setup cost, the setup cost per unit would be S/Q. To calculate the holding cost per unit, we must account for the fact that each lot covers Q/d periods of demand. Formulate the per unit cost function and solve for Q.

17. Using information system terminology, the part number master file is stored under an indexed organization using part numbers and the record key. Describe what such a system would look like.

18. Using information system terminology, the product structure master file is often implemented under a list organization. Describe what such a system would look like.

19. Consider the following problem:

	0	*1*	*2*	*3*	*4*	*5*	*6*	*7*	*8*	*9*	*10*
GR		35	30	45	0	10	40	30	0	30	55
OH	115										
POR											

With a lead time of one period and using a POQ of three periods, develop a POR schedule using an electronic spreadsheet. Set up an MRP table to experiment with changes in requirements. We give only the rudiments here and leave the rest to your own creativity:

Set the cursor at A1.
  Type in the label: Gross Req.
Set the cursor at A2.
  Type in the label: On Hand.
Set the cursor at A3.
  Type in the label: POR.
Set the cursor at A4.
  Type in the label: Sched. Rec.
Now move the cursor to B1, C1, etc.
  Type in the gross requirements 0, 35, 30, using column B as period 0.
Now move the cursor to B2.
  Type in the on-hand quantity: 115 units.
Now move the cursor to C2.
  Type in the formula: +B2+B3−C1.

Now replicate this formula in locations D2 through L2. Use the *relative* option.
Now enter PORs as needed in row 3.
Try again with the period 7 gross requirement changed to seventy units from thirty.

20. Use an electronic spreadsheet to replicate tables 8.36 through 8.38 and then experiment with changes in gross requirements. We give only a general hint here: Suppose that row 5 represents gross requirements for the standard component. Then you need to move the cursor to location C5 and enter a formula such as +C3 where location C3 contains the POR from the standard parent. Now replicate this formula from D5 through L5 using the *relative* option. Calculate the tables with the original gross requirements and with the revised gross requirements.

REFERENCES AND BIBLIOGRAPHY

1. R. C. Carlson, J. V. Jucker, and D. H. Kropp, "Less Nervous MRP Systems: A Dynamic Economic Lot-Sizing Approach," *Management Science*, Vol. 25, No. 8 (August 1979), pp. 754–761.
2. J. Forrester, *Industrial Dynamics* (Cambridge, Mass.: MIT Press, 1961).
3. J. Orlicky, *Material Requirements Planning* (New York: McGraw-Hill, 1975).
4. A. Sloan, *My Years with General Motors* (Garden City, N.Y.: Doubleday, 1964), p. 128.
5. A. Vaszonyi, "The Use of Mathematics in Production and Inventory Control," *Management Science*, Vol. 1, No. 1 (October 1954), pp. 70–85.
6. U. Wemmerlov, "Design Factors in MRP Systems: A Limited Survey," *Production and Inventory Management* (Fourth Quarter 1979), pp. 15–34.
7. D. C. Whybark and J. G. Williams, "Material Requirements Planning under Uncertainty," *Decision Sciences*, Vol. 7, No. 4 (October 1976), pp. 595–600.

appendix 8A

Material Requirements Planning Systems: The State of the Art

John C. Anderson
Roger G. Schroeder
Sharon E. Tupy
Edna M. White
University of Minnesota

Abstract

This article reports on an extensive survey of 679 APICS members, Material Managers and Production Inventory Control Managers, regarding the use of Material Requirements Planning Systems. The study is the largest survey of MRP Practice ever undertaken. This article describes the study and presents findings with regard to the nature of MRP systems in practice, the extent of growth of MRP, the role of computerization, and the benefits achieved in practice.

More complete information can be obtained in *MRP: A Study of Implementation and Practice**, available through the American Production and Inventory Control Society.

Introduction

Material requirements planning (MRP) systems have been the target of thoughtful speculation on the part of managers not having MRP systems,

---

* Funded by the APICS Educational and Research Foundation.

From *Production and Inventory Management*, Fourth Quarter, 1982. Reprinted by permission of the American Production and Inventory Control Society, Inc.

the source of stability and discipline for managers who have MRP systems, and the subject of much presentation and discussion in literature. It is generally felt that MRP systems, when properly implemented, can be a tremendous asset to management. In fact, it has been said that MRP holds the promise of the future for manufacturing management [4].

Hundreds of companies throughout the United States have entered into the development of Material Requirement Planning systems. Conference after conference provides testimony regarding MRP design and experience. However, remarkably little has been done to observe the state of the art of MRP systems from a wider perspective. Most information that is available today comes from personal observation and remarks from active consultants in the field.

A few research studies exist which look at the practice of MRP. A survey by Baer and Centamore [3] of 106 manufacturing companies regarding their use of MRP focused on the degree of acceptance of materials management, the company's reasons for adopting materials management, how it was organized, what functions were included, and finally, the advantages and disadvantages of adopting materials management. Vollmann and Hall [7] have provided some interesting observations regarding MRP practice through case study research. Perhaps the largest survey to date was the APICS sponsored survey [2] conducted in 1973. This survey focused on a variety of techniques used in the production inventory control area and further contrasted the MRP and Reorder Point approaches. Davis [5] provides a comparison of this study with earlier studies in the area. Several other localized studies have been made; however, few studies have viewed the breadth of MRP practice.

Given the interest in MRP and the large commitment that industry is currently making and planning to make in MRP systems, we felt it appropriate to thoroughly examine the practice of MRP from a broad perspective. This article will highlight some of the results of such a study, focusing on a description of the study itself, the nature of the companies involved, and the MRP systems themselves. Particular attention will be placed on the growth and extent of MRP system development, the level of commitment to computerization, and a brief assessment of benefits achieved.

Description of the Study

We decided early to examine collective experience; that is, to obtain information from as many companies as possible. A primary aim was to provide a wide assessment of the state of the art of MRP systems. This premise shaped our approach to the study. While personal interview or case study research can provide useful results, these approaches severely limit the number of respondents that can be included. Consequently, we chose a mail survey approach.

A six-page survey form was developed which included questions to identify the nature of the company involved, the current status of the MRP system, the benefits and costs incurred, the nature of implementation problems and implementation approaches used. Based upon a pilot study, the questionnaire took about 45 minutes of the manager's time to complete.

Survey questionnaires were sent to approximately 1,700 APICS members in APICS Regions III and V. This area includes the Upper Midwest as far west as North Dakota and South Dakota, and as far east as mid-New York, Pennsylvania and West Virginia. As such, the geographic sample included a highly industrialized section of the country. Particular care was taken to send only one questionnaire per firm represented. The recipient of the questionnaire was asked to complete the questionnaire or forward it to the materials manager or the individual responsible for production and inventory control, or simply to the individual most knowledgeable about the MRP system in the firm.

The response of the APICS members was excellent. It might be argued, however, that using APICS members, and more specifically material requirements/production inventory control people as respondents to the survey clearly biased the results. We certainly concur with the observation. The results are biased. They represent a unique perspective: the perspective of the material managers or production inventory control managers throughout a large geographic section of the United States. We can think of no better set of individuals to ask regarding MRP practice.

The Survey Response

Of the survey questionnaires sent to 1,700 different firms, 679 or 40 percent of the sample population responded. This is considered to be an excellent response to a mail survey. In a typical survey, response rates are often considerably lower. Of those 679 companies reporting, 433 (or 64%) indicated that they had MRP systems in place or in some stage of development.

Figure 8A.1 exhibits the profile of sales volume for the responding companies. As can be observed, there was a wide range of sales volume reported, from under \$10 million to over \$100 million in sales.

A wide variety of industries were represented in the study, as exhibited in table 8A.1. The greatest representation came from the electronic, instrument, fabricated metals, machinery, transportation industries and miscellaneous manufacturing companies. As might be expected from the population surveyed, the majority of the response was from manufacturing type firms with few non-manufacturing firms responding.

Tables 8A.2 and 8A.3 provide additional information regarding the plant characteristics and company size within the survey response. A large majority of the firms (70.4%) followed a policy of both making-to-order and to stock. Similarly, a large percentage of the firms (83.2%) was involved in

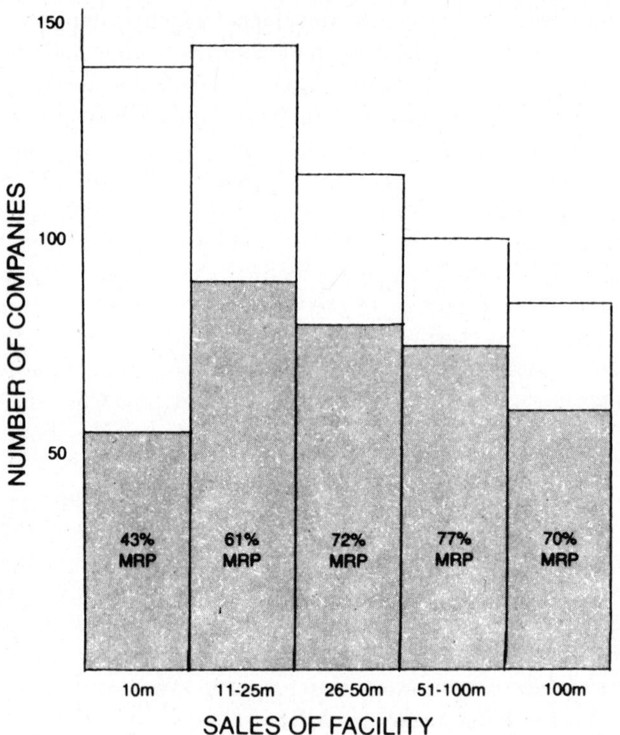

FIGURE 8A.1 MRP and non-MRP companies profile of sales volume

both assembly and fabrication processes. While there was a variety of processes involved (i.e., job shop, continuous process, assembly line, etc.), a majority of firms reporting were job shop oriented. As with sales volume, a wide variety of other size characteristics was observed in the responding firms. The mean levels of a number of characteristics of the process and the number of employees are shown in table 8A.3. While these values may look large on average, it should be remembered that a few extremely large firms increased these values.

The foregoing discussion has described the overall survey response. A wide range of firms reported in the survey—large and small companies, with varied manufacturing configurations, and a variety of industrial orientations. An important observation is whether we see a difference in the kinds of companies reporting between MRP and non-MRP companies. The foregoing figures [and tables] are helpful as we examine this question. It would appear that some industries are more heavily involved in MRP than others. For example, electric-electronic instrument, transportation equipment, and miscellaneous manufacturing industries appear to be most highly committed. Others appear to be less involved; i.e., lumber and wood, paper,

TABLE 8A.1 Industry Representation

	Total Companies	*MRP Companies*	*% MRP*
Food	16	8	50
Tobacco	1	0	0
Lumber and wood	5	1	20
Paper	12	4	33
Chemicals	15	8	53
Petroleum and coal	5	1	20
Rubber and plastic	15	7	47
Primary metal	1	0	0
Fabricated metals	95	47	49
Machinery	166	108	65
Electric-electronic	90	68	76
Instruments	34	24	71
Transportation equipment	67	50	75
Misc. manufacturing	61	46	75
Apparel	5	2	40
Furniture	10	5	50
Printing and publishing	6	3	50
Leather	0	0	0
Stone, clay, glass	4	2	50
Other manufacturing	54	24	44

petroleum and coal, and apparel. The prime characteristics of MRP companies and non-MRP companies with respect to type of product, type of manufacturing and type of process don't reveal any startling differences. The only observation that one might draw is that as the process becomes more complex—if the firm manufactures both to order and to stock, if the manufacturing includes assembly and fabrication, and if there is a combination of processes involved, then it appears that there may be a higher level of commitment toward the use of MRP.

Size characteristics of reporting companies revealed evidence of varied commitment to MRP. As a firm increases in size, as measured by sales volume, the number of parts and components, and by the number of employees, it would appear that there is a greater commitment to MRP. Figure 8A.1 exhibited the profile of sales volume by responding firms. A more careful look at the figure reveals the degree of commitment of MRP. Within each sales level, the shaded area indicates the proportion of companies involved with MRP systems. For example, 43 percent of the companies with sales less than $10 million per year have MRP systems. On the other hand, 70 percent of the companies with sales greater than $100 million per year had MRP systems. The figure reveals that the degree of commitment to MRP appears to increase with the size of the firm as measured by sales volume. Above $26 million in sales, the percentage of companies using MRP is always 70 percent or above. The conclusion one can draw is that

TABLE 8A.2 Plant Characteristics

	Total Response	*MRP Companies*	*Non-MRP Companies*
Type of products			
Make to order	16.3%	14.1%	20.1%
Make to stock	13.3%	13.7%	12.9%
Both	70.4%	72.2%	67.0%
	100.0%	100.0%	100.0%
Type of manufacturing			
Assembly	7.1%	7.2%	7.5%
Fabrication	9.7%	6.3%	17.0%
Both	83.2%	86.5%	75.5%
	100.0%	100.0%	100.0%
Type of process			
Job shop	41.3%	38.8%	45.8%
Continuous process	11.5%	9.1%	17.6%
Assembly line	22.8%	22.4%	24.5%
Combination	24.4%	29.7%	12.1%
	100.0%	100.0%	100.0%

TABLE 8A.3 Company Size Representation

	Mean Values		
	Total Response	*MRP Companies*	*Non-MRP Companies*
# End items	3,169	3,002	3,000
# Parts/components	24,378	25,782	13,821
# Levels in BOM	6.71	6.9	5.84
# Employees	957	1,064	578
# P&IC employees	17	19	12.5

as the company becomes more complex, and larger, the need and opportunity for MRP systems appears to increase.

MRP . . . What Is It?

Up to this point we have designated some companies as MRP companies and others as not being MRP companies without clarifying this distinction. For a moment we should reflect on the definition of MRP. At first it might seem a bit facetious that we should examine the definition of materials requirements planning today. In the simplest sense, two extreme views of MRP could be offered: First that MRP is a narrow concept involving the parts explosion process, i.e., the process of exploding the demand for independent demand items into their necessary components. In this sense,

MRP has facilitated order launching. At the other extreme is a broad definition which says that Material Requirements Planning is a concept that involves the entire manufacturing control system. It starts with parts explosion and order launching, but it goes far beyond that to capacity planning, purchasing, shop floor control, costing, and interfaces with a variety of other necessary functions to effectively operate the manufacturing business. Historically, it is fair to say that a majority of people have used the narrower definition, but today diversity exists. Of the MRP companies reporting, 34 percent of the companies used MRP in the broad sense; 57 percent used MRP in the narrower sense. This use of the definition doesn't appear to depend on the size of the company or the plant characteristics or their number of years of MRP experience. The non-MRP companies responding were about equally split between the broad and the narrow definitions of MRP, but as you might expect, many had not formulated their definition of MRP.

It is clear that a variety of definitions exists. In fact, Oliver Wight's definition of Class A through D encompasses both the broad and the narrow sense of MRP. In this study a modified definition of these classes was used as shown below.

Class A: Closed-loop system used for both priority planning and capacity planning. The master production schedule is leveled and used by top management to run the business. Most deliveries are on time, inventory is under good control, and little or no expediting is done.

Class B: Closed-loop system with capability for both priority planning and capacity planning. However, the master production schedule is somewhat inflated. Top management does not give full support. Some inventory reductions have been obtained, but capacity is sometimes exceeded and some expediting is needed.

Class C: Order launching system with priority planning only. Capacity planning is done informally with a probably inflated Master Production Schedule. Expediting is used to control the flow of work. A modest reduction in inventory has been achieved.

Class D: The MRP system exists mainly in data processing. Many records are inaccurate. The informal system is largely used to run the company. Little benefit is obtained from the MRP system.

It is not surprising that a company's definition of MRP becomes broader as they mature toward a Class A user. The issue of definition may seem somewhat academic. Someone might say, "Who cares, let's just get MRP up and running." The point is the confusion regarding meaning inhibits defining the scope of the development. Many definitions exist; what is important is that a definition be chosen, and project goals set.

We might accept the broadest definition offering a variety of degrees of sophistication in the process. But for purposes of analysis of results, we classified a company as being an MRP company by their own statement of existence or nonexistence of MRP. Consequently, our MRP companies represent a wide variety of sophistication and complexity of the MRP system, as will be seen in the discussion to follow.

How Recent Is This MRP Phenomenon?

Given the recent upsurge in interest in Material Requirements Planning today, it is hardly surprising to see the marked increase in the development of MRP systems in industry. Figure 8A.2 exhibits a growth curve showing the number of companies starting MRP systems in a particular year, from 1955 to 1978. It shows that the earliest development in our sample occurred in 1957 with a large increase, almost an exponential increase, in the development of MRP since that time. Industrial commitment to MRP is dramatically increasing.

Our results revealed few determinants of the particular time of MRP development. Plant characteristics, industry, etc., appeared to have little bearing on whether a company stated MRP early or late. However, study results revealed that early developments were dominated by larger companies and later developments involved smaller companies. Certainly, computer software and computer hardware play an important role in making MRP systems more feasible for smaller companies today.

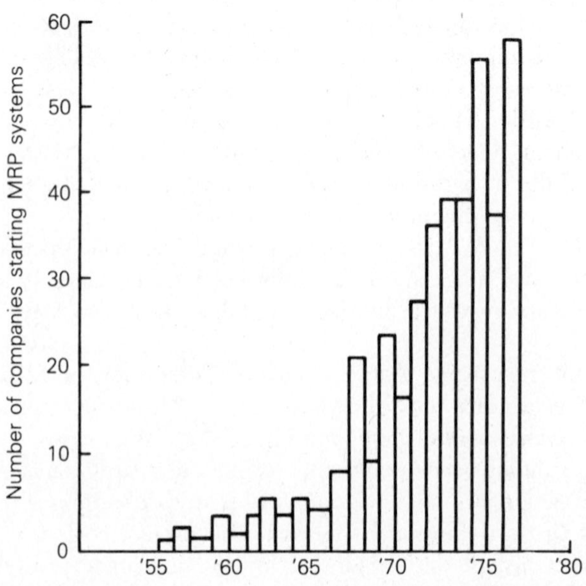

FIGURE 8A.2 The growth of MRP systems

How Extensive Is MRP Development Today?

What percent of the firms in the United States are using MRP? We might answer that question by saying that since 433 out of 679 companies reporting were MRP companies, 64 percent of the firms in the U.S. are using MRP. However, to do so would be misleading. It is true that 64 percent of the companies reporting in this survey were MRP companies. However, we are confident that a number of the firms not responding to the questionnaire have little or no interest in MRP and the nonrespondents may have a larger percentage of non-MRP companies than our respondent sample. Consequently, what must be said is that out of the original sample population of 1,700 firms, at least 433 of these firms have MRP in some stage of development. That alone is a respectable number.

But what is the stage of development of these systems? As might be expected, a variety of sophistication exists, Class A users to Class D users. Table 8A.4 outlines the Class levels reported by the respondents. As indicated in the table, 9.5 percent or 38 of the firms reporting MRP usage claim to be Class A users. However, over 60 percent of the firms reporting MRP usage identify themselves as Class C or Class D users. There appears to be much room for improvement of these systems. Another way of looking at level of sophistication of an MRP user is by the degree to which they feel they have integrated the various elements of the system. These elements include a variety of things from Forecasting End Items to Shop Floor Control as listed in table 8A.6. Only 27 percent of the respondents with MRP systems indicated that they had 80 percent or more of these elements fully integrated.

As might be expected, the length of time or longer experience with MRP seems to be related to Class A usage at a statistically significant level. Furthermore, Class A users have more integrated systems. Although Class A users are comprised of both small and large companies, smaller companies appear to report more Class D usage.

Common Features of MRP Systems

Table 8A.5 illustrates the common features of MRP systems reported by respondents in the survey. The majority of the MRP systems appear to be

TABLE 8A.4 Class Usage of MRP

Number of Companies	*Percent*	*Class Usage*
38	9.5	A
117	29.2	B
195	48.6	C
51	12.7	D

TABLE 8A.5 Common Features of MRP Systems

A. Update method	Net change, 30.3%, regenerative, 69.7%
B. Pegging	Yes, 55.1%, No, 44.9%
C. MPS update frequency	Weekly, 56.7%, Daily, 16.37%, Other, 27.0%
D. Cycle counting	Yes, 61.4%, No, 38.6%
E. Allocation of inventory	Yes, 71.3%, No, 28.7%
F. Automatic lot sizing	Yes, 44.5%, No, 55.5%
G. Time bucket size	Weekly, 70.4%, Monthly, 12.5%, Other, 17.0%
H. Number of weeks in MPS	40 Weeks Average

of a regenerative nature, apparently avoiding the nervousness and anxiety experienced with some net change systems. Pegging does not appear to be as prevalent as some might believe—only 55 percent used pegging. The master production schedule update frequency is predominantly weekly. As many apostles of MRP would hope, the majority of MRP companies employ cycle counting. Even a larger majority employ allocation of inventory in an effort to stabilize the production process. Firms appear to split with regard to the use of automatic lot sizing. By far the predominant time bucket size is weekly, and the number of weeks on the master production schedule planning horizon averaged about 40 weeks.

One might say that the variety of features of MRP systems within the survey reflect to some extent varied maturity in the development process. However, the particular features did not seem to depend upon length of MRP experience. Some of the features did appear to be related to the size of the firm as measured by sales volume, and to the class of usage and finally to the level of computerization. As sales volume increased, the commitment to regeneration versus net change was clearly evident. Similarly, automatic lot sizing appeared to increase as sales volume increased. Both pegging and cycle counting increased as a company moved toward Class A usage. Finally, as might be expected, cycle counting and automatic lot sizing increased at a statistically significant level as computerization increased.

The Extent of Computerization of MRP System Elements

Many have contended that MRP requires a large commitment to computerization. Certainly, some firms that claim to be MRP users have little computerization. However, by and large, our survey results bore out the contention that computerization is necessary for effective MRP utilization. Table 8A.6 exhibits the extent of computerization of possible elements of an MRP system for both MRP and non-MRP companies. In every instance,

TABLE 8A.6 Extent of Computerization of System Elements

	% Companies Computerized	
	Current MRP Companies	*Current Non-MRP Companies*
A. Forecasting end items	42.5	15.7
B. Bill of materials	86.7	48.5
C. Inventory stock system	84.4	54.4
D. Master production schedule	52.2	15.9
E. Parts explosion	86.9	40.9
F. Order release	49.6	17.6
G. Purchasing	43.1	8.9
H. Capacity planning	37.7	6.1
I. Operations scheduling	35.9	8.5
J. Shop floor	30.5	9.9

MRP companies had more computerization. The bill of materials, inventory stock system, and parts explosion were among the highest levels of computerization, while capacity planning, operations scheduling and shop floor control were the least computerized. These same elements were generally the most and least computerized for non-MRP companies. However, as stated, the level of computerization for non-MRP companies was substantially less.

Another way of looking at the computerization issue is to see the development of computerization over time. In other words, are there some elements of an MRP system which appear to be more quickly computerized than others? The data revealed that the three which are most highly computerized in their own right—bill of materials, inventory stock system and parts explosion—were the elements most quickly computerized by a firm developing MRP. Similarly, it appeared that computerization of capacity planning, operations scheduling and shop floor control were elements which became computerized much more slowly. Clearly, this data reveals a commitment to computerization on the part of firms employing MRP and there appears to be precedent regarding the order in which particular MRP elements are computerized.

MRP . . . Is It Worth It?

Past experience tells us that development of successful MRP systems requires a commitment to concept, a commitment of management, and finally a commitment of resources and dollars. The analysis of problems, benefits, and costs involved and how they relate to the approaches used and to organizational characteristics is a subject by itself (see [6], [8]). However, it is important to conclude with some assessment of benefits reported by MRP companies in the study.

Several benefits of MRP systems deserve mentioning. The first is the effect the MRP system has on the accuracy of information with which management deals; the second, a more subjective assessment of the benefits of the process; the third, a look at some of the critical factors that management may use in assessing the performance of their particular operations.

A primary benefit of the implementation of MRP would appear to be improved accuracy of information. Table 8A.7 compares the accuracy of data from non-MRP and MRP companies in the survey sample. As shown, on a scale from 1 to 4, from poor to excellent, the MRP companies indicate that they generally have more accurate data than non-MRP companies. As might be expected, the areas of greatest improvement appear to be in the accuracy of the bill of materials, master production schedule, inventory, and production leadtime data. A word of caution must be made, however, with regard to the interpretation of these results. We are not sure whether the implementation of MRP creates this additional accuracy, or, in fact, if increased accuracy is a necessary precondition for successful MRP implementation. Certainly, these two possibilities are intertwined. What is apparent is that those companies with MRP systems have greater accuracy of information, particularly in those areas which must be accurate for effective application of material requirements planning systems. It would appear that the structure and discipline of MRP are synonymous with more accurate information.

As the table shows, however, these are some types of data accuracy which are still quite low even after MRP implementation: the accuracy of market information, shop floor control and capacity data. These are the areas of future challenge in both MRP and non-MRP companies and additional resources and effort must be placed in these areas. It is interesting to note that the areas of highest accuracy are, in fact, the areas of highest computerization, while those areas of lowest accuracy are the least computerized.

A number of subjective benefits were reported by the respondents. The material managers felt that the MRP system had resulted in substantially

TABLE 8A.7 Average Accuracy of Information[a]

	MRP Companies	*Non-MRP Companies*
Bill of materials	3.2	2.4
Inventory	2.7	2.1
Master production schedule	2.7	2.0
Vendor lead times	2.5	2.3
Production lead times	2.6	2.2
Market forecasts	2.0	2.3
Shop floor control	2.0	1.9
Capacity	2.0	1.9
Composite accuracy (32 possible)	19.7	17.1

[a] 4 = excellent, 1 = poor.

improved production scheduling and a better handle on inventory control. They did feel, however, that the MRP system had little impact, at least to date, regarding improved competitive position, better cost estimating, or improved morale in production. On the whole, the material managers felt better about their operation and the structure which MRP added to the decision-making process. However, potential for further improvement clearly exists.

While subjective benefits provide some indication of success, more objectively measurable benefits show startling improvement. Table 8A.8 exhibits some performance measures examined within the study. The table speaks well for MRP implementation. It shows the material managers' estimate of what performance would have been under the same economic circumstances prior to the implementation of MRP. It shows the current estimate of those measures, and finally indicates the material managers' estimate of what these measures will be when they complete the development of their particular MRP system. In each instance, the companies reported substantial improvement in these performance measures. On average, inventory turnover has increased by 34 percent. Average delivery leadtimes have been reduced by 17 percent. The percent of time meeting delivery promises increased by 24 percent. The percent of orders requiring a split has decreased by 41 percent. Finally, the average number of expeditors has been decreased by 40 percent. While this shows progress, the results indicate that material managers feel that further improvement is possible.

Certainly, the bottom line of benefit assessment of MRP systems would be from a cost benefit ratio. We, unfortunately, cannot report such a figure. Production costs are clearly a proprietary item for the respondents. In addition, cost benefit ratios may be uniquely defined for particular organizations and one overall figure may not be readily estimated. Suffice it to say that the improvements in data accuracy and the benefits that we have observed speak well of material requirements planning systems.

TABLE 8A.8 MRP Performance Measures

	"Pre-MRP" Estimate	*Current Estimate*	*Future Estimate*
a. Inventory turnover	3.2 (2.4)	4.3 (3.1)	5.3 (3.8)
b. Delivery lead time (days)	71.4 (65.8)	58.9 (59.6)	44.5 (43.3)
c. Percent of time meeting delivery promises	61.4 (21.4)	76.6 (18.2)	88.7 (13.8)
d. Percent of orders requiring splits because of unavailable material	32.4 (22.0)	19.4 (17.3)	9.1 (8.8)
e. Number of expeditors	10.1 (16.0)	6.5 (9.2)	4.6 (6.0)

Average value in the table, standard deviation below in parentheses.

Conclusion

Interest is growing in MRP system development across the country in a variety of firms and industries. The demands, complexities, and critical interdependencies of our productive systems appear to require a more informed, disciplined, planned and controlled approach which MRP systems can, in part, facilitate.

The recent growth rate of MRP system developments is remarkable. Each year more and more companies join the ranks of MRP system users. Early MRP developments comprise a varied constituency of large and small firms in a variety of industries. This would indicate the impetus for MRP is not necessarily size, industry, or particular production configuration; rather the impetus may be more simply the complexities management perceives in trying to plan and control production operations.

The design of the MRP system varies widely in breadth of definition and particular features incorporated. Both definition and system features seem to depend more upon particular company characteristics and needs rather than maturity of usage. This reveals the importance of seriously analyzing individual company requirements and carefully defining the scope of the MRP system development. Some commonality appears to exist, however, with regard to computerization of system elements. Computerization is an important part of the MRP system. MRP planners should envision a heavy investment for computerization of, at least, the basic areas of bill of materials, inventory stock status and parts explosion and for improvements in areas such as capacity planning, shop floor control, etc. This will require a commitment of computing resources and a commitment of time and effort in designing underlying system structure to meet these challenges.

The benefits of MRP systems are real. On the whole, accuracy of information is improved either as a result of or as a prerequisite to successful MRP implementation. Material managers appear pleased with the added structure and discipline that MRP can bring to bear on the decision-making process. Finally, substantial improvements have been realized in several critical performance measures including inventory turns, delivery leadtime, delivery promises, and order splitting. While these benefits have already been obtained, material managers are also optimistic regarding further improvements.

This survey research is the first large-scale study of its type focusing on MRP practice. Much has been learned. Yet more detailed field study, longitudinal study, and survey research must be accomplished which focuses on the MRP implementation process. The growth of system development, the possible breadth of system scope, and finally the growing diversity of users warrant more analysis and understanding.

REFERENCES

1. Anderson, John C., Schroeder, Roger G., Tupy, Sharon E., and White, Edna M. *MRP: A Study of Implementation and Practice,* Monograph published by APICS, 1981.
2. APICS, "State-of-the-Art Survey: A Preliminary Analysis," *Production and Inventory Management,* Fourth Quarter, 1974, pp. 1–11.
3. Baer, R. and Centamore, J. "Materials Management: Where it Stands . . . What it Means . . . ", *Purchasing Magazine,* January 8, 1970, pp. 53–58.
4. Bevis, George. "The Bright Promise of the Future in Manufacturing," Speech given at University of Minnesota Operations Management Seminar, Minneapolis, Minnesota, January 1977.
5. Davis, Edward W. "A Look at the Use of Production-Inventory Techniques: Past and Present," *Production and Inventory Management,* Fourth Quarter, 1975, pp. 1–19.
6. Schroeder, Roger G., Anderson, John C., White, Edna M., and Tupy, Sharon E. "A Study of MRP Benefits and Costs," Working Paper, Graduate School of Business Administration, University of Minnesota.
7. Vollmann, Thomas E., and Hall, Robert W. "MRP Implementation: How Tough Is It at Your Company," Proceedings of MRP Implementation Conference, September 24–26, 1978, pp. 116–128.
8. White, Edna M., Anderson, John C., Schroeder, Roger G., and Tupy, Sharon E. "A Study of the MRP Implementation Process," Working Paper, Graduate School of Business Administration, University of Minnesota.

chapter nine

Aggregate Planning

In an earlier chapter, we explained that demand forecasting can be for the long, medium, or short range. Long-range forecasts help management formulate capacity planning strategies. Managers ask many policy-related questions: Do we need to increase or curtail our operations at various locations? Do we need to build or expand facilities at existing or new locations? Do we need to negotiate or renegotiate our supply of parts from vendors? Once long-range capacity decisions are made, intermediate-range plans should be made that are consistent with long-range policies. Management must work within the resources allocated by long-range decisions. The plans do not necessarily have to be so detailed as to provide specific instructions for daily or weekly operations, such as loading, sequencing, expediting, and dispatching. These specifics will be dealt with in later chapters.

The Nature of the Aggregate Planning Decisions

As explained earlier, inventories provide a means of storing excess capacity during intermediate slack periods and assist us in smoothing the impact of demand fluctuations on manpower levels. In most productive systems, we must be concerned with scheduling equipment and the work force in addition to managing inventories. Given the sales forecast, the factory capacity, aggregate inventory levels, and the size of the work force, the manager must decide at what rate of production to operate the plant over the intermediate term. Intermediate-range planning is generally known as *aggregate planning*. Aggregate plans and master schedules provide common points at which capacity and inventories are considered jointly in the light of firm's long-range plans, and they provide inputs to the financial plan, the marketing plan, and requirements planning and detailed scheduling decisions. Several crucial decisions have to be made while generating an aggregate plan. Management may ask many inventory and work force-related questions: To what extent should inventories be used for absorbing changes in demand that might occur during the intermediate term? Should we absorb the flucuations by varying the size of the work force? Should we keep the work force constant and absorb fluctuations by overtime, shorter time schedule hours, and part-time work force? Should we maintain a fairly stable work force, as well as production rate, and subcontract the fluctuating order rates? Should we vary the prices to counterinfluence the demand pattern? Generally, a mixture of strategies is preferred and is feasible. We will briefly discuss the effects of various policies next. In this chapter, we will first cover various aggregate planning strategies and associated costs. Then we will present some qualitative and quantitative methods to solve these problems. Finally, we will compare these methods and evaluate their advantages and limitations.

Aggregate Planning Defined

Aggregate output planning generally consists of planning a desired output over an intermediate range of three months to one year. The aggregate plan needs some logical unit of measuring output—for example, gallons of paint in a paint factory, number of dresses in a garment factory, cases of beer in a brewery, and perhaps equivalent machine hours in manufacturing industries. Product group forecasts are generally more accurate than individual item forecast. The further the forecast goes into the future, the less likely it is to be accurate. Recognizing this, planning and control of production is done on the basis of group demand over the intermediate and long range. In the short range, however, as better forecasts become available for individual products, disaggregation and detailed scheduling become feasible. Choosing meaningful groups requires a thorough knowledge of the products as well as manufacturing processes. The groups are not necessarily the same as those used by the marketing/sales department or the inventory control system department. The chosen groups must be meaningful in terms of, for example, demand on manufacturing facilities for products that go through similar manufacturing operations or that are processed in common manufacturing facilities. Comparable Ford and Mercury cars, for example, require the same capacity for body construction, although assembly department requirements may vary. The disaggregation of product groups and the master scheduling process is dealt with in another chapter.

Aggregate Planning Strategies

Many aggregate planning strategies are available for the manager. These strategies involve the manipulation of inventory, production rate, manpower needs, capacity, and other controllable variables. When we vary any one of the variables at a time to cope with changes in product output rates, we use what are known as *pure strategies*. *Mixed strategies,* in contrast, involve the use of two or more pure strategies to arrive at a feasible production plan. We will briefly discuss, first, the effect of adopting pure strategies—that is, changing the level of individual variables.

PURE STRATEGIES

Changing Inventory Levels

If we accumulate inventories during slack periods of demand, working capital and costs associated with obsolescence, storage, insurance, and handling will increase. Conversely, during periods of increasing demand, changes in inventory levels or backlogs might lead to poorer customer service, longer lead times, possible lost sales, and potential entry of new competitors in the market.

Changing Work Force Levels

The manager may change the size of the work force by hiring or laying off production employees to match the production rate in order to meet the demand exactly. In many instances, new employees require training and the average productivity is temporarily lowered. A layoff frequently results in lower worker morale and lower productivity, and the remaining employees may retard output to protect themselves against a similar fate.

In some instances, it is possible to maintain a constant work force and vary the working hours. However, during upswings of demand, there is a limit on how much overtime is practical. Excessive overtime may wear workers out, and their productivity may go down. The incremental costs associated with shift premium, supervision, and overhead may be significant. In periods of slack demand, the firm also faces the difficult task of absorbing the workers' idle time.

Subcontracting

As an alternate to changing work force or inventory, perhaps the company could subcontract some work during the peak demand periods and increase the capacity to satisfy the demand. Again, a potential danger exists of opening doors to competition.

Influencing Demand

Since changing demand is a chief source of aggregate planning problems, the management may decide to influence the demand pattern itself. For example, the telephone companies level their loads by offering evening rates; and some utility companies are experimenting with similar strategies. It is also an old game in the airline industry to offer weekend discounts and winter fares. It is not always possible, however, to balance the demand pattern and the desired production plan.

MIXED STRATEGIES

We see that every pure strategy has a countervailing cost associated with it, and pure strategies are often infeasible. Therefore, a combination of strategies, or a mixed strategy, is often used. Mixed strategies involve the use of two or more controllable variables to arrive at a feasible production plan. Such strategies could include, for example, a combination of subcontracting and overtime or overtime and inventory, as illustrated by some examples later in this chapter. When one considers the possibility of mixing these strategies—the infinite variety of ratios for blending various strategies—one can realize how challenging the problem is. In any case, it is the responsibility of top management to set guidelines for aggregate planning activity, because these planning decisions frequently involve company policies. The production control department, in conjunction with the marketing department, should generate master schedules commensurate with company policies and specific operating prodedures. The complexity of the decision process leads us to a discussion of the value of decision rules for solving aggregate planning problems.

The Value of Decision Rules

Determining when to change production level is a difficult decision. It involves a great deal of time and money, as millions of strategies are available to the decision maker. By establishing decision rules, the production control manager, in conjunction with the operations manager, is in effect setting the rules of the game once, rather than each time it is played. Once a policy is established regarding what justifies a change, weekly decisions can be concerned with the specific actions to be taken to accomplish the change in the most economical and effective manner. The aim of these rules is to help the manager keep out of trouble, rather than get out of trouble. Industry experience indicates that having some kind of rule, even if it is not optimal, significantly improves operations.

To optimize any production plan, we need to review the behavior of cost structures. After a brief exposition of these costs, we will present some important approaches and techniques for solving aggregate planning problems.

Costs

REGULAR PAYROLL AND OVERTIME COST

Detailed empirical cost studies by Holt, Modigliani, Muth, and Simon [12] examined regular payroll, overtime, hiring and layoff costs, and inventory

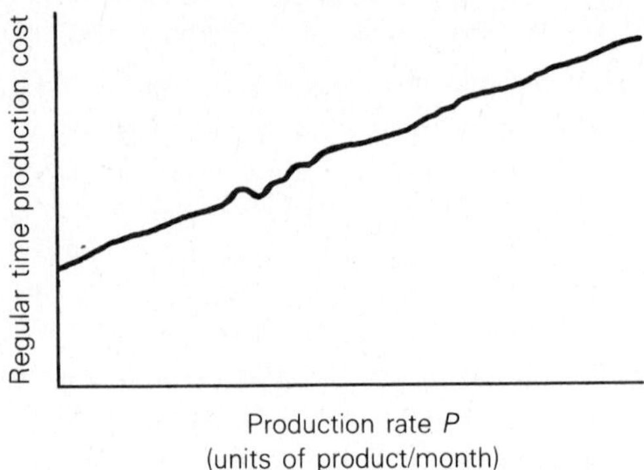

FIGURE 9.1 Costs of regular time production

and backorder costs. These studies covered several years' operation of a paint factory. The typical regular time production cost versus production rate relationship was found to be a monotonic increasing curve, as shown in figure 9.1. The sudden jump in cost could be attributed to the cost of additional equipment acquired for achieving higher production rates. A significant portion of regular time production cost is spent as wages to the full-time work force. Such costs can be approximated to increase linearly with the size of the work force. However, industry surveys [23] indicate that firms attempt to maintain a constant work force size because of social pressures, public opinion, union contracts, and the high cost of training and severance associated with changes in the work force. Under these circumstances, the cost of the work force becomes a constant, as illustrated by the dotted line in figure 9.2.

The general shape of overtime costs for a given work force size is shown in figure 9.3. The costs are kept to a minimum when the facilities

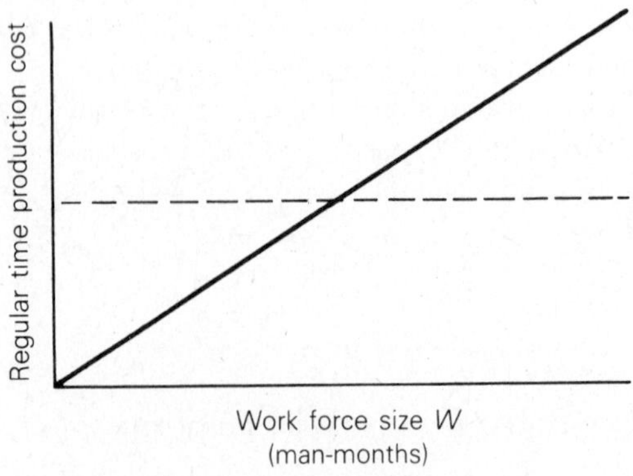

FIGURE 9.2 Cost of work force

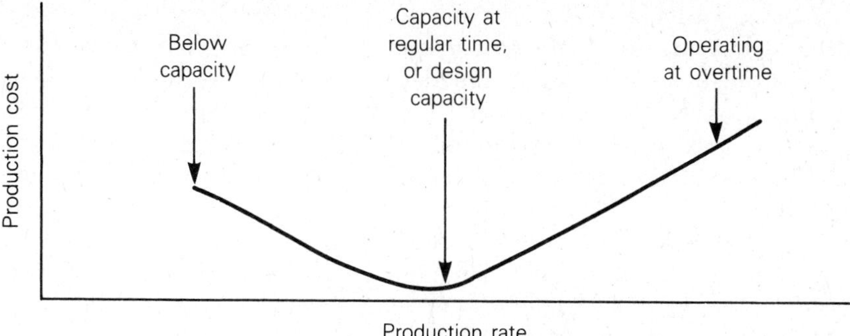

FIGURE 9.3 Cost of overtime and idle time

are operated at optimum level. The cost increases when the plant is operated below the designed capacity. With continued increases in demand, more and more production is scheduled, and the cost curve rises sharply at higher levels of production. The increases can be attributed to shift premium, supervision, and the decrease in productivity of workers as they toil through long hours.

THE COST OF CHANGING THE PRODUCTION RATE

These costs can be attributed primarily to changes in the size of the work force. The typical incremental cost of hiring and layoff is depicted in figure 9.4. When the size of the work force is increased, the firm incurs costs of hiring, training, and possible reorganization, resulting in lower productivity in the initial periods. Similarly, when employees are laid off, terminal pay, decreased morale in the remaining employees, and possible decreased productivity from the fear of losing their jobs increases the cost of production. Rarely is a laid off worker rehired for the same job. In

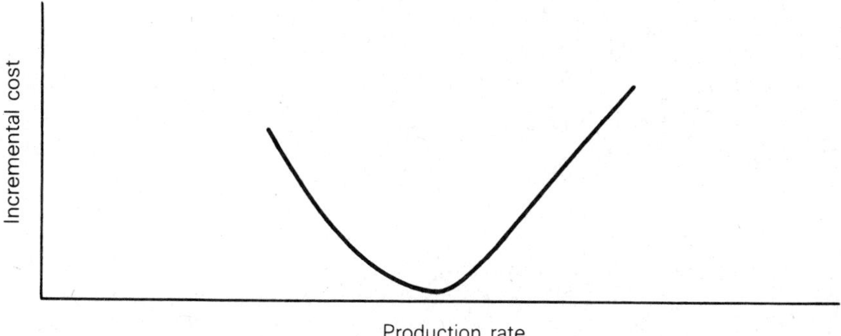

FIGURE 9.4 Cost of changing work force level

addition, social pressures, company image, and other factors prevent excessive hiring and firing. In many instances, union contracts and supplemental unemployment benefits (SUB) programs make it very costly for a firm to lay off workers. The incremental cost of increasing the production rate could be different from the incremental cost of decreasing the production rate, as illustrated by the shape of the curve along the vertical axis in figure 9.4.

In responding to changes in production levels, management should consider the costs of hiring and training and other associated layoff costs against the costs of overtime and undertime and the possible decrease in productivity caused by prolonged working hours.

INVENTORY, BACKORDER, AND SHORTAGE COSTS

There is a cost associated with funds used for inventories. The optimal aggregate inventory level may be approximated by the sum of the average safety stock plus half the optimal batch size, as determined for individual items. The aggregate inventory for an item is shown in figure 9.5. If $\bar{I}_t$ represents the amounts of inventory tied up in inventory at time t, and r is the unit cost of inventory for item i, then the total cost of inventory (C_I) for n periods is

$$C_I = \bar{I}_1 r + \bar{I}_2 r + \bar{I}_3 r + \ldots + \bar{I}_n r = r \sum^{n} \bar{I}_t$$

The cost per year of carrying inventory typically ranges from 5% to 50% of the value of items. The total inventory for all items is obtained by summing individual item inventory costs.

The cost of backordering and lost sales could also be treated in the same manner. If lost sales occur too often, it might provide an easy path to competition, and hence its cost could be high. The cost of lost sales is

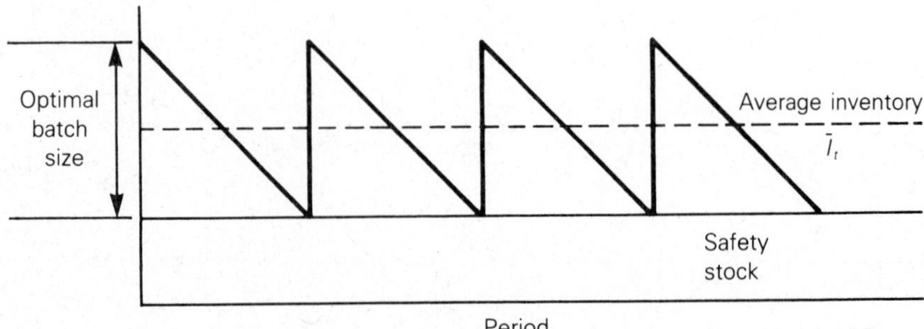

FIGURE 9.5 Aggregate inventory level

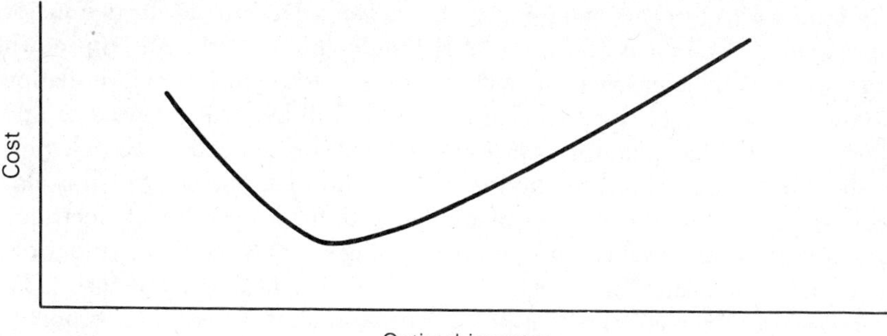

FIGURE 9.6 Cost of inventory and shortage

very difficult to estimate. For any given sales forecast (demand), the cost of inventory, backorder, and shortage can be approximated by the curve exhibited in figure 9.6.

We have discussed the determination of cost curves pertaining to optimal inventory associated with a sales forecast S_t. In fact, a whole set of such curves can be drawn, one for each value of S_t, as discussed by Holt et al. [12].

SUBCONTRACTING COSTS

As an alternative to changing production levels and carrying inventory, a firm may elect subcontracting to meet peak demands. Subcontracting may not be profitable, however, since the contractor may charge a much higher price. Subcontracting may also open the doors for competition. It is also hard, in many instances, to find a reliable supplier who delivers on time. Difficulties in forecasting the right quantities could result in excessive inventory or shortage costs.

So far, we have discussed various costs that could be used in a cost model; the costs are quantified in a later section of this chapter. It is important to keep in mind, however, that cost structures change over time. Hence, these cost models (estimates) must be continually updated to reflect ongoing changes.

Aggregate Planning Approaches

Aggregate planning is usually the responsibility of the operations manager. He or she must devise a strategy to meet changing needs so that total cost is minimized. Aggregate planning methods can be grouped into two major approaches. The first is the traditional top-down approach. The top-down approach uses the concept of an average or composite product in formulating the overall plan. The composite product plan will be disaggregated in due course for detailed planning purposes, which is discussed in the chapter on the MPS. The second method is the bottom-up approach, which is also known as capacity requirements planning. With the availability of electronic computers and material requirements planning systems, it becomes feasible to compile the plans for a total product line in one overall picture. The overall aggregate plan can then be evaluated in light of available resources and can be revised if necessary. This approach is dealt with in detail in the chapter on MRP. As we discussed earlier, production planning involves a great deal of time and money, and millions of combinations of resources are possible. In the next section we deal with some decision rules that have significant practical value in industry.

Aggregate Planning Methods

There are several methods for solving aggregate planning problems, including both qualitative and quantitative methods. The qualitative methods include consensus among groups and inventory ratios, among others. The quantitative methods consist of heuristic rules, explicit mathematical solutions, simulation, and other sophisticated search procedures. First, we will briefly summarize the qualitative methods of solving the problem. Second, we will describe the graphical and charting techniques. Finally, a detailed discussion will be provided of some viable quantitative approaches to the aggregate planning problem.

NONQUANTITATIVE OR INTUITIVE METHOD

In almost all organizations, there are always conflicting goals and views. The marketing department desires many product varieties and large buffer inventories. The manufacturing department prefers to keep as few products as possible and thus avoid any unneccessary setup costs. The financial controller would like as few inventory items as possible to minimize the investment in inventory and the carrying cost, whereas marketing desires to increase the service level by increasing safety stock inventories. The actual policy is usually dictated by the most persuasive individual, rather than according to economic measures. In general, this method is not desirable. In many industry situations, the management takes the previous plan and adjusts it slightly upward or downward to meet the present situation. Such a decision is not dependable if the previous plans were not close to optimal.

Unfortunately, in many instances they are not, and hence the management is locked into a series of poor plans.

INVENTORY RATIOS

Turnover ratio is a concept that is often used in production planning because the performance of managers is often measured by the turnover ratios their facility achieves. The ratio is defined as follows:

Turnover ratio = average sales/average inventory

However, using turnover ratios for controlling production capacity has a drawback. It leads to large gyrations in the inventory level for a fluctuating demand pattern [25], as illustrated by the following example. For simplicity, we shall consider the economic order quantity (EOQ) formula:

$$\text{Optimum inventory} = \left(\frac{1}{2}\right)\sqrt{\frac{2SD_t}{h}}$$

$$= K\sqrt{D}$$

where K is a constant, S is the setup cost, h is the holding cost and D_t is the demand during period t. Based on the optimum inventory model, the best turnover ratio is

$$\frac{D_t}{K\sqrt{D_t}} = \frac{\sqrt{D_t}}{K}$$

which is a function of demand. Since the demand is fluctuating, the turnover ratio is not a constant, and hence it is fallacious.

CHARTING AND GRAPHICAL METHODS

Charting and graphical techniques are easy to understand and convenient to use. These techniques basically work with a few variables at a time on a trial-and-error basis. They require only minor computational effort; a clerk can usually be trained to perform the calculations. The essence of an aggregate planning problem is best illustrated by means of production requirements charts and cumulative workload projections.

Example 9.1

ABC Corporation has developed a forecast for a group of items that has the following seasonal demand pattern:

Quarter	*Demand*	*Cumulative Demand*
1	220	220
2	170	390
3	400	790
4	600	1,390
5	380	1,770
6	200	1,970
7	130	2,100
8	300	2,400

1. Plot the demand as a histogram. Determine the production rate required to meet average demand, and plot the average demand forecast on the graph.
2. Plot the actual cumulative forecast requirements over time and compare them with the available average forecast requirement. Indicate the excess inventories and backorders on the graph.
3. Suppose that the firm estimates that it costs \$100 per unit to increase the production rate, \$150 to decrease the production rate, \$50 per quarter to carry the items on inventory, and an incremental cost of \$80 per unit if subcontracted. Compare the cost incurred if pure strategies are used.
4. Given these costs, design a mixed strategy solution for this problem.

The histogram and the cumulative requirements graph show how the forecast deviates from the average requirements (see figures 9.7 and 9.8). Using pure strategies, it is possible to come up with several plans as follows.

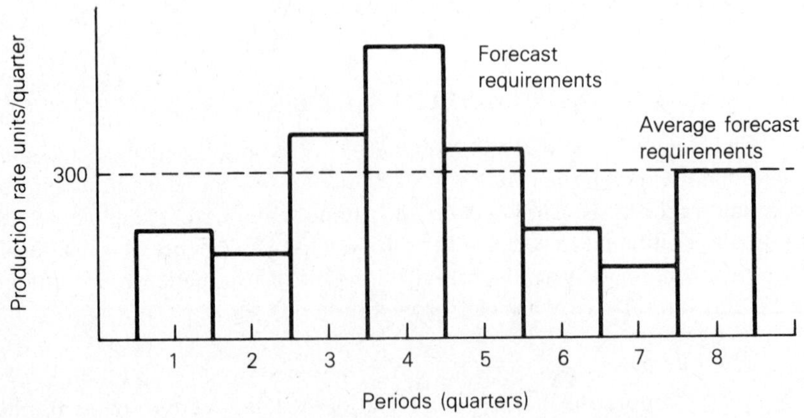

FIGURE 9.7 Histogram of forecast and average requirements

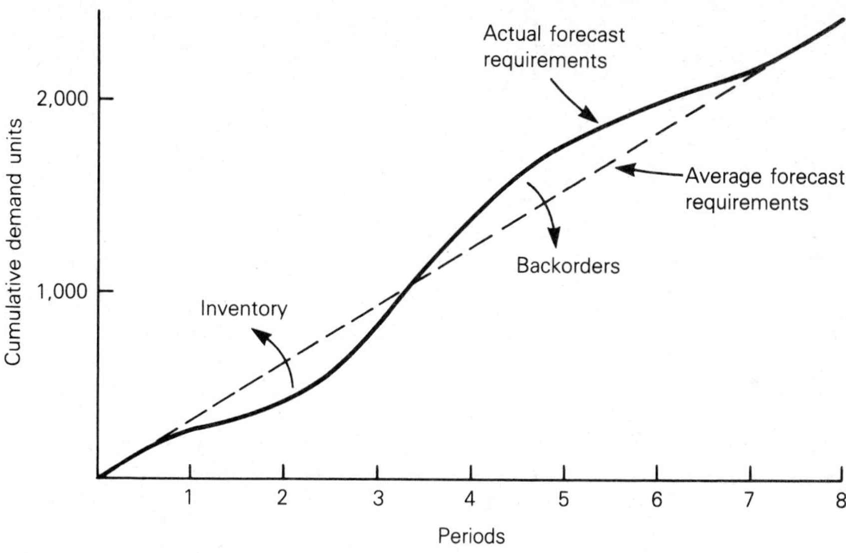

FIGURE 9.8 Cumulative and average forecast graph

Plan 1: Varying the Work Force Size. Demand can be met exactly by varying the work force size. The plan involves hiring and firing as necessary. The production rate will equal the demand. The cost of this plan is $138,000, as computed in table 9.1.

Plan 2: Changing Inventory Levels. Suppose that the firm wants to avoid frequent hiring and layoffs. The firm might choose a production level equal to its average demand and meet the variations in demand by holding inventory. The cost of such a plan is computed in table 9.2. The plan incurs a maximum shortage of 270 units during period 5. Since a certain amount

TABLE 9.1 Varying the Work Force Size to Meet the Demand

Quarter	*Demand Forecast*	*Cost of Increasing Production Level: Hiring ($)*	*Cost of Decreasing Production Level: Layoff ($)*	*Total Cost of Plan ($)*
1	220	—	—	—
2	170	—	7,500	7,500
3	400	23,000	—	23,000
4	600	20,000	—	20,000
5	380	—	33,000	33,000
6	200	—	27,000	27,000
7	130	—	10,500	10,500
8	300	17,000	—	17,000
Total				138,000

TABLE 9.2 Changing Inventory Levels to Meet the Demand

Quarter	*Demand Forecast*	*Cumulative Demand*	*Production Level*	*Cumulative Production*	*Inventory*	*Adjusted Inventory with 270 at Beginning of Period 1*	*Cost of Holding Inventories ($1000s)*
1	220	220	300	300	80	350	17.5
2	170	390	300	600	210	480	24.0
3	400	790	300	900	110	380	19.0
4	600	1,390	300	1,200	−190	80	4.0
5	380	1,770	300	1,500	−270	0	0
6	200	1,970	300	1,800	−170	100	5.0
7	130	2,100	300	2,100	0	270	13.5
8	300	2,400	300	2,400	0	270	13.5
Total							96.5

of uncertainty is involved in any forecast, the firm might decide to carry the inventory from the beginning of period 1. Adjusted inventories and cost of carrying inventories are shown. The total cost of the plan is $96,500. Notice, however, that if the item in question is high-fashion apparel, the firm might not want to carry unnecessary inventory, even though Plan 2 is less costly than Plan 1.

Plan 3: Subcontracting. The firm might prefer to produce an amount equal to its lowest requirements and meet the rest of the demand by subcontracting. The cost of such a plan amounts to $108,000, as computed in table 9.3. Again, it may not always be feasible or desirable to subcontract. This decision leads us to a fourth plan, involving a mixed strategy.

Plan 4: Mixed Strategy. As a compromise, a firm might combine the pure strategies, thus designing a mixed strategy. This mixed strategy varies production capacity slightly up or down as aggregate demand varies. Drastic changes in production capacity are curtailed, and frequent hiring and layoff situations are avoided. For example, based on past experience and available manpower, the management may decide to maintain a constant production rate of 200 per quarter and permit 25% overtime when the demand exceeds the production rate. To meet any further demand, it chooses to hire and lay off workers. Remember, in a mixed strategy, a host of other alternatives exist. Trial-and-error computations of such a plan can be carried out step by step, as shown in table 9.4.

Our results show that the mixed strategy incurs an incremental cost of $101,500. However, a smart manager would notice that subcontracting would be cheaper than hiring and layoffs in this situation. The manager might also analyze the effect of constant overtime production, if permissible. These variations are left as exercises for the reader in a problem at the end of this chapter. Several combinations of pure strategies are possible. In many instances, policies are dictated by upper management. Although mixed strategies using graphical methods are not optimal, they do provide lower management with practical guidelines for day-to-day operations. In

TABLE 9.3 Subcontracting Costs

Quarter	*Demand Forecast*	*Production Units*	*Subcontract Units*	*Incremental Cost at $80 per Unit ($)*
1	220	130	90	7,200
2	170	130	40	3,200
3	400	130	270	21,600
4	600	130	470	37,600
5	380	130	250	20,000
6	200	130	70	5,600
7	130	130	0	0
8	300	130	170	13,600
Total				108,800

TABLE 9.4 Mixed Strategy

Quarter	Units of Demand Forecast	Regular Time Production Units	Additional Units Needed After Regular Time	Overtime Production	Additional Units Needed After Regular Time + Overtime		Cost of Inventory ($)	Cost of Overtime ($)	Cost of Changing Work Force ($)	Total Cost ($)
1	220	200	20	50	−30	(−30)[c]	1,500	1,000	0	2,500
2	170	200	−30	—	−30[a]	(−60)	3,000	0	0	3,000
3	400	200	200	50	150[b]	(90)	0	1,000	9,000	10,000
4	600	200	400	50	350	(350)	0	1,000	26,000	27,000
5	380	200	180	50	130	(130)	0	1,000	33,000	34,000
6	200	200	0	—	—	—	0	0	19,500	19,500
7	130	200	−70	—	−70	(−70)	3,500	0	0	3,500
8	300	200	100	50	50	(−20)	1,000	1,000	0	2,000
Total										$101,500

[a] Note that the inventory in period 2 is sixty units.

[b] If the existing inventory of sixty units is used, an increase of only ninety units is required.

[c] Negative quantities in parentheses indicate inventories, and positive quantities in parentheses denote the quantities to be produced by changing the capacity.

the real world, firms that have some guidelines operate much more efficiently than those that do not.

MATHEMATICAL PROGRAMMING AND TABULAR METHODS

Several versions of mathematical programming models can be formulated, depending on the complexities of the assumptions that are made. Many models have been proposed by Bowman [3], Hanssmann and Hess [10], Von Lanzenauer [28], and others for solving aggregate planning problems. A few notable examples will be discussed in this section.

Transportation Model: Absorbing Demand Fluctuations with Regular Capacity and Overtime

The problem described here, originally formulated by Bowman [3], is a special case of a linear programming model. The transportation method can be used to analyze the effects of holding inventories or backordering, using overtime, and subcontracting. When more factors are introduced, such as hiring and layoffs or the cost of changing production level, the more flexible simplex method of linear programming must be used. The transportation models are relatively easy to solve with available computer routines. We will also see from the structure of the model that the full power of the transportation algorithm is not needed. We will elaborate on an algorithm proposed by Land [15] and on another shortcut tabular method for solving the special case of the transportation model. We will find from the following example that the tabular method is a convenient worksheet for these approaches.

Example 9.2: Absorbing Demand Fluctuations with Regular Capacity, Overtime, and Subcontracting

Warren Rogers Associates produces minicomputers that have a seasonal demand pattern. We are required to plan for the optimum production rates and inventory levels for the next four quarter periods. The available production capacities during regular time and overtime, as well as other cost data, are as follows:

Supply Capacity				*Demand Forecast*	
PERIOD	REGULAR TIME	OVERTIME	SUBCONTRACT	PERIOD	UNITS OF DEMAND
1	700	250	500	1	500
2	800	250	500	2	800
3	900	250	500	3	1,700
4	500	250	500	4	900

Available initial inventory: 100 units
Desired final inventory: 150 units
Regular time cost/unit: $100/unit

Overtime cost/unit: $125/unit
Subcontract cost/unit: $150/unit
Inventory cost/unit/period: $20/unit

Table 9.5 formulates the problem in the desired tabular format. The supply consists of beginning inventory and units that can be produced using regular time, overtime, and subcontracting. Demand consists of the individual period requirements and any desired final inventory. The costs of producing and carrying inventory until a later period are entered in the small boxes inside the individual cells of the matrix. The problem can now be solved utilizing the standard transportation algorithm or a computer software package. Land [15] apparently has been working on the same problem. He suggests an alternative easier method of arriving at the solution (see table 9.6). To facilitate easy understanding of the computations shown in table 9.6, we define the source codes as follows: 1 = regular time production, 2 = overtime production, 3 = subcontracted production. Columns 1 and 2 are self-explanatory; column 3 denotes the source of supply and its associated period. For example (1, 1) means that during period 1, from source 1 (regular time production), at a cost of $100 per unit (column 4), 700 units are available (column 6). A comparison of availabilities during period 1 indicates that source 1 is the least costly, source 2 the next least costly, and so on (column 5). Naturally, if all requirements were met by the least costly source, there would be no need to use other sources. However, these units can be made available for the next period if necessary, incurring an inventory carrying cost. The new cost is shown in column 9. Notice that the subcontractor does not charge an inventory cost. No matter how far in advance we order them, the subcontractor could deliver for the same price. During period 2, we list all available sources (1, 2, and 3) as well as the unused capacities from period 1, with the associated new cost. All sources are ranked for cost, and the iteration is repeated until demands for all periods are met. The total cost of such allocation amounts to $445,750.

Tabular Method

We suggest a much simpler approach. We deviate from the transportation procedure after the small boxes in each cell are posted with costs (see table 9.5). We inspect each forecast period column and select the source that costs the least, the next least, and so forth. In column 1, the beginning inventory is the cheapest source; in column two, procuring through regular time is next cheapest. Therefore, these allocations are made. Once the source is exhausted, we simply draw a dash in all cells corresponding to the source. During period 3, the allocation exhausts all current production sources. Three hundred units are obtained from the regular time production during period 1 and stored until period 3. Similarly, all other cheaper sources have been utilized, as we can see in table 9.5. The cost of this program is $445,750. The total is obtained by multiplying the quantity in each cell by the corresponding cost and then adding all costs.

Modifications to the Standard Transportation Method

We assumed in table 9.5 that products can always be stored and used during succeeding periods. However, a backorder situation was not considered. Since backordering assumes that current demand can be satisfied at a future time, appropriate cost figures can be entered in the boxes. Then the problem is solved in the usual manner. In many instances, there is a cost associated with the unused regular time capacity. If such costs are known, they should be posted in the corresponding cells. In table 9.5, notice that we have posted $40 per unit for the unused regular time production. The total cost of a program would be higher if the regular time capacity during any period were not used.

The problems illustrated so far started with initial inventory that was used during the first period. Because of uncertainties in demand, a firm may want to carry safety stocks. In such instances, the safety stocks should be added to the demand, and total production requirements for the periods should be computed as follows:

$$p_t = I_t + D_t - I_{t-1}$$

Once the initial tableau is formulated with correct requirements instead of demands, the problem may be solved in the usual manner. Problems at the end of this chapter illustrate this concept. Note that the inventory requirements are implicitly included in the demand function.

THE LINEAR PROGRAMMING METHOD

The tabular methods assumed that production capacities can be changed within the specified upper bounds. If hiring and layoffs were employed, the model ignored the penalty costs associated with those activities. Also, desired inventories were expressed implicitly in the demand row. In a linear programming (LP) formulation, however, all these variables and their associated costs can be stated explicitly. The LP algorithm provides a solution with a mixed strategy, so that the total cost of the program is minimized.

The use of the LP model implies that a linear function adequately describes the variables for the firm studied. Hanssmann and Hess [10] developed a comprehensive LP model for production planning that was followed by many others. Excellent discussions of various LP models are found in Buffa and Miller [5]. Groff and Muth [9], Lasdon and Terjung [16], Narasimhan and Gruver [20], and Shore [24]. For illustration purposes, we present here a variation of a simpler model formulated by Shore. We will start the discussion by listing many common assumptions; then we will present a specific model.

Assumptions

1. Demand rate D_t is known and is assumed to be deterministic for all future time periods.

TABLE 9.5 Transportation Method of Solving Aggregate Production Problem

Period	*Source of Supply/Production*	*Period in Which Product Is Forecast to Be Sold* 1	2	3	4	*Unused Capacity*	*Total Available Capacity*
	Beginning inventory	0 (100)	20 (—)	40 (—)	60 (—)	0 (—)	100
1	Regular time	100 (400)	120	140 (300)	160 (—)	40 (—)	700
	Overtime	125	145	165	185	0 (250)	250
	Subcontract	150	150	150	150	0 (500)	500
2	Regular time		100 (800)	120 (—)	140 (—)	40 (—)	800
	Overtime		125	145 (250)	165 (—)	0 (—)	250
	Subcontract		150	150	150	0 (500)	500
3	Regular time			100 (900)	120 (—)	40 (—)	900
	Overtime			125 (250)	145 (—)	0 (—)	250

	Subcontract			150	150	0 (500)	500
4	Regular time				100 (500)	40 (—)	500
	Overtime				125 (250)	0 (—)	250
	Subcontract				150 (300)	0 (200)	500
	Demand	500	800	1,700	1,050	1,950	6,000

Note: The cost of unused capacity during regular time costs $40 per unit. The solution provided inside the circles is explained by the tabular method.

TABLE 9.6 Solution to the Aggregate Production Problem Using Land's Algorithm

(1)	(2)		(3)		(4)	(5)	(6)	(7)	(8)	(9)	(10)
			Supply					*Used*	*Available*	*Cost at*	
Period	*Demand*		*Period*	*Source*	*Cost at t*	*Rank*	*Available at t*	*During t*	*at t − 1*	*t − 1 ($)*	*Total Cost ($) [(4) × (7)]*
	Initial inventory	100									
1	Demand	500	1	1	100	1	700	400	300	120	40,000
	Net requirement	400	1	2	125	2	250		250	145	
			1	3	150	3	500		500	150	
2	800		2	1	100	1	800	800	0		80,000
			2	2	125	3	250		250	145	
			2	3	150	5	500		500	150	
			1	1	120	2	300		300	140	
			1	2	145	4	250		250	165	
			1	3	150	5	500		500	150	
3	1,700		3	1	100	1	900	900			90,000
			3	2	125	2	250	250			31,250
			3	3	150	5	500		500	150	
			2	2	145	4	250	250			36,250
			2	3	150	5	500		500	150	
			1	1	140	3	300	300			42,000
			1	2	165	6	250		250	185	
			1	3	150	5	500		500	150	
4	Demand	900	4	1	100	1	500	500			50,000
	Inventory	150	4	2	125	2	250	250			31,250
	Total	1,050	4	3	150	3	500	300	200	150	45,000
			3	3	150	3	500		500	150	
			2	3	150	3	500		500	150	
			1	2	185	4	250		250	205	
			1	3	150	3	500		500	150	
Total cost											445,750

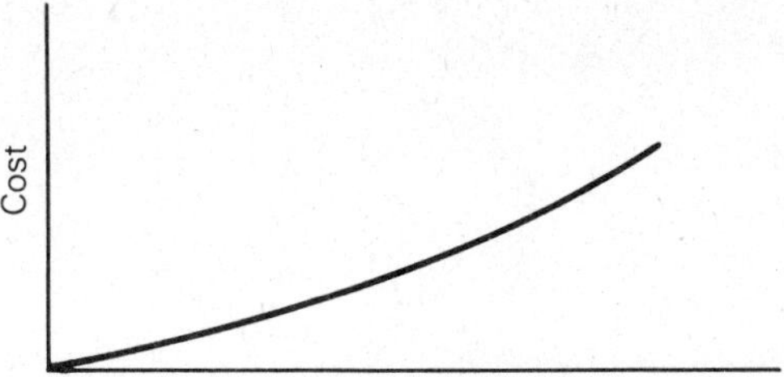

FIGURE 9.9 Regular time production rate

2. The costs of production during regular time are assumed to be piecewise linear, as exhibited in figure 9.9. To ensure that the regular time capacities are fully utilized before using overtime, and to avoid subcontracting before using all available overtime, the following cost assumption is made:

$$c_3 > c_2 > c_1$$

where c_1, c_2, and c_3 are the production costs during regular time, overtime, and subcontracting, respectively.

3. The costs of changes in production level are approximated by a piecewise linear function, as shown in figure 9.10.

4. Lower and upper bounds are usually specified on production quantities and on inventory levels, representing the limitations on capacities and available space, respectively.

5. A cost is always associated with inventory/backlog levels, although the unit cost could vary each period.

The Model

The objective function and constraints of a general linear model follow. In this model, it is assumed that the manager is interested in minimizing the total costs of production, hiring, layoffs, overtime, undertime, and inventory. Minimize

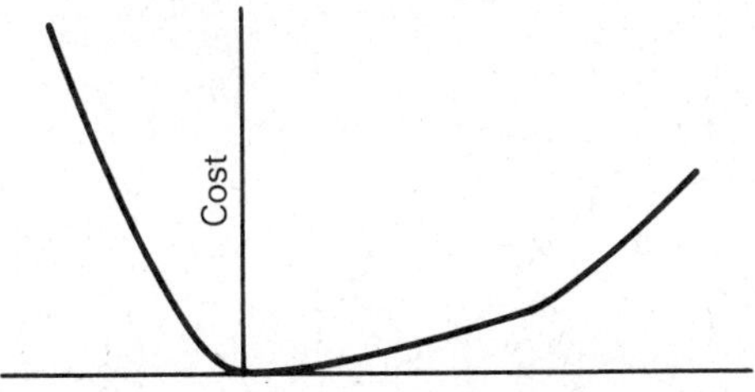

FIGURE 9.10 Changes in production level

$$C = r \sum_{t=1}^{k} P_t + h \sum_{t=1}^{k} A_t + f \sum_{t=1}^{k} R_t$$

$$+ v \sum_{t=1}^{k} O_t + c \sum_{t=1}^{k} I_t$$

Subject to constraints

$$P_t \leqslant M_t; \qquad t = 1, 2, \ldots, k \tag{9.1}$$

$$O_t \leqslant Y_t; \qquad t = 1, 2, \ldots, k \tag{9.2}$$

$$I_t = I_{t-1} + P_t + O_t - D_t; \qquad t = 1, 2, \ldots, k \tag{9.3}$$

$$A_t \geqslant P_t - P_{t-1}; \qquad t = 1, 2, \ldots, k \tag{9.4}$$

$$R_t \geqslant P_{t-1} - P_t; \qquad t = 1, 2, \ldots, k \tag{9.5}$$

and all

$$A_t, R_t, I_t, P_t, O_t \geqslant 0 \tag{9.6}$$

where r, v = cost/unit produced during regular time and overtime, respectively
P_t, O_t = units produced during regular time and overtime, respectively
h, f = hiring and layoff costs per unit, respectively
A_t, R_t = number of units increased or decreased, respectively, during consecutive periods
c = inventory costs per unit per period
D_t = sales forecast

The constraints (9.1) and (9.2) mean that the maximum production during regular time P_t and overtime O_t cannot exceed the available capacities M_t and Y_t, respectively. The third constraint expresses the inventory relationship. By defining the inventory variables as nonnegative, along with other variables in equation (9.6), we impose a no-backorder condition in the model. The constraints (9.4) and (9.5) expresses the hiring and layoffs when the production rate is increased or decreased during consecutive periods. Given the information required, the problem can be solved using any standard linear programming computer code.

Example 9.3

The following data were obtained from Joyce Manufacturing Company. Using the foregoing linear programming model, find the optimal production and work force levels. Backorders are not allowed.

$$\begin{array}{lll}
D_1 = 200 \text{ units} & M_1 = 180 & Y_1 = 30 \\
D_2 = 50 \text{ units} & M_2 = 120 & Y_2 = 20 \\
D_3 = 75 \text{ units} & M_3 = 120 & Y_3 = 20 \\
v = \$15/\text{unit} & f = \$10/\text{unit} & I_0 = 0 \\
c = \$5/\text{unit} & r = \$10/\text{unit} & \\
h = \$30/\text{unit} & P_0 = 150 &
\end{array}$$

Solution. The problem can be formulated as follows. Minimize

$$\begin{aligned}
C = {} & 10(P_1 + P_2 + P_3) + 30(A_1 + A_2 + A_3) \\
& + 10(R_1 + R_2 + R_3) + 15(O_1 + O_2 + O_3) \\
& + 5(I_1 + I_2 + I_3)
\end{aligned}$$

Subject to

$$\begin{aligned}
P_1 &\leqslant 180 \\
P_2 &\leqslant 120 \\
P_3 &\leqslant 120 \\
O_1 &\leqslant 30 \\
O_2 &\leqslant 20 \\
O_3 &\leqslant 20 \\
P_1 + O_1 - I_1 &= 200 \\
P_2 + O_2 + I_1 - I_2 &= 50 \\
P_3 + O_3 + I_2 - I_3 &= 75 \\
P_1 - A_1 &\leqslant 150 \\
-P_1 + P_2 - A_2 &\leqslant 0 \\
-P_2 + P_3 - A_3 &\leqslant 0 \\
P_1 + R_1 &\geqslant 150 \\
-P_1 + P_2 + R_2 &\geqslant 0 \\
-P_2 + P_3 + R_3 &\geqslant 0
\end{aligned}$$

and

$$P_t,\ O_t,\ A_t,\ R_t,\ I_t \geqslant 0$$

The linear programming problem is also exhibited in the tableau (figure 9.11). We can also solve the problem using any linear programming software package (we used the IBM-MPS package). The solution is as follows:

$$\begin{array}{lll}
P_1 = 170 & P_2 = 62.5 & P_3 = 62.5 \\
O_1 = 30 & O_2 = 0 & O_3 = 0 \\
I_1 = 30 & I_2 = 12.5 & I_3 = 0 \\
 & & \\
A_1 = 20 & A_2 = 0 & A_3 = 0 \\
R_1 = 0 & R_2 = 107.5 & R_3 = 0
\end{array}$$

$$C = \$5137.50$$

Obj. Fcn.	10	10	10	15	15	15	30	30	30	10	10	10	5	5	5			
Deci. Var.	P_1	P_2	P_3	O_1	O_2	O_3	A_1	A_2	A_3	R_1	R_2	R_3	I_1	I_2	I_3	Sign	RHS	Remarks
	1															≤	180	
		1														≤	120	
			1													≤	120	
				1												≤	30	
					1											≤	20	
						1										≤	20	
	1			1									−1			=	200	
		1			1								1	−1		=	50	
			1			1								1	−1	=	75	
	1						−1									≤	150	
	−1	1						−1								≤	0	
		−1	1						−1							≤	0	
	1									1						≥	150	
	−1	1									1					≥	0	
		−1	1									1				≥	0	

FIGURE 9.11 Linear programming tableau for Example 9.3

In this model the inventories were assumed to be nonnegative variable. However, if backorder is desired, the variable I_t can be replaced by an expression $I_t^+ + I_t^-$, where I_t^+ and I_t^- represent inventory and backlog, respectively, during period t. The modified inventory equation (9.3) is as follows:

$$I_t^+ - I_t^- = I_{t-1}^+ - I_{t-1}^- + P_t + O_t - D_t$$

Similarly, if the desired final inventory is given, we can substitute its value in the appropriate equation. For example, suppose that the desired final inventory was $I_3 = 25$ in the foregoing example. We would simply modify the relevant equation by substituting 25 for I_3. With these modifications, we can solve such problems using an LP computer software package. Several problems involving these modifications are given at the end of this chapter.

THE LINEAR DECISION RULE

The linear decision rule was developed by Holt, Modigliani, Muth, and Simon [12] (and thus is popularly known as the HMMS rule), followed by their extensive study in the paint factory. When the costs discussed earlier can be approximated by U-shaped quadratic functions, the resulting decision rule formula turns out to be of simple linear form. The HMMS rule is intended to make possible routine calculations of the volume of production and size of work force needed to be scheduled next period—month or week. The results are based on four cost factors: regular production costs, hiring and layoff costs, overtime and undertime costs, and inventory and shortage costs.

Regular Production Costs

The cost of regular time production is the function

$$C_t(1) = c_1 W(t) \tag{9.7}$$

It is assumed that the cost of production is linearly related to the size of the workforce W_t in period t, as shown in figure 9.12. Although a term involving an additional fixed cost could be added, it would not alter the optimal solution. The cost parameters here and in the following equations were determined from the company cost data.

Hiring and Layoff Costs

The cost of increasing and decreasing work force level is assumed to be a quadratic function:

$$C_t(2) = c_2[W_t - W_{t-1}]^2 \tag{9.8}$$

where $W_t - W_{t-1}$ is the change in the work force level from period $t - 1$ to period t. The function signifies that an increase or decrease in work force level means the same cost for the given amount. Differences in costs can be introduced by including a constant in expression (9.8). However, the optimal decision rule will not be affected.

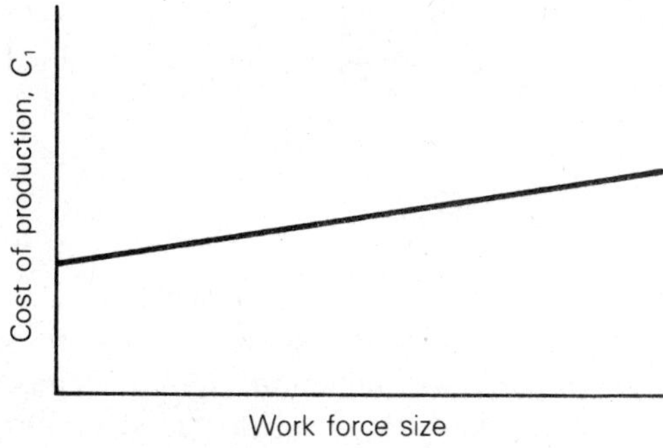

FIGURE 9.12 Regular production costs

Overtime and Undertime Costs

For any given work force size W_t, it is assumed that there is a desirable production rate KW_t. A lower production level means that workers are idling, and a higher production level signifies that overtime is required. The cost function is given by

$$C_t(3) = c_3[P_t - c_4 W_t]^2 + c_5 P_t - c_6 W_t \tag{9.9}$$

where P_t is the production rate and W_t is the size of the work force, as defined previously. The equation is quadratic in P_t and W_t. Note that the cost function is for a particular value of W_t and that a whole family of curves exists, one for each value of W_t.

Inventory and Shortage Costs

If the inventory level at the end of the period t is I_t, then

$$I_t = I_{t-1} + P_t - S_t \tag{9.10}$$

where I_{t-1} is the inventory at the end of period $t-1$ and S_t is the sales forecast of the actual shipments from the facility in period t. The total cost of inventory, including holding costs and shortage costs, is assumed to take the quadratic form:

$$C_t(4) = c_7\,[I_t - (c_8 + c_9 S_t)]^2 \tag{9.11}$$

Since the value of S_t is unknown, a whole family of curves based on each value of S_t can be drawn.

The Decision Rule

The total cost for any period t is given by

$$C_t = C_t(1) + C_t(2) + C_t(3) + C_t(4) \tag{9.12}$$

and total cost over t periods is given by the sum of individual period costs:

$$C_T = \sum_{t=1}^{T} \sum_{i=1}^{4} C_t(i)$$

It is important to note that we are attempting to minimize the expected costs. Since the exact demand is not known in advance, we deal in terms of average or expected costs. The minimization of the foregoing mathematical equation in terms of differentiation leads to the simple linear rules for W_t and P_t:

$$P_t = a_0S_t + a_1S_{t+1} + a_2S_{t+2} + \dots + g_1W_{t-1} - h_1I_{t-1} + c_1 \qquad (9.13)$$

$$W_t = b_0S_t + b_1S_{t+1} + b_2S_{t+2} + \dots + g_2W_{t-1} - h_2I_{t-1} + c_2 \qquad (9.14)$$

These equations are known as the production and employment linear decision rules. All lowercase coefficients are constants. Notice that each equation consists of a series of terms that include the forecasts for a given number of future periods, and that each expression considers the present levels of inventory and manpower as well as the weighted forecast of sales. The optimal decision rules for the paint factory were derived by Holt, Modigliani, Muth, and Simon [12] as follows:

$$P_t = \begin{bmatrix} 0.463S_t \\ 0.234S_{t+1} \\ 0.111S_{t+2} \\ 0.046S_{t+3} \\ 0.013S_{t+4} \\ -0.002S_{t+5} \\ -0.008S_{t+6} \\ -0.010S_{t+7} \\ -0.009S_{t+8} \\ -0.008S_{t+9} \\ -0.007S_{t+10} \\ -0.005S_{t+11} \end{bmatrix} + 0.993W_{t-1} - 0.464I_{t-1} + 153 \qquad (9.15)$$

$$W_t = 0.743W_{t-1} + 2.09 - 0.010I_{t-1} + \begin{bmatrix} 0.0101S_t \\ 0.0088S_{t+1} \\ 0.0071S_{t+2} \\ 0.0054S_{t+3} \\ 0.0042S_{t+4} \\ 0.0031S_{t+5} \\ 0.0023S_{t+6} \\ 0.0016S_{t+7} \\ 0.0012S_{t+8} \\ 0.0009S_{t+9} \\ 0.0006S_{t+10} \\ 0.0005S_{t+11} \end{bmatrix} \qquad (9.16)$$

The total cost of the program is given by

$$\begin{aligned} C_N = \sum_{t=1}^{n} \{&(340W_t) + [64 \cdot 3(W_t - W_{t-1})^2] \\ &+ [0.20\,(P_t - 5.67W_t)^2 + 51.2P_t - 281W_t] \\ &+ [0.0825\,(I_t - 310)^2]\} \end{aligned}$$

To determine the aggregate production rate, equations (9.15) and (9.16) would be used at the beginning of each month. They are easy to compute using a calculator; a trained clerk can accomplish this job easily.

MANAGEMENT COEFFICIENT MODEL

Models discussed in previous sections attempted to capture the important trade-offs required by complex analytical structures. Difficulties arise, however, when we estimate the esoteric costs required for complex mathematical models. As an alternative, Bowman [4] developed the management coefficient model on the premise that management's past decisions can be incorporated into a system for improving present decisions. Based on his extensive consulting experience, Bowman reasoned that managers are aware of and sensitive to the variables that are important in the aggregate planning decisions. Managerial decisions might be improved by making them consistent from one time to another rather than by using optimal solution approaches, especially for problems where intangibles, such as runout cost or delay penalties, must be estimated or assumed. Using statistical regression analysis, rules can be developed that are generally of the following form:

$$P_t = a_1 S_t + a_2 W_{t-1} - a_3 I_{t-1} + a_4$$

$$W_t = b_1 S_t + b_2 W_{t-1} - b_3 I_{t-1} + b_4$$

where parameters a and b are constants derived from the regression techniques according to the past experience of the firm. These equations are based on the managerial decisions with the current workforce W_{t-1} and inventory level I_{t-1}, as well as the demand forecast S_t for the period t. Many multiple regression models may also be derived. For example, the model may account for the forecast in period $t + 1$, taking the form

$$P_t = a_1 S_t + a_2 S_{t-1} + a_3 W_{t-1} + a_4 I_{t-1} + a_5$$

Bowman [4] remarks, however, that as the number of forecast periods in the model increases, the regression gives poor results because of the high correlation between the forecast estimates. We note that as the number of forecast periods increases to eleven, Bowman's model becomes similar to the HMMS model. Using the cost equation provided by the HMMS model, however, we can predict the cost of implementing the decisions. Bowman's model also implies that the number of demand forecasts incorporated in the HMMS model is relatively unimportant. This is true in the sense that these constants are small and are uncertain. Neglecting these forecasts would not alter the solution significantly.

DIRECT SEARCH METHODS AND SIMULATION

The linear decision rule assumes that a quadratic equation can be fitted to an organization's cost data. The relationships and cost functions between variables are assumed to be linear in the linear programming approach. It may be an inaccurate oversimplification, in many instances, to assume that these relationships are quadratic or linear. Linear decision rule and linear programming procedures also place restrictions on the mathematical structure necessary for the functions to be optimized, although they provide an optimum solution to the assumed model. The true cost, however, might need a higher order equation. The mathematical complexity of the problem increases greatly when equations of higher order or step functions are present. Simulation and search methods can be used to obtain optimal solutions. Using computers, we can find many possible relationship values of the variables, select one that is acceptable, and provide a near optimal solution.

Three such models gained prominence in the 1960s. The structures of the cost equations and the methods used to obtain the optimum decision varied in these models. In 1966, Vergin [27] formulated a model that he called "scheduling by simulation." This computer simulation procedure used a search procedure to seek the minimum cost combination of values for the size of the work force and the production rate.

In 1967, Jones [14] published a method he called "parametric production programming" (PPP). The PPP method used a computer search routine to examine various possible values for four parameters within the decision rule equations. Once the equation parameters were obtained satisfactorily, the decision rule could be applied as in the linear decision rule model. The advantage of the PPP model, however, was that it didn't restrict the cost equations to any specific form, as linear decision rule or linear programming methods do.

In 1968, Taubert [26] published a procedure called the "search decision rule" (SDR) using the paint company data with the linear decision rule optimum solution as a test function. The SDR approach does not restrict the mathematical form of the cost equation and hence it is superior to any linear, quadratic, or dynamic programming approach designed so far for this purpose. Taubert used a pattern search technique, which starts at a base point with a trial set of values for the work force size (W_t) and production rate (P_t) for, say, the ten periods in the planning horizon. The model works with these twenty variables to arrive at a best combination. Small movements (variations in magnitude) are tested in a pattern around their base point, and the most promising direction is selected. A new trial point is selected by moving in the most promising direction. If this new trial point decreases the cost, it becomes the new base point, and the search continues for the new trial point. If the trial point does not improve the solution, however, the search goes back to the old base point and moves in a different direction to check whether the solution can be improved. The search terminates if no improvement can be found in any direction. The values for W_t and P_t of the current base point are recommended by the decision rule.

A flow chart of Taubert's search procedure is exhibited in figure 9.13. Taubert points out that the pattern search method is adaptive and heuristic. For example, if the best direction to move in is the one that would be expected from the last move, the search proceeds in larger steps. If the solution doesn't improve, then a smaller step is taken from the base point. The adaptive search feature reduces the computer time necessary to complete the minimization process. It is important to note that the SDR approach does not guarantee optimality of solutions, although it facilitates specification of a realistic cost model. For practical purposes, however, this will be one of the satisfying solutions.

Summary

The function of an intermediate-range aggregate plan is to anticipate forthcoming changes in work force and production and to set overall goals for output rates. The overall goals may be translated into a detailed schedule, at least for the first planning period. Therefore, it is important to obtain the best possible information for generating the plans. We have discussed many aggregate planning techniques that are suitable for either hand computation or computer-assisted methods. Table 9.7 compares the advantages and limitations of the various methods discussed in this chapter. The selection of an alternative plan is a trade-off between the desired accuracy and the cost of implementing such a program. Regardless of the method used, implementation of the plan is what matters. One problem could be obtaining necessary data. Cost data are usually obtained by using cost accounting methods; demand data from marketing and other sources; and capacity data from shop records. It is important to realize that many of the restrictions imposed on the plan are subjective. It is also essential to include as many constraints as possible when developing and evaluating alternate plans. In certain instances, very elaborate forecasting methods may be justified. For example, sophisticated methods may be used for demand forecasting, or learning curves could be used for calculating exact capacities. Although our discussion of aggregate plans centered on the manufacturing environment, plans for service systems are not much different. For some systems that supply standardized services to customers, aggregate planning may be even simpler than it is for production systems. Service industries include trucking firms, automotive services, fast-food stores, and banks and savings associations. Developing aggregate plans for these systems poses no additional problems beyond those faced by most manufacturing systems.

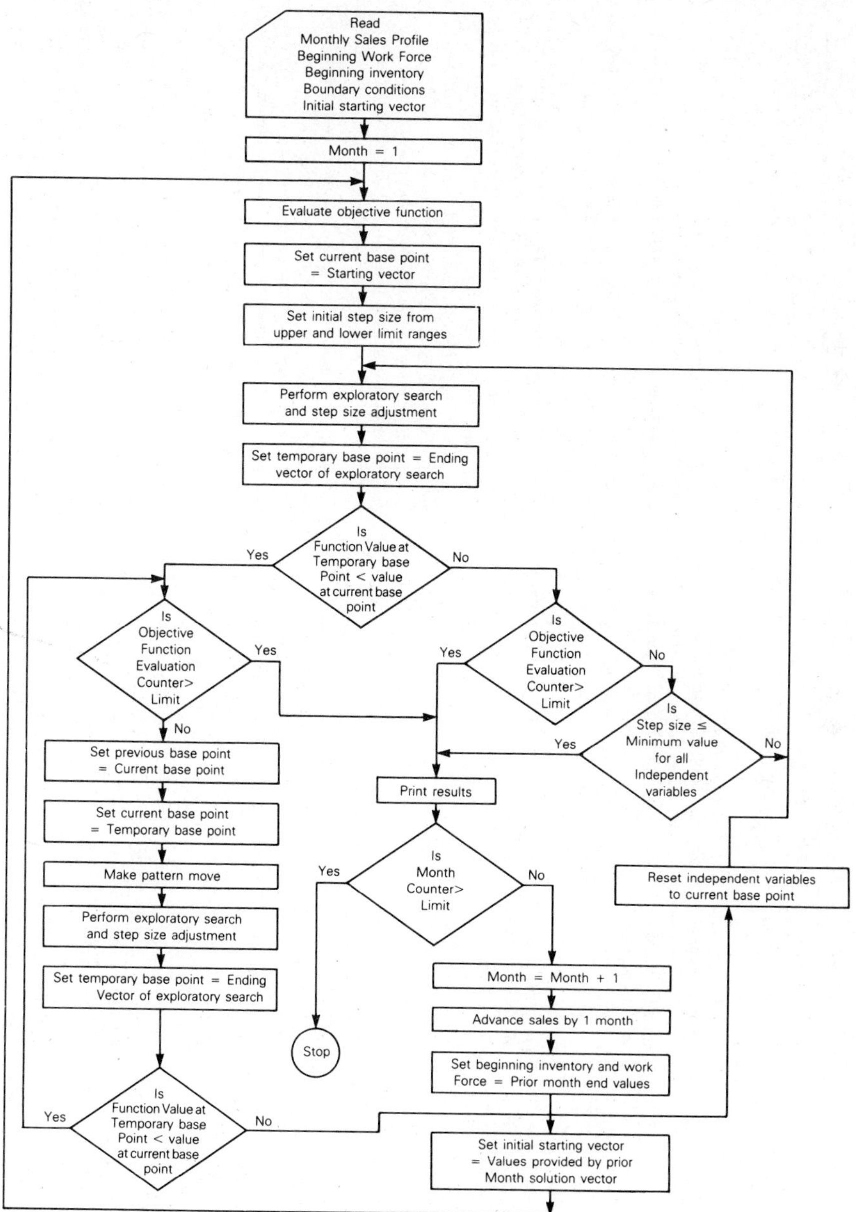

FIGURE 9.13 Flow chart of the search decision rule heuristic

Source: From W. H. Taubert, "A Searcg Decision Rule for the Aggregate Scheduling Problems," *Management Science*, Vol. 14, No. 6 (February 1968), pp. 343–359. Reprinted with the permission of *Management Science*.

TABLE 9.7 Comparison of Aggregate Planning Methods

Technique	*Advantages*	*Limitations*
1. Graphical methods	Simple to understand and easy to use	Millions of solutions; chosen solution need not be optimal
2. Linear programming	Provides an optimal solution; several LP computer routines available; a popular tool in business and industry, and many managers seem to understand; sensitivity analysis easy to do; easy to add constraints on the availability of resources, warehouse space limitation, etc.; dual solutions provide shadow prices and help determine maximum allowable warehouse space, etc.	Mathematical functions must be linear; may not be realistic in real-world situations, although all right in most situations; ignores economic lot sizes for production runs; may plan for less than full capacity in some periods Demand is deterministic, but studies indicate it is acceptable so long as the data are updated periodically
3. Linear decision rule	Demand patterns need not be deterministic; provides an optimum solution to the given problem	Model development takes 1–3 months; incorporates some complex costs that are not available in a standard accounting system; ability to translate data into quadratic relationships needs very skilled personnel, and the quadratic relationship need not be true; model is insensitive to errors in cost estimates; values of variables are unconstrained; feasible solution is not guaranteed, although it is optimal
4. Management coefficients model	Attempts to duplicate managers' decision-making process; simplest, least disruptive, and easiest to implement, since it was developed from the past experience of management; when managers have limited information of forecasts, a plan based on past decision behavior is very useful for production planning	Solution need not be optimal; assumes past decisions are good, which may not be true; takes a few man days to come up with a model; built on individual's behavior; any changes in personnel invalidate the model; selection of the rule is subjective
5. Search decision rules	Permits any realistic modeling by allowing all types of cost functions; alternative decisions can be tested; sensitivity analysis can be performed; modifications and variations to cost functions easily incorporated	Not absolute global optimum; takes 3–6 months' effort to develop a model; solution could be different depending on search routine used; cannot predict which search routine is more efficient for the given function; number of variables restricted because of response surface limitations, and cost of search cycle is expensive; requires expertise to use

PROBLEMS

1. Warren Rogers Associates has the following expected production capacity and demand:

Quarter	*Capacity*	*Demand*
1	300	300
2	400	600
3	450	300
4	550	500

The company does not accept any backorders and wishes to fulfill demand by letting inventories absorb all fluctuations. How many minicomputers must they have on hand on January 1 in order to meet the forecast demand throughout the year?

2. The vice-president of the Koza Company has estimated the following demand requirements for the forthcoming periods:

Period	*Forecast*	*Period*	*Forecast*
1	1,400	5	2,200
2	1,600	6	2,200
3	1,800	7	1,800
4	1,800	8	1,400

The operations manager is considering the following plans:

Plan 1: Maintain a stable work force that is capable of producing 1,800 units per period, and meet the demand by overtime at a premium of $50 per unit. Idle time costs are equivalent to $60 per unit.

Plan 2: Produce at a steady rate of 1,600 units per period, and accept a limited number of backorders during periods when demand exceeds 1,600 units. The stockout cost of lost sales is $100 per unit. Inventory costs per period are $20 per unit.

Plan 3: Produce at a steady rate equal to minimum requirements of 1,400 units, and subcontract the additional units at a $75 per unit premium.

Plan 4: Vary the work force level, which is currently capable of producing 1,600 units per period. The cost of additional work force per 100 units is $5,000, and the cost of layoffs per 100 units is $7,500.

Plan 5: Vary inventory levels, but maintain a stable work force level by maintaining a constant production rate equal to the average requirements. The company can accumulate required inventory before period 1 at no additional cost. The inventory cost per period is $20 per unit. Plot a histogram for the demand and show the average requirements on your graph.

Discuss the merits and disadvantages of these plans. Which plan would you recommend?

3. The operations manager at Koza Company is considering the following mixed strategies. The costs given in problem 2 are also applicable to this problem.

   Plan 6: Maintain the current stable work force level, which is capable of producing 1,600 units per period. Permit a maximum of 20% overtime at a premium of $50 per unit. Warehouse space constrains the maximum allowable inventory to 200 units.

   Plan 7: Maintain the current work force level, which is capable of producing 1,600 units per period. Subcontract the rest of the requirements. A current inventory of 400 units is available.

   Compare these strategies with the solutions obtained in problem 2 and make your recommendations.

4. Triden maintains a steady work force of 40 men per month. The company wants to analyze the cost of a mixed strategy employing inventories, overtime, and subcontracting as a means of absorbing demand. The cost per unit during regular time is $60, during overtime, $70; the cost of carrying is $5 per month; the cost of unused regular time capacity is $15. Find the optimum production cost for the plan, given the monthly demands and capacities shown in table 9.8.

5. The OBS Company has a regular time production capacity of 30 units per period, and the subcontractor can supply a maximum of 50 units per period. The management forecasts the demand for the next four periods at 35, 20, 50, and 40 units. Given a production

TABLE 9.8 Monthly Demands and Capacities, Problem 4

	January	*February*	*March*	*Unused*	*Capacity*
January					
Regular time					600
Overtime					300
Subcontracted					500
February					
Regular time					300
Overtime					300
Subcontracted					500
March					
Regular time					200
Overtime					300
Subcontracted					500
Demand	900	300	700		

cost of \$100 per unit, a subcontract cost of \$130 per unit, an inventory cost of \$2 per unit per period, and an unused production capacity cost of \$50 per unit, provide a production plan for the company.

6. Giant Factory, Inc., found the following modified HMMS model to be very useful in aggregate planning:

$$P_t = \begin{bmatrix} 0.50S_t \\ 0.25S_{t+1} \\ 0.10S_{t+2} \\ 0.05S_{t+3} \\ 0.01S_{t+4} \end{bmatrix} + W_{t-1} + 150 - 0.50\, I_{t-1}$$

$$W_t = 0.75\, W_{t-1} + (2.0 - 0.01 I_{t-1}) + \begin{bmatrix} 0.012S_t \\ 0.010S_{t+1} \\ 0.008S_{t+2} \\ 0.006S_{t+3} \\ 0.004S_{t+4} \end{bmatrix}$$

Given a forecast demand for the next six months of 621, 415, 380, 763, 845, and 550 and an initial inventory and work force size of 350 and 85, respectively, find the production plan for the next two months.

7. Determine the optimal production rates and work force levels for the next four quarterly periods. The forecast demands for the next four quarters are 1,600, 2,100, 1,800, and 1,950 units (a final inventory of 300 units is desired at the end of the fourth quarter). The following information is available from the company records.

   Current work force: 600 workers
   Current inventory level: 200 units
   Inventory holding cost: \$50/unit/quarter
   Backorder cost: \$100/unit/quarter
   Cost of hiring: \$1,000/person
   Cost of layoff: \$1,200/person
   Regular time payroll cost: \$5/hour
   Overtime payroll cost: \$7.50/hour

   Each unit requires 160 man hours to produce. Assume that each quarterly period consists of 480 regular time hours.

8. Dannon Company produces several types of slacks for retailing through department stores. The aggregate forecast (in thousands) for the next eight months is as follows:

	1	*2*	*3*	*4*	*5*	*6*	*7*	*8*
Forecast	100	200	200	150	200	250	100	125

Regardless of the type of material and the size, all of the slacks take approximately the same amount of time to manufacture. The total cost of producing one unit during regular time and overtime is \$3 and \$4, respectively. With the current regular time capacity they can produce 150,000 slacks per month. Each person can produce 400 and 80 slacks per month during regular and overtime, respectively. The cost of hiring and laying off per worker amounts to \$200 and \$300, respectively. If the demand is not met during the month, the sales are lost. Inventory carrying cost amounts to 2% per month. The present inventory is 50,000 slacks.

a. Set up the equations for the linear programming problem.
b. Solve, using an LP code.

9. For the Dannon Company, which one of the following plans would maximize their gross margin if their slacks are sold at \$4.25?

   Plan 1: Maintain the present work force and use overtime for additional needs.

   Plan 2: Vary the work force to meet the needs of the month by hiring and laying off workers, and work during regular time only.

   Plan 3: Maintain a work force approximately equal to the minimum requirements. Subcontract the rest at \$1.10 incremental cost.

   Graph the production and requirements for all the plans.

10. For the ABC Corporation example in this chapter (Example 9.1), the manager decides that he can have two hours of overtime per day. If it is not sufficient, he will add an eight-hour Saturday as overtime. Based on this information, design a strategy, assuming that it costs \$50 more per unit for overtime.

11. In problem 8, if the Dannon Company were able to hold back orders at 5% per month, what would be your solution?

12. In problem 4, suppose that Triden has an initial inventory of 50 units and requires 200 units of safety stock at the end of March. What is the new optimum solution?

13. Clarkson Company is a producer of microwave ovens. A schedule of their expected production capacity and demand is as follows:

Month	*Capacity*	*Demand*
1	700	650
2	700	650
3	750	850
4	780	800
5	800	750
6	800	900

The company does not accept backorders and wishes to absorb all fluctuations through their inventory. How many ovens must they have on hand on January 1 to meet the forecast demand for the first six months?

14. A producer of display panels expects the following production capacity and demand for its product:

Month	*Capacity*	*Demand*
1	400	400
2	400	450
3	450	450
4	460	500
5	480	500
6	500	500
7	550	520
8	550	530
9	550	600
10	600	650
11	550	600
12	550	600

Assuming that the company lets its inventory absorb demand fluctuations, and with a January 1 inventory on hand of 300 units, what can it expect its December 31 inventory balance to be? Assuming an inventory cost of $2 per unit per period, calculate the total and average inventory costs.

15. The operations manager at Jarrett, Inc., has received estimates for demand requirements for the next six months, as follows:

Month	*Forecast*
1	1000
2	1200
3	1400
4	1800
5	1800
6	1600

The following plans are being considered:

Plan 1: Maintain a stable work force that is capable of producing 1,500 units per month, and meet the demand by overtime at a premium of $50 per unit. Idle time costs are equivalent to $60 per unit.

Plan 2: Produce at a steady rate of 1,300 units per period, and accept a limited number of backorders during periods when demand exceeds 1,300 units. Stockout costs of lost sales are $100. Inventory costs per period are $25 per unit.

Plan 3: Produce at a steady rate equal to minimum requirements of 1,000 units, and subcontract the additional units at a $60 per unit premium.

Plan 4: Vary the work force level, which is at a current production level of 1,300 units per period. The cost of additional work force per 100 units is $3,000, and the cost of layoffs per 100 units is $6,000.

Plan 5: Maintain a stable work force, and vary inventory levels by maintaining a constant production rate equal to average requirements. Inventory required before January 1 has no additional cost. The inventory cost per month after January 1 is $25 per unit. Plot a histogram for the demand, and show the average requirements on your graph.

Discuss the merits and disadvantages of these plans. Which plan would you recommend?

16. In addition, the operations manager at Jarrett, Inc., will consider the following mixed strategies. The costs in problem 15 apply to this problem also.

    Plan 6: Maintain the current work force level capable of producing 1300 units per period. Subcontract the rest of the requirements. A current inventory of 300 is available.

    Plan 7: Maintain the current work force level capable of producing 1300 units per period. Permit a maximum of 20% OT at a premium of $40 per unit. Warehouse space constrains the maximum allowable inventory to 180 units. Subcontract the rest of the requirements at $60 per unit incremental cost.

    Compare these strategies with those in problem 15 and make your recommendations.

17. Crandell Co. maintains a steady work force of 30 men per month. The company desires to analyze the cost of a strategy employing inventory/overtime as a means of absorbing demand. The cost per unit during regular time is $50; during overtime it is $60; the cost of carrying is $5 per month; the cost of unused regular time capacity is $10. Find the optimum production cost for the plan, given the following monthly demands and capacities: the initial inventories amount to 100 units in January; regular time capacity is 500 units; overtime capacity is 300 units; and the demand for the next three months is 500, 700, and 900.

18. Conrad Corporation has a regular time production capacity of 50 units per month, and the subcontractor can supply a maximum of 40 units per month. Forecast demand for the next six months is 60, 40, 65, 70, 35, and 65 units. Given that production cost is $150 per unit, inventory cost is $5 per unit per month, and unused capacity cost is $75 per unit, provide a production plan for the company.

19. Determine optimal production rates and work force levels for the next four quarters. The forecast demands are 2,200, 2,700, 2,300, and 2,500 units, and a final inventory of 500 units is desired at the end of the fourth quarter. The following information is available from the company's records.

    Current inventory level: 300 units
    Current work force: 700 workers.
    Inventory holding cost: $75/unit/quarter
    Backorder cost: $125/unit/quarter
    Cost of hiring: $1,500/person
    Cost of layoffs: $1,600/person
    Regular time payroll cost: $10/hour
    Overtime payroll cost: $15/hour

    Each unit requires 200 man hours to produce. Assume that each quarterly period consists of 600 regular time hours.

20. Determine optimal production rates and work force levels for the next six months. Forecast demands are 800, 900, 1,200, 1,000, 1,600, and 1,400 units. Final inventory desired is 250. The following information is available:

    Current inventory level: 200 units
    Current workforce: 300 workers
    Inventory holding cost: $50/unit/month
    Backorder cost: $75/unit/month
    Hiring cost: $800/person
    Layoff cost: $1000/person
    Regular time payroll cost: $7.50/hour
    Overtime payroll cost: 10.00/hour

    Each unit requires 120 man hours to produce. Assume that each month consists of 240 regular time hours.

21. Develop the objective function and the constraint equations for the following aggregate output problem. Assume an eight-hour, twenty-day month. Man-hour demands for the next six months are 35,000, 25,000, 40,000, 45,000, 40,000, and 30,000. The costs are as follows:

    Inventory holding cost: $0.30/manhour/month
    Regular time cost: $6/manhour

Overtime cost: \$9/manhour
Hiring cost: \$300/worker
Layoff cost: \$500/worker

The initial status consists of a current work force of 220 workers, and a current inventory of 10,000 manhours.

22. MBI, Inc., manufactures snowmobiles. The company uses the management coefficient model for their aggregate planning;

$$P_t = 2.05_t + 1.75W_t - .05I_{t-1} + 25$$

$$W_t = 0.9W_{t-1} + 0.3S_t - 0.1I_{t-1} + 10$$

At present, MBI has 150 workers and an initial inventory of 500 units. Determine the production level and work force necessary for the next six months. The forecast demands for the next six months are 1,000, 800, 1,500, 1,200, and 1,150. Comment on the quality of the production and work force equations based on your results. Can you come up with a better set of equations?

23. Consider the HMMS model given in this chapter. Given the following information, find the production level, work force, and total cost for the next two periods.

Period	*Forecast*	*Period*	*Forecast*
1	1,000	8	1,300
2	1,500	9	1,500
3	2,000	10	1,600
4	1,750	11	1,400
5	2,000	12	1,300
6	1,800	13	1,700
7	2,200	14	1,600

The current workforce is 200 workers, and the initial inventory is 850 units.

24. Given the following additional data, design a mixed strategy for Example 9.1 in the text:
    a. Use a constant overtime of 50 units per period.
    b. Increase the initial output by 10% and a constant overtime of 50 units per period.

REFERENCES AND BIBLIOGRAPHY

1. G. L. Bergstrom and B. E. Smith, "Multi Item Production Planning—An Extension of the HMMS Rules," *Management Science*, Vol. 16, No. 10 (June 1970), pp. 614–629.

2. A. B. Bishop and T. H. Rockwell, "A Dynamic Programming Computational Procedure for Optimal Loading in a Large Aircraft Company," *Operations Research*, Vol. 6, No. 6 (November–December 1958), pp. 835–848.
3. E. H. Bowman, "Production Scheduling by the Transportation Method of Linear Programming," *Operations Research*, Vol. 4, No. 1 (February 1956), pp. 100–103.
4. E. H. Bowman "Consistency and Optimality in Managerial Decision Making," *Management Science*, Vol. 9, No. 2 (January 1963), pp. 310–321.
5. E. S. Buffa and J. G. Miller, *Production-Inventory Systems: Planning and Control*, (Homewood, Ill.: Richard D. Irwin, 1979).
6. R. J. Ebert, "Aggregate Planning with Learning Curve Productivity," *Management Science*, Vol. 23, No. 2 (October 1976), pp. 172–182.
7. S. Eilon, "Five Approaches to Aggregate Production Planning," *AIIE Transactions*, Vol. 7, No. 1 (June 1975), pp. 118–131.
8. J. H. Greene (Ed.), *Production and Inventory Control Handbook*. (New York: McGraw-Hill, 1970).
9. G. K. Groff and J. F. Muth, *Operations Management: Analysis for Decision*. (Homewood, Ill.: Richard D. Irwin, 1972).
10. F. Hanssmann and S. W. Hess, "A Linear Programming Approach to Production and Employment Scheduling," *Management Technology*, Vol. 1 (January 1960), pp. 46–52.
11. A. Hax and H. Meal, "Hierarchical Integration of Production Planning and Scheduling," in M. A. Geisler (Ed.), *Studies in Management Sciences: Vol. 1. Logistics*, (New York: North Holland, 1975).
12. C. C. Holt, F. Modigliani, J. F. Muth, and H. A. Simon, *Planning Production, Inventories and Workforce*. (Englewood Cliffs, N.J.: Prentice-Hall, 1960).
13. R. E. Johnson and L. B. Schwarz, "An Appraisal of the Empirical Performance of the Linear Decision Rule for Aggregate Planning," *Management Science*, Vol. 24, No. 8 (April 1978), pp. 844–849.
14. C. H. Jones, "Parametric Production Planning," *Management Science*, Vol. 15, No. 11 (July 1967), pp. 843–866.
15. A. H. Land, "Solution of a Purchase Storage Programme: Part II," *Operational Research Quarterly*, Vol. 9, No. 3 (1958), pp. 188–197.
16. L. S. Lasdon and R. C. Terjung, "An Efficient Algorithm for Multi Item Scheduling," *Operations Research*, Vol. 19, No. 4 (July–August 1971), pp. 946–965.
17. W. B. Lee and B. Khumawala, "Simulation Testing of Aggregate Production Models in an Implementation Methodology," *Management Science*, Vol. 20, No. 6 (February 1974), pp. 903–911.
18. T. G. Mairs et al., "On Production Allocation and Distribution Problem," *Management Science*, Vol. 24, No. 15 (November 1978), pp. 1622–1630.
19. R. E. McGarrah, *Production and Logistics Management: Text and Cases*. (New York: Wiley, 1963).
20. S. L. Narasimhan and W. A. Gruver, "Integrated R&D Production and Inventory System," *AIIE Transactions*, Vol. 11, No. 3 (September 1979), pp. 198–205.
21. R. Peterson and E. A. Silver, *Decision Systems for Inventory Management and Production Planning*. (New York: Wiley, 1979).
22. G. W. Plossl and O. W. Wight, *Production and Inventory Control*. (Englewood Cliffs, N.J.: Prentice-Hall, 1967).
23. W. T. Shearon, "A Study of the Aggregate Production Planning Problem."

Unpublished doctoral dissertation, The Colgate Darden Graduate School of Business Administration, University of Virginia, 1974.

24. G. Shore, *Operations Management.* (New York: McGraw-Hill, 1973).
25. E. A. Silver, "A Tutorial on Production Smoothing and Work Force Balancing," *Operations Research*, Vol. 15, No. 6 (November–December 1967), pp. 985–1010.
26. W. H. Taubert, "A Search Decision Rule for the Aggregate Scheduling Problem," *Management Science*, Vol. 14, No. 6 (February 1968), pp. 343–359.
27. R. C. Vergin, "Production Scheduling under Seasonal Demand," *Journal of Industrial Engineering*, Vol. 17, No. 5 (May 1966), pp. 260–266.
28. C. H. Von Lanzenauer, "Production and Employment Scheduling in Multistage Production Systems," *Naval Research Logistic Quarterly*, Vol. 17, No. 2 (July 1970), pp. 193–198.
29. U. P. Welum, "An HMMS Type Interactive Model for Aggregate Planning," *Management Science*, Vol. 24, No. 5 (January 1978), pp. 564–575.

appendix 9A

The Production Plan—The Top Management Interface

Romeyn Everdell, CMC (The Concepts and the Process)
Executive Vice President
Rath & Strong, Inc.

Judith A. Ryde, CPIM (Case Study)
Harvard University
Graduate School of Business

The Concepts and the Process

INTRODUCTION

In the year of 1982, we are being reacquainted with the importance of production planning as companies endeavor to manage their way through a recession. We are still finding too many companies that do not really understand the process. It is also a fact that manufacturing planning and control systems can only be as good as the process that develops a production plan. That process is often called "business planning" and has been identified as "management's handle on the business." We need to redouble our efforts to make sure that management grabs this handle and provides a firm and wise guiding force. As more computer-based systems go on the air, remember that a modern MRP system will "explode" a bad plan overnight! The output of the system can be only as good as the production plan that guides it.

THE CONCEPT

The concept is, like many good management techniques, an old one that predates our current development of improved production and inventory control systems.

Reprinted with permission, American Production and Inventory Control Society, Inc., *25th Annual International Conference Proceedings*, October, 1982.

A company, like an airliner, needs a flight plan to know where it is going. For a manufacturing facility, the production plan is that flight plan since it expresses the desired rate of production in aggregate terms for each month in the future. However, top management's view of the flight plan is generally expressed in terms of total dollar revenue to be generated each month—actually a "shipping plan." The problem in generating production and shipping plans is that only for special situations are they the same. Both a production plan and a revenue/shipping plan are needed from the process of business planning as two related but different outputs.

Management planning starts with a sales forecast, except in those few cases in which the company works from a backlog of orders out beyond the cumulative lead time. However, stating that planning starts with a sales forecast creates an immediate semantics problem. Consider some of the variations around the sales forecast theme:

- Booking forecast—forecast of orders by entry data.
- Shipping forecast—forecast of orders by promise date.
- Demand forecast—forecast of orders by request date.

To make it worse, some fail to distinguish between the tracking of sales—a moving average of actual bookings, and therefore, historical data—with the projection of an estimate into the future. To add confusion, most of the content of a management plan can be called a forecast as each individual output is a projection into the future. In addition to the various forms of a sales forecast, companies may also have production forecasts, inventory forecasts, profit forecasts, cash forecasts, shipping forecasts, etc.

Because of this confusion, it is important to clear up the semantics, define some terms, and understand key relationships. Traditionally, management has been taught to be concerned about "bookings, billings, and backlog." In the interest of alliteration, two critical elements were left out of this jingle: production and finished inventory. Bookings and backlog cover the demand side of planning and unfortunately too many companies concentrate only on planning demand. Equally important is how to satisfy that demand—the supply question, resolved by a production plan which determines how best to meet the demand, using finished inventory to the extent it is necessary and can be justified. The shipping plan (billings) is influenced by demand, supply, and inventory. It cannot be generated by merely looking at bookings and backlog.

Before we can deal with the planning process, it is necessary to understand the five key ingredients:

- *Bookings*—a measure of the *rate* of incoming order intake (net business taken).
- *Backlog*—the *status*, at a moment in time, of the amount of unshipped customer orders (orders booked but not shipped).
- *Production*—a measure of the *rate* of product completions (transfers

to finished goods and/or shipments to customers directly from production).

- *Shipments*—a measure of the *rate* of shipments to customers (billings or invoicing of customer orders).
- *Inventory*—the *status*, at a moment in time, of the amount of finished (ready for sale) product in inventory.

The objective of a production plan is to express, in aggregate terms, a supply plan expressed as a rate projected out into the future—usually at least a year out by months—that will assure the proper level of shipments, consistent with customer service objectives and appropriate levels of finished inventory where they apply, giving consideration to production constraints and costs.

To understand the five ingredients and their relationships, consider two examples. For simplicity, assume that top management at the end of each month is given operating data all in aggregate cost dollars. Figure 9A.1 presents an example involving products that are exclusively sold out of inventory (there is no significant backlog—merely orders in the process of being picked and shipped). This example shows an actual situation of a company coming off several years of increased demand into a recessionary period. Several issues are apparent:

1. Forecast of Bookings is not consistent with actual bookings.
2. Production Rate is above rate of incoming orders (actual booking rate).
3. Shipping Target (set several months earlier) is unrealistically high.
4. Finished Inventory is excessive.

In terms of meeting the shipping target, shipments in a make-to-stock situation depend on bookings and available inventory.

FORECAST OF BOOKINGS (next month)	**$ 900,000**
ACTUAL BOOKING RATE (last 3 months)	**750,000**
PRODUCTION RATE (current month)	**1,000,000**
SHIPPING TARGET (next month)	**1,250,000**
FINISHED PRODUCT INVENTORY (month ending)	**5,000,000**

FIGURE 9A.1 Production planning: make-to-stock
All figures in cost $ in monthly terms.

If we have the correct items and quantity in inventory, a shipping target and a bookings forecast are one and the same. In this case the inventory is well balanced, but even so the shipping target is seriously overstated. Neither the customers (actual booking rate) nor the sales department (forecast of bookings) indicate that shipments of $1,250,000 are attainable.

In terms of managing inventory, recognize that production is input to and shipments (actual bookings) are output from finished inventory:

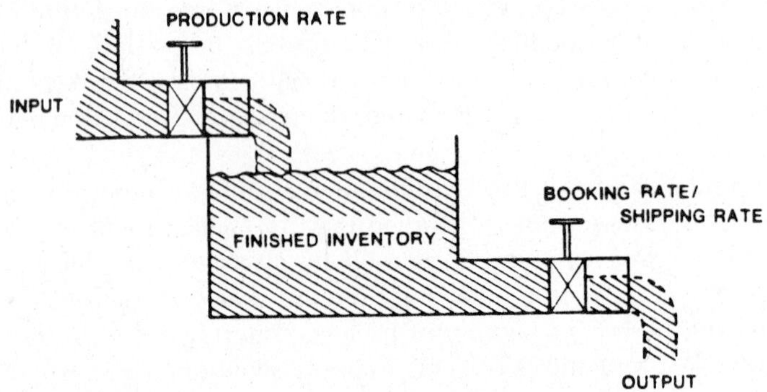

Obviously, inventory at more than 6 months of supply even at the forecast rate of bookings, is excessive. Worse yet, inventory will continue to increase as long as we make more than we ship (sell). No material requirements planning system or other inventory management technique will reduce the inventory build until the production rate is set at the proper level—in this case below the booking forecast. It is surprising how many management people believe that MRP will reduce that finished inventory!

The problem in this case lies with management for not having recognized that the production rate is the controllable variable and adjusted it earlier. An additional problem is the difference between actual bookings and the booking forecast. Such a situation usually causes lower level personnel to "second-guess" the sales forecast, each following their own interpretation. Since planning starts with a sales forecast, part of the planning process is to reconcile any differences between actual vs. forecast demand and, if necessary, modify (second-guess) the forecast at the highest level of management and avoid low level confusion.

Once the decision is made as to what the bookings are most likely to be, the solution to the problem should be obvious: the production plan must be reduced below the expected booking rate until inventory is worked off. This plan must be expressed quantitatively, and there are corollary implications, such as revising the shipping target (and rebudgeting to protect profits at lower operating levels). Note that any delay in responding to a drop in sales increases the problem as inventory builds, causing production to be reduced lower and for longer periods to regain control.

Figure 9A.2 represents an example involving products made-to-order. The business situation is reversed in this case, reflecting a company trying

FORECAST OF BOOKINGS (next month)	**$ 750,000**
ACTUAL BOOKING RATE (last 3 months)	**1,250,000**
CUSTOMER ORDER BACKLOG (month ending)	**6,000,000**
PRODUCTION RATE (current month)	**900,000**
SHIPPING TARGET (next month)	**1,000,000**

FIGURE 9A.2 Production planning: make-to-order
All figures in cost $ in monthly terms.

to keep up with a growth in demand. In this example, there is no significant finished product inventory—merely completed production in the process of being shipped—so that backlog of orders becomes the major concern. Again, several issues show up:

1. Forecast of Bookings is not consistent with actual bookings.
2. Production Rate is below the actual booking rate, although above the forecast.
3. Shipping Target is optimistic.
4. Customer Order Backlog is high. New orders would have to be promised out 6 months at the existing production rate.

In terms of meeting the shipping target, shipments in a make-to-order situation depend on the production rate. The production rate and shipping target should but do not coincide. In Figure 9A.2, the shipping target is too high, but in contrast to Figure 9A.1, it is related to the production rate, not the actual or forecast bookings. Since there is no finished inventory, bookings are an input to *backlog* and production (and shipments) are output from the backlog as well as the plant:

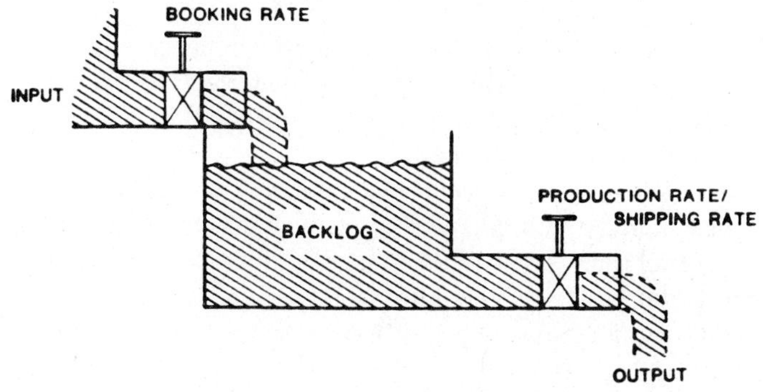

The problem in this example is that the backlog is growing while competitors are delivering in three months. The reason for the low forecast in relation to past order intake is due to the concern on the part of the sales department that non-competitive delivery would start to adversely affect sales. The obvious solution is to increase production, but this decision must be quantified and time-phased because there are constraints on how fast production can be increased and how far above the rate of booking it is to be set before the backlog is brought back to the desired level. It should be obvious that the booking rate would have to be carefully reviewed each period to strike the proper demand (booking)/supply (production) balance.

THE PROCESS

The process of production planning is all about achieving and maintaining that demand/supply balance in as realistic and cost-effective way as possible. It takes constant attention and review, at least on a monthly basis, and must involve the top management group:

1. The Chief Executive Officer
2. Senior Sales/Marketing Executive
3. Senior Manufacturing/Operations Executive
4. Senior Financial Executive
5. Senior Engineering Executive (optional in a make-to-stock environment).

The top materials (production and inventory control) executive should be present as "secretary" of the group to:

1. Put the data together and present the problems.
2. Evaluate the quality of the inventory and/or backlog.
3. Suggest alternatives in quantitative terms.
4. Convey the decision to the materials group.

Two overriding principles must be recognized:

1. The *production plan* is the key independent, control*lable* variable. Bookings are influenced by the sales force, but we can only deal with orders that actually materialize. In other words, demand is only partially controllable.
2. The material and capacity plans must be driven by the production plan, not the shipping plan or the bookings forecast. To order more material than the production plan requires will increase inventory, to order less will generate shortages and fail to utilize available capacity (assuming capacity is reconciled to the production plan).

INFORMATION REQUIRED AND FORMAT OF PRESENTATION

To allow the management planning process to proceed, it is important that the information be presented and formatted carefully. Planning is a "numbers game" and the arithmetic is very simple, but the information display and reconciliation is critical to success.

The initial consideration is how best to display, relate, and reconcile the five components: Bookings, Backlog, Production, Shipments, and Finished Inventory. All of these components must be able to be added up to a single aggregate number per division, company, and manufacturing unit. Before dealing with the various "levels" of planning, let us first look at the relationships. The unit of measure is the first issue. To reconcile and relate the numbers, the various elements must be in the same terms. To start, let us assume that all five are expressed in cost dollars; dollars because they are additive as well as being the language of management, and cost since that is close to a standard or constant dollar basic unit of measure free of margin differences and price discounts, allowances, and escalation problems. Some few companies can plan in units, pounds, feet, or volumetric terms where product is homogeneous (i.e., items are additive without significant distortion in relation to throughput volume), but even then it is desirable to convert to and evaluate the dollar impact.

Figure 9A.3 is a recommended format for planning and takes care of the problem that most companies are not purely make-to-stock or make-to-order but have product in both categories. To combine and consolidate

Unit of Measure: $ **BUSINESS PLAN** as of 6/30 **Date Issued:** 7/5

Month	APR	MAY	JUNE	Quarter Totals	JULY	AUG	SEPT	Quarter Totals
Working Days	19	19	20	58	10	20	24	54
Booking Forecast	824,000	847,000	793,000	2,464,000	722,000	838,000	850,000	2,410,000
Actual Orders	759,073	1,177,515	806,566	2,743,154				
Actual Daily Order Rate	39,951	61,975	40,328	47,296				
Order Backlog	1,051,475	909,250	1,191,500		340,124	860,875	714,000	
Production Plan	988,000	1,045,000	1,100,000	3,133,000	550,000	1,100,000	1,320,000	2,970,000
Planned Daily Rate	52,000	55,000	55,000	54,000	55,000	55,000	55,000	55,000
Actually Produced	906,000	871,750	1,093,125	2,870,875				
Actual Daily Rate	47,684	45,882	54,656	49,498				
Shipping Forecast	1,085,000	1,045,000	1,191,500	3,321,500	533,250	860,875		
Actual Shipments	841,017	945,125	1,075,096	2,861,238				
Actual Daily Ship Rate	44,264	49,743	53,775	49,332				
Month Ending								
Fin. Inv. Planned	649,823	817,448	652,573	X	822,848			X
Fin. Inv. Actual	817,448	744,073	806,098	X				X

FIGURE 9A.3

the information shown in Figures 9A.1 and 9A.2, consider that all production closes out to finished goods whether or not it goes to a stockroom or directly to a customer. The model is as follows:

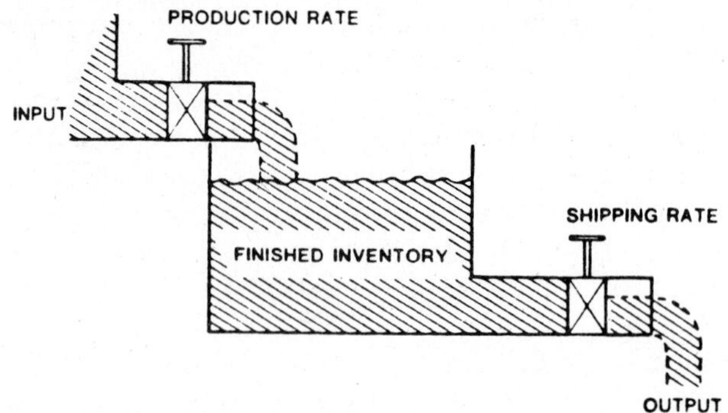

Bookings in this case become only a guide and not an input or output whereas the backlog is *part* of the output. The backlog cannot exceed the production plan although it is possible to ship more than produced if the additional amount comes from finished inventory. The production output is made up of two "streams," one shipping against the backlog and the second replenishing inventory that has been shipped out of the stockroom, even though mathematically we pass both streams through finished inventory.

With these principles in mind, examine Figure 9A.3. Planning requires both a look back at history and a projection ahead. The provision in this format is to be able to enter the plan and track the actuals. With a sheet for each six months, it is possible to keep as much history *and* forward planning as required. The time phasing is by month, subtotaled by quarter. To be able to take out the effect of the variable number of production days per calendar month, the number of working days in each period is displayed in the heading.

The first section of the report deals with the Bookings—the first line is the bookings forecast (projection), the second line is the actual orders booked, the third line is the daily rate of actual bookings. The purpose of this section is to determine the rate of incoming demand. Usually the forecast line is a forecast of orders by entry date, but it may be by request date. We recommend not trying to look at it by promise date as the purpose of this line is to project the *rate of order flow* and not to use it as a precisely timed piece of data. The bookings section will deal with the promise date. Forecasts are not that accurate, and the data will only be used as output for the make-to-stock items where the difference between entered, requested, and promised is usually insignificant. The primary function of this Bookings section is to provide a *guide* in evaluating the production and shipping rates. However, it is also used to project seasonal demand patterns to help in determining the degree of production leveling, and the resulting inventory effect.

The next section shows the customer order Backlog. This is a "hard" number pulled from the order entry file. It is a time-phased display at the beginning of each month of all unshipped orders collected and accumulated by the month in which they are *promised* for shipment. The past due would be included in the current month but is often broken out and displayed as an addition line in this section. The quantity for each month changes with time until the month is closed. History data is the final amount scheduled for the month when that month was current (e.g., April's backlog in the July report was the quantity originally promised for April shipment as of April 1). The purpose of this section is to determine:

1. Realism of promising—is the quantity promised in any month greater than the production for that month?
2. The extent of the backlog—how far out in time is the production plan "sold out"?
3. How much production is available for inventory replenishment?

The third section is the Production section showing the monthly plan, the planned daily rate, the actual each month, and the actual daily rate. The quantity projected is the result of the planning group's decision. The quantity is based on several considerations.

1. Is the rate of production consistent with the rate of demand?
2. Is the rate of production consistent with the desired inventory levels and forecast rate of demand for items that are stocked?
3. When the rate of production is changing, are the new rates achievable and is the daily rate smooth—steadily increasing or decreasing or holding level?
4. Is the production rate and the backlog consistent and rational? Is it necessary to increase the rate and "pull in" the backlog because it is extended out beyond the competitive delivery policy, or should it be reduced because the backlog is less than production and "available to promise" is earlier than necessary?
5. Are projected changes in demand (seasonal patterns, promotion, product phase-in/phase-outs) or production interruptions (shutdowns, maintenance schedules, plant moves, vacations) properly anticipated and production rates leveled to the correct degree?

The fourth section is the Shipping section, including the plan (revenue plan), the actual shipments, and the actual daily rate. In the case of a pure make-to-stock situation, this section would merely be a repeat of the Bookings section and unnecessary. If the company was purely make-to-order, this section would be virtually the same as the Production section (unless there were a significant number of items that were built ahead of time or finished and held for credit, export, customer decisions, etc.). However, in most cases there is a combination of stock and make-to-order products. In this case the shipping forecast is an estimate based on first the orders in the backlog for each month plus what additional business is expected to be booked which can be shipped that month. This type of estimation is not easy and is generally done on the basis of first laying in the backlog and then by evaluating what percentage of the forecast (after deducting the backlog) will materialize that can be shipped in each month:

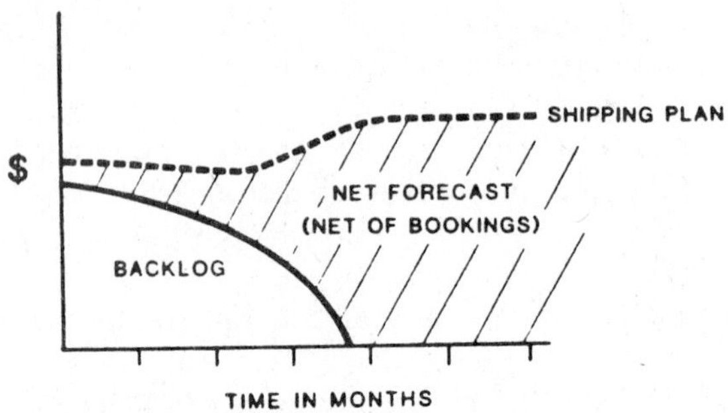

Unless the inventory level is being changed or the backlog is being pulled in or pushed out, the shipping plan should be close to the same rate as the production plan and the booking forecast. For the purpose of comparison, the section shows the daily shipping rate. The main reason for showing a separate production plan and shipping plan is:

1. To separate the two when inventory and/or backlog levels are being changed.
2. To differentiate between actual production and actual shipment, which even when not planned to be different, usually are.
3. To be able to determine the cause of shipping failures (i.e., were low shipments due to not making enough, not selling enough, or too many "holds").
4. To have proper figures for input to and output from finished inventory and determine reasons for any failure to meet inventory plans.

The final section deals with Finished Inventory. The projected inventory plan always starts with the last actual inventory and, month by month, adds planned production and subtracts planned shipments. Each month a new actual is entered and inventory projected. In a true sense, the management process of production planning is controlling the level of finished inventory.

OTHER CONSIDERATIONS

Level of Detail

The generation of a business plan must always produce a production plan for each operating unit. The purpose is to set the activity level of the manufacturing facility or facilities. However, it is more common to plan at a product category level and then summarize (or roll up) to an overall plan for a division and/or company. Generally, the initial planning involves between 5 to 12 logical product groups—normally distinguished by market category. For example, a bearing company might look at distributor products, original equipment sold to machine tool, aircraft and automotive, and a special products group. A computer company may look at manufacturing, financial and banking, laboratory and university, and communication systems. In this fashion, the aggregate forecast can be more readily defined and evaluated in the light of each market segment. Once the plan has been generated for each, the preparation of the overall is merely a roll up to the aggregate summary.

However, there is a complication that product/market categories do not correspond to manufacturing/operating facilities. High volume or large size items may make up part of several product categories whereas the high volume items are made in one facility and the large low volume items in another. This kind of situation would require a matrix of product vs. facility with percentage factors for each product by facility. To develop such a matrix it is advisable to source and product code all the products produced in each facility of a multi-plant operation and add up the detail by product for each facility. This kind of summarization of sales, shipping, and production data can generate the percentage data for the matrix to permit reconciling plans by facility to plans by product. The key is to be able to read in by product and read out by facility for projection and to reverse the process for actuals.

Unit of Measure

Up to this point we have assumed that the planning would be done in cost dollars or with "homogeneous" product, in units. In many cases this is not appropriate. Forecasts and Bookings are usually expressed in sales dollars; Inventory is almost never expressed in any terms other than cost dollars; whereas production people think in units or hours. Teaching everyone to talk in the same terms is a lesson in frustration and an evolving approach, particularly with computer assist, is the bilingual or "Rosetta Stone" concept. Basically this approach shows each line in three units:

Sales dollars
Cost dollars
Units

In some cases not all three are available, but if all can be expressed in at least one category, usually cost dollars, there is an ability to relate each section of the plan. For forecasts, an average profit margin is used to generate cost dollars. For production and inventory an average billing price can be used to generate sales dollars. Shipments and backlog can be directly expressed in all three terms. Units may only be necessary for production and shipments but can be expressed for the actuals on all categories.

Under this concept exciting opportunities for reconciliation open up. Management has always been frustrated by the virtual impossibility of reconciling the various financial reports that are required for planning. For example, actual bookings, after adjusting for discounts, allowances, cancellations, returns, etc., are difficult to compare to a forecast. The difference between gross and net sales figures can be significant. It is possible, however, to show the adjusted and unadjusted figures so that financial data can be included in the actuals of the planning sheets. The same problems exist in looking at shipments and inventory. The format of the report begins to look "busy" as the operating statistics and the financial data are both displayed, but the usefulness and credibility of the report increases as management begins to work to "one sheet of music" without confusion.

RESOURCE PLANNING

The production plan should be looked at as both a schedule (how much in total to make) and a capacity plan (what resources are required). However, to read a plan expressed in dollars or units and recognize its impact on capacity is difficult. Most companies develop capacity-related factors that allow the production plan to be converted to resource terms:

1. Manpower Plan—Using an average labor dollar in cost of sales to generate direct labor requirements.
2. Facilities Plan—Using a maximum manufacturing cost output per facility (usually based on a key or pacing production units within each facility).
3. Energy Plan—Using energy consumption per dollar of cost.
4. Cash Flow—Combining average labor and material content in cost of production plus or minus changes in finished inventory.

Once these conversion factors have been generated and maintained, the aggregate resources required to support a production plan become readily available. This by-product starts the first level of capacity planning, which becomes further refined and detailed at subsequent lower levels of planning.

PRINCIPLES AND PRACTICES

In putting together a Production Plan, there are several key principles we can extract:

- Management involvement must be one of total commitment. Successful companies do not tolerate any higher priority to displace or allow absenteeism from the planning meetings.

- Successful planning makes relatively small adjustments frequently, rather than delaying decisions and making large adjustments. Meetings should be at least once a month.
- A rigorous discipline must be established to develop a single set of numbers. There may, as an example, be two forecasts—one the initial plan at the outset of the fiscal year for reference as well as the latest revision that is used in the current plan. But there can be no confusion as to which is guiding the current plan.
- To the extent possible financial data is used, showing adjustments if it is necessary to reconcile financial and operating data.
- Use the "roll-up" concept to reconcile and control detail planning such as Master Scheduling to the Production Plan and vice-versa.
- Always express the plan in dollars and where desirable express it in more than one unit of measure. It is important in the "roll-up" to be able to convert detail Master Schedules in units to dollars to allow adding up and reconciling to a Production Plan.
- Use history to develop integrity, realism, and "doability" in the planning process. There can be no discontinuities or anomalies in the projection as compared to the actuals.
- Require the materials manager (production and inventory control manager) to:
  —Pull the data together.
  —Present the problems and suggested alternatives.
  —Qualify the quality of the inventory and backlog.

  The meeting should be a decision making session, not a data gathering or "number crunching" one.
- Use the various elements of the plan as objectives to hold top functional executives accountable:
  —Marketing/Sales should be measured on actual bookings vs. forecast.
  —Manufacturing/Operations should be measured on actual production vs. plan.
  —Materials management should be accountable for explaining inventory variance from plan and assuring integrity between the Production Plan and the Master Schedule.

A well-conceived Production Plan:

- Initiates the planning process from the top, moving the company from a reactive, fire-fighting mode to a mode of setting objectives and influencing the future.
- Sets the tone for clarity in expressing objectives and intuition by communicating in quantitative clarity.
- Avoids the need for lower level interpretation or second-guessing.
- Provides a basis for feedback from lower levels when detail decisions suggest the plan is in some way flawed.
- Allows the dependent systems in terms of manufacturing control,

financial and cost control, and demand management to operate to their maximum potential.
- Reduces the number and magnitude of "surprises" and severe year-end adjustments.

Case Study

INTRODUCTION

This talk is to be given in conjunction with R. Everdell's on the concept of production planning. In this session, we will review one year's worth of production planning in an actual company. The firm is a metal stamping operation which manufactures about 200 different parts. The product line includes both make-to-stock and make-to-order items. We will follow this company's planning efforts beginning with the creation and implementation of its planning function in the first quarter of 1981. A master scheduling system was implemented at the same time, and data for both functions is provided manually.

We shall see that production planning is the means by which management establishes the plan which controls the levels of finished inventory and customer service, and which provides factual information pertinent to top-level decision making for both the short- and long-term goals of the company. Reviewing an entire year of real production planning enables us to see how it has been a key element in managing this company through dramatic variations in business conditions.

START-UP OF PROJECT

To set up the production planning function, the following actual historical data (in common units) is gathered in order to examine the current situation within the company:

- Bookings
- Backlog of Orders
- Production
- Shipments
- Finished Goods Inventory

To enable comparison between months on equal terms, the actual monthly figures for bookings, production, and shipments are divided by the number of days in each particular month. This provides comparable actual daily rates of bookings (incoming customer demand), production (flow within the factory), and shipments (items leaving the factory and going out to customers), as shown in Figure 9A.4.

Unit of Measure: $ | **BUSINESS PLAN** as of 2/28 | **Date Issued: 3/3/81**

(1980) | (1981) History ← | → Plan

Month	OCT	NOV	DEC	Quarter Totals	JAN	FEB	MAR	Quarter Totals
Working Days	24	17	22	63	20	19	25	64
Booking Forecast								
Actual Orders	1,191,395	718,070	1,177,650	3,087,095	818,263	1,006,002		
Actual Daily Order Rate	49,641	42,239	53,530	49,001	40,913	52,895		
Order Backlog								
Production Plan								
Planned Daily Rate								
Actually Produced	777,125	620,250	751,750	2,149,125	655,500	637,000		
Actual Daily Rate	32,380	36,485	34,170	34,113	32,775	33,526		
Shipping Forecast								
Actual Shipments	1,015,150	631,470	858,327	2,504,947	952,080	714,989		
Actual Daily Ship Rate	42,298	37,145	39,015	39,761	47,604	37,631		
Month Ending				X				X
Fin. Inv. Planned				X				X
Fin. Inv. Actual	1,201,818	1,210,698	1,161,948	X	866,323	823,823		X

FIGURE 9A.4

In addition, the current finished goods inventory and order backlog figures must be qualified by analyzing how much of each is actually usable or shippable. Inventory which is slow-moving or obsolete or which cannot be shipped (due to customer or credit hold) must be removed from the finished goods total, in order to give an accurate picture of the amount of usable inventory. In a similar fashion, orders in the backlog which cannot be shipped due to either customer or internal hold (for credit, awaiting specifications, etc.) are removed from the total backlog figure so that the volume of orders which could actually be shipped (the "hard" demand, or shippable backlog) can be determined. This is an important step in the production planning analysis. In our case study, a significant portion (46%) of finished goods fell into the hold/obsolete category initially, as can be seen in Figure 9A.5. This data pointed out some order entry problems related to customer-imposed holds and international orders (requiring letters of credit prior to shipment). A full 23% of finished goods was made up of items which had been manufactured in anticipation of shipment in the preceding months. In effect, almost one-quarter of our company's finished goods inventory investment was tied up in customers' stock, although no such formal arrangement had been reviewed or planned for, and no premiums were charged to these customers.

The usable inventory and shippable backlog are then quantified in terms of week's worth, by dividing each by the weekly production rate. The backlog "spread," or distribution of orders by promise dates, is shown

PRODUCTION PLANNING DATA

February 1981 (19 working days)

Booked	$\frac{1,005,002}{19}$	=	52,895 per day
Produced	$\frac{637,000}{19}$	=	33,526 per day
Shipped	$\frac{714,989}{19}$	=	37,631 per day

Added to backlog in February	290,013		
Total backlog	2,483,912	(12.4 weeks at 40,000 per day)	
Scheduled for March	1,189,026		
Scheduled for April and May	711,750		
Balance beyond	583,136		
Total on hold	684,763		
Actual finished goods inventory	823,823	Percent of inventory:	
In stock, no letter of credit	111,000	23%	
In stock, credit or customer hold	80,250		
Slow-moving or obsolete	186,595	23%	
Total unshippable inventory (February)	377,845	46%	
Usable inventory	445,978	54%	
	(2.2 weeks at 40,000 per day)		

FIGURE 9A.5

across the next few months, and the data in Figure 9A.5 is complete for review at this company's first production planning session.

The above steps provide the aggregate information required to assess the current actual position of the company, to determine if steps should be taken to change that position, and to agree upon a course of action.

INITIAL ASSESSMENT

The first production planning meeting in our case study was held in February, 1981. We examined the aggregate data shown in Figure 9A.4 and 9A.5, and came to the following conclusions.

Booking rate (approximately 50,000 per day) and production rate (40,000 per day planned; 34,000 average actual) are far out of synchronization. Compounding the imbalance, we have not yet shown that we can actually average 40,000 per day in production.

To make matters worse, backlog is out too far (12 weeks instead of the 3–6 desired for customer lead time), and inventory is too low (2.5 weeks of usable stock). Backlog appears to be increasing and inventory decreasing, as the booking rate is higher than the shipping rate, and the production rate lower than the shipping rate. In other words, the flow of demand into the company is greater than the flow of filled orders out; the remaining unfilled orders add to the size of the backlog. Since shipments exceed the volume of production, we know that some orders are being shipped from inventory that will not be replaced. Simply put, the company has not been producing enough to keep up with customer demand, and has been falling further and further behind.

Capacity is a problem. The numbers indicate that production must exceed 50,000 per day to bring the backlog down to 3 to 6 weeks and to raise inventory to at least 4 weeks of usable stock.

Until the backlog is reduced and inventory replenished, customer service will suffer. Inquiries and complaints from customers unhappy with poor delivery performance is going to make life uncomfortable, and some business may be lost.

Almost half (46%) of the total finished goods inventory is unshippable, due to either obsolescence or various holds. Revisions of order entry and of obsolescence policies are needed to improve the efficiency of the investment in inventory. It is advisable under these conditions to schedule into production only what can be shipped and invoiced, and not release to production anything on hold or without a letter of credit (for international payment).

Production plans were set up for February (40,000 per day to total 720,000) and for March (41,000 per day to total 1,025,000). The group agreed to meet monthly to review and discuss the plan, and to attempt to extend the planning horizon to six months, and, later, to one year.

Top management must perform the production planning function on a monthly basis. Once the plan can be extended to cover a period of six months to a year, each monthly session will involve reviewing the last month's data, making any appropriate changes to the existing production plan, and establishing a plan for one additional future month. What follows is a general guideline which was designed to aid in carrying out this process.

STANDARD MONTHLY AGENDA

1. Review current backlog and inventory levels. Qualify these figures—how much of the backlog is actually shippable? How is the backlog distributed (by promise date) over the next months? How much of the inventory is usable?
2. Examine the booking, production, and shipment actual rates. How do they differ from one another? Should they differ in order to reach an aggregate inventory or customer service goal of the company? Remember that the production rate is the element over which management has direct control.
3. Analyze the demand. Is it "normal," or are we seeing a one-time rise or drop in the monthly rate due to some unusual, unique

occurrence, or some artificial inflation in demand? Is there any "soft" demand which is not in the backlog figure (not in the master production schedule) which should be taken into consideration?

4. Are there any new product introductions, promotions, or other market factors which may also require a change to the booking forecast?
5. Review master schedule performance. Was the production plan we set up last month realistic? Too high? Too low? What needs to be done to improve?
6. Identify the first amount available-to-promise by finding the first month where the production plan exceeds the backlog. How much is available-to-promise?
7. Review shipping performance relative to service goals. Are the goals still realistic? Are we meeting the goal (or moving toward it) successfully? If the shipping plan was not met, was this because the expected orders for which we have inventory did not come in, or because of problems in getting authorization to ship items produced for firm orders in the backlog?
8. Review target inventory goal for various inventory categories, and compare to actual inventory levels for these categories. Are the goals still appropriate? If actual inventory levels differ significantly from target levels, what are the reasons?
9. What are the realistic plant capacities (output) for the next months? What is involved in changing the capacities of the factory?
10. What is the company's strategy for the short-term? For the long-term?
11. Agree upon a production plan and average daily production rate for the next month. Also update the longer range plans, and extend by one month.

LEARNING TO PLAN

Notice that the standard agenda always includes questioning whether or not the plan made last month was a good one. The distinction between good planning and good execution of a plan is an important one which is often difficult to make, especially during the initial months of production planning when the group is new to the concept. It is tempting to automatically blame problems on poor execution of the production plan, when in fact the plan itself may not have been a good one. As with any new management function, the process of good production planning takes practice to perfect. Any new planning group will go through a learning curve, during which some of the plans generated may fail to meet the production planning objectives of providing the best *realistic*, agreed-upon plan designed to enable the company to meet its goals in light of its current actual position.

Particularly when a major change in production rate is called for, the realism element in planning is difficult to maintain. Significant changes in production rate are best accomplished gradually over time, as they require considerable planning of staffing, overtime, machine scheduling, subcontracting, layoffs, etc. in order to adjust output. We saw above that our case company needed a dramatic increase in output in order to begin to cut into its large order backlog before it grew further out of control. However, a jump of 50% (from 33,000 to 50,000 plus daily production) is a major undertaking, and in most industries would require careful planning, significant lead time, and an incremental "ramp-up" as opposed to a sudden jump in production rate.

We can see in Figure 9A.6 that the planning group in our case generated several unrealistically optimistic plans. The group hoped to jump from a 41,000 daily rate in March to 52,000 in April, and in spite of a much lower actual April rate (48,000) further increased the plan for May to 55,000 per day. In fact, during 4 of the 6 months from April to September, the actual production was well below the planned figures. However, it is important to recognize that the actual production rate *did* increase dramatically once the need was revealed by production planning efforts, and probably increased as much as was possible given the constraints on capacity of this particular factory. Production jumped from a first quarter average of 36,000 to 47,000 in April, maintained a two quarter average of about 48,000. The point is that the *plans* appear to have been unrealistic, but the underlying problem was that the bottleneck operation had not been identified and resolved. Unless there is a clear strategy to achieve higher levels, neither the *plan* nor the *execution* is satisfactory.

Unit of Measure: $ (1981) **BUSINESS PLAN** as of 10/5 **Date Issued: 10/8/81**

Month	APR	MAY	JUNE	Quarter Totals	JULY	AUG	SEPT	Quarter Totals
Working Days	19	19	20	58	10	20	24	54
Booking Forecast	824,000	847,000	793,000	2,464,000	722,000	838,000	850,000	2,410,000
Actual Orders	759,073	1,177,515	806,566	2,743,154	371,710	423,112	693,423	1,488,245
Actual Daily Order Rate	39,951	61,975	40,328	47,296	37,171	21,156	28,893	27,560
Order Backlog	1,051,475	909,250	1,191,500		340,124	860,875	714,000	
Production Plan	988,000	1,045,000	1,100,000	3,133,000	550,000	1,100,000	1,080,000	2,730,000
Planned Daily Rate	52,000	55,000	55,000	54,000	55,000	55,000	45,000	50,555
Actually Produced	906,000	871,750	1,093,125	2,870,875	512,375	1,012,750	1,058,375	2,853,500
Actual Daily Rate	47,684	45,882	54,656	49,498	51,238	50,638	44,099	47,842
Shipping Forecast	1,085,000	1,045,000	1,191,500	3,321,500	533,250	860,875	740,500	2,134,625
Actual Shipments	841,017	945,125	1,075,096	2,861,238	438,500	901,115	890,515	2,230,130
Actual Daily Ship Rate	44,264	49,743	53,775	49,332	43,850	45,056	37,105	41,299
Month Ending				X				X
Fin. Inv. Planned	649,823	817,448	652,573	X	822,848	1,119,323	1,331,573	X
Fin. Inv. Actual	817,448	744,073	806,098	X	880,198	992,073	1,157,948	X

FIGURE 9A.6

REGAINING CONTROL

Although the actual production rates fell below the production plans, the benefits of the planning process become evident within a short time. The company became accustomed to monitoring the relationships between flow of bookings, production, and shipments and the impact of those relationships on backlog and inventory levels, and learned how to adjust backlog or inventory sizes by altering the production rate. As greater amounts were produced the oversized backlog slowly began to shrink. What had been a 12-week-and-growing pile of unfilled orders in March was down to a more manageable 9 weeks at the beginning of May, and continued to decrease to 7 weeks' worth of work by September. Customer service improved correspondingly, with significant lead time reductions, much more accurate promise-dating of orders, and an increase in the percentage of line items shipped on time from an estimated 45% in March to around 80% by August.

Because the company was regaining control of its situation, the number of close-range master schedule changes decreased, and the shop was able to be much more efficient due to more stable systems for scheduling ahead.

Obsolete inventory was cleaned out, and revised order entry policies helped to prevent most make-and-hold situations which had previously been tying up inventory. Finished goods finally began to grow from the dangerously low March level of 2 weeks' worth of usable stock.

FINE TUNING

As the company's backlog decreased and the initial sense of near-panic gave way to feeling in control, it became more and more evident that the inventory management functions required fine tuning. When production can be scheduled based directly on a large backlog of actual customer orders, the importance of accurate demand forecasting is reduced. Specific items are scheduled into production based on firm customer orders. However, since two of our company's stated objectives called for a reduction of the order backlog and a related improvement in customer service (reduction of delivery lead times), demand forecasting and inventory management became increasingly critical. In order to build appropriate inventories of selected items and/or to be able to deliver some items to customers on short notice (less than manufacturing lead time), some production has to be scheduled based on forecasts of demand rather than on actual customer orders. Our case company undertook a target inventory analysis (items are categorized and goal inventory levels calculated based on usage and desired coverage) and began to work with demand forecasting.

DIFFERENT BUSINESS CONDITIONS

By July 1981, demand had begun to drop off, as seen in the booking rate (Figure 9A.6). Because of unfamiliarity with demand forecasting and because of feelings that the decrease in bookings was a single occurrence as opposed to a trend, the planned production rate was held at 55,000 for July and August. By the end of August, it became evident to the planning group that inventory would be likely to grow too much if bookings remained low and the production rate high. In fact, inventory would have been quite a bit higher at the end of August had the improved inventory management skills not taken effect. Because more careful planning and the parallel effort in Master Scheduling had determined what quantities of which items should be produced and stocked, the Inventory Manager found that he was able to keep the shipping total up even though bookings were very low. The same thing was possible in September—as many orders as possible were "pulled in" and shipped out of stock. Figure 9A.7 indicates that by October, however, the prior decreases of booking rate had "caught up" with the shipping plans, which had to be reduced significantly.

The production rate was reduced in September to 45,000, where it remained through December. However, actual production performance was considerably lower than this planned rate in October through December. We may again question whether or not this was a good plan. In this instance, it appears that the production plan was too high and that Manufacturing began second-guessing the production rate, reducing it to avoid excessive inventory buildup as bookings dropped off. By January the planned production rate was reduced further, and lowered again in February and March 1982, so that for that quarter the second-guessing appeared to stop as planned and actual production rates converged.

Unit of Measure: $ | BUSINESS PLAN as of 3/1 | Date Issued: 3/3/82

Month	OCT (1981)	NOV	DEC	Quarter Totals	JAN (1982)	FEB	MAR	Quarter Totals
Working Days	19	17	22	58	20	19	25	64
Booking Forecast	845,000	814,000	828,000	2,487,000	1,078,000	987,000	1,335,000	3,400,000
Actual Orders	671,975	1,028,334	665,284	2,365,593	744,667	611,468	820,432	2,176,567
Actual Daily Order Rate	35,367	60,490	30,240	40,786	37,233	32,183	32,817	34,009
Order Backlog	424,000	354,875	544,125		548,375	336,250	625,750	
Production Plan	855,000	765,000	990,000	2,610,000	825,000	760,000	750,000	2,335,000
Planned Daily Rate	45,000	45,000	45,000	45,000	41,250	40,000	30,000	36,484
Actually Produced	777,079	609,000	886,750	2,272,829	702,250	800,407	771,944	2,274,601
Actual Daily Rate	40,899	35,823	40,307	39,186	35,113	42,127	30,878	35,541
Shipping Forecast	575,000	510,000	580,000	1,665,000	750,000	650,000	675,000	2,075,000
Actual Shipments	620,954	771,016	835,217	2,227,187	821,925	698,153	823,396	2,343,474
Actual Daily Ship Rate	32,682	45,354	37,964	38,399	41,096	36,745	32,936	36,617
Month Ending								
Fin. Inv. Planned	1,437,948	1,575,198	1,614,586	X	1,331,119	1,263,598	1,340,352	X
Fin. Inv. Actual	1,320,198	1,204,586	1,256,119	X	1,153,598	1,265,352	1,217,223	X

FIGURE 9A.7

Because of the improved planning and flexibility which resulted from the production planning process, the inventory level remained fairly stable over this period of major change in business conditions. Had the company not been production planning, finished goods would have undoubtedly grown significantly, as too much would have been produced relative to the demand.

Summary

Booking, production, and shipping rates and backlog and inventory levels are the five key variables which indicate the true situation within any manufacturing concern. The production rate is the variable which can be directly and independently planned and controlled. The production rate, in turn, has direct impact upon the inventory level and the size of the order backlog, which determine the level of customer service that is attainable.

We have seen how one company learned how to production plan. This company began the process when it was in serious trouble due to a growing backlog and shrinking inventory which had caused customer service to deteriorate. The company had not kept up with its increasing rate of customer demand. Production planning enabled the company to regain control of its operation, reduce the backlog, and improve customer service and plant efficiency significantly.

As the desired planned reduction to backlog took effect, the impact of the 1981/1982 recession caused the demand to drop off, so that backlog was further reduced. Demand continued to decrease, but because of improved flexibility and visibility, the company was able to maintain a fairly high shipping plan and to keep finished goods from inflating. Delivery times became very short, and the company was able to "run tight" to make the best of the unfortunate business conditions.

In summary, production planning was initiated when the company had more business than its managers thought it could handle, and has continued to be a critical management function as business turned to the other extreme and demand fell off. The setting of, planning for, and monitoring of a production rate is a critical function of management in any manufacturing company. Production planning is the vehicle by which top management chooses and subsequently plans for the direction in which the company is headed.

chapter ten

Capacity Planning and Control

Introduction

In the last chapter, we saw how aggregate output plans—popularly known as production plans—are formulated. Within the framework of a production plan, we create a master production schedule (MPS), which specifies amounts and need dates for specific items. The MPS can be exploded to determine implied loads on work centers, which generally consist of a group of machines or workers who can perform similar operations. A comparison of these implied loads and existing capacities can lead to a revision of the MPS or an increase in capacity. The capacity planning and control cycle extends from the MPS to activities at individual work centers, and the results of the capacity decision analysis are fed back to the master schedule, as illustrated in figure 10.1. In short, capacity planning and control involves establishing, measuring, monitoring, and adjusting limits or levels of capacity to facilitate smoother execution of all manufacturing schedules, including the MPS, material requirements planning (MRP), and shop floor control (SFC).

CAPACITY PLANNING AND CONTROL DEFINED

Capacity planning is the process of determining the necessary people, machines, and physical resources to meet the production objectives of the firm. *Capacity* is the maximum rate at which a system can accomplish work. Consider two people washing and drying dishes after a banquet. The washer can wash 80 dishes per hour, and the dryer can dry 100 per hour. The system capacity of 80 per hour is determined by the "bottleneck"—the person washing the dishes. Obviously, the person drying the dishes will be idle fairly often while waiting for the washer. But what is the load on this system? That depends on how many people attended the banquet—how many dishes there are. At our present capacity, 400 guests would

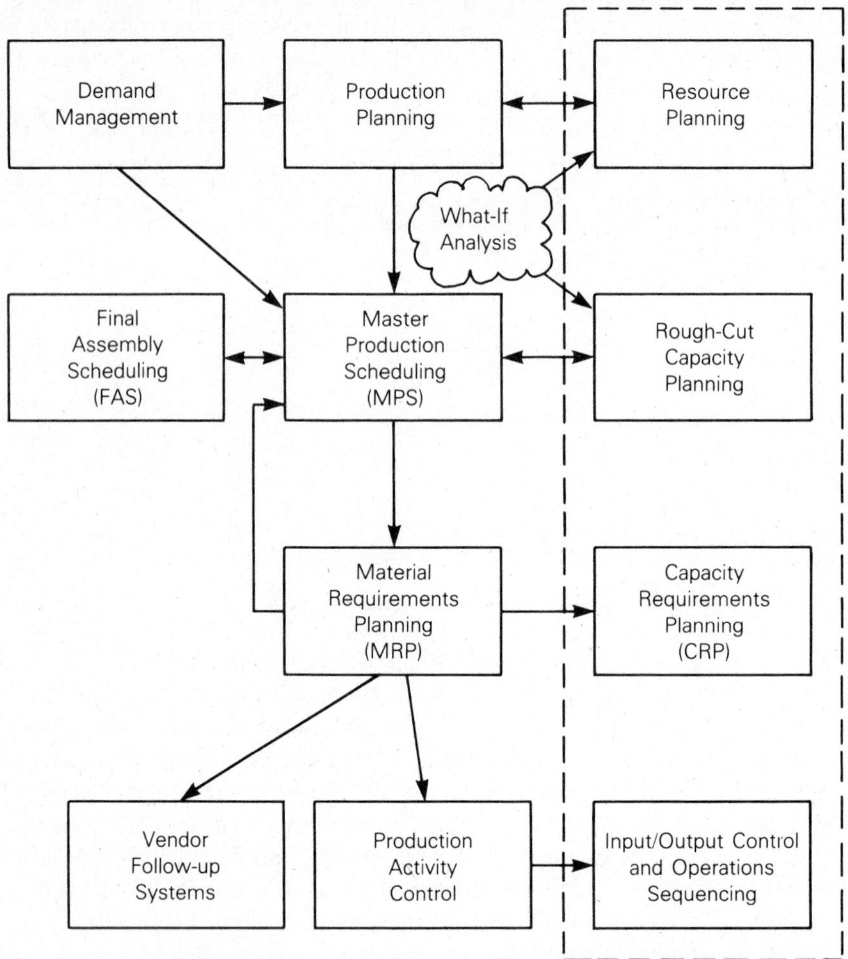

FIGURE 10.1 Capacity management techniques

represent a five-hour load. Suppose, however, that we were renting the hall and that we had to clear out two hours after the banquet. What choices do we have? There are only two ways: reduce the load or control the capacity. Either we allow fewer guests at the banquet or we increase the system capacity by renting a dishwashing machine or by adding extra people to the washing and drying. Thus, *capacity control* can be defined as the process of monitoring output, comparing it with the capacity plan, determining if variations exceed preestablished limits, and taking corrective actions.

MACHINE UTILIZATION AND OPERATOR EFFICIENCY

In determining effective capacity, machine utilization and operator efficiency considerations complicate the situation only slightly. Downtime or repair time on equipment reduces capacity; so does labor inefficiency. Machine utilization factors indicate the percentage of scheduled time a machine actually runs. On the labor side, operation efficiency is the ratio of standard hours to actual hours ($E = S/A$). Although the load imposed on a work station is usually calculated with standard times, workers on an incentive system often beat the standard. If it usually takes a worker only 2 minutes to perform an operation with a 2.5-minute standard, his or her efficiency rating would be 1.25. Such a worker would have an effective daily capacity of $1.25 * 8 = 10$ hours. If the machine utilization factor were 90%, the effective daily capacity would be reduced to $10 * 0.9 = 9$ hours.

Example 10.1

A drilling work center has three drills, three operators per shift, one shift per day, five days worked per week, and eight hours worked per shift. Records indicate that machine utilization is 95% and operator efficiency is 85%. What is the effective work center capacity per week? Three drills times eight hours per day times five days per week times 95% utilization times 85% operator efficiency gives approximately 97 hours of effective capacity per week.

In a manufacturing concern, capacity planning looks ahead to predicted loads to determine whether available capacity is sufficient. Expanding the plant, purchasing equipment, and hiring personnel are options for matching long-term capacity to a long-term forecast load on the plant. Shifting the load to off-peak seasons through pricing policies would also help. In the short term, capacity can be increased through overtime and subcontracting; the forecast load can be met by making judicious delivery promises or by building up a backlog of past-due orders.

TIME HORIZONS

In the APICS capacity planning literature, long-, medium-, and short-term planning have meanings that are specific to materials management. True long-range planning answers the question of what the company wants to be doing five to ten years hence. Decisions about products to be offered, plants to be built, and major equipment to be purchased are the main issues. This is where manufacturing policy contributes to the company's future. Materials managers, however, are not usually involved in true long-range planning. Hence, the term *long-range planning* in this chapter refers to a one- to five-year horizon—long from the perspective of the materials manager.

The time horizons for capacity planning match the three major decisions to be made for materials planning. Long-range capacity planning extends a year or more into the future, where only gross estimates of capacity requirements are available. Vital long-range capacity planning activities include both resource planning and rough-cut capacity planning.

Medium-range capacity planning generally extends as far into the future as detailed production planning data are available. The master production schedule will specify amounts and dates for all end items. When these have been chained back through subassembly and parts requirements and dates, using lead times of purchased or manufactured parts, the load on each work center can be determined. Capacity requirements planning (CRP) is the major tool used for medium-term capacity planning.

Once adjustments have been made so that we have a feasible master schedule, it is the job of the short-term capacity control system to meet schedules. Input control prevents too much work from being released to the plant, and output control ensures that work centers are producing at the expected rates. Dispatching specifies the sequence in which jobs are to be handled. The finite loading technique is used for short-term planning of actual jobs to be run in each work center, based on capacity, priority, and other relevant information about the status of the shop.

Long-Range Capacity Planning

Long-range capacity planning extends beyond the range of the master production schedule. We seek to match the long-range capacity factors (facilities, work force, and capital equipment) and the long-range production plan. The terms *rough-cut capacity planning*, *resource planning*, *resource requirements planning*, and *long-range capacity planning* are used interchangeably for this type of approximation.

The basic idea of long-range capacity planning is quite simple. The production plan gives production rates that raise or lower inventories or backlogs. This plan is exploded through the bill of labor (bill of capacity) to give requirements on the resources. Resource requirements planning is performed on a macro level, using rough estimations of load, and a precise fit is not required. The resource requirements are then compared to resource capacities, and attempts are made to match the two. Generally, this is an iterative procedure, and these reviews lead to changes in the production plan and/or the capacities.

TRUE LONG-RUN CAPACITY DECISIONS

Long-run capacity decisions are essentially sequential. Given a projection of long-term growth, what capacity should we set? Would it be better to add capacity in small increments as the growth materializes, or should we obtain economies of scale by overexpanding now to a capacity level that will be adequate for many years to come. Because of the sequential nature of the problem, dynamic programming [3] and decision tree techniques [8] have been widely advocated for capacity decision making.

Long-term capacity decisions involve facility size and location, work force size, and capital equipment. Such "bricks and mortar" decisions tie us down for at least five to ten years into the future. Therefore, it is very important to understand the implications of long-range planning. The uncertainty inherent in our forecasts over this horizon heightens the utility of the simulation approach.

Example 10.2

Virts and Garrett [15] reported a capacity expansion simulation at Eli Lilly. Because it is simple, yet representative, we present its rudiments here. When the article was written in 1970, Eli Lilly had more than a thousand products, principally prescription drugs and agricultural chemicals. New product forecasts were uncertain, especially products that had to be accepted by regulatory agencies and customers. Not only were the product forecasts uncertain, but so were the yields from machines. Sometimes manufacturing plants were designed and even built during the development stage of new products.

To determine the number of machines needed, we could simply estimate:

$$\text{Required machines} = \frac{\text{forecasted sales}}{\text{forecasted yield/machine}}$$

From basic probability, however, we know that the expected value of the ratio of two random variables is *not* the ratio of their expected values. Therefore, simulation is in order. Basically, we use subjective probability distributions to model both sales and yields (see figures 10.2 and 10.3). After generating sales and yields for a large sample of trials, we produce an equipment requirements curve (figure 10.4).

Once we have the equipment requirements curve, it is relatively easy to settle on an optimal number of machines. Let the annual revenue generated by the machine when employed be R, and let the annual fixed charge for owning a machine be C. The contribution is $R - C$. Using marginal analysis, we have the payoff matrix shown in table 10.1.

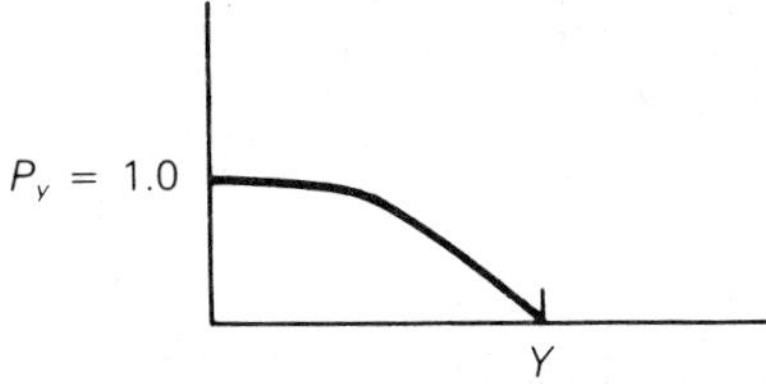

FIGURE 10.2 Yield

P_y is the probability that yield will be Y or greater

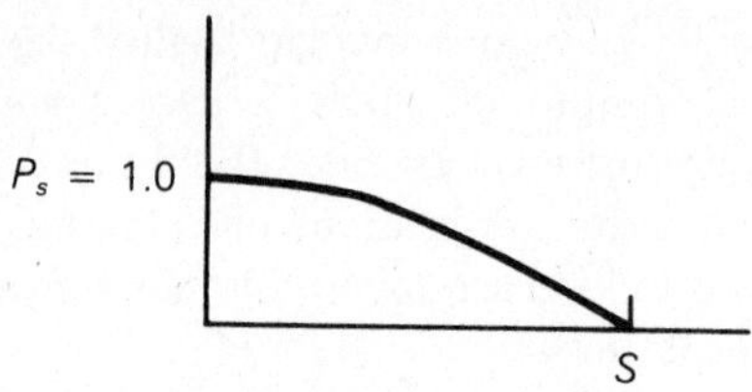

FIGURE 10.3 Sales
P_s is the probability that sales will be S or greater

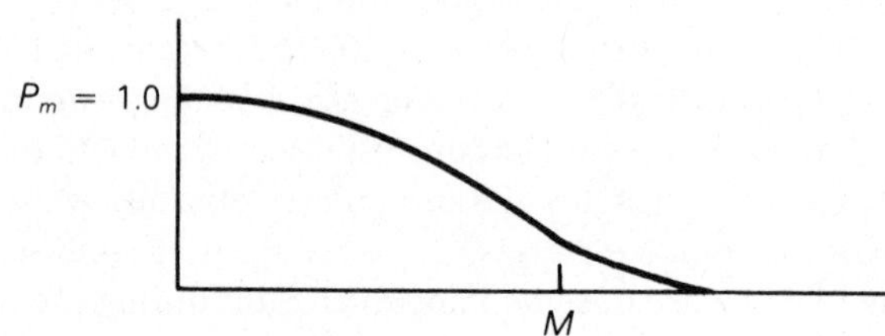

FIGURE 10.4 Machines
P_m is the probability of needing M or more machines

TABLE 10.1 Payoff Matrix for Machine Decision

Decision	*Probability P, Machine Needed*	*Probability 1 − P, Machine Not Needed*
Buy	$R - C$	$-C$
Don't buy	0	0

Hence, we would buy, provided that we had

$$P(R - C) + (1 - P)(-C) \geq 0$$

or $P > C/R$.

Virts and Garrett [15] give an example of a particular product being manufactured and a process being employed for which R = \$1,000,000 and C = \$571,000. According to our analysis, we would continue purchasing machines up to the point on our equipment requirements curve where $P = C/R = 0.571$. (Unfortunately, Virts and Garrett became confused over the concept of opportunity costs and developed the formula $P > C/(2R - C)$, which in this case would give $P = 0.4$ and an expected loss from purchasing the machine!)

ROUGH RELATIONSHIPS FOR LONG-TERM MATERIALS PLANNING

For long-range materials planning, we use only rough-cut procedures. After all, the long-run future is uncertain enough to make detailed planning rather pointless. Furthermore, trying out various detailed plans through simulation takes a great deal of computer storage and time. Both can be minimized by building a rough-cut model of our system.

The model converts the five-year production plan into required capacities, which can then be compared to available capacities. What we need is a bill of labor or resources to indicate the work center man-hour requirements generated, not only by the end product but also by all its subassemblies and components. Three main simplifications allow us to estimate roughly the capacity needed for the products and thus facilitate the use of a model, termed the *bill of labor*. First, we use product groups rather than stock keeping end items as input. Just as a work center is a collection of machines and/or people with similar capabilities, so a product group is a collection of items with similar shop routings and operation times. Sometimes such a group is called a product family, but we prefer to reserve the term *family* for a collection of parts (or end products or subassemblies) that share a major setup. The second simplification concerns the use of key work centers rather than all machines. Since work centers that never cause bottlenecks are of little interest in requirements planning, we consider as key work centers those that might cause trouble. Furthermore, we want rough estimates of critical work centers, not individual machines. Finally, we choose a typical product in the product group and use its bill of materials, route sheets, and standard hours to determine capacity requirements for the planned production for the entire product group. The master production schedule associated with this group will be referred to hereafter as the *gross MPS*.

Example 10.3

Two product groups, A and B, have product trees (bills of materials) as shown here. In a company producing batteries, product group A might be watch batteries and group B might be photographic batteries.

The process sheets in table 10.2 give the sequence of operations (route) for each item, along with setup and run time standards. In addition, our inventory records show economic order quantities for these items as A, 15; B, 10; C, 25; D, 20; and E, 30. From this information, we can calculate standard run hours in each work center:

$$\text{Standard run hours} = \frac{\text{setup}}{\text{EOQ}} + \text{run time}$$

For item C in the milling work center (operations 0010 and 0030), for example:

TABLE 10.2 Process Sheets, Example 10.3

Item	*Operation Number*	*Work Center*	*Operation Description*	*Setup Hours*	*Run Hours*
A	0010	1030	Assembly	0	2.00
B	0010	1030	Assembly	0	3.00
C	0010	1012	Milling	0.3	0.14
	0020	1020	Drilling	2.4	0.40
	0030	1012	Milling	2.7	0.23
	0040	1018	Grinding	1.0	0.21
D	0010	1012	Milling	0.4	0.15
	0020	1020	Drilling	2.8	0.35
	0030	1018	Grinding	2.2	0.24
E	0010	1012	Milling	0.3	0.18
	0020	1020	Drilling	2.1	0.39
	0030	1012	Milling	2.5	0.26
	0040	1020	Grinding	1.3	0.23

$$\text{Standard run hours} = \frac{0.3 + 2.7}{25} + 0.14 + 0.23 = 0.49 \text{ hours}$$

Intermediate run time tables can be created for each item by this procedure:

Item	*Work Center*	*Work Center Standard Run Hours per Unit*
C(Q^* = 25)	Milling	0.49
	Drilling	0.50
	Grinding	0.25
D(Q^* = 20)	Milling	0.17
	Drilling	0.49
	Grinding	0.35
E(Q^* = 30)	Milling	0.53
	Drilling	0.46
	Grinding	0.27
A(Q^* = 15)	Assembly	2
B(Q^* = 10)	Assembly	3

The bill of labor, which follows readily from the intermediate run time tables, is shown in table 10.3. Product group A requires C and D, giving total milling requirements of 0.49 + 0.17 = 0.66.

Now, taking the production plan presented in table 10.4, we can generate a resource requirements plan, as shown in table 10.5, given the presently available capacity of 5,000 standard run hours. We now see, for example, that producing 3,000 units of A and 2,000 units of B in 1985 will require 3,000 * 0.66 + 2,000 * 1.02, or 4,020 hours of milling time.

TABLE 10.3 Bill of Labor or Resources

	Standard Run Hours per Unit	
Work Center	*Product Group A*	*Product Group B*
1012 milling	0.66	1.02
1020 drilling	0.99	0.96
1018 grinding	0.60	0.52
1030 assembly	2.00	3.00

TABLE 10.4 Production Plan for Product Groups A and B

	Units per Year				
Item	*1985*	*1986*	*1987*	*1988*	*1989*
A	3,000	4,000	3,000	3,000	3,000
B	2,000	2,000	3,000	3,500	4,000

TABLE 10.5 Rough-Cut Requirements Plan for Milling Center (Rough-Cut Capacities)

	Standard Run Hours per Year				
	1985	*1986*	*1987*	*1988*	*1989*
Required	4,020	4,680	5,040	5,550	6,060
Available	5,000	5,000	5,000	5,000	5,000
Cumulative deficit	—	—	40	590	1,650

Table 10.5 shows that beginning in 1987, requirements exceed capacity. Our response can only be to reduce the planned production in line with the capacity constraint or to add more machines and/or people.

LONG-TERM RESOURCE REQUIREMENTS PLANNING

So far, we have used only gross estimates of long-run capacity requirements for making decisions regarding facilities and equipment needs. Now we turn to the more specific long-term planning process of testing the feasibility of various gross master production schedules. Although we still use work centers and product groups to gain rough approximations of load, we now want these estimates in specific time buckets for a particular master schedule.

The resource requirements planning concept thus facilitates balancing long-range needs and maintaining a reasonably level load on a company's resources. Resource requirements planning consists of the following steps:

1. Compute the load profile for each product group. The load profile is based on one unit of an average product.
2. Determine the total load needs on each resource for the proposed MPS. This determination is called the resource requirement profile.

3. Simulate the effect of an alternative MPS on resource requirements, and finalize on an acceptable MPS.

Computing the Load Profile

We can develop a product load profile by choosing a typical product in a product group. The product load profile displays the time-phased requirements of a machine load report to produce one unit of the typical product. To compute the profile, simply run one unit of the product through the MRP system, using no lot sizing and no beginning inventories for any item. The gross requirement of one unit of the typical product is exploded through all levels of the product structure in the usual fashion to generate planned order releases (PORs). The computations are made only once against each resource for each product group, and the load profile is stored in the computer for future use. Although the concept of the load profile is simple, the computations could become cumbersome for a complex product. Example 10.4 illustrates the development of a load profile for product group A (from Example 10.3) in the milling work center.

Example 10.4

Recall from Example 10.3 that product group A has a bill of materials and lead times as follows:

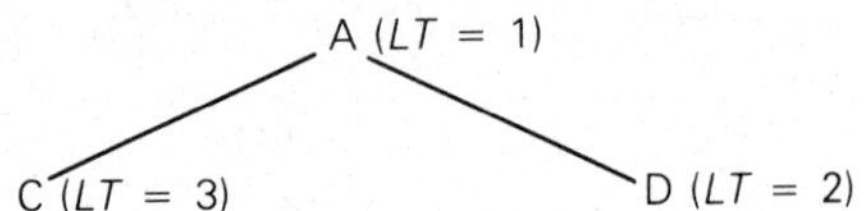

To locate the gross requirement for group A, we take an arbitrary future time bucket beyond our total manufacturing lead time—for example, bucket 10. Then we would have the typical MRP time phasing shown in table 10.6. The process file is shown in table 10.7.

If we could schedule and load the planned order releases, we could determine where and when the per unit workload would fall, as follows:

Item A (POR in week 9): The end item has a one-week lead time. Therefore, it requires a load of two hours during the ninth week.

Item C (POR in week 7): Item C has a two-week lead time. We will assume that operation 0010 milling and operation 0020 drilling are performed during week 7 and that operation 0030 milling and operation 0040 grinding are performed during week 8. Standard run hours per operation for each item can be calculated in any machine center and assigned to specific time buckets, as shown in table 10.8. For example, operation 0030 milling, which is performed during period 8 for item C, consists of a setup time of 2.7 hours, with a lot size of 25 and a run time of 0.23 hours per unit:

$$\text{Load} = \frac{2.7}{25} + 0.23 = 0.338 \text{ hours/unit}$$

TABLE 10.6 Time-Phased Requirements (POR) Table for Product Group A

	Weeks									
	1	2	3	4	5	6	7	8	9	*10*
End Item A (*LT* = 1 week)										
Gross requirements (GR)										1
Planned order release (POR)									1	
Item C (*LT* = 2 weeks)										
GR									1	
POR							1			
Item D (*LT* = 3 weeks)										
GR									1	
POR						1				

TABLE 10.7 Process File, Example 10.4

Item	*Operation Number*	*Work Center*	*Setup Hours*	*Run Hours*	*Operation Standard Run Hours per Unit*[a]
A	0010	Assembly	0	2.00	2.000
B	0010	Assembly	0	3.00	3.000
C (Q^* = 25)	0010	Milling	0.3	0.14	0.152
	0020	Drilling	2.4	0.40	0.496
	0030	Milling	2.7	0.23	0.338
	0040	Grinding	1.0	0.21	0.250
D (Q^* = 20)	0010	Milling	0.4	0.15	0.170
	0020	Drilling	2.8	0.35	0.490
	0030	Grinding	2.2	0.24	0.350

[a] This column of information is not provided by the process file but has been calculated specifically for this example. We will use these standard run hours in table 10.8: (Setup hours/lot size) + run time.

Item D: Item D has three operations, with a lead time of three weeks. Assume that operation 0010 milling is performed during week 6, operation 0020 drilling during week 7, and operation 0030 grinding during week 8. Standard run hours for each machine center are assigned to each time bucket. To compute the load profile, simply add all loads in each machine center for every week, as shown in table 10.8.

The Resource Requirements Profile

What requirements are generated by a gross master production schedule? A resource requirements profile gives a rough estimate of expected loads on key resources. To generate a resource requirements profile, we extend the load profile for each product group in the gross master production schedule.

GR on A in period 10 ↓

TABLE 10.8 Load Profile Computations, Product Group A

	Weeks									
Machine Center	*1*	*2*	*3*	*4*	*5*	*6*	*7*	*8*	*9*	*10*
Assembly										
Load in Hours									2.000	
Milling										
Load for C							0.152	0.338		
Load for D						0.170				
Total						0.170	0.152	0.338		
Drilling										
Load for C							0.500			
Load for D							0.490			
Total							0.990			
Grinding										
Load for C								0.250		
Load for D								0.350		
Total								0.600		

GR on A in period 6 ↓

		1	2	3	4	5	6
Assembly						2	
Milling	Load on C			.152	.338		
	Load on D		.170				

GR on A in period 6 places a 0.17 hour per unit load or milling in period 2.

Example 10.5

Compute the resource requirements profile for the milling machine center. The gross master production schedule for product groups A and B is as follows (assume 150 standard hours of existing capacity):

Gross Master Production Schedule

	6	7	8	9	10
Group A	200		200		200
Group B		150		150	

A load profile for product group B in the milling center can be calculated to match the load profile exhibited in figure 10.5 for product group A. Multiply the load profile data by appropriate POR quantities to obtain the total resource requirements in each time bucket for every lot, as shown in table 10.9. For example, consider lot 5 for product group A—gross MPS requirements of 200 in period 10. For the milling work center, Table 10.8

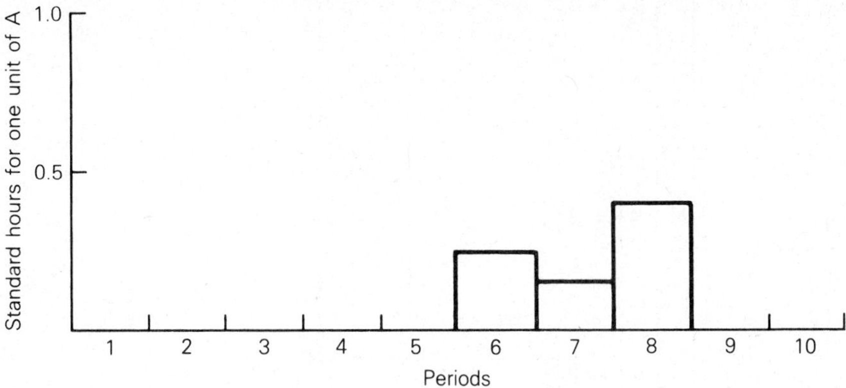

FIGURE 10.5 Product group A load profile for milling work center in real time periods

indicates that 0.152 hours per unit would be required in week 7; but 200 units of A then require 30.4 hours of milling time.

The computations for lot 5 in milling machine requirements are as follows:

Period 8: (200)(0.338) = 67.6 hours

Period 7: (200)(0.152) = 30.4 hours

Period 6: (200)(0.170) = 34.0 hours

All other requirements are similarly calculated and summarized. The totals represent the resource requirements profile, as exhibited in figure 10.6.

Choosing an Acceptable Gross MPS

Resource requirements profiles are prepared especially for critical machine centers and are compared with the available capacities to gain insight into potential capacity problems. If a problem is detected, then alternative gross master schedules are used to generate new resource requirements profiles. This information helps management decide how much additional capacity will have to be added and when.

Medium-Range Capacity Planning and Control

In medium-range capacity planning, we generally accept the physical facilities and location as they are and add capacity by arranging alternative routings, additional tooling, subcontracting, overtime, and so on. We develop a

TABLE 10.9 Resource Requirements Profile Computations, Milling Machine Center

	Period									
	1	*2*	*3*	*4*	*5*	*6*	*7*	*8*	*9*	*10*
				Lot 1, Group A 200	Lot 2, Group B 150	Lot 3, Group A 200	Lot 4, Group B 150	Lot 5, Group A 200		
Lot 1, Group A		200 * 0.17 = 34.00	30.40	67.60						
Lot 2, Group B				64.80	102.15					
Lot 3, Group A				34.00	30.40	67.60				
Lot 4, Group B						64.80	102.15			
							30.40 = 0.152 * 200			
Lot 5, Group A						34.00		67.60 = 0.338 * 200		
Total		34.00	30.40	166.40	132.55	166.40	132.55	67.60		

GR	6	7	8	9	10
Group A	200		200		200
Group B		150		150	

GR of 200 units of A in period 6 places a 0.17 * 200 = 34 hour load on milling in period 2.

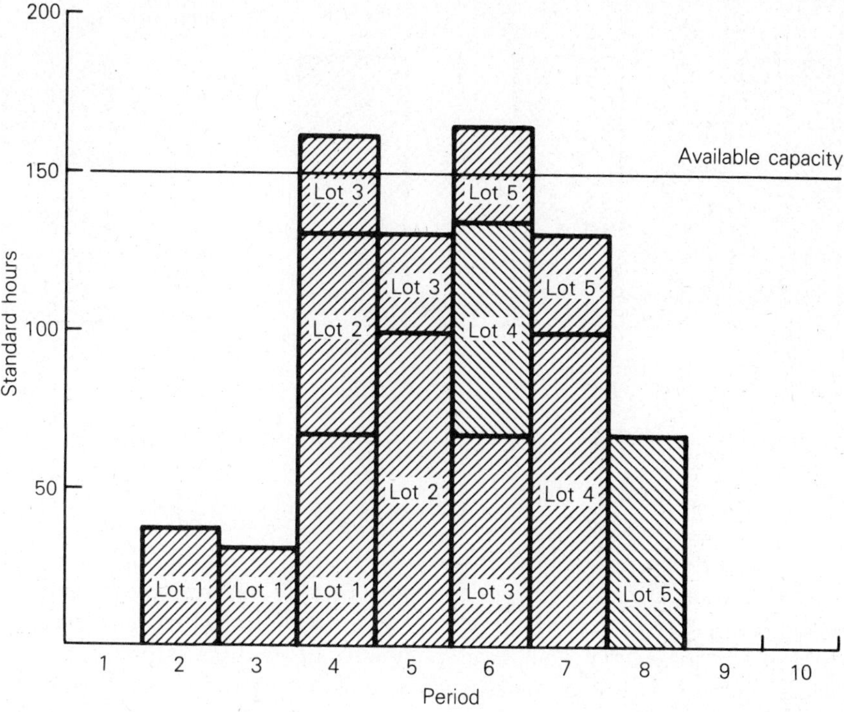

FIGURE 10.6 Resource requirements profile, milling machine center

capacity requirements plan from the master production schedule for specific end items. No longer do we use gross estimates and product groups. A detailed master production schedule can be tried out by exploding it through MRP to give planned orders. When these planned orders are added to released orders, a work center load report can be constructed for each work center in much the same way that we earlier developed a resource requirements profile (see figure 10.7). This capacity requirements report must then be compared with available capacity at the work center.

MEDIUM-TERM CAPACITY REQUIREMENTS PLANNING

Essentially, capacity requirements planning differs from resource requirements planning only in the level of detail considered. Resource requirements planning converts from a gross master schedule of product groups to estimates of time required on major departments, such as fabrication and assembly, or on key resources, such as a specific work center. The input to capacity requirements planning is a master schedule that shows actual model numbers, as advertised in a catalog. When exploded through the MRP system, this schedule will give capacity requirements on individual work centers.

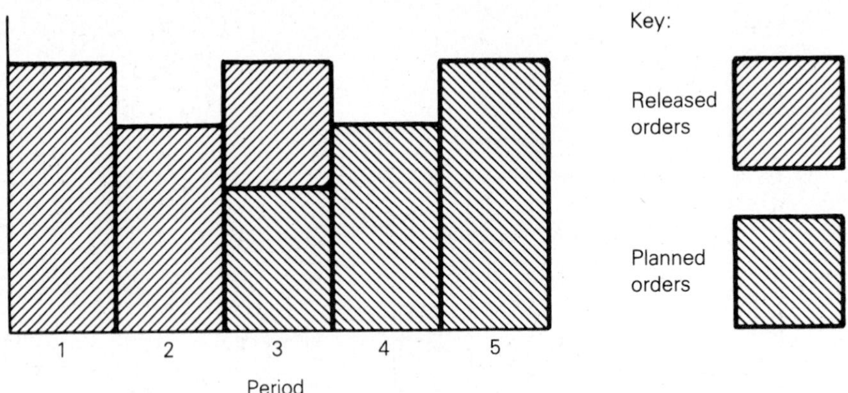

FIGURE 10.7 Capacity requirements report, milling work center

The task of formulating a detailed master schedule consistent with the schedule for product groups will be studied in the next chapter, on the MPS. For the present, we only note that the master scheduler must disaggregate the product group plan by applying individual model popularity percentages or rule-of-thumb computations. In the case of products with major options, such as automatic versus standard transmissions, the option assemblies are often promoted to end item status in a planning bill of materials. Thus, the master production schedule may include specific major assemblies rather than model numbers. The complexities of developing feasible master schedules are reserved for a separate chapter.

Staying with the simple case of exploding a master schedule with end item models only, we observe that the corresponding capacity requirements or load projections are calculated with no consideration of individual work center capacities.

In calculating the loads on the work centers, we have implicitly used the technique of backward scheduling, or backloading. From the due date for the end item, we back off by lead times through planned order release to estimate the timing of requirements on the work centers. Time buckets are essential. In performing this backloading, we abide by scheduling rules, such as allowing two days between operations in different departments. These rules are dealt with in detail in a later chapter on shop floor control (SFC).

This process of preparing load projection without any regard to capacity has received the unfortunate name "infinite capacity loading"—unfortunate because we know that capacities are finite. Infinite capacity loading or capacity requirements planning, whatever it is called, seeks only to show the load implied by a master production schedule.

What happens if the capacity requirements plans show overloaded work centers? Our first reaction might be to shift the load around—that is, level the load. To do this, we must take a closer look at lead times to see whether standard lead times can be compressed to allow some operations to start later and some, perhaps, earlier. The details of this process lead us to a discussion of strategies for leveling loads.

STRATEGIES FOR LEVELING LOADS

Total manufacturing lead time is defined as the average time between the release of an order to the shop floor and its delivery to stores or assembly. Usually, 10% to 20% of lead time is operation duration time—that is, setup and run time. The other 80% to 90% of lead time includes time the job is being moved, being inspected, in queue for an operation, or waiting to be moved. The estimated operation run times depend on the lot size. Interoperation time depends on the conditions in the shop, the backlog of orders on the floor, and the priority of the job.

Strategies for leveling the load depend heavily on changing lead times. Also, backward scheduling sometimes yields a start date in the past; that is, we do not have enough time to meet the due date. To change the lead time, three popular tactics are available. *Overlapping*, which reduces the lead time, entails sending pieces to the second operation before the entire lot is completed on the first operation. *Operations splitting* sends the lot to two different machines for the same operation. This involves an additional setup but results in shorter run times, since only half the lot is processed on each machine. Finally, *lot splitting* involves breaking up the order and running part of it ahead of schedule on an expedited basis. This, of course, involves extra setup but allows us to expedite a few items. We will reserve lot splitting for short-term capacity planning and control, but operations splitting and overlapping properly belong to medium-range planning, where these techniques can be used to reschedule orders and level the load requirements to finite capacity.

FINITE CAPACITY LOADING FOR LEVELING THE LOAD AT A WORK CENTER

Finite capacity loading uses simulation procedures to schedule and load orders automatically within the given capacity constraints at each work center. Visualize a complex simulation program that reiterates between the master production schedule and capacity requirements in an attempt to piece together a jigsaw puzzle within work center constraints.

A basic feature of such a simulation program is the ability to forward schedule. Starting with the earliest possible start date for an operation, forward loading routines project the load for future periods and indicate the completion time for the entire job. For example, a planned delay in the start of an operation because of an overloaded time bucket will cause delays to all subsequent operations and hence will shift much of the load forward. Forward loading, the reverse of backloading, might then predict an order completion date beyond the due date.

In leveling the load, we might also want to perform certain operations ahead of schedule if an early time period has surplus capacity. The chief restrictions on starting operations earlier are the availability of materials and the completion of prior operations on the part or subassembly.

In the medium term, standard load times are used as the simulation attempts to level the released loads to the planned loads. Just as capacity requirements planning indicates where capacity adjustments must be made, finite loading indicates where changes should be made in the master schedule. In the next section, we examine short-term scheduling, where we must control jobs at work centers and shift released loads according to priority rules. In the short term, finite loading routines help determine the timing of order releases to the machine centers.

Short-Term Capacity Planning and Control

The capacity plan is finalized in the medium-range planning cycle. In the short term, most of our options have been exhausted. Our capacity adjustment alternatives are overtime, work force reallocation, and, to some extent, alternative routings, operation splitting, and the like. The next step is to ensure that the output measured is equal to the required capacity. For this comparison, we will study input/output rate concepts at the work center level and detailed operations scheduling (short-term finite loading).

INPUT/OUTPUT CONCEPTS AT WORK CENTERS

George Plossl and Oliver Wight [12] have popularized the bathtub model of an input/output system (see figure 10.8). Although their model

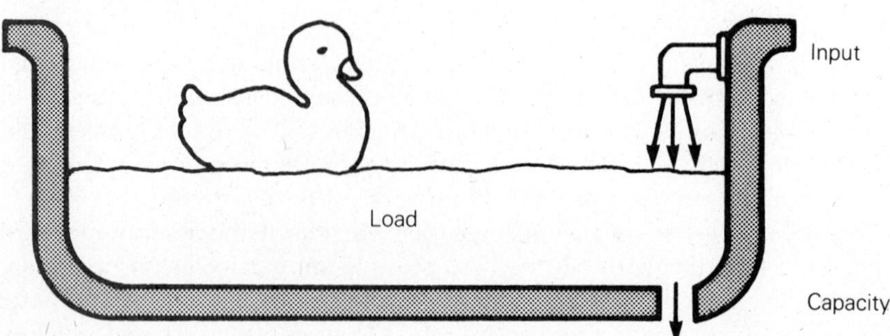

FIGURE 10.8 Bathtub model of an input/output system

(the ducky is ours) portrays the situation very well, we believe that the human body also provides an interesting example of input/output concepts. Caloric intake represents the orders released on the body. Suppose that we consume 3,500 calories a day. Calories burnt in a day would be our capacity—say, 3,000 calories per day. Clearly, we will build up a load—a pot belly or a backlog of fat—at a rate of 500 calories per day. Since a backlog of 3,500 calories equals one pound of excess weight, we would gain one pound every seven days. Now assume that we have built up a five-pound backlog (call it our work-in-process inventory) and that we decide to go on a crash diet. By judiciously cutting out one candy bar and one piece of cake per day, we reduce our caloric intake to 3,000 per day. What happens? We live with our five-pound rubber tire. Only by reducing our intake below 3,000 calories will we work off the backlog. In a manufacturing situation, the output rate must exceed the input rate to reduce the work-in-process inventory. In our biological example, a caloric intake of 2,650 per day would allow us to work off the fat at the rate of 350 calories per day, so that the five pounds could be gone in ten days.

Input/output concepts help explain the dilemma of the lead time–late order cycle. A company suffering poor due date performance decides to increase lead times. If only we had two more weeks for the job, we could complete it on time! Increasing the lead time only aggravates the situation, however, because orders are released earlier, and this puts a larger load on the plant. Inevitably, queues get longer, lead times are increased further, and the revised due dates are missed.

If increasing the lead time does not solve the problem, what will? Rephrasing the question—if the water level (queue or backlog) in the bathtub is too high, how can we reduce it? We can reduce the backlog only by increasing the work center capacity or by reducing the rate of orders released to the factory. This means that we must lower our expectations of quantities to be produced, increase the work center capacity, or subcontract. In our biological example, we must jog more or eat less. Unfortunately, we can't subcontract the jogging.

FINITE LOADING FOR SMOOTHING THE LOAD AT WORK CENTERS

The input/output model focuses attention not only on the capacity or possible output rate but also on the input rate—the rate of releasing orders to the plant. Even the most finely tuned master schedule will probably produce lumpy loads at some work centers—overloads in some periods and underloads in others. Finite loading, or detailed operations scheduling, attempts to ameliorate this situation by smoothing the load at work centers.

Finite loading means simulating the factory operations to determine exactly when orders should be released, how orders will move through the plant, and what order completion dates will result. As in any simulation, we have a model of the system, measures of effectiveness, and decision variables.

In addition to such obvious factors as the number of machines, the number of shifts, and the like, the model of the plant includes priority rules that govern the flow of orders and the time each order spends in queue. Our goal is to reproduce actual job conditions in the face of the orders for the next few weeks.

Priorities determine the time an individual order will spend in queue, just as capacities determine overall queue sizes or work-in-process amounts. The order due date, the size of the order, and management's feelings about the importance of the customer all contribute to order priority. Clearly, orders with higher priority will be released to the shop first. Once released to the shop, the order must find its way out through the queues at various operations. Here, the operation priority takes over. At each work center, a priority index or a critical ratio (CR) might be calculated to decide which job should go on the machine next. Critical ratios, like babies, come in various sizes and shapes, and those responsible for them always claim that theirs are the best. Most critical ratios hinge on some measure of the time remaining to due date, divided by the time or number of operations remaining:

$$\text{CR} = \frac{\text{time to due date}}{\text{required time for remaining operations}}$$

In general, critical ratios are constructed so that lower ratios represent higher or more urgent priority and ratios less than unity indicate orders that will be late. In some companies, the critical ratio is further modified by a weighted measure of order priority to ensure that very important orders get high operation priorities. These aspects are fully explored in a later chapter on job shop production activity control.

For our simulation, the measures of effectiveness are quite simple: How smooth are the input rates at the work centers, and how close are the predicted completion dates to the due dates generated by the master production schedule? To achieve good performance on these effectiveness measures, several decision alternatives are available: order release planning decisions and operations sequencing decisions.

Order Release Systems

The order release planning module of a finite loading program or system might be run every few days. Order priorities are calculated for released and planned orders. Then orders are released according to these priorities and at the latest possible start dates, as determined by the lead time offsetting routine in the capacity requirements planning module. When an order runs up against a capacity constraint at a work center, the order release planning system tries some alternatives. First, the previous and the following week are checked out to see whether the operation could be handled then. Also, alternative work centers or routings might be possible. Furthermore, some orders might be released earlier to take advantage of underload situations. Early release of orders depends on material availability. As a last resort, if no alternatives can be found that allow all operations to be completed by the due date, the master production schedule will have to be changed.

Various computer software packages handle order release planning in different ways. Indeed, many companies have created their own systems. Nevertheless, the underlying procedures rest on order scheduling and operation shifting: releasing the order earlier or shifting one of its operations forward or back. The forward loading procedures mimic company operations. How do we fit the puzzle together?

Example 10.6

Jobs A and B are waiting to be released. Both will go to work center 1. Then A will continue on to work center 3 while B will go to center 4. Suppose that A has a higher priority on the first work center but that work center 3 is backlogged and center 4 is idle. Which order should be released first? Job B should be first, of course, even though it has a lower priority on the first work center.

Operation Sequencing Systems

At an even more detailed level than the order release planning system, we might run an operation sequencing system daily. The IBM Communications Oriented Production Information and Control System (COPICS) [3] uses a work sequence list rather than a standard priority list at each work center. Essentially, a work sequence list gives the work center foreman a sequence of jobs based on coordinated priorities between work centers. A job with a low priority on the first work center might get a top priority on the second work center in the usual priority list. Yet the job will not arrive at the second work center for quite some time because of its low priority at the first center. By contrast, the work sequence list at the second work center will show jobs in an order that *combines* the usual priority at the second work center and the priority at the first work center. Hence, the list takes into account both priority and probable arrival at the second work center.

An operation sequencing system uses the work sequence concept, and such options as operations splitting, overlapping, and lot splitting are used in simulating the performance of the factory. A prime purpose of this simulation is to generate feasible, not optimal, work sequence lists for the foremen.

The complexity of finite loading does not suit everyone's taste or needs. Many companies simply do finite loading manually as problems arise, without resorting to simulation. Indeed, the simulation programs are generally designed to model the usual behavior of people who are scheduling and loading the plant.

INPUT/OUTPUT CONTROL

The simplicity and usefulness of input/output control make this technique appealing. Wight [16] developed the approach of monitoring work centers with input/output control reports. Released and planned orders appear as man-hour requirements in the capacity requirements plan. Since these loads may be rather lumpy, we might calculate an average rate of orders arriving at the work center and show this as our planned input at the work center, as in table 10.10. The input in table 10.10 comes as planned for the first three weeks. Our planned output rate, 50 hours in excess of the planned input rate, indicates an attempt to reduce the backlog to 200 units by the end of week 4. Even so, our actual output shows that we have not been entirely successful. At the end of four weeks, the released backlog has been reduced by only 170 units, to 230.

In working with input/output tables, several related tables are extremely useful. We encourage the reader to draw these up to help in creating an input/output report like table 10.10. First, planned input versus planned output can be displayed as a planned backlog or planned queue report. Similarly, actual input versus actual output presents the most important information—what's happening to the actual queue.

Input/output control tables are useful in both production to order and production to stock. In production to stock, forecast sales become planned inputs. Planned versus actual sales, production, and inventory are then displayed in three tables, yielding a production/sales/inventory report. In production to order, the manufacturing lead time takes center stage, as *released* backlogs are closely monitored. Of course, total lead time through the plant also depends on the size of the *unreleased* backlog. The assumption must be made that total lead time can be reduced by careful management of manufacturing lead times.

TABLE 10.10 Input/Output Report, Work Center 20

	Standard Hours per Period					
	1	2	3	4	5	6
Planned input	350	350	350	350	350	350
Actual input	350	350	350	350		
Cumulative deviation (actual − planned)	0	0	0	0		
Planned output	400	400	400	400	350	350
Actual output	410	395	405	360		
Cumulative deviation	+10	+ 5	+10	−30		
Backlog reduction by week						
Planned backlog	350	300	250	200	150	100
Actual backlog	340	295	240	230		

Released work backlog = 400 hours. Planned and actual backlogs show the status at the end of each period.

Input/output tables focus attention where it should be—where we can actually make decisions. This view of the world says that backlogs and lead times can be controlled by close monitoring.

Example 10.7

Most of us accept the idea that some queue is necessary to act as a buffer between succeeding operations. Suppose that we have been working with an average queue size of 400 man-hours, with a standard deviation of 100 man-hours. Further, we want only a 1% chance of ever running out of work at our work center. What queue size should we maintain, assuming that the queue size is normally distributed? Using the normal tables, 99% of the curve will be to the right of the average queue size minus 2.34 standard deviations. Hence, the average is 2.34 * standard deviation = 2.34 * 100 = 234.

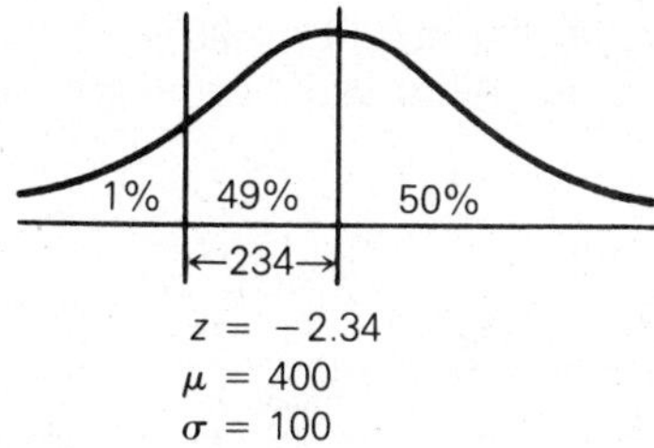

Having determined that we could be satisfied with an average queue size of 234 man-hours, compared with our current average of 400 man-hours, how do we go about reducing the queue? Simply set the planned output rate at 10 man-hours more than the planned input rate for the next sixteen weeks. This is our "diet." Of course, as the weeks go by, we may find that it takes fewer weeks than planned.

Summary

This chapter has examined the capacity planning and control cycle. Production plans are checked against key resource capacities through the use of the bill of labor. Resource requirements planning and capacity requirements planning are methods for determining the capacities needed by trial master schedules. Given an infeasible schedule, adjustments to capacity or revisions in the schedule can alleviate bottlenecks.

Matching requirements to capacities becomes a juggling maneuver. Methods for compressing lead times and rescheduling orders can help meet customer needs with the capacities available. Finite capacity planning can be accomplished by planners either manually or with computer algorithms.

Input/output control techniques help monitor the release of orders and the output rates at work centers. Reductions in backlogs occur only when output rates are greater than input rates.

PROBLEMS

1. Clark Company makes three products on three different types of equipment. The matrix of operating times and job setup times (in decimal hours), demand per month, and economical lot sizes for manufacturing are given in table 10.11. The machine utilization factor is approximately 90%, and operator efficiency of the shop is believed to be 105%. How many of each of the machines will be needed if the plant works a forty-hour week?
2. Using the information in table 10.12, a machine utilization factor of approximately 80%, and operator efficiency of the shop of 105%, how many of each machine will be needed if the plant works a forty-hour week?
3. A work center has the input/output table shown below. The starting backlog is 150 hours. What will be the backlog at the end of the third week?

TABLE 10.11 Matrix for Problem 1

Equipment	*Job A*	*Job B*	*Job C*
Punch			
Set-up hours	0.750		0.600
Run hours	0.040		0.060
Grind			
Setup hours		0.750	
Run hours		0.020	
Screw			
Setup hours	0.400	0.520	
Run hours	0.030	0.050	
Demand per month (units)	1,500	2,000	1,000
Economical batch quantity (units)	300	500	250

Standard Hours per Week

	1	2	3	4	5
Planned input	400	400	400	400	400
Actual input	410	410	380	310	310
Planned output	420	420	420	420	420
Actual output	380	380	380	320	300

4. What would the backlog be at the end of the third week if planned output rates had been met in problem 3?
5. What will the actual backlog be at the end of week 5?

TABLE 10.12 Matrix for Problem 2

Equipment	*Job 1*	*Job 2*
Turn		
Setup hours	0.800	
Run	0.070	
Press		
Setup hours		0.450
Run hours		0.020
Die		
Setup hours	0.550	0.600
Run hours	0.040	0.030
Demand per month (units)	800	1,500
Economical batch quantity (units)	400	400

6. At a particular work center, our average queue has been 250 hours, with a standard deviation of 50 hours. Should we reduce our queue length? If so, by how much?
7. At a particular work center, our average queue has been 400 hours, with a standard deviation of 75 hours. Should we reduce our queue length? If so, by how much?
8. Using the following bill of materials and data, determine whether the given production plan is feasible.
   a. Bill of materials:

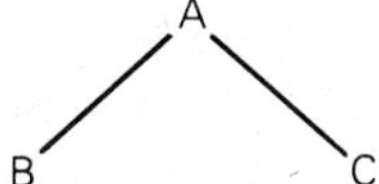

   b. Route sheet:

Product or Subassembly	Work Center	Unit Hours
A	Assembly	3
B	Milling	2
	Drilling	1
C	Milling	2
	Drilling	3

   c. Work center capacities:

Assembly: 250 hours per month
Milling: 150 hours per month
Drilling: 120 hours per month

d. Production plan:

	Month								
PRODUCT	1	2	3	4	5	6	7	8	LOT SIZE
A	20	25	30	35	40	45	45	45	10

If the plan is not feasible, explain the difficulty.

9. Using the following bills of materials and data, determine whether the given production plan is feasible.
   a. Bills of materials:

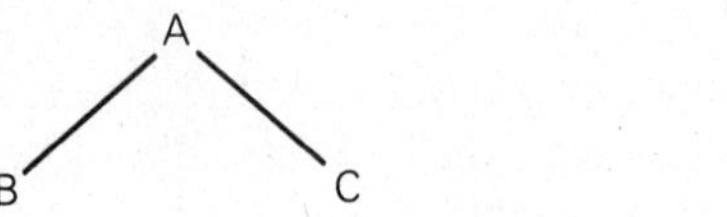

   b. Route sheet:

Product or Subassembly	Work Center	Unit Hours
A	Assembly	4
B	Assembly	4
C	Turning	1
	Tapping	2
D	Milling	4
	Tapping	4
E	Turning	3
	Tapping	4

   c. Work center capacities:

   Assembly: 350 hours per month
   Milling: 150 hours per month
   Turning: 150 hours per month
   Tapping: 120 hours per month

   d. Production plan:

	Month								
PRODUCT	1	2	3	4	5	6	7	8	LOT SIZE
A	30	30	30	30	30	40	40	40	15
B	15	15	20	20	25	25	25	25	15

   If the plan is not feasible, explain the difficulty.

10. Using the data in problem 9, suggest a better production plan.

11. Using the following data and the technique of backward scheduling, determine whether we can meet the due dates on products Y and Z.

a. Route sheet (times in hours):

	Product Y		*Product Z*	
OPERATION NUMBER	WORK CENTER	TIME	WORK CENTER	TIME
I	1	50	2	50
II	3	60	3	55
III	2	70	1	50

b. Work center capacities:

Work Center	*Hours per Day*
1	60
2	70
3	80

c. Due dates:

Job	*Day*
Y	3
Z	3

12. Using the following data and the technique of backward scheduling, determine whether we can meet the due dates on products A and B.

a. Route sheet (times in hours):

	Product A		*Product B*	
OPERATION NUMBER	WORK CENTER	TIME	WORK CENTER	TIME
10	1	35	2	40
20	4	35	4	50
30	3	40	1	50
40	2	50	3	55

b. Work center capacities:

Work Center	*Hours/Day*
1	50
2	40
3	40
4	40

c. Due dates:

Job	*Day*
A	3
B	3

13. Given the data in problem 12, level the load as much as possible.

14. A company makes five products on four different types of equipment. The matrix of operating times and job setup times (in decimal hours), the demand per month, and the economical lot sizes for manufacturing are given in table 10.13. The machine utilization factor is approximately 90% and operator efficiency of the shop is believed to be 105%. How many of each of the machines will be needed if the plant works a forty-hour week?

15. Would it make more sense to change the EOQs in problem 14 rather than to purchase machines?

16. The bills of material for products A, B and C are as follows (items 1, 2, 4, and 5 are those in problem 14):

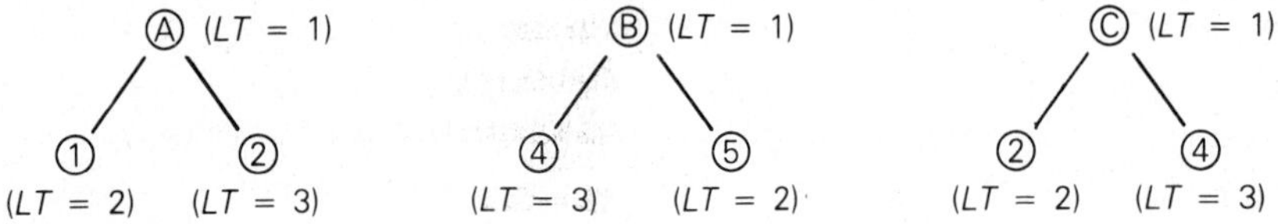

Exhibit the bill of labor for products A, B, and C.

17. Generate load profiles for product A in problem 16.

TABLE 10.13 Matrix for Problem 14

Equipment	*Item 1*	*Item 2*	*Item 3*	*Item 4*	*Item 5*
Lathe					
Setup hours	0.800			0.500	
Run hours	0.050			0.070	
Forge					
Setup hours		0.550		0.750	
Run hours		0.060		0.040	
Mill					
Setup hours	0.320	0.750			0.450
Run hours	0.010	0.020			0.015
Grind					
Setup hours			0.500		0.600
Run hours			0.050		0.060
Demand per month (units)	1,000	2,000	1,500	500	800
Economical batch quantity (units)	250	500	300	200	400

TABLE 10.14 PSI Report for Problem 21

	Units per Period				
	1	2	3	*4*	5
Production					
Planned	350	450	360	460	400
Actual	300	500	400	450	480
Sales					
Forecast	350	460	475	500	390
Actual	400	500	450	420	475
Inventory					
Starting inventory = 1,500 units					

18. Given the following MPS, generate a resource requirements profile for the forge.

	Gross Requirements per Week				
PRODUCT	5	6	7	8	9
A	1000	2000	1500	2000	
B	500	800	600	400	200
C		1100	1200	1100	1100

19. Generate load profiles for products B and C in problem 16.

20. Generate resource requirements profiles for the lathe, mill, and grinding centers, given the product information in problem 14 and the MPS in problem 18.

21. One of the common uses of an input/output control report is in creating a production/sales/inventory (PSI) report. Table 10.14 shows the planned and actual production and sales data. Expand the PSI report to include planned and actual inventories.

22. At a particular work center, our average queue has been 200 hours, with a standard deviation of 30 hours. Should we reduce our queue length? If so, by approximately how much?

23. At a particular work center, our average queue has been 200 hours, with a standard deviation of 100 hours. What does this indicate? What should be done?

24. Using the following bills of materials and data, determine whether the given production plan is feasible.
    a. Bills of materials:

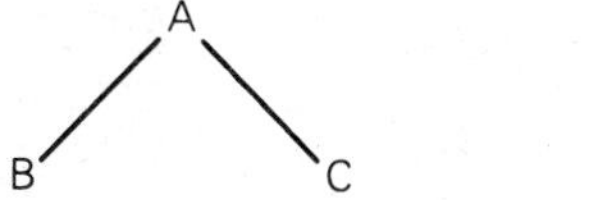

D

b. Route sheet:

Product or Subassembly	*Work Center*	*Unit Hours*
A	Assembly	4
B	Milling	3
	Drilling	2
C	Turning	1
	Drilling	4
D	Turning	3
	Drilling	3

c. Work center capacities:

Assembly: 300 hours per month
Milling: 150 hours per month
Drilling: 120 hours per month
Turning: 120 hours per month

d. Production plan:

	Month								
PRODUCT	1	2	3	4	5	6	7	8	LOT SIZE
A	20	20	25	30	40	40	40	40	10
D	15	15	15	15	15	15	15	15	15

If the plan is not feasible, explain the difficulty and suggest a better production plan.

25. Using the following data and the technique of backward scheduling, determine whether we can meet the due dates on products A, B, and C.

a. Route sheet (times in hours):

	Product A		*Product B*		*Product C*	
OPERATION NUMBER	WORK CENTER	TIME	WORK CENTER	TIME	WORK CENTER	TIME
I	2	30	1	40	1	35
II	3	30	3	30	4	20
III	4	40	2	40	2	35
IV	1	50	4	30	3	40

b. Work center capacities:

Work Center	*Hours per Day*
1	60
2	40
3	50
4	30

c. Due dates:

Job	*Day*
A	5
B	4
C	5

26. Work center 17 has the following input/output table and a starting backlog of 130 hours. What will the backlog be at the end of the third week?

	Standard Hours per Week					
	1	2	3	4	5	6
Planned input	300	300	300	300	300	300
Actual input	305	305	305	150	155	150
Planned output	310	310	310	300	300	300
Actual output	290	290	290	290	190	150

What would the backlog be at the end of the third week if planned output rates had been met?

27. An industrial engineer has been complaining that the workers in work center 17 (in problem 26) are lazy. As evidence, he displays data showing that they are working at half their capacity. What would be your explanation?

REFERENCES AND BIBLIOGRAPHY

1. J. T. Clark, "Capacity Management," *Twenty-second Annual APICS Conference Proceedings*, 1979, pp. 191–194.
2. J. T. Clark, "Capacity Management—Part 2," *Twenty-third Annual APICS Conference Proceedings*, 1980, pp. 355–341.
3. D. Erlenkotter, "Capacity Expansion with Imports and Inventories," *Management Science*, Vol. 23, No. 7 (March 1977), pp. 694–702.

4. R. Everdell, *Master Production Scheduling*. APICS Training Aid (Washington, D.C.: American Production and Inventory Control Society, 1974).
5. *IBM Communications Oriented Production Information and Control Systems* (COPICS), Vol. 5 (1st ed.). Form No. G320-1978. (White Plains, N.Y.: International Business Machines Corporation, 1972).
6. R. L. Lankford, "Short Term Planning of Manufacturing Capacity," *APICS Conference Proceedings*, 1978, pp. 37–68.
7. R. L. Lankford, "Input/Output Control: Making It Work," *Twenty-third Annual APICS Conference Proceedings*, 1980, pp. 419–420.
8. J. F. Magee, "How to Use Decision Trees in Capital Investment," *Harvard Business Review*, Vol. 2, No. 5 (September–October 1964), pp. 79–96.
9. J. Orlicky, *Materials Requirements Planning*, (New York: McGraw-Hill, 1975).
10. G. W. Plossl, *Manufacturing Control: The Last Frontier for Profits*. (Reston, Va.: Reston, 1973).
11. G. W. Plossl and W. E. Welch, *The Role of Top Management in the Control of Inventory*, (Reston, Va.: Reston, 1979).
12. G. W. Plossl and O. W. Wight, *Production and Inventory Control*. (Englewood Cliffs, N.J.: Prentice-Hall, 1967).
13. G. W. Plossl, and O. W. Wight, "Capacity Planning and Control," *Production and Inventory Management*, Vol. 14, No. 3 (Third Quarter, 1973), pp. 31–67.
14. A. Rao, *Capacity Management*. APICS Training Aid. (American Production and Inventory Control Society, 1982).
15. J. R. Virts and R. W. Garrett, "Weighting Risk in Capacity Expansion," *Harvard Business Review*, Vol. 48, No. 3 (May–June 1970).
16. O. W. Wight, "Input/Output Control: A Real Handle on Lead Time," *Production and Inventory Management*, Vol. 11, No. 3 (Third Quarter, 1970), pp. 9–31.

appendix 10A

Job Shop Scheduling: A Case Study

Ray Lankford
Plossl & Lankford

Tom Moore
Remmele Engineering, Inc.

Even though Remmele Engineering, Inc. had virtually no prior experience with computer-based manufacturing systems, they recognized that better management of capacity could help them achieve a significant competitive advantage. In this case study, the Vice President of Operations of Remmele describes their implementation of a capacity management system with exceptional capabilities, and he assesses the performance improvements they achieved. To provide a perspective on capacity management systems, the consultant on the Remmele project evaluates developments of the last decade in an effort to define what is the "state-of-the-art" today.

Capacity Systems in Perspective (Ray Lankford)

Ten years ago, in the early 1970's, the revolution in systems of manufacturing planning and control had just begun. Not only did the innovators of those years bring to the attention of the world the power of MRP and the importance of master scheduling, but they also stimulated thought and development in major aspects of capacity management. The formative paper on Input/Output Control appeared in 1970 [1]; a redefinition of what was thereafter called Capacity Requirements Planning occurred at APICS Conference of 1971 [2]; and at the Conference of 1973, I spoke about the feasibility of what we now call Operation Sequencing [3].

Reprinted with permission, American Production and Inventory Control Society, Inc., *25th Annual International Conference Proceedings*, October, 1982.

Interestingly enough those three papers are still in the reprints offered by APICS for study for the certification examination. They represent pioneering thought and are still useful for the study of basic concepts, but they come from an early period in the "systems revolution" of the 1970's and 1980's. As chairman of the APICS Certification Committee on Capacity Management, I am involved now in the search for and examination of new papers which will replace the earlier ones for our study—new works which portray what we have learned and what we have developed in the intervening decade.

There have been significant developments in recent years, which I will describe and evaluate. At the same time, there is a tremendous gap today between what we *know* about capacity management and how we *apply* the techniques available to us. This "proficiency gap" between what we know and what we accomplish in capacity management is one of the most serious problems of manufacturing control today. It is the root of failure of many firms to derive benefits from their installation of MRP. It is a major impediment to increasing productivity in countless manufacturing companies. Without a doubt, improving the management of capacity offers for most companies the greatest single opportunity for improving performance of any sector of manufacturing planning and control. And because of this common "proficiency gap", the fact that a company relatively inexperienced with systems implemented and is successfully using an advanced capacity management system makes the Remmele story interesting and significant.

Remmele's capacity management system consists of Capacity Requirements Planning and Operation Sequencing. They elected not to use Input/Output Control because of characteristics of the production environment which Tom Moore will explain. In this perspective on capacity management, I will not focus on Input/Output Control, since that was done in a paper at the 1980 Conference [4]. We will look, however, at the "state-of-the-art" today in CRP and Operation Sequencing.

In 1971, George Plossl and Oliver Wight wisely proposed the term "Capacity Requirements Planning" to replace what was previously called "infinite loading" or "loading to infinite capacity". They pointed to two weaknesses of traditional machine loading:

1. a typically high past-due load; and
2. a misleading decay of load derived from released orders only.

A solution was proposed for each of these defects:

1. improve priority planning with MRP, so as to reschedule late but unneeded jobs to their time of actual need; and
2. use planned orders from MRP to portray future loads over the entire CRP horizon.

Thus Capacity Requirements Planning took its place as a major module of the integrated manufacturing system.

Despite the demonstrated effectiveness of the technique, however, a "proficiency gap" still exists today. A minority of companies are using CRP effectively—not unlike the situation ten years ago when a relatively few companies had mastered MRP. Moreover, the capacity planning modules of commercial software are usually the weakest part of the packages, making CRP unnecessarily difficult to use effectively. Finally there are some extraordinary misconceptions regarding CRP which may cause confusion to potential users. One such misconception is that CRP is expensive. One consultant has written, "It probably consumes more computer capacity than any other single step within MRP". Leaving aside the semantic confusion of this reference to MRP, this commentator is simply misinformed.

In a plant handling 6,420 manufacturing jobs using the same software as Remmele, total processing time for MRP, CRP, and Operation Sequencing (with networking) is about four hours, with CRP requiring about 60% of the time of MRP. In terms of actual CPU time, excluding file manipulation and printing time, CRP loading requires about one minute.

Certainly, when compared to the benefits of having advance visibility of capacity overloads and underloads, the cost of CRP is acceptable and should not deter anyone from using it.

Some other misconceptions about CRP will be dispelled in a later section.

When the manufacturing people at Remmele Engineering decided to improve their ability to schedule their shop, the specific technique they wanted was Operation Sequencing. As Tom will explain later, they arrived at this conclusion independently, without the advice of any so-called "expert" advisor. This was probably fortunate, because no technique in manufacturing control is more misunderstood by consultants and practitioners alike than Operation Sequencing.

Operation Sequencing is sometimes thought of as "finite loading" because it loads work centers only to their known capacity—i.e., to "finite" capacity. Just, however, as the term "infinite" loading was a disservice to the perfectly valid technique we now call Capacity Requirements Planning, so the term "finite loading" bestows confusion and even animosity on what is really an extremely powerful and useful technique of capacity control.

Correctly understood, Operation Sequencing is a technique of *simulation.* It simulates in advance, inside the computer, the sequence in which manufacturing jobs will flow through the various work centers of the plant. Unlike some of the more complex mathematical methods sometimes applied to real-world problems, computer simulation has proven effective in many applications. In their classic book of 1967, Plossl and Wight devoted a section to Job Shop Simulation, which concluded, "Simulation will undoubtedly become one of the most important tools for controlling shop operations efficiently." [5] Indeed, at that time a number of companies, especially in Europe, were already using simulation successfully. One of my clients in Scandinavia has had the technique in continual use with good results since 1968.

The development of manufacturing systems in Europe has been very different from that in the United States. Because of the damage sustained by manufacturing plants during World War II, European industry in the post-war years concentrated on the management of critical capacity. In the United States, by contrast, capacity was plentiful and readily expandable, but materials were frequently critical in a booming economy. It is not surprising that the thrust of systems development was toward materials planning and inventory control. Of course, the eventual development of MRP improved priority planning for both purchased and manufactured items. Nevertheless, capacity management received far less emphasis in the United States than in Europe.

Recently, a group of manufacturing system specialists came from Europe to review several major U.S. software packages for potential purchase. Their conclusions were that the U.S. uses bills of materials far more expertly than they do, and that Master Scheduling and MRP software are highly developed here. They were, however, appalled at the crudity of the capacity management modules which they examined and, in particular, they were shocked at the infrequent use of Operation Sequencing, which they regard as commonplace.

That Operation Sequencing became both misunderstood and controversial in the United States is one of the major misfortunes of the generally productive past decade of system evolution. Several factors contributed to the confusion:

1. the "infinite" versus "finite" debate carried over from prior years tended to polarize opinions before real analysis could begin;
2. the development of MRP concentrated thought and effort, and rightly so, on priority planning methodology;
3. companies implementing MRP were so totally occupied with the demands of data integrity, master scheduling, rough-cut capacity planning, and MRP utilization that they were slow to develop beyond MRP to capacity management; and
4. some of the major opinionmakers in the field, for a variety of reasons, quickly denounced Operation Sequencing as unworkable.

It is both interesting and useful to examine this last factor and ask whether some of these early denunciations were valid then or remain valid now. Certainly Remmele Engineering went into their implementation of Operation Sequencing fully aware of the reasons given by some "experts" as to why the technique will not work. Remmele simply concluded that the objections of a decade ago are no longer valid today.

Criticism of Operation Sequencing derives from that fundamental misconception referred to earlier, that *it is the same as finite loading*. Let's look at the facts.

Oliver Wight has described finite loading in this way: "It automatically revises the need priorities—that is, the priorities developed by MRP, for example, in order to level the load." [6]

Does Operation Sequencing do this? Absolutely not! It uses the required dates developed by MRP to prioritize all jobs and *does not revise them*.

The definition of Operation Sequencing is: " . . . a simulation of what is likely to happen on the shop floor, given the *current production plan* and existing man power and machine availability." [7] (. . . emphasis was added by the author.)

By "current production plan" is meant the Master Schedule converted into manufacturing jobs with required dates developed by MRP. As will be seen later, Operation Sequencing at Remmele uses the required date of each job to state its priority and always endeavors to schedule to that date.

Although Operation Sequencing loads work centers to finite capacity, it clearly is something different from "finite loading".

As a result of the confusion over finite loading, some of the defects of that limited technique have been linked to Operation Sequencing.

In the early 1970's, four specific problems were attributed to any system using "finite" loading:

- *Assumes predictable job arrival.* This alleged defect of simulation is ironic, in that the prediction of job arrivals by simulation is far more accurate than it is with backward planning, upon which CRP and conventional Dispatch Lists are based. Some early ultra-sophisticated simulators pretended to predict events to fractions of an hour, which deserved the ridicule of practical manufacturing people. The objective of Remmele's system is to do better—much better—than backward planning which uses "planned" queue allowances, which frequently do not prevail in the plant. This will be illustrated in the section on the mechanics of Operation Sequencing.
- *Component priorities are usually dependent.* Here the objection was that getting all components of an assembly scheduled to complete at the same time required endless reiterations of the loading process. This is really a "paper tiger" in that the purpose of simulation is not to schedule all components equally late, but rather to identify those which will probably be late so that early action can be taken to solve the problem.
- *Automatic master scheduling is risky.* Nothing could be more true! However, no practical proponent of simulation ever advocated letting

the computer have the final say in determining the schedule. All simulation purports to do is to make a reasonable estimate of completion dates, to highlight potential problems in advance, and to allow production controllers and master schedulers to decide if problems can be solved or if the Master Schedule must be revised. Again, this will be demonstrated in a later section.

- *There are easier, better ways to do the job.* In some production environments, this is unquestionably true. But for the complex network of thousands of manufacturing jobs competing for capacity at hundreds of work centers in a job shop with non-uniform routings, the alternatives of CRP, Input/Output Control, and conventional MRP pegging are grossly inefficient in the solution of the enormous number of daily problems confronting the production controller.

In addition to these alleged problems, there are two other misconceptions which often perplex critics of Operation Sequencing:

- *One must use either Capacity Requirements Planning or Operation Sequencing.* In reality, of course, these techniques are used together, as was recognized by Plossl and Wight fifteen years ago when they advised, "Orders are first . . . loaded to infinite capacity to see where overloads will occur, then orders are rescheduled . . . based on available capacity after corrective actions have been taken . . . " [5]
- *It requires enormous amounts of computer time.* Here, two things have happened in the last ten years: simulators have become simpler and computer power has become cheaper. Tom Moore will address this issue in his remarks.

Where, then, does the "state-of-the-art" stand today?

On this matter Oliver Wight has proposed: "Since we've abolished infinite loading, if we're going to continue with our progress, in my opinion, we should abolish finite loading, and if necessary replace it with some kind of a shop simulator that tells the planner what he might want to do in order to do some load leveling on the vital few, rather than having the computer automatically do the load leveling on everything." [6]

This is sound advice. "Finite loading" is a dead issue. But what about simulation? Wight goes on: "I would have no objection to somebody using the basic logic of finite loading in simulation mode, where they showed the planner what would happen if jobs flowed through different work centers at the current production rate." [6]

Remmele Engineering is doing *exactly that.* They call it Operation Sequencing, and Tom Moore is here to tell you how they got started.

The Manufacturing Environment (Tom Moore)

Remmele is in three basic businesses: 1. contract machining, 2. fabrication, and 3. designing and building special machines. Manufacturing operations are located in five plants comprising a total of 271,000 square feet. Each plant is individually designed and equipped to offer a specialized type of precision machining or machine building and fabrication service.

Each of these basic businesses presents a somewhat different manufacturing environment.

Contract machining—Remmele's contract machining or general machining activities encompass a broad spectrum of part sizes and lot quantities. At the top end of the size range are a number of large boring mills. The largest is capable of machining a work piece 100 feet long by 14 feet high and weighing up to 75 tons. At the lower end, equipment such as small jig bores handles very small precision work to tolerances of .0001″ on a production basis. Lot sizes vary from single piece parts to quantities of 1,000 per week in continuous runs.

Fabrication—Fabrication activities are targeted at jobs requiring both machining and fabrication. These jobs have ranged from the complete fabrication of large paper-making machinery on a one-of-a-kind basis to producing pumps used in the oil fields in quantities of several a month.

Special machinery—The special machines activity consists of designing and building special purpose equipment ranging from individual units to complete production lines. Applications have included the automation of: assembly, fabrication, packaging, testing, processing, machining, and web-handling functions. Although these machines are primarily one-of-a-kind, there are occasional repeat orders for a previously-built machine. In addition to designing machines, this activity also includes building machines to a customer's design.

It should be evident from the above description that the manufacturing process in all three product areas meets a number of the criteria of a classic job shop. These criteria can be grouped generally into demand and processing characteristics as follows:

Demand characteristics—Production is initiated with a customer's order. There is no production to a forecast and no inventory is kept at any level. Demand is predominantly independent demand. Because of the non-repetitive nature of the special-machine business, the bill of materials is approached as a simple, minimum-level bill without emphasizing assemblies and subassemblies and their relationships. Further, since materials and purchased components are bought to order, there is no need to net against inventory levels to determine required production quantities. These demand characteristics led to the conclusion that Materials Requirements Planning was not essential at the present time. Unexpected demands and the rapidly changing nature of the product mix require frequent and rapid rescheduling. The one-of-a-kind or low-volume, nonrepetitive production may result in more frequent changes to the process and to estimated run times than would be the case with repeat production. Repair orders, which may be time-and-materials, and other types of emergencies are part of the business.

Process characteristics—Batch-mode processing with complex routings across a variety of general purpose machine tools characterizes the small lot or one-of-a-kind production. Overlapping operations are the rule in high-volume parts production. Machine assembly operations, such as mechanical, hydraulic, and electrical, are seldom sequential but tend to be in parallel. The plant load at the outset of the project consisted of 3,000 manufacturing jobs requiring 15,000 operations. This load was spread over approximately 150 work centers, including outside processes.

In the contract machining and fabrication business, there are three major features of the service that are being sold: 1. quality or conformity to the customer's specifications; 2. *the timeliness and predictability of deliveries*; and 3. the cost. In the special-machine design business, the added dimensions of engineering and a solution to the customer's problem are present. However, timely production of machine parts, which are competing with all other parts in the shop, is also essential to satisfactory performance.

With all of the above characteristics of the manufacturing process to deal with, two primary business objectives need to be accomplished:

1. improve the ability to set accurate delivery dates; and
2. once these delivery dates are set, improve the on-time delivery performance.

To accomplish these objectives, it was imperative to deal with capacity as a finite resource. Infinite loading did not seem to be a complete solution.

What was needed was the ability to simulate the manufacturing process on each of the jobs to give a realistic delivery estimate. This simulation needed to deal with the complexities of the routings and the diversity of the work centers. It also needed to recognize the finite capacity that existed in all the work centers. This led us to Operation Sequencing.

Capacity Requirements Planning (Ray Lankford)

The five segments of an integrated manufacturing system are:

- Demand Management
- Priority Planning
- Capacity Management
- Production Activity Control
- Inventory

These correspond to the five subdivisions of the body of knowledge defined by APICS. An idea of the relationship among these segments may be gained by reference to figure 10A.1.

The software installed by Remmele is designed to do all the necessary functions of the Capacity Management segment of the integrated system. In addition, it provides some of the most important outputs needed for Production Activity Control, the most notable of which is the prioritized Dispatch List.

The purpose of Capacity Requirements Planning is to disclose the amount of work which must be performed by each work center in each time period in order to produce the products in the Master Schedule.

Master Scheduled items are normally exploded through MRP into time-phased requirements for subassemblies and components. The need for future capacity is then derived from two sources:

1. released manufacturing jobs resident in the open job file; and
2. jobs planned by MRP, but not yet released.

Because the great majority of Remmele's work consists of single piece parts, with customer stipulated required dates, they do not use MRP; because they do not forecast, their Master Schedule is their backlog of customer orders. Thus, there are no "planned jobs", and the only constituent of future load is the open job file.

The process of CRP has been described in the literature [8], but will be summarized here to illustrate technical features of the Remmele system.

The first step in CRP is backward planning, in which each job has operation start and finish dates calculated using planned values for move and queue times. Remmele utilizes a Move Time Matrix to specify transit time. Planned values of queue are specified for each work center in the Work Center Master file.

The second step in CRP is infinite loading, in which each future demand for capacity is registered on each work center for each future time period. These demands are totaled and a report is produced showing the

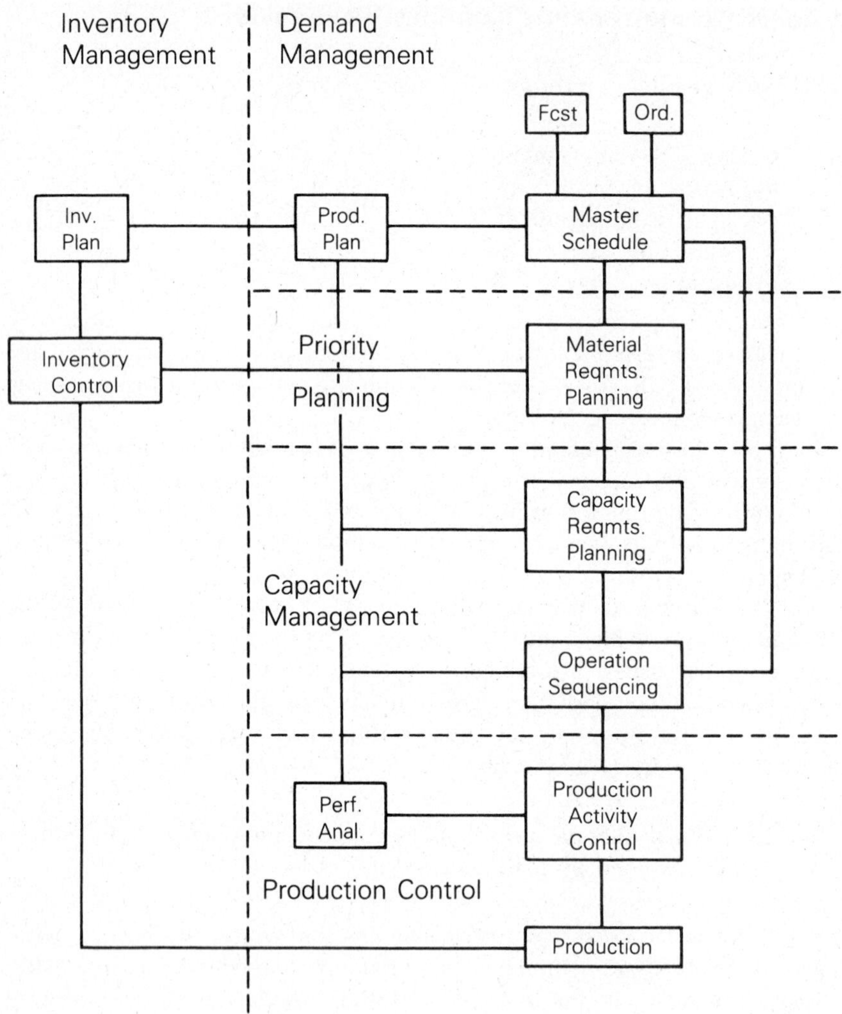

FIGURE 10A.1

overloads and underloads. Let's examine the information contained in a CRP report and be certain we understand the significance of the numbers.

An extremely useful feature of the Remmele CRP report is that it shows the action plan from which the work center's output will be derived. This *action plan*, which portrays how we intend to operate the work center in the weeks ahead, consists of two parts:

1. the Work Schedule in shifts per day, days per week, and hours per shift; and

2. the number of productive units (machines or people) which will be operational each shift.

The CRP report can thus be used as a working document to plan adjustments to schedules or to staffing and at all times show the planner such things as planned overtime, personnel shifts, and scheduled holidays. It is apparent to the planner *where* the capacity is coming from to meet the requirements of the Master Schedule.

It is sometimes said that the "capacity" to be used for CRP must be "demonstrated" capacity. This is provided in the case of Remmele by using the *demonstrated productivity* of the work center during the recent past. The reason for calculating capacity from the productivity ratio, instead of using some "normal" capacity in standard hours, is so that planned outputs for different operating schedules can be readily obtained. For example, there is a capacity of 809 standard hours in a week when six days are scheduled, but only 675 standard hours in a five-day week.

It is important to recognize this fact that capacity is not static, but rather adjustable. What is contained in the "Capacity" field of a CRP report is the *planned output* based on a demonstrated capability from actual output tracking in the recent past.

The "Load", on the other hand, is the *required output*, which must be achieved if the Master Schedule is to be accomplished.

When "output needed" is compared to "output planned", it may be necessary to adjust the capacity plan. Remmele's software will accept this adjustment to the Work Schedule and/or the Units in any period and will calculate and display the expected capacity.

Another important, but poorly understood, fact is that the required output in any period will, in fact, be required *only* if the jobs comprising it arrive in time to be worked on that period. That will occur only if these jobs wait in queues in various preceding work centers a total time equal to the planned queues at those work centers. If queues are longer or shorter than planned, the timing of required capacity may be quite different from that shown by CRP.

A CRP load profile by itself is of limited usefulness. Also required is a Detailed Load Report listing the jobs which comprise the load in each period. With this information, jobs may be routed to alternate work centers, shifted to other time periods, or pegged to end items which are to be rescheduled in the Master Schedule.

When Remmele first implemented CRP, they found some surprising maldistributions of load. Separate salespeople had sold the same machine time, causing unsuspected problems with promised delivery dates. Changes to personnel assignments would clearly be required in the future, but had not been foreseen. And perhaps most important of all, the amount of unsold capacity on each machine could be quantified for focusing the sales engineer's efforts on machine time that could be converted to revenues.

Tom Moore will tell you about how they applied the system, but first he will review how they got the company prepared for a new way of operating.

Preparations for Capacity Management (Tom Moore)

Focusing on operation sequencing as the major system feature, an extensive software search was undertaken including:

- Visists to a number of companies around the country
- Contacts with all major computer vendors either for references or their own software
- Independent software firms
- Custom development programs were discussed with several systems consultants and software firms

The overriding conclusion was that Operation Sequencing applications were relatively few in number and none were found in a business similar to Remmele's.

Most manufacturing systems were MRP oriented and involved a master schedule. One commercially-available system that was found was judged to be too complex. A "black box" solution complete with dedicated stand-alone hardware was discarded because we couldn't find out, to our satisfaction, the logical basis of the programs and how they worked. We were unwilling to turn our manufacturing process over to this type of systems solution.

With the findings above and the lack of alternatives, a program to develop in-house software was begun. Working with two mathematics professors from the University of Minnesota, the development of a prioritizing algorithm for use in operation sequencing was started. Although a workable program was ultimately completed and tested, the question arose as to whether Remmele had the experience or the resources to design or even manage the design of a total system by ourselves.

An article on job shop scheduling, written by Ray Lankford when he was responsible for production control for an oil-field equipment manufacturer, ultimately led us to our consultant.

At the time we discovered the article, Ray was in the consulting business. Contact with him led to a visit by Remmele's top management group to the company featured in his article. In addition, the management group attended a Plossl and Lankford seminar on top management's role in manufacturing.

Seeing the complexities of an actual systems application and drawing on this seminar for background, we concluded that the assistance of a consultant would be very valuable, even necessary to implement a system in a reasonable period of time.

After a visit by Ray and a review of Remmele's operations, we agreed to work together on the implementation of a capacity management system.

Although the search for software had not produced any solutions considered acceptable, we continued our efforts, and ultimately became aware of a new capacity management package that had been successfully implemented, but was not, as yet, commercially released. This package, developed by Manufacturing Management Systems, Inc., incorporated both Capacity Requirements Planning and Operation Sequencing. We judged it to be suitable to our needs.

During implementation, the final documentation was completed and we had the opportunity to incorporate some features that were required to suit our operation.

The software, as it had been developed, did not operate on the computer we had selected. However, the vendor agreed to make the required conversion.

At the time this project began, the Data Processing Department consisted of a manager and two data entry people. Remmele had outgrown its small, punched card batch-processing computer and faced the need to expand due to needs for improved financial and general management systems, as well as manufacturing systems requirements.

No major manufacturing systems existed, except for a job-status reporting system that was driven by time cards. In the financial area, payroll and cost accounting were the major systems in place.

The first objective in the selection process was to select a computer that would meet the company's needs for the next five years. There were a number of key issues that emerged in this selection process:

- The computational requirements of the scheduling system required a certain minimum capability.
- As we examined the upper end of computing capability that we thought we might need, the cost and perceived complexity of large main frames pushed us in the direction of large mini-computers with 32-bit architecture.
- Except for the question of our scheduling requirements, other system needs could have been met by a comfortable, more evolutionary step to an interactive 16-bit mini-computer.
- Substantial differences of opinion existed within our management group over which course to take since there was no commercially-available software to benchmark; however, some tests run on the Operation Sequencing programs developed by the university professors led to a decision in favor of the large computer.

- As it turned out, the purchased software was more computer efficient than we anticipated, but initially it had not been converted to the type of computer under consideration.

The conversion process was accomplished via a remote terminal tied into the new computer. The process went very smoothly and approximated the following timetable:

New computer fully operational	January, 1981
Software conversion completed	May, 1981
CRP in production	July, 1981
Operation Sequencing in production	August, 1981

A project team was established with the Plant Manager of the largest plant designated as the project manager. Also assigned to this team were the Plant Superintendents from two other plants, the Production Control people from each of the plants, the Data Processing Manager, and a representative from the Sales Department. As Vice President of Operations, I worked in a dual capacity: working with the consultant and the project manager, and also working on individual tasks as a team member.

To get the initial direction for the project and to bring the tasks into focus, we concentrated on the major files that we needed to build to get the scheduling system working.

Work center master file—This file contains all the capacity and schedule data for each work center.

Open job file—This consists of both the job master file (information about the job) and the job detail file (specific routing information).

Job chaining file—This file links the bill of materials of an assembly by job numbers.

For each of these files, it was necessary to determine the who, when, and how for all the pieces of information that were required. Certain general task groupings emerged:

Numbering system—After considering a change to a non-significant six-digit job number, we decided to retain our significant job numbering system. In retrospect, this was a good decision because the added complications of introducing this change along with the new system implementation would have outweighed the benefits. It was necessary, however, to establish a common definition of terms for the complete numbering system including sales orders, manufacturing jobs, part numbers, and detail numbers.

Purchasing system interface—Reliable material availability dates are essential to effective scheduling. In our situation, this meant the availability dates of raw materials, purchased components, or customer-supplied materials, such as castings or forgings, are necessary. Some consideration was given to finding a commercially-available purchasing system, but the idea was dismissed when a quick solution was not available. Instead, Remmele developed its own material-control system, which focused narrowly on meeting the needs of the scheduling process and left the implementation of an expanded purchasing system for a future date.

Labor reporting—The existing procedures for labor reporting had to be expanded substantially and formalized to support the requirements of the scheduling system. This was a lengthy process as the requirements of the system led to the development of new procedures to permit accurate execution on the shop floor. The approach we selected involved the use of three individual time cards: on-line operations, off-line operations, and attendance. Although we expect to streamline this process in the future, it was functional and met the necessary requirements of our scheduling and cost accounting systems.

Routings—When the system was first implemented, the quality and thoroughness of the routings varied widely, dependent largely upon the individual writing them. To meet the needs of an accurate scheduling system, it was necessary to include more detail in many cases. The existing route sheets were essentially complete, but it was necessary to make revisions to include additional information. Although the changes were not substantial, this represented a major educational effort given the large number of people involved in writing route sheets.

Networking—This task consisted of developing simple procedures for linking the bill of materials together at the time a special machine or any form of assembly was released to the shop. The goal here was to collect and present in meaningful form all the relevant scheduling information on a project, as well as to take advantage of the feature in the system that relates priorities to the relationship of jobs in the network.

Data integrity—The initial task was to measure the accuracy of the information collected off the shop floor. The target was set at a 95% accuracy level; Remmele was initially confident that it would be close to this figure. The issue was interpreted too narrowly, however, and the initial results were much worse than expected. The more detailed information requirements of the scheduler, the lack of consistent procedures, and poor file maintenance were major problems. With the aid of some very comprehensive audit programs generating time-card error messages, the target level has been achieved for information going into the system. Work is continuing on the reduction of errors and the resulting time-card rejections. Substantial improvement, primarily through education, has been made.

Data processing operating routine—The new computer, followed shortly by this new scheduling system, necessitated a dramatic change in data processing operations. The change in hardware from the batch-processed punched cards to a more interactive environment with the new system changed the whole data processing mentality. Before the scheduling system implementation, a job status run was made on Wednesdays with the previous Friday's time cards. Now, the new system is run at night with the day shift's time cards, and the foremen's work lists are ready at 6:30 AM the following morning.

Interface programming—This task consisted of formatting the data files which the Capacity Management System needed from our work-in-process master files. This was done on a part-time basis over a period of two months by the Data Processing Manager. In addition, a number of custom reports were created that would integrate the Capacity Management System results with the work-in-process data. On-line access has also been provided to display results generated by the system.

System documentation—Our response to this task was slow in spite of the consultant's continual stressing of the need to fully document policies and procedures. In addition to the uncertainties of feeling our way, our team, almost to the man, did not like to write nor had we much experience at it. After solving a couple of the same problems twice, however, we did begin to write down our conclusions with the objective of developing a Production Control Manual. With the focus on procedures, policy issues emerged for resolution, and this manual evolved into what would more appropriately be called a "business guide".

Project planning—As the project began, the breadth of these tasks was not apparent in all cases, nor was the interdependence of these tasks. The plan started using a simple, milestone-planning technique. As progress was made and learning occurred, the milestone chart was updated. This proved to be a very valuable tool to help manage the project.

Education—Implementation of systems of this magnitude are difficult because they introduce new concepts, and they involve almost everyone in the organization. A substantial amount was invested in education and communication to help overcome these difficulties. The major efforts were:

- *Company newsletter*—Even before a system was found to implement, the President of the company began to talk about the need for a system and its importance to the company. He continued to comment at various points throughout the implementation process and left no question as to his commitment to the project.

- *Top management briefing*—All members of the top management group attended an appropriate seminar.
- *Capacity management seminar*—After the project team was selected, all team members attended.
- *System newsletter*—The project team wrote a series of newsletters to all employees on different aspects of the system and its impact on them.
- *Consultant*—Ray Lankford conducted a number of educational sessions for the top management group, foremen, sales engineers, design engineers, and office people. In addition, his periodic visits during the implementation process provided necessary education and problem-solving aids for the project team.
- *Production control meetings*—Ray Lankford also attended these in all of the plants after the system was running. Focus then began on the effective utilization of the system output—actual on-the-job training.
- *Employee meetings*—Departmental meetings for all employees were conducted by the project team to explain portions of the system and introduce new procedures.

In addition to the above, there has been a lot of one-on-one training and small group sessions with all users and project team members.

Operation Sequencing (Ray Lankford)

Let's review the capacity planning process which has taken place before Operation Sequencing:

- The Master Schedule has been tested against a rough-cut capacity plan on critical work centers, so there are no gross errors in Master Schedule content.
- MRP has planned the quantity and timing of manufacturing jobs; some jobs have been released, while others are still at the "planned" stage.
- Capacity Requirements Planning has, for all work centers, displayed the "output needed" in each time period to accomplish the Master Schedule.
- An aggressive and resourceful Production Control Department has taken a myriad of actions to match the "output planned" for each

work center to the "output needed", overtime has been scheduled, subcontracting has been arranged, personnel have been shifted, and jobs have been re-routed.

At this point, one thing is certain: *A lot of problems still remain!*

- Some work centers are still overloaded in some time periods and underloaded in others.
- Because each job takes a different route through the plant, it is impossible to predict the size of queues at all work centers in the future; hence, lead times are uncertain.
- Since queues at some work centers will undoubtedly differ from the "planned" levels assumed by CRP, the load profiles may contain significant errors.
- We are working to averages, but specifics are killing us!
- As each "problem" work center is recognized, the planners start trying to work their way up through the pegs to the end items to communicate with Master Scheduling. But there are hundreds of problems and several thousand jobs to deal with.
- The changes keep coming!

In short, as one knowledgeable realist recently observed, "No matter how carefully Master Scheduling has been executed (rough-cut cycles included), the planner cannot possibly foresee all manufactured-part shortages generated by standard lead time offsets." [9]

Before we conclude that the quality of life in Production Control is not likely to improve, let's look at what we have to work with.

The action plans for altering capacity devised by our energetic planner have been entered into the computer, so as to portray planned output for comparison with required output. In actuality, this data, derived from practical planning work, constitutes a mathematical model of the factory.

Moreover, we have a file of all current and future jobs with their priorities expressed by their required dates.

We also know from production labor reporting those jobs currently working in the plan, with their status of completion.

Common sense might tell us that we could see how our jobs, sequenced according to priority, might fit the capacity produced by our action plans. However, conventional wisdom in this body of knowledge says, "Don't do it! Ignore what you know about capacity and priorities."

The common-sense approach of simulating the processing of jobs in order of priority using replanned capacity is, of course, Operation Sequencing. This is what Remmele uses to schedule their shop.

The particular software at Remmele is significantly different from other simulation-mode scheduling routines. While it has some very powerful capabilities, it is much simpler and, hence, more practical than some of the elegant, highly-sophisticated simulators which have been used in the past. For example:

1. Time resolution is a half-shift, not a fraction of an hour.
2. It does not try to solve problems automatically. Instead, it reports problems to the human scheduler so that judgement and experience may be applied to the solution.

Because of these and other simplifications, the simulation program requires only a modest amount of computer time, meaning it can be run frequently enough to recognize changed conditions.

The second of the simplifications cited is quite significant! The point was made emphatically in an earlier section that the computer does not "automatically reschedule". What Operation Sequencing does is to produce a manufacturing job schedule which shows for each job the following information:

1. Required Date—from MRP or MPS
2. Planned Start and Finish Date—the standard lead time using planned move and queue times
3. Scheduled Start and Finish Dates—the probable, actual lead time, recognizing available capacity and the job's relative priority

Thus, the planner can see these jobs which will probably be late. From detailed operation dating, bottleneck operations are evident. Using this information, the planner can go to work solving the problems. The computer did not change the required date, nor did it automatically change the plan. It merely reported the degree to which *reality* will probably deviate from the *plan*. It is entirely up to the planner whether to solve the problem or to re-promise.

In cases of dependent demand in which a number of components are required at the same time for assembly, the software used by Remmele will simulate component job completion and the subsequent start and completion of subassembly and assembly jobs. This process is called "networking". It identifies any component jobs which will not be completed in time to support the Master Schedule, but it does not automatically reschedule all other component jobs equally late. It allows the planner to solve the problems causing lateness or to decide that rescheduling is, indeed, required.

Most make-to-order plants like Remmele require the ability to identify the manufacturing jobs which are providing components to the final assembly. Unfortunately, much MRP software provides only single-level pegging, whereby a demand for an item is linked to the next higher level part causing that demand. This linking is part number to part number. When a component job is going to be late, it is necessary to trace upwards through the pegs to identify all other jobs at all levels which will be affected. This is a time-consuming and laborious process.

The networking option in Remmele's software utilizes "job chaining", a form of multi-level pegging, which links requirements to sources by *job number*. Thus, for every sales order, Remmele can, at any time, see each job which is producing parts, subassemblies, and assemblies for that specific sales order; this is an enormously useful capability when answering customer inquiries or considering revision of the Master Schedule.

Since a simulation-mode scheduling system utilizes priorities to sequence operations at work centers, the manner in which priorities are designated is of some interest. Remmele's software offers a choice of two alternatives, each based on slack time: Critical Ratio and Index Number. The former is well-known, and the latter is described elsewhere in the literature. [3]

Tom Moore will now discuss this point and some other special requirements of Remmele's scheduling system.

Applying the System (Tom Moore)

Given the nature of Remmele's organization and it's business, we recognized a number of special problems that would require us to evolve our own particular solutions.

Remmele's decentralized organization had implications in two areas. First, there were three separate plants, each with an individual Plant Manager. The plants differed in size and somewhat in mission. The need for a "better" way was recognized in the largest plant, but was less apparent in the two smaller plants. We resisted the temptation to implement in the larger plant first and, instead, brought everyone through the process together. The result was a smoother implementation and broader acceptance in all plants when the switch was turned.

A second concern centered on the widely dispersed responsibilities for process engineering and production control. The routings for many of the jobs are the responsibility of the Sales Engineers, as is the responsibility for establishing required dates with the customers. These Sales Engineers, as well as the Design Engineers, function as project managers for their jobs, and in doing so, performed much of the production control function, working closely with the foremen. This "decentralization" or dispersion of responsibility required the involvement of many people in the process of changing our procedures and, to some degree, even the changing of key roles as a more concentrated production control function evolved.

In addition to the dynamic characteristic of demands, the one-of-a-kind or non-repetitive nature of much of the manufacturing means a minimum of up-front investment in process, design, and standard setting. While striving to constantly improve this, estimates and processes that change when the job reaches the shop floor are always present. Added operations and revised routings and estimates are a way of life on many of our jobs, and we had to find a convenient way of making these changes as well as getting the people involved to recognize the need to change our computer files.

We promoted the adage "You don't have to do things differently because of the system, just tell someone when you make a change." Most of the changes involved the route sheet file, so on-line file maintenance procedures were developed for use by the Production Control Department to make this task easier.

Operation overlapping—or as we call it "flowing"—was not in the software as we purchased it initially, but we knew this to be a requirement for effectively scheduling any of the volume-production jobs. This practice was also found useful with our small-lot production to reduce lead times in emergencies or to get work to open downstream work centers.

Working with the consultant and software vendor, this capability was brought on-line six months after the initial implementation.

Two options for expressing job priorities are available in the software: Critical Ratio and Index Number. Index Number was chosen. Based on the *required date*, a number between "0" and "999" is derived from the time remaining and the work remaining. An external priority or management factor can also be applied to intensify the priority in an emergency.

Initially, the idea of structuring or formalizing the decision of which job to work on first was a difficult concept to become comfortable with. However, experience has shown that it has a sound basis in logic and, while not perfection, it does satisfactorily handle the vast majority of jobs.

The quantity and quality of information received from this system far exceeded what existed in the past. Initially there was more information than we could digest, and we had to learn how to efficiently use the system output to pinpoint problems and take the necessary actions.

Lacking the ability to accurately "benchmark" the system in advance, estimates of the computer resources required were made. Processing time remained a concern until the actual operation began; however, the results turned out to be fairly close to the estimates.

At shop workload peaks, the CRP and Operation Sequencing phases were both run within an hour. Report printing was a large time-consumer, but we are printing less and using the CRT's more. Currently our total cycle from building the work files to printing the reports takes less than three hours at night.

The User's Appraisal (Tom Moore)

The value of this system to Remmele and the primary results achieved to date can be summarized as follows:

1. In terms of the primary objective of improving on-time deliveries, steady progress has been made. The system has contributed to this, but it can't take sole credit. With the impact of the recession and the resulting reduced work load, contention for scarce capacity hasn't been as pronounced as in normal times. It is expected, however, that when the demand for absolutely full capacity resumes, the system will make possible much more reliable delivery promising.
2. We have achieved the required level of accuracy in work-in-process reporting. Jobs don't get lost and the information as to their status is realistic. In addition to benefiting the scheduling process, this has paid dividends in cost accounting as well.
3. Capacity bottlenecks are visible, and the response to them is more timely.

The system has proven to be very well designed and a highly-effective tool. It has contributed substantially to Remmele's ability to manage its capacity.

Implications of This Case Study (Ray Lankford)

Ten years ago, the type of capacity management system being used today by Remmele was considered very sophisticated. Simulation-mode scheduling, what we now call Operation Sequencing, was regarded as extremely complex. Software was of limited availability, computer requirements were large and expensive, and applications were confined to relatively large companies.

Today, Tom Moore has described how his company, a relatively small firm with limited systems experience, is successfully using Operation Sequencing. Software, while not abundant, is more readily available; computer power is no longer the obstacle it once was. There are a number of other companies of various sizes using similar systems. Two examples are especially interesting. One large, aircraft-equipment manufacturer has been so impressed by the results of Operation Sequencing that for some years after its installation in 1973, no publicity about the system was permitted because management regarded it as a major competitive advantage. Only recently one of my clients, smaller than Remmele, programmed in-house for a mini-computer a simulator which is producing schedules enthusiastically endorsed by shop foremen, production controllers, and salespeople alike.

Another major improvement of the past ten years is the increase in knowledge about capacity management systems. And with knowledge has come understanding that some of the controversies of the formative years are behind us. Infinite loading and finite loading are obsolete concepts. True to the prediction of Plossl and Wight in 1967, simulation has developed into a technique of genuine usefulness. Today, it is the "sleeping giant" of manufacturing control.

Using simulation—Operation Sequencing, as we now call it—companies like Remmele are closing the "proficiency gap", applying with skill and enthusiasm the "state-of-the-art" in capacity management.

REFERENCES

1. Wight, Oliver, "Input/Output Control: A Real Handle On Lead Time", *Production & Inventory Management*, Volume II, Number 3, Third Quarter, 1970.
2. Plossl, George W. and Oliver W. Wight, "Capacity Planning and Control", Proceedings of the Fourteenth Annual Conference of the American Production and Inventory Control Society, 1971.
3. Lankford, Ray, "Scheduling the Job Shop", Proceedings of the Sixteenth Annual Conference of the American Production and Inventory Control Society, 1973.
4. Lankford, Ray, "Input/Output Control: Making It Work", Proceedings of the Twenty-third Annual Conference of the American Production and Inventory Control Society, 1980.
5. Plossl, George W. and Oliver W. Wight, *Production and Inventory Control*, Prentice-Hall, Inc., Englewood Cliffs, New Jersey, 1967.
6. Wight, Oliver, "Finite Loading", *Managing Inventories and Production*, Oliver Wight Video Productions, Inc., Audio Tape Number 9, Copyright 1976 ASI.
7. *Communications Oriented Production Information and Control System*, Volume V, IBM Corporation, White Plains, New York, 1972.
8. Lankford, Ray, "Short-Term Planning of Manufacturing Capacity", Proceedings of the Twenty-first Annual Conference of the American Production and Inventory Control Society, 1978.
9. Thomas, Gene, "Real-Time, Behind Schedule Replanning", *Production & Inventory Management Review*, April, 1982.

chapter eleven

The Master Production Schedule

Introduction

A master production schedule (MPS) represents a plan for manufacturing. When a firm uses an MRP system, the MPS provides the top-level input requirements. It develops the quantities and dates to be exploded for generating per period requirements for subassemblies, piece parts, and raw materials. The MPS is not a sales forecast, but it is a feasible manufacturing plan. It also serves as a customer order backlog system. It considers changes in capacity or loads, changes in finished goods inventory, and fluctuations in demand. A detailed MPS also determines the economics of production by grouping various demands and making lot sizes. Thus, the MPS maintains the integrity of the total system backlogs, anticipated backlogs, and lower-level component requirements.

The MPS should be consistent with the aggregate production plan (APP) from which it is derived. It should consider, in detail, the unit of measure, such as pounds of steel or number of phones per period, the efficiency, and the utilization factors of the system. The relationship of the MPS to other manufacturing and control activities is shown in figure 11.1. The output of the aggregate planning process is a set of parameters indicating aggregate inventory or backlog levels, the number of shifts to be operated, the number of employees to be hired or laid off, the anticipated amount of subcontracting, and the aggregate amount to be produced within certain time periods. The APP provides a basis for decision making regarding specific production dates, available capacity, total demand, lead time, or inventory constraints that cannot be reconciled within the company policy objectives. Although this information is necessary, it is not sufficient for the smooth functioning of a firm. What is necessary is a plan stated in terms of specific products that are to be produced in certain quantities by certain dates. The process of deriving such an MPS that is consistent with the overall APP is called disaggregation.

It is important to recognize that the MPS is not a control technique or a system. Rather, it is a logical representation of information for decision making. The MPS highlights conflicts that can be solved only by people. If the MPS is done properly, the rest of the system can be harnessed to reach the desired objectives of management.

THE EFFECT OF CAPACITY ON THE MPS

The importance of an accurate and feasible schedule cannot be overemphasized. The MPS is an important input in deriving rough-cut capacity planning, as exhibited in figure 11.1. The existing capacity and changes to it over the planning horizon become a major constraint. Considerations to capacity should include actual number of shifts scheduled, number of days scheduled in a week, overtime policy, available equipment, and work force levels. The capacity should be expressed in terms of what is feasible, rather than in theoretical possibility estimates. In addition to scheduling hours, factors such as efficiency and utilization should be included.

When the total requirements specified by the inputs exceed available capacity, the MPS should indicate a need for corrective action. The alternative decisions may involve extending the delivery date, changing capacity, finding ways to divert parts from other activities, and so forth, which may need critical inputs from management, especially when policy guidelines are inadequate.

Example 11.1

Suppose that the milling machine center represented in table 10.9 in the capacity planning and control chapter (chapter 10) has two machines. The center operates two eight-hour shifts per day, five days per week. Records indicate machine utilization at 95% and operator efficiency at 99%. What is the effective work center capacity per week? Is the master production schedule feasible?

Solution: Effective capacity is calculated by multiplying two machines times eight hours per day times five days per week times 95% utilization times 99% operator efficiency. This gives approximately 150 hours of effective capacity per week. Since the required capacities in periods 4 and 6 exceed the available capacity, the master schedule should be revised if additional capacity is not found.

Suppose that we make 100 units of product A and 75 units of product B every week instead of 200 units of A and 150 units of B in alternate weeks. The required milling machine capacities are summarized in table 11.1. Note that the required and available capacities match. Other machine

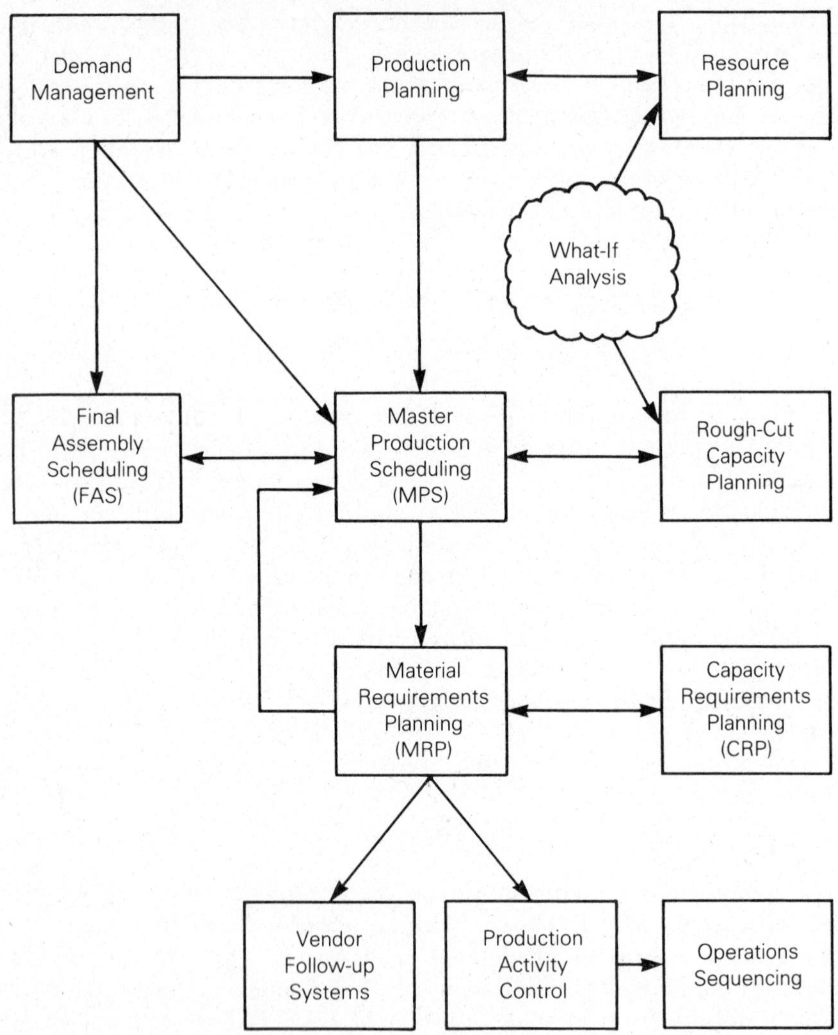

FIGURE 11.1 Relationship of MPS to other manufacturing planning and control activities

centers should similarly be checked for feasibility. The MPS may have to be revised several times before arriving at a feasible schedule.

LEAD TIME CONSTRAINTS

The computation of lead times for MRP purposes is a complicated procedure. When end items, assemblies, subassemblies, and components are involved, the cumulative lead time, known as the *critical path lead time*, determines the earliest time that the end products could be built

TABLE 11.1 Capacity Requirements Plan, Milling Machine Center

	Period								
	1	*2*	*3*	*4*	*5*	*6*	*7*	*8*	*9*
POR									
Group A				100	100	100	100	100	100
Group B				75	75	75	75	75	
Grp. A, Period 4		17.0	15.2	33.8					
Grp. B, Period 4			32.4	51.1					
Grp. A, Period 5			17.0	15.2	33.8				
Grp. B, Period 5				32.4	51.1				
Grp. A, Period 6				17.0	15.2	33.8			
Grp. B, Period 6					32.4	51.1			
Grp. A, Period 7					17.0	15.2	33.8		
Grp. B, Period 7						32.4	51.1		
Grp. A, Period 8						17.0	15.2	33.8	
Grp. B, Period 8							32.4	51.1	
Total				149.5	149.5	149.5			

from the time an order is received. Orders cannot be accepted if the days remaining are less than the cumulative lead time. Tables 8.32 through 8.35 of the MRP chapter (chapter 8) illustrate this point. One way to shorten the lead time is to carry inventory of long lead items. Unfortunately, this defeats the purpose of material requirements planning. In certain cases where a chemical process is involved, such as the distillation of beer, it is not possible to reduce the lead time.

INPUTS TO THE MASTER SCHEDULE

Major inputs to the master schedule are customer order backlog and product sales forecast. The MPS requirements should also include (1) interplant requirements, (2) service parts requirements, and (3) distribution warehouse requirements. The backlogs are input as the firm or hard portion of the schedule, which has been committed through specific customer orders. The inputs should be very specific, such as the number of beer cases or pounds of steel. If specified in terms of dollar value, these inputs would still need to be translated to measurable quantities or units, using conversion factors. The sales forecast provides the basis for extending the master schedule to generate the uncommitted or planned portion of inventories in anticipation of customer demand. This forecast leads directly into the order entry system. These inventories could fill seasonal peaks, promotional periods, or new product introductions, which create capacity overloads that could affect customer service. When the orders or bookings are temporarily below production capacity, inventories help prevent underutilization and declining productivity.

Example 11.2

Given the following product structure tree and the associated MPS, compute the net requirements, using LFL rule.

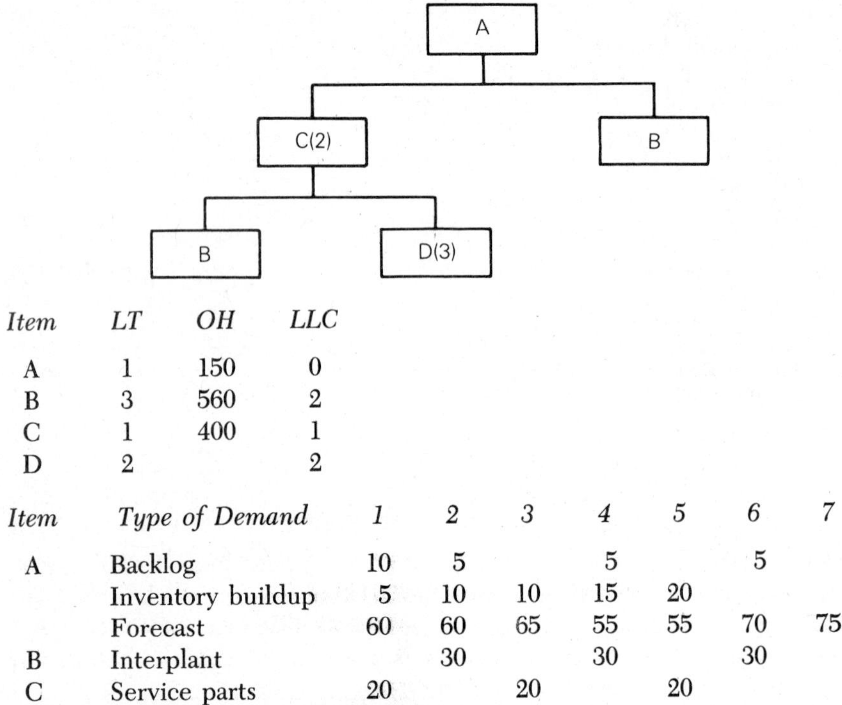

Item	*LT*	*OH*	*LLC*
A	1	150	0
B	3	560	2
C	1	400	1
D	2		2

Item	*Type of Demand*	*1*	*2*	*3*	*4*	*5*	*6*	*7*
A	Backlog	10	5		5		5	
	Inventory buildup	5	10	10	15	20		
	Forecast	60	60	65	55	55	70	75
B	Interplant		30		30		30	
C	Service parts	20		20		20		

Solution: The critical path lead time for the product is five weeks. The inventory buildups are planned whenever the total of backlog and forecast for item A is below seventy-five units. Table 11.2 includes interplant and service part requirements for items B and C. For example, the requirements for B come from items A and C as well as interplant needs.

PLANNING (TIME) PERIODS

For production planning purposes, we want to consider intervals that are different from the forecast intervals. The objective of any system is to smooth the production process, enabling uniform production of items over the period and thus avoiding production of a month's quota during the last week of the month. The length of the planning period is a matter of convenience and compromise. Smaller periods facilitate a precise production schedule, but at the cost of extra data processing. Computational costs are more economical for longer periods, but at the loss of some precision. In auto assembly plants, for example, the orders and quantities are so large that the natural scheduling period involves a shift of production. A Boeing

TABLE 11.2 MRP Table for Example 11.2

Item A	*0*	*1*	2	3	*4*	5	6	*7*
GR		75	75	75	75	75	75	75
OH	150	75	0	0	0	0	0	0
PR				75	75	75	75	75
POR			75	75	75	75	75	

Item C	*0*	*1*	2	3	*4*	5	6	*7*
GR		20	150	170	150	170	150	
OH	400	380	230	60	0	0	0	
PR					90	170	150	
POR				90	170	150		

Item B	*0*	*1*	2	3	*4*	5	6	*7*
GR			105	165	275	225	105	
OH	560	560	455	290	15			
PR						210	105	
POR			210	105				

Item D	*0*	*1*	2	3	*4*	5	6	*7*
GR				270	510	450		
OH	0	0	0					
PR				270	510	450		
POR		270	510	450				

factory that produces 747 aircraft might find that a month is a short enough increment of time. For most manufacturing firms, a week or a fortnight is a satisfactory length of time. The MPS should be extended to cover at least twice the critical path lead time of the product. The total time horizon usually consists of twelve weekly periods, followed by months. As the fourth month moves into the twelfth weekly period, it must be broken down. This process is called a *rolling schedule*. An example of a rolling schedule is given in table 11.3. The requirements for the tenth period were rolled over from the following period.

DUE DATE VERSUS NEED DATE

The *due date* is the scheduled completion date associated with the order, whereas the *need date* is the time at which the order is actually needed. These two dates need not be the same. The need date depends on the customer requirements, whereas the due date is the result of priority planning. An MRP system has the ability to make these dates coincide at

TABLE 11.3 Example of a Rolling Schedule

Initial MRP Table	0	1	2	3	4	5	6	7	8	9	10
GR		15	15	15	25	25	10	10	10	10	25
SR			90								
PR									90		
OH	30	15	90	75	50	25	15	5	85	75	50
POR							90				
MRP Table After One Period	0	1	2	3	4	5	6	7	8	9	10
GR		15	15	25	25	10	10	10	10	25	30
SR		90									
PR								90			
OH	15	90	75	50	25	15	5	85	75	50	20
POR						90					

the time of order release. The system also monitors changes in the status of orders and signals the inventory planner, if necessary, to take action. Accordingly, the scheduler can expedite or deexpedite the order by scheduling it to an earlier or later date, as shown in table 11.4. Of course, capacity should be available to replan activities.

Bill of Material Types

A bill of material (BOM) is a key input document in production planning for establishing a proper inventory control system. The BOM can best be described as a list that specifies the quantity of each item, ingredient, or material needed to assemble, mix, or produce an end product. Since inventory records (status) are an important part of MRP, an accurate BOM becomes a vital input to MRP systems. A collection of these bills—one for each assembly and one for each of its components, which are sometimes assemblies themselves—describes the flow of material through the manufacturing process in the plant. Thus, a BOM also describes the relationships among parts.

TABLE 11.4 Rescheduling a Scheduled Receipt

	Period										
	0	*1*	*2*	*3*	*4*	*5*	*6*	*7*	*8*	*9*	*10*
GR		60	40	0	10	10	0	15	25	30	10
SR				20[a]							
PR											
OH	100	40	0	20	10	0	0				
POR											

[a] Scheduled receipts of twenty units in period 3 are too early. They should be rescheduled to period 4.

Consider the Taj Mahal, with all its gorgeous marble domes and embedded precious stones, or the tower of Pisa. Could they have been completed without a BOM? Consider, too, your grandmother's secret recipe for your favorite dish. Do you remember her ever consulting a cookbook for the dish that was gobbled up by everyone instantaneously? She probably used an informal BOM.

The BOM has several other uses. As an example, suppose that an item or part is delayed, and the manager wants to know the effects of the delay on the MPS. He or she has to know what actions are necessary to keep the shop going. A complete and accurate bill of material is needed to summarize parts requirements if an MRP system is to be used efficiently. The number and complexity of parts in most businesses today necessitates the use of computerized BOMs. It is important to note that the computations are only as accurate as the information you provide to the computer. However, the real value of computers in manufacturing BOMs comes from three sources: (1) its ability to store massive amounts of data, (2) the speed with which information can be retrieved, and (3) the availability of software packages that organize and retrieve this information.

The relationships among parts can be represented in many ways, including the cross-classification chart, the product structure tree, and indented bills of material. In this section, we will illustrate these methods and show how the MPS calculations could become cumbersome even for a few products when they are extended to several planning periods.

THE CROSS-CLASSIFICATION CHART

The earliest and simplest method of representing the relationships among parts was by a matrix that is known as the cross-classification chart. It exhibits the subassemblies, parts, and raw materials that are used in each of the primary products. For example, row 1 in table 11.5 represents product 1, which requires one unit of subassembly 4 and one unit of subassembly 6. One unit of subassembly 4, in turn, requires one unit of part 9 and two units of part 10; one unit of part 9 needs two units of raw material 12 and one unit of raw material 13. Thus, the cross-classification chart shows the complete explosion of a product line.

Example 11.3

Prepare a list of the parts and raw materials required to manufacture the following:

Product	*Quantity*
Item 1	10
Item 2	20
Item 3	30

TABLE 11.5 Cross-classification Chart

	Subassembly (SA)				*Part (P)*				*Raw Material (RM)*			
Item	*4*	*5*	*6*	*7*	*8*	*9*	*10*	*11*	*12*	*13*	*14*	*15*
Finished Product												
1	1		1									
2		2										
3		1		2								
Subassembly (SA)												
4						1	2					
5					3							
6					1		1					
7						2		2				
Part (P)												
8									1			
9									2	1		
10										1	1	
11										2		3

Solution: For clarity, we can represent the requirements for each item by means of a tree diagram. The tree diagram in figure 11.2 shows, for example, that we need two units of raw material 12 to make one unit of part 9, that each subassembly 4 requires one unit of part 9, and finally that each item 1 requires one unit of subassembly 4, and so forth. We can compute the requirements for one branch at a time by multiplying all the quantities on that branch. The material requirements for producing ten units of item 1

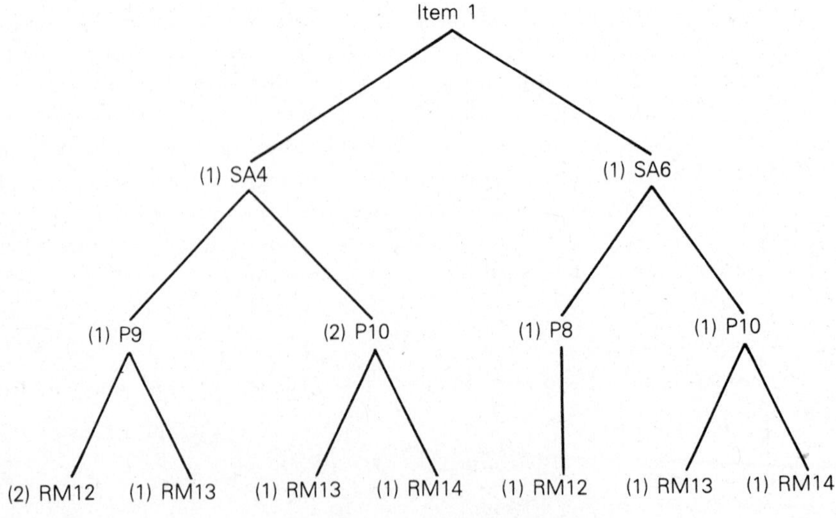

FIGURE 11.2 Tree diagram

TABLE 11.6 Material Requirements for Ten Units of Item 1 (Example 11.3)

Part	*Raw Material*	*Quantity*	*Where Used*
P8	RM12	10	SA6
P9	RM12	20	SA4
P9	RM13	10	SA4
P10	RM13	20	SA4
P10	RM13	10	SA6
P10	RM14	20	SA4
P10	RM14	10	SA6

are exhibited in table 11.6. We can summarize these requirements as follows:

Raw Material	*Quantity*
RM12	30
RM13	40
RM14	30

Using the data in table 11.5, we can also summarize the requirements for items 2 and 3. The overall material requirements for the three items are given in table 11.7.

It is obvious that the calculations can become astronomical when hundreds of products (each product having many assemblies, subassemblies, and raw materials) are considered for several periods.

PRODUCT STRUCTURE TREE

The product structure tree is commonly used to display the total makeup of a particular product. An example for a bicycle is given in figure 11.3. The highest level is zero, which represents the end item. Wheel and frame assemblies make up the next level, level 1. Similarly, tires and rim assemblies, seat, handlebars, and so forth, make up level 2. The tree can be extended to the raw material level, level 4. The quantity of each subassembly or component used in producing one unit of a higher-level item is shown beside the item.

TABLE 11.7 Overall Raw Material Requirements (Example 11.3)

Raw Material	*Item 1*	*Item 2*	*Item 3*	*Total*
RM12	30	120	330	480
RM13	40	—	360	400
RM14	30	—	—	30
RM15	—	—	360	360

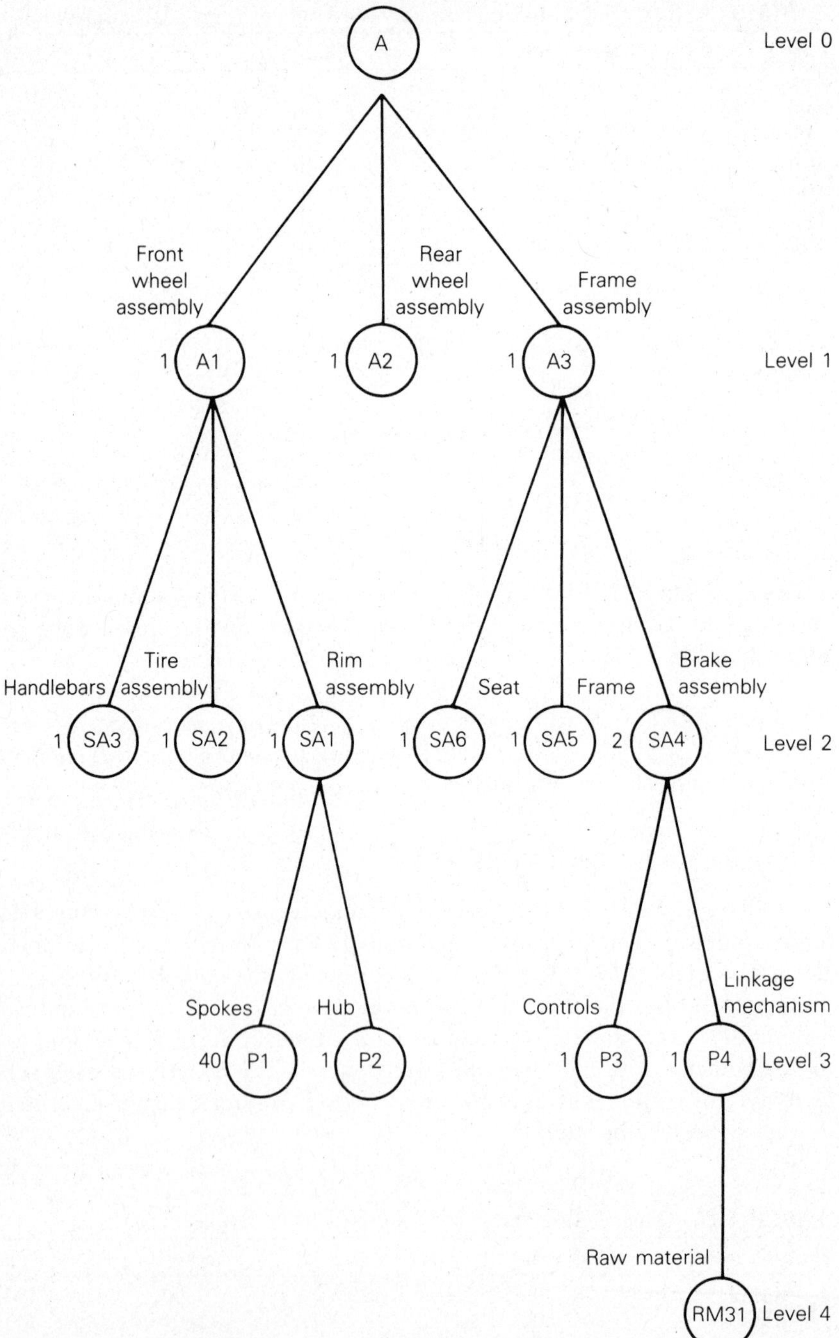

FIGURE 11.3 Product structure tree for a bicycle

INDENTED BILL OF MATERIAL

The most convenient way to represent the BOM so that it is easy to retrieve for use in MRP and in MPS computation is the indented BOM. Table 11.8 highlights the product structure complexity of an end product. It shows concisely how many levels of components the end product has and how many different components exist on each level. It has precisely the same type of information contained in the product structure tree and in the cross-classification chart. In short, it exhibits how much of what material is required, and in what order an end product is manufactured.

Structuring the Bill of Material

Bill of material processor programs are generally used to load the computer disk files when an MRP system is implemented in a firm. The BOM processor assumes that the bill is accurate and properly structured for computing material requirements. Therefore, it is important to check all features of a BOM file [11].

DESIRABLE FEATURES OF THE BOM

A bill of material should include the following features:

1. For the purpose of material requirements planning, the bill should be useful for forecasting optional product features. All items should have individual identities.
2. The bill should facilitate statement of the master schedule planning in a small number of end items, thus reducing the total number of end item assemblies, subassemblies, and so forth.

TABLE 11.8 Indented Bill of Material for Bicycle

Level	*Quantity*	*Part Number*	*Description*
. 1	1	A1	Front wheel assembly
. . 2	1	SA1	Rim assembly
. . . 3	40	P1	Spokes
. . . 3	1	P2	Hub
. . 2	1	SA2	Tire assembly
. . 2	1	SA3	Handlebars
. 1	1	A2	Rear wheel assembly
. 1	1	A3	Frame assembly
. . 2	1	SA4	Brake assembly
. . 2	1	SA5	Frame
. . 2	1	SA6	Seat assembly

3. The bill should be helpful in planning the release of lower-level items at the right time with valid due dates. The BOM should reflect the material flow in and out of the raw materials stock, subassemblies, and assemblies.
4. The BOM should permit easy order entry by translating customer orders into a language that the MRP system can operate efficiently, such as recognizing the model numbers or a configuration of option features.
5. The BOM should be usable for final assembly schedule purposes—for example, showing which assembly numbers and how many of the assemblies are required to build individual units of end products.
6. Finally, the BOM should provide a basis for product costing.

DEFINITION OF END ITEM

Given the foregoing desirable features of a BOM, one of the most difficult and confusing aspects of developing an MRP system is the definition of an end item, which varies from firm to firm.

The specific product configuration used for the MPS varies considerably among firms. For example, in the make-to-stock companies, the MPS is often stated in terms of end products. In the make-to-order companies, it is usually stated in terms of actual customer orders. If the total number of products is less than 100, then all products are included in the master schedule. When the number of products grows over 300 to 500, it becomes more difficult to deal with all products in the master schedule. The MPS may then work best with product group rather than end products. In assemble-to-order firms, an abnormal combination of products can be made from relatively few component building blocks. In such cases, the MPS is often stated in terms of options. Thus, how to structure the BOM for a product becomes an important topic.

BILL OF MATERIAL STRUCTURES

There are three basic structures for bills of material, as shown in figure 11.4. It is important to determine the point of greatest commonality, which is represented by the narrowest part of the BOM structure. The narrowest point determines the end item for the purposes of the MPS [9].

Modular Bills of Material

Modularization consists of breaking down the bills of material of high-level items, such as products or end items, and reorganizing them into product modules. For example, consider the manufacture of bicycles. A bicycle is actually an assembly of many optional features. Because of the large number

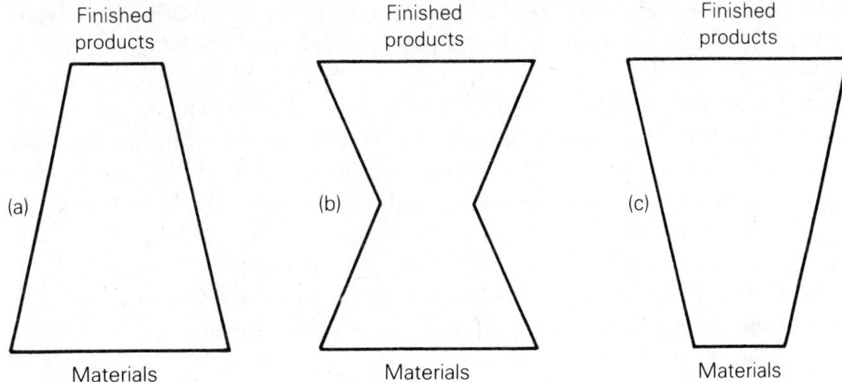

FIGURE 11.4 Three types of product structures: (a) limited number of standard items assembled from components (examples: telephones, radios); (b) many items made from common subassemblies (examples: automobiles, computers); (c) many items made from limited number of base materials (examples: chemicals, paper).

Reprinted with permission, American Production and Inventory Control Society, Inc., *Master Production Scheduling Training Aid*, 1973, p. 15.

of option combinations that are available in each product line, a phenomenal number of possible end products exist. Table 11.9 exhibits eight different options available for a bicycle, taken from a manufacturer's catalog. With all the possible choices, it is possible to build 1,024 different bicycles. Each bike represents a unique combination of optional product features. Having a multitude of model designations in the sales catalog looks impressive, but the various designations merely point out differences among products belonging to the same family. Also, model identities are not fully meaningful for the purpose of forecasting and material requirements planning, because

TABLE 11.9 Bicycle Options

Options	*Choices*
1. Wheel size	24-inch
	26-inch
2. Frame size	52 cm
	64 cm
3. Handlebars	Steel
	Alloy
4. Saddle	King: leather, vinyl
	Super: leather, vinyl
5. Brakes	Side-pull, center-pull
6. Derailleur	12-speed: touring, racing
	18-speed: touring, racing
7. Chainlink finish	Silver
	Gold
8. Gear assembly	Front: 2 sprockets for 12-speed, 3 sprockets for 18-speed
	Rear: 6 sprockets

they fail to provide a precise and complete product definition. Separate BOMs for each item would be impractical and too costly to store and maintain.

To simplify master scheduling and material requirements planning, the number of models must be reduced. Instead of forecasting by finished products, we must forecast by product groups and then divide the groups into component assemblies and subassemblies. This process, known as modularization of the BOM, consists of two important steps [11]:

1. Disentangling combinations of optional product features.
2. Segregating common parts from unique or peculiar parts.

DISENTANGLING OPTION COMBINATIONS

Instead of maintaining bills of material for individual end products, the bills are restated in terms of the building blocks or modules from which each final product is put together. Thus, disentangling makes forecasting feasible when there are numerous product variations. Many of the 1,024 possible bicycle combinations, for example, may be sold only rarely. Furthermore, design changes and engineering improvements could increase bills for the file. The disentangling procedure can best be illustrated by the bicycle example.

The solution to this problem lies in forecasting each of the high-level components (i.e., major assembly options, such as wheel sizes and number of speeds) and not attempting to forecast by end products at all. Specifically, suppose that 5,000 bicycles of the type in question are to be produced in a given month. If there are two choices of speeds and if the past demand averaged 65% twelve-speeds and 35% eighteen-speeds, then by applying these percentages to the bicycle speed option, we could schedule 3,250 and 1,750 units, respectively, as discussed in chapter 3. Actual orders may not exactly coincide with the forecast, however, and hence safety stock would be necessary. Under this modular approach, the total number of bills of material would be as follows:

Basic bicycle	1
Wheel size	2
Frame size	2
Handlebars	2
Saddle	4
Brakes	2
Derailleurs	4
Gear assembly	2
Chainlink	2
Total	21

This total of 21 bills compares with 1,024 bills if each bicycle configuration had a BOM of its own. If the manufacturer added three different colors and two types of trims, it still would give a total of 26 BOMs instead of $3 * 2 * 1{,}024 = 6{,}144$ BOMs. Therefore, the manufacturer would forecast major assembly units, such as wheel assemblies and frames, not a specific module, such as a Royale 18-speed.

To illustrate the concept, a more simplified model will be used. First, a bill of material will be constructed for bikes with only two optional features: (1) the number of speeds and (2) styles. The customer can choose between twelve-speed and eighteen-speed and between touring and racing styles. Two options with each two choices will provide us with five BOMs (1 basic or common + 2 speeds + 2 styles). These four possible combinations are considered end items at level 0, and the options available are level 1, as shown in figure 11.5. Descriptions of the parts are given in table 11.10. The next step consists of restructuring these bills into modular bills.

SEGREGATING COMMON PARTS FROM UNIQUE PARTS

To restructure these bills into modules, it is necessary to segregate the level 1 components and to determine which items are common to all bike models, which are unique to a specific number of speeds, and which are unique to a specific style. Some of the items will be unassigned because they are unique to a product combination. Each item has seven assemblies at level 1, as exhibited in figure 11.5. For simplicity of illustration, we will deal primarily with level 1. First, we segregate all components shown in figure 11.5 according to their use and group them into different categories, as shown in table 11.11.

We see that items D1, D2, D3, and D4 are unique and cannot be assigned to any group option combination. For these unique components

TABLE 11.10 Descriptions of Parts Used in Figure 11.5

W—wheel size: This option varies only when the frame size varies. For example, there is a standard wheel size for touring style W1 and a standard wheel size for racing style W2.

H—handlebars: Racing handlebars are used for all of the combinations previously discussed, but there are options for other models. A suboption would be the material of which the handlebars are made.

B—brakes: Brakes vary according to the number of speeds. All 18-speeds have side-pull brakes, B1, and all 12-speeds have center-pull brakes, B2.

S—saddle: The saddle type also varies with the number of speeds. All 18-speeds have kings, S1, and all 12-speeds have supers, S2. A suboption would be a vinyl or leather saddle.

D—derailleurs: The derailleur varies with every product option combination. Subassemblies are based on the number of component parts.

C—chainlink size: There is one standard chainlink size for all of the assemblies previously discussed, although both silver and special gold finishes are available.

G—gear assembly: The number of gear wheels varies with the number of speeds.

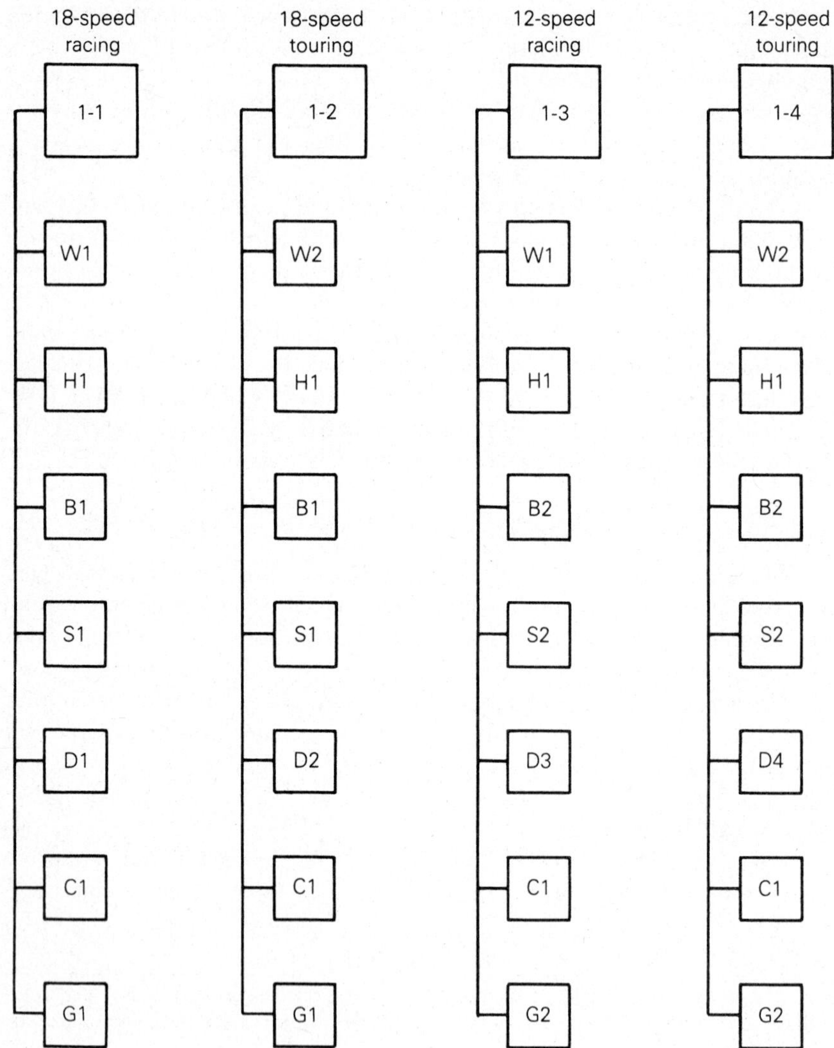

FIGURE 11.5 Bills of material for four bike models

TABLE 11.11 Components Grouped in Categories

Categories	*Components*
All models	H1, C1
18-speed only	B1, S1, G1
12-speed only	B2, S2, G2
Racing only	W1
Touring only	W2

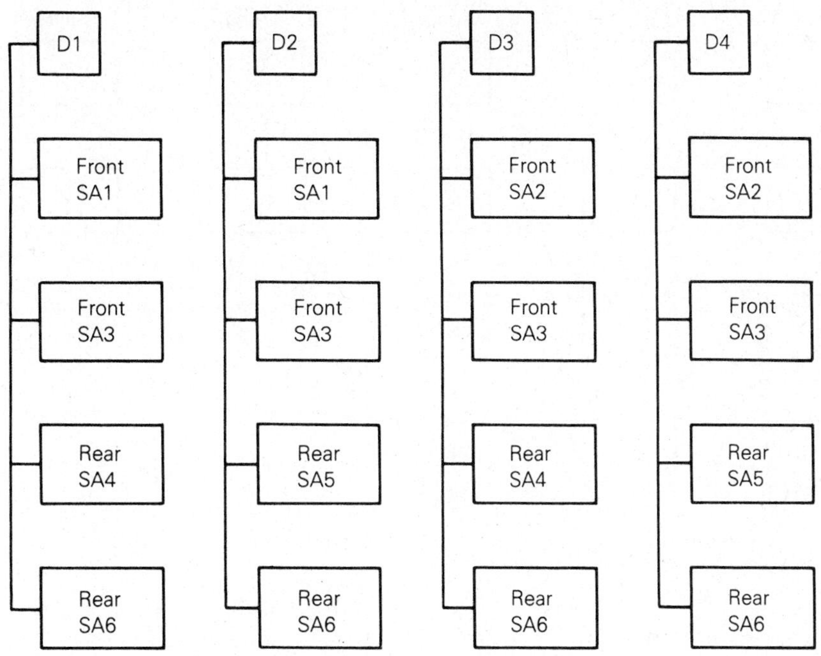

FIGURE 11.6 Subassemblies of derailleurs

only, we carry out the same procedure at one more level (level 2) in the BOM. The breakdown of item D, the derailleurs, is shown in figure 11.6. The derailleur assembly is composed of many common items at level 2. The level 2 items have now been elevated to level 0, as shown in figure 11.7. These items now become a part of the manufacturing bill (M-bill) file, to be accessed whenever a particular assembly is not found in the common items of level 0. In this example, a complete modularization has been achieved. The MPS will treat these bills as though we have only five (superficial) items, as will be described in the later discussion of S-bills. If we had been unable to decompose the four components D1, D2, D3, and D4, then we would have achieved only partial modularization. In such instances, we can either forecast these items separately (resulting in more than five BOMs), or they can be assigned to more than one grouping during the modularization process. The latter approach is particularly desirable for inexpensive items, since it would prevent us from running out of stock.

Example 11.4

The Pymex Clock Company manufactures several lines of clocks. Every line consists of many models and options, which can be summarized as follows:

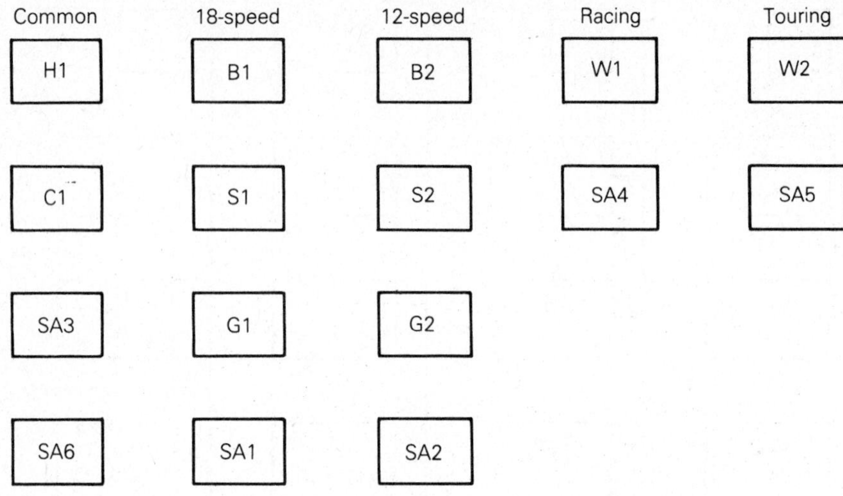

FIGURE 11.7 Complete modular (planning) bill of materials

Components	*Types*
Basic clock	1
Motor assembly	2
Operating mode	2
Dial color	3
Hand color	3
Frame color	7
Reflector type	2

(a) Based on the variations available, calculate how many models Pymex can advertise in their sales catalog. (b) How many BOMs would be necessary to cover all models? (c) Under the modular approach, how many BOMs will be necessary? (d) What are the savings?

Solution: (a) The number of models that can be made is calculated by multiplying one basic clock times two motor assemblies times two operating modes times three dial colors times three hand colors times seven frame colors times two reflector types. Thus, a total of 504 models can be advertised in the catalog. (b) One BOM would be necessary for every model. Therefore, 504 BOMs are needed. (c) Under the modular approach, we need only twenty BOMs. This quantity is obtained by adding the basic model to all other options available for manufacturing. (d) Total savings amounts to 504 − 20 = 484 BOMs.

PLANNING BILLS

The modularization process elevates level 1 items and, in some instances, level 2 items to level 0. This process eliminates the former level 0 items—that is, end products. The new modular bills of material—known as planning bills—are used for forecasting and master scheduling that express the material requirements for a product without showing the final configuration of the product. Planning bills are exhibited in figure 11.7. As we explained earlier, the planning, or modular, bills are particularly useful for material requirements planning where the final configuration of the end product is extremely difficult or cumbersome to forecast.

Example 11.5

As the new production planning analyst for Pymex Clock Company, you are responsible for simplifying the system. The following table lists the four possible combinations of battery types and motor assemblies and the components necessary to make these clocks:

Battery-Operated, Regular	*Battery-Operated, Heavy-duty*	*Electrical-Operated, Regular*	*Electrical-Operated, Heavy-duty*
A1	A1	A1	A1
B2	C3	B2	C3
D1	D1	E2	E2
T3	T3	X4	X4
F1	G1	H1	J1

The subassembly components are as follows:

Subassembly	*Component*
F1	K1, M3
G1	K1, N5
H1	L7, M3
J1	L7, N5

Is it possible to achieve a complete modularization in this case? List all planning bills.

Solution: We restructure these bills into the components that belong to all models and those that are unique to specific models:

Categories	*Components*
All models	A1
Battery-operated	D1, T3
Electrical-operated	E2, X4
Regular	B2
Heavy-duty	C3

We find that items F1, G1, H1, and J1 are each unique to one model, but by studying their second-level components, we can list the following planning bills in each category.

Common	*Battery-operated*	*Electrical-operated*	*Regular*	*Heavy-duty*
A1	D1	E2	B2	C3
	T3	X4	M3	N5
	K1	L7		

Thus, a complete modularization is achieved in this case.

M-BILLS

The manufacturing bills, or M-bills, represent another technique of structuring bills of material. Notice that when the planning bills were structured, we no longer identified items such as D1, D2, and so on, since they were abolished during modularization. However, they are needed for the production control system so that the sales department can place orders, the industrial engineering department can use the information for standards and product costing, and the production department can schedule manufacturing properly. Therefore, we should keep their identity for manufacturing purposes, as exhibited in figure 11.6.

An M-bill item can be a component only of another M-bill item or of an end product. Since the components of the M-bill are included in the planning bill, it is not necessary for the computer to access M-bills for generating material requirements. These bills are coded in such a way that the MRP system bypasses them. When an order is received from a customer or warehouse, it also includes options. These options are specified in their original identities, such as D1, D2, and so on. The order entry procedure, finding that these items are not a part of the planning bill, calls out the M-bill file and reconstructs the appropriate planning bills for manufacturing proper assemblies. Since the M-bills are not used for component requirements planning by MRP, they are segregated in a separate M-bill file. The M-bills are used for final assembly, ordering, scheduling, and costing only.

Example 11.6

In the Pymex problem, is it necessary to maintain a file of M-bills? Exhibit these M-bills.

Solution: The original items F1, G1, H1, and J1 no longer exist in the planning bills. Therefore, it is necessary to have an M-bill file, which would contain the following:

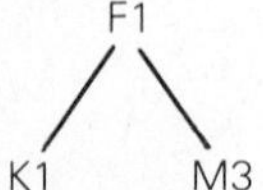

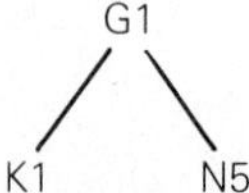

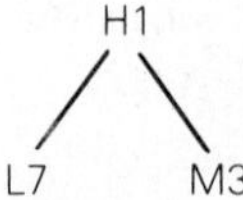

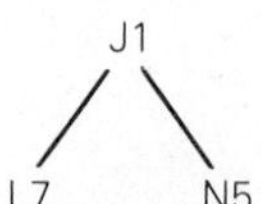

PSEUDO BILLS OF MATERIAL (S-BILLS)

Planning bills facilitate easier forecasting and requirements planning when numerous end items are involved. The modularization process also creates problems, however. When assemblies, and in some cases subassemblies, are promoted to end item level, a large number of end items remain in the MPS without a parent item. In some instances, there may be too many to work with, and the modularization must be further simplified. For example, we notice in figure 11.7 that the items are grouped in terms of options. By assigning a superficial (artificial) parent to each group—such as eighteen-speed or touring styles—we can create a pseudo bill. These pseudo bills, also known as super bills or S-bills, and the restructured bills of material are assigned a number with the suffix S, such as S-101 (see figure 11.8). In figure 11.8, the S-bills reduced the sixteen items of the planning bill to only five end items, thus enabling easier material requirements planning. Keep in mind that an assembly such as S-103 will never be built; the S-bill numbers are nonengineering part numbers. Using these S-bills in the BOM file, the MRP system will explode the requirements. (Note that *S-bills* and *S-numbers* are not standard terminology in the industry). These bills are treated as end items or level zero items in the MPS.

Example 11.7

High Wheeler Bike Shop wishes to forecast the numbers and types of bikes to be sold in the upcoming summer season as input to the production

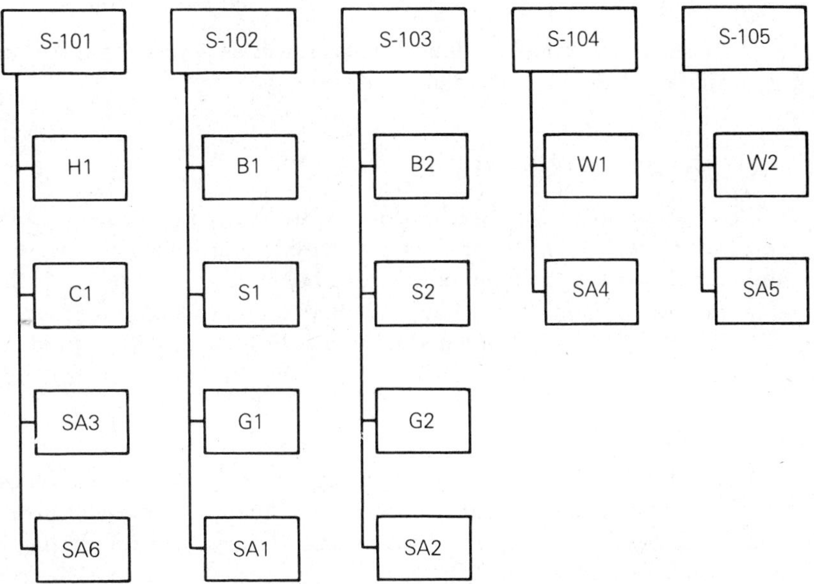

FIGURE 11.8 Super bills

process. In the past, High Wheeler sold 500 bikes, on the average, during this period. The breakdown is as follows:

18-speed	30%
12-speed	70%
Touring	60%
Racing	40%

The amount of each assembly and subassembly to be produced can be determined by referring to the S-bill in figure 11.8. The breakdown is as follows:

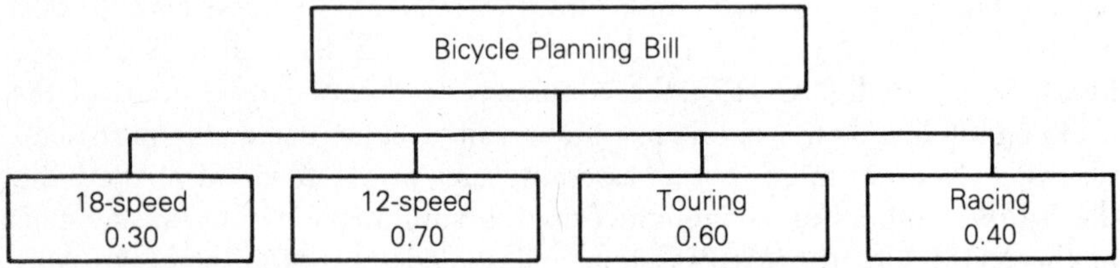

From the S-bill, we determine that 500 units of assembly S-101 (items common to all) will be produced. This will require 500 units of H1, C1, SA3, and SA6. Similarly 150 units (500 × 0.30) of S-102 (items common to eighteen-speeds) will be produced. The progression is similar for S-103, S-104, and S-105:

Common	*18-speed*	*12-speed*	*Touring*	*Racing*
500	150	350	300	200

Forecasting of options within options—such as a vinyl or a leather saddle—would be done by the same method.

KIT NUMBERS (K-NUMBERS)

When there are many small, loose parts—such as fasteners, nuts, and bolts—at level 1 in the product structure, some companies use the kit number (K-number) technique. The idea behind the kit numbers is the same as that for pseudo bills. The K-numbers merely identify a group of unrelated items; as such, an engineering item does not exist. Kit numbers create a more convenient way of planning, forecasting, and master scheduling.

Example 11.8

Beanie Garage Door Opener Company manufactures several types. Although the parts could be added in the BOM, their cost does not justify the action. However, it is important to keep track of them for requirements planning. How would you handle the situation? The three do-it-yourself models require the following loose parts:

Quantities

ITEM	REGULAR	DELUXE	HEAVY-DUTY	MAXIMUM QUANTITY
3351 Bolt	3	4	5	5
1151 Washer	3	4	5	5
4151 Nuts	3	4	5	5
101 Cotterpin	3	2	3	3
3021 Fastener	5	4	5	5
425 Clips	6	6	6	6

Solution: Find the maximum quantity of each item required, regardless of the model. For all models, include a kit containing these quantities of each item. The kits are generally identified as K-101, K-102, and so forth; the same kit number will be included in all models. The inclusion of a kit number simplifies requirements generation for forecasting. Also, the consumer is assured of receiving sufficient loose parts.

ADVANTAGES OF THE MODULAR BOM

As mentioned earlier, the modular bill accomplishes two important goals: (1) disentangling combinations of optional product features and (2) segregating common parts from unique or peculiar parts. Disentangling makes forecasting feasible when numerous product variations are encountered. Segregating facilitates the reduction of inventory investment in components that are common to optional units. The optional units must be forecast separately, thus making it necessary to carry safety stock. In all cases, safety stock should be considered as a buffer against unexpected increases in demand. It must be emphasized that the bicycle example is a very simplified model, for illustrative purposes. As Orlicky [11] indicates, we do not generally modularize the BOM for bicycles. However, this concept can be used for highly engineered items, such as trucks, automobiles, cranes, and the like.

FINAL ASSEMBLY SCHEDULE VERSUS MPS

The final assembly schedule (FAS) can serve as an MPS when the number of end products manufactured is small. These products could be simple ones—such as lawn mowers, hand tools, and vacuum cleaners—or complex ones—such as aircraft or missiles. When the number of end items becomes very large, however, the modularization process elevates assemblies and subassemblies to higher-level items for deriving the MPS. The actual customer order entry system interfaces with the MPS through the final assembly scheduling system. The FAS calls on the MRP system for components and the M-bill file, which is under its own control for options to facilitate manufacture of end items. Therefore, we can say that the MPS represents management's commitment for procurement of raw materials and production of component items in support of the FAS. The FAS, however, is constrained by the availability of components provided by the MPS via the MRP system. Thus, the FAS represents management's commitment to deliver specific end products either to the customer or to the finished goods inventory. Another distinction is that the MPS could be based on anticipated customer demand, whereas the FAS generally represents actual customer demands. Therefore, the FAS needs to cover only the time span that starts when all component items are available for final assembly and ends when the items are completed. The development of the FAS also represents a critical time fence. When this time fence is crossed, all unsold products go to the finished goods inventory.

Disaggregation Techniques

The entire process of translating top-level aggregate plans to more detailed bottom-level decisions of inventory control and scheduling is referred to as *disaggregation*. The master schedule is the result of disaggregation. It specifies (1) the sizing and timing of production orders for specific items, (2) the sequencing of individual jobs, and (3) the short-term allocation of resources to individual activities and operation. Krajewski and Ritzman [6], in their survey article on disaggregation, point out the need for more concentrated research in this area, so that the various aggregate planning techniques can be implemented more easily. We can broadly categorize the existing disaggregation techniques into (1) cut and fit methods, (2) mathematical programming methods, (3) heuristic methods, and (4) others. We will briefly explain the cut and fit methods, which are popular in industry. To illustrate the use of mathematical programming in disaggregation, we will also present a linear programming model. In many cases, heuristic methods are tailored for special situations, as illustrated by Hax and Galovin [5], who claim that these methods are implemented in industry. Other methods, such as the "knapsack" algorithm, are limited in their applicability to real-world problems.

CUT AND FIT METHODS

Generally, firms try out various allocations of capacity for the products in a group until a satisfactory combination is determined. Such an approach is called a cut and fit method. For example, the master schedule shown in table 11.12 is satisfactory in the sense that it indicates when the plant should plan to start and stop the production of individual items. The amount of capacity required to support the plan is consistent with the capacity that the aggregate planning process had indicated as appropriate. However, we

TABLE 11.12 Aggregate Forecast Plan

	Initial Inventory	Week								
		1	*2*	*3*	*4*	*5*	*6*	*7*	*8*	*Total*
Aggregate forecast		100	100	100	150	150	200	200	200	1,200
Production		150	150	150	150	150	150	150	150	1,200
Aggregate inventory	400	450	500	550	550	550	500	450	400	—
Item Forecast										
Product A		60	60	60	90	90	120	120	120	720
Product B		40	40	40	60	60	80	80	80	480
Total		100	100	100	150	150	200	200	200	1,200
Master Production Schedule										
Product A		150	150	150				120	150	720
Product B					150	150	150	30		480
Total		150	150	150	150	150	150	150	150	1,200
Aggregate plan capacity		150	150	150	150	150	150	150	150	1,200
Deviation		0	0	0	0	0	0	0	0	0

do not know whether the schedule is satisfactory in terms of the number of setups and the associated setup costs or the in-process inventory for the production line. Only the use of several alternative master schedules or the use of optimizing methods can guarantee that the MPS is feasible. Unless carefully planned, the use of aggregation may lead to infeasibilities. The product types concept is merely an abstraction that makes the aggregation process possible. Inventories and demand have physical meaning only at the end item level. When calculating product type inventories, we cannot add all items that belong to a product type. That would assume complete interchangeability of inventories among all items in a product type, which is not the case. As an example, consider a product type that consists of items A and B. Table 11.12 shows that we have adequate capacity and inventories for the given forecast and production goals of the product family. However, when we derive the inventories of items A and B separately, we find that item B is short twenty units during period 3, as exhibited by table 11.13. The aggregate inventories are also compared with the total inventories for items A and B. The deviation is visible only when we deal with individual items, rather than with a family of products. Therefore, the MPS may have to be revised several times until a feasible schedule is obtained. This is the cut and fit method of arriving at a schedule. The same procedure can be used for checking capacity requirements.

LINEAR PROGRAMMING METHOD

Krajewski and Ritzman [6] propose a linear programming version of a disaggregation model that can be used for combined aggregate–disaggregate planning in service as well as manufacturing organizations. In service organizations, we cannot store up services (inventories), and hence it becomes difficult to smooth the production rate. Disaggregation in service amounts to assigning available manpower, and possibly other resources, optimally. The general disaggregation model to be presented here minimizes the total costs of output, subcontracting, inventory, backlog, hiring, firing, overtime, and wages for T periods. Basically, this model combines aggregate planning, inventories, and scheduling decisions in one integrated problem. Optimize

$$Z = \sum_t \sum_i [C_1 X_{it} + C_2 S_{it} + C_3 I_{it} + C_4 B_{it} + C_5 H_{jt} + C_6 F_{jt} + C_7 O_{jt} + C_8 W_{jt}] \tag{11.1}$$

subject to

$$X_{it} + I_{i,t-1} - I_{it} + S_{it} + B_{it} - B_{i,t-1} = D_{it} \quad \text{for all } i \in L \tag{11.2}$$

TABLE 11.13 Inventory Status

	Initial	*Week*								
	Inventory	*1*	*2*	*3*	*4*	*5*	*6*	*7*	*8*	*Total*
Product A										
Forecast		60	60	60	90	90	120	120	120	720
Production		150	150	150	0	0	0	120	150	720
Inventory	300	390	480	570	480	390	270	270	300	
Product B										
Forecast		40	40	40	60	60	80	80	80	480
Production					150	150	150	30		480
Inventory	100	60	20	−20	70	160	230	180	100	
Total inventory	400	450	500	570	550	550	500	450	400	
Aggregate plan inventory	400	450	500	550	550	550	500	450	400	
Deviation	0	0	0	−20	0	0	0	0	0	

$$\sum_{m=1}^{li} [r_{imj} + X_{i,t+m} + r'_{imj}\,\phi_{i,t+m} = P_{ijt} \qquad \text{for all } i \in N_j \quad \text{and} \quad j \in J \tag{11.3}$$

$$\sum_{i \in L} P_{ijt} - W_{jt} - O_{jt} \leqslant 0 \qquad \text{for all } j \in J \tag{11.4}$$

$$W_{jt} - W_{j,t-1} - H_{jt} + F_{jt} = 0 \qquad \text{for all } j \in J \tag{11.5}$$

$$O_{jt} - \theta W_{jt} \leqslant 0 \qquad \text{for all } j \in J \tag{11.6}$$

$$\phi_{it} = \begin{cases} 1 & \text{if } X_{it} > 0 \\ 0 & \text{if } X_{it} = 0 \end{cases} \qquad \text{for all } i \in L \tag{11.7}$$

where C_i = costs associated with variables
X_{it} = output to product (service) i in period t
I_{it} = on-hand inventory level of product i in period t (manufacturing setting only)
S_{it} = subcontracted output of product (service) in period t
D_{it} = market requirements for product (service) i in period t
l_i = production (or procurement) lead time for product (service) i (in service settings, l_i would normally equal one time period)
B_{it} = amount of product (service) put on backorder in period t
r_{imj} = number of man-hours required per unit of product (service) i at operation j in the mth period before production is finished on i (in service settings, r_{imj} is usually 0 or 1 for all i,m,j, since output is normally measured in man-hours)
r'_{img} = total setup time required by product i at operation j in the mth period before production is finished on i (in service settings, r'_{imj} is 0 for all i,m,j)
ϕ_{it} = binary variable that assigns a setup time for product i whenever $X_{it} > 0$
P_{ijt} = production output of product (service) i at operation j in period t expressed in man-hours
W_{jt} = regular man-hours assigned to operation j in period t
O_{jt} = overtime man-hours assigned to operation j in period t
H_{jt} = man-hours of labor hired for operation j at the start of period t
F_{jt} = man-hours of labor released from operation j at the start of period t

θ = proportion of the regular time work force that can be used on overtime

L = set of all end items (services) to be controlled (in manufacturing settings.

T = length of the planning horizon

J = set of all operations where we assume there is only one type of skill at each operation

N_j = set of all products (services) that require resources at operation j

The constraint equation (11.2) represents the basic inventory identity relationship, with the added feature of the recognition of demands placed on the inventory of product i by higher-order components and subassemblies in manufacturing. In the service section, constraint equation (11.2) defines the service i backordered in period t. Constraint equation (11.3) identifies the output in terms of product or service i at operation j in period t. Constraint equation (11.4) ensures that the work planned for operation j in time period t does not exceed the manpower capacity planned for department j in period t. Hiring and releasing of manpower is represented by equation (11.5). The amount of overtime θ as a fraction of regular time man-hours is represented in equation (11.6). The term ϕ_{it} in equations (11.3) and (11.7) is a binary variable. If a setup is necessary, $\phi_{it} = 1$; otherwise, it is equal to zero.

In service sectors, variables such as X_{it}, B_{it}, and S_{it} are expressed in terms of man-hours rather than units of products. In a manufacturing setting, the X_{it} values determine the planned production of specific products from master schedule through component production, along with the manpower capacities to support these schedules. In a service setting, however, these values represent the planned output of each service. The selection of manpower capacities becomes paramount.

Example 11.9

Consider a firm that provides two different services. Given the following data, find an optimum production schedule using the linear programming technique.

	Demand Hours per Period		
	1	2	3
Service type 1	100	150	125
Service type 2	300	100	200

Available man-hours currently amount to 300, and the maximum allowable overtime is limited to 20% of the work force. In addition, (1) setups are not required; (2) inventories or backorders are not feasible; and (3) subcontracting is not possible. We also have $C_1 = 10$, $C_5 = 20$, $C_6 = 15$ and $C_7 = 15$.

Solution: Since setups are not required,

$$\phi_{1t}, \phi_{2t} = 0, \quad \text{for } t = 1, 2, 3$$

Since inventories and backorders are not allowed,

$$I_{1t}, I_{2t}, B_{1t}, B_{2t} = 0 \quad \text{for } t = 1, 2, 3$$

Since subcontracting is not possible,

$$S_{1t}, S_{2t}, = 0 \quad \text{for } t = 1, 2, 3$$

The linear programming problem can now be formulated as follows: Minimize

$$C = \sum_{t=1}^{3} 10\,(X_{1t} + X_{2t}) + 20\,(H_t) + 15(F_t) + 15(O_{1t} + O_{2t})$$

subject to

$$X_{11} + O_{11} = 100$$

$$X_{21} + O_{21} = 300$$

$$X_{12} + O_{12} = 150$$

$$X_{22} + O_{22} = 100$$

$$X_{13} + O_{13} = 125$$

$$X_{23} + O_{23} = 200$$

$$O_{11} + O_{21} - 0.2X_{11} - 0.2X_{21} \leqslant 0$$

$$O_{12} + O_{22} - 0.2X_{12} - 0.2X_{22} \leqslant 0$$

$$O_{13} + O_{23} - 0.2X_{13} - 0.2X_{23} \leqslant 0$$

$$X_{11} + X_{21} - H_1 + F_1 = 300$$

$$X_{12} - X_{11} + X_{22} - X_{21} - H_2 + F_2 = 0$$

$$X_{13} - X_{12} + X_{23} - X_{22} - H_3 + F_3 = 0$$

X_{11}	X_{12}	X_{13}	X_{21}	X_{22}	X_{23}	O_{11}	O_{12}	O_{13}	O_{21}	O_{22}	O_{23}	H_1	H_2	H_3	F_1	F_2	F_3		RHS
1						1												=	100
	1						1											=	300
		1						1										=	150
			1						1									=	100
				1						1								=	125
					1						1							=	200
−0.2			−0.2			1			1									≤	0
	−0.2			−0.2			1			1								≤	0
		−0.2			−0.2			1			1							≤	0
1			1									−1			1			=	300
−1	1		−1	1									−1			1		=	0
	−1	1		−1	1									−1			1	=	0

FIGURE 11.9 Linear programming tableau for Example 11.9

and

$$X_{it},\ O_{it},\ H_t,\ F_t \geqslant 0$$

The problem was solved using a linear programming software package. The solution is as follows:

Period (t)	X_{1t}	X_{2t}	O_{1t}	O_{2t}	H_t	F_t
1	100.	100.	0.	0.	0.	100.
2	229.17	125.	70.83	0.	154.17	0.
3	150.	200.	0.	0.	0.	4.17

The total cost of the program is

$$\begin{aligned} C &= 10(100 + 229.17 + 150) + 10(100 + 125 + 200) \\ &\quad + 15(70.83) + 20(154.17) + 15(100 + 4.17) \\ &= \$14{,}750.10 \end{aligned}$$

Maintenance of the MPS

The master schedule requires constant monitoring and revisions to reflect new orders, new problems, and new decisions. These functions may take one to five man-days over a period of a month [7]. The frequency of revisions depends on the type of system in operation—that is, net change versus regeneration. The details of these systems are explored in the MRP chapter.

The revisions are made quarterly, monthly, and weekly or daily. Quarterly revisions encompass new sales forecasts. Major revisions could also occur between the quarterly ones, but not frequently. Monthly revisions involve adding more new weeks in the future and rescheduling past due orders. Weekly or daily revisions include the loading of new orders and revisions on an exception basis. The key to success is to keep the master schedule up to date. The basic MPS maintenance steps [7] are as follows:

1. Load and level the capacity, using the most accurate MPS available, out through the combined lead time. Use backlogs as necessary to satisfy the forecast.
2. When new orders cannot be shipped from inventory, supply them from the first available planned lots.
3. If planned quantity is not available for a new order, schedule the order at the end of the combined lead time (freeze period) if capacity is available. If this is not feasible, extend the due date to the nearest future period that has capacity or reschedule a lower priority order in the earliest period to provide capacity.
4. If items were not met from inventory and quantities were not planned, determine whether capacity is available earlier than the combined lead time. If it is available, special handling will be required to coordinate long-lead items to meet an assembly date that is shorter than the freeze period.
5. Finally, fill up any unused capacity with standard items to obtain a full and level load for all future periods.

While keeping the MPS up to date, some basic rules must be followed for revisions.

1. *Reschedule past due orders*. Suppose that the output capacity is 500 units. If a backlog of 200 units exists, do not schedule 500 additional units without planning for additional capacity. If we lie to the MPS, it will lie back to us! There is no sense in claiming that the system is no good! The master scheduler is always blamed for the failure of the system. Unfortunately, this is the rule most frequently violated in industry.
2. *Make changes as soon as the need is recognized*. All major revisions should be done as soon as possible. This facilitates recognition of problems and issues to be dealt with—such as long lead times, capacity adjustments, and inventory adjustments—in advance.
3. *Never reschedule a component*. The component due date provided by the MPS is a firm requirement in manufacturing. If components are not available on time for some reason, such as equipment breakdown or strike, do not reschedule only the affected components.

As a first priority, find other ways to get the component in time. Alternative scheduling may sometimes be feasible if safety time is built into the system or if low-priority items that use the same components can be rescheduled. If nothing is feasible, always reschedule the highest-level item, using the where-used list provided by pegging. (Details of pegging are fully explored in the MRP chapter.) Otherwise, you might be left with unnecessary in-process inventory in the system.

4. *Maintain integrity*. Never lie to your MPS. Do not close your eyes and hope that problems will go away! If you overstate your MPS without additional capacity, you will end up with many past due orders. If you understate, the efficiency of the system may be impaired. A good understanding between the master scheduler and the management is very important. If you (the master scheduler) budge for everyone in the system, you might be in the wrong job.

Summary

Master scheduling includes a variety of activities involved in the preparation and maintenance of the MPS. The master schedule is stated in terms of specific product configurations and usually indicates the quantities to be produced in specific time brackets (weekly) for the next twelve months or longer. The unit of production selected for the MPS varies considerably among firms. In make-to-stock companies, the MPS is stated in terms of end items. As discussed in the section on BOM structuring, it can also be stated in terms of lower-level requirements, such as major assemblies or component parts. In make-to-order firms, the actual customer orders can be used as the unit of the MPS. Assemble-to-order firms generally have a very complex problem in defining the unit. Modularization and planning bills are often a great help to the scheduler. One important criterion is selecting the units so that the total number of units in the MPS is minimized, which generally improves the forecast and reduces the administrative costs. Another important criterion of the MPS is that it represents a disaggregation of the production plan into specific items, whereas the final assembly schedule represents the production plan with specific buildable end products. The importance of keeping the MPS feasible and up to date cannot be overemphasized.

This chapter also discussed some techniques used for disaggregation. The concepts learned in this chapter will help you appreciate and understand material requirements planning better.

PROBLEMS

1. a. Using Table 11.5 in this chapter, compute weekly raw material requirements for the following schedule. Write a computer program if necessary.

	Period					
	5	6	7	8	9	10
Product 1	100		150		200	
Product 2		200		200		150
Product 3			300		300	

   b. Assuming that the following lead times apply to these products, prepare a table to show what, when, and how much to order in a distribution requirements planning environment. Use LFL rule.

Product	*Lead Time*
1, 12	2 weeks
2, 13, 14	3 weeks
3, 15	2 weeks

   c. How will the answer differ if the lead times of raw materials are included for product 1? Assume that all assemblies and subassemblies require one week of lead time. Comment on your results.

2. Brown, Inc., a hoist manufacturer, offers customers a number of options, totaling 2,400 configurations of hoists:

Options	*Choices*
Motors	10
Drums	30
Gear boxes	4
Pendents	2
Hooks	1

Smart Alex, who is being interviewed for the production control manager's job, claims that forecasting can be made much easier if the modularization process is used. To prove his point, he uses the information in Figure 11.10. In addition, he is able to describe the following items more fully:

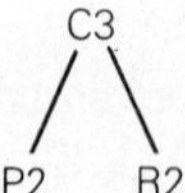

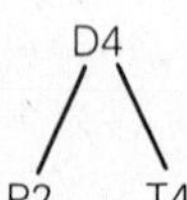

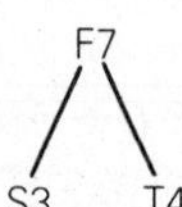

   a. From the given data, can you prove that it is possible to obtain 2,400 configurations of hoists?

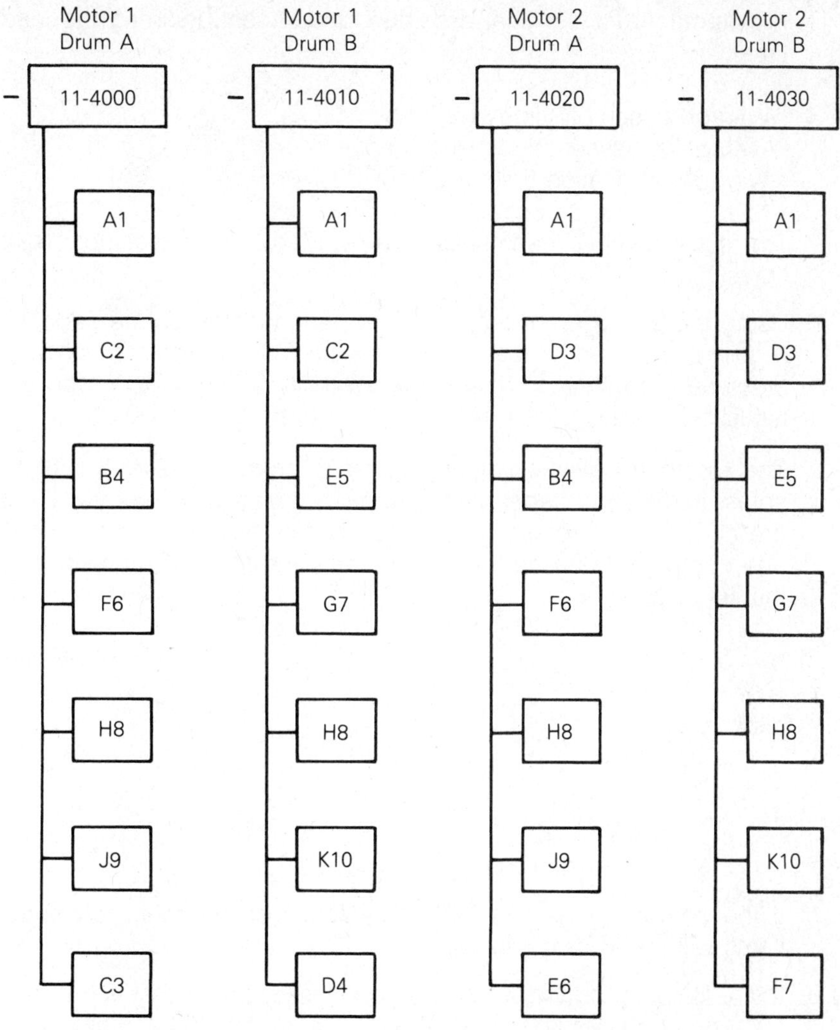

FIGURE 11.10 Data for problem 2

b. Illustrate the modularization process, providing examples of the planning bill, manufacturing bill, and super bill.

3. After modularization, how many end items exist in your solution of problem 2?

4. Figure 11.4 exhibits different types of product structures. What structure does the hoist example have? Why?

5. Explain how MRP, the MPS, and the FAS are related in the hoist manufacturing example.

6. Given the master schedule in problem 1, calculate the capacity

requirements for the final assembly department, ignoring the lead times.

Average assembly time: 1.2 hours
Average subassembly time: 0.8 hour
Average fabrication time: 0.2 hour

The subassembly lead times are included in the assembly lead times.

7. Using the average requirements per period, establish the capacity required for every department. Assume that a maximum of 20% overtime is permitted. Check the feasibility of the MPS for the established capacity. Use the data given in problems 1 and 6.

8. The Chethan Ballan Company currently produces several lines of sofas. Items vary, depending on the size and style. Currently, there are hundreds of sofas listed in the catalog as well as in the MPS. The company is taking steps to simplify the MPS. The following is the list of options:

Options	*Choices*
Widths	2
Lengths	3
Base heights	2
Arm styles	6
Rear finish	3
Trim	4
Fabrics	15

If the company has one BOM for each possible sofa, how many items will the MPS contain?

9. In the Ballan problem, if modularization is feasible, what is the least number of BOMs required? What savings would be realized by modularization?

10. Consider only the choices of width and base height (BH) combinations of sofas in the Ballan Company. The level 1 items that make up the sofas are as follows. Check whether complete modularization of BOM is feasible.

Width A, BH X	*Width A, BH Y*	*Width B, BH X*	*Width B, BH Y*
1010	1010	1020	1020
1030	1040	1030	1040
1050	1050	1050	1050
1053	1054	1053	1054
1701	1702	1703	1704

11. If complete modularization is not feasible in the Ballan sofa problem, explore whether it is possible with the following information:

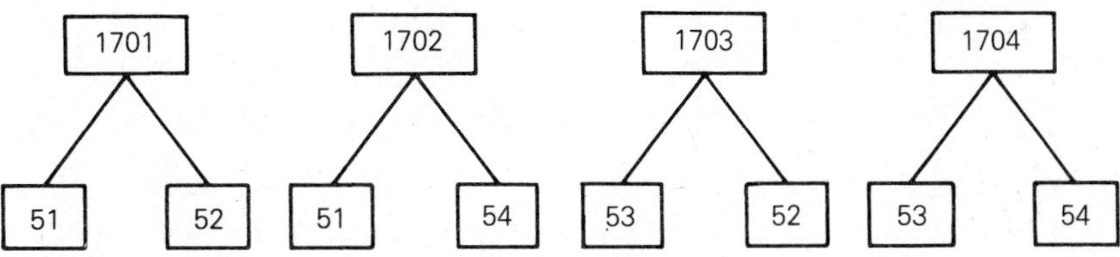

Here, 51, 52 and so forth, represent level 2 of items 1701, 1702, and so forth.

12. The Ballan Company expects to sell 5,000 sofas during the next month. The breakdown, based on the width and base heights, is as follows:

Width *A*:	40%
Width *B*:	60%
Base height *X*:	70%
Base height *Y*:	30%

Provide a forecast for sofas based on these proportions of choices.

13. Using the planning bills created for the Ballan Company and the forecasts for the given options, (a) exhibit the minimum number of super bills required; (b) provide the forecasts for level 1 items, based on the super bills.

14. The Lears Company markets several types of lawn mowers that require customer assembly. Depending on the type and size of the model, different sets of small, loose parts are required. To simplify the number of items on level 1, the company would like to create a kit that would satisfy the requirements of all models. Based on the following information, set up a kit number and list its contents.

	Quantities Required		
ITEMS	MODEL 1	MODEL 2	MODEL 3
Nuts 3562	3	4	2
Bolts 4531	4	4	4
Cotter pins 210	2	4	3
Washers 3251	2	2	1
Lock washers 4251	1	2	1

15. The Brown Company forecasts total sales of 5,000 hoists for the next month. Based on past sales information, the following breakdowns were obtained for the options:

Motor 1: 50%
Motor 2: 50%
Drum A: 35%
Drum B: 65%

Using S-bills, indicate how many of each item would be manufactured.

16. The aggregate MPS for product group X is as follows. Check whether the MPS is feasible. Backorders are not permissible; initial inventory of the product group amounts to 200 units; and the capacity of the manufacturing facility is listed as 250 units per week.

Weeks

1	2	3	4	5
250	300	300	200	300

Is the demand met?

17. Suppose that product group X in problem 16 is made up of items A and B. Given the following additional information, check whether the item MPS is feasible. Are the demands met?

Forecasts

ITEM	1	2	3	4	5	INITIAL INVENTORY	ALLOCATED CAPACITY UNITS/WK
A	50	100	150	150	150	100	150
B	200	200	150	50	150	200	100

18. Using the cut and fit method, develop a master production schedule for items A and B such that the inventory constraints are met. The following data are known regarding the capacity requirements:

Item A: 1.0 hours/unit
Item B: 0.8 hours/unit

Based on the capacity requirements, is your MPS feasible? If the cost of inventory amounts to $1.00 per item per month, calculate the average inventory cost. A total of 230 hours/week of capacity is available.

19. The Keysinger Corporation makes two different flash guns for cameras. The forecasts for the next three months are as follows:

	Oct	*Nov*	*Dec*	*Initial Inventory*	*Final Inventory*
Flash 310	1,500	1,500	2,500	350	250
Flash 311	900	1,300	1,500	200	200

In addition, the following data were accumulated from various departments in the company:

	Flash 310	*Flash 311*
Production cost/unit	$20	$25
Inventory cost/month/unit	$0.50	$0.70
Cost of increasing capacity	$15/unit	$15/unit
Cost of decreasing capacity	$10/unit	$10/unit
Existing capacity/month	200 hours	150 hours
Assembly hours/unit	0.10	0.125

Assuming that backorders are not permitted, write the equations for the problem, using linear programming.

20. In the Keysinger problem, suppose that the available manpower is limited to 175 and 125 hours in departments 310 and 311, respectively. Since the production involves only assembly, would this alter your equations?

21. The Highwheeler Bicycle Company assembles racing and touring models. The current forecasts for the next two months are 300 touring, 500 racing; and 400 touring, 450 racing. In addition, the following information is known:

	Racing	*Touring*
Production cost/unit	$50	$40
Fabrication hours/unit	4	3
Assembly hours/unit	1	1
Current inventory	200	150
Inventory/cost/month/unit	$1.50	$1.25
Final inv. desired	250	200

The total labor hours last month were 2,000 man-hours. The cost of increasing or decreasing the production level amounts to $5 per unit. Establish an optimum production schedule for Highwheeler. What is the total cost of your program? (*Hint*: Combine fabrication and assembly hours for solving this problem. Assume an 8-hour-per-day schedule for changes in man-hour calculations.)

REFERENCES AND BIBLIOGRAPHY

1. G. R. Britan and A. C. Hax, "On the Design of Hierarchical Production Planning Systems," *Decision Sciences*, Vol. 8, No. 1 (1977), pp. 28–55.
2. R. G. Brown, *Decision Rules for Inventory Management* (New York: Holt, Rinehart and Winston, 1967).
3. *Communications Oriented Production Information and Control System* (COPICS) (White Plains, N.Y.: IBM Publications, 1972).

4. A. C. Hax and H. C. Meal, "Hierarchical Integration of Production Planning and Scheduling." In M. A. Geisler, ed., *Studies in Management Science: Vol. 1, Logistics* (New York: North Holland–American Elsevier, 1975).
5. A. C. Hax and J. J. Galovin, "Hierarchical Production Planning Systems." In A. C. Hax, ed., *Studies in Operations Management* (New York: North Holland–American Elsevier, 1978).
6. L. J. Krajewski and L. P. Ritzman, "Disaggregation in Manufacturing and Service Organizations: Survey of Problems and Research," *Decision Sciences*, Vol. 8, No. 1 (1977), pp. 1–18.
7. *Master Production Schedule*, APICS Training Aid. (Falls Church, Va.: American Production and Inventory Control Society, 1973).
8. *Master Production Scheduling: Principles and Practice*, W. L. Berry, T. E. Vollmann and D. C. Whybark, eds. (Falls Church, Va.: American Production and Inventory Control Publications, 1979).
9. *Master Production Schedule Reprints* (Falls Church, Va.: American Production and Inventory Control Society, 1977).
10. *MITROL: An Introduction to MRP* (Lexington, Mass.: Mitrol, Inc., 1978).
11. J. Orlicky, *Material Requirements Planning* (New York: McGraw-Hill, 1975).
12. G. W. Plossl and W. E. Welch, *The Role of Top Management in the Control of Inventory* (Reston, Va.: Reston, 1979).
13. H. J. Zimmerman and M. G. Sovereign, *Quantitative Models for Production Management* (Englewood Cliffs, N.J.: Prentice-Hall, 1974).

appendix 11A

The Planning Bill of Material—All It's Cracked Up to Be?

F. John Sari, CPIM
Richard C. Ling, Inc.

The planning bill of material has long been a standard solution to a wide variety of master scheduling problems, especially for make-to-order and assemble-to-order manufacturers. There are many situations in which it works very well. There are also, however, many conditions under which it really does not work well, if at all. The objective of this paper is to identify some of the common pitfalls in the use of planning bills of material.

Bill of Material Terminology

The terms used to describe various forms and types of bills of material seem, to the author, to be one of the *least* standard areas of APICS terminology. Paraphrasing the 1980 APICS Dictionary, we have several to understand.

1. Planning bill (of material)
   Artificial grouping of items, in bill of material format, used to facilitate master scheduling and/or material planning.

(This definition was surely kept very general in order to cover the wide variety of bills of material in use to accomplish planning. We've got to push further to understand the various types.)

2. Super bill (of material)
   Type of planning bill, located at the top level in the structure,

Reprinted with permission, American Production and Inventory Control Society, Inc., *25th Annual International Conference Proceedings*, October, 1982.

which ties together various modular bills (and possibly a common parts bill) to define an entire product or product family.
"Quantity per" relationship of super bill to modules represents forecasted % popularity of each module.
Master scheduled quantities of the super bill explode to create requirements for the modules which also are master scheduled.

3. Modular bill (of material)
   Type of planning bill which is arranged in product modules or options.
   Often used where products have many optional features, e.g., automobiles.
4. Common parts bill (of material)
   Type of planning bill which groups all common components for a product or family of products into one bill of material.

This paper will focus on proper use of the type of planning bill described above as a "Super Bill." The terms "planning" and "super" will be used interchangeably.

The classic example used in existing literature is the hoist example (see Figure 11A.1) popularized by Messrs. Orlicky, Plossl and Wight. With 2400 possible combinations of modules (options, features, attachments, etc.), planning bills are very useful for forecasting this type of product. One needs to know the forecast of total number of hoists to be produced and the forecasted mix of options. Although frequently discussed as "two-level" master scheduling, the process is really a "two-level" forecasting procedure initially.

Planning Bill Nervousness

One of the significant pitfalls of this planning bill process is the potential for generating nervousness in our formal planning systems, especially the MPS. The actual mechanics of planning bills generate different results.

Figure 11A.2 illustrates the typical 3-zoned master schedule situation of make-and-assemble-to-order companies. The planning process involves

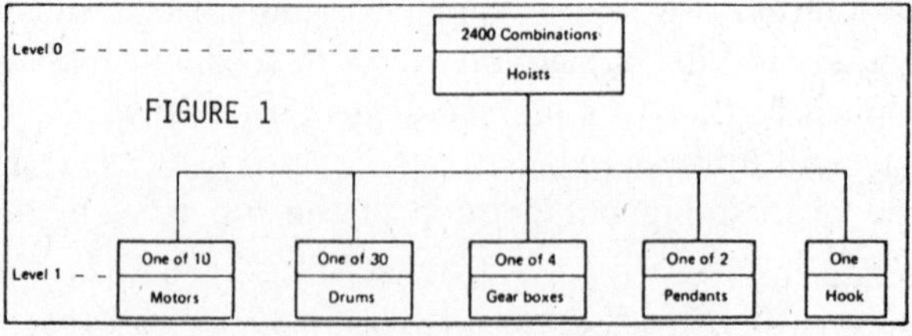

FIGURE 11A.1

FORECAST NERVOUSNESS

HOISTS 40 PER MONTH	PERIOD 1	2	3	4	5	6	7	8
PROD. PLAN / MPS		20		20		20		20
ACTUAL DEMAND		20		16		8		0
AVAILABLE-TO-PROMISE			36	44				

PENDANT 1 (50%)		1	2	3	4	5	6	7	8
FORECAST									
PRODUCTION FORECAST			10		10		10		10
ACTUAL DEMAND			12		7		5		0
PROJECTED AVAILABLE BALANCE						24			
AVAILABLE-TO-PROMISE				19					
MPS									

PENDANT 2 (50%)		1	2	3	4	5	6	7	8
FORECAST									
PRODUCTION FORECAST			10		10		10		10
ACTUAL DEMAND			8		9		3		0
PROJECTED AVAILABLE BALANCE					20				
AVAILABLE-TO-PROMISE				17					
MPS									

FIGURE 11A.2

setting a Production Plan (40 per month) for hoists which considers marketplace needs, desired backlog levels, staffing required, etc. With a forecasted split of 50/50 between pendants 1 and 2 (P1 & P2) the second level forecast for P1 & P2 becomes 20 per month or 10 every other week as shown. (The examples all assume 4-week months for simplicity.)

Zone 1 covers weeks 1–3 in which we are completely sold out. Second-level forecasts for P1 & P2 are no longer needed since actual backlog fully describes Zone 1. Zone 3 covers weeks 7 and beyond. There is no customer backlog beyond week 6 and we must deal with pure 2-level forecasts. Zone 2 is in the middle, weeks 4–6, where we must plan with a mixture of backlog and actual demand.

The actual demand in the example indicates the 50/50 forecasted mix isn't bad. Of 36 hoists sold through week 4, 19 went P1, 17 went P2.

Three basic types of mechanics are used to develop second-level forecasts. Type 1 mechanics (see Figure 11A.3) explode the available-to-promise (ATP) of the hoist family. In week 4, (Zone 2) 16 of 20 hoists have sold. Of the 4 ATP, our best estimate is two P1's and two P2's. In week 2 (Zone 1), this approach produces a zero second-level forecast which is desirable. In week 8 (Zone 3), it produces the desired 10. Potential for nervousness exists with each sale in Zone 2. In week 4, the original forecast of 50/50 has now been changed to a 45%/55% split between P1 and P2.

MECHANICS

1. EXPLODE AVAIL-TO-PROMISE

HOISTS 40 PER MONTH

		PERIOD 1	2	3	4	5	6	7	8
PROD. PLAN / MPS			20		20		20		20
ACTUAL DEMAND			20		16		8		0
AVAILABLE-TO-PROMISE			0		4		12		20

PENDANT 1 (50%)

		1	2	3	4	5	6	7	8
FORECAST									
PRODUCTION FORECAST			0		2		6		10
ACTUAL DEMAND			12		7		5		0
PROJECTED AVAILABLE BALANCE									
AVAILABLE-TO-PROMISE									
MPS									

PENDANT 2 (50%)

		1	2	3	4	5	6	7	8
FORECAST									
PRODUCTION FORECAST			0		2		6		10
ACTUAL DEMAND			8		9		3		0
PROJECTED AVAILABLE BALANCE									
AVAILABLE-TO-PROMISE									
MPS									

FIGURE 11A.3

The combination of remaining P1 forecast and 7 actual P1 demand totals 9. 9 of 20 is 45%. A responsive MPS tool might be recommending a reschedule or de-expedite of PI material in week 4 since the original forecast of 10 has been reduced to 9. The opposite is true in week 6 for P1. The original forecast of 10 has been replaced by requirements for 11, 6 remaining forecast and 5 actual demand.

People who understand the theory of flipping coins prefer Type 1 planning bills. 16 tosses have been made in week 4 of Figure 11A.3. 4 tosses remain. The best estimate of results in those 4 tosses is a 50/50 split.

Type 2 planning bill mechanics (see Figure 11A.4) consume second-level forecasts week-by-week with actual demand. Originally, all P1 forecasts were 10. As 7 sold in week 4, 7 of the forecast of 10 were consumed, leaving 3. In week 2, all 10 were consumed by 12 actual demand, etc.

Type 2 mechanics must deal with the P2 situation in week 2. Even though only 8 sold, the 2 remaining forecast must be eliminated. Otherwise, the MPS would call for 10 sets of P2 material, 2 of which are not required. Type 2's must also deal with situations where forecasts and the actual demands don't fall in the same week.

MECHANICS

2. CURRENT PERIOD FORECAST CONSUMPTION

HOISTS 40 PER MONTH	PERIOD 1	2	3	4	5	6	7	8
PROD. PLAN / MPS		20		20		20		20
ACTUAL DEMAND		20		16		8		0
AVAILABLE-TO-PROMISE								

PENDANT 1 (50%)	1	2	3	4	5	6	7	8
FORECAST								
PRODUCTION FORECAST		0		3		5		10
ACTUAL DEMAND		12		7		5		0
PROJECTED AVAILABLE BALANCE								
AVAILABLE-TO-PROMISE								
MPS								

PENDANT 2 (50%)	1	2	3	4	5	6	7	8
FORECAST								
PRODUCTION FORECAST		2*		1		7		10
ACTUAL DEMAND		8		9		3		0
PROJECTED AVAILABLE BALANCE								
AVAILABLE-TO-PROMISE								
MPS								

FIGURE 11A.4

Type 2 planning bills do a better job of protecting the original 50/50 forecast split than Type 1's. The assumption made is that 20 hoists will sell 50/50 in the end.

Type 3 planning bills extend the thought process of Type 2. (See Figure 11A.5.) Examine P1. Type 3 mechanics recognize that through week 4, 19 of the original 20 forecast for P1 have sold and 1 unconsumed forecast remains in week 4. Through week 6, 24 of 30 have sold and 6 remain—1 in week 4 and 5 in week 6. Type 3 tries to hold to the 50/50 split projected on a cumulative basis. It potentially generates less MPS nervousness than either Type 1 or 2. Type 3 is also slowest to respond to a changing mix.

Which type is best? The answer for any given company is a function of several factors:

1. Family rate of sales or volume (hoists).
2. Customer order size relative to family volume.
3. Stability of mix.
4. Percentage of option forecast, i.e., 50% options would prove more stable than 5% options.

Which is least nervous—Type 3.

MECHANICS

3. CUMULATIVE FORECAST CONSUMPTION

HOISTS 40 PER MONTH

	PERIOD							
	1	2	3	4	5	6	7	8
PROD. PLAN / MPS		20		20		20		20
ACTUAL DEMAND		20		16		8		0
AVAILABLE-TO-PROMISE								

PENDANT 1 (50%)

	1	2	3	4	5	6	7	8
FORECAST								
PRODUCTION FORECAST		0		1		5		10
ACTUAL DEMAND		12		7		5		0
PROJECTED AVAILABLE BALANCE				Σ 24 OF 30				
AVAILABLE-TO-PROMISE								
MPS		Σ 19 OF 20						

PENDANT 2 (50%)

	1	2	3	4	5	6	7	8
FORECAST								
PRODUCTION FORECAST		0		3		7		10
ACTUAL DEMAND		8		9		3		0
PROJECTED AVAILABLE BALANCE				Σ 20 OF 30				
AVAILABLE-TO-PROMISE								
MPS		Σ 17 OF 20						

FIGURE 11A.5

Major Customer Situations and Planning Bills

Major customers frequently impact planning bill forecasting techniques. (See Figure 11A.6.) It describes the situation of a major customer who buys 200 hoists per year with P1 pendants on a 4-week shipment schedule. Including this customer, total hoist sales are 600 per year and the P1/P2 split is forecast at 50/50. The actual demands of 15 in week 4 and 16 in week 8 are the major customer's orders.

The alternative planning bill approach is to exclude this major customer. (See Figure 11A.7.) The hoists which will be sold (400 per year) to normal, unknown customers split 25/75 between P1 and P2. The major customer for P1 is included through a standalone forecast. The 15 originally forecast in week 4 has been consumed by an order in week 4. The 16 in week 8 remains a forecast in Figure 11A.7. The customer has not yet provided a firm order.

The Figure 11A.7 approach does a better job of describing the family forecast. Two separate and distinct demand patterns exist. The planning bill does a good job for the normal customer demand but poorly describes the major customer.

MAJOR CUSTOMER
1. INCLUDED IN
PLANNING BILL

HOISTS
600 PER YEAR

	PERIOD 1	2	3	4	5	6	7	8
PROD. PLAN / MPS	12	12	12	12	12	12	12	12
ACTUAL DEMAND								
AVAILABLE-TO-PROMISE								

PENDANT 1 (50%)

	1	2	3	4	5	6	7	8
FORECAST								
PRODUCTION FORECAST	6	6	6	6	6	6	6	6
ACTUAL DEMAND				15M				16M
PROJECTED AVAILABLE BALANCE								
AVAILABLE-TO-PROMISE								
MPS								

PENDANT 2 (50%)

	1	2	3	4	5	6	7	8
FORECAST								
PRODUCTION FORECAST	6	6	6	6	6	6	6	6
ACTUAL DEMAND								
PROJECTED AVAILABLE BALANCE								
AVAILABLE-TO-PROMISE								
MPS								

M- MAJOR CUSTOMER BUYS 200 PER YEAR,
ALL PENDANT 1 CONFIGURATIONS,
MONTHLY SHIPMENTS

FIGURE 11A.6

MAJOR CUSTOMER
2. EXCLUDED FROM
PLANNING BILL

HOISTS
* 600 PER YEAR

	PERIOD 1	2	3	4	5	6	7	8
PROD. PLAN / MPS	8	8	8	8	8	8	8	8
ACTUAL DEMAND								
AVAILABLE-TO-PROMISE								

PENDANT 1 (25%)

	1	2	3	4	5	6	7	8
* FORECAST (MAJOR CUST.)				~~15~~				16
PRODUCTION FORECAST (UNKNOWN CUST.)	2	2	2	2	2	2	2	2
ACTUAL DEMAND				15M				
PROJECTED AVAILABLE BALANCE								
AVAILABLE-TO-PROMISE								
MPS								

PENDANT 2 (75%)

	1	2	3	4	5	6	7	8
FORECAST (MAJOR CUST.)								
PRODUCTION FORECAST (UNKNOWN CUST.)	6	6	6	6	6	6	6	6
ACTUAL DEMAND								
PROJECTED AVAILABLE BALANCE								
AVAILABLE-TO-PROMISE								
MPS								

* 200 HOISTS PER YEAR FOR MAJOR CUSTOMER,
400 PER YEAR FOR NORMAL OR UNKNOWN
CUSTOMERS SPLIT 25/75 PENDANT 1 VS. 2.

FIGURE 11A.7

Lumpy Demand Situations and Planning Bills

Master scheduling to cover lumpy demand patterns is difficult at best. Planning bills probably won't help and may in fact hurt. (See Figure 11A.8.) Even though the warehouse uses P1 and P2 equally, it should be forecast separately rather than included in a planning bill. Although the planning bill forecasts P1 and P2 in aggregate, it assumes a smooth rate of usage of each. Once again, a separate forecast of warehouse replenishment (see Figure 11A.9) does a better job of describing the real situation. Distribution Requirements Planning is useful in projecting warehouse replenishment patterns.

Small Numbers and Planning Bills

Planning bills can generate a lot of planning nervousness when family (hoists) rates are small or when an option percentage is small. (See Figure 11A.10.)

LUMPY DEMAND

1. INCLUDED IN PLANNING BILL

HOISTS 600 PER YEAR		PERIOD							
		1	2	3	4	5	6	7	8
PROD. PLAN / MPS		12	12	12	12	12	12	12	12
ACTUAL DEMAND									
AVAILABLE-TO-PROMISE									
PENDANT 1 (50%)		1	2	3	4	5	6	7	8
FORECAST									
PRODUCTION FORECAST		6	6	6	6	6	6	6	6
ACTUAL DEMAND					25W				
PROJECTED AVAILABLE BALANCE									
AVAILABLE-TO-PROMISE									
MPS									
PENDANT 2 (50%)		1	2	3	4	5	6	7	8
FORECAST									
PRODUCTION FORECAST		6	6	6	6	6	6	6	6
ACTUAL DEMAND									25W
PROJECTED AVAILABLE BALANCE									
AVAILABLE-TO-PROMISE									
MPS									

W - REMOTE WAREHOUSE USES 200 PER YEAR, 50/50 SPLIT ON PENDANT 1 VS. 2, REPLENISHES QUARTERLY

FIGURE 11A.8

LUMPY DEMAND

2. EXCLUDED FROM PLANNING BILL

HOISTS
* 600 PER YEAR

		PERIOD							
		1	2	3	4	5	6	7	8
PROD. PLAN / MPS		8	8	8	8	8	8	8	8
ACTUAL DEMAND									
AVAILABLE-TO-PROMISE									

PENDANT 1 (50%)

		1	2	3	4	5	6	7	8
FORECAST (WHSE)					~~25~~				
PRODUCTION FORECAST (NORMAL)		4	4	4	4	4	4	4	4
ACTUAL DEMAND					25W				
PROJECTED AVAILABLE BALANCE									
AVAILABLE-TO-PROMISE									
MPS									

PENDANT 2 (50%)

		1	2	3	4	5	6	7	8
FORECAST (WHSE)									25
PRODUCTION FORECAST (NORMAL)		4	4	4	4	4	4	4	4
ACTUAL DEMAND									
PROJECTED AVAILABLE BALANCE									
AVAILABLE-TO-PROMISE									
MPS									

* 200 HOISTS PER YEAR FOR WAREHOUSE REPLENISHMENT (LUMPY DEMAND) - 400 PER YEAR NORMAL (NON-LUMPY) DEMAND VIA PLANNING BILL

FIGURE 11A.9

SMALL NUMBERS

HOISTS
* 78 PER YEAR

		PERIOD							
		1	2	3	4	5	6	7	8
PROD. PLAN / MPS		2	2	1	1	2	2	1	1
ACTUAL DEMAND									
AVAILABLE-TO-PROMISE									

PENDANT 1 (50%)

		1	2	3	4	5	6	7	8
FORECAST									
PRODUCTION FORECAST		1	1	1	0	1	1	1	0
ACTUAL DEMAND									
PROJECTED AVAILABLE BALANCE									
AVAILABLE-TO-PROMISE									
MPS									

PENDANT 2 (50%)

		1	2	3	4	5	6	7	8
FORECAST									
PRODUCTION FORECAST		1	1	1	0	1	1	1	0
ACTUAL DEMAND									
PROJECTED AVAILABLE BALANCE									
AVAILABLE-TO-PROMISE									
MPS									

* 78 PER YEAR = 6 PER 4 WEEKS

FIGURE 11A.10

A smooth sales rate of 78 per year equates to 6 units each 4 weeks. The sales of one hoist thus represents 16% of the hoist forecast and 33% of a pendant forecast in any month. Since customer order size is so large relative to either forecast, any variation from expected means a large percentage miss.

The real problem may be that one simply cannot forecast small numbers very well. If that's the case, planning bills won't help. You may be forced to accept some risk inventory maintained by safety stock or firm planned order techniques.

Planning Bills in Perspective

The planning bill of material is a powerful tool when used properly. There are many firms who effectively utilize planning bills for selected products. It has, however, been "a solution in search of a problem" for some.

Planning bills make certain assumptions and apply selectively. One must understand those assumptions as well as the mechanics in use. Foremost, however, make sure the solution fits the problem.

chapter twelve

High-Volume Production Activity Control

Shop floor control (SFC) includes the principles, approaches, and techniques that are necessary to plan, schedule, control, and evaluate the effectiveness of production operations. Shop floor control integrates the activities of the so-called factors of production of a manufacturing facility, such as workers, machines, inventory, and material handling equipment. The SFC plan facilitates efficient execution of the master production schedule, control of processing priorities, improvement of operating efficiency through proper worker–machine scheduling, and maintenance of minimum quantities of work in process and finished goods inventories. In the final analysis, SFC should lead to improved customer service. This chapter covers the major functions of an efficient SFC and its relationships to MRP, capacity planning, and inventory status that are applicable to make-to-stock continuous-flow manufacturing for high-volume, standardized products.

The Production Environment

Major differences exist in the management of production activities in make-to-order and make-to-stock firms. In make-to-order situations, due dates are important, and hence the sequencing of customer orders at various machine centers is an essential function. This involves both planning and control of activities. Make-to-stock products are generally high-volume consumer goods, such as telephones, automobiles, and wrist watches. The manufacture of standardized, high-volume items, which involves flow shops, is the subject of this chapter. Differences in the production environment could also represent technological differentiation, such as manual versus automated, chemical reactions or materials forming, and the like. The cost and quantity of production determines the degree of automation in industries.

Chemicals, drugs, petroleum, and other process industries fall in the special category of high-volume production industry. Management of these industries generally requires trained technical professionals, a high degree of automation, and special materials management techniques. Production control techniques for such industries are discussed in Bensousson, Hurst, and Nasland [2]; Gruver and Narasimhan [8]; Paul [26]; and Sethi and Thompson [29]. The unique characteristics of various types of such shops are exhibited in table 12.1.

FLOW SHOPS

A flow shop consists of a set of facilities through which work flows in a serial fashion. The same operations are performed repeatedly in every work station, thus requiring lower-level skilled workers. The flow shop generally represents a mass production situation, and hence the operations become very efficient. For example, an operator might be installing car doors on an automotive assembly line or assembling dials on the handset of a telephone.

In flow shops, items enter the finished goods inventory one after another, often in the same order they were input, leaving very low in-process inventories. Since the items are mostly made to stock, forecasting is a difficult job, and hence the finished goods levels carried in terms of

TABLE 12.1 Comparison of Flow Shop and Job Shop Characteristics

Item	*Flow Shop*	*Job Shop*
Equipment	Special-purpose	General or multipurpose
Investment amount	Medium to high	Low to medium
Manpower	Low-skilled	High-skilled
Product	Make-to-stock	Make-to-order
Demand volume	High	Low
Number of end items	Few	Many
Production control systems	Fixed layout and continuous flow; uses assembly line balancing	Variable flow pattern controlled by batch, order, or service needs; uses sequencing rules and simulation
Efficiency of production	Most	Least
Finished goods inventory	High	Low
In-process inventories	Low	High
Raw material inventories	High	Low
Component demand type	Dependent	Predominantly independent

anticipation inventories are very high. For the same reason, raw materials are carried at higher inventory levels. Machines in flow shops tend to have a special-purpose design, and hence the initial investment level is generally high for heavily automated plants.

The production control system for continuous production is called *flow control*. Specialization, high volume, division of labor, and efficiency are built into the design of assembly lines. Hence, flow shops generally require repetitive and low skills only. The repetitive nature of the manufacturing environment also creates monotony and affects worker morale. To deal with this problem, industrial engineers and social scientists have developed job enrichment programs. Although we will not dwell on these issues in detail, they should be kept in mind when designing assembly lines.

JOB SHOPS

Job shops follow different flow patterns through a facility in batches. The operations need not be repetitious. Job shop facilities are made up of general-purpose machines that are capable of using various tools, dies, and fixtures to perform many different jobs at the same facility. The jobs may be unique and hence may never be repeated. Variations in sequencing of jobs on different machines, processing time requirements, priorities, and number of operations make management of job shops very challenging. These factors also necessitate highly skilled workers. Unfortunately, this leads to a production system that is not very efficient. Job shops accumulate large amounts of in-process inventories. Many end items are made to customer specifications, requiring low amounts of raw materials and low end item inventories. The production control system for a job shop is called *order control*. Hospitals, restaurants, and service stations are classic examples of job shops in the service sector. Management of job shops will be addressed in later chapters.

INTERMITTENT FLOW SHOPS

An intermittent flow production shop is useful when high production volumes are needed on a periodic basis. Examples include the production of refrigerators, air conditioners, and heat pumps. Such systems are known as *batch processing*. This chapter also discusses several techniques for managing such systems. When batches of several items are to be manufactured in a job shop environment, the process is dominated by serial production. The volume may not justify special-purpose machines because of recurrent use. For production and inventory system purposes, such shops can be treated as flow shops. These systems are treated in chapter 13, which covers job shop activity planning.

Controlling Continuous Production

The major flow shop problem is to attain the desired production rate, such as 60 cars per hour or 600 telephones per day, with maximum possible efficiency. The total work content of the job is divided into elementary operations, and these operations are grouped together at work stations. The job moves successively, and in many instances continuously, from one station to another. All work stations are occupied with jobs that are at different stages of completion. The speed of the assembly line is controlled by the required output rate, the space between stations, and the time requirements for each work station. By controlling the speed of the conveyor or the cycle time, we can essentially control the output rate on the production line.

Table 12.2 exhibits all operations involved in the assembly of a calculator, which requires 120 seconds of total work. Suppose that we allocate operations 1 through 7 to station A; operations 8 through 14 to station B; and, finally, operations 15 through 20 to station C. The workload at stations A, B, and C would be 43 seconds, 43 seconds, and 34 seconds, respectively. The maximum output of such a system could only be 83.7 units per hour, even though individual output rates of 83.7, 83.7, and 105.8 units per hour at stations A, B, and C, respectively, are possible. This can be explained by

TABLE 12.2 Calculator Assembly

Station	*Operation*	*Duration* t_i *(seconds)*	Σt_i *for Station*	*Maximum Output Rate per Hour*
A	1	5		
	2	14		
	3	6		$\frac{60 \times 60}{43}$
	4	3		
	5	8		
	6	5		= 83.7
	7	2	43	units
B	8	5		
	9	7		
	10	12		$\frac{60 \times 60}{43}$
	11	2		
	12	7		
	13	4		= 83.7
	14	6	43	units
C	15	3		
	16	4		$\frac{60 \times 60}{34}$
	17	9		
	18	10		
	19	3		= 105.8
	20	5	34	units
Total		120	120	

the following. Stations A and B each have a total of 43 seconds of work, and hence a job arrives at station C every 43 seconds. Station C has only 34 seconds of work, and hence the station will be idle for 43 − 34 = 9 seconds during every cycle.

For an efficient layout and production operation, therefore, all stations should be loaded with equal amounts of work. Several aspects of manufacturing make it difficult to assign equal work assignments to all stations. Generally, most operations must be done in a particular sequence, which is specified by a precedence diagram. Also, the capacity of equipment and the efficiency of people on the assembly line differ. The interaction of these aspects complicates the balancing of workload among stations. Generally we must ask the following questions: How do we determine the sequencing of operations? How do we determine the ordering of stations? How many stations are necessary? How well balanced will the flow shop be? The answers to the first two questions are given by the process sheet released by the manufacturing process engineer. Very few choices may exist to alter the operation times or assembly sequence. The answer to the last question, and other questions, depends on the required production rate, feasible cycle times, and available facilities. A brief discussion of these issues follows.

PRECEDENCE DIAGRAM

A precedence diagram specifies the order or sequence in which the activities must be performed. As an example, figure 12.1 shows the precedence relationship for the calculator assembly. Each circle is a node, and the numbers inside the circles identify particular operations. The number outside the circle represents the duration of the operation. We have specified them in seconds; it is also popular to specify them in hundredths of minutes. Arrows indicate which operations should be completed first. For example, operation 14 cannot be started until operations 3 and 7 are completed.

CYCLE TIME

Cycle time (c) is directly related to the production rate of the assembly line:

$$c = \frac{\text{productive time}}{\text{demand}}$$

For example, if 2,400 calculators are required per day, then the cycle time, based on an eight-hour day, would be $(8 \times 60 \times 60)/2{,}400 = 12$ seconds. This cycle time tells us that the items must be spaced at least 12 seconds apart on the assembly line and that each station has that amount of time. Referring to table 12.2, we notice that operation 2 exceeds twelve seconds. Thus, a cycle time of twelve seconds is not feasible in this case. Therefore,

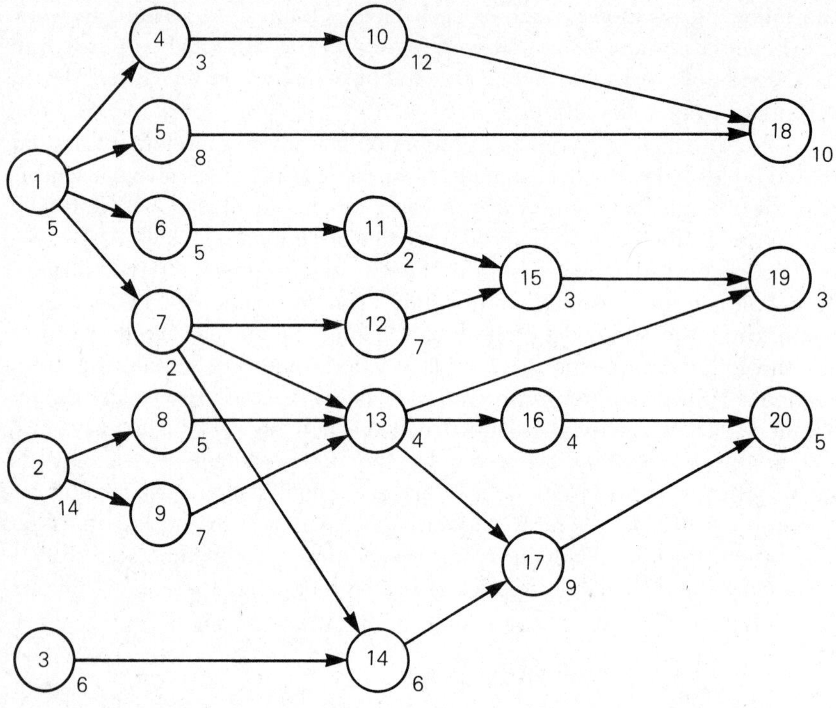

FIGURE 12.1 Precedence diagram for calculator assembly

we can state that the cycle time should be larger than the longest duration, t_{max}. It is also evident that c need not be greater than the total time Σt_i to complete all operations. Therefore,

$$t_{max} \leqslant c \leqslant \sum_i t_i$$

where t_i represents the duration for operation i.

NUMBER OF WORK STATIONS

The total number of work stations (n) must always be an integer. The value of n is dependent on c, and vice versa. That is,

$$n = \frac{\sum t_i}{c} \quad \text{or} \quad c = \frac{\sum t_i}{n}$$

Table 12.3 exhibits several alternative cycle times and production rates for many possible numbers of stations. The results are based on perfect balance,

TABLE 12.3 Relationship Between Cycle Time and Production Rate

Number of Work Stations (n)	*Cycle Time* $(c = \Sigma t_i/n)$	*Daily Production*	*Remarks*
1	120	240	
2	60	480	
3	40	720	
4	30	960	
5	24	1,200	
6	20	1,440	
7	17.1	1,685	Not feasible
8	15	1,920	
9	13.3	2,165	Not feasible
10	12	2,400	

which may not be feasible in all cases. A layout is said to have a perfect balance when the total work content in all stations are equal, and only a limited number of combinations satisfy the precedence constraints. For example, it is not possible to obtain exactly 17.1 seconds per station for a seven-station layout, since elementary operations are not divisible.

BALANCE DELAY

The quality of the solution is measured by the balance delay (d) equation:

$$d = \frac{\left(nc - \sum t_i\right)100}{nc}$$

The ratio indicates the inefficiency of the system, which is induced by the idle time. In our calculator example, the ratio would be

$$d = \frac{[(3)(43) - 120]100}{(3)(43)}$$

$$= 6.98\%$$

The proposed solution does not meet the required production of 720 units per day. Management may explore the use of overtime or the addition of another station, or they may find other ways of increasing the productivity of assembly operations. Although this layout resulted in an imbalanced solution, we will see later that it is possible to achieve a perfect balance for this example. In a perfectly balanced layout situation, $nc = \Sigma\ t_i$, and hence the balance delay will be equal to zero.

We see that cycle time (c) is a function of the required output rate and the total number of work stations (n). We also know that the required basic output rate depends on demand, available inventory, and capacity of the facility. Therefore, we see that many aspects of production are interrelated and, hence, that the design of an assembly line is a complex problem. Assuming that a suitable production schedule is stated, a feasible cycle time and an acceptable number of work stations can be determined using one of the several balancing methodologies discussed in this chapter.

Sequencing and Line Balancing Methodologies

Line balancing concepts have been implemented in a number of industries, such as automobile, telephone, and consumer electronic goods manufacturing. These are generally large-scale problems involving perhaps 75 to 100 tasks or more, with ten to fifteen or more stations. Line balancing methods and techniques include (1) linear programming, (2) dynamic programming, (3) heuristic methods, and (4) computer-based sampling techniques. The size of the problems (number of operations) that can be successfully and economically tackled by optimizing methods such as linear programming and dynamic programming is limited. Further, complexities inherent in manufacturing, as will be described later, make heuristics and other computer-based techniques very attractive for solving large-scale line balancing problems. In this section, we will explain the basic concepts of a heuristic method that was developed by Kilbridge and Wester [18] and a computer-based sampling technique, COMSOAL, that was developed by Arcus [1].

Heuristic Techniques in Line Balancing

A heuristic, or rule of thumb, is a shortcut solution procedure that searches for a satisfactory, rather than optimal, solution. Analogous to the human trial-and-error process, heuristics reach acceptable solutions to problems for which optimizing solutions are not feasible or are too costly to employ. There is no way to guarantee that an optimal solution will be found with the heuristic techniques; rather, the best of the arrangements considered has been found.

THE TRIAL-AND-ERROR TECHNIQUE

The trial-and-error technique merely groups work elements so as not to violate the cycle time, starting with precedence diagram and activity times. For example, suppose that 1,400 units of the product shown in table 12.2 are required per day. This translates to approximately twenty seconds of cycle time with six work stations, as shown in Table 12.3. The ease of rearrangement of existing facilities, economics, and quality reasons lead the management to consider two assembly lines, each producing 720 units. This layout will have a cycle time of forty seconds, with three work stations in each assembly line.

Assuming that activities may be combined within a given zone without violating the precedence relationship, we can designate work zones/stations on the precedence diagram. When we obtain the theoretical minimum number of work stations, the optimum assignment is made. The solution need not be unique. One such solution is exhibited in figure 12.2. In this case, a perfect balance was achieved, since all work zones have exactly the same workload of forty seconds. Hence, the balance delay is 0%. This can also be shown by use of the balance delay formula discussed earlier:

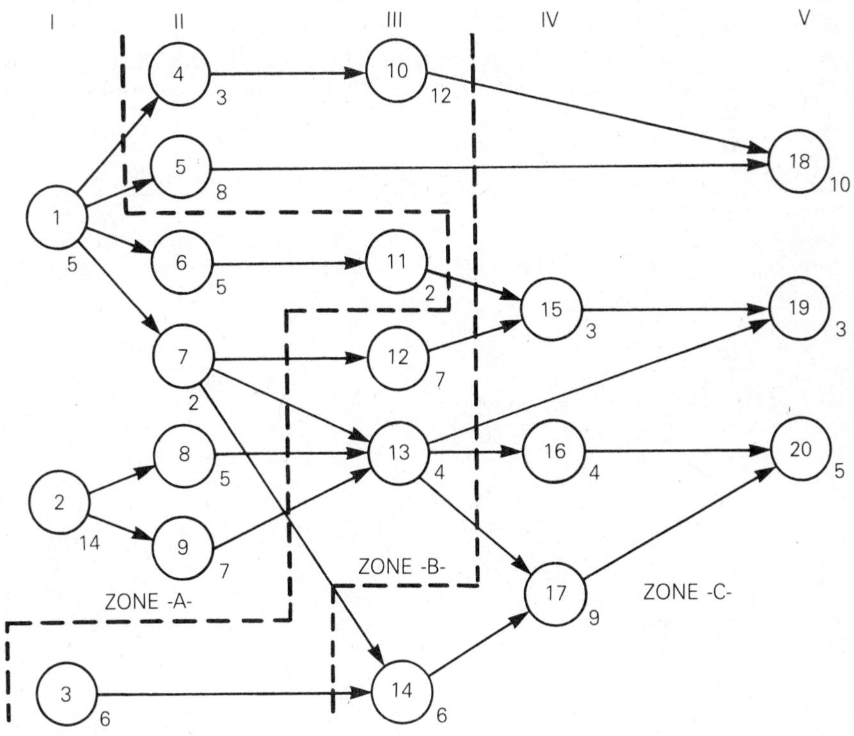

FIGURE 12.2 A three-station solution by the trial-and-error procedure for the problem shown in table 12.2

$$d = \frac{(nc - \sum t_i)100}{\text{nc}}$$

$$= \frac{[(3)(40) - (120)]100}{(3)(40)} = 0$$

THE KILBRIDGE-WESTER HEURISTIC TECHNIQUE

Suppose that the calculator production needs to be increased. The demand leads the management to consider a capacity using a four-station layout with a thirty-second cycle time and two production lines. We will use this example to illustrate a heuristic line balancing method developed by Kilbridge and Wester [18]. As described earlier, the circled numbers in figure 12.2 represent operations, and the numbers outside the circles represent the task time in seconds. The tasks in column I of figure 12.2 have no predecessors, and column II tasks follow column I tasks. Thus, the columns represent the precedence relationship among tasks. Since the total time to complete all operations amounts to 120 seconds, it is theoretically possible to attain a perfect balance with four stations, with thirty seconds of workload in each work station. Table 12.4 summarizes the information

TABLE 12.4 Summary of Information for the Calculator Assembly

Precedence Diagram Column (A)	*Operation (B)*	*Remarks (C)*	*Duration (D)*	*Sum Duration for Columns (E)*	*Column Cumulative Times (F)*
I	1		5		
	2		14		
	3		6	25	25
II	4	10 → III	3		
	5	→ III, IV	8		
	6		5		
	7		2		
	8		5		
	9		7	30	55
III	10	→ IV	12		
	11		2		
	12		7		
	13		4		
	14		6	31	86
IV	15		3		
	16		4		
	17		9	16	102
V	18		10		
	19		3		
	20		5	18	120

contained in the precedence diagram. All columns are self-explanatory except column C, which describes the flexibility that will be useful while assigning tasks to specific work stations. For example, although operation 5 is in column II on the precedence diagram, it can also be done in column III or column IV without violating the precedence relationships. Similarly, operations 4 and 10 can be moved together to column III; the completion of operation 10 in column IV satisfies precedence relationships. We can describe the Kilbridge-Wester assembly line balancing procedure in three logical steps.

Step 1

Since the cycle time (c) is equal to thirty seconds, scan through column I and check whether any combinations of operation durations sum to thirty seconds. If yes, station 1 is obtained. If more operations are left over, assign them to station 2. On the other hand, if cumulative time is less than c, scan through column II and add one or more operations to station 1. In our problem, operation 6 can be moved ahead without violating the precedence relationship, as shown in table 12.5. Repeat step 1 for station 2, if possible. We see that column II has twenty-five seconds of workload remaining, which means that we need one or more operations amounting to five seconds from column III. Since this is not possible, we go to step 2.

TABLE 12.5 Heuristic Line Balancing Method, Step 2

Precedence Diagram Column (A)	*Operation (B)*	*Remarks (C)*	*Duration (D)*	*Sum Duration for Columns (E)*	*Column Cumulative Times (F)*
I	1		5		
	2		14		
	3		6		
II	6		5	30	30
	4		3		
	5		8		
	7		2		
	8		5		
	9		7	25	55
III	10		12		
	11		2		
	12		7		
	13		4		
	14		6	31	86
IV	15		3		
	16		4		
	17		9	16	102
V	18		10		
	19		3		
	20		5	18	120

Step 2

Consider the unassigned tasks in columns II and III. The operation times total 25 + 31 = 56 seconds. Check whether a set of tasks sum to 56 − 30 = 26 seconds and can be moved to the next station without violating the precedence relationships. We see that tasks 5, 10, and 14 total twenty-six seconds and can be moved to the next station, as exhibited in table 12.6. If it were not possible to find tasks that sum to twenty-six seconds, we would add another column totaling 25 + 31 + 16 = 72 seconds and see whether a combination of tasks totaling 72 − 30 = 42 seconds is feasible to move, and so forth. Thus, we would repeat step 2 as many times as necessary. Note that it was not necessary to repeat step 2 to obtain station 2 in our problem.

Step 3

Repeat steps 1 and 2. Add the unassigned operation in column III, which sums to twenty-six seconds. Is there any combination of tasks in column IV that sums to 30 − 26 = 4 seconds? We see that operation 16 can be moved up at station 3 without violating the precedence relationship. The results are exhibited in table 12.7. Since the remaining tasks add up to thirty, they automatically comprise station 4. Figure 12.3 shows the new

TABLE 12.6 Heuristic Line Balancing Method, Step 1

Precedence Diagram Column (A)	*Operation* (B)	*Remarks* (C)	*Duration* (D)	*Sum Duration for Columns* (E)	*Column Cumulative Times* (F)
I	1		5		
	2		14		
	3		6		
	6		5	30	30
II	4		3		
	7		2		
	8		5		
	9		7		
III	11		2		
	12		7		
	13		4	30	60
	5		8		
	10		12		
	14		6	26	86
IV	15		3		
	16		4		
	17		9	16	102
V	18		10		
	19		3		
	20		5	18	120

TABLE 12.7 Heuristic Line Balancing Method, Step 3

Precedence Diagram Column (A)	*Operation (B)*	*Remarks (C)*	*Duration (D)*	*Sum Duration for Columns (E)*	*Column Cumulative Times (F)*
I	1		5		
	2		14		
	3		6		
	6		5	30	30
II	4		3		
	7		2		
	8		5		
	9		7		
III	11		2		
	12		7		
	13		4	30	60
	5		8		
	10		12		
	14		6		
	16		4	30	90
IV	15		3		
	17		9		
	18		10		
	19		3		
	20		5	30	120

layout. Note that the layout need not be unique and that several alternative combinations of operations are feasible in most cases.

Wester and Kilbridge [36] discuss the technique as applied to television assembly. In a mass production situation, the sets move on an assembly line. Some operations can be done only from the front of the set and some can only be done from the rear. A group of operators facilitated the assembly from either side. To accommodate the worker positions on the assembly line and other constraints, Wester and Kilbridge modified their algorithm. The algorithm was further modified by Thomopoulos [33] for problems involving the balance of an assembly line that produces several different television models on the same line.

THE COMSOAL ALGORITHM

The computer method of sequencing operations for assembly lines (COMSOAL) was developed by Arcus [1]. The procedure generates a large number of feasible solutions using a biased sampling method. We can then choose the solution that most satisfies our needs. In general, the procedure assigns a number to each operation that represents the number of predecessors

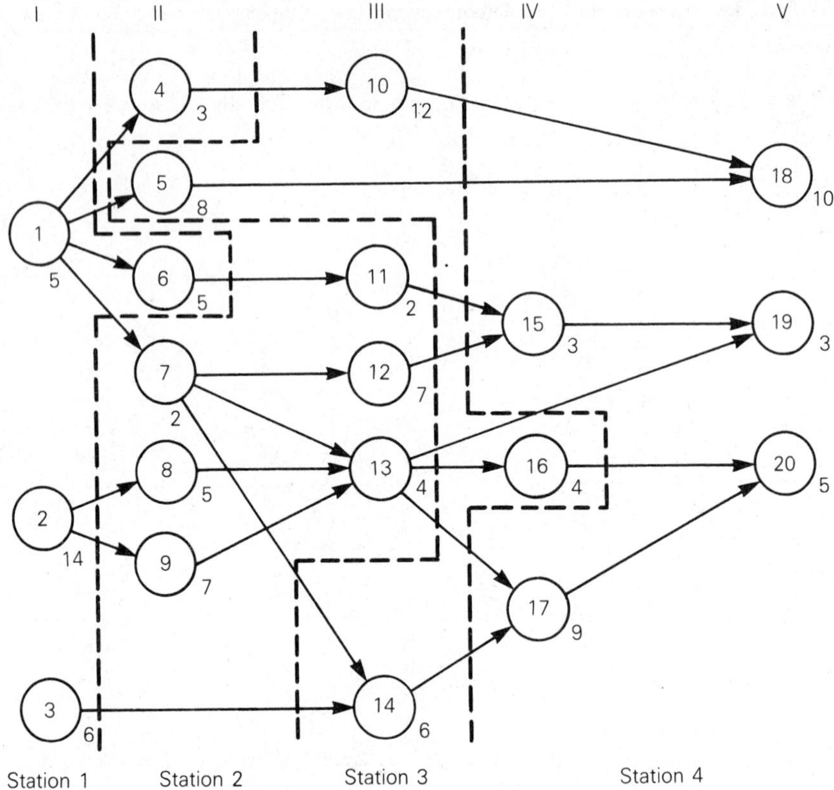

FIGURE 12.3 Four-station layout, $c = 30$ seconds, using Kilbridge and Wester algorithm

that operation has. The principle can best be described by an example. Suppose that we need to design a four-station layout with $c = 30$. Referring to the precedence diagram in figure 12.1, we see that operations 1, 2, and 3 have no predecessors; hence, they are assigned a zero weight. Operations 4, 5, 6, 7, 8, 9, and 14 have one predecessor, and so forth. The operations' numbers of predecessors and operation times are given in table 12.8. The COMSOAL procedure is described by the following steps.

Step 1

Scan list A in table 12.8. Create list B by listing all tasks that do not have preceding tasks. In our example, tasks 1, 2 and 3, whose operation times are 5, 14, and 6, respectively, have no predecessors. Create list C, which is made up of all eligible jobs from list B. A job becomes eligible to be assigned to a station if the task time is less than the cycle time or if it is less than the time remaining to complete the work station. Since all

TABLE 12.8 Solution Procedure for COMSOAL Algorithm, Steps 1 and 2

LIST A

Operation Number	*Maximum Number of Preceding Tasks*	*Duration* t_i
1	0	5
2	0	14
3	0	6
4	1	3
5	1	8
6	1	5
7	1	2
8	1	5
9	1	7
14	1	6
10	2	12
11	2	2
12	2	7
13	2	4
15	3	3
16	3	4
17[a]	3	9
18	3	10
19	4	3
20	4	5

[a] Operation 17 has three predecessors 2 → 8 → 13 or 2 → 9 → 13.

LIST B

Operation	*Duration*
1	5
2	14
3	6

(FIT) LIST C

Operation	*Duration*
1	5
2	14
3	6

jobs in list B are less than cycle time $c = 30$, they also constitute list C, which is also known as a *fit list*.

Step 2

Tasks from fit list C are assigned to station 1 until they total $c = 30$ using very general rules: (1) larger tasks have greater probability of being assigned than smaller ones; (2) tasks with more followers have more probability of being assigned first; and (3) operations are chosen at random. According to these rules, operation 2 will be assigned first to station 1, since it is the longest task and it has the largest number of followers. Total operation time assigned to station 1 so far amounts to fourteen seconds. As this is lower than $c = 30$, operation 3 will be assigned to station 1 next, since operation 3 has a longer duration than operation 1. If they had the same duration, one of them would be assigned first in random manner. After assigning tasks 2, 3, and 1, the load at station 1 is twenty-five seconds, which is less than $c = 30$ seconds. Now, lists A, B, and C are revised.

Step 3

Update list A by deducting 1 from all jobs immediately following tasks 1, 2, and 3. The new list B consists of tasks 4, 5, 6, 7, 8, 9, and 14, as shown in table 12.9. Since list C should include all tasks that are less than or equal to 30 − 25 = 5 seconds, it consists of only tasks 4, 6, 7, and 8. Since the longest operation, task 6, uses five seconds, it is assigned to station 1, and station 1 is now fully packed. Note that operation 8 was equally likely to be assigned.

Step 4

Continue the process, repeating steps 1 and 2 for all remaining stations and thus generating revisions to lists A, B, and C. For example, the revised

TABLE 12.9 Solution Procedure for COMSOAL Algorithm, Step 3

LIST A

Operation Number	*Maximum Number of Preceding Tasks*	*Duration* t_i
4	1 − 1 = 0	3
5	1 − 1 = 0	8
6	1 − 1 = 0	5
7	1 − 1 = 0	2
8	1 − 1 = 0	5
9	1 − 1 = 0	7
14	1 − 1 = 0	6
10	2 − 1 = 1	12
11	2 − 1 = 1	2
12	2 − 1 = 1	7
13	2 − 1 = 1	4
15	3 − 1 = 2	3
16	3 − 1 = 2	4
17	3 − 1 = 2	9
18	3 − 1 = 2	10
19	4 − 1 = 3	3
20	4 − 1 = 3	5

LIST B

Operation	*Duration*
4	3
5	8
6	5
7	2
8	5
9	7
14	6

(FIT) LIST C

Operation	*Duration*
4	3
6	5
7	2
8	5

TABLE 12.10 Revised Lists for COMSOAL Algorithm Solution

LIST B		*(FIT) LIST C*	
Operation	*Duration*	*Operation*	*Duration*
4	3	4	3
5	8	5	8
7	2	7	2
8	5	8	5
9	7	9	7
14	6	14	6

list B will not have operation 6, and the revised fit list C will be the same as the revised list B, as exhibited in table 12.10. All operations are eligible to be assigned to station 2, since they are all smaller than $c = 30$ seconds. Tasks 5, 9, 14, 8, and 4 make up station 2, with a total of twenty-nine seconds. Task 7 cannot be assigned to station 2, since its inclusion will exceed $c = 30$ seconds, and hence it is assigned to station 3. The revised lists B and C, exhibited in table 12.11, consist of operations 10, 11, 12, and 13. Now the total load at station 3 is twenty-seven seconds. After assigning task 15 to station 3 in the next iteration, we will have a total load of thirty seconds. The remaining tasks—operations 16, 17, 18, 19, and 20—make up station 4, with a load of thirty-one seconds. This configuration thus results in a cycle time of thirty-one seconds, instead of a planned thirty-second cycle time. The daily production will be 929 units, instead

TABLE 12.11 Solution Procedure for COMSOAL Algorithm, Step 4

LIST A

Operation Number	*Maximum Number of Preceding Tasks*	*Duration* t_i
10	$1 - 1 = 0$	12
11	$1 - 1 = 0$	2
12	$1 - 1 = 0$	7
13	$1 - 1 = 0$	4
15	$2 - 1 = 1$	3
16	$2 - 1 = 1$	4
17	$2 - 1 = 1$	9
18	$2 - 1 = 1$	10
19	$3 - 1 = 2$	3
20	$3 - 1 = 2$	5

LIST B		*(FIT) LIST C*	
Operation	*Duration*	*Operation*	*Duration*
10	12	10	12
11	2	11	2
12	7	12	7
13	4	13	4

of the 960 units originally planned. The layout is exhibited by figure 12.4. It should be noted that the COMSOAL algorithm generates many solutions. One of them could have generated a four-station layout with a perfect balance. It should also be noted, however, that the algorithm provides a near optimal solution for line balancing problems. Since manual adjustments can improve these solutions, a near optimal solution is acceptable for large industrial problems.

In addition to the precedence constraints, however, other constraints could exist in the real world. For example, an exhaust system can be installed on an automobile only when a pit exists; undercoating and painting can be done only where the facilities are located; engines or doors can be installed only where the conveyor line carrying these parts is accessible; and more than one person may be required to install an engine on the chassis. Also, the work content on particular stations could vary according to the options ordered by the customer. To accommodate these and other types of constraints, Arcus [1] incorporated refinements in the COMSOAL algorithm. The model has been implemented successfully by the Chrysler

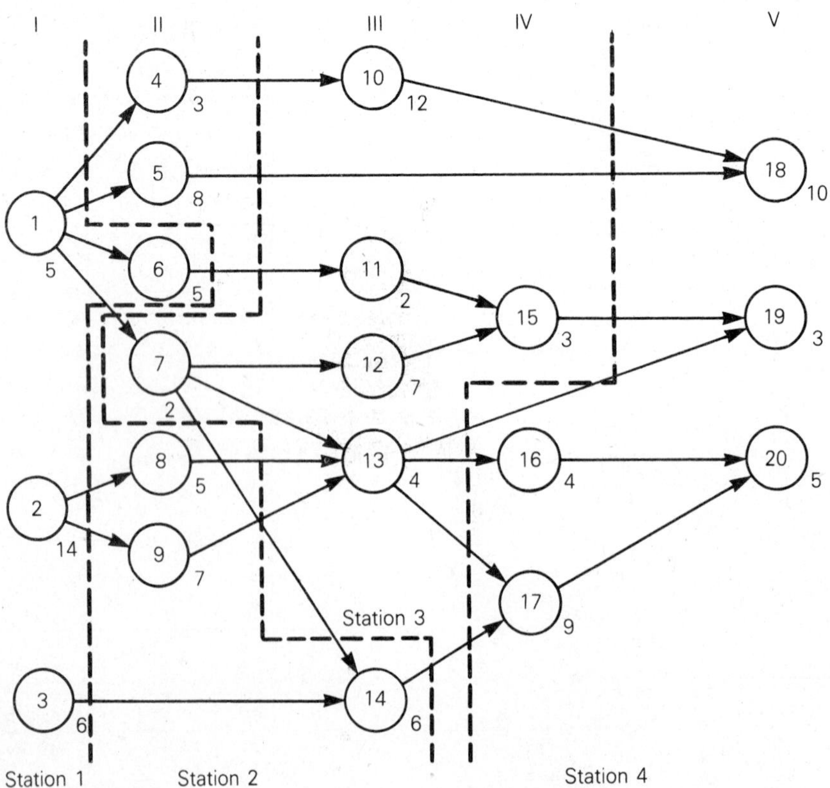

FIGURE 12.4 Four-station trial solution using the COMSOAL algorithm

Corporation with 200 stations, and Arcus reports that approximately 1.5% balance delay was incurred. The COMSOAL procedure is capable of providing computer solutions quickly and inexpensively, which is helpful for testing the effect of alternative production rates on manpower and other planning procedures.

THE RANKED POSITIONAL WEIGHT TECHNIQUE AND MALB

The ranked positional weight technique was developed by Helgeson and Birnie [13]. This method assigns those jobs first whose followers have the largest total time—that is, $\Sigma\ t_i$ of all successors—including the time to perform that task. The technique, as refined and computerized in 1973 for large-scale problems by Dar-El [5], is known as the model for assembly line balancing (MALB). We will describe the original method with an example and point out the refinements made by Dar-El. We will use the example exhibited in figure 12.1.

This method ranks operations in descending order of positional weights, as shown in table 12.12. For example, operation 4 with a duration of 3 seconds is followed by operations 10 and 18 with durations of 12 and 10, respectively. Therefore, the positional weight is obtained by adding all durations of operations including operation 4, which is 25. For a four station layout, the procedure follows.

TABLE 12.12 Ranking by Positional Weight

Operation, in Ranked Order	*Time*	*Positional Weight*	*Immediate Predecessor*
1	5	88	4,5,6,7
2	14	51	8,9
7	2	43	12,13,14
9	7	32	13
8	5	30	13
3	6	26	14
4	3	25	10
13	4	25	16,17
10	12	22	18
14	6	20	17
5	8	18	18
17	9	14	20
6	5	13	11
12	7	13	15
18	10	10	—
16	4	9	20
11	2	8	15
15	3	6	19
20	5	5	—
19	3	3	—

Step 1

Select the task with the highest positional weight and assign it to the first available work station (see table 12.13). We assign operation 1 to station 1. Continue the procedure until unassigned time is zero, making sure that the precedence relationship is satisfied. Thus, we have assigned tasks 1, 2, 7, and 9 to station 1. If the addition of the next task exceeds cycle time, then assign that task to the next available station. An attempt is made to find a feasible operation farther down the list that can be included. No other feasible operation can be assigned to station 1; hence, a cycle time of twenty-eight seconds is achieved. The process is repeated for the remaining stations. If a perfect balance is achieved, the problem has an optimal solution, but this is not guaranteed. In our example, stations 2 and 3 obtain perfect balances. Stations 1 and 4 have a load of twenty-eight and twenty-nine seconds, respectively. The remaining task, operation 19, is assigned to station 5.

Step 2

If the cycle time is allowed to increase slightly, operation 4 can be combined with station 1, with a new cycle time of thirty-one seconds, and

TABLE 12.13 Ranked Positional Weight Technique

Station	*Operation*	*Station Time*	*ΣStation Time*	*Unassigned Time*	*Remarks*
1	1	5	5	25	Assigned
	2	14	19	11	Assigned
	7	2	21	9	Assigned
	9	7	28	2	Assigned
	No other feasible operation can be assigned				
2	8	5	5	25	Assigned
	3	6	11	19	Assigned
	4	3	14	16	Assigned
	13	4	18	12	Assigned
	10	12	30	0	Assigned
3	14	6	6	24	Assigned
	5	8	14	16	Assigned
	17	9	23	7	Assigned
	6	5	28	2	Assigned
	12	7	35		$>c$
	18	10	38		$>c$
	16	4	32		$>c$
	11	2	30	0	Assigned
4	12	7	7	23	Assigned
	18	10	17	13	Assigned
	16	4	21	9	Assigned
	15	3	24	6	Assigned
	20	5	29	1	Assigned
	No other feasible operation can be assigned				
5	19	3	3	27	Assigned

the problem can be reworked. An attempt would be made to obtain a better balance.

We notice that with four stations and a cycle time of thirty seconds, the balance delay for the assigned operations is

$$\frac{[(4)(30) - 117]100}{(4)(30)} = 2.5\%$$

The solution is exhibited in figure 12.5. The computerized version of this procedure, MALB, attempts to improve the initial solution provided by the ranked positional weight technique. The MALB procedure permits backtracking after initial assignments have been made. It takes other combinations of tasks to determine whether an improvement is possible. The details of the MALB procedure are given in Dar-El [5].

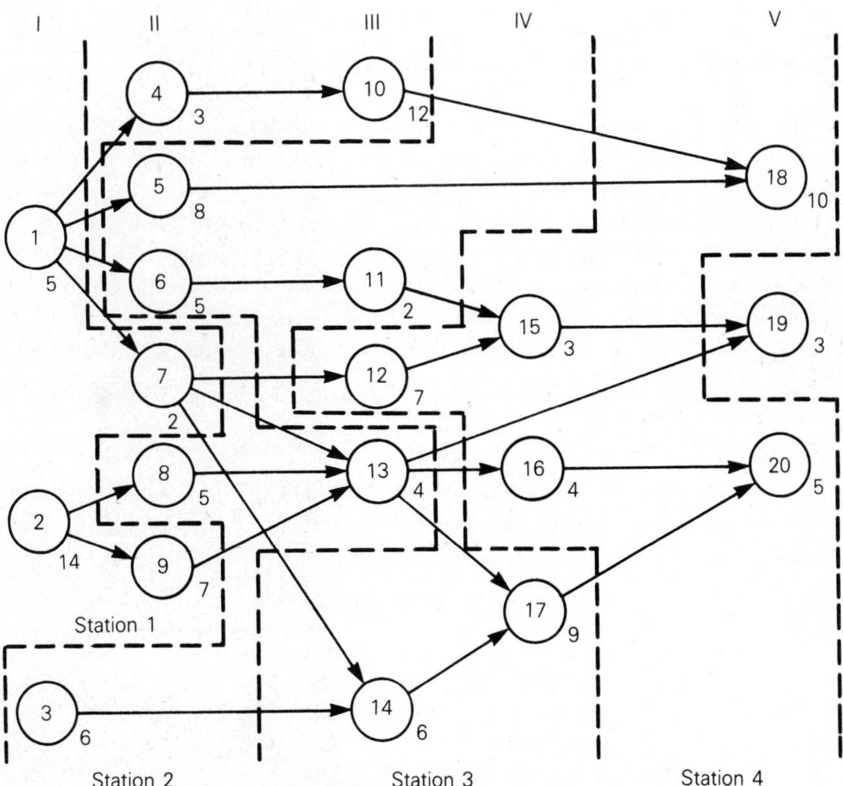

FIGURE 12.5 Four-station solution using the ranked positional weight technique

COMPARISON OF BALANCING TECHNIQUES

We have now discussed several heuristic assembly line balancing techniques. Although we have not dealt with any analytical techniques, we would like to remark on a notable algorithm by Held, Karp, and Sharesian [12]. Their algorithm combines the best of heuristic methods and dynamic programming. We will refer to this algorithm as the *combined heuristic*. Mastor [23] compared the effectiveness of these techniques on the basis of the computational time required to provide a feasible solution and the resulting balance delay for the solutions. The COMSOAL and combined heuristic techniques consistently performed better than others. Held et al. [12] report that the combined heuristic procedure yielded the least balance delay, followed by the COMSOAL algorithm. Since the combined heuristic procedure used dynamic programming, the size of the problem that could be economically solved was a limitation. It also took considerably more computer time compared to the COMSOAL algorithm. Mastor concluded, however, that the magnitude of computational time was still moderate.

Relationship to Aggregate Planning

It is important to realize that assembly line balancing is a component of overall scheduling. It was indicated earlier that cycle time is a function of many variables, such as the output rate, the speed of conveyors, the distance between stations, and, of course, the number of stations. We also know that the required output rate is designed by aggregate planning. The aggregate plan, in turn, depends on demand, inventory, and the capacity of the available facility. Thus, we see that many of these factors are interrelated and that the design of an assembly line is a complex problem, as illustrated by the following example.

Example 12.1

The demand for calculators is seasonal. During the school opening and Christmas seasons, the demand is heavy. The Nikity Company needs a plan to produce calculators according to the following schedule:

Month	*Production Rate*
August	2,400
September	1,920
October	1,200
November	1,920
December	2,400
January	960

Solution: To accommodate this production schedule, we would need two parallel lines, each with five stations, for August; two parallel lines, each with four stations, or a single line with eight stations for September; and so forth—as exhibited by table 12.3. It is important to note that frequent changes in the number of work stations lead to a loss of productivity, since these changes would lead to reassignment of activities, which generally requires a learning period. Rather than changing the production rate drastically every month, the firm might want to smooth the schedule or explore other strategies, as explained in chapter 9, on aggregate planning.

Batch Processing Techniques

In assembly line situations, we have assumed that the same item is manufactured continually. In many instances, however, several items belonging to the same product family are produced in the same line. A setup may or may not be required between batches of production. A problem involving a setup is called an economic lot size problem (ELSP) in the literature [7] [24]. Hax and Meal [11] developed a method involving a major setup for the family and a minor setup for individual items in the family. These methodologies find the economic batch quantities by analyzing the tradeoff between setup and inventory costs. In addition to the economic batch sizes, if we want to determine their best sequence along with capacity considerations, mathematical programming techniques can be used to solve these problems. However, if we include the uncertainty in demand, we would need a dynamic method of sequencing and scheduling items. In this section, we will illustrate some simple but effective batch processing techniques.

THE RUNOUT TIME (ROT) METHOD WITH LOT SIZE CONSIDERATIONS

The runout time (ROT) method is based on the depletion times for different items in the family. For example, a family may contain linens, pillow cases, and fitted sheets with the same design. The ROT of an item is expressed as the ratio of the current inventory to the demand forecast for the period [27]:

$$ROT_i = \frac{\text{current inventory of item } i}{\text{demand per period for item } i}$$

With the ROT method, the ROT for each item in the family is computed, and the items are ranked in the ascending order of their ROTs. The item with the lowest ROT is scheduled for production first, followed by the item with the next lowest ROT. This process is repeated for the remaining items.

As we discussed in the capacity planning chapter, problems involving a setup generally specify the lot size, setup time, and run time. Based on the given data, we can calculate the required standard hours per unit for every item in the family. The following example illustrates the ROT method.

Example 12.2

Table 12.14 gives the data on current inventory, production lot sizes, standard hours per unit, and the forecast of demand for all items in a product family. Using the ROT method, determine the sequence of production. The available production capacity is stated as eighty hours. Analyze the effect of capacity on your schedule.

Solution: As a first step, we calculate the runout time for each item by dividing the current inventory by the forecast demand per week (see table 12.15). This process provides the sequence D, B, A, C. Given the available capacity of eighty hours, the effect of capacity on the sequence is analyzed in table 12.16. We thus find that the capacity is inadequate to produce the desired units of all items in the family.

TABLE 12.14 Data for Example 12.2

Item	*Standard Hours per Unit*	*Lot Size*	*Forecast per Period*	*Current Inventory*	*Machine Hours per Order*
A	0.10	100	35	100	10
B	0.20	150	50	120	30
C	0.15	100	40	130	15
D	0.20	200	60	80	40
Total					95

TABLE 12.15 ROT Determination, Example 12.2

Item	*Current Inventory*	*Demand per Week*	*ROT (weeks)*	*Sequence*
A	100	35	2.86	3
B	120	50	2.40	2
C	130	40	3.25	4
D	80	60	1.33	1

TABLE 12.16 Capacity Analysis, Example 12.2

Scheduled Sequence	*ROT*	*Lot Size*	*Machine Hours Required*	*Remaining Capacity*
D	1.33	200	40	40
B	2.40	150	30	10
A	2.86	100	10	0
C	3.25	100	15	−15

THE AGGREGATE RUNOUT TIME METHOD

In many cases, we may be able to remove the lot size restrictions. In some other cases, however, we may be forced to delineate from the lot size considerations. For instance, in the previous example, although we found ourselves short of the required capacity, we might be forced to produce all items in a family so that a shortage of any single item does not occur. Such problems can be solved by the aggregate runout time (ART) method [4]:

$$\text{ART} = \frac{\begin{array}{c}\text{Machine hours inventory} \\ \text{for all items in the family}\end{array} + \begin{array}{c}\text{total available} \\ \text{machine hours}\end{array}}{\begin{array}{c}\text{machine hour requirements forecasted} \\ \text{for all items in the family}\end{array}}$$

We will extend the previous example to illustrate this method.

Example 12.3

Suppose that the firm wants to prevent any anticipated stockouts caused by the lack of capacity. How would we devise a new schedule for Example 12.2?

Solution: As a first step, we compute the available and required capacities and determine the value of ART (see table 12.17). We obtain

$$\text{ART} = \frac{69.5 + 80}{31.5} = 4.746$$

As a second step, we calculate the schedule, assuming the same ART for all items in the family (see table 12.18). The gross and net requirements are calculated using the following formulas:

$$\text{Gross requirements} = \text{forecast per period} \times \text{ART}$$

$$\text{Net requirements} = \text{gross requirements} - \text{current inventory}$$

TABLE 12.17 ART Determination, Example 12.3

Item	*Standard Hours per Unit*	*Forecast per Period*	*Machine Hours for the Forecast*	*Current Inventory*	*Machine Hours Inventory*
A	0.10	35	3.5	100	10.0
B	0.20	50	10.0	120	24.0
C	0.15	40	6.0	130	19.5
D	0.20	60	12.0	80	16.0
Total			31.5		69.5

TABLE 12.18 Schedule Requirements, Example 12.3

Item	*Standard Hours per Unit*	*Forecast per Period*	*ART*	*Gross Require-ments*	*Current Inven-tory*	*Net Require-ments*
A	0.10	35	4.746	166	100	66
B	0.20	50	4.746	237	120	117
C	0.15	40	4.746	190	130	60
D	0.20	60	4.746	285	80	205

TABLE 12.19 Capacity Requirements, Example 12.3

Item	*Standard Hours per Unit*	*Net Requirements*	*Machine Hours Required*	*Remaining Capacity*
A	0.10	66	6.6	73.4
B	0.20	117	23.4	50.0
C	0.15	60	9.0	41.0
D	0.20	205	41.0	0

Using the net requirements, and with the given available capacity of eighty hours, we can check the capacity requirements, as exhibited in table 12.19. The use of the ART formula facilitated the production of all items in the family, thus avoiding any shortages of any individual items in the family.

Summary

In this chapter, we have discussed the functions of shop floor control in a make-to-stock manufacturing environment. Table 12.20 shows the useful techniques according to manufacturing environment, which can be broadly classified as continuous flow shops, intermittent flow shops, and job shops. Controlling a flow shop involves successfully manipulating cycle time, number of stations, and idle time without violating precedence relationships.

We also discussed in detail several useful heuristic assembly line balancing techniques. Many of these algorithms have been computerized for easier implementation of real-world problems. One such program is

TABLE 12.20 Classification of SFC Techniques

	Make-to-Stock	*Make-to-Order*
High volume	Assembly line balancing Process planning techniques	Intermittent flow shops scheduling techniques
Low volume	ROT, ART Batch/intermittent processing techniques	Job shops planning and control techniques

General Electric's ASYBL$ (assembly line configuration), which is based on the ranked positional weight technique. Schofield [28] also reports that NULISP (Nottingham University Line Sequencing Program) has been successfully implemented in many industries. We also dealt with the ROT and ART methods for scheduling and sequencing intermittent or batch processing environments. As these plans are being implemented, there may be cases where wide fluctuations in demand occur for certain items, requiring adjustments to the run quantities. It is also important to realize that planning and control of flow shop activities are an integral part of aggregate planning and master scheduling. The management of make-to-order systems, known as job shops, is discussed in later chapters.

PROBLEMS

1. Rago, Inc., manufactures radios. The company wishes to make approximately 290 radios per day. The following table lists all basic tasks performed along the assembly line:

Task	*Operation Time (min.)*	*Immediately Preceding Tasks*
A	0.20	—
B	0.30	A
C	0.40	A
D	0.60	B, C
E	0.80	—
F	0.80	E
G	0.60	D, E
H	1.20	F, G
I	1.20	H
J	1.00	I
K	1.90	J

   The shop operates five days per week and two shifts per day. The company provides two coffee breaks of ten minutes each during an eight-hour day.
   a. Group the activities into the most efficient arrangement.
   b. What is the cycle time of your arrangement?
   c. What is the balance delay percentage?

2. Rago's market research department forecasts the following demand (in thousands) for the next eight quarters:

	1	*2*	*3*	*4*	*5*	*6*	*7*	*8*
Demand	200	250	350	100	200	250	350	100

Assume that each quarter has approximately thirteen weeks. There is an initial inventory of 100,000 radios. The company desires a final inventory of 100 thousand radios.

a. Given the following data, what manufacturing strategy should Rago follow?

Plan 1: Vary the labor force from an initial capacity of 200 units to whatever is required to meet the demand.

Amount of Change	*Incremental Cost of Labor*	
(000)	*Increase*	*Decrease*
50	$ 5,000	$ 5,000
100	10,000	10,000
150	15,000	15,000
200	25,000	25,000
250	35,000	35,000

Plan 2: Produce at a steady rate of 200,000 and sub-contract for excess requirements at an additional cost of $1/unit. Inventory cost amounts to .50/unit/quarter.

b. Give station layouts and balance delay ratios for your solution.

c. Discuss the effect of changes in production rate on productivity and meeting the desired production goals.

3. Kilbridge and Webster [18] use a heuristic method to solve assembly line balancing. Their original problem has been modified, as shown in figure 12.6. Using the data in the figures, design a six-station layout.

4. With the data given in problem 3, obtain a solution using the COMSOAL algorithm.

5. With the data given in problem 3, obtain a solution using the ranked positional weight technique.

6. Using the calculator assembly example given in figure 12.1 and table 12.2, generate a three-station solution using the COMSOAL algorithm.

7. Using the data given in figure 12.1 and table 12.2, design a six-station layout using the ranked positional weight technique.

8. The Easy Corporation manufactures light fixtures. Subassemblies are produced and packed in cartons. The durations of operations and their sequence are given in the following table:

Task	*Operation Time (min.)*	*Immediately Preceding Tasks*
A	1.1	—
B	0.4	A
C	0.5	A
D	1.2	A
E	1.1	A,D
F	0.3	B,C
G	0.4	D
H	1.1	F
I	0.8	E,G
J	0.7	H,I
K	0.3	J
L	1.2	K

Draw the precedence diagram for the assembly. What is the total time of manufacture for this light fixture?

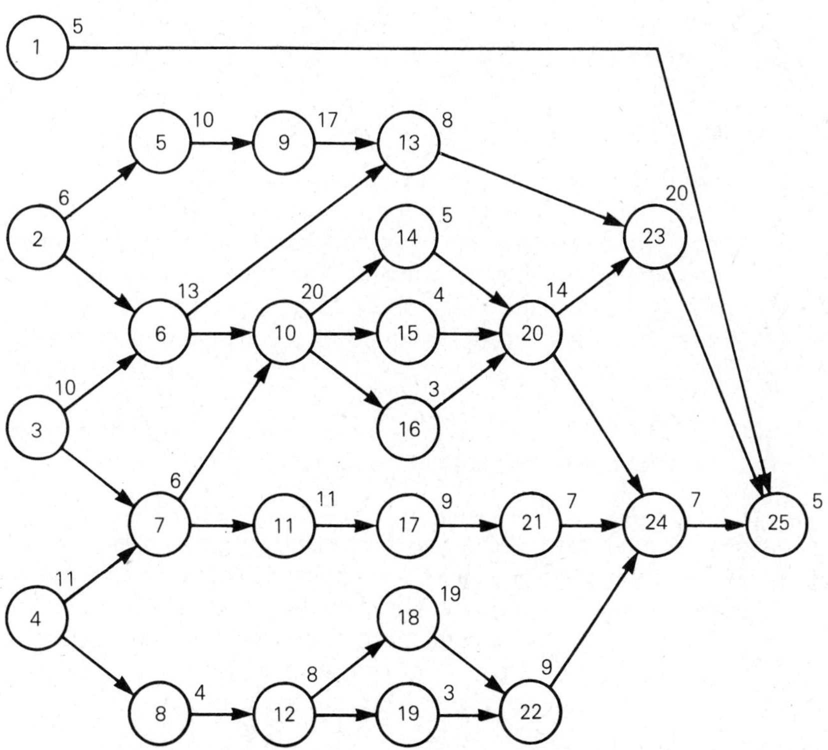

FIGURE 12.6 Precedence diagram for problem 3

9. The facility given in problem 8 is operating on an eight-hour, two-shift, five-day schedule. Each shift consists of two ten-minute coffee breaks. The assembly schedule calls for approximately 700 units per day. If the shop operates at 95% efficiency, how many work stations should we need to obtain the desired production rate? Group the activities into appropriate work stations using the Kilbridge-Wester heuristic algorithm.

10. Solve problem 9 using the COMSOAL algorithm. Calculate the balance delay for your solution. Suppose that the Easy Corporation needs to double the output. What changes would you make on the cycle time and output rate to accommodate the new forecast?

11. The following table exhibits the assembly time assigned to the respective work stations. The efficiency percentages of workers presently allocated to the corresponding work stations are also exhibited.

Station	*Production Time (sec.)*	*Efficiency Percentage*	*Operator*
1	25	95	A
2	30	100	B
3	20	90	C
4	35	110	D
5	25	90	E

   a. What is the cycle time of this layout?
   b. If the shop operates an eight-hour shift, five-day work schedule, what is the average hourly production rate? Assume that the company provides two 15-minute rest periods every day.
   c. What is the balance delay percentage?
   d. If these workers can be assigned to any station without any loss of efficiency, can you increase the production rate by switching them among stations?
   e. What is your new hourly production rate, and what percentage productivity increase was accomplished?

12. The necessary activities and their durations in seconds required to assemble the Krown Blunder are shown in figure 12.7. Given a cycle time of thirty seconds, balance the assembly line stations using the COMSOAL algorithm. How many stations would you have in your layout? Assuming that the company provides two fifteen-minute breaks during an eight-hour shift, what production rate would you expect from the assembly line? Would your answer vary if the efficiency of the workers is stated as 95%?

13. The Krown Blunder Company currently has four assembly lines in parallel. It needs to increase its total production by 50% soon. The company has the following alternatives:

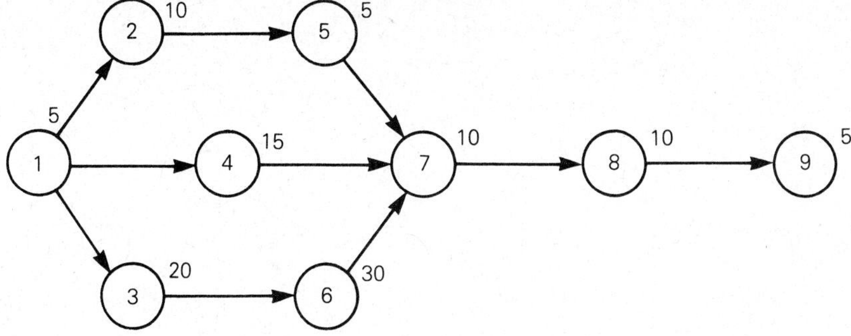

FIGURE 12.7 Precedence diagram for problem 12

Alternative 1: Establish new production lines at a cost of $100,000 per line.

Alternative 2: Increase the production rate by decreasing the cycle time. Operation 6 can be divided into 6A and 6B, with fifteen and twenty seconds, respectively. Rearranging each line will cost $20,000. Assume that labor costs amount to $10 per hour, including benefits.

Based on the data, which alternative would you recommend? Show all your calculations. Use the ranked positional weight technique for balancing the assembly line work stations. Assume that operation 4 can be divided into two operations: 4A = 5 seconds, 4B = 10 seconds.

14. Find a five-station balance for the assembly line shown in figure 12.8, using the trial-and-error technique. (The performance times for the tasks are given above the nodes.) What is the balance delay percentage in your layout?

15. Is a four-station layout feasible in problem 14? Provide a solution using the Kilbridge-Wester heuristic. What is the balance delay for your solution?

16. Find a five-station balance for the assembly line shown in figure 12.9, using the ranked positional weight technique. (The performance of corresponding tasks is also shown in the precedence diagram.)

17. The Taylor Company needs to produce items A and B. The production times, lot sizes, current inventories, and weekly forecasts are as follows:

Item	*Production Time (hrs.)*	*Current Inventory*	*Weekly Forecast*	*Lot Size*
A	0.25	100	60	200
B	1.00	50	40	100

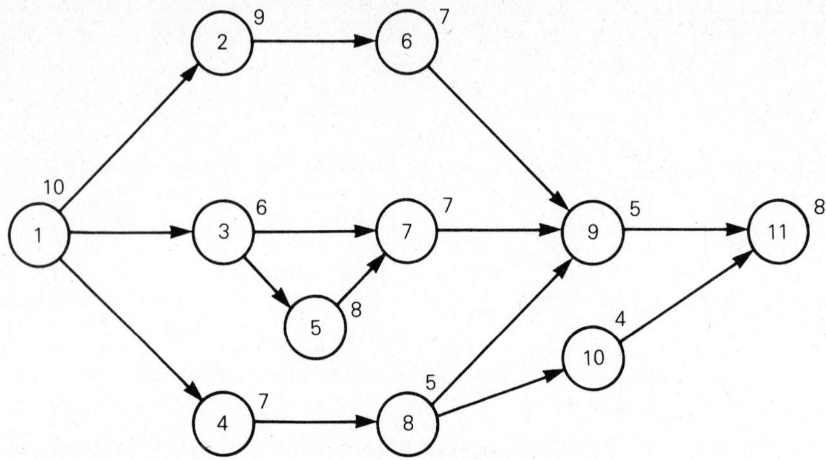

FIGURE 12.8 Precedence diagram for problem 14

Assuming that 120 hours are available for scheduling these items, find the production quantities for items A and B using the runout time method.

18. Ignoring the lot sizes and using the aggregate runout time method, find the production quantities for items in problem 17.

19. The Barry Mojena Corporation bottles three different types of wines. Since retailers order them periodically, they are made to stock for

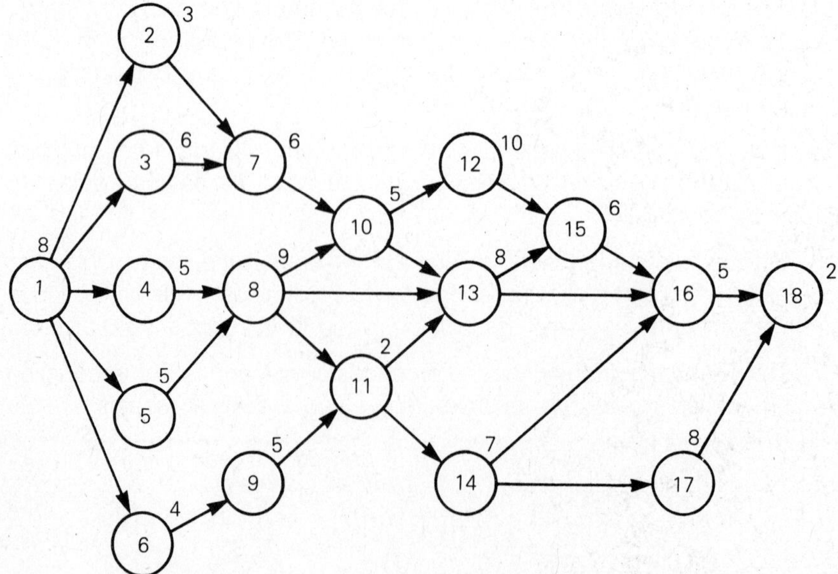

FIGURE 12.9 Precedence diagram for problem 16

satisfying the demands. The company operates two eight-hour shifts, five days per week. The filling times, current inventories, and demand forecasts are as follows:

Type, Size	*Filling Time per 100 Bottles (min.)*	*On-hand Inventory (000)*	*Lot Sizes (000)*	*Demand Forecast per Week (000)*
Rosé, 16 oz.	8	70	40	20
Rosé, 24 oz.	10	60	40	30
Chablis, 16 oz.	8	50	40	35
Chablis, 24 oz.	10	40	40	25
Chablis, 1 qt.	12	30	40	20

Using the runout time method, schedule the winery for bottling these varieties.

20. If the Barry Mojena winery has only 330 hours of filling time left next week, determine the sequence for bottling these wines, using the aggregate runout time method.

21. The White Radar Company produces components for electronic equipment. These components are made to stock to meet anticipated customer demands. Currently, sixty-six hours of machine capacity are available for the next week. Using the aggregate runout time method, establish the sequence for the given data:

Items	*Machine Hours per Unit*	*Lot Size*	*On-hand Inventory*	*Demand Forecast*
W	0.07	300	240	200
X	0.10	200	225	150
Y	0.05	500	400	250

Calculate the projected inventory at the end of two weeks.

22. Suppose that the White Radar Company has only forty hours of machine time available in the planning period and that lot sizes can be modified without any sacrifice in capacity. Assuming that the data given in problem 21 are still valid, establish the sequence of items to be produced, using the aggregate runout time method. Project the anticipated inventories at the end of two weeks.

23. The following formula establishes the economical production run quantities when a family of items is to be produced:

$$\text{EOQ} = \sqrt{\frac{2\,\Sigma A\,\Sigma S}{(1 - \Sigma d/\Sigma p)}}$$

where ΣA = sum of yearly dollar volumes of all items in the family
ΣS = sum of all setup times in dollars
Σd = sum of daily usage in dollars for all items
Σp = sum of daily production rates in dollars for all items

Given the following data, find the dollar values of items to be produced:

Items	*A($)*	*S($)*	*d($)*	*p($)*
1	3000	3	12	90
2	6000	5	20	120
3	1200	5	6	110
4	15000	3	60	100
5	1500	3	5	95

Assume that the cost of a major setup is $100.

REFERENCES AND BIBLIOGRAPHY

1. A. L. Arcus, "COMSOAL: A Computer Method of Sequencing Operations for Assembly Lines." In Elwood S. Buffa, ed., *Readings in Production and Operations Management* (New York: Wiley, 1966).
2. A. Bensousson, E. Hurst, and B. Nasland, *Management Applications of Modern Control Theory* (New York: North Holland–American Elsevier, 1974).
3. E. S. Buffa and J. G. Miller, *Production-Inventory Systems: Planning and Control,* 3rd ed. (Homewood, Ill.: Richard D. Irwin, 1979).
4. R. B. Chase and N. J. Aquilano, *Production and Operations Management* (3rd ed.) (Homewood, Ill.: Richard D. Irwin, 1981).
5. E. M. Dar-El (Mansoor), "MALB—A Heuristic Technique for Balancing Large-Scale Single Model Assembly Lines," *AIIE Transactions,* Vol. 5, No. 4 (December 1973), pp. 343–356.
6. E. M. Dar-El, "Mixed Model Assembly Line Sequencing Problems," *OMEGA,* Vol. 6, No. 4 (1978), pp. 313–323.
7. S. Elmaghraby, "The Economic Lot Scheduling Problems (ELSP): Review and Extensions," *Management Science,* Vol. 24, No. 6 (February 1978), pp. 587–598.
8. W. A. Gruver and S. L. Narasimhan, "Optimal Scheduling of Multistage Continuous Flowshops," *INFOR,* Vol. 19, No. 4 (November 1981), pp. 319–330.
9. P. G. Gyllenhammer, "How Volvo Adapts Work to People," *Harvard Business Review,* Vol. 55, No. 4 (July–August, 1977), pp. 102–113.
10. L. Gutjahr and G. L. Nemhauser, "An Algorithm for the Line Balancing Problem," *Management Science,* Vol. 11, No. 2 (November 1964), pp. 308–315.
11. A. Hax and H. Meal, "Hierarchical Integration of Production Planning and Scheduling." In M. Geisler, ed., *TIMS Studies in the Management Sciences, Logistics* (Amsterdam: North Holland, 1975).
12. M. Held, R. M. Karp, and R. Sharesian, "Assembly Line Balancing—Dynamic

Programming with Precedence Constraints," *Operations Research*, Vol. 11, No. 3 (May–June 1963), pp. 442–459.

13. W. B. Helgeson and D. D. Birnie, "Assembly Line Balancing Using the Ranked Positional Weight Technique," *Journal of Industrial Engineering*, Vol. 12, No. 6 (November–December 1961), pp. 394–398.
14. T. R. Hoffman, "Assembly Line Balancing with a Precedence Matrix," *Management Science*, Vol. 9, No. 4 (July 1963), pp. 551–562.
15. E. J. Ignall "A Review of Assembly Line Balancing," *Journal of Industrial Engineering*, Vol. 16, No. 4 (July–August 1965), pp. 244–254.
16. J. R. Jackson, "A Computing Procedure for a Line Balancing Problem," *Management Science*, Vol. 2, No. 3 (April 1956), pp. 261–271.
17. L. A. Johnson and D. C. Montgomery, *Operations Research in Production Planning, Scheduling and Inventory Control* (New York: Wiley, 1974).
18. M. D. Kilbridge and L. Wester, "A Heuristic Method of Assembly Line Balancing," *Journal of Industrial Engineering*, Vol. 12, No. 4 (July–August 1961), pp. 292–298.
19. M. D. Kilbridge and L. Wester, "The Balance Delay Problem," *Management Science*, Vol. 8, No. 1 (October 1961), pp. 69–84.
20. M. D. Kilbridge and L. Wester, "A Review of Analytical Systems of Line Balancing," *Operations Research*, Vol. 10, No. 5 (September–October 1962), pp. 626–638.
21. M. Klein, "On Assembly Line Balancing," *Operations Research*, Vol. 11, No. 2 (March–April 1963), pp. 274–281.
22. E. M. Mansoor (Dar-El), "Assembly Line Balancing—An Improvement on the Ranked Positional Weight Technique," *Journal of Industrial Engineering*, Vol. 15, No. 2 (March–April 1964), pp. 73–77.
23. A. A. Mastor, "An Experimental Investigation and Comparative Evaluation of Production Line Balancing Techniques," *Management Science*, Vol. 16, No. 11 (July 1970), pp. 728–746.
24. W. L. Maxwell, "The Scheduling of Economic Lot Sizes," *Naval Research Logistics Quarterly*, Vol. 11 (1964), pp. 89–124.
25. J. O. McClain and L. J. Thomas, *Operations Management* (Englewood Cliffs, N.J.: Prentice-Hall, 1980).
26. R. J. Paul, "A Production Scheduling Program in the Glass Container Industry," *Operations Research*, Vol. 27, No. 2 (March–April 1979), pp. 290–302.
27. G. Plossl and O. Wight, *Production and Inventory Control* (Englewood Cliffs, N.J.: Prentice-Hall, 1967).
28. N. A. Schofield, "Assembly Line Balancing and the Application of Computer Techniques," *Computers and Industrial Engineering*, Vol. 3 (1979), pp. 53–69.
29. S. P. Sethi and G. L. Thompson, *Optimal Control Theory: Application to Management Science* (Boston: Martinus-Nijhoff, 1981).
30. H. A. Simon and A. Newell, "Heuristic Problem Solving: The Next Advance in Operations Research," *Operations Research*, Vol. 6, No. 1 (January–February 1958), pp. 1–10.
31. M. K. Starr, *Operations Management* (Englewood Cliffs, N.J.: Prentice-Hall, 1978).
32. N. T. Thomopoulos, "Mixed Model Line Balancing with Smoothed Station Assignments," *Management Science*, Vol. 16, No. 9 (May 1970), pp. 573–603.

33. N. T. Thomopoulos, "Some Analytical Approaches to Assembly Line Balancing Problems," *Production Engineer*, July 1968, pp. 345–351.
34. F. M. Tonge, "Summary of a Heuristic Line Balancing Procedure," *Management Science*, Vol. 7, No. 1 (October 1960), pp. 21–39.
35. F. M. Tonge, "Assembly Line Balancing Using Probabilistic Combinations of Heuristics," *Management Science*, Vol. 11, No. 7 (May 1965), pp. 727–735.
36. L. Wester and M. Kilbridge, "Heuristic Line Balancing: A Case," *Journal of Industrial Engineering*, Vol. 13, No. 3 (May–June 1962), pp. 139–149.

appendix 12A

Integrating Material and Product Control Systems into a Tightly Regulated Processing Environment

John Burt and Bob Kraemer
McCormick and Company, Inc.

Introduction

Problems of product traceability, lot control, product structure flexibility, and yield variability are not recognized in most manufacturing resource planning systems. While the systems framework and basic principles are quite similar across many types of industries, techniques to deal with the problems mentioned above create the need for varied approaches to implementation for tightly regulated processing businesses such as foods, drugs, and chemicals.

This paper addresses two such implementations within the same corporation but involving two distinct segments. These segments have in common the fact that they are both food processors but, as we will see, the approaches they had to take to reach similar goals were somewhat controlled by the environment within which each operated.

We first describe the company and the major segments with which we deal. Next is a description of the principles on which the manufacturing resource planning systems were built in each case. Then the application of these principles is described for each and comparisons are made where the implementations differed. Finally, we offer some suggestions for implementing manufacturing resource planning systems for a tightly regulated processing environment.

Reprinted with permission, American Production and Inventory Control Society, Inc., *22nd Annual International Conference Proceedings*, October 1979.

The Company

McCormick and Company is a world wide processor and distributor of food flavorings for consumer, food service and industrial markets. 1978 sales were $400,357,000 which placed McCormick 487th on Fortune's 500 list. The two segments with which we deal here are the Grocery Products Division, Salinas Plant, and Gilroy Foods, Inc. (a wholly owned subsidiary). The Grocery Products Division manufactures and markets spices, extracts flavorings, tea, foil-packed seasoning and sauce mixes, food colors, cake decorating products, popcorn, and convenience dinners to retail customers through chain stores, independent retailers, wholesalers, co-operatives, specialty shops, and government installations. Their products carry the McCormick label in the East and Schilling in the West. There are four

TABLE 12A.1 Comparisons and Contrasts

Schilling Plant—GPD	*Gilroy Foods, Inc.*
1. Less than 400 finished goods	1. 12,600 potential finished goods
2. Forecast by end item relatively reliable	2. Forecast at finished goods level unreliable (much better at family level)
3. Pack to stock (some pack to order)	3. Pack to order (some pack to stock)
4. Heavy emphasis on MRP	4. Heavy emphasis on production planning
5. 40 processable spice raw materials and 910 other ingredients	5. Two raw materials and 15 other ingredients
6. 1400 pkg material items (uniform labeling)	6. 150 pkg material items (specialized labeling)
7. Consumer products	7. Industrial/food service products
8. Batch processing flow (some continuous)	8. Continuous processing flow (some batch)
9. Batch computer ops (weekly regeneration)	9. On line, real time computer operations
10. Steady growth company	10. Rapid growth then level
11. IMS developed from formal manual system	11. IMS developed from informal manual system
12. Systems staff and computer on site prior to project	12. No systems staff or computer prior to project
13. Modified a purchased software package	13. Developed computer systems in house
14. Product coded as produced	14. Product coded after 7 to 10 day testing hold
15. Relatively fixed finished product flow	15. Many options for finished product flow
16. Locator important	16. Locator vital
17. Convenient plant layout	17. Poor plant layout
18. Implemented 1975/76	18. Implementing 1978-80
19. Production moderately seasonal and weekday operation	19. Production highly seasonal and 7 day/3 shift operation
20. Sales moderately seasonal	20. Sales moderately seasonal

manufacturing plants and six main distribution centers. This division provides the majority of the company's sales. Gilroy Foods, Inc. is a major dehydrator of onion and garlic products for food service and industrial markets. They are the largest contributor to McCormick's industrial sales. There is one plant which is also the main distribution center.

The reasons for choosing these two company segments for our paper are best illustrated by reviewing comparisons and contrasts shown in Table 12A.1. It should be noted that the Grocery Products Division was one of the first food processing companies to have successfully implemented an MRP system and Gilroy Foods, Inc. is one of few now installing such systems. Also, there are slight operational variations among Grocery Products Division plants and we will cite the Schilling Plant in our illustrations for this report.

The System

As noted above these factors caused us to take different approaches to implementation in the two company elements but the framework on which each is based is similar. That framework is illustrated in Figure 12A.1, which also shows the current status of the Gilroy Foods implementation.

Figure 12A.1 differs only in minor respects from the Standard Processing Industry System Framework developed at the June, 1979 Processing Industry Workshop in Denver. In fact, it is not dramatically different from the common job shop framework. This is consistent with our contention that we differ mainly in technique rather than principle.

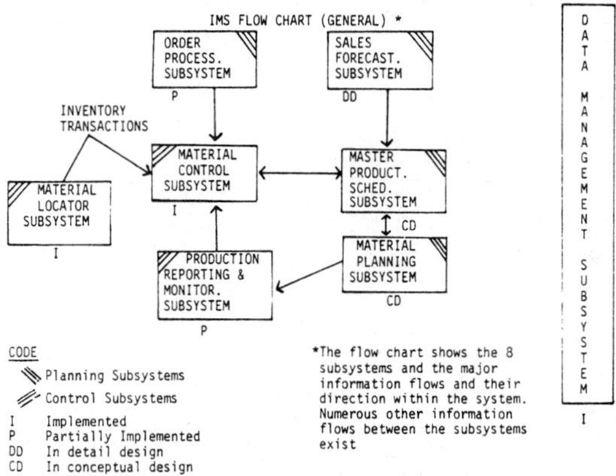

FIGURE 12A.1 The inventory management system

The projects began in each element of the company for similar reasons. In the case of the Schilling Plant, the main goals were to reduce inventory and increase production efficiency while maintaining customer service at the 97% level. At Gilroy Foods all three of these classic elements were targeted for improvement but the primary emphasis was on the establishment of a formal system of controls.

In each case, the goals have been met. The Schilling Plant has maintained its 97% customer service goal while reducing inventories at least 40% and increasing production efficiencies as much as 25%. Although Gilroy Foods is still in the implementation stage, early benefits have been noted as follows: Customer service up from a pre-implementation level of 65% to the present 85%, inventory record accuracy as measured by product code by location up from 60% to 97%, year-end work in process inventory down from 18% of total inventory to 2%, and production efficiency up an estimated 5% simply from greater reliability of supply to the lines. This improvement has been accomplished at Gilroy Foods even without the majority of the new planning systems which will be implemented soon and which will have at least a similar if not greater impact on service and efficiency.

Approaches to the task of installing an Inventory Management System (cf. Manufacturing Resource Planning System) were also similar in the two company segments. Gilroy's use of the team concept was in fact based on its success at the Salinas Plant. Figure 12A.2 shows this organization.

In both cases the feeling persisted that the team concept with user leadership and membership was vital to the success of the project for two prime reasons. The first was that broad support was needed since an endeavor of this magnitude made it essentially a company rather than simply an inventory project. Along similar lines, it was apparent that the knowledge and experience of a diverse group was needed in order to achieve common goals. The second reason was management education. Involvement and commitment had to start at the top and be transmitted through line management to the people who had to operate the system. At the same time,

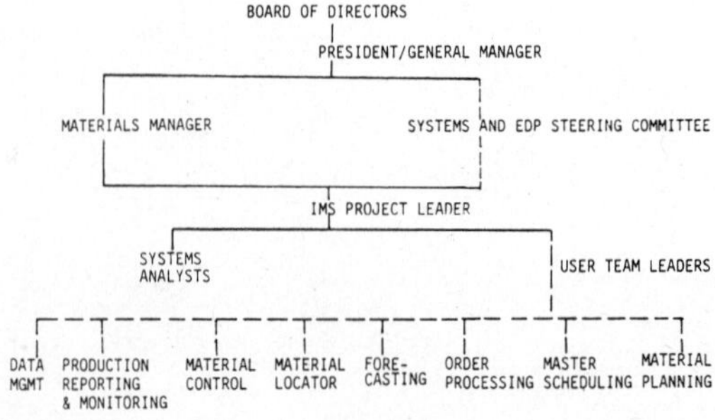

FIGURE 12A.2 The inventory management system (IMS) organization

the information that these operations people had to offer in terms of practical systems application had to reach the decision makers in a relatively unfiltered manner. In other words, education had to be a two way communication process—the system requirements in one direction and the operational needs in the other. It is in the area of these operational needs that a tightly regulated processing industry encounters problems in implementation that are different from job shop/hardware industries. The following two sections provide case studies that illustrate this point.

The Application at the Schilling Plant

System application at the Schilling Plant was in many ways more straightforward than that at Gilroy. Reasons for this can be picked up from Table 12A.1. There are relatively few finished goods and they can be forecasted at that level and packed to inventory. There are a relatively large number of raw ingredients and packaging materials that lend themselves to a standard MRP logic. The computer system evolved from a formal manual system within a stable growth environment. The facility itself is new and well laid out. Finally, production operations are only moderately seasonal and involve mainly weekday operations with only a limited 2nd shift.

However, on closer examination there are a number of similarities with Gilroy Foods. Both are tightly regulated by Good Manufacturing Practices necessary in the food industry as well as by federal and state food and drug laws. This requires extensive lot control and product traceability procedures. Both have a need for formulation or bills of material that allow for substitute or alternate ingredients. Finally, both must take into account large variations on yield from at least some of their primary raw materials. We will concentrate in these areas of commonality relative to system development to show how, even within the same industry or company, different means may be required to reach the same end. A simplified processing flow diagram is shown for the Schilling Plant in Figure 12A.3. Note that raw materials, in process products, and finished goods each have their own separate storeroom. Product codes are assigned to the raw materials based on broad family categories such as spice type and country of origin. Lot numbers are also assigned by using the purchase order number and delivery sequence number in case of multiple loads. The product is lab tested for such things as physical defects, color, oil content, and bacteriological levels. Raw material input is then scheduled by both product code and lot number.

When the product is milled, it again receives a product code. Unlike the raw material code, however, the in-process code more accurately describes the physical characteristics of the material. However, it again receives a lot number based on the batch and date processed. For the most part, this material is scheduled by the product code only, but it is important to note

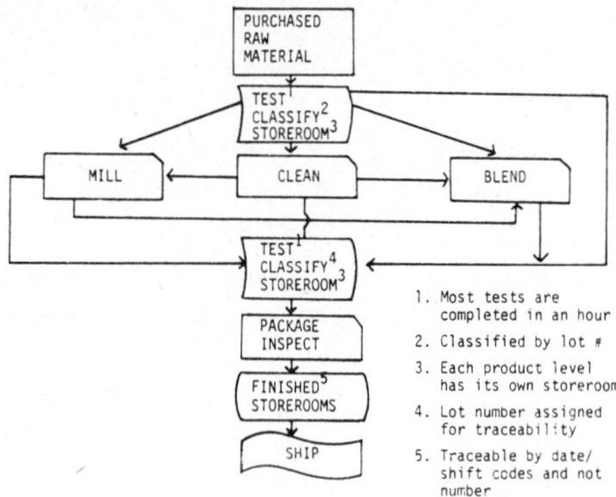

FIGURE 12A.3 Schilling plant simplified processing flow

that usage is recorded by both product code and lot number for traceability purposes.

As the product is then packaged it receives a product code once again. Also, it is given a date/shift number as a lot number. Thus, a given individual finished container can be traced by production date and shift through an in-process code (or codes in the case of multiple process items) with associated lot numbers, back, if necessary, to the specific raw material lots used in producing that finished product. These lot number/product code linkages were vital to establish in our system. They are generally not recognized as a problem in most current literature or software packages.

Another implementation problem not often dealt with in descriptions of a standard system is that of substitute or alternate formulations often used in our business. Figure 12A.4 shows examples of two levels of a product structure/bill of materials technique that was developed at Schilling to deal with this problem. The technique revolves around the use of sequence numbers and start/stop usage dates within the bills. The sequence numbers show the order in which product is assembled and priority of usage for the substitute or alternate material. In using this technique within MRP, only the high priority sequence numbers (designated by a 0 in the third digit) are normally exploded. The exception is that where start/stop usage dates are shown, the lower priority sequence items will be exploded to reflect their demands in the appropriate time phase relationship.

The problem of yield variations are handled at Schilling in basically two ways. One is to use an average yield figure in the bills of materials. Second is to create safety stock in certain raw materials where yield is most variable. It should be noted that purchasing is measured against targeted raw materials inventory levels as well as shortages. This helps keep safety stocks realistic.

BILL OF MATERIAL - SCHILLING
CREATED ON 06/05/79

PRODUCT INFORMATION

ITEM NUMBER	DESCRIPTION OF ITEM	UNIT OF MEASURE	BATCH SIZE
8C1230	Cinnamon, 4.00 Oz	Oz	12.00

INGREDIENT INFORMATION

ITEM NUMBER	SEQ NUMBER	DESCRIPTION OF ITEM	UNIT OF MEASURE	QUAN-TITY	STD. OVRFIL	LOSS SPILL	USAGE-DATES START STOP
780568	100	Cinnamon-GPD REG	LB	36.000	.000	.070	
550078	110	Can Cinnamon, 4 Oz	EA	144.000	.000	.080	05/04 08/06
550072	119	Can Cinnamon, 4 Oz new	EA	144.000	.000	.080	08/06 05/04
550205	120	Action Metal, 4 Oz can	EA	144.000	.000	.080	05/04 08/06
550210	129	Top plastic,4 Oz can, twin-top	EA	144.000	.000	.080	08/04 05/04
551228	130	Transwrap can/ext 4W4, 22 inch	EA	12.000	.000	.080	
551324	140	Case 12 Oz Blank, 4 Oz, 1040	EA	1.000	.000	.080	

Sequence for substitution

Substitution Dates

BILL OF MATERIAL - SCHILLING
CREATED ON 10/11/78

PRODUCT INFORMATION

ITEM NUMBER	DESCRIPTION OF ITEM	UNIT OF MEASURE	BATCH SIZE
750868	Cinnamon Grd Reg	LB	1.00

INGREDIENT INFORMATION

ITEM NUMBER	SEQ NUMBER	DESCRIPTION OF ITEM	UNIT OF MEASURE	QUAN-TITY	STD. OVRFIL	LOSS SPILL	USAGE-DATES START STOP
780581	100	Cinnamon Cln Kor Brkn	LB	.600	.000	.020	
781998	101	Cinnamon Cln Kor C	LB	.600	.000	.000	
780646	109	Cinnamon Cln China Brkn	LB	.600	.000	.000	
780677	110	Cinnamon Cln China Thin	LB	.400	.000	.000	
780581	111	Cinnamon Cln Kor Brkn	LB	.400	.000	.000	
780646	119	Cinnamon Cln China Brkn	LB	.400	.000	.000	

Sequence for alternative formulation

FIGURE 12A.4

Application—Gilroy Foods, Inc.

Systems application at Gilroy Foods presents a number of additional challenges. As noted, there are some common problems, but Table 12A.1 shows that there is a different environment to be addressed. Gilroy has over 12,000 potential finished goods codes (at least half of which are active at any one time) that must be structured against essentially two raw materials. Consequently, forecasting and master scheduling at this level is impractical. Figure 12A.5 illustrates the conceptual differences—numbers in parentheses indicate the number of codes to be tracked. In the case of raw material, these are shown as basic raw materials/other ingredients.

Note the use of Inverted Product Structure Bills and Planning Bills. These are concepts that could be common tools in process industries once their use is fully developed. Planning bills are often used by companies whose end products offer a number of optional configurations, e.g., automobile companies. Figure 12A.6 shows how the concept of Inverted Bills is to be utilized at Gilroy.

Product coding at Gilroy is quite complex. An example of the coding scheme used is shown in Figure 12A.7, which is a printed drum tag with a bar code or source sequence label. The latter identifies the source of the material (by line, system, and spout) in the first three digits while the last

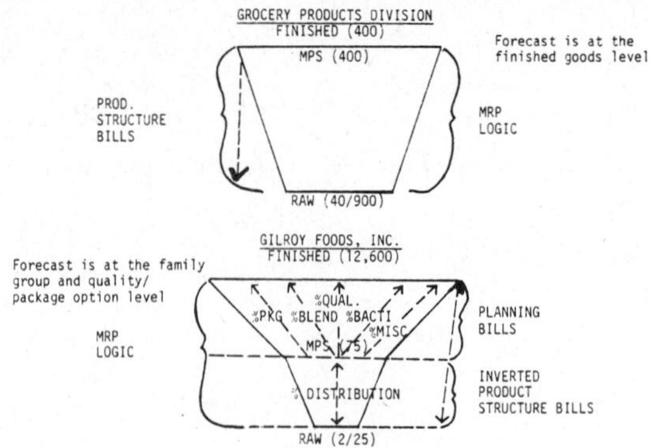

FIGURE 12A.5 Master production scheduling

seven are simply sequential in order to uniquely identify that drum in the system for reasons outlined below in discussions on product control.

The coding scheme, as shown by the large numbers (for warehouse visibility) is unique in itself. The code is determined by applying lot numbers against a quality matrix. There are several major categories that determine this code, e.g., background color, level of physical defects, bacteriological and analytical results and density. The first two digits indicate finished or in-process onion or garlic. The middle five reflect the quality based on the categories noted above and the last three indicate the package type. Very early it became apparent that a method was needed to identify material that was off quality in some respect(s) without losing the basic information about the product. This was handled by creating an in-process code that was identical to the finished code except in two respects: the first two digits were changed to identify it as in-process and detail codes were added that showed the reason for this change in category. This enabled us to identify product needing rework while retaining quality information that enabled us to rework the product in logical batches according to overall quality characteristics. Furthermore, by doing it this way, we avoided the need to create thousands of additional product codes.

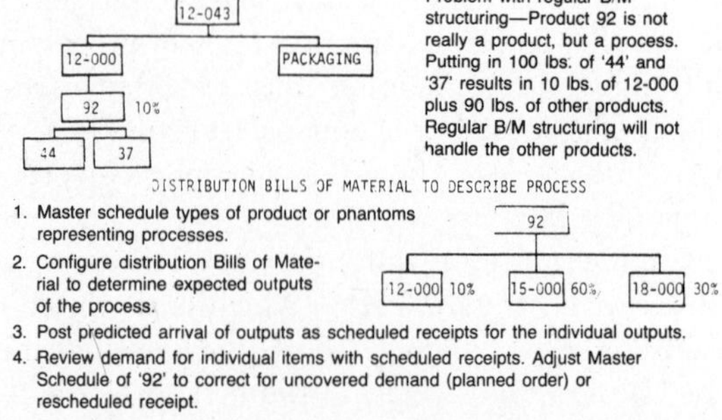

FIGURE 12A.6 Regular bill structure

FIGURE 12A.7 Computer printed drum tags

Reports have been created that summarize the quality of our production output and the quality of our total inventory. The need for summary information can be seen by reviewing a sample of our product code book shown in Figure 12A.8. This is just one of 75 families. Notice how quickly the matrix can become complicated by quality, bacteriological, density (bulk index), and special test requirements.

Even the concept of what constitutes finished product caused definition problems for Gilroy. Figure 12A.9 illustrates finished product flows at Schilling and Gilroy Foods. Notice that while Schilling finished product is nearly all shipped directly, only 40% of the "finished" drums at Gilroy are labeled, inspected and shipped. The balance follow at least four alternate routes. The coding and planning concepts outlined above allows us to neatly address this problem.

Other environmental differences are evident in Figure 12A.9 that provide opportunities for innovative approaches to material and product control at Gilroy Foods. The necessity for holding material for up to 8 days for bacteriological and analytical testing created the need for a product hold area. This also means unique disciplines in product control since the exact product made and its attendant code is not known for some time.

This problem is accentuated by a poor plant layout which was influenced by the company's rapid growth in the late 60's and early 70's. The highly seasonal nature of production operations as compared with the moderately

00 Rept 100

PRODUCT BOOK
--SPECIFICATIONS--
GILROY FOODS, INC.

FAMILY CODE 07-94000 GROUND ONION

* * * BACTI GROUPS * * *

TEST PLAN F015

GROUP	SPC	Y&M	COLIFORMS
1.0	50000	100	100
2.0	100000	100	100

FINISHED PRODUCTS

Product Code	Bacti Except	Bacti Grp	Bulk-Index Lo	Bulk-Index Hi	Hot-Water Lo	Hot-Water Hi	Qual/ Color	Calc Ster	Fum	Test Grp
09-08973		1.0	130	150			A			
09-08974		1.0	130	150			B			
09-08976		1.0	151	170			A			
09-08977		1.0	151	170			B			
09-08985		2.0	130	150			A			
09-08986		2.0	130	150			B			
09-08988		2.0	151	170			A			
09-08989		2.0	151	170			B			

FIGURE 12A.8

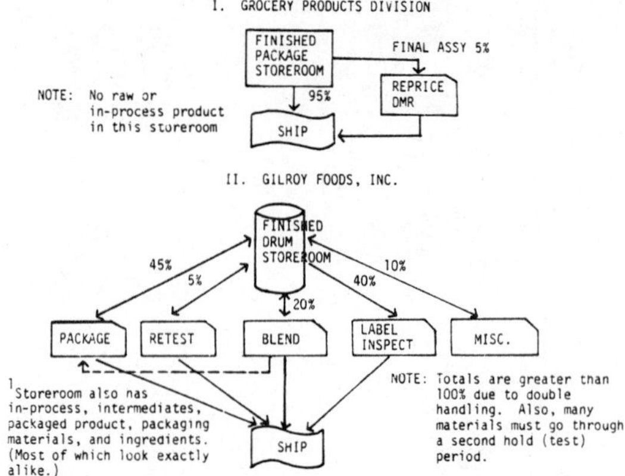

FIGURE 12A.9 Finished product flow

seasonal nature of sales further contributes to the need for extensive controls due to the cycle of building large inventories then working them down to low levels. Seasonality of production also leads to high worker turnover and low experience levels which must be taken into account in operating systems.

Material control problems are aggravated by the fact that all material must be kept within a single storeroom operation. It should be emphasized that virtually all the material looks identical. Finished product, in-process material, and quality rejects are all in 55 gallon fiber drums. There are from 60,000 to 300,000 of these drums in three separate, local warehouses that total 500,000 square feet. They are stacked six to a pallet, five to six high, in rows six to ten deep for a total of 180 to 360 to a row. The predictability of product codes to be released for storage is low due to the variability of raw material quality and the precise testing requirements. Material control in terms of location and space planning systems is vital to Gilroy. Storekeepers are used to verify transactions at appropriate points in the product flow. In addition, they insure product is put away in the proper location by reviewing check digits given to them by the driver who put the material away. These check digits are painted on the floor along with the aisle and row locations. Even though the plant works three shifts/seven days, the warehouse workload is structured to allow most activities to take place during the day shift for better supervision. Warehouse workers are responsible for all activities within a defined area of the storeroom. This zonal concept allows for a feeling of accountability for the worker's area. Picking lists are batched by location to maintain the integrity of the zonal concept. Cycle counting is used to maintain accuracy and identify control problems. It has worked well enough that our accounting people are pressing the auditors to discontinue physical inventories.

The simplified product classification and coding flow diagram shown as Figure 12A.10 indicates the ways we are dealing with the material and

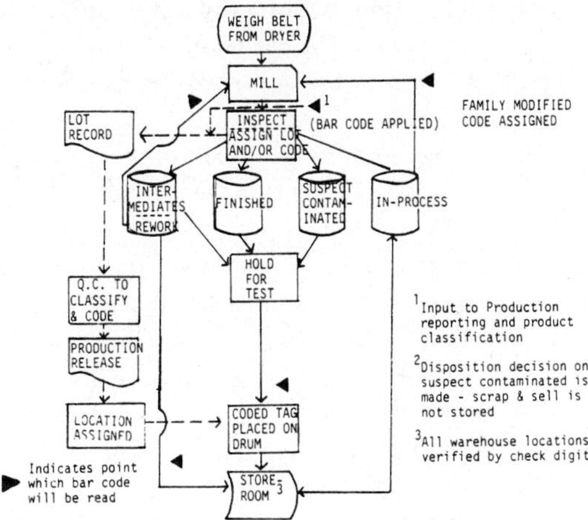

FIGURE 12A.10 Gilroy Foods, Inc., product classification and coding flow

product control problems outlined above. The inventory management system as presently structured starts with output from the mill, although material can be manually tracked through lot numbers to truck deliveries and ultimately to the field from which it was harvested. Light readable bar codes are used to uniquely identify each drum as it is produced in the mill. This greatly increases the accuracy of inventory transactions and provides real time status for the total inventory. Queries can be made to the drum level if necessary, but most reports require only product code information.

Production Control schedules material from the warehouse for both shipping and manufacturing by product code. Bar code readings at critical points again allow for real time status. Usage of this material is then reported against each open order by both product code and lot number for traceability purposes. This material usage information is also utilized to report such management information as input/output ratios, product yields and machine throughputs against budget.

Implementation Suggestions

Our experience at Schilling and Gilroy Foods illustrate that the same means cannot always be used to reach a similar end. However, we can at least avoid some of the problems encountered and errors made by others through learning from their experiences when the opportunity arises. It is in this spirit that we offer the following suggestions which may not always be consistent with the prevailing literature, but which certainly evolve from sometimes painful experience.

1. Management education must include their comprehension of what a formal system *requires them* to do.
2. Look objectively at how the company operates now and determine how it *actually* works.
3. The shortest distance between two points is not always a straight line—allow time for people to adapt to change; this may involve interim design steps.
4. If you have informal manual systems, don't create formal manual systems—go directly to computer systems.
5. With apologies to Ma Bell, the system is not always the solution—realize what can be changed by systems versus what cannot and develop systems accordingly.
6. Have an adequate staff in place (in terms of both quantity and training) prior to implementation.
7. Recognize and prepare for implementation trauma.
8. Make certain that the data processing people have the same objectives as the users.
9. Data processing people should work directly with user departments during design and in user departments during implementation.
10. Standard packages don't always meet your needs, particularly in the control area—be prepared to do the work yourself.

Note that most of these suggestions deal directly with the people impact on systems. The people at every level must be committed to the formal disciplines imposed by inventory management systems. Clerical employees particularly seem to be often taken for granted. Attitudes and actions have got to be transitioned from doing what is expedient to doing what will maintain accurate information for all. This could mean some tough personnel decisions in terms of transferring or terminating people who have difficulty adapting. While these decisions are often the toughest, there are a number of others that will come up that are also quite difficult, e.g., organizational definitions, job descriptions and evaluations, product structuring and methods of changing structures. If management is not prepared to make these critical decisions and then stand by them through the difficulties of implementation, then the idea of a manufacturing resources planning project should be abandoned.

However, once these tough lessons are learned and the commitment is made, implementation can go on in a reasonably smooth manner. The positive impact on the company is soon apparent to top management and is typically greater than could have been envisioned in the early project proposals. Management then realizes that they have the tools to control the company and its future.

chapter thirteen

Job Shop Production Activity Planning

The job shop is the most widely used production organization. It represents a variety of industries that produce goods as well as service industries such as restaurants, repair shops, hospitals, and colleges. In high-volume production systems, idle facility time and excessive in-process inventories can be controlled by the proper use of assembly line balancing techniques. In a job shop, however, every order is different, and each job could be unique. Work stations are grouped together according to their functions. The job shop production control system should schedule the incoming orders in a way that does not violate the capacity constraints of individual work stations or processes. The system should check the availability of materials and tools before releasing an order to departments. It should establish milestones or due dates to measure progress against need dates and lead times for each job. It should check work in progress as the jobs progress through the shop and should provide feedback on plant and production activities. The system should also provide work efficiency statistics and should collect operator times, thus satisfying payroll and labor distribution objectives.

In general, an effective production activity control system should cover many activities, such as planning, executing, monitoring, and control, as shown in figure 13.1. In doing so, the system interfaces with the overall objectives of the production plan, the inventory systems, and other activities in manufacturing.

In this chapter, we will see how various functions of the production activity system are executed as the job shop manager attempts to run the shop in a balanced and efficient manner—like assembly line production. If the system is unable to execute the overall objectives, what choices do we have? What are the possible corrective actions we can take to assure that the job is completed on time? To answer these and other questions, we will organize this subject into three stages: (1) planning, (2) execution, and (3) monitoring and control. The planning stage consists of scheduling, machine loading, and operation sequencing. (In figure 13.1, comparable activities in a high-volume production system are given in parentheses.) This chapter will discuss the planning stage of the system, which interfaces with demand management, material control, and capacity management. The second stage—execution—involves the production releasing activity, which is also known as dispatching. The final phase includes production reporting and status control as well as plant monitoring and control activities. The execution and control phases of the system are the subject of the next chapter. To fully understand how these functions are carried out in a job shop, it is important for us to know what information is available from which sources. We will briefly discuss these aspects before we delve into the details of production activity system functions.

Data Base Information Requirements

The production activity system may be manual, mechanized, or a combination. Regardless of the type of system used, it is important to set up the framework for planning and reporting. We are all familiar with the expression GIGO (garbage in, garbage out). Not only do we need *accurate* information, but *all* relevant information must be available for successful implementation of any production activity control system. The production system data base can be broadly categorized into planning and control files [1].

THE PLANNING FILES

The planning files consist of (1) the part master file, (2) the routing file, and (3) the work center master file. Each work center should be uniquely identified (e.g., lathe #15), and its capacity should be given in terms of units per hour or per day, its utilization factor in terms of periods it is active, and its output efficiency in comparison to specified time standards. Routing information indicates the plan of an order's flow through the shop. It also describes the operation that should be performed on each work center and the standard for how long the operation should take for completion. The contents of each file are as follows.

The Part Master File

The purpose of this file is to store all relevant manufacturing and inventory data related to a part or item in a single location. It contains the part number and description; the manufacturing lead time; and on-hand, allocated, and on-order quantities. It also has lot sizing requirements. As explained in the MRP chapter, the allocated quantities refer to the amount

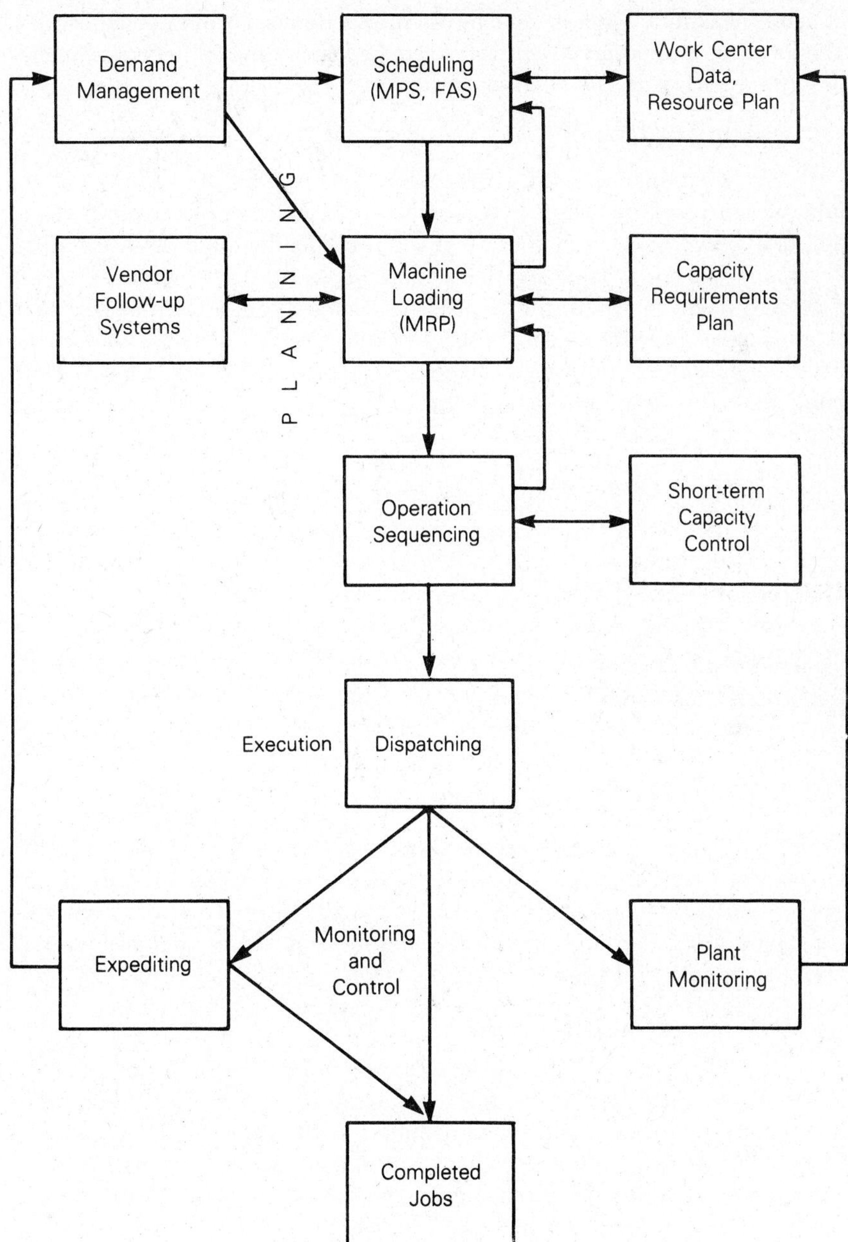

FIGURE 13.1 Job shop production activity system

of material assigned to a specific future production order but not yet cashed. The lot sizing requirements are determined by one of the lot sizing techniques described earlier in the MRP chapter.

The Routing File

This file contains all important operations required to manufacture an item. Each record consists of a specific operation number, operation description, setup hours, run hours, and codes to identify the type of operation. A separate record is kept for each operation, and they are arranged in the exact sequence in which the item is produced. Special instructions, such as alternative operations and subcontracting, may also be included in the data file. In determining how elaborately defined a file should be, keep in mind that a well-defined manufacturing process is a potential control application, even if only in the form of a simple routing.

The Work Center Master File

This file consists of all data relevant to a work center, such as capacity, efficiency, utilization, and so forth. Every work center is uniquely identified. The capacity data include the number of shifts worked per week, the number of machine hours utilized per shift, and the number of labor hours used in the work center. The master file also contains the average queue time of the work center and an identification of alternative work centers if the specific work center becomes overloaded.

THE CONTROL FILES

These files perform both monitoring and control functions once the job is released for production. They measure the actual progress made against the plan. The control file consists of all information pertaining to a particular order: (1) the shop order master file, and (2) the shop order detail file. The contents of these files are as follows.

The Shop Order Master File

This file stores all data related to a shop order, such as order quantity, reference data, priority, status information, and cost data. Each shop order is uniquely identified in the file. Included in the file are total number of units completed, quantities scrapped, and actual quantity disbursed for any given order quantity specific to the order. The shop order master file also contains the due date on which the order is scheduled for completion. Of course, MRP systems may revise these data files during replanning. Priority may be specified in terms of a critical ratio. In case of shortages of raw material or interruption of operation, the balance due will also be recorded. The balance due quantity obviously affects the quantity disbursed, unless actions such as alternative routing or subcontracting are taken.

The Shop Order Detail File

This file consists of all information that pertains to the planning, scheduling, actual progress, and priority related to an operation of a shop order. This file is similar to the master file except that the master file data refer to the entire order, whereas the detail file consists of all information necessary for each operation. Each operation is uniquely identified by a number. The progress data include reported actual setup hours, run hours, and quantity disbursed as each operation is recorded. The detail file also includes the operation due date or the lead time remaining prior to completion of the operation, which permits dynamic calculation of the critical ratio.

THE SHOP PLANNING CALENDAR

This calendar is also referred to as the *shop calendar* or the *planning calendar*. When the production control system is computerized, use of the regular Gregorian calendar creates scheduling difficulties, since months have varying numbers of days and the pattern of holidays is irregular. Therefore, it becomes necessary to develop a planning calendar. The typical planning calendar consists of two-digit week designations (00–99) and three-digit day designations (000–999), resulting in a 100-week or 1,000-day scheduling horizon, as exhibited in figure 13.2.

Scheduling

The purpose of scheduling is to optimize the use of resources so that the overall production objectives are met. In general, scheduling involves the assignment of dates to specific jobs or operation steps. As mentioned earlier, many jobs on the shop floor compete simultaneously for common resources. Machine breakdowns, absenteeism, quality problems, shortages, and other uncontrollable factors further complicate the manufacturing environment. Hence, the assignment of a date does not ensure that the work will be performed according to the schedule. Developing reliable schedules for completion of jobs on time requires a method or discipline to determine the sequence in which scheduled work will be performed.

A good scheduling approach should be simple, unambiguous, easily understood, and executable by the management and by those who must use it. The rules should set tough but realistic goals that are flexible enough to resolve unexpected floor conflicts and allow replanning, as priorities may continually change. When people trust and use these rules, scheduling becomes a reliable and formal means of communication.

Many scheduling techniques can be employed to schedule a job shop. The type of technique used depends on the volume of orders, the nature

January

Sunday	Monday	Tuesday	Wednesday	Thursday	Friday	Saturday
					1 New Year's Day	2
3	4 001	5 002	6 003	7 004	8 005	9
10	11 006	12 007	13 008	14 009	15 010	16
17	18 011	19 012	20 013	21 014	22 015	23
24 / 31	25 016	26 017	27 018	28 019	29 020	30

February

Sunday	Monday	Tuesday	Wednesday	Thursday	Friday	Saturday
	1 021	2 022	3 023	4 024	5 025	6
7	8 026	9 027	10 028	11 029	12 030	13
14 Valentine's Day	15 Presidents' Day	16 031	17 032	18 033	19 034	20
21	22 035	23 036	24 037 Ash Wednesday	25 038	26 039	27
28						

FIGURE 13.2 Shop planning calendar

of operations, and the overall job complexity. The selection of the technique also depends on the extent of control required over the job while it is being processed. For example, we would try to minimize or eliminate idle time in costly machine operations, and we might want to minimize the cost of in-process inventories at the same time. Scheduling techniques can generally be categorized as (1) forward scheduling and (2) backward scheduling. In practice, a combination of forward and backward scheduling is often used.

FORWARD SCHEDULING

Forward scheduling, which is also known as set forward scheduling, assumes that procurement of material and operations start as soon as the requirements are known. The events or operations are scheduled from this requirements point of view. Forward scheduling is used in many companies, such as steel mills and machine tools manufacturers, where jobs are manufactured to customer order and delivery is requested as soon as possible. Forward scheduling is well suited where the supplier is usually behind in meeting schedules. The set forward logic generally causes a buildup of in-process inventory, which costs money. Figure 13.3 provides an example of forward scheduling.

BACKWARD SCHEDULING

In backward scheduling, which is also known as set backward scheduling, the last operation on the routing is scheduled first. Then the rest of the operations are offset one at a time, in reverse order, as they become necessary. Finally, by offsetting the procurement time, the start date is obtained.

Set backward scheduling is used primarily in assembly-type industries.

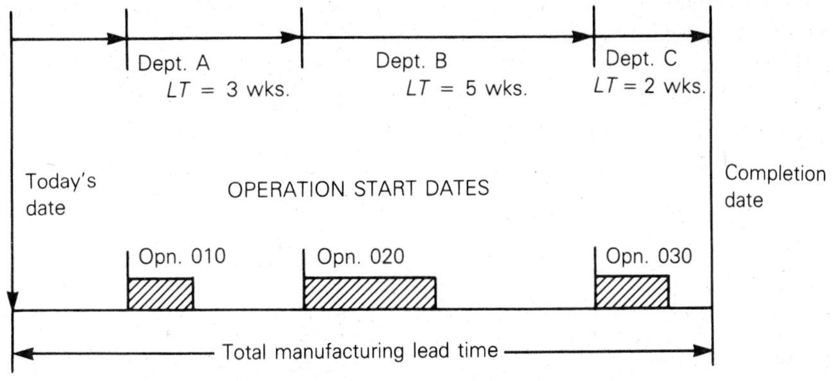

FIGURE 13.3 Forward scheduling

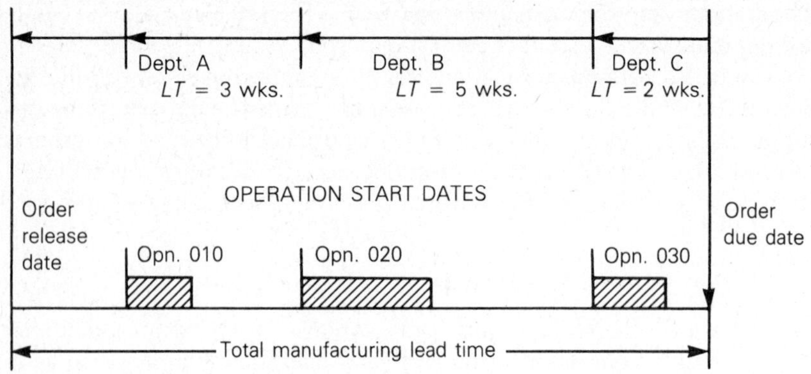

FIGURE 13.4 Backward scheduling

After determining the required schedule dates for major subassemblies, the schedule uses these required dates for each component and works backward to determine the proper release date for each component manufacturing order. Backward scheduling minimizes the in-process inventory. It works well in the MRP environment and is used for establishing shop order start and due dates using the lead time offset. Figure 13.4 provides an example of backward scheduling.

SIMPLE AND BLOCK SCHEDULING RULES

Simple scheduling rules roughly estimate the total operation times (O), move times (M), wait times (W), queue times (Q), and transit times (T) for each job in number of days and schedule them approximately on a calendar for computing the completion times. The simple scheduling rules are exhibited in table 13.1. These rules generally are not detailed enough to be implemented. Block scheduling rules are even worse. They estimate operation times in weeks for every department and express the scheduled completion dates in week numbers. Table 13.2 portrays the block scheduling rules. We will present an example to illustrate simple and block scheduling rules [9].

TABLE 13.1 Simple Scheduling Rules

1. Compute operation time to the nearest day.
2. Allow one day for successive operations in the same department, two days if they are in different departments.
3. Allow two days for inspection.
4. Allow two days to withdraw material from stock room and one day to deliver completed material to stock room.
5. Allow five extra days for certain specified bottleneck operations.

TABLE 13.2 Block Scheduling Rules

1. Express operation times in weeks; combine short operations.
2. Allow one week of inspection time for piece parts, two weeks for equipment.
3. Allow one week for releasing order, withdrawing material from stock room, and delivering completed products into stock room.
4. Allow one extra week for certain specified bottleneck operations.

Example 13.1

The XYZ Company is required to quote a completion time for a possible job to a preferred customer. The job has four operations, with estimated durations of operations as follows:

Operation	*Description*	*Duration (days)*
01	Make patterns	5
02	Pour casting (Bottleneck)	2
03	Grinding	15
04	Milling and assembly	10

Table 13.3 illustrates how completion times are derived. The codes indicate the type of activity. The simple scheduling rules allot a certain

TABLE 13.3 Simple and Block Scheduling, Example 13.1

		Simple Scheduling		*Block Scheduling*	
Operation	*Code*	*Days Allowed*	*Day Number*	*Weeks Allowed*	*Week Number*
Release date			394		80
Withdraw material		2	396	1	81
Opn. 01	O	5	401	1	82
	MWQ	2	403	1	83
	I	2	405	1	84
Opn. 02	O	2	407	1	85
	MWQ	2	409	1	86
	I	2	411	1	87
Bottleneck		5	416	1	88
Opn. 03	O	15	431	3	91
	MWQ	2	433	1	92
	I	2	435	1	93
Opn. 04	O	10	445	2	95
	MWQ	2	447	1	96
Inspection and delivery	I, D	3	450	1	97
Time to complete			56 days		17 weeks

Note: O refers to the operation time, I is the inspection time, and MWQ refers to the move, wait, and queue times, as described in Chapter 14. Sequence of activities within the operation is not important because we are in the planning range.

number of days for each activity in the department, whereas the block scheduling rules round the days into the approximate number of weeks, thus providing a much worse schedule. (Compare fifty-six days for simple scheduling versus seventeen weeks, or eighty-five days, for block scheduling rules.) Note that these rules provide examples for the forward scheduling technique. Many problems may arise while using forward or backward scheduling. For example, in forward scheduling, the completion date may fall beyond the due date; in backward scheduling, the start date may turn out to be a past date. In such cases, the schedule becomes infeasible. Also, we didn't pay any attention in our scheduling to the available capacities of facilities. Such problems may be resolved by the judicious use of capacity control techniques.

Shop Loading

As orders are released to the shop according to a schedule, individual jobs are assigned to work centers. The process of determining which work center receives which jobs is known as *loading*. Loading procedures are categorized as infinite or finite. In finite loading procedures, the jobs are assigned by comparing the required hours for each operation with the available hours in each work center for the period specified by the schedule. In infinite loading, jobs are assigned to work centers without regard to capacity. The procedures for generating load reports were discussed earlier, in the capacity planning chapter. In the job shop environment, capacity requirements and availability are rarely equal. When the number of jobs is limited, the jobs can be allocated to machines where the operations can be done more efficiently, and hence the loading becomes manageable. However, when the same job can be performed by many work centers, with varying time periods (for example, job A can be done at work center 1 in ten hours, whereas it needs only eight hours in work center 2), the choice of work centers becomes very complex. When we consider the costs of operations and available capacities, it becomes a more complex problem. In addition to the trial-and-error technique described in the preceding chapter, graphical and analytical techniques such as charts, the index method, the assignment method, and the transportation method of linear programming can be applied. Each of these techniques is suited to particular situations.

THE GANTT LOAD CHART

Several charts, graphs, tables, and boards are available for projecting machine center loads in a department. They can be either manual or computerized. The Gantt chart is a visual aid that is commonly used in job shops. It is also used in maintenance and service industries. Figure

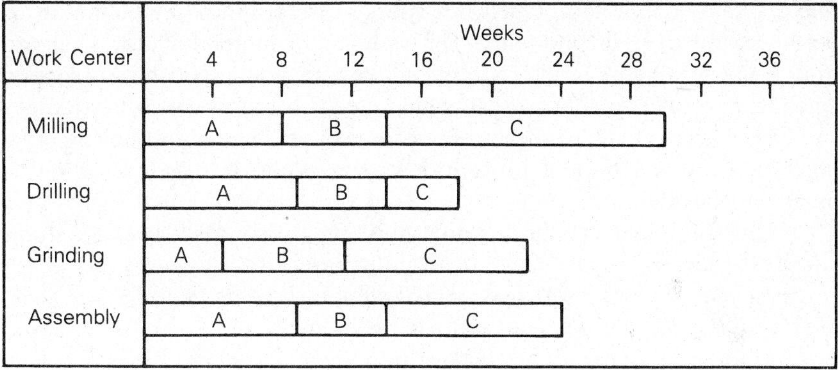

FIGURE 13.5 Gantt load chart for one department

13.5 shows a Gantt load chart. In the figure, the department has four machine centers, and each machine center may have more than one machine. The cumulative hours assigned to each machine center are plotted on the chart, which then displays the relative workloads in the system. When a center is overloaded, it is easy to identify the problem areas and to develop corrective action by reassigning workloads to alternative machines.

Gantt charts are simple to devise and easy to understand. Many commercial schedule boards are available, using magnetic strips, pegs, plastic inserts, and other devices. There are several limitations to the Gantt chart, however. For example, the sequence of operations is not considered in detail. Also, since the machines are grouped together, the wait times of individual jobs and the idle times of machines are not apparent. In addition, the charts do not reflect maintenance and breakdown times of machines, operator performance variables, and other details.

THE ASSIGNMENT METHOD OF LINEAR PROGRAMMING

Consider the problem of assigning three jobs to three machines. Jobs A, B, and C, for example, can be done on machines I, II, and III in 3! = 6 different ways, as exhibited in Table 13.4. Similarly, problems involving ten jobs may be done in 10! ways. These are typical combinatorial problems, and all possible solutions may need to be enumerated to find an optimal solution. Thus, enumeration methods are impractical for large problems.

TABLE 13.4 Possible Ways of Assigning Three Jobs to Three Machines

Machines			*Assignments*			
I	A	A	B	B	C	C
II	B	C	C	A	A	B
III	C	B	A	C	B	A

The assignment method, which is a special case of linear programming, is better suited to such problems. The assignment method allocates jobs to work centers, workers to jobs, salespeople to territories, contracts to bidders, and the like. The procedure can minimize such objectives as cost, time, and efficiency or can maximize profit or some other single-criterion objective functions. The assignment procedure known as the *Hungarian method* is presented here.

This solution procedure involves forming a square matrix and systematically developing relative costs of assigning projects to work centers, which is called *matrix reduction*. An optimal solution is obtained when at least one zero appears in each row and each column.

As an example, consider Andy's Auto Shop, where the manager needs to assign three different jobs to Tom, Dick, and Harry. Based on the workers' past experience, the required duration for completing a job varies among them. The manager would like to minimize the total hours spent by all three employees, since their hourly wages are the same. The effectiveness of assigning workers to various jobs can be presented in a tabular form, known as the *effectiveness matrix*, which is presented in Table 13.5. The Hungarian method transforms the effectiveness matrix into the desired matrix, with one zero in each column and each row, by adding or subtracting constants to columns or rows without changing the set of optimal assignments.

This method requires that the number of jobs equals the number of work centers. Otherwise, a dummy row or a column would be added to the matrix to make it a square matrix. A zero cost coefficient is assigned to the dummy to identify which job would be eliminated. If a particular assignment for a worker is not feasible, then either the corresponding cell would be blocked out or a high cost would be assigned. The solution procedure consists of the following three steps:

Step 1: Subtract the smallest element in each row from every element in that row. Then subtract the smallest element in each column from every element in that column. This is called the matrix reduction. The resulting matrix is exhibited in Table 13.6b.

Step 2: Find the minimum number of straight lines required to cover all zeros in Table 13.6b. The straight lines can be horizontal or vertical. If the maximum number of lines is equal to the number of columns or rows in

TABLE 13.5 Hours Required by Three Employees on Three Different Jobs

Employee	*X*	*Y*	*Z*
Tom	11	12	17
Dick	7	11	21
Harry	5	8	15

TABLE 13.6 Matrix Reduction, Step 2

(a) Row Reduction

	X	Y	Z
Tom	0	1	6
Dick	0	4	14
Harry	0	3	10

(b) Column Reduction

	X	Y	Z
Tom	0	0	0
Dick	0	3	8
Harry	0	2	4

the given problem, then an optimal solution has been obtained. Otherwise, go to Step 3. We need only two lines to cover all zeros in Table 13.6b. We have a situation in which we can assign any job to Tom and in which job X can be done by anyone. Suppose that we assign job X to Dick and job Y to Tom; then Harry will not have an optimum assignment. Regardless of how we reassign these jobs, the situation remains the same. We want to move any one of the zeros to another position on the matrix in order to remove this deadlock situation. Therefore, we go to Step 3.

Step 3: Find the smallest uncovered number in the new matrix exhibited in table 13.6b. In our example, it is 2. Subtract this number from every row that is not covered with a horizontal line (see table 13.7a). Since this gives us some negative elements in the first column, add the number to the first column. The resulting matrix is shown in table 13.7b.

Since we need three lines to cover all zeros in table 13.7b, the problem is solved. It must be possible to assign a zero for each row-column combination, as shown by squares in Table 13.7b. The solution to the assignment can be found by referring to the original problem and adding the corresponding times associated with the optimal solution. A total of thirty-two hours are necessary to complete all jobs. Suppose that we still needed fewer than three lines to cover all zeros in table 13.7b; then we would repeat Steps 2 and 3 as often as necessary until an optimum solution was found.

What if you cheat in step 2—for example, just drawing three horizontal lines and looking for an optimal assignment? Unfortunately, you will not find an optimal solution, which just shows that cheating does not pay! You must do it again—right.

There are limitations to this procedure. First, it uses a static approach. When jobs arrive continually, however, loading decisions may have to be checked continually. Also, there is no provision for checking capacity in this method; hence, the most efficient machine may be overloaded while

TABLE 13.7 Matrix Reduction, Step 3

(a) Removing Deadlock

0	0	0
−2	1	6
−2	0	2

(b) Final Solution Matrix

2	0	[0]
[0]	1	6
0	[0]	2

other machines are lightly loaded. We might need a Gantt chart or some other mechanism to balance the load among machines. In addition, an important assumption in this method is that several choices (machines, workers, or processes) exist for each job. This may not be true in many cases, and this procedure is not very valuable when choices do not exist. Although the transportation method of linear programming can overcome these difficulties, it has very restrictive applications.

THE INDEX METHOD

The index method overcomes many of the problems inherent in the assignment method. The index method is better suited, in fact, for shop loading purposes. This heuristic procedure uses opportunity cost, time, or some other single criterion as a variable. The index number represents the ratio of opportunity cost or time to the value of the best assignment.

As an example, consider a situation in which seven jobs, A to G, need to be completed. The capacity, in hours, needed for each job at every interchangeable machine center is as follows:

	Alternative Work Centers		
JOB	1	2	3
A	25	35	70
B	50	60	40
C	300	200	450
D	180	160	120
E	60	90	150
F	90	45	60
G	75	220	250
Available capacity	140	235	250

It is desirable to assign a job to the work center that takes the shortest amount of time or has the lowest cost. It may not always be possible to assign jobs to the most efficient work center because of capacity limitations. If we assign job A to work center 1, job B to work center 3, and so on, we would have a shortage in work centers 1 and 2 and excess capacity at work center 3, as shown in table 13.8. The hours assigned to each machine are shown in parentheses, and the total assigned capacities are compared to the available work center capacities. Since all jobs cannot be done by the most efficient work center, some jobs need to be shifted to the next most efficient center. The steps involved in the index method are as follows:

Step 1: Find the lowest process time for each job among the alternative work centers. Divide the lowest process time of each job into the other

TABLE 13.8 Calculation of Index

	Alternative Work Centers					
	1		2		3	
Job	*Hours*	*Index*	*Hours*	*Index*	*Hours*	*Index*
A	(25)	1.00	35	1.40	70	2.80
B	50	1.25	60	1.50	(40)	1.00
C	300	1.50	(200)	1.00	450	2.25
D	180	1.50	160	1.33	(120)	1.00
E	(60)	1.00	90	1.50	150	2.50
F	90	2.00	(45)	1.00	60	1.33
G	(75)	1.00	220	2.93	250	3.33
Assigned	160		245		160	
Available	140		235		250	
Excess	−20		−10		90	

alternative process times and obtain index numbers. Show the index numbers next to the process times, as in table 13.8.

Step 2: Allocate the jobs with the lowest index numbers to the corresponding work centers. If sufficient capacity exists, the problem is solved. Otherwise, go to Step 3. We already know that the available hours and assigned hours do not match in our example; therefore, we proceed to Step 3.

Step 3: Shift some jobs to the next most efficient center—that is, to the center with the next lowest index number. After moving job A to center 2, we find that center 1 has adequate capacity for completing jobs E and G, as shown in table 13.9. However, center 2 is in a worse situation, needing thirty-five more hours. Therefore, we repeat Step 3 to shift some jobs from center 2 to center 3.

TABLE 13.9 Index Method, Step 3: Moving Job A to Center 2

	Alternative Work Center					
	1		2		3	
Job	*Hours*	*Index*	*Hours*	*Index*	*Hours*	*Index*
A	25	1.00	(35)	1.40	70	2.80
B	50	1.25	60	1.50	(40)	1.00
C	300	1.50	(200)	1.00	450	2.25
D	180	1.50	160	1.33	(120)	1.00
E	(60)	1.00	90	1.50	150	2.50
F	90	2.00	(45)	1.00	60	1.33
G	(75)	1.00	220	2.93	250	3.33
Assigned	135		280		160	
Available	140		235		250	
Excess	5		−45		90	

TABLE 13.10 Index Method, Repeat Step 3: Moving Job F to Center 3

	Alternative Work Center					
	1		*2*		*3*	
Job	*Hours*	*Index*	*Hours*	*Index*	*Hours*	*Index*
A	25	1.00	(35)	1.40	70	2.80
B	50	1.25	60	1.50	(40)	1.00
C	300	1.50	(200)	1.00	450	2.25
D	180	1.50	160	1.33	(120)	1.00
E	(60)	1.00	90	1.50	150	2.50
F	90	2.00	45	1.00	(60)	1.33
G	(75)	1.00	220	2.93	250	3.33
Assigned	135		235		220	
Available	140		235		250	
Excess	5		0		30	

We notice that job F can be moved to center 3, which has the next lowest index number. The solution found in table 13.10 is feasible, and so we need not continue the iterative procedure any longer. In some instances, we may be forced to move a partial load to another center. For example, suppose that we need to shift only twenty hours of job A from center 1 to center 2. The additional hours needed at center 2 can be computed as (20) (index) = (20)(1.4) = 28 hours. However, if a setup time is included, these hours would vary.

There are limitations to the index method. In complex situations, especially when several job splits are included, several iterations would be needed to complete the loading. Although this heuristic solution procedure doesn't always provide an optimal solution, it generally gives reasonably good loads.

Sequencing

We know that scheduling provides a basis for following jobs as they progress through succeeding manufacturing operations. Machine loading is a detailed capacity control technique that highlights daily or weekly overloads and underloads. However, we still need to determine the priorities of operations at each machine to meet schedule dates of individual jobs. In many factories, also expediters, known as stock chasers, follow jobs through the shop, attaching red tags to indicate urgent jobs. Expediting is the real production control system in these factories. The expediter works with the shop floor foreman to complete jobs that are due. In due course, the expediter discovers shortages and rushes important jobs through production by establishing priorities. Alas, very soon almost all jobs have red tags, and then the expediter is told what the real job priorities are! Fortunately, in most cases, such situations can be prevented by using a reliable MRP system in conjunction with priority rules for sequencing jobs on the floor.

Sequencing specifies the order in which jobs should be done at each center. For example, suppose that ten patients are assigned to a medical clinic for treatment. In what order should they be treated? Should the first patient to be served be the one who arrived first or the one who needs emergency treatment? Sequencing methods provide such detailed information. These methods are referred to as priority rules for dispatching jobs to work centers.

Priority Rules for Dispatching Jobs

Priority rules are used for preparing dispatch lists of jobs or lots in job shops. They provide simplified guidelines for the sequence in which the jobs should be worked when the machine center or facility becomes available. Numerous rules have been developed; some are static and others are dynamic. The rules are especially applicable for intermittent and batch processes with independent demands. The priority rules attempt to minimize mean flow time, mean completion time, and mean waiting time and to maximize throughput and so forth. Several simulation experiments have been conducted to compare the performance of priority rules [7]. In this section, we will discuss some well-known rules and their effectiveness in sequencing.

PRIORITY SYSTEM

Many properties are desirable in a good priority system. The system should be relative, and it should specify the order in which the jobs should be processed—first, second, third, and so on. A priority system should be dynamic, so that the priority rule permits regular updating of priorities if necessary. This is particularly true for items with long lead times whose demand is uncertain. Finally, a priority system should truly reflect the due dates. Properly maintained MRP systems can provide priority planning information that meets these specifications and can supply valid input to a priority control system. A discussion of how an MRP system can be used in job shop situations is explored by Teplitz [21].

PRIORITY RULES

The following priority decision rules are commonly used:

FCFS (first come, first served): By this rule, jobs are scheduled for work in the same sequence as they arrive at the facility. This is used particularly in service firms, such as automotive repair shops, barber shops, and restaurants.

EDD (earliest due date): This rule sequences the jobs waiting at the facility according to their due date, and they are processed in that order. This does not guarantee that all jobs will be completed on time, as will be illustrated by Example 13.2.

SPT (shortest processing time): This rule, which is also known as the shortest operation time rule, selects first the job with the shortest operation time on the machine. Many simulation experiments have demonstrated that this rule minimizes in-process inventories. This is accomplished, however, at the expense of keeping the bigger jobs longer.

LPT (longest processing time): This rule selects first the job with the longest operation time on the machine.

TSPT (truncated shortest processing time): This rule sequences jobs according to the SPT rule, except for jobs that have been waiting longer than a specified truncation time. Those jobs go to the front of the waiting line in some specified order (using, for example, the FCFS rule).

LS (least slack): This rule selects first the jobs with the smallest slack. Slack is defined as the number of days remaining before the due date minus the duration of the job.

COVERT (cost over time): This rule computes the ratio of expected delay cost to processing time. The job with the largest ratio is selected first.

Example 13.2

The AMX Company has received the following jobs and wishes to use priority decision rules for sequencing. All dates have been translated according to shop calendar days; assume that today is day 120.

Job Number	*Production Days Required*	*Date Order Received*	*Date Order Due*
117	15	115	200
118	10	120	210
119	25	121	185
120	30	125	230
121	17	125	150
122	20	126	220

Assuming a five-day work week, determine the sequence in which the jobs should be performed according to each of the seven priority rules. For the TSPT rule, assume that jobs cannot be delayed more than sixty-five days.

Solution: The sequences according to the priority rules are as follows:

Priority Rule	*Sequence*
FCFS	117, 118, 119, 120, 121, 122
EDD	121, 119, 117, 118, 122, 120
SPT	118, 117, 121, 122, 119, 120
LPT	120, 119, 122, 121, 117, 118
TSPT	118, 117, 121, 119, 120, 122
LS	121, 119, 117, 122, 120, 118
COVERT	121, 122, 117, 118, 119, 120

The first four sequences, as given by the FCFS, EDD, SPT, and LPT rules, are obvious. For the TSPT rule, we specified that jobs cannot be delayed more than sixty-five days. If none of the jobs in the SPT sequence violate the constraint, the sequence provided by rules SPT and TSPT will be identical. Let us now check the wait time of the jobs according to the SPT sequence:

Job Sequence	*Duration (days)*	*Date Order Received*	*Start Date*	*Wait Time (days)*
118	10	120	120	—
117	15	115	130	15
121	17	125	145	20
122	20	126	162	36
119	25	121	182	61
120	30	125	207	82

The SPT sequence results in a delay of eighty-two days for job 120, which is more than the sixty-five days specified. Therefore, the TSPT rule would schedule job 122 after job 120. The slack for each job is computed as follows:

Job Number	*Duration (days)*	*Days Remaining*	*Slack (days)*	*Sequence*
117	15	85	70	3
118	10	90	80	6
119	25	64	49	2
120	30	105	75	5
121	17	25	8	1
122	20	94	74	4

If, by chance, one of these jobs were already being processed, the rest of the jobs would be arranged using the least slack rule. The COVERT rule computes possible delays for individual jobs, using rules such as FCFS. If one or more jobs are delayed, the ratio is computed, as shown in table

TABLE 13.11 COVERT Priority Rule Ratio Calculation, Example 13.2

Job Number	*Duration (T)*	*Completion Date*	*Due Date*	*Delay*	*Cost (C)*	*C/T*
117	15	135	200	No	—	0
118	10	145	210	No	—	0
119	25	170	185	No	—	0
120	30	200	230	No	—	0
121	17	217	150	Yes	680	40
122	20	237	220	Yes	500	25

13.11. Then we can sequence the jobs such that the largest C/T is completed first. We have explained the concept of the COVERT rule in its simplest form. In its original version, C/T ranges from zero to one. The priority rules are fully described by Carroll [5] and Buffa and Miller [3].

DYNAMIC SEQUENCING RULES

The following rules are often used for sequencing:

DS (dynamic slack): When the LS rule is used repeatedly at each machine center for sequencing jobs, it is known as the dynamic slack rule. This rule, however, does not consider the duration of the job.

DS/RO (dynamic slack per remaining operation): This rule computes a ratio for each job waiting. The ratio is obtained by dividing the total slack time available for the job by the number of operations remaining (including the current machine). Obviously, the job with the smallest ratio is scheduled first. The DS/RO rule suffers from the same shortcoming as the DS rule.

CR (critical ratio): This dynamic priority rule constantly updates priorities according to most recent conditions. It has been found effective in MRP for review and revision of the existing schedule. The rule develops a comparative index of any job in relation to others at the same facility. The CR is designed to give priority to jobs that have the most urgently needed work to meet the shipping schedule. The CR is the ratio of the time period left prior to the shipping date to the time period needed to complete the job:

$$\text{CR} = \frac{\text{need date} - \text{today's date}}{\text{Days Required to Complete the job}}$$

$$= \frac{\text{days remaining}}{\text{days required}}$$

As a job gets further behind schedule, its CR becomes smaller, and jobs with low CR take precedence over others.

Example 13.3

The AMX Company has a list of jobs to be started on day 358. The jobs' durations and due dates are as follows:

Job Number	*Duration (days)*	*Due Date*
150	25	360
151	17	372
152	35	367
153	19	377
154	29	370
155	10	390

Using the critical ratio technique, find the sequence of jobs to be done.

Solution: We can calculate the days remaining by subtracting today's date from the due date. Assuming that none of the jobs have been started, we can say that the time remaining for each job is equal to its duration. If a certain portion of the work was completed on a job, we would merely subtract that amount from the duration of that job. The critical ratio is found by dividing the days remaining by the days required (see table 13.12). Ratios range from zero to one for jobs that are behind or on schedule. Smaller ratios signify more urgent jobs. Ratios that are greater than one represent noncritical jobs. By the CR rule, then the sequence of jobs is 150, 152, 154, 151, 153, and 155.

We have described many rules for dispatching jobs. These rules can be useful for generating the start dates of the jobs or operations on a particular machine as the job progresses. Obviously, dynamic rules are superior to static rules. The effectiveness of these rules in the job shop environment was studied by Conway, Maxwell, and Miller [7], Nanot [14], and others. The critical ratio technique has been the most highly acclaimed by industry practitioners, including Plossl and Wight [17], Orlicky [16], and others.

TABLE 13.12 Critical Ratio Calculation, Example 13.3

Job Number	*Duration (days)*	*Due Date*	*Days Remaining*	*Critical Ratio*	*Sequence*
150	25	360	2	2/25 = 0.080	1
151	17	372	14	14/17 = 0.824	4
152	35	367	9	9/35 = 0.257	2
153	19	377	19	19/19 = 1.00	5
154	29	370	12	12/29 = 0.41	3
155	10	390	32	32/10 = 3.2	6

Mathematical Programming, Heuristics, and Simulation

Several techniques have been presented for scheduling, loading, and sequencing in job shops. We have pointed out that many jobs in job shops are unique and that they move through work centers as specified by the route sheets. The sequences of operations often are different. In many instances, however, the sequences of operations are the same, but the orders may require varying loads in different work centers. Note that the job shop is different from an assembly line environment, in which most operations, their durations, and the sequence are essentially the same. Many mathematical programming and heuristic techniques for job shop production control can be found in the literature [10], and several efficient heuristic techniques have been developed to solve special cases encountered in job shop situations. These solution techniques can be classfied as (1) series machines, (2) parallel machines, and (3) series-parallel machines. They are referred to as "*N* job, *M* machine problems" or simply *n*/*m* problems in the scheduling and sequencing literature. We will discuss the solution procedures for some configurations which are popularly known as flow shops.

N JOBS, ONE MACHINE

This configuration consists of several jobs waiting to be processed by a single facility:

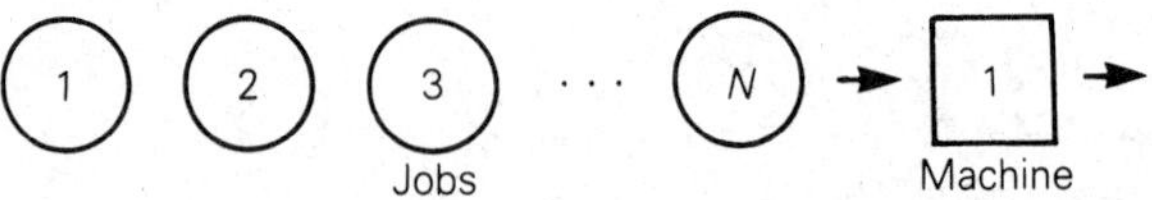

Many of the priority rules discussed in this chapter can be used to solve problems in this category. They provide the sequence in which the jobs are to be processed by a single facility.

N JOBS, TWO MACHINES IN SERIES (NO PASSING)

In this case, each job has to go through two facilities in the same order. "No passing" means that no job is allowed to pass any other job while the first job is waiting between facilities and that no job can be started before the previous job is completed.

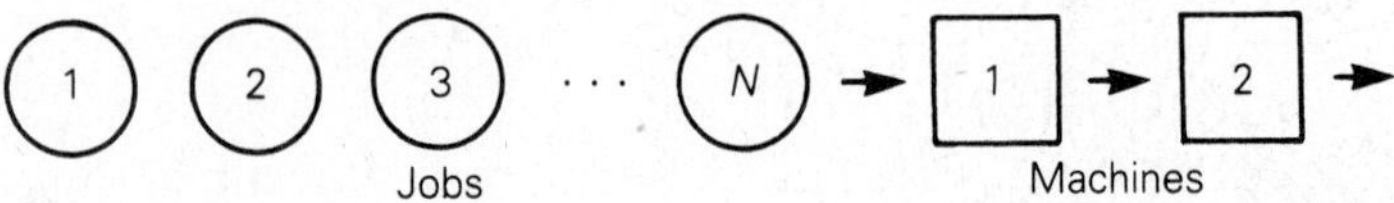

Johnson's rule [11] can be used to obtain an optimal solution to this problem. The rule minimizes the total make span. Given a set of jobs and their associated operation durations in corresponding machines, Johnson's rule consists of the following steps:

Step 1: Select the shortest operation duration.

Step 2: If the shortest duration requires the first machine, schedule the job in the first available position in the sequence. If the shortest duration is on the second machine, schedule the job in the last available position in the sequence.

Step 3: Remove the assigned job from further consideration and return to Step 1 for the next job.

Example 13.4

The Bracken Company tests laboratory specimens. The testing department must perform two consecutive operations for each job. The following table lists jobs and their corresponding durations of operations:

	Duration (hours)	
JOB	MACHINE 1	MACHINE 2
A	3	6
B	5	2
C	1	2
D	7	5

1. Use Johnson's rule to set the sequence of processing the shipments.
2. Using a Gantt scheduling chart, determine how much time is required to complete all jobs listed.

Solution: The shortest duration is one hour on machine 1. Schedule job C first in the sequence and remove it from further consideration. Now the shortest duration is two hours on machine 2. Schedule job B last in the sequence and remove it from further scheduling. Since the next smallest duration of three hours is on machine 1, schedule job A as the second job in the sequence. Finally, job D is scheduled in third place. We now have the optimal sequence: C, A, D, B.

The Gantt chart for the sequence is shown in figure 13.6. The chart is constructed by scheduling job C first on machine 1. Job C on machine 2 can be started as soon as it is completed on machine 1. The succeeding job, job A, can be started on machine 1 as soon as job C is completed there. Similarly, upon job A's completion on machine 1, it can be started on machine 2, provided that the previous job has been completed. Otherwise, it will wait in the in-process inventory until the previous job is finished.

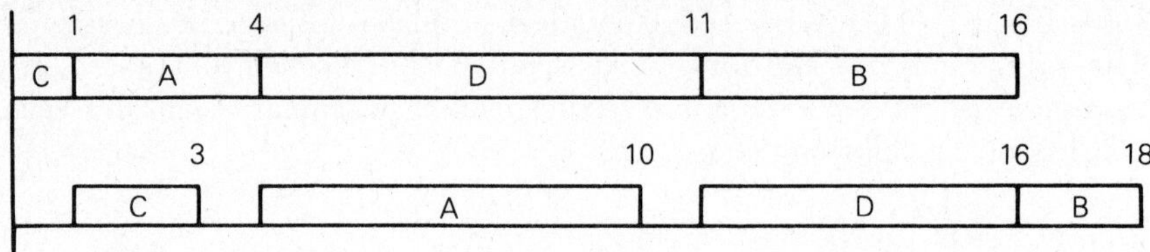

FIGURE 13.6 Make span for the optimum sequence, Example 13.4

The make span, or throughput time, for these jobs is given by the schedule chart as eighteen hours. It is not hard to explain how this algorithm works. The smaller jobs are scheduled on machine 1 first, so that machine 2 is not kept waiting too long. Once the machines are busy, the situation reverses at the end of the sequence. Machine 2 has all small jobs left, which again helps complete all jobs quickly.

N JOBS, THREE MACHINES IN SERIES (NO PASSING)

The optimal solution for a general case is quite complicated. However, if either or both of the following conditions are met, the solution is given by the *N*/3 Johnson's rule [11]:

1. The smallest duration on machine 1 is at least as great as the largest duration on machine 2.
2. The smallest duration on machine 3 is at least as great as the largest duration on machine 2.

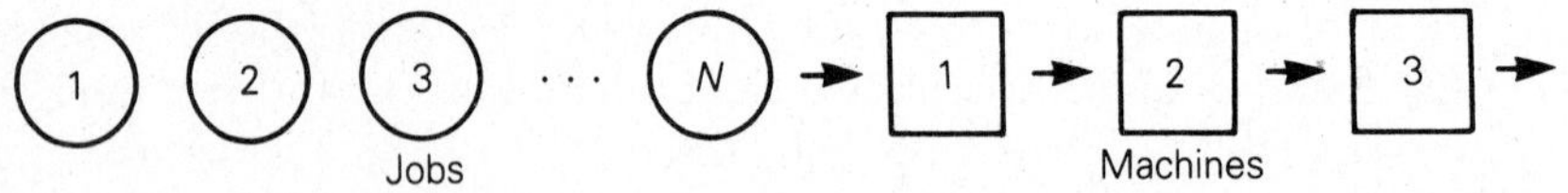

We will explain the algorithm with the following example.

Example 13.5

Consider the following jobs and their processing times at corresponding machines:

Duration (hours)

JOB	MACH 1 t_{i1}	MACH 2 t_{i2}	MACH 3 t_{i3}
A	13	5	9
B	5	3	7
C	6	4	5
D	7	2	6

Using Johnson's rule, find the optimal sequence.

Solution: Since both conditions of Johnson's rule are met, we can apply the algorithm. First, form a new matrix, as follows:

Job	$t_{i1} + t_{i2}$	$t_{i2} + t_{i3}$
A	18	14
B	8	10
C	10	9
D	9	8

Now, using Johnson's rule for the $N/2$ problem, we get the optimal sequence: B, A, C, D.

Essentially, Johnson's rule converts an $N/3$ problem into an $N/2$ problem, provided that certain conditions are met. Even if these conditions are not met, the rule still provides a near optimal solution, as we will soon see.

N JOBS, *M* MACHINES IN SERIES (NO PASSING)

When several jobs have to be processed through many facilities, finding an optimal sequence requires a combinatorial search procedure.

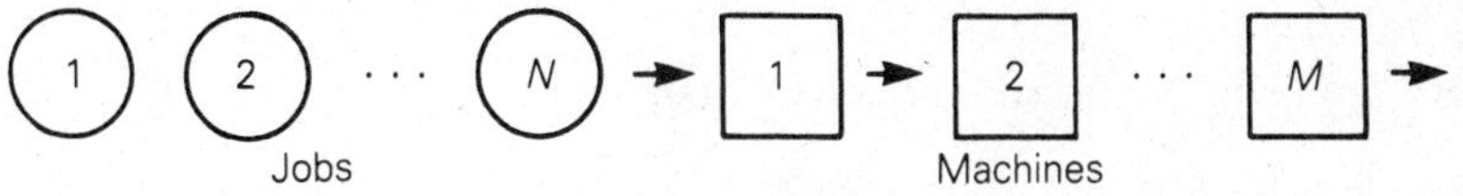

An efficient heuristic procedure, suggested by Cambell, Dudek, and Smith [4], is known as the CDS algorithm. The CDS algorithm extends the $N/3$ Johnson's rule to a general N/M problem and provides a near optimal solution.

Example 13.6

The following table provides jobs and their durations on respective machines:

	Duration (hours)			
JOB	MACH 1	MACH 2	MACH 3	MACH 4
A	3	1	11	13
B	3	10	13	1
C	11	8	15	2
D	5	7	7	9
E	7	3	21	4

The algorithm generates $m - 1 = 4 - 1 = 3$ two-machine (M1, M2) solutions. The sequence that yields the minimum make span is chosen.

Solution 1: From the foregoing table, consider only the durations on the first and last machines:

Job	*M1*	*M2*
A	3	13
B	3	1
C	11	2
D	5	9
E	7	4

Applying Johnson's rule, we obtain the sequence A, D, E, C, B.

Solution 2: From the original data, add the durations of the first two machines for M1 and add the durations of the last two machines for M2 for every job:

Job	*M1*	*M2*
A	4	24
B	13	14
C	19	17
D	12	16
E	10	25

Again applying Johnson's rule, we obtain the sequence A, E, D, B, C.

Solution 3: In this solution, the process times for M1 and M2 are obtained from the original data by adding the first three and the last three durations, respectively, for each job. This concept can be extended to any number of machines in a series.

Job	*M1*	*M2*
A	15	25
B	26	24
C	34	25
D	19	23
E	31	28

Using Johnson's algorithm, we get the sequence of A, D, E, C, B.

We can now find the make span for the solutions generated, as shown in figure 13.7. Since the sequences obtained in solutions 1 and 3 have the smallest make span—seventy-two hours—we would probably choose A, E, D, C, B.

N JOBS, *M* MACHINES IN PARALLEL

In this configuration, the *N* available jobs may be processed by any one of the *M* machines available. A simple yet effective heuristic solution is given by the LPT rule [2].

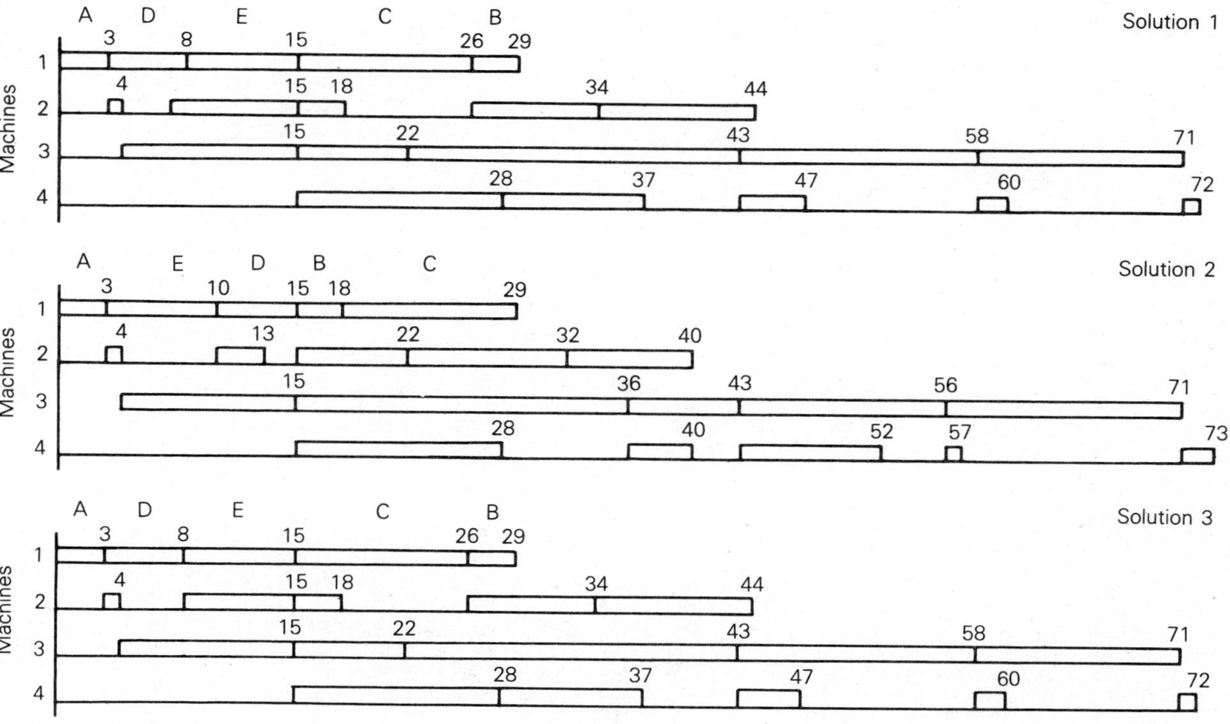

FIGURE 13.7 Calculating make spans for Example 13.6

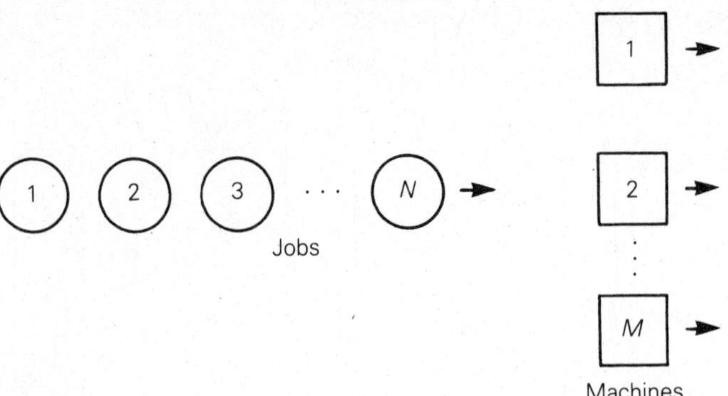

Example 13.7

The following table provides the data for an $N=8/M=3$ problem. Assign the jobs using the LPT rule.

Job	*Duration*
A	11
B	18
C	4
D	13
E	2
F	7
G	5
H	3

Solution: As a first step, using the LPT rule, we obtain the sequence B, D, A, F, G, C, H, E. The second step consists of assigning jobs to each machine in an order such that the least amount of total processing is already assigned. Ties are arbitrarily resolved. The solution is shown in figure 13.8.

This procedure assumes that all parallel machines have identical capacities. Several elaborate algorithms for minimizing make spans are discussed in Baker [2].

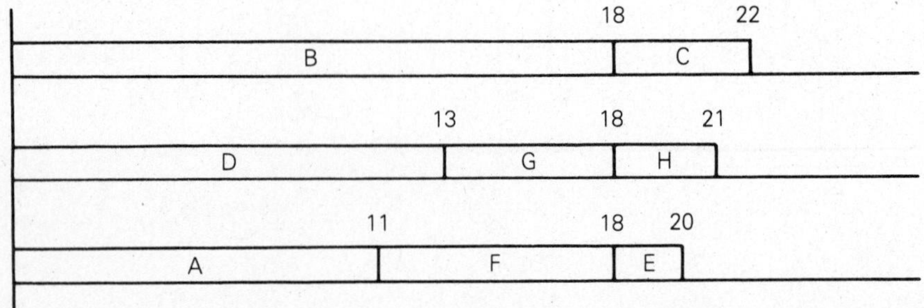

FIGURE 13.8 LPT sequence for Example 13.7

N JOBS, *M* MACHINES IN SERIES AND PARALLEL

In this case, the jobs may be processed by any one of the machines at stage I. Once the operation at stage I is completed, the job is then served by any one of the machines at stage II.

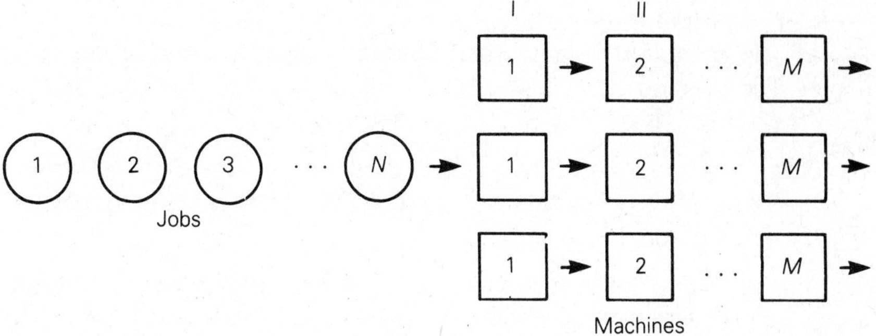

This is probably the most difficult type of scheduling problem to solve. Zangwill [22] presented a mathematical programming model to solve multiproduct, multifacility production and inventory problems. However, as indicated earlier, mathematical programming techniques for solving such problems are not yet practical. So far, computer simulation techniques have been found to be the most effective tools.

Summary

This chapter has focused on job shop activity planning. We have discussed many aspects of scheduling, loading, and sequencing. The details and the extent of planning depend on the situation, but planning alone doesn't get the job done. Executing the job involves issuing actual shop orders, following through on the job progress, and delivering goods to the customer on time. These factors are fully explored in the next chapter.

PROBLEMS

1. Job A has the following five operations:

Operation	*Description*	*Duration (hours)*
010	Casting	15
020	Milling	28
040	Drilling	18
050	Finishing	8

The due date on the planning calendar is day 235.

Using the simple scheduling rules in table 13.1, find the following:

a. The completion date, using forward scheduling; today is day 198 on the planning calendar. Assume a five-day work week.
b. The starting date, using backward scheduling.

2. For problem 1, apply the block scheduling rules specified in table 13.2 and find the following:
   a. The completion date (week number), using forward scheduling.
   b. The starting date, using backward scheduling; the due date is week 47. Note that 235 days is 47 weeks.

3. Operations required for completing jobs A, B, and C are given by the route sheet information in table 13.13. Draw a Gantt load chart for each machine center.

4. A scheduler in the Mary Mont Hospital needs to assign four technicians to four different jobs. Estimates of the time to complete every job were provided by each technician and are summarized as follows:

Hours to Complete Job

TECHNICIAN	1	2	3	4
A	20	36	31	17
B	24	34	45	12
C	22	45	38	18
D	37	40	35	18

   a. Using the assignment method of linear programming, how would you assign jobs to technicians to minimize the total work time?
   b. Assuming that the estimates are fairly accurate, can these jobs be completed in three eight-hour days? If not, give a schedule for completion of all jobs.

5. Suppose that, in problem 4, it is not desirable to assign technician A to job 1 and technician D to job 3. How will this affect your results?

6. A scheduler has five jobs that can be done on any of four machines, with respective times (in hours) as shown here. Available capacities in each machine center are also given.

TABLE 13.13 Route Sheet for Problem 3

	Job A		*Job B*		*Job C*	
Operation Number	*Work Center*	*Time (hrs.)*	*Work Center*	*Time (hrs.)*	*Work Center*	*Time (hrs.)*
I	2	30	1	40	1	35
II	3	30	3	30	4	20
III	4	40	2	40	2	35
IV	1	50	4	30	3	40

JOB	Machines 1	2	3	4
A	50	60	80	70
B	100	120	110	70
C	100	80	130	60
D	80	70	40	30
E	75	100	70	120
Available capacity	70	120	70	120

Determine the allocation of jobs to machines that will result in minimum hours.

7. Prepare a Gantt chart schedule based on the criterion of the shortest total processing time per order, using problem 3 data.

8. Using the techniques learned in this chapter, solve problem 9 in chapter 10.

9. The following jobs are waiting to be processed at the same machine center. Jobs are logged as they arrive:

Job	*Due Date*	*Duration (days)*	*Cost*
A	313	8	100
B	312	16	100
C	325	40	200
D	314	5	50
E	314	3	75

In what sequence would the jobs be ranked according to the following decision rules: (a) FCFS, (b) EDD, (c) SPT, (d) LPT, (e) TSPT, (f) LS, and (g) COVERT? All dates are specified as manufacturing planning calendar days. Assume that all jobs arrive on day 275. No job is allowed to wait more than fifty days.

10. Suppose that today is day 300 on the planning calendar and that we have not started any of the jobs given in problem 9. Using the critical ratio technique, in what sequence would you schedule these jobs?

11. Job B has the following five operations:

Operation	*Description*	*Duration (hours)*
01	Casting	10
02	Reaming	21
03	Milling	14
04	Finishing	6

Apply the simple scheduling rules specified in table 13.1 and find the following:

a. The completion date, using forward scheduling.
b. The starting date, using backward scheduling; the due date is 310.

Assume a total procurement lead time of ten days. Today is day 257.

12. For problem 11, apply block scheduling rules specified in table 13.2 and find the following:
   a. The completion date, using forward scheduling.
   b. The starting date, using backward scheduling; the due date is 320. Today is day 257. Assume a five-day work week.
13. The operations required for completing the jobs A and B are given by the route sheet information in table 13.14.
   a. Draw a Gantt schedule chart for each machine center.
   b. Calculate the percentage of the time that the machines are idle prior to the completion of operations in individual work centers.
14. The operations required to complete Jobs X, Y and Z are given by the route sheet information in table 13.15. Draw a Gantt load chart for each machine center. Assume two machines at Center 2.
15. A manager at Paul's laboratories must assign three engineers to three different duties. Estimates of the time to complete each duty for every engineer have been determined from historical data and are summarized as follows:

TABLE 13.14 Route Sheet for Problem 13

	Job A		*Job B*	
Operation Number	*Work Center*	*Time (hrs.)*	*Work Center*	*Time (hrs.)*
010	2	30	1	40
020	3	30	3	30
030	1	40	2	50

TABLE 13.15 Route Sheet for Problem 14

	Job X		*Job Y*		*Job Z*	
Operation Number	*Work Center*	*Time (hrs.)*	*Work Center*	*Time (hrs.)*	*Work Center*	*Time (hrs.)*
Release order		40		40		40
010	2	80	1	60	2	120
020	1	40	2	100	1	160

ENGINEER	Hours to Complete Job 1	2	3
A	10	12	16
B	12	24	20
C	14	20	24

a. Using the assignment method of linear programming, how would you assign jobs to the engineers to minimize the total work time?
b. Assuming that the estimates are fairly accurate, can all three duties be performed completely in two eight-hour days? If not, give a feasible schedule for completion of all jobs.

16. The scheduler at CPA Company needs to assign four accountants to four different projects. Estimates of the time to complete every job were determined by the scheduler and are summarized as follows:

ACCOUNTANT	*Hours to Complete Job* 1	2	3	4
A	16	29	34	19
B	11	43	32	23
C	17	36	43	21
D	17	33	40	36

a. Using the assignment method of linear programming, how would you assign projects to minimize the total work time?
b. Assuming that the estimates are accurate, can these jobs be completed in three regular days? If not, give a feasible schedule for completion of all jobs.

17. For problem 16, suppose that it is not desirable to assign accountant A to job 4 and accountant D to job 2. Will this affect your results; if so, how? (*Hint*: Block off unwanted squares or assign very high costs to those squares and recompute the problem.)

18. A scheduler has four jobs that can be done on any of five machines, with respective times (in hours) as shown here. Determine the allocation of jobs to machines that will result in minimum hours.

MACHINES	*Jobs* 1	2	3	4
A	60	110	70	50
B	70	40	100	80
C	70	80	100	120
D	100	70	80	110
E	30	120	60	70

(*Hint*: Add a dummy column with zero values for job 5 and proceed as usual. One of the machines will be allocated to a dummy job in the final solution; that is, the machine is idled.)

19. Using the index method, find the allocation of the following six jobs to four machines that will result in minimum hours.

	Machines			
JOB	I	II	III	IV
1	40	50	60	70
2	100	40	80	30
3	50	60	20	100
4	110	80	100	120
5	120	60	70	80
6	60	30	80	50
Available capacity	100	80	120	40

20. The following jobs are waiting to be processed at the same machine center:

Job	*Due Date*	*Duration (days)*	*Per Day Cost*
010	260	30	100
020	258	16	100
030	260	8	200
040	270	20	75
050	275	10	100

In what sequence would the jobs be ranked according to the following decision rules: (a) FCFS, (b) EDD, (c) SPT, (d) LPT, (e) TSPT, (f) LS, and (g) COVERT? All dates are specified as manufacturing planning calendar days. Assume that all jobs arrive on day 210. No job is allowed to wait more than fifty days.

21. The following jobs are waiting to be processed at the same machine center:

Job	*Date Order Received*	*Production Days Needed*	*Date Order Due*	*Cost of Delay ($)*
A	110	20	180	500
B	120	30	200	1,000
C	122	10	175	300
D	125	16	230	500
E	130	18	210	800

In what sequence would the jobs be ranked according to the following rules: (a) FCFS, (b) EDD, (c) SPT, (d) LPT, (e) TSPT, (f) LS, and (g)

COVERT? All dates are according to shop calendar days. No job is allowed to wait more than seventy days. Today on the planning calendar is day 130.

22. Suppose that today is day 150 on the planning calendar and that we have not yet started any of the jobs in problem 21. Using the critical ratio technique, in what sequence would you schedule these jobs?

23. Dotmat Data Processing Company estimates the data entry and verifying times for four jobs as follows:

Job	*Data Entry (hours)*	*Verify (hours)*
A	2.5	1.7
B	3.8	2.6
C	1.9	1.0
D	1.8	3.0

In what order should the jobs be done if the company has one operator for each job? Using a Gantt chart, show how long it will take to complete all four jobs.

24. Six jobs are to be processed through a two-step operation. The first operation involves preparation and the second involves painting. Processing times are as follows:

Job	*Opn 1 (hours)*	*Opn 2 (hours)*
A	10	5
B	7	4
C	5	7
D	3	8
E	2	6
F	4	3

Determine a sequence that will minimize the total completion time for these jobs. Using a Gantt chart, find the make span time.

25. Consider the following jobs and their processing times at the three machines. No passing of jobs is allowed.

Job	*Machine 1 (hours)*	*Machine 2 (hours)*	*Machine 3 (hours)*
A	6	4	7
B	5	2	4
C	9	3	10
D	7	4	5
E	11	5	2

Using Johnson's rule, find the sequence in which the jobs are to be processed.

26. Given the processing times for three consecutive operations: (a) find the optimal sequence for machines 1 and 2; (b) find the optimal sequence for machines 2 and 3; and (c) find the optimal sequence for the $N=5/M=3$ problem. If all sequences are the same, we have an optimal sequence for the $N/3$ problem. Verify the solution.

Job	*Machine 1*	*Machine 2*	*Machine 3*
A	3	6	7
B	5	3	2
C	1	2	4
D	6	8	9
E	7	5	4

27. Suppose that, in problem 25, a fourth operation was just added, with processing time on machine 4 given as 5, 7, 15, 3, and 4 hours, respectively, for jobs A through E. Using the CDS algorithm, find a near optimal solution. What is the make span time?

28. A list of jobs and their respective job durations is given here. The jobs can be processed by any one of three identical machines. Using the LPT rule, sequence these jobs.

Job	*Duration*
A	17
B	25
C	50
D	10
E	15
F	9
G	35
H	28
I	5
J	13

REFERENCES AND BIBLIOGRAPHY

1. *APICS Training Aid—Shop Floor Control* (Falls Church, VA.: American Production and Inventory Control Society, 1979).
2. K. R. Baker, *Introduction to Sequencing and Scheduling* (New York: Wiley, 1974).
3. E. S. Buffa and J. G. Miller, *Production-Inventory Systems: Planning and Control,* 3rd ed. (Homewood, Ill.: Richard D. Irwin, 1979).

4. H. G. Campbell, R. A. Dudek, and M. L. Smith, "A Heuristic Algorithm for the *n* Job, (*m*) Machine Sequencing Problem," *Management Science,* Vol. 16, No. 10 (June 1970), pp. 630–637.
5. D. C. Carroll, "Heuristic Sequencing of Single and Multiple Component Jobs." Unpublished Ph.D. dissertation, Sloan School of Management, MIT, 1965.
6. E. G. Coffman, ed., *Computer and Job Shop Scheduling Theory* (New York: Wiley, 1976).
7. R. W. Conway, W. L. Maxwell, and L. W. Miller, *Theory of Scheduling* (Reading, Mass.: Addison-Wesley, 1976).
8. S. E. Elmaghraby, "The Machine Sequencing Problem-Review and Extensions", *Naval Research Logistics Quarterly,* Vol. 15, No. 2, pp. 205–232.
9. J. H. Greene, ed., *Production and Inventory Control Handbook* (New York: McGraw-Hill, 1970).
10. L. A. Johnson and D. C. Montgomery, *Operations Research in Production Planning, Scheduling, and Inventory Control* (New York: Wiley, 1974).
11. S. M. Johnson, "Optimal Two- and Three-Stage Production Schedules with Setup Times Included," *Naval Research Logistics Quarterly,* Vol. 1, No. 1 (March 1954), pp. 61–68.
12. R. McNaughton, "Scheduling with Deadlines and Loss Functions," *Management Science,* Vol. 6, No. 1 (October 1959), pp. 1–12.
13. L. G. Mitten, "Sequencing *n* Jobs on Two Machines with Arbitrary Time Logs," *Management Science,* Vol. 5, No. 3 (April 1959), pp. 293–298.
14. Y. R. Nanot, "An Experimental Investigation and Comparative Evaluation of Priority Disciplines in Job Shop-Like Queueing Networks." Unpublished Ph.D. dissertation, UCLA, 1963.
15. S. L. Narasimhan and S. S. Panwalker, "A Heuristic Solution Procedure to Process Industry." Paper presented at the ORSA/TIME Annual Meeting, Detroit, April 1982.
16. J. Orlicky, *Material Requirements Planning* (New York: McGraw-Hill, 1975).
17. G. W. Plossl and O. W. Wight, *Production and Inventory Control* (Englewood Cliffs, N.J.: Prentice-Hall, 1967).
18. A. A. B. Pritsker, L. W. Miller, and R. J. Zinkl, "Sequencing *n* Products Involving *m* Independent Jobs on *m* Machines," *AIIE Transactions,* Vol. 3, No. 1 (1971), pp. 49–60.
19. A. O. Putnam, et al., "Updating Critical Ratio and Slack Time Priority Scheduling Rules," *Production and Inventory Management,* Vol. 12, No. 4 (1971), pp. 51–73.
20. M. K. Starr, *Operations Management* (Englewood Cliffs, N.J.: Prentice-Hall, 1978).
21. C. J. Teplitz, "MRP Can Work in Your Job Shop," *Production and Inventory Management,* Vol. 19, No. 4 (4th quarter, 1978), pp. 21–26.
22. W. L. Zangwill, "Deterministic Multiproduct, Multifacility Production and Inventory Model," *Operations Research,* Vol. 14, No. 3 (1966), pp. 486–507.

appendix 13A

"Factory of the Future": A Manufacturing Viewpoint

William J. Ehner
Manager

Frans R. Bax
Manager (retired), Process Technology
Motor Group Technology Operation
General Electric Co.
Fort Wayne, IN

Both practicing and theoretical experts have described the evolution or revolution which is about to reindustrialize the nation and perhaps many portions of the industrialized world.

Such descriptions all tend to have three characteristics:

First, the descriptions almost go beyond what can be accomplished in the real world of manufacturing.

Second, descriptions of the future are based on history, where current conditions are dissected as to the past causes and then extrapolations are made.

Third, all descriptions of the future are centered around the computer, and the chip revolution for integrating, linking, data analyzing and control.

If a manufacturing person were to begin to plan his own "plant of the future" based on those three precepts, he might well throw his hands in the air in despair. Let's take just the last item, for example. The impact of computers is clearly profound and pervasive. It has brought new concepts, such as flexible automation, and has sharply increased optimization of decisions by improving available data in quantity, quality and timeliness.

From *Production*, April, 1983. Reprinted with permission.

But to the practicing manufacturing people, this plethora of ideas, concepts, processes, hardware and software is often mind-boggling, and it tends to leave one even more unsure of which direction to take. One senses the gulf between these ideal factories described and those factories that we now have. Most of the concern for today and for tomorrow with most of us is with our existing factories and not the "then" or "sometime" factories—the new greenfields. One can suspect that the many shortfalls of forecasts for factories of the future are because the forecasts deal with new factories, not today's factories.

Today's Factories

The "now" factories can generally be divided into two types, each with its own characteristics. They are:

- **High Volume, fully/semi-dedicated with**

1. Narrow scope/mission, where the building, material handling facilities, special processes, etc., are directed to single, product-type manufacturing as with autos, lamps, appliances, etc., and with
2. High, fixed investment for one of a kind specializations of production facilities, such as fixed transfer lines, rolling mills, metal melting, dedicated conveyors or storage. They are
3. Subject to cloning when capacity demands, since capacity is rarely added sufficiently ahead of demand to allow basic innovations in manufacturing.
4. Plants of this type are usually built for predetermined fixed outputs, but are rarely operated at such levels. Upward or downward shifts in output require disproportionate factory personnel levels.
5. The negotiated pay rate system, with 8 hours pay for 6 hours work, resulted from many years of labor contract negotiations in which plant work concessions were made in the past but are no longer applicable with current manufacturing processes.

- **Low Volume, non-dedicated factories with**

1. High flexibilities directed to customized product manufacturing of a wide variety, only limited by available in-plant process technology usually consisting of standard machinery.
2. High inventories. Throughput of orders slow due to customized orders. Raw material stocks consist of a wide variety of basic materials (steel, aluminum, copper, etc.) and industrial components.
3. Long cycle times evolve because of upfront required engineering and design, and long leadtime of special components and material not carried in inventories.

4. High cost is caused by large engineering and design content per order, usually higher skilled and paid factory workforce, and substantially less "learning curve" productivity gain. Each order is a separate entity.
5. The "one of a type" customized order and less well defined business and factory load forecasting make detailed information systems suspect and often too costly.

PEOPLE

To all of this can be added such people phenomena as:

1. Indiscriminate layoff bumping in factories where seniority of workers is the only or predominant decision rule for employment rather than basic skills.
2. Finite and narrow maintenance crafts based on craft distinctions and training of ages ago (for example, iron worker, welder, machinist, bench repairman, toolmaker, etc.) and very often further divided in A, B or C classes.
3. Non-optional or non-flexible pay plans resulting from many years of company, or even industry-wide, labor contract negotiations where broad uniformity of pay scales was considered the only practical way of fairly dealing with large numbers of employees.
4. Simplistic man/machine systems to minimize training cost and expense of a very volatile factory workforce, jobs were broken down to the smallest and simplest activity.

The Factory of the Future

Contrast the characteristics of the "now" plant with what will be needed to operate tomorrow's plant:

1. High uptime plans of high investment, sophisticated process equipment requiring intensive training of operators, and employment stability or at least selection of employees based on skills and prior training.
2. Lots of instant care by maintenance specialists of broad capability and authority for the expensive and complicated new process technologies when malfunctions occur, doing whatever is necessary to get going again.
3. Higher people knowledge will be needed, using the broader societal educational base of the "new" workforce, to provide extensive

specialist training in new manufacturing concepts and processes with commensurate pay recognition for skill differentiation.

4. Sophisticated man/machine systems with fewer people are needed. Each operator will supervise numerous processes and equipments and has to be part of the total factory decision-making process.

SIMPLIFICATION BEGETS CONFUSION

What today's manufacturing person is looking for is the "renaissance" of existing factories, which may be very different from how to go about the "greenfields" of tomorrow.

Articles in many trade and business magazines on the "reindustrialization of America" base the futuristic factory on a progression of automation development but using current existing factory processes as a base.

First, there comes process automation or spot automation. This is followed by line or cell automation whereby specific individual, automated processes are combined in one package. To carry this to the next step, the concept of area or factory floor automation is defined. This involves the tie-in of multiple, automatic lines into one automatic system.

From here it is realized that the progression of factory automation can be attained only if the necessary factory data in itself is automated, which then constitutes the final dimension of automation. It is generally believed that this will lead to the unmanned, ultimately efficient "factory of the future."

This evolution is easy to perceive in the abstract macro view. It becomes much more difficult when viewed in the micro-step-after-micro-step that most factories will transition through. Independent relationships traded-off against interdependent relationships within hardware and software, combined with data bases that span factories—all this leaves a large gap between the visionaries and the practitioners. This simplification tends to put the manufacturing practitioner in a more, not less, confused state and questioning whether instant information is all that's really necessary to secure the elusive productivity targets.

Three Axes of Activity

We have found it helpful to break out all of our manufacturing activities into three categories. We call them "axes" and we use these three axes to help us sort out activities and areas of greatest potential benefit.

We also feel very strongly that any attempt to plan manufacturing improvements must begin with knowledge of the plant's product plans two, five and ten years out.

Here are the three categories of manufacturing activities, or "axes":

AXIS X—PARTSMAKER

Activities to change the condition, nature or function; includes such processes as stamping, forming, casting, molding, welding, chip cutting, chemical and other metallurgical processes, near-net-shape processes, painting, coating, and activities related to control, improve, speed up, combine or replace above common processes.

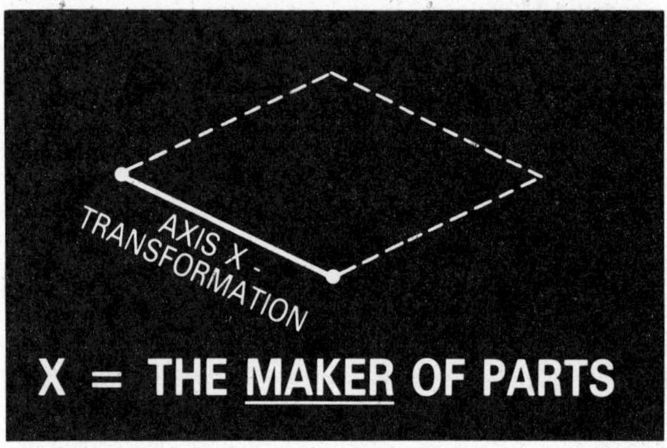

AXIS Y—MOVER/ASSEMBLER

Activities to bring to completion the entire endeavor; includes all material handling from tote pans and material mover to automatic stacker system, automatic guided vehicle system, forklifts, synchronous and non-synchronous conveyors, all assembly activities of any kind, and all storage activities.

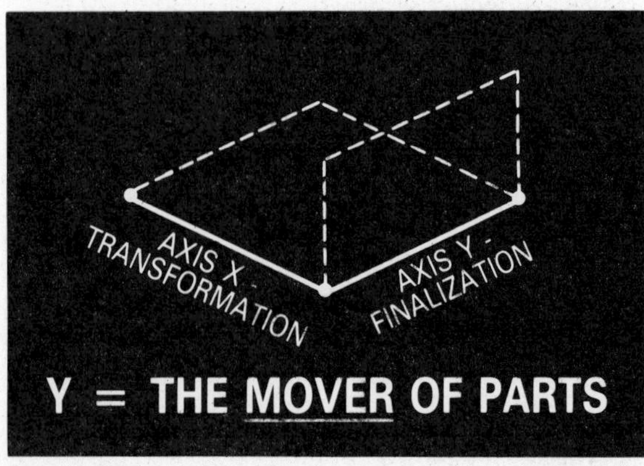

AXIS Z—INFORMATION

Activities to acquire, store, retrieve, and analyze data; includes all test, inspection functions, vision, sensors, all data-gathering functions from expeditor with clipboard to electronic part recognition, from MRP to production control, to inventory control, to cost control. This axis can also be viewed as the factory timer. It sets the speed at which Axis X can flow through Axis Y, and has as a role the economical minimization of time between order and shipment.

There are obviously many more commonly known manufacturing activities, but we believe all of them can be assigned to their predominant function on the X, Y or Z axis.

It should be noted that product engineering and design activities are not specifically mentioned in this matrix. Examination of those activities will show a preponderance in the Z axis.

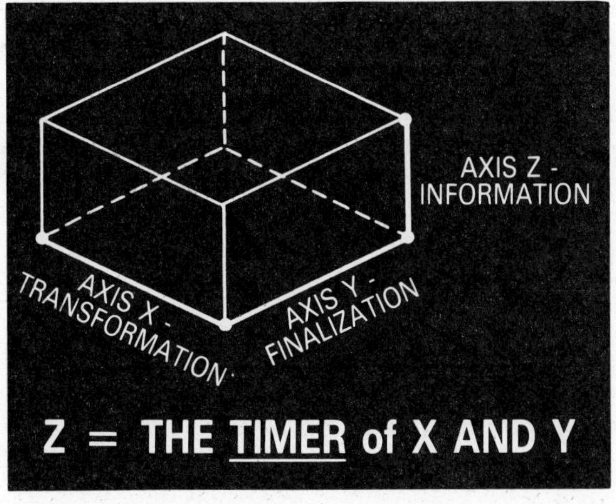

TWO AXIOMS

A further study of the factory model indicates two distinct axioms in its application.

First, the X, Y and Z axes are *not* mutually exclusive but as new technologies emerge and are applied, X, Y and Z become increasingly interdependent. Metal turning and boring manufacturing processes have fundamentally not changed much (X growth) over the years (mostly higher speeds and new cutting tool materials). However, process economics were enhanced considerably by Z growth through NC, CNC and now DNC in past decades. More recently, Y growth occurred for again increased productivity by the addition of robotic material handling and making the X process part of a manufacturing cell. Recently popularized "machining cell" concepts resulted from very low X growth (relatively stable processes) with modest Y growth (use of commercially available material handling), and with enormous Z growth (all phases of computer dependent programs—CAD/CAM).

Secondly, the X, Y and Z axes are mutually competitive and trade-offs between X, Y and Z, in particular between Y and Z, are available to arrive at the same desired goal of efficiency and productivity. The Japanese industries, in particular their automotive component industries, have a heavy emphasis on flexible automation with minimum inventories. Their approach to flexible automation runs about as follows: Raw material in the form of metal strips, bulk plastic molding material, other steel components, fasteners feed into the system through multiple flexible partmaking processes (X), and from there move directly to the nonsynchronous assembly lines (Y). At specific points test and adjust operations are performed to assure optimum end of line quality (Z). Such production processes are targeted at very high outputs with one or few operators for the total system. Ergo, modest X (again stable known processes), very large Y (intricate material handling, short cycle, flexible assembly) and very low Z (few people, continuous flow, simple production, inventory and cost control).

WASTE CONCEPT IN KANBAN

- SETUP
- MAINTENANCE
- INVENTORIES
- MATERIAL HANDLING/STORAGE

AND

- FACTORY INFORMATION

Assuming relatively stable X process conditions, some general statements can be made relative to Y and Z interdependence and competition:

- Mediocre Y plus exquisite Z = highly undesirable
- Exquisite Y plus mediocre Z = attractive
- Exquisite Y plus exquisite Z = highly desirable

Of course, all within the norms of economical application.

WHAT ADDS VALUE?

Still another way of looking at X, Y and Z would be their effect on value added to the end product. By definition, all X processes add to the targeted product value. Only part of Y processes (assembly and finishing) add to the targeted product value. All remaining Y processes and all Z processes do *not* add to product value but do, however, control the speed by which the parts move through a factory. This concept is very elegantly expressed by the Japanese Kanban System denoted by Mr. Kiichiro Toyoda. In this approach the concept of waste includes (other than the normal scrap, rework and extra cost operations):

- Setup activities
- Maintenance activities
- Inventory activities
- Material handling and storage activities, and to this list can be added
- Factory information

All of these activities should be driven to zero as best as could be done to gain optimum efficiency and productivity.

It is, of course, not possible to drive setup, maintenance, inventory, material handling, storage, software and information to zero since they are all interdependent. It does, however, demonstrate that none adds value to the product, and none is obviously more or less desirable than another. In essence, Y and Z functions are to be regarded as "service" activities to the X function. The extraordinary emphasis on Z activities in recent years is, in part, the phenomena of transition to a service economy. They are all speed controllers—all in place to get the desired part transformation (X axis) through the factory's Y axis as fast as possible in an economical manner.

OPPORTUNITIES FOR IMPROVEMENT

The rate of technological change in each axis is of great interest both to the technologist and to the business planner. Synergistic opportunities by blending axis changes are also of interest.

The segregation by axis of high change areas defines three lists of potentials that must be monitored and acted upon.

In the X axis all commonly known processes probably can be eliminated from the list of high changes in technology. However, the assumption that X is fairly stable should be challenged in the light of worldwide energy and material supply conditions and trends. So, potential high technology change rates for Axis X are:

- *Massive Fast Material Removal* such as continuous creep feed grinding or laser (assisted) machining.
- *Minimal Material Removal*—Near-net-shape processes, such as scrap metal extrusion, powder metallurgy, liquid phase sintering, fast plastic molding, directional/controlled flow casting.
- *Composites* such as graphite/glass reinforced high-performance material.

X THE PARTSMAKER

Basic processes used to transform materials and semi-finished parts into the end products of your plant

YOUR NOW PLANT

Process	Present Applications	% of End Product Costs
1. Metal Removal	a. ______	______
	b. ______	______
	c. ______	______
	d. ______	______
	e. ______	______
	f. ______	______
2. Metal Forming	a. ______	______
	b. ______	______
	c. ______	______
	d. ______	______
3. Casting	a. ______	______
	b. ______	______
	c. ______	______
4. Molding	a. ______	______
	b. ______	______
5. Welding/Joining	a. ______	______
	b. ______	______
	c. ______	______
6. Cleaning	a. ______	______
	b. ______	______
	c. ______	______
7. Painting/Plating	a. ______	______
	b. ______	______
	c. ______	______
8. Heat Treating	a. ______	______
	b. ______	______
	c. ______	______
9. Other	a. ______	______
	b. ______	______
	c. ______	______
	d. ______	______

Note: Evaluations of X processes, and the potentials for improvement, are vital in determining priorities for near and long-term effectiveness. Equally vital is knowledge of what changes your plant will be making in products, product sizes, product mixes, etc., over the next two, five and ten years. This knowledge will directly affect your process decisions and progress toward your factory of the future.

OPPORTUNITIES TO IMPROVE All improvements must be evaluated in combination with their impact on Y and Z variables. Also, look for ways to *eliminate* processes; e.g., near-net shape might eliminate chipmaking.

YOUR FUTURE PLANT

Potential Improvements/ New Applications	**Estimate Productivity/Cost Contribution in Percentage (total of 3 stages = 100%)** 2 Years	5 Years	10 Years
E.G.: Better machines, cutting tools, EDM, ECM, laser, etc. ______	______	______	______
______	______	______	______
E.G.: Machine developments, near-net shape processes, tooling, closer-tolerance fine blanking, etc. ______	______	______	______
E.G.: Permanent mold, lost wax, automatic processes, etc. ______	______	______	______
E.G.: Closer-tolerance processes, better mold design, thinner walls, etc. ______	______	______	______
E.G.: More automatic power sources, wire improvements, etc. ______	______	______	______
E.G.: Mechanical cleaning, new chemicals, elimination of contamination, etc. ______	______	______	______
E.G.: New coatings, powders, material which does not require coating, etc. ______	______	______	______
E.G.: Vacuum, material change, other processes, etc. ______	______	______	______
______	______	______	______

Y PARTS MOVERS HANDLERS/ASSEMBLERS

Activities that support and bring the manufacturing operation to completion

YOUR NOW PLANT

Activity	Present Applications	Time/Cost Receiving to Shipping
1. **Material Handling:** lift truck, hand trucks, conveyors, cranes, tote pans, pallets, feeders, robots, automatic guided vehicles, etc.	a. ______ b. ______ c. ______	a. ______ b. ______ c. ______
2. **Storage:** Bins, skids, tote pans, retrieval systems, stacker cranes, etc.	a. ______ b. ______ c. ______	a. (include cost of inventory) b. ______ c. ______
3. **Assembly:** Manual, power tools, power assists, synchronous line, semi-automatic, automatic, etc.	a. ______ b. ______ c. ______	a. (% of total mfg. cost) b. ______ c. ______

Note: While many plants are adequate in X and much attention is being paid to Z ("getting control"), many plants will find their best opportunities here, in handling, storing and assembly. Excellent control of a mediocre operation is futile.

OPPORTUNITIES TO IMPROVE All improvements must be evaluated in combination with their impact on X and Z variables. Also, look for ways to *eliminate* processes; e.g., inventories or buffer storage ahead of machines can be cut if a catastrophic breakdown is handled as such rather than being anticipated and expected.

YOUR FUTURE PLANT

Potential Improvements/ New Applications	**Estimated Productivity/Cost Contribution in Percentage (total of 3 stages = 100%)**		
	2 Years	5 Years	10 Years
E.G.: Re-layout/rearrangement of plant equipment, manufacturing cells, robotics, flexible systems, automated vehicles, system technology, etc. ______	______	______	______
E.G.: Stacker systems, automatic MRP and retrieval, etc. ______	______	______	______
E.G.: Equipment/methods change; processes to eliminate; closer tolerances to simplify; more automatic equipment, etc. ______	______	______	______

Z THE TIMER/ INFORMATION

Activities for controlling the rate at which and the accuracy with which plant operations are performed and coordinated. The controller of costs, output, quality and time.

YOUR NOW PLANT

Process	Present Method	Impact on X & Y
1. Inspect/Test	a. ______	______
	b. ______	______
	c. ______	______
	d. ______	______
2. Process/Machine Control	a. ______	______
	b. ______	______
	c. ______	______
	d. ______	______
3. Production Control	a. ______	______
	b. ______	______
	c. ______	______
	d. ______	______
4. Inventory Control	a. ______	______
	b. ______	______
	c. ______	______
	d. ______	______
5. Materials Planning (requirements & scheduling)	a. ______	______
	b. ______	______
	c. ______	______
	d. ______	______
6. Operations Reporting (including shop floor control)	a. ______	______
	b. ______	______
	c. ______	______
	d. ______	______

Note: New and developing information technologies (especially with computers) become truly significant only when they help to get control of already good performance of X (partsmaking) and Y (handling and inspection).

Maxim: Mediocre Y plus exquisite Z — Undesirable
Exquisite Y plus mediocre Z — Attractive
Exquisite Y plus exquisite Z — Desirable

OPPORTUNITIES TO IMPROVE Assuming a competitive process (X) and efficient material movement (Y), an objective might be to have the minimum amount of control/information (Z) to assure that the other two function superbly.

YOUR FUTURE PLANT

Potential Improvements/ New Applications	Estimate Productivity/Cost Contribution in Percentage (total of 3 stages = 100%)		
	2 Years	5 Years	10 Years
E.G.: Integrated gaging systems; sensors; semiautomatic, automatic gaging ______	______	______	______
E.G.: CNC, adaptive control, etc., Flexible Manufacturing Systems ______	______	______	______
E.G.: Computerized data collection, analysis, communication ______	______	______	______
E.G.: Computerization, etc. ______	______	______	______
E.G.: Computerization, etc. ______	______	______	______
E.G.: Computerization, etc. ______	______	______	______

- *Recycle/Recovery* examples of which are scrap metal extrusion, cold flow casting, ultra high pressure steel forging.
- *New Metal Forming* such as spin forming or flow turning.
- *Metal Conversion* as with amorphous metals.
- *Process Equipment Miniaturizations*.

In the Y Axis, the high technology area develops from the trends toward product proliferation, shortened product design life and rapid customer response. Probable areas are:

- *Flexible Assembly Systems* with nonsynchronous conveyances and robots, station skipping, parallel spurs, kit formations, instantaneous setup changes.
- *Robotics* with emphasis on grippers, compliance, fixturing, speed, response.
- *Component Identification* with new sensors as vision, laser, position orientation in physical state, part feeders.
- *System Technology* including robot modules, servo devices and controls, product structuring, process capability vs. compatibility, simulators and optimization, nondestructive shutdown (soft landing) component quality, risk assessments.

It is felt that the degree of change in flexible automation is profound and virtually impossible to overstate.

The Z axis is currently receiving the most attention because of the seemingly limitless opportunity presented by the chip revolution. It is, however, sobering to remember that Axis Z does not contribute to the product value in a factory, but rather establishes the speed of Axis X movement through Axis Y. Undoubtedly, the enormous emphasis on the "service" response of manufacturers to meet the new consumer demands in product variety makes the factory speed a critical issue to success of the enterprise.

The Z axis consists of both hardware and software segments, hardware to accumulate, transmit and display data and software to analyze and digest data.

Areas of particular interest are:

- *Testing* with all its new emphasis on quantification and classification, calibration and feedback, nondestructive test, data retention/retrieval, self-diagnostics, signature analysis.
- *Sensing* in its full scope with optics, tactile, acoustics, thermal, pressure, dimensional, chemical, electrical, laser.
- *Controls*, not so much the X process controls but architecture, algorithm, computer compatibility, actuator compatibility, distributed systems.

- *Communications* with emphasis on interface definition, data discipline, display apparatus, networking, real time integration, system security, hardware reliability and self-diagnostics.
- *Processing* with its scope of algorithms, computer compatibility, data compression, architecture, data retention/retrieval.
- *System* in all of its sophistication including architecture and manufacturing strategy, data base structure, data flow and integration, generic software for manufacturing, systems modeling, diagnostic and prognostic analysis.
- *Hardware* and systems compatibility, factory environment compatibility, hardware/software trade-offs, communication linkage.

FOUR EVOLUTIONS

The X, Y, Z analysis suggests what might well happen to the renaissance of today's factories to tomorrow's factories of the future. This change is seen as four distinct evolutions introducing "state-of-the-art" technologies in the "now" factories.

FOUR EVOLUTIONS FOR CURRENT FACTORIES

1. ESTABLISHMENT OF MFG. CELLS
   EMPHASIZE Y
2. OPTIMIZE REMAINING & GENERIC MFG. UNITS
   EMPHASIZE X
3. INFORMATION INTEGRATION OF CELLS AND UNITS
   EMPHASIZE Z
4. UNMANNED OPERATION OF CELLS AND UNITS
   EMPHASIZE Y,X,Z

1. **Establishment of Manufacturing Cells** with integration of X, Y, and Z and ranging from
—Robots between machining equipments to
—Large flexible transfer lines to
—Part fabrication directly coupled to
—Assembly and test
And having as predominant characteristics:
—Excellent material movement

—Low inventory
—Fast throughput and cycle times
—Automatic scheduling
—Automatic setup between models
Or in other words:

- Superb Y
- Excellent Z
- It is hoped good-excellent X

With prime emphasis on Y—the mover of the factory.

2. **Optimization of Remaining, Generic Manufacturing Units** ranging from part fabrication to assembly in those activities where synergistic use of investments (punch press, casting, molding, heat treat) provide maximum utilization. This is also the area where the new "X" will play the heaviest role and having as predominant characteristics:
—Minimum material use and content
—Minimum labor content
—Minimum inventory
Or in other words:

- Optimum X
- Modest Y in move and assembly
- Excellent Z for scheduling and control

With prime emphasis on X—the maker of the factory.

3. **Information Integration of Cells and Units**—the arena where the "timer" of the factory makes its biggest productivity contribution. It is here that all cells and units have information tie-in with the complete and total factory, where cells and units, each with their particular computer control configuration are brought together in a system of data handling and control hierarchy, if necessary with human interfaces as a start and having as predominant characteristics:
—Minimum time between cells/units
—Optimum schedule realization
—Minimal inventory backup
—Centralized plant-wide control
Or in other words:

- Exquisite Z—the timer of the factory.

4. **Fully Unmanned Operation of Cells and Units**—This is where our manufacturing people finally have the resolve to turn the lights off in the

factory, full of the noise of operating equipment, and go home. Ranging, probably selective at first, from parts fabrication to assembly, with characteristics of:
—Human and equipment safety controls
—Reliable material handling
—Safe shutdown features (soft landing)
—Substantially reduced labor
—Optimum utilization of fixed investment
—Continuous off-shift operations
Or in other words:

- Optimum Y
- Reliable X
- Expanded Z (sensors)

With prime emphasis on Y but supported by strong X and Z.

It is suggested that the change from "now" to "then"—from today's factories to tomorrow's factories—will follow this evolutionary path of progress. It will require full emphasis on X, Y and Z. It will be different in time and progression between different factories and different product lines but this renaissance will include all features at some time. It is up to the manufacturing people of today to define this strategy and lay a program to accomplish their own vision of the "factory of the future." But we must start now.

chapter fourteen

Job Shop Production Activity Control

The production activity planning chapter dealt with many important aspects of planning, such as scheduling, loading, and sequencing. The rules learned in that chapter can be used to calculate how long it will take to complete any job and to specify start and want dates. Remember, however, that rules and computer systems cannot cut chips and will not get jobs through the shop. A basic function of any planning system is to identify the necessary materials, tooling, and labor skill levels. Once this is done, the control functions must coordinate the production effort and communicate the results effectively to all concerned. This results in good customer relations and savings for the firm.

Dispatching

Dispatching is a production control function that is performed by a dispatcher—a production control person who coordinates with the manufacturing department. The dispatcher maintains a file of all open orders related to his or her department, whether or not they are released. This file is known as the *dead load file*. Once a job is released to the dispatcher's department, that order is kept in the *live load file*. Between the time the order reaches the department and the time the material arrives, the dispatcher issues a dispatch list, which authorizes the manufacturing department to produce the item. Subsequently, a shop packet is issued, consisting of detailed drawing specifications, a bill of materials, a route sheet, a shop order, tickets for materials and tools, and any other information deemed necessary. The dispatcher is also responsible for maintaining an accurate and up-to-date shop order file, using forms or computer terminals.

Dept.:		310					Date:	10/1/82
Work Center:							Capacity:	40 hrs./wk.
Part No	Start Order No	Opn No	Description	Qty	Hours	Operation Start	Dates Due	Order Due Date
A112	110	0100	Drilling	100	10.0	10/1/82	10/4/82	10/9/82
C315	98	0040	Milling	100	10.0	10/5/82	10/6/82	10/13/82
B512	117	0020	Reaming	400	20.0	10/5/82	10/10/82	10/15/82
							Priority	
		Total Standard Hours			40.0			

FIGURE 14.1 Sample dispatch list

The dispatch list, which is the key document for priority control, is generally prepared by computer. This list consists of all jobs that are available to run. They are ranked by priority, using rules such as the critical ratio technique. The dispatch list is the vehicle used for formal communication; a sample is exhibited in figure 14.1. Many commercial devices are available to assist the dispatcher in preparing the dispatch list. The simplest device, of course, is a Gantt load chart. In addition, modern electronic communication equipment, such as the teletype, data collection terminals, and other data transmission devices is also available.

Corrections to Short-Term Capacity

The dispatch list is generally prepared for a short period of time. We should never schedule (input) more than what we can complete (output) within the time frame specified by the dispatch list. If a capacity shortage is detected, corrective actions must be taken. The most common corrective actions [2] are (1) scheduling overtime, (2) selecting alternative routings, (3) reallocating work force, (4) operation overlapping, (5) lot splitting, (6) order splitting, and (7) subcontracting. Some of these tactics are exhibited in figure 14.2, and we will discuss them briefly here.

ALTERNATIVE ROUTINGS

Generally, we schedule jobs through the most efficient machines and methods so that the due dates are met. This approach might lead to overload

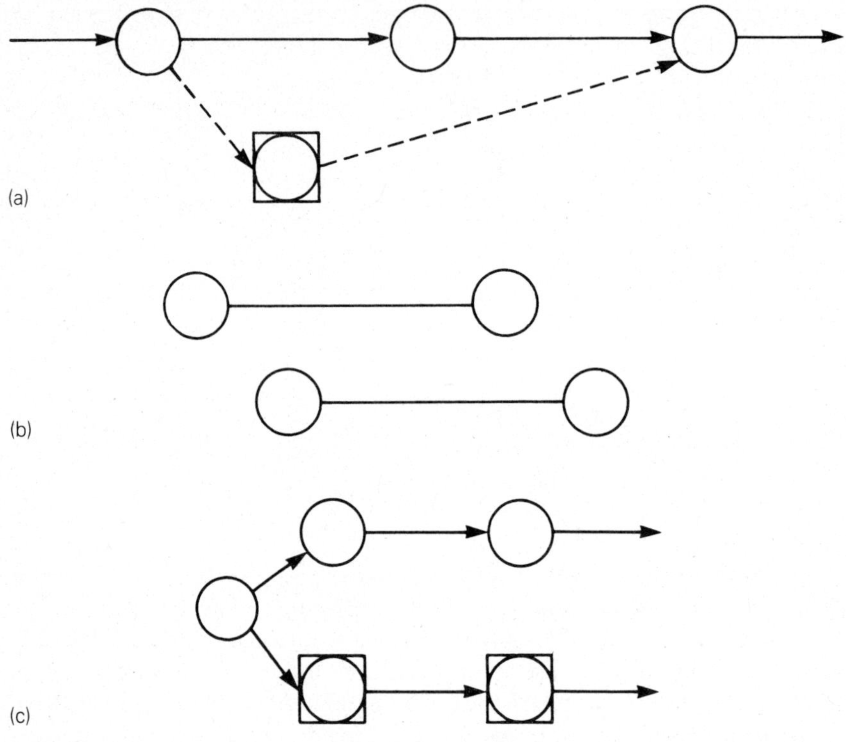

FIGURE 14.2 Corrective actions: (a) alternative routings; (b) overlapping; (c) lot splitting

situations at some critical work centers, however. By routing some jobs to alternative machines, we might be able to gain additional capacity, even though it may not be the most efficient procedure. The trade-offs involved in alternative routing should be fully explored. The route sheet may already indicate alternative routings for accommodating emergency situations.

OVERLAPPING

Overlapping involves sending part of the first lot to the next machine center immediately, so that the second machine center can get a head start. Then the lot sizing rules may be followed as usual. This approach reduces the total lead time of the job. Overlapping may be designated as standard for certain operations, especially when additional setups can be avoided.

LOT SPLITTING

Jobs are completed in lots, and they generally are not moved to the next work station until the entire lot is completed. In many instances, it is possible to send a partial lot ahead of time, thus preventing idle time in the succeeding machine centers. Decreasing idle time essentially increases capacity. For example, suppose that ten additional pieces are scrapped during an operation but that an order quantity of fifty is being produced in the previous operation, which cannot be expedited. As an alternative, the order quantity of fifty can be split into ten and forty, and ten pieces can be expedited ahead of time. This reduces the delay for the order that had ten excess scraps and effectively prevents idle time of machines. Note that overlapping generally occurs at the beginning of a job, whereas lot splitting can occur at any time prior to completion of the job.

Example 14.1

Consider the following jobs on a dispatch list.

Job	*Opn 10, Milling (hours)*	*Opn 20, Drilling (hours)*	*Due Date*
A	40	24	140
B	80	16	141
C	24	40	146

Assuming a forty-hour work week, determine whether it is possible to meet the due dates. If not, what alternative actions can the manager, Smarty, take to complete the jobs on time?

Solution: Assuming that the machines are available right away, the schedule chart would be as exhibited in figure 14.3.

Smarty finds from the process sheet that the first operation of job A can be done by an alternative machine, but it will take fifty-six hours. Based on this additional information, he develops the schedule chart shown in figure 14.4.

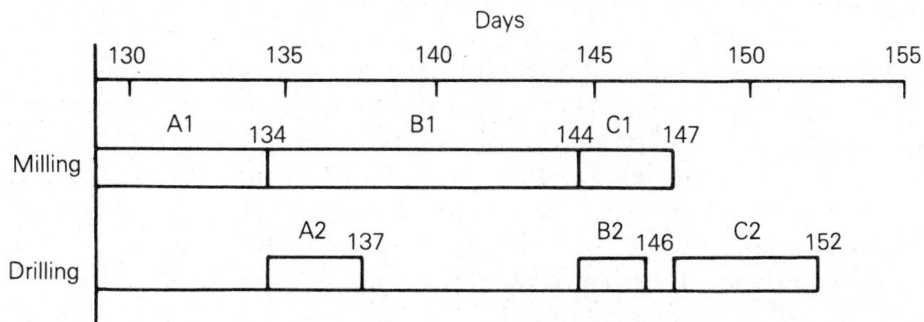

FIGURE 14.3 Schedule chart for Example 14.1

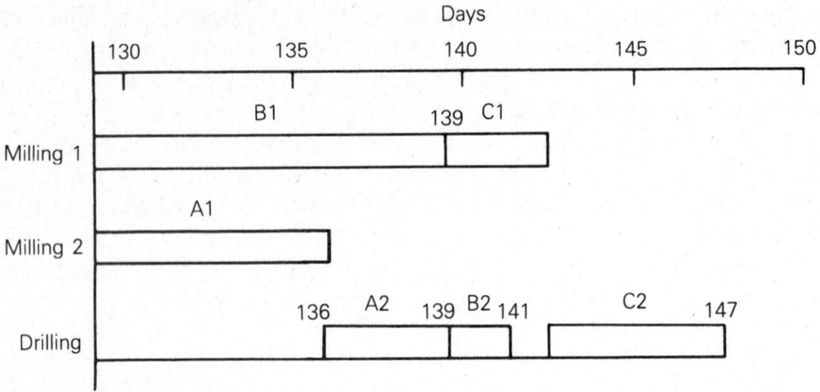

FIGURE 14.4 Revised schedule chart for Example 14.1

He finds that jobs A and B meet the due dates but that job C would be a day behind. Realizing that the process sheet is an important source of information, he finds out that part of job C can be sent ahead to a drilling machine. The lot splitting and overlapping not only eliminate idle time on the drilling machine but also result in completing all jobs on or before the due dates. Note that lot splitting and overlapping generally contribute to additional materials handling costs.

ORDER SPLITTING

Large orders can be split and run on several machines simultaneously, thus reducing the processing lead time. Such decisions are generally made during activity planning stages, and each split order is rescheduled as a separate order.

Production Reporting and Status Control

Manufacturing feedback to the production schedule is done by production reporting. Production reporting helps manufacturing take corrective actions on maintenance of valid priorities of on-hand and on-order jobs. The reporting covers delays in scheduled performance, the efficiency of the shop, the productivity of the workers, and the utilization of capacity. The information is derived from schedules, job authorizations, and job documents, such as the move ticket and the labor ticket, the scrap and rework reports, inventory receipts, and material usage reports, as shown in table 14.1. The reporting also includes operation completions, order closings, and necessary information to assist the payroll department.

TABLE 14.1 Status Reports and Information Sources

Information	*Sources*
Delays	Schedules
Capacity utilization	Job authorizations
Schedule performance	Job documents
Machine efficiency	
Operator productivity	

Factors Affecting the Completion Time of Jobs

The fact that the dispatch list is issued and the operational sequence is defined does not guarantee the completion of jobs on time. Many unplanned and unforeseen circumstances arise in the real world. Machines can break down. A key operator can be absent. A rush order from a preferred customer may force us to reschedule, and when we try to reschedule, we might find that we do not have enough capacity or that our lead time is too high to satisfy so valuable a customer. Reporting the delay does not solve the problem. Therefore, it is important for us to understand how to reduce the lead time of jobs and to learn how to accommodate many emergency situations. A detailed discussion of manufacturing lead time and in-process inventories (queues) will help us in mapping a strategy for coping with such situations [5].

Example 14.2

Friendly Company uses a block scheduling rule for calculating estimated completion dates. Usually, the durations of operations are rounded up to the nearest week. One week is allowed for releasing the order and withdrawing material from the stock room. Two weeks are permitted between operations and one week for final inspection and delivery. Calculate the feasible promise dates for jobs A and B, for which the route sheet is as follows:

	Job A		*Job B*	
OPERATION	WORK CENTER	TIME (HOURS)	WORK CENTER	TIME (HOURS)
I	3	160	3	40
II	4	120	2	200
III	1	200	4	80

This is week 28 on the planning calendar. Given the due dates for jobs A and B as week 44 and week 38, respectively, can we complete them on time?

Solution: Assuming a five-day, forty-hour work week, the number of weeks required for every operation in all departments can be calculated. Using

TABLE 14.2 Block Schedule for Example 14.2

	Job A		*Job B*	
Operation	*Weeks Allowed*	*Week Number*	*Weeks Allowed*	*Week Number*
This week		28		28
Release date	1	29	1	29
I	4	33	1	30
Interoperation	2	35	2	32
II	3	38	5	37
Interoperation	2	40	2	39
III	5	45	2	41
Inspect and deliver	1	46	1	42

the block scheduling rule, we estimate the completion dates for jobs A and B as week 46 and week 42, respectively. Thus, according to the schedule (table 14.2), jobs A and B cannot be completed by the due date.

MANUFACTURING LEAD TIME

The manufacturing lead time of a job is the interval between its release to the shop floor and its delivery to stores or higher-level operations. Although lead times are made up of several time elements, they fall into two major categories: (1) operation duration and (2) interoperation time. Operation duration is the time the job actually spends on the machine. It consists of setup time and run time, which is also referred to as production time (see figure 14.5):

$$\text{Operation duration} = \text{setup time} + \text{run time}$$
$$= S + R$$

Interoperation time refers to the interval between the completion of one operation and the start of the subsequent operation. It is defined as

$$\text{Interoperation time} = \text{wait time} + \text{move time} + \text{queue time}$$
$$= W + M + Q$$

Thus, total lead time can be defined as

$$\text{Total lead time} = \text{operation duration} + \text{interoperation time}$$
$$= S + R + W + M + Q$$

Operation Duration

Operation duration is the actual production time of the job. It depends on the lot size. The necessary data for calculating operation times are given

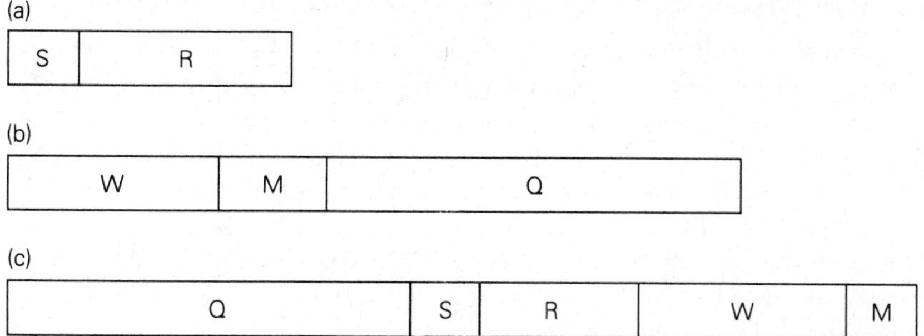

FIGURE 14.5 Elements of manufacturing lead time: (a) operation duration; (b) interoperation time; (c) lead time

by the manufacturing route sheet, which is also known as the process sheet. The calculation of operation duration was dealt with in detail in the chapter on capacity planning.

Interoperation Time

Interoperation time is the time the job waits in the work center queue after the completion of any operation and before the start of the next operation on the same job or order. In high-volume assembly lines, work flows from station to station continuously, and hence the accumulation of in-process inventory between work centers is minimal or negligible. The interoperation times in assembly lines usually are very short. In the job shop environment, however, the work centers are farther apart. Depending on the work content of jobs, the loads among machine centers vary considerably. Overloads at work centers increase interoperation time. The interoperation time is the primary determinant of the lead time. In fact, up to 85% of manufacturing lead time is interoperation time. Therefore, the total lead time can be reduced by cutting the fat from the interoperation time [10].

Queue Time

Queue time is the time that a job spends at a machine waiting to be worked on because there are other jobs ahead of it. Recall that the priority of each job is specified by a sequencing rule. Regardless of the shuffling of the sequences of jobs at work centers, however, the total work load at each center remains the same. The queue time of an individual job is affected by the priority assigned to it.

Move Time

Move time is the actual time a job spends in transit between operations. It is also referred to as transport time. Move time depends on the location of the two work centers involved. Time values for it can be provided in a matrix format.

Wait Time

The term *wait time* is usually applied to the time a job spends waiting before being transported to the next operation and after completion of the prior operation. Note that all elements of lead time except move time are work center-dependent. It is not necessary to specify all time elements for every work center. However, it is desirable to specify all elements as accurately as possible for critical work centers where close control is needed. In other instances, all elements can be lumped as a single value, such as one day or one week. Once a time estimate has been specified, it should be monitored for accuracy periodically.

Example 14.3

Even though the block schedule indicates that the jobs can not be completed on time (see Example 14.2), Friendly Company wants to review the situation in detail. Since the shop is not usually busy at this time of the year, the manager decides that he can get by with one week between operations. Draw a finite forward schedule chart based on this additional information, given the due dates as weeks 44 and 38 for jobs A and B, respectively, and this is week 28 on the planning calendar.

Solution: Table 14.3 summarizes all available data pertaining to the route sheet and the machine center capacities. Next, we develop a Gantt schedule chart. Since jobs A and B need machine 3 simultaneously, we calculate the critical ratios (CR) for these jobs:

$$\text{CR(A)} = \frac{44 - 28}{\frac{160}{40} + \frac{120}{40} + \frac{200}{40}} = \frac{16}{12} = 1.33$$

$$\text{CR(B)} = \frac{38 - 28}{\frac{40}{40} + \frac{200}{40} + \frac{80}{40}} = \frac{10}{8} = 1.25$$

Since job B has a smaller critical ratio, we schedule it on machine 3 first. It is followed by job A, as exhibited in figure 14.6. In the figure, BI, for example, represents the first operation of job B. As they are completed

TABLE 14.3 Load and Capacity Data, Example 14.3

	Job A			*Job B*		
Operation	*Work Center*	*Load (hrs.)*	*Capacity (hrs./wk.)*	*Work Center*	*Load (hrs.)*	*Capacity (hrs./wk.)*
I	3	160	40	3	40	40
II	4	120	40	2	200	40
III	1	200	40	4	80	40

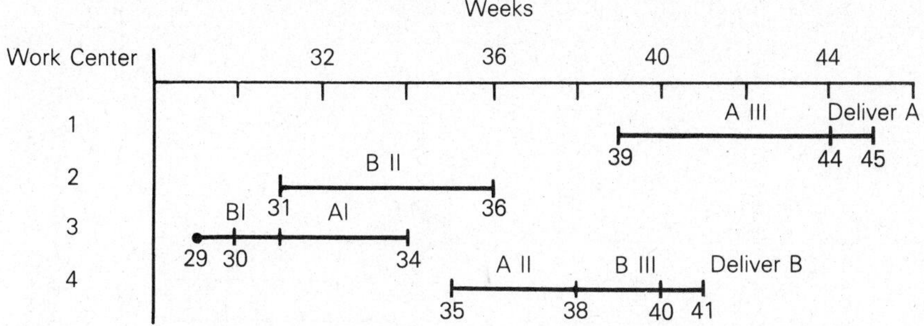

FIGURE 14.6 Gantt schedule chart for Example 14.3

on machine center 3, job B is moved to machine center 2, whereas job A is moved to machine center 4. Note that we permit one week between operations. Then job A goes to machine center 1, whereas job B goes to machine center 4 for the final operations. We see that jobs A and B are completed by weeks 45 and 41, respectively. Unfortunately, Friendly Company is still unable to complete these jobs before their respective due dates.

QUEUE LENGTH (IN PROCESS INVENTORY)

Many managers ask what the optimum length of a queue is. They all know that a queue serves as insurance against idle time. Queues absorb changes in efficiency, randomness in job length, scrap, product mix, and changes in job arrival time. Queues will fluctuate as a result of (1) over- and understatements of the master production schedule, (2) excess or inadequate capacity, and (3) changes in product mix. Therefore, in a job shop situation, it is very difficult to specify or attain an optimum queue length. In practice, however, it is possible to graph the distribution of queue length as the number of work hours waiting at intervals. Some typical distributions are shown in figure 14.7. Diagram (a) portrays a situation with a desirable queue. The distribution of queue length is approximately normally distributed. It indicates that various factors influencing the queue size occur randomly. Note that the queue size is rarely zero, amounting to a very small idle time. Diagram (b) indicates the situation in which a persistent backlog exists. The queue size is always above ninety hours. If this center produces thirty hours of work per day, then the manufacturing lead time can be reduced by three days (90/30) by reducing the average queue size by ninety hours, still resulting in a negligible amount of idle time. Reducing the unnecessary buffer would reduce the lead time of all future orders. The queue represented by diagram (c) is short. It could contribute to a persistent underload situation. Finally, diagram (d) portrays a work center with a highly variable queue length. It indicates frequent overload situations [5]. Using such diagrams, it is possible to calculate the approximate amount of desirable queues for particular machine centers.

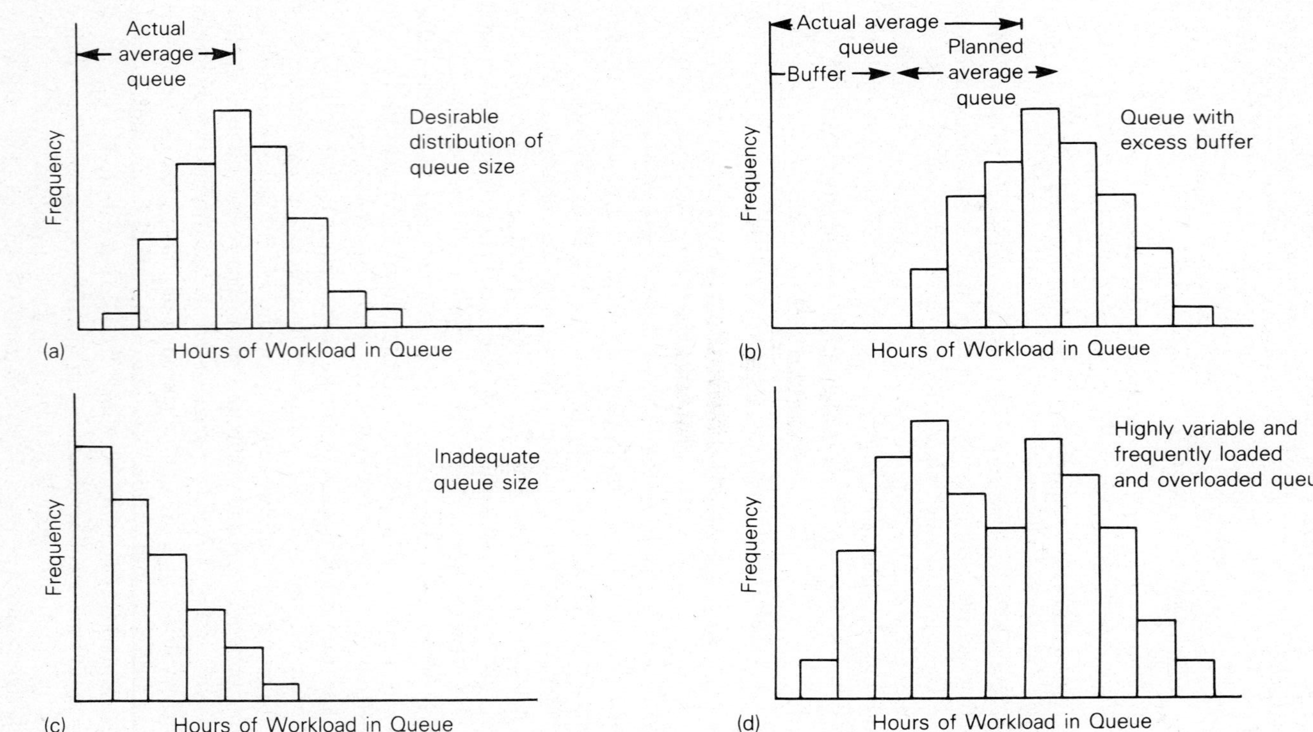

FIGURE 14.7 Queue distributions: (a) controlled queue; (b) excessive queue; (c) underloaded center; (d) uncontrolled queue Adapted by permission from *COPICS*, Volume 5, First edition, p. 16. © 1972 by International Business Machines Corporation.

Example 14.4

Suppose that a work center has an average queue size of 600 hours, with a standard deviation (σ) of 80 hours. The manager is a very conservative individual, who does not want to run out of work more than one in two hundred chances. The capacity of the work center is 160 hours per week. Assuming that the queue size is normally distributed, what queue size should we recommend? By how much can we safely afford to reduce the queue size? What alternatives do we have to attain the desired queue level?

Solution: The queue out risk is specified as one in two hundred, or $\alpha =$ .005 probability. Using normal probability tables, we find the value of $z = -3.29$. The desired average queue length (μ) can then be calculated using the following formula:

$$z = \frac{0 - \mu}{\sigma}$$

That is,

$$-3.29 = \frac{-\mu}{80}$$

or

$$\mu = (80)(3.29) = 263 \text{ hours}$$

The excess queue size = 600 − 263 = 337 hours (see figure 14.8). The buffer is approximately equal to two weeks of workload. The excess queue size can be reduced by increasing the capacity by using overtime or by

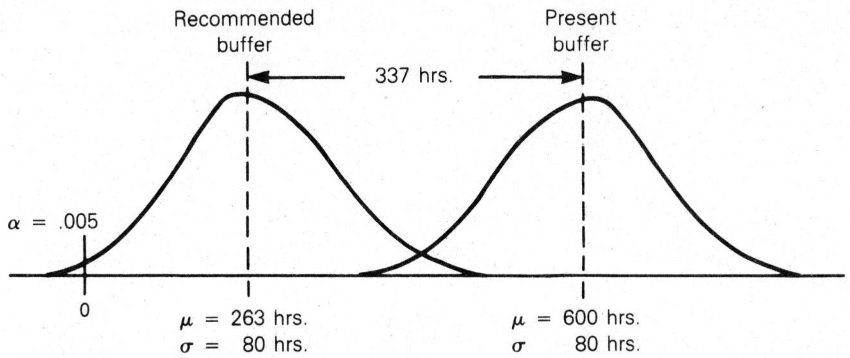

FIGURE 14.8 Queue size, Example 14.4

reducing the amount of work input to the work center. Alternative routing and subcontracting are other options.

Techniques for Aligning Completion Times and Due Dates

The importance of delivering goods on time cannot be overemphasized. When some jobs are ahead of due dates and others are behind, corrective actions are taken with the help of dispatch lists. Jobs that are ahead of schedule can easily be delayed until a future date, but jobs that are behind schedule need attention. Essentially, we need to complete these jobs in less than normal lead times. Some techniques for reducing the lead times are discussed in this section.

LEAD TIME CONTROL

Lead time can be reduced by decreasing the interoperation time. Although the interoperation time consists of wait time, move time, and queue time, it is no secret that queue time is the most difficult one to control. The queue length or the queue time can be reduced by increasing the capacity of critical work centers or reducing the workload to specific work centers. In the short term, capacity can be increased by using overtime or additional shifts or by subcontracting operations. Some of the techniques discussed for short-term capacity corrections, such as overlapping and lot splitting, are also applicable here. They are depicted in figure 14.9. Operation splitting is another way to reduce the lead time. For example, if the operation is labor-oriented, several workers can be assigned to the job. Or, if the operations are machine-controlled, they may be performed on several machines. It is important that the scheduling department be informed of the new routing and its impact on lead times and loads at affected machine centers. Additional setups may be incurred when several machines are employed instead of one. Unfortunately, that is the price we pay to reduce the lead time and keep our customers happy.

Example 14.5

Suppose that the supervisor in Example 14.3 manages to obtain additional forty-hour capacities at machine centers 1 and 2. Can we complete the jobs on time?

Solution: Based on the new information, we first tabulate the machine center loads and capacities, as shown in table 14.4.

Recall that the due dates for jobs A and B are weeks 44 and 38, respectively, and that this is week 28 on the planning calendar. We know

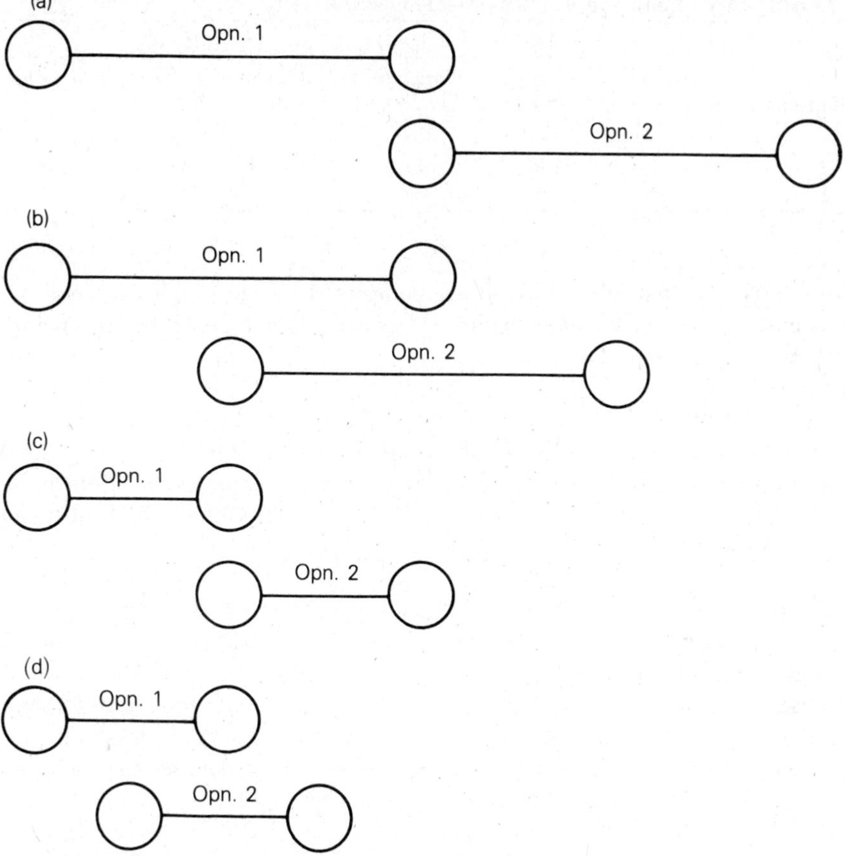

FIGURE 14.9 Techniques for reducing lead time: (a) standard production routing; (b) overlapping; (c) doubling the number of shifts; (d) shift doubling and overlapping

that jobs A and B compete for machine center 3 simultaneously, and hence we calculate their critical ratios:

$$\text{CR(A)} = \frac{44 - 28}{\frac{160}{40} + \frac{120}{40} + \frac{200}{80}} = \frac{16}{9.5} = 1.68$$

$$\text{CR(B)} = \frac{38 - 28}{\frac{40}{40} + \frac{200}{80} + \frac{80}{40}} = \frac{10}{5.5} = 1.82$$

Job A has a smaller critical ratio, and hence we schedule job A at machine center 3, followed by job B. Upon their completion, they are moved to machine centers 4 and 2, respectively, as shown in figure 14.10.

TABLE 14.4 Load and Capacity Data, Example 14.5

	Job A			*Job B*		
Operation	*Work Center*	*Load (hrs.)*	*Capacity (hrs./wk.)*	*Work Center*	*Load (hrs.)*	*Capacity (hrs./wk.)*
I	3	160	40	3	40	40
II	4	120	40	2	200	80
III	1	200	80	4	80	40

We see that jobs A and B are completed by the middle of week 42; that is, job A can be done before its due date, but job B is still late by approximately four weeks.

Example 14.6

The manager at the Friendly Company finds out that lot splitting and overlapping can be done on job A. Based on this information, determine whether it is possible to meet the due dates in Example 14.5. If not, can you suggest an alternative method to solve this problem?

Solution: We notice in Example 14.5 that splitting job A does not hasten the completion of job B in any work center. Instead of using the critical ratio technique, we try the SPT rule at machine center 3. The detailed schedule chart is exhibited in figure 14.11. We see that Jobs A and B can be completed by weeks 44 and 38, respectively. This example shows the complexity of solving job shop problems. Hence, many commercial packages resort to simulation for obtaining a satisfactory schedule.

QUEUE CONTROL

When queue sizes are too large, the associated cost of in-process inventories is high. Large inventories not only increase shop floor congestion, they also increase materials handling costs. Since queues control the lead

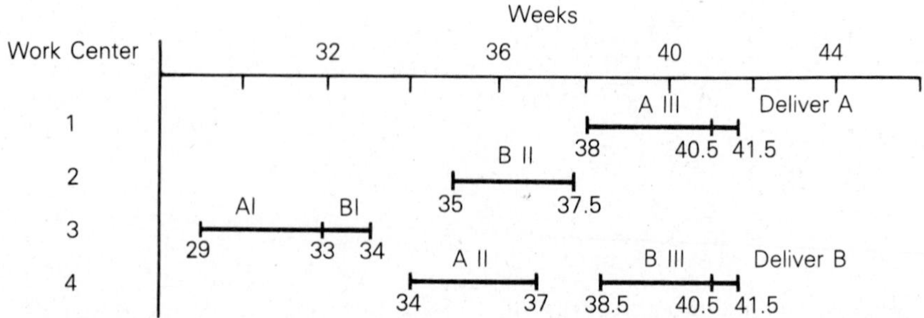

FIGURE 14.10 Gantt schedule chart for Example 14.5

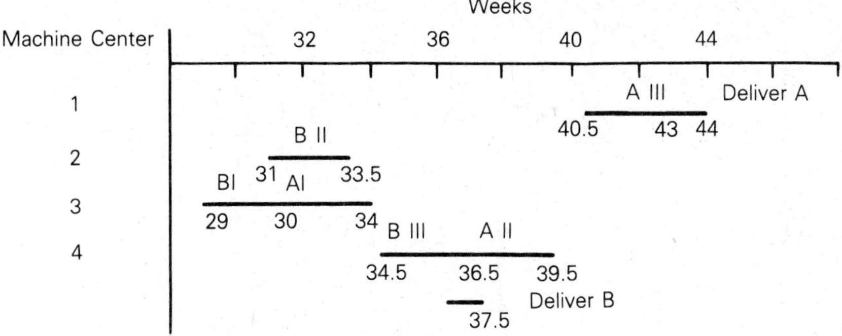

FIGURE 14.11 Gantt schedule chart for Example 14.6

time, the reduction of queue size provides better customer service through decreased lead time. Overall, this increases productivity. Queue control consists of (1) measuring the present queue size, (2) establishing the optimum queue size, and (3) adjusting the capacity of machines or controlling the input to the work center [10].

Measuring Present Queue Size

Queue sizes fluctuate for various reasons, as discussed earlier. By measuring queues regularly, they can be plotted, as was shown in figure 14.7. For example, the following are the buffer inventories in a work center for the past thirty weeks:

450, 500, 700, 540, 320, 750, 650, 870, 930, 400,
730, 550, 610, 850, 890, 930, 650, 710, 550, 850,
660, 750, 690, 350, 450, 630, 620, 640, 650, 580,

We can group these inventories into different classes and draw a frequency distribution diagram, as exhibited in figure 14.12. The calculation of mean and standard deviation, as found in most elementary statistics books, can be calculated as follows:

Range of Queues (hours)	*Queue Size* (x_i)	*Frequency* (f_i)
300–399	350	2
400–499	450	3
500–599	550	5
600–699	650	9
700–799	750	5
800–899	850	4
900–1000	950	2

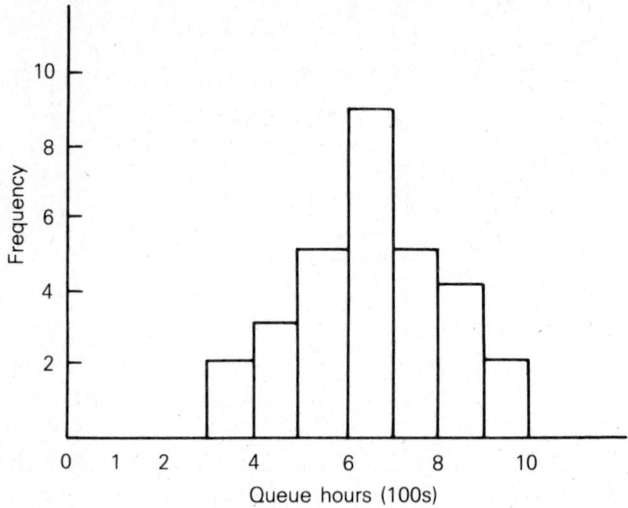

FIGURE 14.12 Frequency distribution diagram

$$\mu = \frac{\Sigma f_i x_i}{\Sigma f_i} = \frac{19{,}700}{30} = 656.67 \text{ hours}$$

$$\sigma = \sqrt{\frac{\Sigma x_i^2 f_i}{N} - \frac{(\Sigma x_i f_i)^2}{N^2}}; \; N = \Sigma f_i$$

$$= \sqrt{455{,}833.33 - 431{,}211.11} = 156.91 \text{ hours}$$

Establishing the Optimum Queue Size

Suppose that the manager does not want to exceed the queue out risk more than 1% of the time. We can calculate the maximum buffer necessary to meet the goals:

$$\text{Required Buffer} = z\sigma$$

$$= (2.33)(156.91)$$

$$= 365.6 \text{ hours}$$

Therefore, the excess queue, or the unnecessary buffer, is equal to 656.67 − 365.6 = 291 hours.

Controlling Queue Size

The final phase consists of reducing the buffer in a planned manner. The input/output control technique described earlier (Chapter 10) is a useful tool for controlling queues. Suppose that the planned input/output table for the work center is as shown in table 14.5. We can anticipate a buffer size of 600 hours at the end of nine weeks. Even through the buffer size is below average, it is above the required queue size of 365 hours. Suppose that we decided to reduce the queue to the optimum value in approximately ten weeks. We should examine the planned jobs (inputs) to see whether it is possible to divert some of them to alternative machine centers. Essentially, we will be reducing the inputs to the overloaded work center. The resulting planned input/output table might be as shown in table 14.6

If we are unable to divert some of the loads to other machine centers, we might plan to increase the output by scheduling overtime for the next ten weeks. Essentially, we are increasing the capacity of the work center. The revised input/output table might be as shown in table 14.7.

Thus, the strategy is either to decrease the input or to increase the output at the particular work center to correct the overload situation. Once the optimum buffer size is achieved, we should monitor the work centers periodically to make sure it stays that way always.

TABLE 14.5 Planned Input/Output Table

		Week								
	Backlog	*1*	*2*	*3*	*4*	*5*	*6*	*7*	*8*	*9*
Planned input	—	75	100	80	90	85	70	90	70	80
Planned output	—	80	80	80	80	80	80	80	80	80
Buffer	580	575	595	595	605	610	600	610	600	600

TABLE 14.6 Planned Input/Output Table After Reducing Queue Size

		Week								
	Backlog	*1*	*2*	*3*	*4*	*5*	*6*	*7*	*8*	*9*
Planned input	—	75	50	85	60	50	50	50	40	60
Planned output	—	80	80	80	80	80	80	80	80	80
Buffer	580	575	545	540	520	490	460	430	390	370

TABLE 14.7 Revised Input/Output Table

		Week								
	Backlog	*1*	*2*	*3*	*4*	*5*	*6*	*7*	*8*	*9*
Planned input	—	75	100	80	95	85	70	90	75	70
Planned output	—	105	105	105	105	105	105	105	105	105
Buffer	580	550	545	520	510	490	455	440	410	375

SHORT INTERVAL SCHEDULING

Short interval scheduling (SIS) is a scheduling and control technique that has met with some success in a variety of manufacturing and service industries, such as fabrication, repetitive manufacturing, warehouses, banks, and mail-order houses. The SIS technique is especially suited to machine-controlled operations. It assists supervisors in periodically auditing worker productivity at short intervals to examine whether the workers are meeting the set output objectives [15]. The first step in SIS is determination of the short interval of time to be used, which varies according to the application. It could be an hour in keypunching or an entire day in the maintenance of large machines. The next step is to schedule a reasonable amount of work that should be completed in the short interval. This step obviously requires established work standards for defining the unit of work, such as the number of pieces per hour or the number of hours and minutes to complete a certain amount of work. Then forms are developed for the supervisor to use in monitoring and taking corrective actions, if needed.

A sample form is exhibited in figure 14.13. The SIS reporting system highlights problem areas and focuses necessary attention on the bottleneck operations, which invariably results in improved productivity.

Summary

In this chapter, we have described many aspects of dispatching and monitoring the progress of jobs through the shop floor. The relationships among major planning, execution, and control activities are exhibited in table 14.8. In

Work Center: 310
Description: Milling

Period:
From 4/1 to 4/5

Machine Number/ Operator		Monday 4/1				Tuesday 4/2				Wednesday 4/3			
		8t 10	10t 12	1t 3	3t 5	8t 10	10t 12	1t 3	3t 5	8t 10	10t 12	1t 3	3t 5
Machine 1	Scheduled	100	100	100	100								
Cap. 100/hr	Actual	100	100	90	100								
Kodale, R.	Variance	0	0	−10	0								
Machine 2	Scheduled	80	80	80	80								
Cap. 80/hr	Actual	80	90	90	70								
Kazmere, T.	Variance	0	10	10	−10								
Machine 3	Scheduled	110	100	110	100								
Cap. 110/hr	Actual	105	105	105	105								
John, P.	Variance	−5	5	−5	5								

FIGURE 14.13 Short interval scheduling: sample performance work sheet

TABLE 14.8 Relationship Among Major Planning and Control Activities

Function	*Purpose*	*Type of Planning/Control Activity*	*Capacity Control Techniques*
Scheduling	Overall output plan	Rough-cut plan	Add land and/or facilities, capital equipment, work force
Machine loading	Calculate order priority; adjust release dates; assign specific jobs to work centers	Capacity requirements plan	Make versus buy; alternative routing; subcontract; reallocate work force; additional tooling
Operation sequencing	Calculate operation priorities; sequence jobs for dispatching; identitfy start/finish dates for each job on each machine	Short-term capacity plan	Determine overtime needs; alternative routing; change work force; operation overlapping; lot splitting; subcontract operations
Dispatching	Issue shop order, move ticket; labor, material and tool orders	Start the ball rolling	Input/output control
Status reporting and control	Report delays; salvage rework and production counts; labor and material utilization	Expediting and lead time control	Reduce interoperation times by overtime, operation splitting, operation overlapping
Plant monitoring	Monitor facilities; report machime utilization; generate productivity reports	Feed back information to data base	Replanning priorities and capacities; updating data files

the short term, resolving overload situations is important. When the available capacity is not adequate, the master schedule should be revised. Low-priority jobs should be rescheduled for a later date. Overload situations can also be overcome by scheduling anticipated jobs in the immediately following periods. As illustrated earlier, the scheduling of job shops is a complex and challenging task. A number of computer programs have been developed for job shop scheduling. The Western Electric Interactive System [7] and the Hughes Aircraft Company Job Shop Control System [3] are examples of in-house programs. In addition, many commercial software packages are available for use. General Electric's GJSCH$ can be used on a time-share basis [6]. The GJSCH$ can handle up to seventy-five work centers and any number of jobs. Sandman Associates have developed a computer simulation approach called Q-control for scheduling job shops [13]. These programs provide several feasible schedules. The manager can choose the one that best satisfies the company's needs.

PROBLEMS

1. The dispatch list contains the following jobs, due dates, and capacities of machines. Allow two days between operations; today is day 130 on the planning calendar. Assume that consecutive jobs can be started on a machine without any delay.

Job	*Opn. 10, Reaming (40 hrs./wk.)*	*Opn. 20, Finishing (40 hrs./wk.)*	*Due Date*
A	40	16	140
B	80	20	145
C	64	24	151

   a. Ignoring the due dates, find an optimal schedule and the completion date. (*Hint:* Use Johnson's rule.)
   b. Using the EDD rule, can we complete these jobs on time?

2. The supervisor finds that a previously scheduled job can be de-expedited and hence that he can get an additional forty hours of reaming during the second week. Based on this information, can the due dates in problem 1 be met? Use EDD rule.

3. With the increase of forty hours in reaming capacity during the second week, the supervisor finds that he still can't meet all due dates. The penalty for not meeting the due dates amounts to $200 per job. He finds that job C can be split into lots. However, an additional materials handling cost of $50 per split is incurred. Is it

economically feasible to split the lot? What is the completion date for your solution?

4. In problem 1, suppose that an alternative machine is available for reaming but that it will take forty-eight hours for job A. Can we meet all due dates? Use EDD rule.
5. With an alternative machine center for job A, the supervisor finds that he still can't meet all due dates. Delays translate to $50 per job per day, but they can be prevented by lot splitting job C, at an additional cost of $50 for materials handling per split. What is the optimum number of splits for this problem? What is the completion date for your solution?
6. If we apply the critical ratio technique in problem 1, how will it be different from the EDD schedule? Which is the more reasonable solution for this problem? Why?
7. The supervisor finds that the shop does not have much in-process inventory to finish in the department. If he allowed only one day between operations, could he complete all jobs in problem 1 on time? If not, which job creates the problems?
8. The buyer has rescheduled job C for day 152. With one-day inter-operation time, can we meet all due dates in problem 1?
9. Work center 364 has an average queue size of 400 hours, with a standard deviation of 60 hours. The manager is willing to take a chance of being out of work 1% of the time. Assuming that the queue size is normally distributed, what queue size would you recommend? By how much should the manager reduce the queue size?
10. The capacity of the work center in problem 9 is eighty hours per week. If the management permits a maximum of 25% overtime, how long will it take to reach the required queue length. Show the existing and the desired queue sizes in a normal probability distribution diagram.
11. The following are the buffer inventories (hours) in a work center for the past fifteen weeks:

    450, 500, 700, 540, 320, 750, 650, 870,
    930, 400, 730, 550, 610, 850, 890.

    Draw a frequency distribution diagram. Calculate the mean and standard deviation of the queue size. If the manager is willing to take a 0.5% chance of running out of work, what queue size would you recommend? (*Hint:* Assume that the queues are normally distributed. Since the sample size is less than thirty, use the student *t* distribution tables.)

12. In problem 11, how long will it take to reach the desired queue size if the capacity of the work center is 120 hours per week?

13. Several priority rules are being considered for dispatching jobs in a job shop. The following table lists the status of all jobs to be processed:

Job	*Days Before Due Date*	*Remaining Work (days)*	*Remaining Number of Operations*	*Order of Arrival*
A	30	25	2	2
B	29	22	3	5
C	25	18	1	1
D	20	15	2	3
E	28	21	1	4

Using the following priority rules, determine the sequence of processing jobs:

a. FCFS
b. LPT
c. SPT
d. Earliest due date
e. Minimum slack per operation
f. Critical ratio technique

14. Which one of the situations illustrated in figure 14.7 do the data in problem 11 describe? Explain.

15. The queue sizes for the past fifty weeks in the milling department of the Extron Company are as follows:

100, 50, 100, 150, 200, 200, 150, 0, 0, 180, 170, 250, 250, 300, 500, 100, 200, 0, 110, 350, 310, 210, 400, 300, 100, 150, 400, 0, 0, 500, 200, 300, 400, 200, 250, 350, 450, 210, 400, 500, 200, 300, 500, 200, 0, 0, 100, 200, 100, 100

Draw a frequency histogram using the data for (a) first twenty weeks, (b) first thirty weeks, (c) first forty weeks, (d) last 40 weeks, (e) all fifty weeks, (f) last thirty weeks, and (g) last twenty weeks. Which one of these diagrams in figure 14.7 does each of these described situations portray?

TABLE 14.9 Data for Problems 16–21

Job (Due Date)	*Operation No.*	*Work Center*	*Duration (hrs.)*	*Alternative Machine Center*	*Overlap*	*Job Splits*
A (190)	0010	1	80	X		
	0020	2	60	X		
	0030	3	24			
	0040	4	40	X		
B (200)	0010	3	80			
	0020	2	40	X		
	0030	1	120		X	X
	0040	4	160	X	X	
C (210)	0010	1	120	X		X
	0020	3	80			
	0030	4	80			
	0040	2	120		X	X

Use the following data for problems 16 through 21. The route sheets and due dates for the following jobs are given in table 14.9. Today is day 141 in the planning calendar. Possible modifications to operations are shown by *X* marks in the table.

The machine center capacities and current backlogs are as follows:

Work Center	*Capacity (hours/week)*	*Current Backlog*
1	80	20
2	40	40
3	40	40
4	80	20

Assume that the capacities of alternative machine centers are not included above.

16. Develop a dispatch list for each machine center, using the critical ratio technique. Assume one week for transport between operations and two days for final inspection and transport to the delivery department. Since the use of alternative machine centers, overlap of operations, and job splits is costlier, can we meet the schedule without utilizing them? Assume a five-day work week.

17. For some operations, alternative machine capacity is available up to forty hours per week, as shown in the table. However, these machines take 50% more time. Does this change your results in problem 16? The interoperation time is five days.

18. As you know, overlapping can sometimes do the trick. The succeeding operation can be started after 25% of the work is done on the

machine center. What effect does overlap of operations have on the results of problem 16? The interoperation time is five days.

19. In problem 17, we gave the additional available capacities. In some instances we can split portions of the operation and allocate them to an alternative machine, but it takes 50% more time. Can this help us meet the due dates?

20. If none of the alternatives given in problems 17, 18, and 19 are helpful, can a combination of these alternatives help resolve the situation? State any additional assumptions necessary to solve the problem.

21. Repeat problem 16 with two days for interoperation time instead of one week (five days).

REFERENCES AND BIBLIOGRAPHY

1. E. E. Adam and R. J. Ebert, *Production and Operations Management*, 2nd ed. (Englewood Cliffs, N.J.: Prentice-Hall, 1982).
2. *APICS Training Aid—Shop Floor Control* (Falls Church, VA.: American Production and Inventory Control Society, 1979).
3. M. H. Bulkin, J. L. Colley, and M. W. Steinhoff, "Load Forecasting, Priority Sequencing, and Simulation in a Job Shop Control System," *Management Science*, Vol. 18, No. 2 (October 1966), pp. 29–51.
4. R. B. Chase and N. J. Aguilano, *Production and Operations Management*, 3rd ed. (Homewood, Ill.: Richard D. Irwin, 1981).
5. *Communications Oriented Production Information and Control Systems* (*COPICS*), Vols. 1–6 (White Plains, N.Y.: IBM Publications, 1972).
6. *General Electric Company Users Guide to General Shop Schedules* (*GJSCH$*) (General Electric Company, 1970).
7. V. Godin and C. H. Jones, "The Interactive Shop Supervisor," *Industrial Engineering*, Vol. 20, No. 11 (November 1969), pp. 16–22.
8. J. H. Greene, *Production and Inventory Control* (Homewood, Ill.: Richard D. Irwin, 1974).
9. F. S. Gue, *Increased Profits Through Better Control of Work In Process* (Reston, Va.: Reston, 1980).
10. N. P. May, "Queue Control: Utopia or Pie in the Sky," *APICS Conference Proceedings*, 1980, pp. 358–361.
11. G. W. Plossl and O. W. Wight, *Production and Inventory Control* (Englewood Cliffs, N.J.: Prentice-Hall, 1967).
12. G. W. Plossl, *Manufacturing Control* (Reston, Va.: Reston, 1973).
13. W. E. Sandman and J. P. Hayes, *How to Win Productivity in Manufacturing* (Dresher, Pa.: Yellow Book of Pennsylvania, 1980).
14. M. R. Smith, *Manufacturing Controls* (New York: Van Nostrand Reinhold, 1981).
15. W. J. Richardson, *Cost Improvements, Work Sampling and Short Interval Scheduling* (Reston, Va.: Reston, 1976).

appendix 14A

Flexible Systems Invade the Factory

Paul Kinnucan

Recently GE invited reporters to its locomotive manufacturing division in Erie, Pa., to show off a new automatic machining system—the centerpiece of a \$300 million program to modernize the division's facilities. A second floor balcony affords a spectacular view of the system which makes frames for traction motors. Nine gigantic milling machines, arrayed on either side of an aisle, spout milky fluids as they bite into massive blocks mounted on steel pallets. Occasionally, a shuttle cart, painted bright yellow, glides down the aisle on a track to snatch a block from one machine and transport it to another. To the left, an idling robot weaves its arm between two vertical milling machines. Suddenly the arm snakes down to one of the machines, twists a tool bit off, and inserts another selected from a large green rack. Off in a corner, two men use a crane to wrestle a rusty block onto a pallet. They are the only humans in sight.

GE's machining system exemplifies a new breed of automated manufacturing system beginning to invade factories in this country and abroad. In contrast to conventional "fixed automation" systems, which follow a preordained sequence of steps in making a product, these flexible manufacturing systems (FMSs) can be programmed to alter their procedures to suit varying production requirements. For example, an FMS can be programmed to produce an assortment of parts simultaneously or quickly reprogrammed to accommodate design changes or new parts.

Such systems have significant advantages over the hard automation systems used in mass production and semiautomated batch processing systems that now turn out most manufactured items. The primary advantage is cost.

Reprinted with permission, *High Technology*, July 1983, pp. 32–42, copyright 1983 by High Technology Publishing Corporation, 38 Commercial Wharf, Boston, MA 02210.

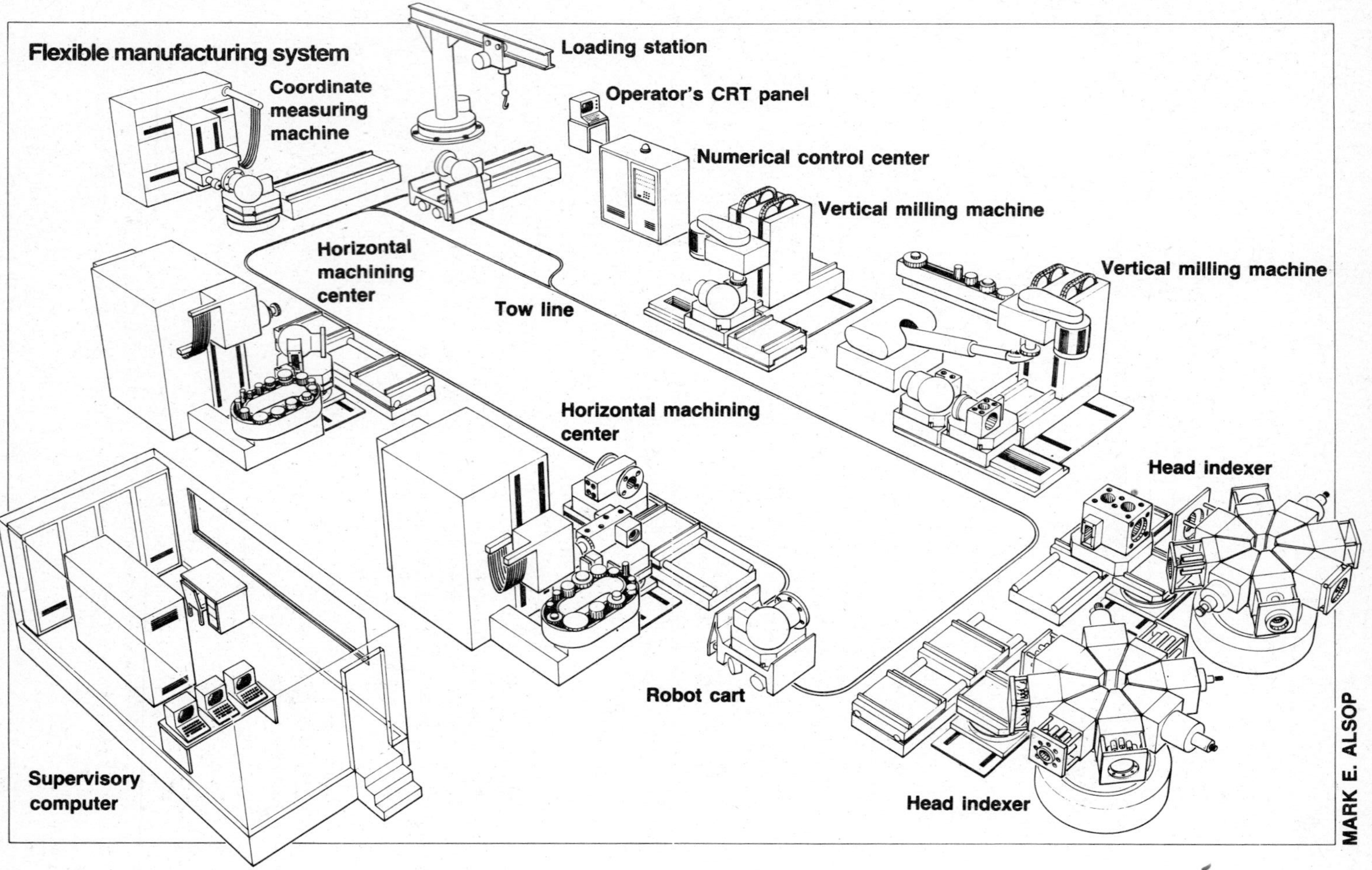
Flexible manufacturing system
Coordinate measuring machine
Loading station
Operator's CRT panel
Numerical control center
Vertical milling machine
Vertical milling machine
Horizontal machining center
Tow line
Horizontal machining center
Robot cart
Head indexer
Head indexer
Supervisory computer
MARK E. ALSOP

This hypothetical FMS starts with the incoming part loaded by crane onto a pallet, where necessary clamps and fixtures are added manually as it rests on the loading platform. After the loaded pallet is moved onto a waiting cart, a recessed wire cable drags it along the floor to the first manufacturing station—a pair of vertical milling machines. One operator supervises these and subsequent automatic steps, and communicates with the main computer control center (bottom of picture) via the CRT station, to report problems and progress.

The pallet is slid automatically from the cart onto one of the vertical mills, into which a robot inserts the proper milling tools. The mills and the other machines are in pairs to supply sufficient manufacturing capacity and backup. A numerical control center supplies instructions to the vertical mills for machining each part. Each semifinished part is placed back on a cart for delivery to the next station, a pair of head indexing machine tools.

The head indexers have eight arms, which are prepared beforehand to perform any required horizontal drilling and boring operation, including multiple drilling. The indexers, and other machine tools, always remain under control of the main computer.

The next station is a pair of horizontal-mill machining centers, each with its own tools and tool changer. They perform specific milling, boring, and drilling operations that are not convenient or possible on the vertical mills or the head indexers.

The final station is a 4-axis automatic measuring machine for inspection of the finished parts. A probe touches each surface of interest and transmits the readings to the main computer, which determines if the parts are in tolerance. The four axes include the X, Y, and Z linear coordinates, and rotation. The inspected part is removed manually from the system.

Hard automation systems are extremely efficient, but they are also expensive and can only turn out one type of part at a time. They require extensive modifications to accommodate new parts or design changes. As a result, they can only be justified for items produced in large quantities.

Flexible systems, on the other hand, radically alter the economics of automation because of their ability to produce multiple parts. Aggregate production volumes can be high enough to justify a flexible system's cost even though individual part volumes are low. "Flexible systems make possible economies of scope as well as scale," observes Robert Johoski, vice president and manager of the manufacturing systems division of Cincinnati-Milacron, a leading U.S. machine tool builder.

Because it is fully automated, the FMS also has strong advantages over the semiautomated batch manufacturing systems now employed to make products in small quantities. These systems move components in batches through machines or processes individually set up by human workers to perform one operation on one type of component.

Batch manufacturing is flexible, and allows diverse products to be produced, but it has drawbacks. It is labor intensive and involves high setup costs, long lead times, and high inventory levels. The components in any batch spend about 90 percent of the time waiting (queuing) for time on a tool. In addition, at each new setup, there is a risk of nonconformance: parts that do not conform with design standards and hence have to be reworked or scrapped. In contrast, the FMS allows automated manufacturing of components on a random basis. The FMS does away with the long setup times, queuing delays, inventory levels, and human errors associated with batch manufacturing.

The result can be a dramatic jump in productivity. The $16 million GE system, installed late last year, turns out a 2500-pound motor frame, in any of six styles, once every hour. By replacing stand-alone machines and human operators with an integrated system, GE has cut a job that once took 16 days to 16 hours.

Flexible systems also improve quality and lower operating and capital equipment costs. Hughes Aircraft recently installed a flexible machining system at a cost of about $7.5 million (1979 dollars)—75 percent of the capital cost of a batch system with comparable capacity, according to William F. Knabb, fabrication manager at the company's electro-optical and data systems group (El Segundo, Calif.). The system, which produces aluminum frames for weapons aiming devices, costs only 13 percent as much to operate as a batch system because of the elimination of operator salaries.

Flexible systems, by enabling the automation of low-volume production, hold the key to the workerless factories of the future. Such factories are already appearing. For example, Mazak Corp., a Japanese machine tool maker, has built a plant in Florence, Ky., based on two flexible manufacturing systems. One turns out frames and beds for Mazak machine tools, and the other makes gear boxes and other small components. Altogether, the two systems make 180 distinct kinds of parts. A plant based on conventional batch systems would have required 240 workers, according to Mac Nakano, vice president for sales at Mazak. However, because of the use of FMS, the new factory, which opened in April and runs three shifts a day, requires only 15 workers on the day shift and only four controllers on the evening shift. At night the factory runs unattended—except for the night watchman. Mazak, which installed its first FMS in 1981, claims to be the only machine tool builder in the world to use FMS in its own operations. It now has FMS systems operating in three plants.

Much Development Needed

But the transition from batch to flexible manufacturing will not come quickly. For one thing, flexible systems still have primitive capabilities that limit the kinds of items they can produce. Many manufacturing jobs require the dexterity, intelligence, and perceptual capabilities of human workers. It will take decades of development for the FMS to reach the point where it can compete with humans.

Still, technology does not appear to be a major barrier to the widespread application of FMS. Stand-alone machine tools have already advanced to where their incorporation into automated systems is fairly straightforward. For example, machines operating under computer numerical control (CNC) have reduced the role of the operator to that of an observer. The machine's computer-based controller can select the proper tool and set the correct tool speed and feed angle. Some CNC machining centers can store as many as 60 different tools in their magazines. A central computer can control these machines by transmitting the appropriate programs via data communications links.

Computer-controlled material handling systems are becoming prevalent. They include robots, towline and wire-guided self-propelled carts, overhead cranes, and power-and-free (asynchronous) conveyors that allow items to be moved at variable speeds between stations. Flexible system builders have barely begun to tap this technology.

Flexible systems based on machining centers and towline carts were first applied in the mid-60s to the machining of prismatic (box-like) parts made of steel, aluminum, magnesium, and other metals. The success of systems installed by such pioneering FMS users as Sundstrand and Ingersoll-Rand have inspired many imitators. In the late 70s, systems for machining round parts appeared, beginning with a semiautomated system installed by Harris at its printing press division in Fort Worth, Texas. Mazak currently is installing a system for rotary parts at its new factory in Minokamo, Japan.

Now manufacturers are beginning to apply flexible manufacturing to other types of processes. For example, Westinghouse is currently putting the finishing touches on a system to forge turbine blade preforms at its turbine components plant in Winston-Salem, N.C. (see HIGH TECHNOLOGY, April 1983). Lockheed-California is developing a system for riveting aircraft structures. A robot equipped with vision selects parts from an automatic storage system and loads them onto a riveting machine. Westinghouse has developed a prototype of a flexible system for assembling electric motors. The system, which can produce six styles of motor bell assemblies, consists of six work stations, four manned by robots, linked by a power-and-free conveyor.

Flexibility is also beginning to appear in mass production applications. Most automobile manufacturers, for example, have installed robot-based spot welding systems capable of handling a variety of body styles.

Lasers Are Ideal

Machine tools based on laser beams, electrical discharge, and other exotic processes could enhance flexible systems. A laser beam can weld, cut, drill, and bore, thus eliminating the need for tool changes. Laser beams never wear out, and hence produce more uniform results while eliminating downtime due to tool breakage. IIT Research Institute (Chicago) has developed a flexible machining system that includes a laser-hardening work station. The computer-controlled system makes plugs for valves and includes a robot that transfers the part from an input station to a lathe, to the laser-hardening station, to an inspection station, and then to an output station. IITRI wants to develop flexible systems based on lasers, electrical discharge, and other advanced machining processes that are inherently flexible.

Automatic inspection and tool compensation would also improve flexible systems. In Avco Lycoming's machining system in Stratford, Conn., for example, operators still stand over many of the machines that could operate unattended. The reason: The operators serve as the eyes and ears and hands of the system's supervisory computer by monitoring tools and the workpiece to detect tool wear or incipient breakage, which they then correct. Human monitoring is especially critical in Avco Lycoming's application: machining very hard stainless steel castings for turbine engines for the M-1 tank. For this reason, Avco's system uses more human workers than is typical in an FMS. However, most companies assign at least a few workers to stroll among the machines as watchers. Automatic systems would eliminate the need for this task.

Many observers argue that the statistical sampling techniques traditionally used for batch manufacturing are not a sufficient safeguard when setups are constantly changing. An FMS should inspect every component it produces. For this reason, some machining systems incorporate inspection stations based on coordinate measuring machines. These computer-comtrolled devices inspect by touch; they use a movable probe to reconstruct an object's shape. Westinghouse's forging system employs machine vision to inspect finished turbine blade preforms.

Such automatic 100 percent inspection allows the detection and correction of errors caused by tool wear and other slowly changing conditions before an unacceptable part is produced. The goal of inspection in flexible systems will not be to winnow good from bad parts but to prevent bad parts from ever being made. In the future, the results of inspection will be fed back to the system's supervisory computer for automatic correction. By monitoring the tool and the piece to detect signs of tool wear, it will be possible to do the compensation automatically. This will allow for real-time adjustment, permitting more uniform production as well as maintaining closer tolerances.

Currently, however, human operators make tool wear adjustments. "Automatic tool compensation is still Star Wars stuff," says Hughes' Knabb, whose system includes a coordinate measuring station for automatic inspection.

There is also a need for in-process inspection to spot dynamic failures, such as a breaking tool. Research organizations, including Carnegie Mellon University and the National Bureau of Standards, are developing techniques for real-time tool and process monitoring that would allow detection and correction of such errors. For example, Paul Wright of CMU is exploring the use of thermal stress monitoring to detect tool breakdown. NBS is taking a different approach. It has developed a microcomputer-based device, called Drill-Up, that detects incipient breakage of a machining center drill by abnormal vibrations (sensed by an accelerometer), and orders the tool's retraction before it breaks. The device allows optimum replacement and prevents damage from broken drills.

But tool monitoring is hardly a prerequisite to FMS operation. Most operational systems include a backup for crucial tools and simply replace them at predetermined times based on average tool lifetimes.

New Control Modes Needed

Existing direct numerical control systems will not be adequate for the flexible systems of the future because they are not equipped to deal with sensory feedback. Modularity and hierarchical organization is key to the control of such systems. NBS, for example, is experimenting with an advanced control system for its automated manufacturing research facility—a flexible machining system comprising eight work stations. The system's data base includes a "world model" that describes the parts to be made and the tools and processes available to make them. The hierarchical control system breaks a manufacturing task into subtasks and assigns them to appropriate subsystems, which may further subdivide the tasks. A sensory system integrates data from sensors and abstracts the information required by each processing module. The modules communicate with each other via mailboxes—locations in common memory where information is dropped and picked up. This makes it easy to add, remove or modify software modules or processors.

A user programs the system by specifying a set of if-then rules describing a task. Rule-based programming languages, an outgrowth of artificial intelligence research, have the advantage of allowing a user to describe not only the action to be taken, but also the conditions under which it is to be taken, such as "Lower the drill head only if the chuck contains a drill." This in turn allows the system to check for error conditions and conflicting commands, thus avoiding catastophe. In addition, rule-based languages simplify program modification: Task descriptions can be altered by adding or deleting rules.

Flexible manufacturing systems demand a new sensitivity to producibility on the part of the designer. Manual or batch systems place very little constraint on design. But even the most flexible automated system will not be as versatile as a bunch of stand-alone machines operated by humans. For example, machining centers can hold at most 70 tools in their magazines; adding another tool requires an expensive setup. As a result, companies will have to set rigid manufacturing constraints on designers to assure effective use of flexible manufacturing. Already this is happening. For example, Hughes Electro-Optical, which once allowed designers to specify any of 400 drill sizes under a half inch, has now standardized on 15 sizes. Rolls Royce has standardized on 100 turning tools for making jet engines compared to the thousands once used.

Effective use of flexible systems will also require companies to master group technology: techniques for identifying parts that can be made by similar processes, and developing processes that can manufacture similar parts. Some companies, such as John Deere and Avco Lycoming, have developed computerized data bases that simplify the procedures. These systems list all the parts made by a company, encoded by their shapes, materials, and production techniques. Such systems allow quick identification of parts families that could be produced by a flexible system. By allowing a designer to quickly find a similar part that can be modified rather than design a new part from scratch, these systems prevent duplication of effort. Moreover, chances are that if the existing part is being made on the flexible system, so can the modified part. A group technology data base thus encourages expansion of existing part families capable of being made by existing flexible systems rather than the design of maverick parts that require additional manufacturing investment.

Cost limits the applications of flexible manufacturing. There are still many applications where production volumes, even when aggregated, are too low to justify the investment. For the moment, the FMS is filling a niche between fixed automation systems used for high volume production, and stand-alone machine tools. The FMS really comes into its own in mid-volume manufacturing. (Mid-volume is a variable figure that depends on the complexity of parts and the type of processes required to make them. 3,000–50,000 parts annually is a typical range.)

The inherent inertia of manufacturers is also slowing the acceptance of flexible manufacturing. They have traditionally been reluctant to adopt automation because of high capital costs, organizational changes, and potential labor problems. Flexible automation does not alleviate these problems. If anything, it exacerbates them. Manufacturers will be very reluctant to junk their existing plants, representing a huge capital investment, in favor of the new technology.

Industry observers point out that fewer than 5 percent of the machine tools installed in the U.S. are numerically controlled, despite the fact that NC tools were introduced more than 30 years ago. It is highly unlikely that an industry so slow to adopt the NC tool will jump to accept the FMS, which is an order of magnitude more complex and sophisticated.

The recession also acted as a brake. Companies slashed capital investment, and the machine tool industry is suffering its worst slump since the Great Depression.

Lack of expertise and resources is also hampering growth. Few potential users have the expertise in all the technologies—computers, machine tools, and automated handling systems—required to design and install a flexible system. But now machine tool makers and users are beginning to assemble the necessary expertise. Kearney and Trecker, Giddings and Lewis, Cincinnati-Milacron, and other leading machinery makers have even begun to form divisions devoted specifically to marketing and integrating flexible systems on a turnkey basis for customers.

Cost is perhaps the biggest barrier, putting flexible systems beyond the reach of most manufacturers. For example, in the discrete parts industry, 87 percent of the manufacturers employ fewer than 50 persons. Such companies cannot afford a multimillion investment. The cost of flexible systems makes even big manufacturers hesitate.

Trend to Modularity

A growing trend toward designing machine tools as modules may mitigate the problem. Modularity facilitates acquisition of an FMS in stages, beginning with an NC tool, adding a robot, another tool, etc., as the company accumulates capital and grows. Because few manufacturers can supply all the components of an FMS, however, modular growth demands standardization of mechanical, electrical, and software interfaces to allow interconnection among devices from diverse sources. The industry, led by NBS, is beginning to develop such standards.

A typical strategy for an evolutionary implementation of a flexible manufacturing system is to begin by grouping tools into cells. The next step would be to add direct numerical control computers for downline loading of programs. Then scheduling and monitoring software is added. Finally, the manufacturer adds the systems needed for transporting, loading, and unloading material among the machines.

GE's aircraft engines business group is following this strategy in its rotating parts manufacturing facilities. It has already installed supervisory computers for its NC lathes. These computers load programs into the lathes via cables, then schedule and monitor production. The next step will be to add robots for loading tools and parts onto the lathes, and automatic material handling systems for transporting parts. The first cell is expected to go into operation later this year at GE's Wilmington, N.C., plant.

Another company that is taking an evolutionary approach is Avco Lycoming. The company, a pioneer in flexible manufacturing systems, now operates two systems, one making aircraft parts and the other making parts for the gas turbine engine used in the Army's M-1 tank. The company is currently modernizing its Stratford turbine engine plant as part of the Army's technology modernization program. The company plans to base its modernization on manufacturing cells—essentially FMS systems with humans serving as tool and part transporters—rather than going immediately to flexible manufacturing systems. The company argues that FMS currently is economically justifiable only for making parts in fairly high volumes and for making fairly large parts. Another company, Sikorsky, is also basing its modernization program on the cellular concept. Sikorsky's vice president of manufacturing claims that cells yield about 75 percent of the productivity gains of FMS for a smaller investment and risk.

The evolutionary approach has drawbacks. It requires retrofitting tools. But more important, it may be too slow in a competitive business. The pay-as-you-go and go-slow approach is fine if your competitors adopt the same strategy, says one observer. But if a competitor opts for a greenfields implementation, the go-slow company may be at a disadvantage. In fact, a more daring competitor can always get an advantage by automating faster. In the aircraft engine business, for example, GE's English competitor, Rolls Royce, appears to be moving into flexible manufacturing at a rapid pace.

Rolls Royce has installed a flexible manufacturing system to produce high pressure turbine blades. It includes an automated vacuum casting line, a flexible turbine blade machining line that uses robots to load blades into creep-fed grinding machines from a conveyor belt, and will soon include automated systems for laser surface hardening and the drilling of cooling holes by spark erosion techniques. An automated factory being built by Rolls Royce in Derby, U.K. will contain: a flexible system to machine compressor and turbine disks, automated part and tool storage systems, wire-guided robot trucks, and robots mounted on overhead gantries. The company is considering building a system to machine large casings; it will feature such advanced devices as standard pallets, laser machining centers, robots, and computer-controlled storage systems.

Competition is serving as the greatest stimulus to the adoption of flexible manufacturing. In the U.S., for example, companies facing foreign competition or stagnant markets have led the way in implementing flexible systems. These include aerospace companies, such as Avco Lycoming, Lockheed-California, Hughes, and Sundstrand, and agricultural and construction equipment makers, such as John Deere, Caterpillar, Allis Chalmers, and International Harvester.

Among the Western industrial nations, Japan and Europe appear to be most receptive to flexible automation, seeing it as a way to gain a

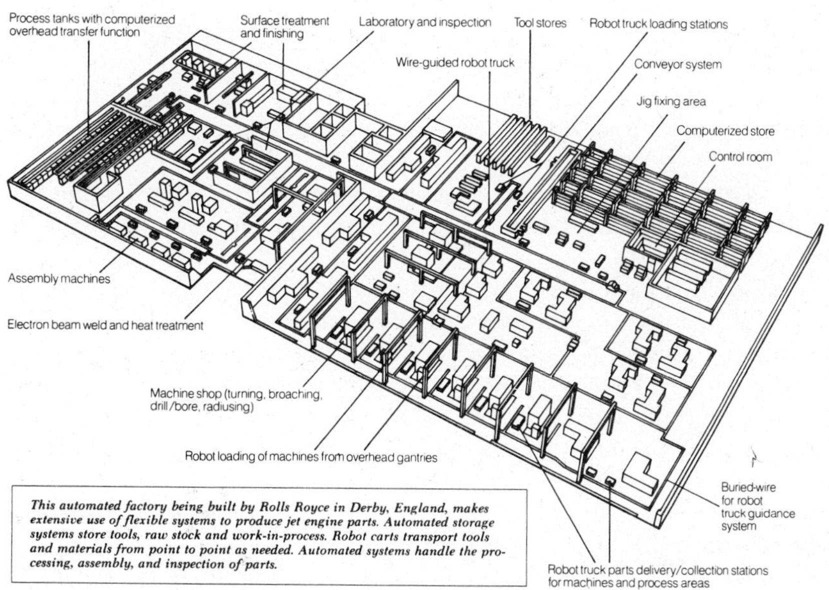

This automated factory being built by Rolls Royce in Derby, England, makes extensive use of flexible systems to produce jet engine parts. Automated storage systems store tools, raw stock and work-in-process. Robot carts transport tools and materials from point to point as needed. Automated systems handle the processing, assembly, and inspection of parts.

competitive edge against U.S. manufacturers who now dominate world markets (see "Flexible manufacturing: where the U.S. lags behind").

Labor opposition could be the biggest barrier to flexible manufacturing. Flexible automation promises to finish the process of job elimination begun with the industrial revolution. Machine tools have already eliminated many jobs in mid-volume manufacturing. Computer-controlled machine tools have reduced humans to little more than watchers. Tool operators route parts, set up tools, load workpieces, inspect finished parts, and observe their tools at work. Flexible systems will eventually eliminate the need for tool operators. For this reason, many companies are proceeding gingerly with the installation of FMS, trying to enlist labor support for automation and transferring displaced employees or allowing attrition and recession to do their trimming for them.

Flexible Manufacturing: Where the U.S. Lags Behind

Although pioneered in the U.S., flexible manufacturing systems seem to be attracting more attention in Japan and Europe than here. Comparative figures are unavailable, but Americans returning from Japan claim that country has installed more systems, which match U.S. systems in sophistication. "I hate to say this, but the Japanese are way ahead of us," says Ralph Patsfall, chief manufacturing engineer at the aircraft engine business group of General Electric and a frequent visitor to Japan, most recently in March.

Chastened by Japanese and European successes, some U.S. companies are looking to flexible systems and other types of automation as a way to combat foreign competition. GE's transportation systems division, for example, is counting on its plant modernization program, in which flexible manufacturing plays a pivotal role, to ensure its survival in the hotly competitive railroad locomotive business. GE does most of its locomotive business abroad, and its principal competitors are foreign companies with access to cheap labor, favorable export financing, and other forms of government support. Without automation, the company says, it will either have to move its manufacturing overseas or withdraw from the business. Either move would devastate the nearly moribund economy of Erie, Pa., where the vast operation has been centered since the turn of the century.

But GE may be an exception that proves the rule. Many American companies are either ignoring flexible systems or opting for a less risky form of automation system: the manufacturing cell in which tools are grouped according to the type of product they make rather than by function (milling, grinding, etc.). Ironically, a flexible manufacturing system is a cell taken to its ultimate conclusion by adding materials handling and supervisory computers. The concept of the cell was introduced by group technology theorists decades ago as a more productive alternative to batch manufacturing. Now when flexible automated systems have become feasible, U.S. manufacturers appear ready to embrace the more primitive concept. "Many U.S. companies are ready to buy a brand new 1959 Cadillac in 1983," says Jim Baker, head of GE's automation group.

Unfortunately, foreign competitors appear to be less timid. "The Japanese appear to be going wild over flexible systems," says Charles Skinner, a consultant with Booz, Allen & Hamilton Inc. A former official with CAM-I, an association of large manufacturers aimed at promoting computer-aided manufacturing, says that the association's European members are active in developing flexible manufacturing but that U.S. companies have shown very little interest.

Foreign competitors appear to have more to gain by flexible automation, and less to lose. The Japanese have suffered from a labor shortage, while the U.S. has chronic high unemployment. Japanese management philosophy, which emphasizes long term performance, seems more attuned to flexible manufacturing. Mazak, for example, is investing huge sums to develop its new automated factory at a time when tool demand is severely depressed worldwide. It wants to be ready for the upturn. Japanese techniques like just-in-time manufacturing, developed without flexible systems, are ideally suited to flexible manufacturing.

The Japanese now are making a bid to seize the lead in development as well as application of the technology. A consortium composed of all of the major Japanese manufacturers and led by the Ministry of Industrial Trade and Technology (MITI) is currently engaged in the single most ambitious FMS development project in the world. The project members are developing a generalized flexible system to make subassemblies. The system will use lasers as well as traditional machine tools, and will include flexible assembly systems.

Observers cite several reasons for the seeming lack of enthusiasm of U.S. firms for flexible automation. For one, U.S. dominance of world markets has provided little incentive for making expensive investments to boost productivity—especially not in flexible manufacturing, which relies heavily on advanced technology and new ways of thinking. U.S. management practice also tends to emphasize short term gains and reduction of risk. This tends to discourage adoption of flexible manufacturing, which requires heavy capital expenditures and long lead times.

But now foreign superiority in flexible manufacturing poses a serious threat. GE's Baker says it is time for U.S. companies to quit crying about the problems they face and the easier time foreign companies have and get on with the business of automation. It is too early to tell whether other U.S. firms are prepared to heed such calls to action.

chapter fifteen

Project Management Techniques

Operations managers must plan, organize, and control a variety of operations. Some of them are repetitive activities, and others are one-shot deals. Routine activities might be continuous or intermittent. The continuous production functions can be managed by assembly line balancing, whereas intermittent or job shop production requires scheduling, loading, and control techniques. The one-shot deals are generally one-time projects, such as constructing a hospital, research and development of a Boeing 747, or building a Polaris missile. A project approach is frequently used to develop and market new products and services. The type of technique required to manage these activities depends on the complexity of the project. For small projects, Gantt charts are adequate, whereas for large and complex projects, the critical path method (CPM) or the program evaluation and review technique (PERT) would be more effective. The problem becomes more complicated when common resources are used to execute multiple projects. For example, NASA launches several space flights from the same facility. Flights must be scheduled so that the capacity of various equipment is not exceeded. Such problems require resource-constrained multiple project scheduling techniques. Other situations may require limited quantities of repetitive production. Line of balance techniques can be used to manage such situations economically. In this chapter, we will discuss a variety of techniques for managing many types of project functions.

Gantt Charts

For small projects, Gantt charts are sufficient. Preparation of Gantt charts was discussed in detail in the chapter on job shop activity planning. A Gantt chart is simply a bar chart that time-phases activities. Every activity should have a start date and a finish date. Figure 15.1 exhibits a typical Gantt chart for a building construction project. All major activities are described.

Gantt charts serve as a record keeping and monitoring tool for projects. The major drawback is that the chart does not show the interrelationships of activities in the project. Gantt charts are frequently used to supplement CPM results.

The Use of CPM and PERT

Large projects present many problems to the manager because of the nonroutine, one-time nature of activities. Planning and coordinating all activities can be very complex for large projects. For example, ship construction involves design, fabrication, purchasing, and building. The total number of activities could easily exceed 5,000. Such projects have a limited time framework and require a host of internal and external approval procedures. Again, in building a Boeing 747, a Polaris missile, or a space shuttle, many technical problems arise. In many instances, new technology emerges. In general, the manager considers all activities of a project and the individual tasks that must be accomplished and relates tasks to one another and to the calendar. For planning and monitoring large projects, network techniques such as CPM and PERT are widely used.

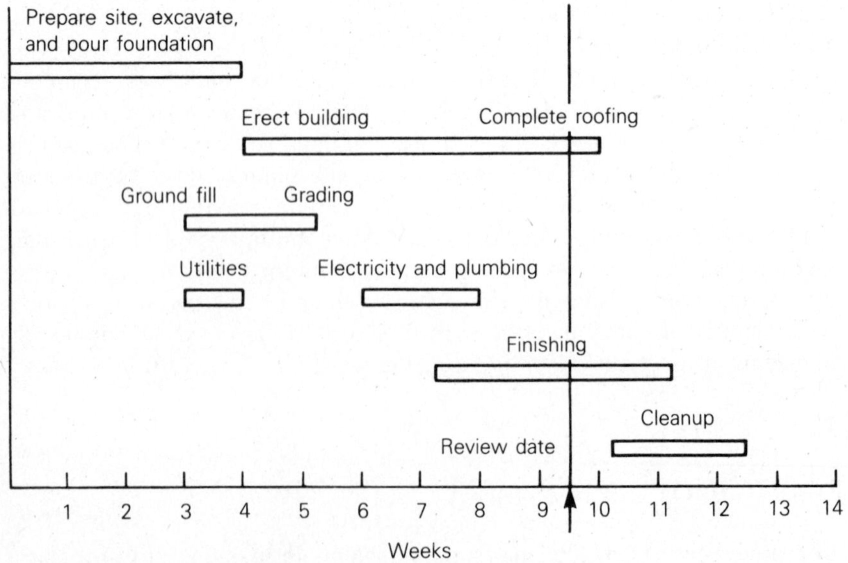

FIGURE 15.1 Gantt chart for construction of a house

CPM was originally developed by J. E. Kelly of Remington Rand Corporation and M. R. Walker of DuPont for planning and coordinating maintenance projects in the chemical industries. PERT evolved from Gantt charts in the late 1950s through the joint efforts of Lockheed Aircraft, the U.S. Navy Special Projects Office, and Booz, Allen and Hamilton, a consulting firm. It was first applied to the U.S. Navy's Polaris submarine project. Although CPM and PERT evolved independently, they have a great deal in common. As users borrowed certain features from each other, the gap narrowed further. These techniques can be used for planning, monitoring, and controlling project activities. CPM and PERT are used to find the minimum expected time to complete a project. By identifying the bottleneck operations, we can monitor the progress of the project to assure project completion on time. In addition, PERT can estimate the probability of meeting certain due dates. As delays occur, certain critical activities may need to be hastened. These techniques are most useful in evaluating the time and cost trade-offs of specific project activities.

ACTIVITY NETWORKS

The main feature of activity networks is the use of a precedence diagram to depict all or major project activities and their sequential relationships to other activities. Each activity must have an associated time estimate and precedence relationship, as shown by the example in figure 15.2. The arrows in the diagram represent activities, and the circles represent nodes. The nodes depict both the completion of one activity and the start of the next activity. The activities may represent steps in building a house, milestones in the construction of a ship, or major steps in an R&D project. One important aspect of a network diagram is that two or more activities

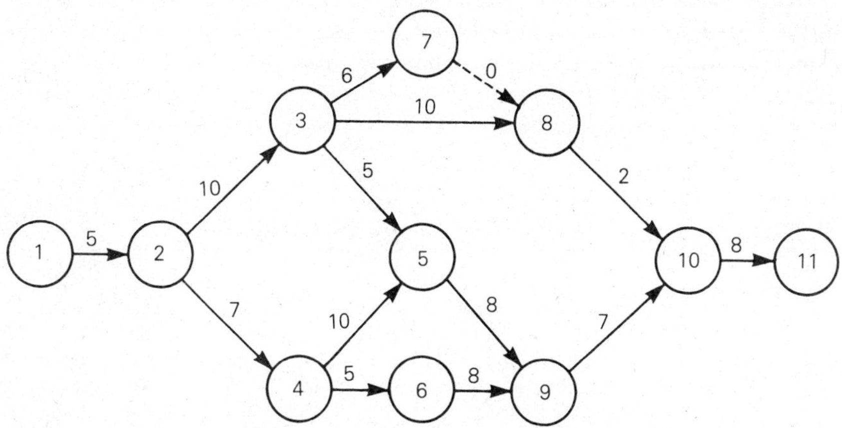

FIGURE 15.2 Precedence diagram

cannot start and finish at the same two nodes. If this did happen in the real world, we would add a dummy activity. For example, see activity 7–8 in figure 15.2; dummy nodes are generally connected by dotted lines. Let us now try to understand what the sequential or precedence relationship means. Activity 5–9, for instance, cannot be started until activities 3–5 and 4–5 are completed. Also, neither activity 2–3 nor activity 2–4 can be started prior to completion of activity 1–2, and so forth.

The Critical Path Method (CPM)

Once the precedence diagram is drawn and the duration of each activity is estimated, the next step involves tracing all paths. A path is defined as the sequence of activities leading from the starting node to the completion node. Table 15.1 lists all possible paths for the network in figure 15.2. In a large network, there wil be several paths. The lengths of individual paths can be calculated by adding the durations of all activities on each path. Path C, for example, consists of activities 1–2, 2–3, 3–5, 5–9, 9–10, and 10–11, with durations 5, 10, 5, 8, 7, and 8, respectively. Summing the durations, we obtain the path length or duration of path C as forty-three weeks. We can see from the table that the longest path is forty-five weeks. Since all other paths are less than forty-five weeks, we know that we need at least forty-five weeks from the start to complete the entire project. The longest path is known as the *critical path*. If there are any delays along the longest path, there will be corresponding delays in the project completion time. Similarly, if the completion time is not acceptable, the management should attempt to shorten the activities on the critical path, which are called the *critical activities*.

Activities that are not on the critical path can experience some delays, to the extent known as *slack,* without affecting the completion time of the project. Slack is the maximum amount of slippage allowed in each path. The slack of any path is obtained by subtracting the length of that path from the critical path length. For example, path C has 45 − 43 = 2 weeks

TABLE 15.1 List of All Paths for the Precedence Diagram

Path Identifier	*Path*	*Length (weeks)*	*Slack (weeks)*
A	1,2,3,8,10,11	35	45 − 35 = 10
B	1,2,3,7,8,10,11	31	45 − 31 = 14
C	1,2,3,5,9,10,11	43	45 − 43 = 2
D	1,2,4,5,9,10,11	45	45 − 45 = 0
E	1,2,4,6,9,10,11	40	45 − 40 = 5

of slack. Obviously, the critical path has zero slack, as exhibited in table 15.1. It is important to understand the difference between the slack of a path and the slack of an activity. For example, activity 2–3 is on paths A, B, and C, where the slacks are ten, fourteen, and two weeks, respectively. Even though path A has ten weeks of slack, activity 2–3 has only two weeks of slack. Thus, the amount of slack for activities on the same path can vary.

DETERMINING THE CRITICAL PATH AND SLACKS

In the foregoing small problem, we were easily able to list all paths and to identify the critical path and the slacks associated with all paths. As the number and the precedence complexity of activities increase, the identification of individual paths by enumeration becomes impractical. A systematic approach is essential. First, we will define the following variables for activity *i–j*. Let t_{i-j} represent the duration of activity *i–j*.

ES_{i-j} = earliest possible start time for activity *i–j*

EF_{i-j} = earliest possible finish time if the activity is started at ES_{i-j}

$= ES_{i-j} + t_{i-j}$

LF_{i-j} = latest feasible finish time for activity *i–j*

LS_{i-j} = latest feasible start time if activity *i–j* needs to be completed by LF_{i-j}

$= LF_{i-j} - t_{i-j}$

Next, we will illustrate how these four variables are generated for each activity, using the example illustrated in figure 15.2.

CALCULATION OF *ES* AND *EF*

All activities that do not have precedence can start at time zero. Thus, activity 1–2 in figure 15.2 can start at time zero, or $ES_{1-2} = 0$. Therefore, the earliest finishing time $EF_{1-2} = ES_{1-2} + t_{1-2} = 0 + 5 = 5$ weeks. Activities 2–3 and 2–4 can be started as soon as activity 1–2 is completed. Therefore,

$$ES_{2-3} = 5$$

$$ES_{2-4} = 5$$

$$EF_{2-3} = ES_{2-3} + t_{2-3} = 5 + 10 = 15$$

$$EF_{2-4} = ES_{2-4} + t_{2-4} = 5 + 7 = 12$$

Similarly,

$$ES_{3-5} = ES_{3-7} = ES_{3-8} = EF_{2-3} = 15$$

$$EF_{3-5} = 15 + 5 = 20$$

$$EF_{3-7} = 15 + 6 = 21$$

$$EF_{3-8} = 15 + 10 = 25$$

$$EF_{7-8} = 21 + 0 = 21$$

and

$$ES_{4-5} = ES_{4-6} = EF_{2-4} = 12$$

$$EF_{4-5} = 12 + 10 = 22$$

$$EF_{4-6} = 12 + 5 = 17$$

The activities at node 5 can be started only after all activities ending in node 5 are completed. We have

$$EF_{3-5} = 20$$

$$EF_{4-5} = 22$$

Therefore, the earliest time that activity 5–9 can be started is week 22; that is, $\max(EF_{3-5}, EF_{4-5})$. Then

$$ES_{5-9} = 22$$

$$EF_{5-9} = 22 + 8 = 30$$

Similarly,

$$ES_{6-9} = EF_{4-6} = 17$$

$$EF_{6-9} = 17 + 8 = 25$$

and

$$\begin{aligned} ES_{8-10} &= \max[EF_{3-8}, EF_{7-8}] \\ &= \max[25, 21] \\ &= 25 \end{aligned}$$

$$EF_{8-10} = 25 + 2 = 27$$

$$ES_{9-10} = \max[EF_{5-9}, EF_{6-9}]$$
$$= \max[30, 25]$$
$$= 30$$
$$EF_{9-10} = 30 + 7 = 37$$

Proceeding in the same way, we obtain

$$ES_{10-11} = \max[27, 37] = 37$$
$$EF_{10-11} = 37 + 8 = 45$$

The calculations of ES and EF are illustrated in figure 15.3 and summarized in table 15.2.

CALCULATION OF *LF* AND *LS*

Determining the latest finish time (LF) and latest start time (LS) follows a similar procedure, but the calculations must start from the end of the network diagram. The procedure is also referred to as the *backward pass*. Once we know the earliest possible completion time of the critical path, we can calculate the latest possible times at which we can start each activity without delaying the project. For example, activity 8–10 can be started as late as week 35 and completed by week 37 without affecting the completion time of the project. That is,

$$LF_{8-10} = 37$$
$$LS_{8-10} = LF_{8-10} - t_{8-10} = 37 - 2 = 35$$

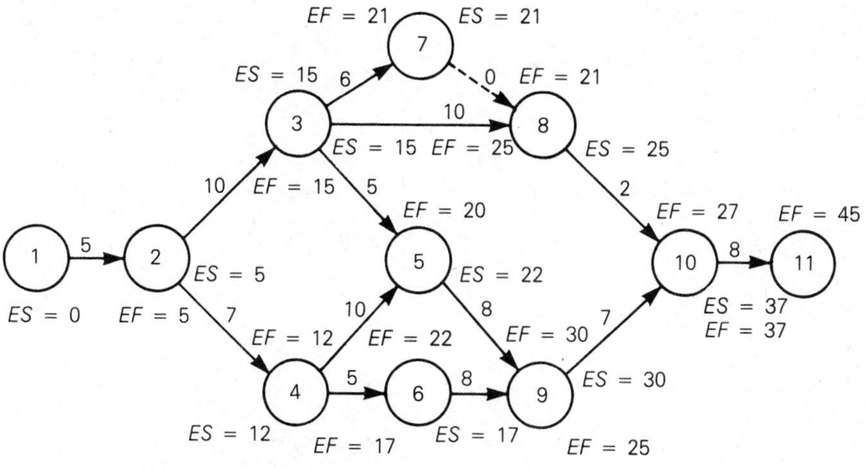

FIGURE 15.3 Calculation of *ES* and *EF*

TABLE 15.2 Summary of *ES*, *EF*, *LS*, *LF*, and Slack and Identification of Critical Path

Activity	*Duration*	*ES*	*EF*	*LS*	*LF*	*Slack*	*Critical Path*
1–2	5	0	5	0	5	0	*
2–3	10	5	15	7	17	2	
2–4	7	5	12	5	12	0	*
3–5	5	15	20	17	22	2	
3–7	6	15	21	29	35	14	
3–8	10	15	25	25	35	10	
4–5	10	12	22	12	22	0	*
4–6	5	12	17	17	22	5	
5–9	8	22	30	22	30	0	*
6–9	8	17	25	22	30	5	
7–8	Dummy	—	—	—	—	—	
8–10	2	25	27	35	37	10	
9–10	7	30	37	30	37	0	*
10–11	8	37	45	37	45	0	*

By subtracting the duration t_{i-j} of an activity from the latest feasible time LF_{i-j}, we obtain the latest feasible start time LS_{i-j}. The *LF* times for the immediately preceding activities are equal to the smallest *LS* times for all immediate successor activities. That is,

$$LF_{3-8} = LS_{8-10} = 35$$

$$LF_{7-8} = LS_{8-10} = 35$$

$$LS_{3-8} = 35 - 10 = 25$$

$$LS_{7-8} = 35 - 0 = 35$$

$$LF_{3-7} = LS_{7-8} = 35$$

$$LS_{3-7} = 35 - 6 = 29$$

Similarly,

$$LF_{9-10} = LS_{10-11} = 37$$

$$LS_{9-10} = LF_{9-10} - t_{9-10} = 37 - 7 = 30$$

$$LF_{5-9} = LS_{9-10} = 30$$

$$LS_{5-9} = 30 - 8 = 22$$

and

$$LF_{3-5} = LS_{5-9} = 22$$

$$LS_{3-5} = 22 - 5 = 17$$

Now we have the latest starts of all activities starting at node 3. They are 25, 29, and 17 respectively, for activities 3–8, 3–7, and 3–5. Therefore, the *LF* for all activities ending at node 3 is 17—that is, min(LS_{3-8}, LS_{3-7}, LS_{3-5}). Then,

$$LF_{2-3} = 17$$

$$LS_{2-3} = 17 - 10 = 7$$

Proceeding in the same way, we calculate

$$LF_{6-9} = LS_{9-10} = 30$$

$$LS_{6-9} = 30 - 8 = 22$$

$$LF_{4-6} = LS_{6-9}$$

$$LS_{4-6} = 22 - 5 = 17$$

and

$$LS_{4-5} = 22 - 10 = 12$$

We now have the latest start times for all activities starting at node 4. They are 12 and 17 for activities 4–5 and 4–6, respectively. Therefore, the *LF* time for all activities ending at node 4 is 12. Now we can complete the calculations for the rest of the activities:

$$LS_{2-4} = 12 - 7 = 5$$

$$LF_{1-2} = \min[LS_{2-3}, LS_{2-4}]$$

$$= \min[5, 7] = 5$$

$$LS_{1-2} = 5 - 5 = 0$$

The calculations are illustrated in figure 15.4 and summarized in table 15.2.

The slack for each activity is obtained by subtracting the *ES* from the *LS* or the *EF* from the *LF* for that activity. Figure 15.5 exhibits the slack (*S*) for all activities. All activities with zero slack are the critical activities, and they make up the critical path.

Any activity with a positive slack can be delayed by that amount of time without delaying completion of the project. Once an activity is delayed by some amount of time, the slack is changed not only for that activity but for all activities on the path. For example, if activity 4–6 is delayed by five weeks, then the slack for activity 4–6 and for activity 6–9 becomes zero. A knowledge of individual activity slack times provides the managers with flexibility for planning and monitoring the allocation of scarce resources.

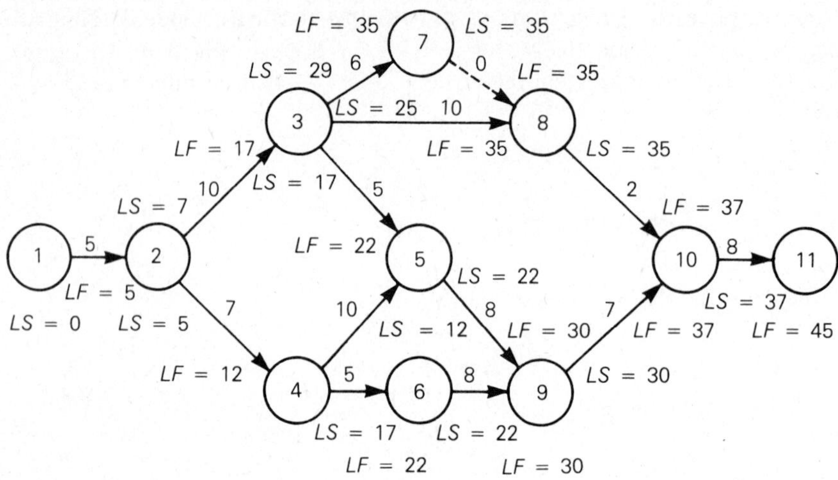

FIGURE 15.4 Calculation of *LF* and *LS*

The Program Evaluation and Review Technique (PERT)

The foregoing discussion of CPM assumed that the durations of activities are known. For most projects, these durations are random variables, and hence many situations require a probabilistic PERT approach. PERT involves three time estimates: optimistic (a), pessimistic (b), and most likely (m). These time estimates are obtained either from past data or from the experience of those who are responsible for completing a specific activity. Once these

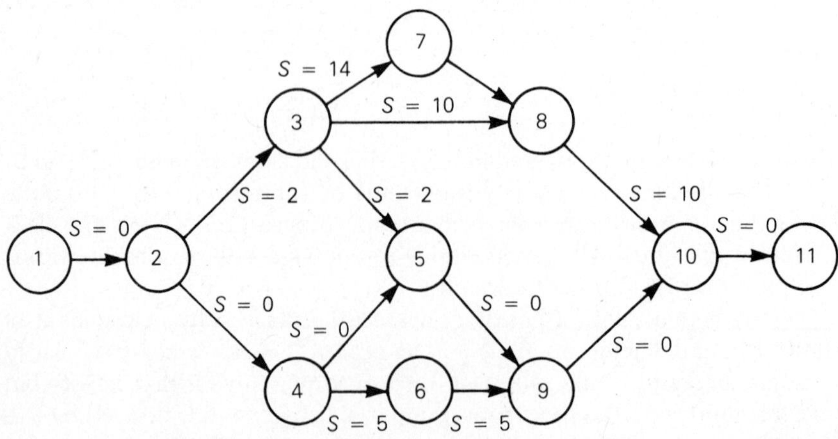

FIGURE 15.5 Calculation of slack and critical path

time estimates are available, the β (beta) probability distribution becomes very handy for computing the expected time t_{i-j} and the variance σ^2_{i-j} of each activity:

$$t_{i-j} = \frac{a + 4m + b}{6}$$

$$\sigma^2_{i-j} = \left(\frac{b - a}{6}\right)^2 = \frac{(b - a)^2}{36}$$

The magnitude of the variance reflects the uncertainty involved in the activity. As the variance gets larger, the uncertainty becomes greater. A knowledge of the variance of the activities on the critical path, and hence the total variance associated with the critical path, facilitate making probability estimates for the project completion dates. The variance of the critical path is given by the sum of the variances of individual activities on the critical path. For example, top management or a government official might like to know the probability of completing an R&D project in forty-two weeks or in a year. Unless we have the probability estimates associated with all activities, we cannot answer these questions. Once we have the probabilistic estimates, the normal probability distribution generally provides a reasonable approximation to the distribution of project completion time, even for a small number of activities. The following example illustrates these concepts.

Example 15.1

The network diagram for a project is shown in figure 15.6. The three time estimates, in weeks, for each activity are shown in table 15.3.

1. Compute the expected time for each activity.
2. Determine the critical path and the expected project duration.

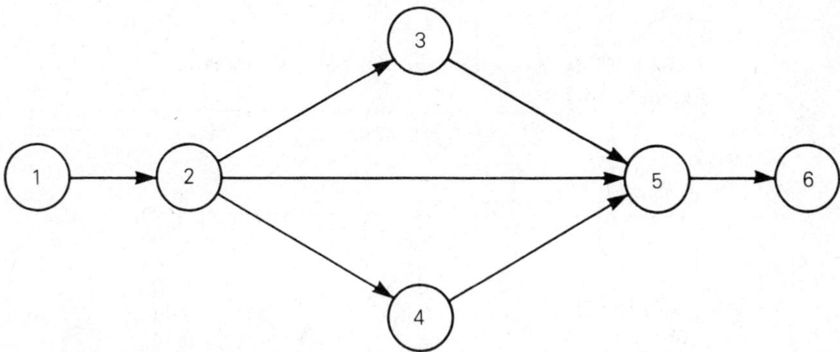

FIGURE 15.6 Precedence diagram for Example 15.1

TABLE 15.3 Time Estimates for Example 15.1

Activity	*Duration (weeks)*		
	a	*m*	*b*
1–2	5	6	13
2–3	2	2	2
2–4	2	5	8
2–5	6	8	10
3–5	3	5	7
4–5	1	3	5
5–6	2	3	10

3. Compute the variance and standard deviation of the critical path.
4. Which activity has the most precise time estimate?
5. What is the probability that the project will be completed in twenty weeks?

Solution: (1) The expected durations and variances of all activities are shown in table 15.4.

(2) We plot the expected times on the network and find *ES*, *EF*, *LS*, and *LF*, for all activities, as shown in figure 15.7. The critical path is depicted by a sequence of activities with slack $S = 0$. Therefore, the critical path in our case is 1, 2, 5, 6. In addition, activities 2–4 and 4–5 are also critical. In other words, we have dual critical paths: 1, 2, 4, 5, 6 and 1, 2, 5, 6. The expected duration T of the critical path is nineteen weeks.

(3) The total variance of the critical path is obtained by summing individual activity variances on the critical path:

$$\sigma^2 = \sigma^2_{1-2} + \sigma^2_{2-4} + \sigma^2_{4-5} + \sigma^2_{5-6}$$

$$= 1.78 + 1 + 0.44 + 1.78 = 5.0.$$

TABLE 15.4 Expected Durations and Variances, Example 15.1

Activity	*Expected Time* $\frac{a + 4m + b}{6}$	*Variance* $\left(\frac{b - a}{6}\right)^2$
1–2	7	1.78
2–3	2	0
2–4	5	1.00
2–5	8	0.44
3–5	5	0.44
4–5	3	0.44
5–6	4	1.78

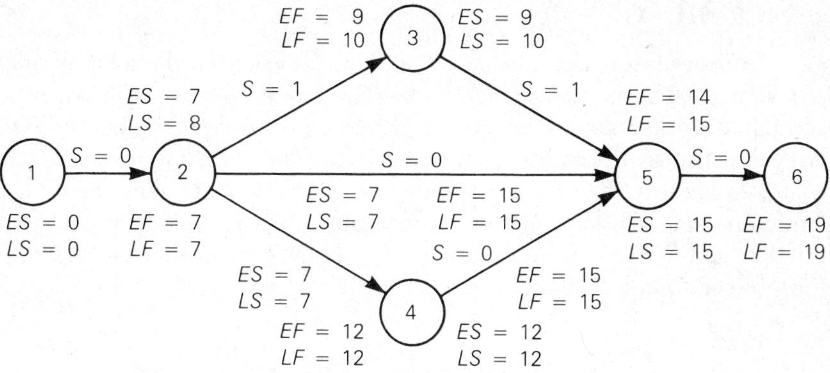

FIGURE 15.7 *ES*, *EF*, *LS*, and *LF* calculations for Example 15.1

or

$$\sigma^2 = \sigma^2_{1-2} + \sigma^2_{2-5} + \sigma^2_{5-6}$$
$$= 1.78 + .44 + 1.78 = 4.0.$$

The variance we use is the larger of the two—that is, 5.0—and the standard deviation is the square root of the variance:

$$\sigma = \sqrt{5} = 2.24$$

(4) Activity 2–3 has the least variance, since its variance is zero.

(5) The normal probability distribution will generally provide a reasonable approximation to the distribution of project durations, and hence it can be used to determine the probabilities for various project completion times:

$$z = \frac{y - T}{\sigma} = \frac{20 - 19}{2.24} = 0.4464$$

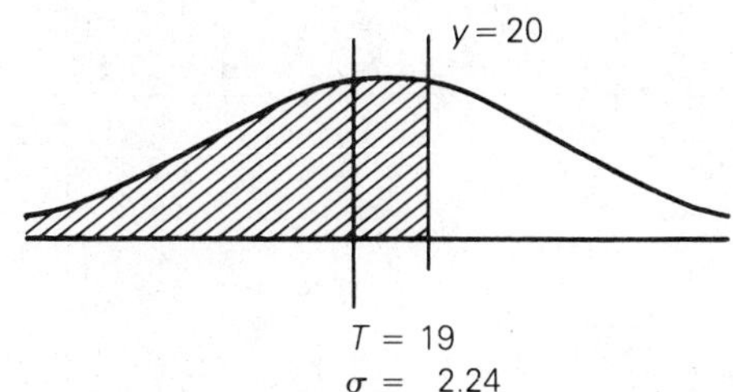

Referring to the normal probability tables, we determine that the shaded area is 0.6736. Therefore, we can state that the probability of completing the project in twenty weeks is 0.6736, or 67.36%.

CRASHING

In many instances, a manager would like to shorten the total duration of a project. The project manager may have some options, such as hiring additional workers and machines or increasing control with supervision on critical projects to expedite their completion time. In these instances, the goal is to identify the time–cost trade-offs and to evaluate alternative plans for minimizing the sum of the indirect and direct project costs. Versions of CPM and PERT can be used to evaluate how best to shorten, or *crash*, the project completion time.

Example 15.2

Suppose that the manager wishes to complete the project shown in figure 15.2 in forty weeks. The crash time estimates—the amount of time it would take to complete an activity if additional resources were allocated—and the costs of allocating resources to corresponding tasks are given in table 15.5. All possible paths are listed in table 15.1. It is evident that we need to expedite activities in paths C and D or activities common to both C and D, since they exceed forty weeks. From table 15.5, we find that the cost of crashing activity 2–4 is the cheapest and 2–3 is next cheapest. By crashing these activities, we can reduce the path by three weeks. By crashing activity 10–11, we gain two more weeks. The total cost associated with this crashing is $16,000. This crashing and an alternative crashing—and their corresponding costs—are as follows:

Alternative	*Activities Crashed*	*Weeks Gained*	*Cost of Crash ($)*
1	2–3, 2–4, 10–11	5	16,000
2	5–9, 10–11	5	16,000

Any other combination yields a higher cost, unless partial crashing is permitted. For example, if we were allowed to reduce two weeks of activity 5–9 for $6,000 in addition to crashing activities 2–3 and 2–4, our total cost of crashing would be only $15,000. In a large network, it is a formidable job

TABLE 15.5 Time–Cost Trade-off Data, Example 15.2

Activity	*Expected Time (weeks)*	*Crash Time (weeks)*	*Cost of Crashing ($)*	*Incremental Cost per Week ($)*
1–2	5	3	10,000	5,000
2–3	10	7	6,000	2,000
2–4	7	4	3,000	1,000
3–5	5	3	4,000	2,000
4–5	10	8	8,000	4,000
5–9	8	5	9,000	3,000
9–10	7	6	10,000	10,000
10–11	8	6	7,000	3,500

to test all combinations and to find all paths that exceed the desired length of duration. Most applications of PERT and CPM use canned computer programs that have been developed to perform the necessary network analysis.

CASH FLOW ANALYSIS

In preceding sections, we have described many techniques for planning and monitoring projects. CPM and PERT can be very useful, not only for scheduling activities but also for monitoring and controlling cash flows. Referring to figures 15.3 and 15.4, we find that CPM and PERT provide a feasible time-phased schedule of activities of the project in either an early start and finish or a late start and finish configuration. Using this information, we can draw Gantt charts. If we were given the cost of completing individual activities, we could find the total cash flow needs for each period according to Gantt chart schedules. For simplicity of calculations, we assume that the cost of an activity is linear. For example, if a project costs $10,000 and it takes four weeks to complete, then we assume that the cost per period is $2,500. However, this assumption is not necessary when working with many CPM/PERT software packages.

Monitoring and controlling project costs involve comparing the expected range of cash flows to the actual costs incurred. If discrepancies are encountered, the project manager can take appropriate action to alleviate the problem.

Example 15.3

The cost of completing each activity in the project represented by figure 15.2 is given in table 15.6. Perform a cash flow analysis. State your assumptions.

TABLE 15.6 Project Activity Costs, Example 15.3

Activity	*Duration (weeks)*	*Cost ($1000s)*	*Cost per Period ($1000s/week)*
1–2	5	20	4
2–3	10	10	1
2–4	7	35	5
3–5	5	10	2
3–7	6	18	3
3–8	10	20	2
4–5	10	30	3
4–6	5	40	8
5–9	8	48	6
6–9	8	48	6
8–10	2	20	10
9–10	7	35	5
10–11	8	40	5

Solution: Based on the data in figure 15.3, we draw a Gantt chart for the earliest possible start (*ES*) and the earliest possible finish (*EF*). Since the duration is expressed in weeks, we assume that a month consists of four weeks. Furthermore, for simplicity of calculations, we assume that activity expenditures are linear. The cash flow for each activity per week is exhibited in table 15.6. For example, activity 1–2 takes five weeks and consumes \$20,000. Based on a four-week month, we show expenses of \$16,000 and

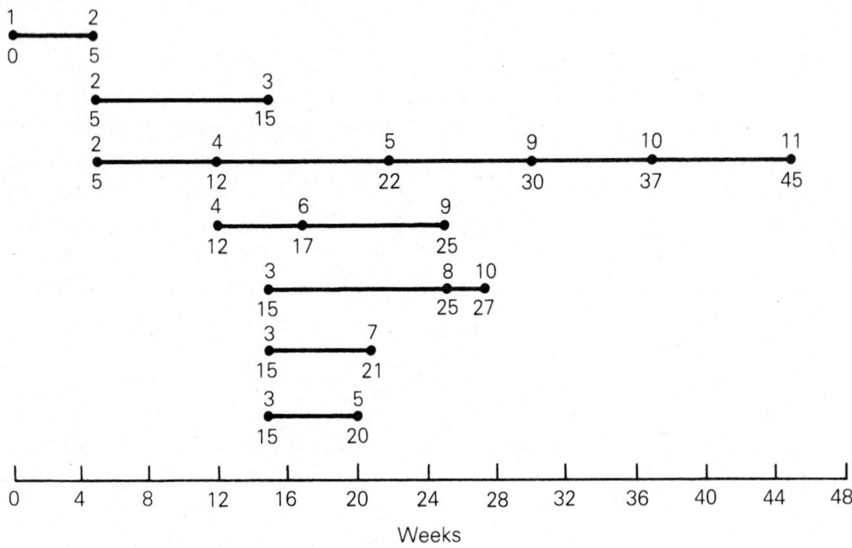

Months

	1	2	3	4	5	6	7	8	9	10	11	12
Activity						($1000s)						
1–2	16	4										
2–3		3	4	3								
2–4		15	20									
3–5				2	8							
3–7				3	12	3						
3–8				2	8	8	2					
4–5				12	12	6						
4–6				32	8							
5–9						12	24	12				
6–9					18	24	6					
8–10							20					
9–10								10	20	5		
10–11										15	20	5
Total	16	22	24	54	66	53	52	22	20	20	20	5

FIGURE 15.8 Gantt chart and cash flow analysis based on the earliest start–earliest finish schedule

$4,000 for months 1 and 2, respectively, in figure 15.8. Total cash flows per month are also exhibited. Similar calculations are shown in figure 15.9 for the latest feasible start (*LS*) and the latest feasible finish (*LF*), as exhibited in figure 15.4. The final step consists of predicting the monthly cash requirements for the project. The ranges are given by the *ES–EF* and *LS–LF* schedule cash flows. Table 15.7 exhibits both the per period and the cumulative expected cash flows for the project.

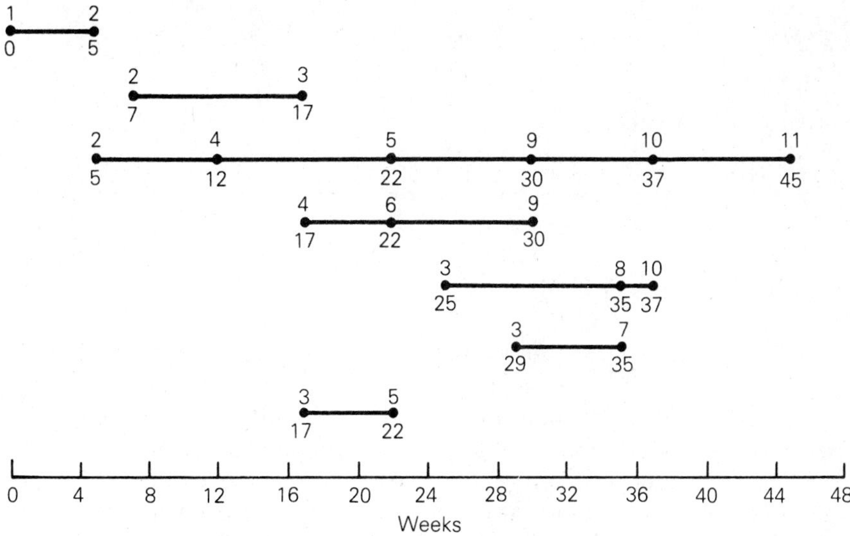

Months

	1	2	3	4	5	6	7	8	9	10	11	12
Activity	($1000s)											
1–2	16	4										
2–3		1	4	4	1							
2–4		15	20									
3–5					6	4						
3–7								9	9			
3–8							6	8	6			
4–5				12	12	6						
4–6					24	16						
5–9						12	24	12				
6–9						12	24	12				
8–10									10	10		
9–10								10	20	5		
10–11										15	20	5
Total	16	20	24	16	43	50	54	51	45	30	20	5

FIGURE 15.9 Gantt chart and cash flow analysis based on the latest feasible start–latest feasible finish schedule

TABLE 15.7 Range of Expected Cash Needs per Month, Example 15.3

	Based on LS Schedule ($1000s)		*Based on ES Schedule ($1000s)*	
Month	*Per Period*	*Cumulative*	*Per Period*	*Cumulative*
1	16	16	16	16
2	20	36	22	38
3	24	60	27	65
4	16	76	51	116
5	43	119	66	182
6	50	169	53	235
7	54	223	52	287
8	51	274	22	309
9	45	319	20	329
10	30	349	20	349
11	20	369	20	369
12	5	374	5	374

Line of Balance (LOB)

An MRP system is very useful when an item containing several production stages and long lead times is mass-produced. However, in many situations, the quantity of items produced is limited, and an MRP system may not be economically feasible. Some examples are the production of aircrafts, missiles, and heavy machinery, where different batches of production could contain different items and there might not be many common parts among products. In such instances, the line of balance (LOB) technique may be more suitable. LOB is a charting and computational technique for monitoring and controlling products and services that are made to meet certain specific delivery dates.

The concept of LOB is similar to the time-phased order-point (TPOP) system and the material requirements planning (MRP) system. We start with the final production date and quantity. Then the product structure tree is laid on the horizontal scale, offsetting lead time on a time scale that reflects the stages of production. The stages could also represent purchased parts, as well as subassembly and assembly operations to support delivery on schedule. The LOB chart depicts the quantity of components, subassemblies, assemblies, and end products produced at every stage and at any given time. It indicates the quantity of goods or services that should be completed at every stage and at any given time in order to meet the delivery date. Therefore, the LOB is the scale against which the progress is measured at any given time. Obviously, actual progress is represented by the LOB chart. We will explain the technique with the following example.

Example 15.4

Amity, Inc., has received orders to deliver beamers, for which the product structure tree and delivery schedule are given here. The test and delivery procedure, which is not shown here, takes a month.

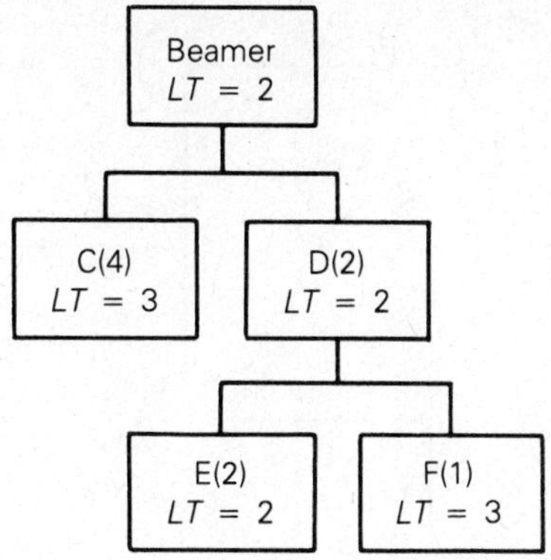

Month	*Quantity*	*Cumulative Quantity*
6	50	50
7	100	150
8	200	350
9	300	650
10	300	950
11	300	1250
12	300	1550

Four months into the shipping schedule, the following cumulative quantities of units have passed through corresponding steps in the production process:

Process Steps	*Cumulative Production*
I	1220
II	1185
III	1150
IV	1125
V	850
VI	720
VII	700

Develop an LOB chart and evaluate the status of production at each production stage, using the line of balance technique.

Solution: As the first step, draw the process plan for producing one unit of beamer (figure 15.10). Second, construct a cumulative delivery schedule and the progress chart on a graph sheet (figure 15.11). Then draw vertical bars on the progress chart to indicate the actual cumulative number of units produced for each production step.

Next, enter the review period—that is, the fourth month—on the graph. We know from the delivery schedule that we should have completed 650 units, and we can also obtain this information by drawing a vertical

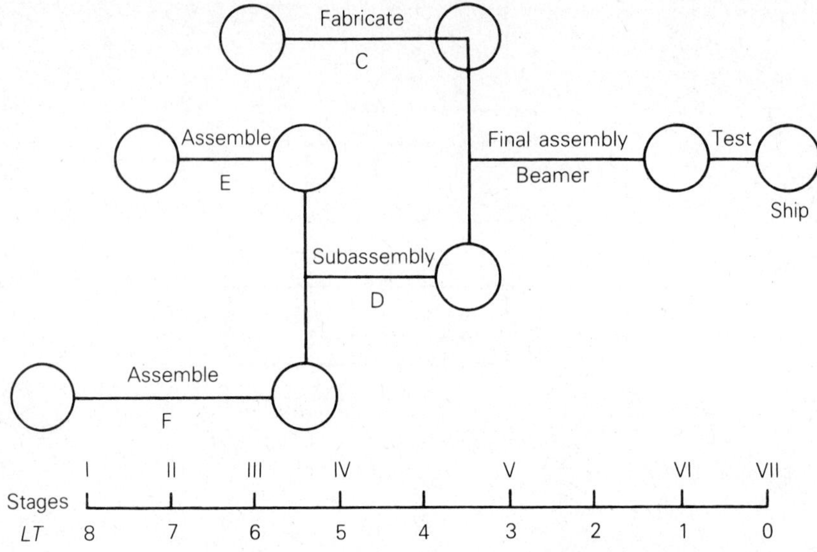

FIGURE 15.10 Process plan, Example 15.4

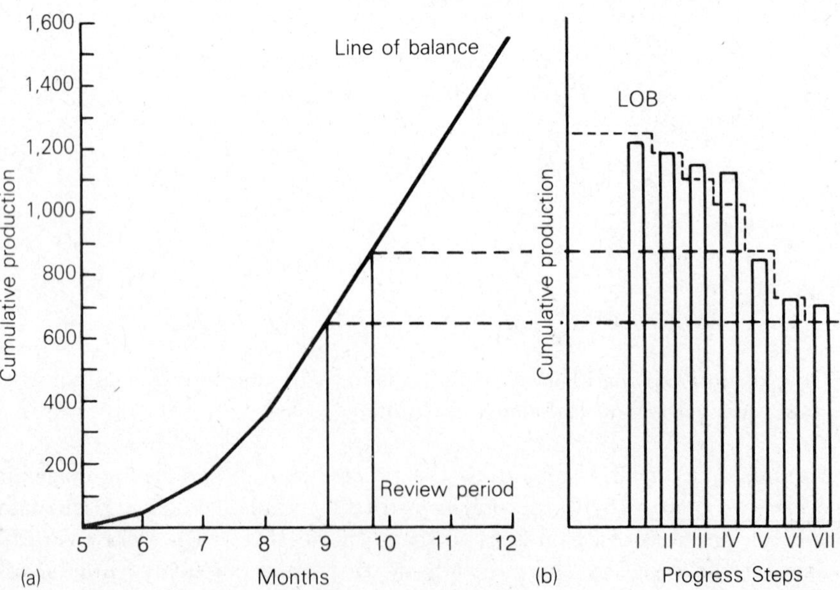

FIGURE 15.11 LOB chart, Example 15.3: (a) cumulative delivery schedule; (b) progress chart

line from the review period to the cumulative delivery schedule curve. Now draw a horizontal line from that point on the curve to stage VII of the progress chart, representing the line of balance for stage VII of production. For other stages, we follow a different procedure. We know, for example, that final assembly and inspection takes three weeks. The cumulative end item production quantity three weeks from the review period will be equal to or less than the cumulative production of part C and subassembly D at stage V now. Therefore, we advance a period of three weeks from the review period—that is, four months and three weeks—and draw a vertical line to the cumulative delivery schedule curve. Now we draw a horizontal line to obtain the line of balance for production at stage V. This means that we should have enough units of C and D to complete 875 units by three weeks from now. In a similar fashion, we can draw the line of balance for every production stage at any given review period. Comparing cumulative production to date and the line of balance, we find that we are behind at stages I and V, whereas we are ahead in stages III, IV, and VII.

A new LOB can be drawn on the progress chart at any given time. Thus, a snapshot evaluation is made of each production stage at regular intervals of weeks or months. These periodic evaluations provide the manager with information about the performance at each stage of the schedule.

Project Scheduling with CPM/MRP

The use of CPM and PERT for cash flow and budgeting decisions were illustrated in an earlier section. The total cost was spread uniformly over the duration of the activity for budgeting purposes. CPM and PERT assume that manpower, machines, and materials are available in the right quantity, at the right time, and in the right place. In the real world, however, material has to be ordered in advance, and adequate capacities of equipment and machinery must be made available when necessary. Suppose that we prepare a master project schedule, list all material requirements, and use an MRP system for procuring them. Essentially, we would have interfaced the CPM and MRP systems. The MRP system can aid in planning and ordering materials according to the current demand obtained from the master project schedule, the amount of inventory on hand, and the quantity of material on order. Inventory records also help in replanning and rescheduling project activities when they are restricted by the capacities of equipment and machinery. Therefore, if we included the procurement of material as part of project planning, the total time necessary to procure materials and complete the activities will be greater than the critical path. Aquilano and Smith [1] stress the importance of an integrated approach in developing a CPM/MRP system. Gessner [6] reports that such a system has been developed by IBM and is used in the ship-building industry.

TABLE 15.8 Project Bill of Material

Parent	*Child*	*Quantity*	*Description*
500–600			
	200–500		
	300–500		
	400–500		
	451	1	Machine
	051	2	Material
300–500	200–300		
	452	1	Equipment
	052	4	Material
400–500	200–400		
	452	1	Equipment
	051	2	Material
200–500	100–200		
	451	1	Machine
	052	2	Material
200–300	100–200		
	451	1	Machine
	052	2	Material
200–400	100–200		
	451	1	Machine
	052	2	Material
100–200	055	3	Labor

THE CPM/MRP MODEL

The CPM/MRP model will be described with the aid of the sample project given in figure 15.6. The project can also be tabulated in the form of an MRP-type indented bill of materials. See table 15.8 for a list of activities, manpower requirements, facilities, and equipment, in addition to the materials usually listed by MRP. Table 15.9 describes the contents

TABLE 15.9 Inventory Status File Description

Description	*Code*	*On Hand*	*On Order*	*Lead Time*	*Activity Duration*
Activity	500–600	0	0		4
Activity	400–500	0	0		3
Activity	300–500	0	0		5
Activity	200–500	0	0		8
Activity	200–400	0	0		5
Activity	200–300	0	0		2
Activity	100–200	0	0		7
Material	051	0	0	2	
Material	052	0	0	5	
Labor	055	0	0	4	
Machine	451	0	0	2	
Equipment	452	0	0	4	

of the inventory status file, including all activities, materials, labor, machines, and equipment and their associated codes. The file also includes the durations of activities and the lead times required to acquire these resources. Figure 15.12 shows the project in the form of a project structure tree. The solid lines connect activities of a path in the CPM diagram. Also shown are the codes for the resources, such as manpower, labor, equipment, and machinery, necessary to complete the task. Activity durations (t) or lead times (LT) are given along with the codes. Since an activity may be common to one or more paths, the project structure tree may show an activity more than once. For example, activity 100–200 is part of three paths, and hence it is listed three times. This may lead to the duplication of resource inputs. To prevent this, an activity is allowed to occur only one time, when it is first needed in the schedule. Duplications of requirements should be ignored by the system as they occur [1].

Using the procedure described earlier, we compute ES, EF, LS, and LF for the project structure tree, as exhibited in figure 15.12. The numbers at the corners of the project structure rectangles represent these variables. For example, activity 200–300, with duration $t = 2$, is exhibited as follows:

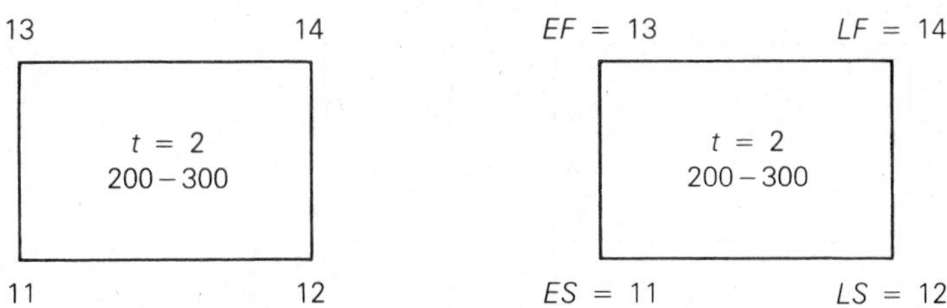

Once the computations are made for all activities and resources, the information can be used in the MRP-like system or in an actual MRP environment. Table 15.10 portrays MRP tables for the project schedule with latest possible starts and table 15.11 gives them with earliest feasible starts. Thus, these two tables provide the lower and upper limits of dates for starting activities or acquiring resources. We see from figure 15.12 that the project needs twenty-three weeks, instead of nineteen weeks, as originally planned.

The CPM/MRP schedules assume that adequate capacities of resources exist. Suppose that we do not have adequate capacity for activity 200–300 either by latest or earliest starts. Then we might have to start the activity one or more periods earlier to complete the project on time. If this is infeasible, the project may have to be prolonged beyond the dates given by the CPM/MRP schedules. In that case, we might end up revising several other activity schedule dates to comply with the new project completion date. Steinberg, Lee, and Khumawala [9] report that they have developed an MRP-type resource-constrained CPM system, which was adopted by NASA for flight operations planning and scheduling.

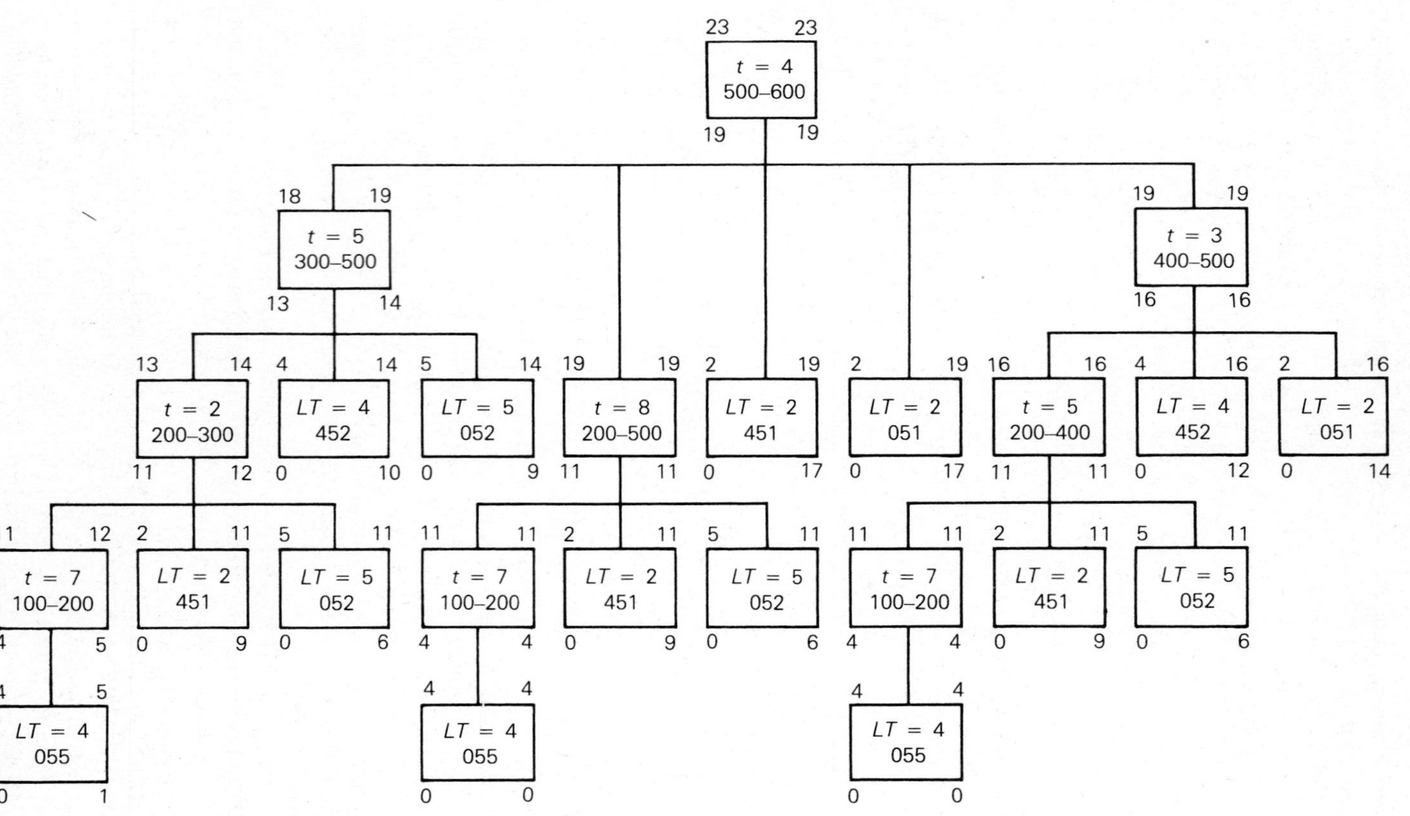

FIGURE 15.12 Project structure tree

TABLE 15.10 CPM/MRP Latest Start Schedule for Branch 055-100-200-300-500-600

Activity 500–600 (LT = 4)

	0	1	2	3	4	5	6	7	8	9	10	11	12	13	14	15	16	17	18	19	20	21	22	23
GR																								1
PR																								1
OH	0																							0
POR																				1				

Activity 300–500 (LT = 5)

	0	1	2	3	4	5	6	7	8	9	10	11	12	13	14	15	16	17	18	19	20	21	22	23
GR																				1				
PR																				1				
OH	0																			0				
POR															1									

Activity 200–300 (LT = 2)

	0	1	2	3	4	5	6	7	8	9	10	11	12	13	14	15	16	17	18	19	20	21	22	23
GR															1									
PR															1									
OH	0														0									
POR													1											

Activity 100–200 (LT = 7)

	0	1	2	3	4	5	6	7	8	9	10	11	12	13	14	15	16	17	18	19	20	21	22	23
GR													1											
PR													1											
OH	0												0											
POR																								

TABLE 15.10 Continued

Labor 055 (LT = 4)

	0	1	2	3	4	5	6	7	8	9	10	11	12	13	14	15	16	17	18	19	20	21	22	23
GR						3																		
PR						3																		
OH	0					0																		
POR		3																						

Equipment 452 (LT = 4)

	0	1	2	3	4	5	6	7	8	9	10	11	12	13	14	15	16	17	18	19	20	21	22	23
GR															1									
PR															1									
OH	0														0									
POR											1													

Machine 451 (LT = 2)

	0	1	2	3	4	5	6	7	8	9	10	11	12	13	14	15	16	17	18	19	20	21	22	23
GR												1												
PR												1												
OH	0											0												
POR										1														

Material 052 (LT = 5)

	0	1	2	3	4	5	6	7	8	9	10	11	12	13	14	15	16	17	18	19	20	21	22	23
GR												1			1									
PR												1			1									
OH	0											0			0									
POR							1			1														

TABLE 15.11 CPM/MRP Earliest Start Schedule for Branch 055-100-200-300-500-600

Activity 500–600 (LT = 4)

	0	1	2	3	4	5	6	7	8	9	10	11	12	13	14	15	16	17	18	19	20	21	22	23
GR																								1
PR																								1
OH	0																							0
POR																				1				

Activity 300–500 (LT = 5)

	0	1	2	3	4	5	6	7	8	9	10	11	12	13	14	15	16	17	18	19	20	21	22	23
GR																			1					
PR																			1					
OH	0																		0					
POR														1										

Activity 200–300 (LT = 2)

	0	1	2	3	4	5	6	7	8	9	10	11	12	13	14	15	16	17	18	19	20	21	22	23
GR														1										
PR														1										
OH	0													0										
POR												1												

Activity 100–200 (LT = 7)

	0	1	2	3	4	5	6	7	8	9	10	11	12	13	14	15	16	17	18	19	20	21	22	23
GR												1												
PR												1												
OH	0											0												
POR					1																			

TABLE 15.11 Continued

Labor 055 (LT = 4)

	0	*1*	*2*	*3*	*4*	*5*	*6*	*7*	*8*	*9*	*10*	*11*	*12*	*13*	*14*	*15*	*16*	*17*	*18*	*19*	*20*	*21*	*22*	*23*
GR					1																			
PR					1																			
OH	0				0																			
POR	1																							

Equipment 452 (LT = 4)

	0	*1*	*2*	*3*	*4*	*5*	*6*	*7*	*8*	*9*	*10*	*11*	*12*	*13*	*14*	*15*	*16*	*17*	*18*	*19*	*20*	*21*	*22*	*23*
GR					1																			
PR					1																			
OH	0				0																			
POR	1																							

Machine 451 (LT = 2)

	0	*1*	*2*	*3*	*4*	*5*	*6*	*7*	*8*	*9*	*10*	*11*	*12*	*13*	*14*	*15*	*16*	*17*	*18*	*19*	*20*	*21*	*22*	*23*
GR			1																					
PR			1																					
OH	0		0																					
POR	1																							

Material 052 (LT = 5)

	0	*1*	*2*	*3*	*4*	*5*	*6*	*7*	*8*	*9*	*10*	*11*	*12*	*13*	*14*	*15*	*16*	*17*	*18*	*19*	*20*	*21*	*22*	*23*
GR						2																		
PR						2																		
OH	0					0																		
POR	2																							

Summary

Many project scheduling techniques, including CPM and PERT, are valuable tools for controlling project times and costs. Several CPM/PERT commercial software packages are available in the market for use in large computers, minicomputers, and microcomputers. It must be realized, however, that CPM/PERT is not a panacea for all the ills of industry and business. If management is poor, if planning efforts are slight, or if the estimates for the project are unrealistic, then CPM/PERT will be of little help. It is important to realize that these are only tools to aid good management in making better decisions.

PROBLEMS

1. The following table lists all activities necessary to procure and build a soda bottling facility:

Activity	*Description*	*Predecessors*	*Duration (weeks)*
1–2	Market research and design building		12
2–3	Site selection	1–2	8
2–4	Supplier selection	1–2	6
2–6	Personnel selection	1–2	6
3–5	Construct building	2–3	8
4–5	Procure machinery	2–4	12
4–6	Prepare procedures	2–4	4
5–7	Install machinery	3–5, 4–5	2
6–7	Personnel training	2–6, 4–6	2
7–8	Launch	5–7, 6–7	4

Construct a CPM diagram and identify the critical path. What is the minimum time required to get the project rolling? Make a table of *ES, EF, LS, LF,* and slack.

2. The following table provides the costs of each activity in problem 1 for normal time and crash time:

Activity	*Normal Time (weeks)*	*Crash Time (weeks)*	*Normal Cost ($1000s)*	*Crash Cost ($1000s)*
1–2	12	8	80	120
2–3	8	6	20	25
2–4	6	4	10	15
2–6	6	4	10	15
3–5	8	5	150	180
4–5	12	8	250	300
4–6	4	3	10	15
5–7	2	2	60	—
6–7	2	2	50	—
7–8	4	2	50	70

The owner feels that the project should be completed in thirty-two weeks. Estimate the additional cost that will be incurred due to crashing.

3. The owner of the soda bottling firm is financing the project through a bank loan. The bank requires a monthly (four week) cash flow statement for the project. Using the *ES* and *LS* approaches, calculate the range of cumulative cash flows required for completing the project using normal time durations.

4. A project has the following schedule:

Activity	*Predecessors*	*Duration (days)*
A	—	10
B	—	3
C	A	7
D	B	10
E	B	12
F	C, D	6
G	E	5
H	E	6
I	G	7
J	H	5
K	I, J	2
L	F	4
M	L, K	10

Construct a CPM diagram and find the critical path. Tabulate *ES*, *EF*, *LS*, *LF*, and slack for each activity. (*Hint:* In this problem, we have specified activity labels instead of node numbers. Make up your own node numbers when you draw the diagram. We have started the diagram; you should not have much trouble in completing it.)

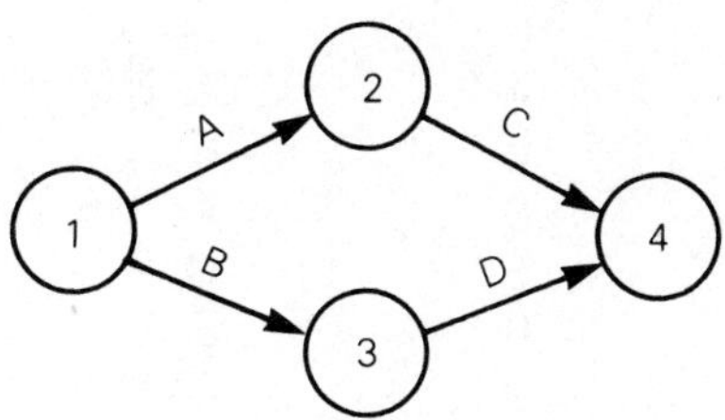

5. The manager feels that the durations given in problem 4 are very tentative. Therefore, he would like to use probabilistic time estimates, as follows:

Activity	*Optimistic Duration (days)*	*Pessimistic Duration (days)*	*Probable Duration (days)*
A	8	15	10
B	2	7	3
C	5	10	7
D	8	15	10
E	8	20	12
F	5	9	6
G	4	6	5
H	5	5	5
I	5	9	7
J	4	8	5
K	2	2	2
L	3	6	4
M	8	12	10

Based on these estimates, calculate *ES*, *EF*, *LS*, *LF*, and minimum duration for completion of the project.

6. What is the probability of completing the project described in problem 5:
   a. In thirty-five days?
   b. In forty-five days?
   c. In the time frame specified by PERT?
   d. Which activity in problem 5 has the most uncertainty?
   e. Which activity has the least uncertainty? Why?

7. The following activities should be accomplished for completing an R&D project:

Activity	*Time (months)*	*Predecessors*	*Cost ($1000s)*
A	3	—	30
B	6	—	40
C	4	A, B	40
D	2	B	30
E	8	A	10
F	6	C	15
G	9	E, F	10
H	9	D, F	20
I	2	G, H	15
J	13	B	30
K	5	I, J	15

Construct a CPM diagram and determine the project duration. Construct a table containing the slack for each activity.

8. Prepare a quarterly cash flow analysis for problem 7, using ES dates.

9. Holland Electric Company installs wiring and electrical fixtures for residential and commercial buildings. The manager generally likes to organize all activities so that she can complete the project on time. The activities and their optimistic completion times (*a*), most likely completion times (*m*), and pessimistic completion times (*b*) are as follows:

Activity	*Days* *a*	*m*	*b*	*Immediate Predecessor*
A	7	9	11	—
B	5	6	9	—
C	3	5	8	—
D	10	20	35	A
E	6	7	8	C
F	7	9	11	B, D, E
G	6	8	10	B, D, E
H	5	7	12	F
I	14	15	17	F
J	6	8	12	G, H
K	4	5	6	I, J
L	9	9	9	G, H

a. Construct a network for this problem.
b. Determine the expected times and variances for each activity.

c. Calculate *ES, EF, LS, LF,* and slack for each activity.
d. Determine the critical path and project the completion time.
e. Determine the probability that the project will require more than 65 days.

10. The costs of completing each activity in problem 9 are as follows:

Activity	*Cost ($)*
A	200
B	300
C	500
D	100
E	200
F	700
G	1500
H	2500
I	1700
J	2000
K	500
L	1000

Assuming a five-day work week and LS schedule, provide a cash flow analysis for problem 9.

11. A manufacturer of stereo equipment has the following information related to activities necessary to procure and build a local facility:

Activity	*Description*	*Predecessor*	*Duration (weeks)*
1–2	Market research/design	—	10
2–3	Site selection	1–2	4
2–6	Personnel selection	1–2	4
2–5	Legal/environmental	1–2	6
2–4	Select vendors	1–2, 2–6	8
3–5	Building construction	2	8
3–6	Purchase equipment	2–4	6
4–5	Establish procedures	2–4	4
4–6	Install test equipment	4–5, 2–5, 3–5	4
6–7	Train personnel	2–6, 4–6	2
7–8	Begin operations	6–7, 5–7	4

Construct a CPM diagram and identify the critical path. What is the minimum time required to get the business started? Construct a table of *ES, FS, LS, LF,* and slack.

12. The following are the costs of each activity in problem 11 for normal time and crash time:

Activity	Normal Time (weeks)	Crash Time (weeks)	Normal Cost ($1000s)	Crash Cost ($1000s)
1–2	10	8	75	100
2–3	4	2	20	30
2–6	4	2	20	30
2–5	6	6	10	10
2–4	8	6	50	60
3–5	8	6	180	220
4–5	6	4	160	200
4–6	4	3	20	30
5–7	4	3	40	—
6–7	2	2	40	40
7–8	4	2	60	90

The owner feels that the project should be completed in thirty weeks. Estimate the additional cost that will be incurred due to crashing.

13. For financing requirements, and using the normal time durations and *LS* approaches, calculate the range of cumulative cash flows required for completing the project in problem 11. (Cash flow statements are due every four weeks.)

14. A manager of a construction company is reviewing the activities in a current project. The schedule is as follows:

Activity	Predecessors	Duration (weeks)
A	—	10
B	—	5
C	A	8
D	A	12
E	B	13
F	B, D	8
G	C	6
H	E, F	4
I	B, D	8
J	G, I	10
K	H, J	6

Construct a CPM diagram and identify the critical path. Tabulate *ES, EF, LS, LF,* and slack for each activity. For this problem, make up your own node numbers.

15. Probabilistic time estimates for the project in problem 14 are as follows:

Activity	*Optimistic Duration (weeks)*	*Pessimistic Duration (weeks)*	*Probable Duration (weeks)*
A	8	14	10
B	2	7	5
C	6	10	8
D	10	15	12
E	10	15	13
F	6	15	8
G	6	6	6
H	4	6	4
I	4	9	8
J	8	15	10
K	4	8	6

Based on these estimates, calculate *ES, EF, LS, LF,* and minimum duration for completion of the project.

16. What is the probability of completing the project in problem 15:
    a. In forty days?
    b. In the time frame supplied by PERT?
    c. Which activity in problem 15 has the most uncertainty?
    d. Which activity has the least uncertainty? Why?

17. Mason Co. has received orders for M-120 terminals, for which the product structure tree and delivery schedule are given. The test and delivery procedure (not shown) takes one month.

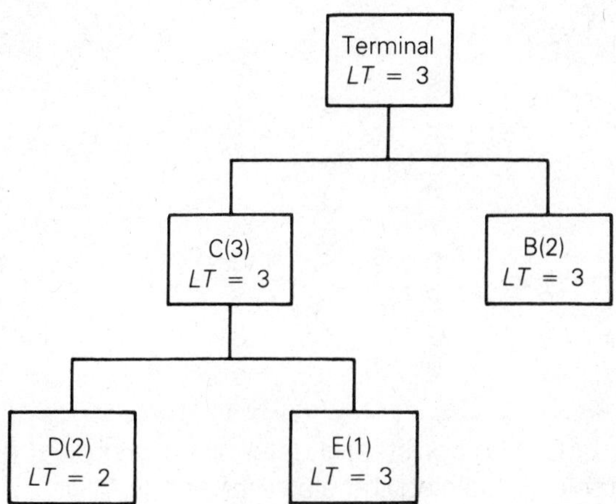

Month	*Quantity*	*Cumulative Quantity*
2	100	100
3	150	250
4	200	450
5	200	650
6	350	1000
7	350	1350
8	350	1700

Five months into the shipping schedule, the following cumulative quantities of units have passed through corresponding steps in the production process.

Process Steps	*Cumulative Production*
1	*1320*
2	*1260*
3	*1220*
4	*1000*
5	*800*

Develop an LOB chart and evaluate the status of production at each production stage, using the line of balance technique.

18. An oil exploration project has been proposed. The following table shows the activities involved in completing the project:

Activity	*Time (months)*	*Predecessors*	*Cost ($10,000s)*
1	4	—	20
2	6	—	30
3	3	1, 2	30
4	9	2	10
5	8	1, 2	10
6	7	3, 4	20
7	8	3, 4	40
8	2	5, 7	40
9	12	8	15
10	4	6, 9	10

Construct a CPM diagram and determine the project duration. Construct a table containing the slack for each activity.

19. Prepare a quarterly cash flow analysis for problem 18, using *LS* dates.

20. For Carter Company, an electrical engineering firm, the project activities and their optimistic (*a*), most likely (*m*), and pessimistic (*b*) completion times are as follows:

Activity	*a*	*m*	*b*	*Immediate Predecessor*
A	5	6	8	—
B	7	9	12	—
C	3	5	7	—
D	6	7	8	*C*
E	10	15	18	*A*
F	5	7	12	*B, E*
G	14	20	24	*A*
H	4	6	8	*D, F*
I	8	9	10	*G, H*
J	4	5	7	*I*

TABLE 15.12 Project Bills of Material, Problem 21

Activities		*Activity Duration (weeks)*	*Quantity (Lead Time)*	*Description*
Parent	*Child*			
500–600		6		
	200–500			
	300–500			
	400–500			
	351		1 (6)	Equipment
	051		2 (2)	Material
400–500		8		
	100–400			
	352		2 (8)	Equipment
	052		4 (3)	Material
300–500		3		
	100–300			
	353		1 (4)	Equipment
	052		2 (1)	Material
200–500		4		
	100–200			
	354		4 (5)	Equipment
100–400		2		
	355		3 (6)	Equipment
	053		2 (1)	Material
100–300		2		
	054		2 (5)	Material
100–200		2		
	055		2 (2)	Material

a. Construct a network for this problem.
b. Determine the expected times and variances for each activity.
c. Determine the critical path and project the completion time.
d. Determine the probability that the project will not be completed in fifty days.

21. A U.S. firm has decided to locate a plant in France. The firm's bills of material are shown in table 15.12.
   a. Based on the parent activities, find the shortest amount of time necessary to complete the project.
   b. Based on the combined parent–child relationship, find the critical path and its duration.

REFERENCES AND BIBLIOGRAPHY

1. N. J. Aquilano and D. E. Smith, "A Formal Set of Algorithms for Project Scheduling with Critical Path Scheduling/Material Requirements Planning," *Journal of Operations Management,* Vol. 1, No. 2 (November 1980), pp. 57–67.
2. T. M. Cook and R. A. Russell, *Introduction to Management Science* (Englewood Cliffs, N.J.: Prentice-Hall, 1981).
3. E. W. Davis, "Project Scheduling under Resource Constraints—Historical Review and Categorization of Procedures," *AIIE Transactions,* Vol. 5, No. 4 (December 1973), pp. 297–313.
4. H. F. Evarts, *Introduction to PERT,* (Boston: Allyn and Bacon, 1964).
5. N. Gaither, *Production and Operations Management* (Hinsdale, Ill.: Dryden Press, 1980).
6. R. Gessner, "Use Networking, MRP, or Both?" *Production and Inventory Management Review and APICS News,* December 1981, pp. 22–23.
7. R. I. Levin and C. A. Kirkpatrick, *Planning and Control with PERT/CPM,* (New York: McGraw-Hill, 1966).
8. L. A. Smith and P. Mahler, "Comparing Commercially Available CPM/PERT Computer Programs," *Industrial Engineering,* Vol. 10, No. 4 (April 1978), pp. 37–39.
9. E. Steinberg, W. B. Lee, and B. M. Khumawala, "A Requirements Planning System for the Space Shuttle Operations Schedule," *Journal of Operations Management,* Vol. 1, No. 2 (November 1980), pp. 69–76.

appendix 15a

Building Block #6: Planning and Control (Part Three)

Eric Peterson

Last month we identified the Master Plan as the primary project Planning document. However, the Master Plan, as its counterpart the Master Production Schedule, is not in sufficient detail to describe work content or control progress and costs. Therefore we must transform this generic master plan to specific detail tasks.

The methodology to accomplish this is the Work Breakdown Structure (WBS). It is a level by level breakdown of the project from complex objective to simple work package—from "Implement MRP" to "assign storeroom availability code". The WBS is similar in structure and intent to the Bill of Material.

In Figure 15A.1, we have followed the breakdown from MRP (The Total Program), through Inventory Control (A project or sub-project), to write manual procedures (TASK), to write Storeroom Procedures (SUBTASK), to a specific transaction—Return to Stock (Work Package). Now some might argue that write Storeroom Procedures or even write Inventory Procedures might have been sufficient detail. Fine, but that depends on how much control you want to exercise. Having written a few manual procedures I know what a time consuming job it can be.

In this case it took five levels to get to a satisfactory level of detail. There is nothing sacred about five. But levels are important. They reduce the span of control, they depict relationship of tasks to sub objectives, they permit categorization, responsibility and cost assignment. By jumping directly from a general objective to a detail task it is inevitable that many tasks will be overlooked. The level by level approach permits us to reveal the enormity of the task at hand in an "easy to take" manner.

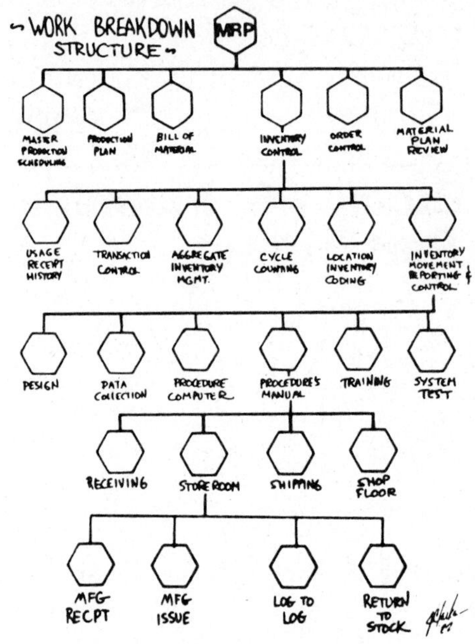

FIGURE 15A.1

There are really very few rules to Work Breakdown Structures. There is no set classification by level. For example, in the first level, I identify the major subsystems (or projects); Next, I decided to break subsystems down by generic activities, and so on. *Some rules:*

- The WBS should be prepared by the Project Manager with each team member. The Project Manager provides the consistency of language and structure throughout.
- It is best to complete the scope at each level for the total project before moving to the next level. In this manner it is easiest to identify common tasks as we get to lower levels. For example, the storeroom transactions will affect Shop Floor Control, MRP and possibly the Purchasing Modules. By reviewing each level and anticipating commonality, duplicate effort may be avoided.
- The sum of the parts at each level must define the total scope of the next higher level.
- Rigorous attention to detail will keep required work from "slipping through the cracks".
- Scope, type and amount of work should be expressed in simple common language.

The Work Breakdown Structure, when completed, is a powerful tool for project control. As in the BOM we are now able to "explode" external changes from the environment through the Master Plan down to the lowest level of work. Furthermore, we may "peg up" through the WBS to depict the impact of schedule shortfalls or cost overruns on the total project.

The Work Breakdown Structure becomes the basis for:

• *Network Scheduling:* relationships, dependencies and common tasks have been defined.

• *Costing:* costs are easiest to define when working with the simple work package. Rolling up costs through subsequent levels of WBS is the same as a Standard Cost Roll.

• *Responsibility:* each level of responsibility may be identified and assigned.

• *Control:* actual performance and its effect on each component of the WBS can be monitored and represented.

The Work Breakdown Structure is the central communication and control tool within the project. In total it describes the sum of work that must be performed, who is responsible and what is affected by performance.

The importance of this tool is best described by Harold Kerzner PhD, author of *Project Management: A Systems Approach to Planning, Scheduling and Controlling:* "Whenever work is structured, understood, easily identifiable and within the capabilities of the individuals, then there will almost always exist a high degree of confidence that the objective can be reached."

Pruning

The Work Breakdown Structure looks like an inverted tree. The tree describes the total effort necessary to accomplish the objective. (Permit me to stretch this analogy a little further). The tree and the project require resources, (Tree: minerals, water/Project: dollars, man hours) to bear fruit. In both instances resources may be limited.

A technique that gardeners use to improve the fruit bearing capability of a tree is pruning. In pruning we cut back marginally producing "live" branches so that nutrients (resources) need not be shared as widely to give more strength to the remaining limbs.

As the project manager realizes that the resources available are not sufficient to cause the multiple sub-objectives to bear fruit; he must cut back, or prune, thereby concentrating resources in critical areas so that they may flourish. The alternative is a slowly growing, possibly dying project unable to bear fruit.

Pruning the project requires that the project manager recognize those objectives most likely to profit by additional resources. Aided by the Work Breakdown Structure the project manager has the tools to select where the cutting must take place.

There are many strategies to pruning. In some cases we may prune one or more sub-objectives such as Requirements Planning, Capacity Planning and Shop Floor control, thereby concentrating resources in Master Scheduling, Bill of Material and Inventory. This results in a healthy but lopsided tree. Another strategy is to maintain all the branches but reduce the project scope. Possibly this would mean implementing the system for a specific product line or manufacturing facility. In this case we end up with a well-rounded but small tree.

In either case we have maintained the life and thrust of the project.

So, when resources are tight, prune for progress.

appendix 15B

Solving Specifics For Today's Management

Towner B. Case

During the 1980's and beyond, manufacturing Management will place increasing emphasis on the financial implications of a manufacturing plan. To do this, clear and concise understanding with regard to the content of Cost of Goods (CGS) and its effect on bottom line profits, will be required. Using computers, managers will be able to measure the effects on CGS of changing forecasts, production schedules and budgeting variances. These measurements will help fine-tune the Forecast and develop a cost, material and capacity sensitive Master Production Schedule.

Understanding the nature of the problem being solved by Manufacturing Resource Planning (MRP II) requires a quick review of the total business control cycle. It is obvious that *planning, analysis* and *control* make up the key phases of a continuing, closed-loop system which requires input and feedback of all functional areas.

Moreover, to understand why CGS is the focal point we can review typical reports which functional manufacturing departments receive today, such as;

- Purchase Price Variance
- Unmatched Labor
- Over and Under Issues of Material
- Actual vs. Standard Labor Variances

These reports provide financial variance information, indicating department performance. Our job is to reconcile the variance and institute changes to improve future periods.

Many times, *Analysis* indicates changes have occurred in marketing forecasts, material costs, engineering changes and normal delays to mention a few.

In the past, manufacturing companies tightened controls and established elaborate measurement tools (e.g., Purchasing and Shop Floor Control), to regulate expenditures for material and labor. This was fairly successful and led to the eventual development of Material Requirements Planning (MRP). This was followed by Capacity Requirements Planning (CRP). These developments produced analytical tools that basically led to an understanding of the cause and effect relationship between planning and control.

Unfortunately, these tools represented a near to intermediate term planning, analysis and control cycle. The "tail is still wagging the dog" and many manufacturing executives would like to more fully understand the financial effect of plans throughout the entire business control cycle. Due to fluctuating dollar values, changing market demands and general improvements in technology, manufacturers are finding a need for more controlled flexibility than ever before.

Definition

To understand the cost ingredients that make up CGS we can examine a typical Manufacturing Cost Flow.

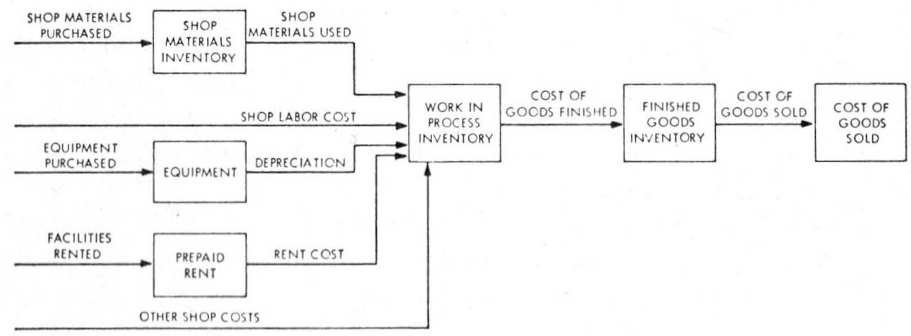

FIGURE 15B.1 Manufacturing cost flows to support annual plan

We can readily see from the manufacturing cost diagram, our product's costs are made up of many independent inputs. Further diagnostics can summarize these costs as *Labor*, *Material* and *Burden*.

Labor is made up of the standard (or actual) labor hours to make one piece multiplied by that work area's labor rate in dollars and cents. This can be described as:

Hrs./piece × Labor Costs/hr. = Labor Costs/Piece

The labor rates are established based on hourly pay and annual increases averaged over a particular department or cost center. The standard hours are engineered, measured and readjusted yearly as technology and product methods change.

Material costs are simply the standard (usually set yearly by Purchasing) or actual prices paid for raw or component materials. Some material costs are expenses (e.g., supplies, hardware) and are not directly tied to a product. These costs will be absorbed in the overhead or burden rate.

Finally, to understand CGS totally, we must analyze overhead, more commonly known as Burden. Burden can be defined as the accumulation of all production/factory costs that cannot be traced specifically to a job or product. This category includes indirect labor and expensed materials, clerical and supervisory salaries, depreciation on buildings and equipment, maintenance, repairs and taxes on property, cost of money, insurance and so forth.

Some costs are treated as overhead because it would be unsound to treat them as direct costs. For example, overtime premiums paid to direct labor should not be charged to the jobs that the foreman or supervisor schedules during overtime hours. Instead, this portion of direct labor cost should be treated as factory overhead.

Each year, at budget time, the entire factory overhead costs are totalled. These costs are separated into budget expenses for manufacturing and averaged over 12 months to establish a burden rate or overhead costing rate. To state this average, we must divide by some measure of the total volume of production activity, such as the estimated direct labor costs to be incurred during that year:

$$\text{Burden Rate} = \frac{\text{Total Factory Overhead Costs}}{\text{Production Volume as Direct Labor Costs}}$$

Some companies will not average burden rates and will instead predict the occurrence of major changes due to labor settlements, technology shifts, etc. Thus, if the total direct labor cost for the period were \$100,000 and the total factory overhead \$80,000, the charge to each job or product would be 80 percent of the direct labor cost incurred on that job or product.

Once the burden rate is established and approved, most companies standard-cost their products through the labor, material and burden components:

$$\text{Labor} + \text{Material} + \text{Burden} = \text{Total Unit Cost}$$

A further breakdown will show that:

$$\begin{gathered}\text{Hrs./piece} \times \text{Labor Rates \$/Hr.}\\ + \\ \text{Material \$}\\ + \\ \frac{(\text{Direct Labor \$} \times \text{Total Factory Costs})}{\text{Direct Labor Costs}} = \text{Total Unit Cost}\end{gathered}$$

It is now clear that the key to controlling costs is measuring the variances between actual costs incurred and the established standard costs. These variances will be apparent in:

- Purchase Price
- Nonproductive Time
- Overtime
- Changes in Budgeted Overhead
- Labor Rate Adjustments

Although all of these variances affect bottom line profits, some companies will attribute gains and losses to a CGS variance through the factory overhead. Typically, these adjustments are overtime and labor rate adjustments.

We can see that the actual-to-standard variances will affect the CGS, on a period by period basis, as do adjustments to the forecast. We will focus our attention on these forecast adjustments in order to understand how and when to measure the effects on CGS and, thus, company income. The adjustments will typically come in the form of product mix changes, which will then affect the amount of direct versus indirect labor, and also material. The changes in labor and material will cause a shift in the burden rate and thereby in CGS. Two exceptions must be noted:

1. Most manufacturers will have multiple labor and burden rates for departments. These will produce an even greater swing in CGS due to product mix.
2. We have described a standard cost approach to aid in defining costing terminology. While this approach considers a majority of modern companies, many companies do costing on a job oriented basis. Some of these methods are:
   A. First In/First Out (FIFO)
   B. Last In/Last Out (LIFO)
   C. Average Cost
   D. Job or Actual Cost
   E. Cost Plus Fixed Fee (CPFF)

Controlling Manufacturing

From the late 1950's to the present, we have developed financial techniques for controlling the business. Inventory systems with Reorder Point were designed and developed to help regulate a major resource. Bills of Material were established, on a gross basis, to help calculate total material needs. Most companies began an avid campaign to measure material and labor variances. With these tools and other management reports, executives began to measure the business on a periodic basis and apply the results quickly and efficiently to help finetune future periods.

Buying techniques and the cost control of materials improved while stock outs and material-sensitive down time became almost nonexistent. Although a limited number of computer-based techniques existed, the logic and approach was fairly fundamental. This allowed companies to institute these tools and reap the rewards.

Unfortunately, in the early 1970's a business downturn caught manufacturers with excess inventory on hand and on order. Again, we struck back with logic and determined that we were working at a detail level and controlling material and labor independently.

Although we now had tools for inventory and order tracking, our timing was off and inventories were not balanced. Too much expediting was a part of normal manufacturing activity and variances were only determined after month end. Order backlogs had dropped and the pressure was on to get a better handle on all phases of the process.

Analyzing Manufacturing

The control phase had produced many valuable pieces of information that could now help to design and implement a better mouse trap. Manufacturers could, for instance, show the effects of:

- Lead Times on purchased and manufactured materials.
- Economic order quantities to help control prices during inflation.
- Work orders in tracing material and labor absorption.
- Open order files for tracking backorders, purchasing and WIP.
- The use of computers to handle large volumes of data to help reduce response time.

With the help of the computer, Bills of Material processors were used in a gross-to-net calculation to determine periodically, by end item, the required quantities of purchased and manufactured materials. Only the question of when to build or buy was left and this final step produced what we know as Material Requirement Planning (MRP). We could now in a near-to-intermediate period define our requirements for one of the major resources in manufacturing–material.

While the introduction of MRP aided many material intensive manufacturing companies, others discovered that another valuable resource—*capacity*—had been ignored. This void has caused a major problem for all manufacturers in our recent inflationary period.

Putting their heads together, professionals in the industry designed Capacity Requirements Planning systems to close this gap and plan for labor requirements. Capacity Planning systems are becoming available as problems and solutions are better defined. Just as MRP evolved, so will CRP.

There are a number of factors that we must consider with CRP such as the level of detail data needed, currently available information and our ability to analyze the resulting output. Many manufacturers have posed the question, "How Rough is Rough with CRP?" The answer to this question is coming with further analysis and development of CRP and Shop Floor Control (SFC) systems. Test results are being documented indicating that Capacity Planning may belong at all stages of the business cycle

With the advent of MRP and CRP, and now the availability of effective software, manufacturers have begun to analyze the all-important "Master Plan" that we refer to as the Master Production Schedule (MPS). Through this analysis process we can now:

1. Test the MPS for capacity and material availability.
2. Review and redefine, make and buy, order policies.
3. Maximize labor utilization.
4. Expedite and de-expedite.
5. Plan and control engineering changes.
6. Improve customer service.
7. Plan short-term cash requirements.

In essence we are now able to test plans, review output and control purchasing and production in a planning rather than reacting mode. The only remaining problem is one of understanding the financial aspects and impacts of our plan and replan decisions.

Planning Manufacturing

Today manufacturing executives are evaluating methods for systematically testing intermediate and long term production plans. With our knowledge of CGS and its impact on profit and loss we are able to begin design of a system that can now represent the full business control cycle.

This system will allow testing of decisions to occur at the levels of Planning, Analysis and Control to provide information which will help the manufacturer maximize the utilization of money through the control of labor and material. Doing this will provide major benefits in all functional areas such as:

- Conversion of Forecasts to Master Schedules.
- Load leveling from the summary plan level to detail work centers.
- Maintenance of Finished Goods Inventory level.
- CGS Variance Analysis.

- Cash Requirements Planning.
- Economic Trend Analysis.
- Economic Build and Buy Analysis.

Many other opportunities exist to close the business planning loop and gain insight into current and future business trends. It must also be recognized that only through the closed-loop approach will we be able to achieve the full benefits possible from the Analysis and Control segments.

As we see, the value is in feeding information in a closed-loop manner into preceding plans. We also note that information is tested top down, on a gross-to-detail basis against data that may have been collected in a bottom-up to detail-to-summary manner. This process solidifies integration of each phase of the business planning cycle. For the computer to manipulate this kind of data we will require modules like:

- Forecasting (Time Series Analysis)
- Economic Trend Analysis
- Operational Budgeting
- Capital Expenditure Budgeting
- Income and Balance Sheets
- Rough Cut and Detail CRP
- MPS
- MRP
- Purchasing
- SFC

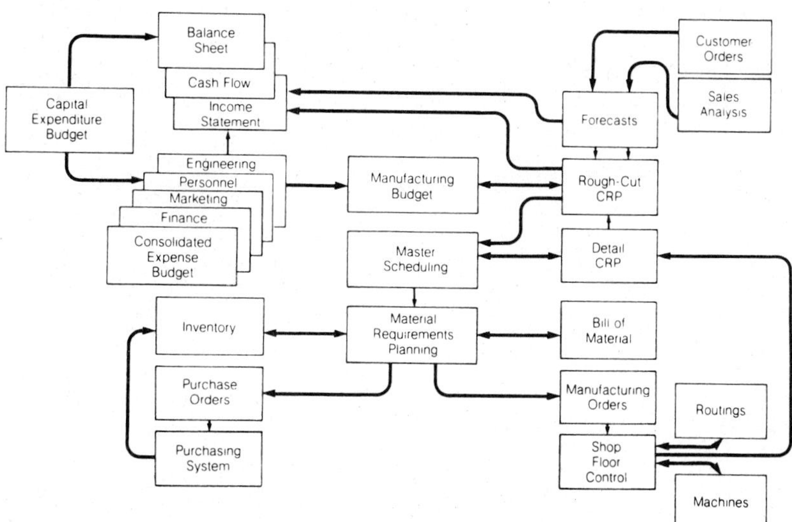

FIGURE 15B.2 Closed loop manufacturing resource planning

The use of computers will help shorten the total cycle, provide integration and summarization of information and allow for continuous dynamic replanning. Assembled, these modules may look like Figure 15B.2.

Conclusion

The values to be obtained by development of a total, closed-loop Resource Requirements Planning system are endless. All functional areas in Marketing, Finance and Manufacturing can plan, analyze and control each segment of the business while utilizing common, continually upgraded information.

Today's manufacturing environment will need to concentrate on technology, marketing and cash flow while maintaining the ability to respond and replan. This flexibility can only be controlled by continuous measurement of our most valuable resource—people. By providing a common set of tools and objectives, manufacturers can expect continued growth and better payback for each invested dollar. When these commitments are made, MRP will again take on a new meaning . . . *Management Relying on People*.

chapter sixteen

What Is Ahead?

We have discussed the usefulness of MRP in capacity planning, priority planning, and material requirements planning. The required and available capacities are matched by an iterative procedure, as shown in figure 16.1. Wight [19] and others refer to this procedure as a closed-loop MRP system. The MPS is determined by the manufacturing and marketing departments. The engineering department participates by providing a valid bill of material. For any system to be successful, it should simulate reality. Unfortunately, some participants are not in the game. For example, the accounting departments have their own inventory records in dollars for financial purposes, while the inventory control department maintains a separate set of records on quantities. In addition there generally is a business plan that top management uses, which consists of their forecasts of sales, inventories, and production for the firm. These forecasts are expressed in dollars, of course. In many instances, the production department duplicates their efforts in units of production. The business plan, of course, is roughly the sum of the production plans expressed in terms of cost of sales, but other expenses, such as R&D, administration, and marketing must be added.

Manufacturing Resource Planning (MRP II)

Recognizing the lack of coordination among departments, manufacturing resource planning, or MRP II, attempts to integrate their functions. By including finance, accounting, and other activities in the planning process, we can make it a truly viable system. Similar to the closed-loop MRP system, MRP II has additional feedback for the financial planning aspects, as shown in figure 16.2. MRP II is also known as business requirement planning (BRP). The manufacturing resource planning system generally results in better coordination of activities among departments of a firm [19], and hence in a more acceptable plan for the firm as a whole. Top management

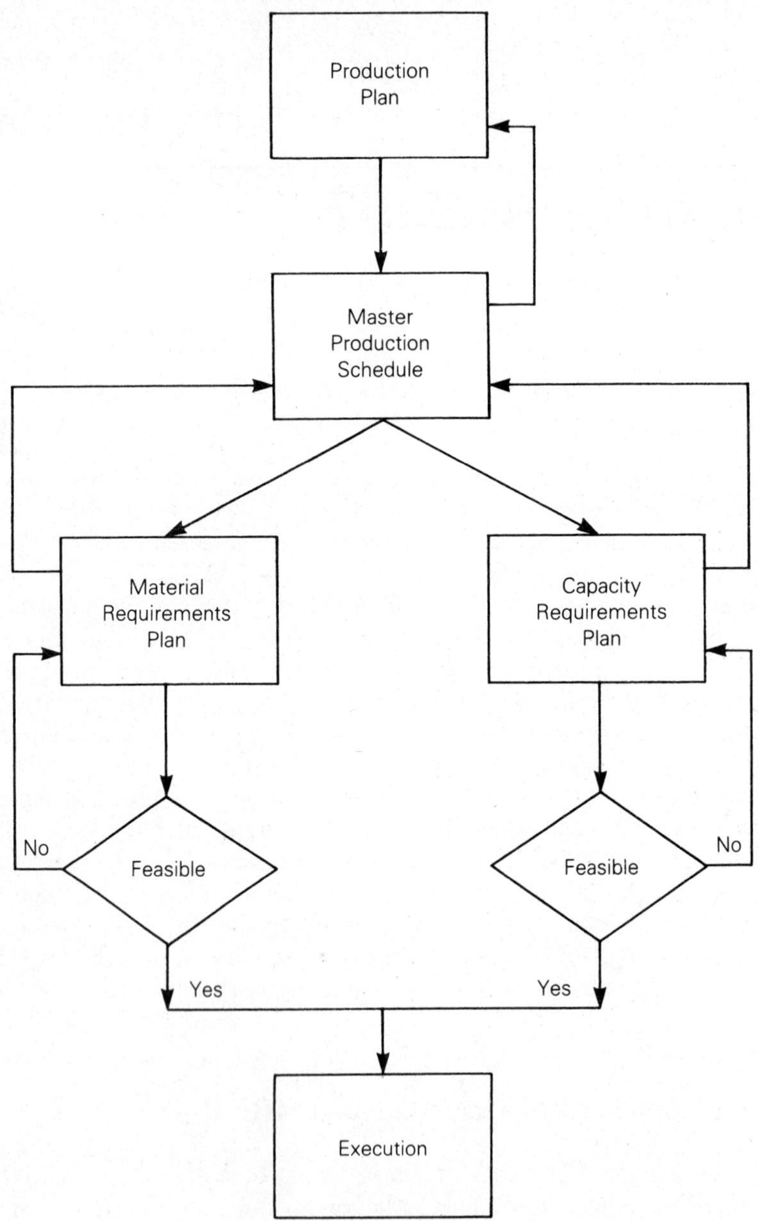

FIGURE 16.1 Closed-loop MRP system

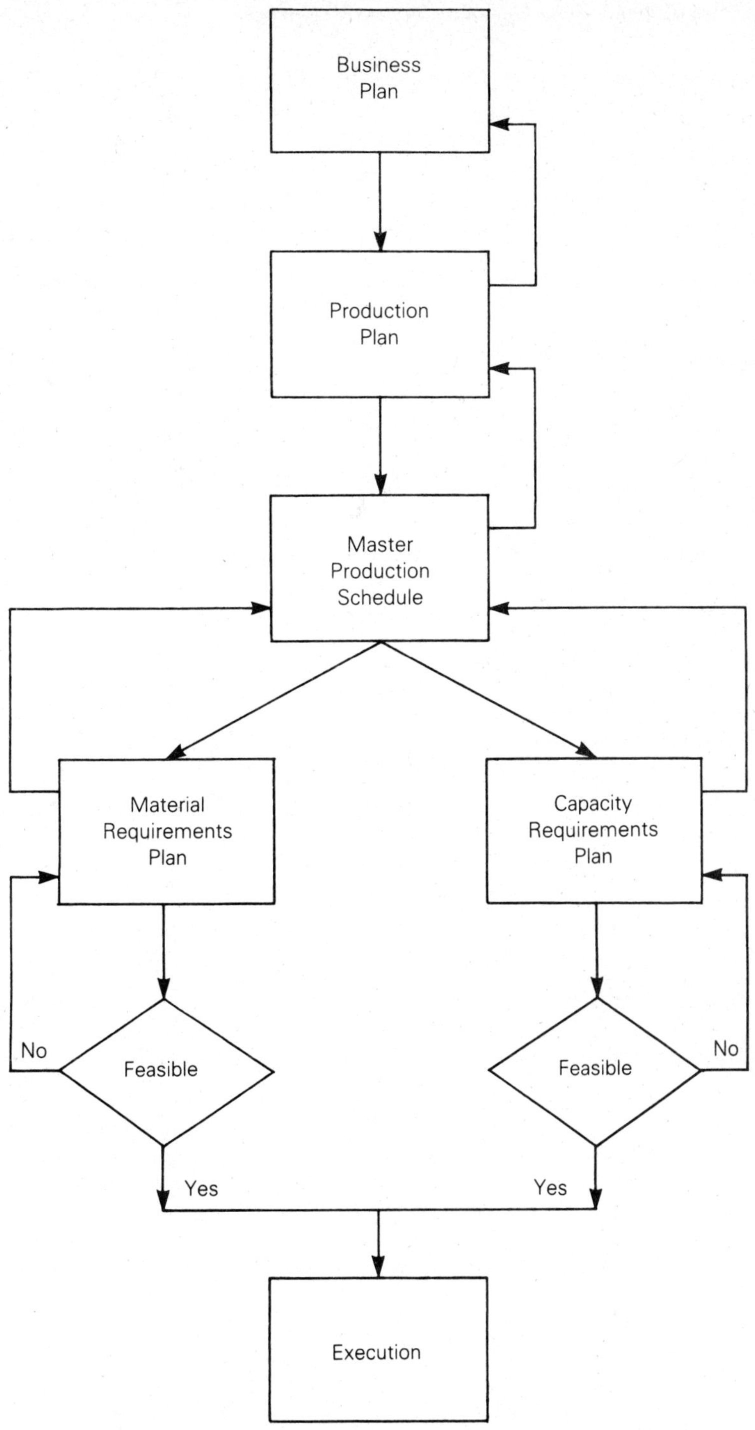

FIGURE 16.2 Manufacturing Resource Planning

has more reliable numbers to work with, since they were arrived at from a very detailed bottom-up approach.

In most instances, management likes to test the effect of alternative business plans on inventory levels, capacities, and other financial variables. With an on-line BRP environment, managers can simulate alternative plans on computers for profitability, due dates, or changing market conditions.

Microcomputers

The advent of high-powered computers has vitalized the use of MRP systems in many large firms. Thanks to the progress made in microcomputer technology, computer manufacturers are widening the marketplace by offering users more computer power at lower prices. It is becoming increasingly more difficult to distinguish between minicomputers and microcomputers, and there has been a steady reduction in mass storage costs. The disks used for mass storage in microcomputers have expanded into the ten- to fifty-megabyte range, approaching the capacity of the hard disks used in mainframes. Sophisticated operating systems and data base management software are no longer scarce commodities. For example, Digital Research markets CP/M and MP/M operating systems; Micro Data Base Systems and Ashton-Tate sell data base management systems; Ryan-McFarland offers the RM/COBOL language for business applications [16]; and Microsoft offers the MS-Assembler, MS-FORTRAN, MS-Pascal compiler, and MS-GW-BASIC compilers.

Now more and more small and medium-sized firms, with sales ranging from $1 million to $50 million can afford very powerful computers at relatively low costs. Newer developments in microcomputers will facilitate storage of up to 100 million megabytes in the near future. These developments in microcomputers and software systems are making MRP systems available even to small and medium-sized firms. Furthermore, the much-heralded gallium arsenide crystal, made in outer space, promises to give more computer power at lower cost in the future, and it will occupy a much smaller space. Research in microcomputers also leads to advances in computer-aided design (CAD), computer-aided manufacturing (CAM), and robotics.

COMPUTER-AIDED DESIGN AND MANUFACTURING (CAD/CAM)

Computer-aided design (CAD) and computer-aided manufacturing (CAM) are among the newest, most comprehensive, and most complex software systems designed to promote efficient planning and production and routing of piece parts and assemblies. CAD/CAM is designed to integrate all aspects of manufacturing and engineering while enabling better communication among them [8].

The CAD element of the system allows an engineer to create, design, draft, and analyze a product model using computer graphics displayed on a screen. An engineer can access a data base that contains engineering data on piece parts as well as other needed information, such as a product structure tree. The engineer can also use the computer terminal as a drawing board. The CAD element not only speeds up slow and tedious drafting but also aids in analyzing various configurations of a product by rotating them on a computer screen. The designer can also look at cross-sections and can request product drawings to different scales. Using CAD, the designer can simulate the effect of field conditions and test their durability. This is accomplished, of course, by a vast and costly computer program. The CAM element transfers the final design of CAD into the assembly stage. CAM facilities range from running machine tools by punched tape to programming sophisticated robots to perform a variety of industrial tasks. CAM provides speed, accuracy, dependability, and timeliness in the production of piece parts and assemblies.

The integration of CAD with CAM magnifies the potentials and permits greater design flexibility in a wide variety of market needs. It reduces the lead time between design and production. In addition, it makes it less costly to make engineering changes in midstream. Using simulation techniques in a central computer network, the system can provide inventory status, process flow control, work station control, assembly control, and manpower control. The future of CAD/CAM lies in its ability to provide cost-efficient and flexible design and manufacturing systems in a rapidly changing technological era. Its greatest benefit is improvement in performance and productivity, which essentially leads to increased profits.

Several obstacles lie ahead. A common data base is essential for smoother functioning of the system. Since this area is still relatively new and specialized, there is a severe shortage of experienced personnel for designing the system. It is also difficult, at present, to find personnel with the broad background necessary for managing a staff and computerized machinery.

In an ideal CAD/CAM environment, many departments should be able to access the common pool of data. Eventually, production planners, schedulers, shop foremen, accountants, and other department personnel should be able to communicate with each other. Such a system should help management in more accurate planning and use of manufacturing resources.

ROBOTS

Robots are computer-operated machines that can work with fantastic precision. At present, there are approximately 5,000 robots at work in the United States. They can do hard, repetitive, dirty, or dangerous work on land or sea, in the air or in space. Many robots are employed in arc welding tasks in automotive body assembly work. For example, robots are used in the world's fastest welding operations at the Dearborn Frame Plant of the Ford Motor Company. They weld many automotive body parts together. They can also paint, inspect parts, and do a variety of monotonous tasks. Robots can work under water and in a polluted, cold, dark, or hot atmosphere.

Once a robot is taught its task, it never forgets. The usual way to teach the robot is actually to "lead it by the hand" by moving its arm and hand through a series of required motions. While the parts of the robot are moving, its sensors are automatically recording the motions in its computer memory. The motions can be played back right away. Currently, robots are programmed in assembly language. The use of higher-level languages, such as BASIC or FORTRAN, will make programming of operations easier and more efficient in the future.

In some instances, robots are slow, weak, bulky, and expensive. They cannot pick a randomly oriented part from a bin, and hence they are not useful in assembly operations. Much research is underway to make robots adaptable to a variety of industrial tasks. They have already proved their worth in many tough, boring, and dangerous tasks in manufacturing.

Group Technology

Modern group technology (GT) is a system that contains electronic card files of parts that a firm manufactures. The system can sort cards according to various physical characteristics, such as size, shape, volume, and materials used. The system can also classify parts according to their manufacturing processes, such as lot sizes and bills of labor in each machine center, and the sequence of operations. When a new requirement arises, the engineer can retrieve a list of existing parts that have similar characteristics and can simply define the new part (file) from the existing files [8] [11].

Group technology identifies and brings together components in order to take advantage of their similarities in function or in the way they are produced. The extent to which the components can be grouped depends on the quantity and variety of individual components being made and the type of manufacturing processes required to produce them. For example, grouping can be done by organizing a large number of diverse components into families that require similar manufacturing facilities. By using a group system, the production of components can be sequenced so that machine tool attachments can be designed to minimize subsequent setup times. The adoption of component group machining can lead to mass production even in small- and medium-batch firms, since it attempts to reduce the total number of parts being produced. Fewer parts result in more efficient process planning, mass production, and less movement in the plant. This obviously reduces the raw materials, in-process inventories, and warehouse inventory investment levels and the documentation associated with them. The type and number of machine tools or attachments are reduced, facilitating mass production and high-technology equipment.

Group technology has been found to be very successful in the packaging industry, in which items were classified according to their physical characteristics. Decisions on standard package designs, construction, strength, and materials were greatly simplified. The items were classified by GT families, and then packaging methods were designed for each family of parts in accordance with that family's procedures. The technique attempts to assign new components to existing categories, thus minimizing the total number of parts. If a part does not fit into any family, or if it requires special handling, packaging specialists can be called upon. A great deal of effort can be prevented by determining whether a physical characteristic of a part is already available, rather than "reinventing the wheel." GT users indicate that part similarities exist in 3% to 10% of their products [4]. Common designs, process methods, packaging methods, and other manufacturing procedures can result in fewer parts, less paperwork, and improved service. Obviously, the planning process of GT can be enhanced through the use of CAD/CAM, and vice versa.

Kanban: Japanese Inventory Control

In Japan, *Kanban* means card. Kanban is a *pull system* [1] [14] [18], which means that work centers that need parts, subassemblies, or assemblies from other producing work centers pull them out. In this way, the materials produced exactly equal requirements. For smooth function of a Kanban system, certain plans have to be followed. The system uses a quarterly planning horizon and a monthly planning cycle. The master production schedule (MPS) is frozen for a period of two to four weeks, and the monthly requirements are broken down into daily requirements. The MPS is exploded to get a list of parts for daily production. The parts list is sent to departments in the form of Kanban. When the MPS is changed, a new set of cards is put into the system.

The cards are used for two purposes: (1) to move parts from one place to another or (2) to authorize the production of parts, subassemblies, and assemblies. The former is known as *conveyance Kanban,* and the latter is known as *production Kanban*. A standard-size container is used, and each card is treated like a coupon and is good for one container. The Kanban system is shown in figure 16.3.

As an example, suppose that a container of item X is required from work center WS-2. As a first step, a production Kanban is issued to work center WS-2. The work center withdraws a container of raw materials RM-

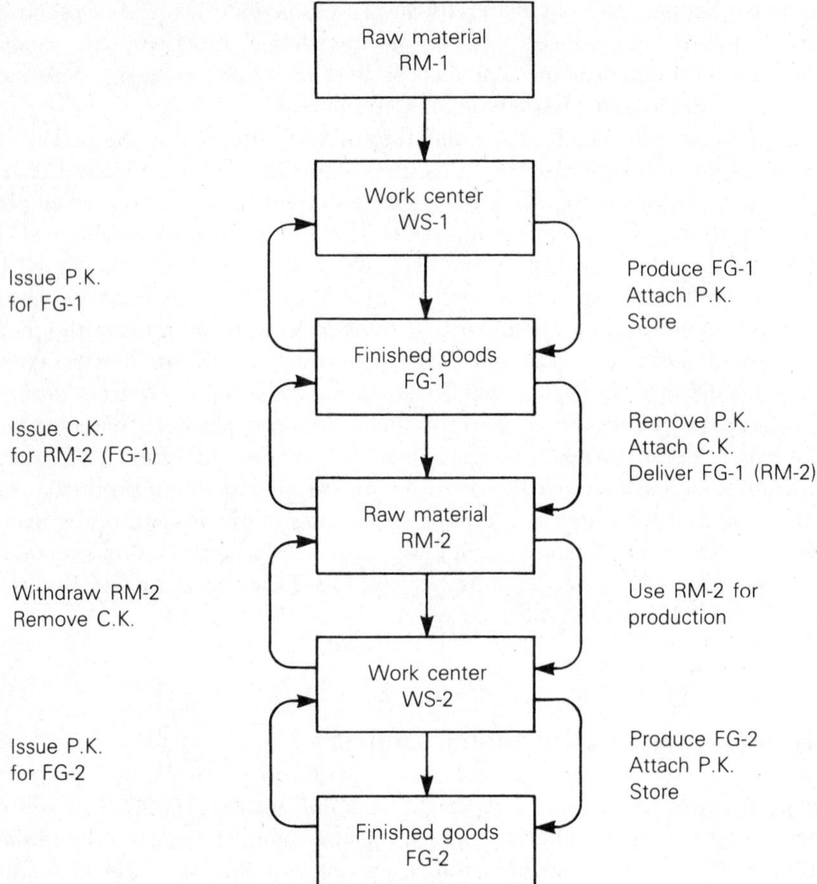

Key: P.K. = production Kanban; C.K. = conveyance Kanban.

FIGURE 16.3 Kanban system

2 from its inventories. The container of RM-2 also includes a move card (conveyance Kanban). Work center WS-2 removes the move card from the container and sends it to the preceding work center, WS-1. The move card serves as an authorization to pick up a container of FG-1. The container of FG-1 also includes a production Kanban for FG-1. Finished goods FG-1 serve as raw material RM-2 at work station WS-2.

When a container of FG-1 is moved to WS-2, the production Kanban is removed from the container and a move card is attached to it. The production Kanban just removed from the container of FG-1 is hung on the board or sent back to work center WS-1. It serves as an authorization to produce another container of FG-1. Then work center WS-1 withdraws a container of raw material RM-1. The entire process is repeated at work center WS-1, with its feeding work center.

When the items are produced, the production Kanban is stuck on the container, and the container is sent to the finished goods inventory.

In Kanban, all operations going to the final assembly are linked together. As parts must follow a specified path, the final assembly gets the right parts at the right time and in the right place. The system forces us to maintain an optimal amount of work-in-process inventories at all times. To make it work more smoothly, daily production is kept constant during the frozen period. This necessitates a large number of setups, which puts a burden on management to keep setup times down. Small quantities of everything must be produced every day. All employees are trained in many different operations. When a slowup occurs in one operation, management has to act fast to shift workers among work centers so that one area doesn't slow down the whole production. If an item is not necessary, the company will stop producing it. The employees will do other things, such as improving the process, housekeeping, auditing, and a variety of other activities. This procedure also aids capacity utilization and holds down idle time. Finally, actual production must be very close to the schedule. The assumption is that having more parts than necessary is as bad as incurring shortages.

JUST-IN-TIME (JIT) PURCHASING

The Kanban system is supported by just-in-time (JIT) purchasing. JIT purchasing requires the products in precisely the necessary units at the required time. Extra quantities of components are discouraged exactly as much as shortages. Japanese plants often coordinate and synchronize supplier production as an extension of their own plant to accomplish this goal. The outside suppliers are generally very small and are dedicated to meeting the requirements of host plants. As they are located in close proximity, it becomes economical to provide just-in-time delivery directly to the production lines in many situations. This concept is very powerful in a repetitive manufacturing process. The idea is to drive all queues to zero in order to minimize inventory investment, shorten production lead time, react faster to customer demand, and identify any quality problems right away. JIT attempts to achieve a stable and predictable flow of materials. Once this is achieved, managers try to reduce the in-process inventories or increase the throughput without changing the existing resources. Essentially, they make every attempt to increase the output and decrease the in-process inventories simultaneously. Thus, productivity is systematically increased in the system.

QUALITY CIRCLES

In the Japanese system, every individual is responsible for the quality of production. Inspection is tailored to be a part of the production process. Jidoka push buttons are installed on the assembly line. (*Jidoka* means "Stop everything when something goes wrong" in Japanese.) When a defective part is found in the assembly line, when a safety hazard is incurred, or when the quantity of production deviates from the specified levels, the worker is obliged to push the button, and the entire assembly line is halted. People from manufacturing, engineering, and management rush to the location and fix the problem on the spot while the workers engage themselves in support activities, such as cleaning and materials handling. This procedure eliminates production of defective parts, which obviously eliminates defective assemblies.

Summary

We have discussed many aspects of production planning and inventory control. The MRP systems play an important role in manufacturing, and the MRP principles can be extended by the inclusion of distribution requirements planning as a part of total planning. Successful implementation of these systems depends on the accuracy of information on bills of material, lead times, and inventory records. The Kanban system has proved to be an effective tool in Japanese manufacturing. Similar techniques, such as optimized production technology (OPT), are being adopted in this country [5]. Still, there is a great concern about U.S. manufacturing technology and productivity. We must take a fresh look at our manufacturing and distribution system. We must attempt to integrate new product planning, design, tooling, construction, manufacturing, and virtually all related activities with basic business decisions. Computer-automated process planning (CAPP) systems are on the way [3] [12]. CAPP attempts to integrate group technology, the manufacturing engineering data base, and MRP to formulate production schedules, to order material, and to plan manpower requirements. The development of various CAPP systems is presently being coordinated by Computer Aided Manufacturing—International (CAMI) with interested individual companies [7]. The diversity of applications and the different levels of details pursued by individual organizations make it difficult to develop a universal CAPP system. As the emphasis on productivity grows, many efficient automated systems are likely to be innovated. In conclusion, we must emphasize that many of the techniques and factors discussed here are not universally applicable. Companies should analyze the merits of new technologies, such as microcomputers, CAD/CAM, and other manufacturing information systems, for individual applications before investing in them.

REFERENCES AND BIBLIOGRAPHY

1. J. Arai, "The Success of the Japanese," *Production and Inventory Management Review,* Vol. 1, No. 12 (December 1981), p. 26.
2. A. B. Bishop and R. A. Miller, "IEs' Expertise Is Well Suited to Role of Integrating CAD and CAM," *Industrial Engineering,* Vol. 13, No. 11 (November 1981), pp. 126–129.
3. Canadian General Electric Company, *Advanced Manufacturing Engineering* (Scarborough, Ont.: Canadian General Electric Company.
4. D. L. Coke and D. C. Hagerman, "GT: A New Concept in Packaging," *Modern Packaging,* Vol. 5, No. 1 (August 1978), pp. 31–34.
5. B. Fox, "OPT—An Answer for America," *Inventories and Production Magazine,* January–February 1983, pp. 18–26.
6. C. C. Gallagher and W. A. Knight, *Group Technology* (London: Butterworth, 1973).
7. M. P. Groover, *Automation, Production Systems and Computer-Aided Manufacturing* (Englewood Cliffs, N.J.: Prentice-Hall, 1980).
8. T. G. Gunn, "The Mechanization of Design and Manufacturing," *Scientific American,* Vol. 247, No. 3 (September 1982), pp. 114–130.
9. R. D. Holtz, "GT and CAPP Cut Work-in-Process Time 80%," *Assembly Engineering,* Part 1, June 1978, pp. 24–27; Part 2, July 1978, pp. 16–19.
10. E. K. Ivano, *Group Production, Organization and Technology* (London: Business Publications, 1968).
11. C. Knox, "CAD/CAM and Group Technology: The Answer to System Integration?" *Industrial Engineering,* Vol. 12, No. 11 (November 1980), pp. 66–73.
12. C. H. Link, "Computer Aided Process Planning (CAPP)," Technical Paper MS77-314 (Dearborn, Mich.: Society of Manufacturing Engineers, 1977).
13. R. A. McNeely and E. M. Malstrom, "Computer Generated Process Routings," *Industrial Engineering,* July 1977, pp. 32–35.
14. Yasuhiro Monden, "What Makes the Toyota Production System Really Tick?" *Industrial Engineering,* January 1981, pp. 36–46.
15. C. New, "MRP and GT, A New Strategy for Component Production," *Production and Inventory Management,* Vol. 18, No. 3 (Third Quarter, 1977), pp. 50–62.
16. E. Pennenale and E. Levy, "MRP and Micro Computers," *Production and Inventory Management Review,* May 1982, pp. 20–25.
17. W. C. Rhodes, Jr., "Computer Graphics Invades Manufacturing," *Infosystems,* Vol. 28, No. 10 (October 1981), pp. 69–72.
18. K. A. Wantuck, "The Japanese Approach to Productivity," *Inventories and Production Magazine,* January–February 1983, pp. 4–13.
19. O. W. Wight, *MRP II: Unlocking America's Productivity Potential* (Williston, Vt.: Oliver Wight Publications, 1982).

appendix 16A

Selling Top Management—Understanding the Financial Impact of Manufacturing Systems

James T. Clark
IBM Corporation
Poughkeepsie, New York

The objectives of this paper are to assist the reader in his efforts to:

- Better understand the motivations, the goals and objectives, of top management
- Relate the goals of production and inventory management to these goals
- Justify production and inventory management systems

The Goals and Objectives of Top Management

Tell me how a man is measured and I will tell you how to sell to him.

The simplest and most direct approach to gaining an understanding of the goals and objectives of top management is to read the manager's written performance plan. A properly developed performance plan should define in very specific numbers and schedules what that person is being measured against. It should also prioritize multiple objectives giving specific weighting factors to individual objectives.

However direct and accurate this approach might be, it is not likely to happen.

Reprinted with permission, American Production and Inventory Control Society, Inc. *25th Annual Conference Proceedings*, October, 1982.

It is often possible though, through interview and discussion, to get a reasonably accurate general description (without confidential data) and ranking of a manager's objectives. It then becomes your responsibility to present your eventual proposal or results in terms that are easily translated by that manager to his specific objectives and measurements.

Another excellent source of information is the formal business plan. This assumes that there is a formal business plan and that you have access to it. Unfortunately, formal business plans are still relatively scarce in industry. Again, an alternative is intelligent questioning of top management for useful information.

The business plan should define the business you intend to be in, the products you intend to sell, and the marketplace you intend to serve. It should also define major strategies and priorities. Strategy examples include: being the low cost and high volume producer; or having the highest service level or shortest lead time; or to service only a unique small portion of the marketplace.

The business plan should provide measureable objectives/targets (quantity and date) for key items such as net sales, net profit, return on investment, return on equity, market share, etc.

Additionally, statements of policies, practices or responsibilities relative to employees, the community or society in general can influence top managements evaluation of your proposal.

The full employment objective and strategy shared by government, management, workers and owners in Japan is an excellent example of a significant influence in justifying and selling projects or ideas.

In well managed companies, the objectives of all managers (and employees) should reflect and support the business plan objectives.

Top management, of course, tends to get a grade or score that is very close to (or exactly the same as) the 'company score'.

The 'company score' is best defined in the company's Annual Report.

The objectives of the next two sections of this paper are to provide an introduction to and a basic understanding of, the company Annual Report or Financial Report. It is presented in layman's terms. A basic understanding of the Financial Report is defined as 'What does the Financial Report tell you?'.

If you are a CPA or are otherwise financially trained, then skip this portion of the paper.

The Annual Report is the summarized set of company books that is shared with the stockholders (assuming a public company). There is a second set of books that is shared with the government. (This is legal.) Differences in these sets of books, for example, could involve depreciation schedules. A third set of books may, or may not be as well defined. This is the set of books for the decision makers. This is the most important set of books in justification and selling to top management. Hopefully these books or something equivalent, are available, at least in part, to employees of the business.

Access to the detailed facts of the business could make this portion of the paper seem too general or broad. The logic, evaluations and comments however, still apply. You should then read this section and consider how you can enhance and expand it with your knowledge of more detailed facts.

An Introduction to a Financial Report

The ABC Manufacturing Company is a durable goods manufacturer. It stocks subassemblies and is vertically integrated (it does some fabrication). It manufactures in an interrupted flow (discrete manufacturing).

ABC's balance sheet consists of Assets (Figure 16A.1) and Liabilities and Stockholders' Equity which represents claims against these assets (Figure 16A.2). The asset side and the liability side of the balance sheet are, as the name implies, always in balance.

Assets are listed in order of decreasing liquidity from top to bottom. In other words, items at the top of the list can be converted to cash sooner

CONSOLIDATED BALANCE SHEET
ABC MANUFACTURING COMPANY

ASSETS In Millions of Dollars - December 31, 1981		% of Total
CURRENT ASSETS		
Cash	$ 1.1	1.0
Short-Term Investments-At Cost (Appx Mkt)	2.5	2.2
Receivables, Less Allowances of $0.7 Million	25.6	22.5
Inventories	35.9	31.6
Other Current Assets	3.6	3.2
Total Current Assets	68.7	60.5
PROPERTY, PLANT AND EQUIPMENT, AT COST		
Land	1.1	1.0
Buildings	12.3	10.8
Machinery and Equipment	40.4	35.6
Construction in Progress	5.0	4.4
	58.8	51.8
Less Accumulated Depreciation	22.0	19.4
Net Property, Plant and Equipment	36.8	32.4
Investments	3.9	3.4
Prepaid Expenses and Deferred Charges	1.3	1.1
Other Assets	2.9	2.6
Total Assets	$113.6	

FIGURE 16A.1

LIABILITIES AND STOCKHOLDERS' EQUITY
In Millions of Dollars - December 31, 1981

		% of Total
CURRENT LIABILITIES		
Short Term Borrowings and Current Maturities of Long Term Debt	$ 9.5	8.4
Accounts Payable	15.2	13.4
Accrued Expenses	6.8	6.0
Income Taxes	4.0	3.5
Total Current Liabilities	35.5	31.3
LONG TERM DEBT	23.9	21.0
STOCKHOLDERS' EQUITY		
Preferred Stock of $2.50 Par Value Per Share. Authorized 22,000 Shares, Issued - None	-	-
Common Stock of $1 Par Value Per Share Authorized 15,000,000 Shares, Issued 9,700,000	9.7	
Additional Paid-In Capital	13.5	
Retained Earnings	31.0	
Total Stockholders' Equity	54.2	47.7
Total Liabilities and Stockholders' Equity	$113.6	

FIGURE 16A.2

and more easily than items further down the list. Current Assets are expected to be converted into cash within one year. Property, Plant and equipment, or fixed assets, as well as certain other investments are not expected to be converted to cash within one year.

Liabilities are listed from top to bottom in order of maturity. Items at the top of the list are expected to be paid off sooner. Current liabilities are expected to be paid within one year. Stockholders' equity is considered permanent capital since it is not paid off like payables or debt. It represents what would be left for the stockholders if the company's assets were liquidated at their balance sheet (or book) value (this is highly unlikely if the company did, in fact, go out of business). The entire liabilities and stockholders' equity side of the balance sheet is referred to as the financial structure of the company. It details how the company's assets are financed.

The capital structure (permanent financing) of the company is represented by long term debt and stockholders' equity. It does not include short term (current) liabilities. The capital structure is a part of the financial structure.

The income statement (Figure 16A.3) is often referred to as the 'P&L' or earnings report. The net profit or loss is simply the difference between the incoming dollars for product sold and the outgoing dollars necessary to cover the costs of running the business.

CONSOLIDATED STATEMENTS OF INCOME AND RETAINED EARNINGS
ABC MANUFACTURING COMPANY

In Millions of Dollars - Year Ended December 31, 1981		% of Sales
NET SALES	$200.00	
COSTS AND EXPENSES		
Cost of Sales	148.6	74.3
Selling, General and Administrative Expenses	34.4	17.2
Interest Expense	3.0	1.5
Depreciation	2.8	1.4
Other (Income) Expense	1.0	.5
	189.8	94.9
INCOME BEFORE INCOME TAXES	10.2	5.1
PROVISION FOR INCOME TAXES	4.6	2.3
NET INCOME	5.6	2.8
RETAINED EARNINGS BEGINNING OF YEAR	27.3	
LESS CASH DIVIDENDS DECLARED	1.9	
RETAINED EARNINGS AT END OF YEAR	$31.0	
NET INCOME PER COMMON SHARE	$ .58	
DIVIDEND PER COMMON SHARE	$ .20	

FIGURE 16A.3

The income statement summarizes the activities of an entire fiscal year. The balance sheet represents the financial position of the company on a single specific date.

The additional columns: % of Total Assets, % of Total Liabilities and Stockholders' Equity, and % of Sales, are not normally a part of the financial report. This % decomposition is included for the reader's convenience and discussion further on.

Following is a brief definition of the items detailed in the Financial Report:

Cash—Money in the cash drawer and money deposited in banks.

Short Term Investments—Temporary investment of idle cash, readily marketable and usually with minimum price fluctuation.

Receivables—Amount due from customers for product shipped, adjusted for bad debt allowances.

Inventories—Raw material, work in process and finished goods.

Property, Plant and Equipment (Fixed Assets)—Assets not intended for sale which are employed in the manufacture and distribution of products.

These assets include land, buildings, machinery and equipment and construction in progress. They are valued at cost minus accumulated depreciation with the exception of land, which is not depreciated.

Accumulated Depreciation—Decline in useful value of fixed assets due to use, wear, passage of time, obsolescence, etc.

Prepaid Expenses and Deferred Charges—Prepaid expenses are expenses paid before they are actually due such as paying insurance premiums or rentals in advance. The asset listed is the amount which is paid but should not be expensed until sometime after the date of the balance sheet. Deferred charges allow the spreading of large one-time expenditures over future time periods. (Assuming benefits from the expenditures will occur over future time periods.)

Short Term Borrowings and Current Maturities of Long Term Debt—Amount which must be paid within the year to banks or other lenders.

Accounts Payable—Amount which must be paid to vendors for purchased goods.

Accrued Expenses—Amount owed for expenses incurred up to the date of the balance sheet which have yet to be paid for, such as salaries, wages, fees, pensions, etc.

Income Taxes—A special category of accrued expenses reported separately because of the relative importance and size of the amount.

Long Term Debt—Debts due beyond one year from the balance sheet date. Examples include notes, mortgage bonds, lease obligations, sinking fund debentures, etc.

Stockholders' Equity—The net worth of the company after subtracting all liabilities.

Preferred Stock and Common Stock (Capital Stock)—Shares in the company owned by stockholders and represented by stock certificates. Preferred stock has preference over common relative to dividends and the distribution of assets in the event of liquidation.

Additional paid-in Capital (often referred to as Capital Surplus)—The amount paid in by stockholders for stock purchases which is in excess of the par value (legal value) of the stock.

Retained Earnings (often referred to as earned surplus)—Net profits less dividend payments. This is reported as an accumulated amount from the origin of the business. The accumulation prior to the current year has been reinvested in the business. These funds are not available for current use. The current year retained earnings reported at the bottom of the income statement were available during the year. (Specifically for the ABC Manufacturing Company that would be \$5.6 million of net income less \$1.9 million in dividend payments or \$3.7 million. This \$3.7 million has been added to the accumulated retained earnings of the previous years financial statement of \$27.3 million resulting in an accumulated retained earnings of \$31.0 million at the end of 1981.)

Net Sales—Money received for goods or services provided adjusted for returned goods and price reductions or discounts.

Cost of Sales—Material, labor and burden costs associated with the procurement of raw material and the factory costs to manufacture products.

Selling, General and Administrative Expenses—'Non-Manufacturing' costs such as office payroll and expenses, executive salaries, salesmen's salaries and commissions, advertising, etc.

Interest Expense—Interest paid during the year to lenders for the use of their money.

Depreciation—Current expense for decline in the useful value of fixed assets.

Net Income (Net Profit)—All income less all costs and expenses.

Cash Dividends—The payout to the stockholders which is declared by the board of directors. It is stated and paid quarterly (at the option of the board) as a per share amount. The total annual amount for ABC Manufacturing was $.20 per share.

Net Income per Common Share—Calculated by dividing net income by the average number of shares outstanding during the year.

It is important to understand that this is a sample financial statement. Many companies have variations and it is essential to gather as much additional information as possible. Some examples of variations are: including physical distribution costs in cost of sales or selling expenses or reporting it separately. Including R&D expenses in cost of sales or general and administrative or reporting it separately.

The first place to look for additional information is in the 'Notes to Consolidated Financial Statements'. An example would be the costing practice applied to inventory and the detailing of the total inventories into finished goods, work in process and raw material. Even with this additional information caution must be exercised because the financial manager's definition of work in process inventory often differs from the manufacturing manager's definition.

Notes cover a wide range of items such as stock option plans, litigation, details of long term debt, and detail sales, profit and asset information by industry segment and geographic area.

Public companies must also file a form 10-K with the Securities and Exchange Commission. This contains additional financial details. Most companies make this available, on request, to stockholders without charge.

What Does the Financial Report Tell You?

ABC Manufacturing Company's financial report displays long lists of specific numbers. Inventories are $35.9 million, net income is $5.6 million, receivables are $25.6 million and stockholders equity is $54.2 million. So what! What does this tell you? Even the % numbers supplied, such as selling, general and administrative at 17.2% of sales tells you little or nothing.

These numbers tell us something; they have value, only if they can be related, compared, or trended relative to other numbers.

The following portion of this paper will develop some basic types of financial ratios where multiple specific items in the financial statement are related to one another, where a company is compared with other companies in a similar business, and where the same item is trended over a period of time.

There are four basic types of financial ratios:

- Liquidity ratios which relate to the company's ability to meet its maturing short term obligations.
- Activity ratios which relate to the effectiveness of asset utilization.
- Profitability ratios which relate to net profits generated on sales and investments.
- Leverage ratios which relate to debt vs equity financing.

In the development of these measurements, particular attention will be paid to areas of current concern. Working capital is one of these. The concern is really with net working capital but unfortunately the words are often improperly interchanged. Working capital is defined as short term assets. Net working capital is defined as current assets minus current liabilities. 'Working Capital Management' includes both current assets and current liabilities.

Working Capital Management is important because:

- Financial managers spend the largest portion of their time in this area.
- Current assets generally represent more than 50% of a company's assets (current assets are 60.5% of ABC Manufacturing's total assets).
- Small firms have limited access to long term capital markets and must rely on the short term which increases current liabilities.
- Interest rate uncertainty is also forcing some companies to increase current rather than long term debt.

Net working capital problems plague many companies today. Some of these companies (Automotive provides an example) have significant potential liquidity problems because current assets can barely cover current liabilities.

Proposals that impact this balance unfavorably in today's questionable economy will surely be rejected in many companies, regardless of the long term benefits.

ABC Manufacturing Company has $33.2 million in net working capital. Is that good or bad? Who knows? Liquidity ratios answer these questions.

LIQUIDITY RATIOS

The current ratio is calculated by dividing current assets by current liabilities. A ratio of 2.0 or better (with few exceptions) indicates a healthy net working capital.

$$\text{Current Ratio} = \frac{\text{Current Assets}}{\text{Current Liabilities}} = \frac{\$68.7 \text{ Million}}{\$35.5 \text{ Million}} = 1.9$$

Generally companies that have small inventories and easily collected receivables can operate more safely than companies with large inventories and extensive credit sales.

The inventories portion of current assets is particularly questionable relative to the ability to sell it quickly and at book value. The quick ratio excludes the inventories in the current ratio calculation, recognizing the importance of the company's ability to pay off short term obligations without relying on the sales of inventory. A safe quick ratio is 1.0 or greater.

$$\begin{matrix}\text{Quick Ratio} \\ \text{(Or Acid Test)}\end{matrix} = \frac{\text{Current Assets} - \text{Inventories}}{\text{Current Liabilities}} = \frac{\$32.8 \text{ Mil}}{\$35.5 \text{ Mil}} = 0.9$$

ACTIVITY RATIOS

Activity ratios relate sales to many different assets giving multiple measurements of the effectiveness of asset utilization.

$$\begin{matrix}\text{Inventory Turnover} \\ \text{(Sales)}\end{matrix} = \frac{\text{Sales}}{\text{Inventory}} = \frac{\$200.0 \text{ Million}}{\$\ 35.9 \text{ Million}} = 5.6 \text{ times}$$

A problem with the sales to inventory ratio is that sales are at market prices and inventory is at cost. An additional calculation of inventory turnover involves cost of sales:

$$\begin{matrix}\text{Inventory Turnover} \\ \text{(Cost of Sales)}\end{matrix} = \frac{\text{Cost of Sales}}{\text{Inventory}} = \frac{\$148.6 \text{ Mil}}{\$\ 35.9 \text{ Mil}} = 4.1 \text{ times}$$

Another potential problem is that sales occur over the entire year and the inventory asset represents one point in time. The best possible inventory turnover calculation would utilize average inventory and cost of sales. It is also possible to measure inventory turnover for individual inventories such as raw material, work in process and finished goods.

A use of the inventory turns ratio is to compare your company's inventory turnover with other companies in your industry utilizing the key business ratios published by Dun & Bradstreet, Inc. But, be cautious in your conclusions. Differing company strategies, for example, can render these comparisons useless.

The best and safest use of the inventory turnover number is to plot it (trend it) over a number of years and use this as a basis for intelligent questioning in identifying or confirming problems.

Caution again is advised because of possible changes in the business, business strategy or inventory costing policy over the time period you are analyzing trend data.

Another activity ratio is collection period which is a measure of accounts receivable turnover. It is calculated by dividing receivables by sales per day. The resulting collection period represents the average amount of time between sales and receipt of payment. It is also defined as the average number of days of sales that is represented by accounts receivable.

$$\text{Sales Per Day} = \frac{\$200.0 \text{ Million}}{365 \text{ Days}} = \$.548 \text{ Million}$$

$$\text{Collection Period} = \frac{\text{Receivables}}{\text{Sales per Day}} = \frac{\$25.6 \text{ Mil}}{\$.548/\text{Day}} = 46.7 \text{ days}$$

This collection period should be compared with the company's selling terms to see if, on the average, customers are paying their bills on time. Trend data should be related to credit policy changes, billing changes, shipping changes, etc.

The aging of receivables (30, 60, 90 days & over) is also important. Large amounts of older receivables which may be from a relatively small number of customers, can cause an unhealthy skew in the aging. Unfortunately, aging information is normally not provided in financial reports.

Fixed asset turnover, particularly when trend data is plotted, is an excellent indicator of capacity utilization.

$$\text{Fixed Assets Turnover} = \frac{\text{Sales}}{\text{Net Fixed Assets}}$$

$$= \frac{\$200.0 \text{ Mil}}{\$\ 36.8 \text{ Mil}} = 5.4 \text{ Times}$$

Total asset turnover is an overall measurement of the company's effectiveness in utilizing all its assets.

$$\text{Total Asset Turnover} = \frac{\text{Sales}}{\text{Total Assets}} = \frac{\$200.0 \text{ Mil}}{\$113.6 \text{ Mil}} = 1.76 \text{ Times}$$

In other words, ABC Manufacturing Company generated $1.76 in sales for every $1.00 of assets.

PROFITABILITY RATIOS

Profit is the 'bottom line' of the business score card. The profitability ratios, therefore, give a good measurement of the net result of the overall management of the business.

Profit margin, the profit for every $1.00 of sales, is calculated by dividing after-tax net income by sales

$$\text{Profit Margin} = \frac{\text{Net Profit After Taxes}}{\text{Sales}} = \frac{\$\ \ 5.6\text{ Mil}}{\$200.0\text{ Mil}} = 2.8\%$$

or $.028 profit per $1.00 of sales. The ABC Manufacturing Company is making a little less than three cents for every sales dollar.

Is that good or bad? Again, it is a function of the type of business and business strategies. After-tax profits can range from less than a penny per sales dollar for a supermarket to over fifteen cents for a computer manufacturer. How do you compare management effectiveness?

This leads us to the return on total assets (return on investment) often called ROI.

$$\text{Return on Total Assets} = \frac{\text{Net Profit After Taxes}}{\text{Total Assets}}$$

$$= \frac{\$\ \ 5.6\text{ Mil}}{\$113.6\text{ Mil}} = 4.9\%$$

This can also be calculated by multiplying total asset turns by profit margin.

$$\begin{aligned} \text{Return on Total Assets} &= \text{Profit Margin} \times \text{Total Asset Turns} \\ &= 2.8\% \times 1.76 \\ \text{ROI} &= 4.9\% \end{aligned}$$

The ROI measurement is the equalizer. It is the result of the management of all the items on the income statement and the asset side of the balance sheet.

Return on equity (net worth) is the critical measurement for the stockholders. ROE measures the return on the stockholders' investment.

$$\text{Return on Equity} = \frac{\text{Net Profit After Taxes}}{\text{Total Stockholders' Equity}}$$

$$= \frac{\$\ 5.6\text{ Mil}}{\$54.2\text{ Mil}} = 10.3\%$$

ROE can also be calculated by dividing ROI by the total stockholder's portion of total liabilities and stockholders' equity. The decomposition of the balance sheet (Figure 16A.2) provides 47.7% or .477 for total stockholder's equity.

$$\text{ROE} = \frac{\text{ROI}}{\text{“Equity \%”}} = \frac{4.9}{.477} = 10.3\%$$

LEVERAGE RATIOS

Debt ratio provides the relationship between the two major categories of items on the liabilities and stockholder's equity side of the balance sheet. The debt ratio relates the total funds provided by creditors/lenders to the funds provided by owners/stockholders.

The decomposition %'s of liabilities and stockholders' equity (Figure 16A.2) show a 47.7% contribution by owners and a 52.3% contribution by creditors.

The debt ratio is specifically defined as the % of total funds that have been provided by creditors. ABC Manufacturing has a debt ratio of 52.3% or .523.

Since total funds supplied equals total assets (the balancing act of the balance sheet) the debt ratio calculation is normally portrayed as:

$$\text{Debt Ratio} = \frac{\text{Total Debt}}{\text{Total Assets}} = \frac{\$\ 59.4\ \text{Million}}{\$113.6\ \text{Million}} = 52.3\%$$

Relating back to the return on equity calculation in the preceding section on profitability ratios, you see that the ROE calculation can now be written:

$$\text{ROE} = \frac{\text{ROI}}{(1 - \text{Debt Ratio})} = \frac{4.9}{(1 - .523)} = 10.3\%$$

This demonstrates vividly why the debt ratio is referred to as leverage. As the debt ratio increases the ROE increases relative to ROI, giving an earnings leverage to the stockholders/owners.

There is a favorable leverage only as long as the company earns more on borrowed funds that it pays in interest. Leverage is a two edged sword however, and if the company earns less on borrowed funds than it pays in interest, the leverage can be just as dramatic, but in an unfavorable direction.

A highly leveraged company (50% to 60% or more) might find it difficult to borrow funds since creditors already share the largest portion of risk. A high debt ratio allows a smaller number of owners to control the business. It might encourage irresponsible speculative activity though, because success brings significantly high returns, but failure means only a moderate loss to the owners.

Production and inventory management practitioners should understand the debt ratio in their business. Projects and proposals are both users and hopefully, future suppliers of funds.

SUMMARY OF FINANCIAL REPORT ANALYSIS

An understanding of the financial report of your business should allow you to better appreciate the concerns and the motivators of top management (it is, after all, their score card).

More importantly, it should help you present and discuss your proposals in a language and fashion that top management can easily relate to.

For example: A proposal for an inventory management system (MRP) has potential impact on:

Total Asset Turns—VIA

1. Improved inventory turnover
2. Improved fixed asset turnover due to better utilization of capacity
3. Increased sales due to better service
4. Increased receivables turns (reduction in collection period) due to more complete order shipment and more on time shipments.

Profit Margins—VIA

1. Reduced cost of sales due to decreased carrying costs, reduced factory burden (expeditors, production control) and reduced material cost (improved vendor communications and scheduling and less vendor associated expediting costs)
2. Reduced selling, general and administrative expenses due to decreased office and marketing costs and reduced physical distribution costs.

Source of Funds

1. Funds released from inventory investment are available for other business purposes.

These improvements in both profit margins and total asset turns provide a multiplication effect in the improvement of ROI and ROE.

In using financial report data, always keep in mind the qualifications and limitations previously mentioned. Also recognize that these represent only a partial list.

The best approach is to use trend data of all the %'s, ratios and other financial measurements presented—and then use this to ask intelligent questions. The management of the many items displayed in the financial report (not to mention voluminous supporting detailed data) and the complex interrelationship of these items suggests prudence in its use.

But—properly understood—the financial reports are an extremely valuable source of meaningful data to aid in selling to top management.

Financial Simulations Using the Financial Report

This section describes how to use portions of the financial report to develop simple, yet powerful financial simulations. The simulations are not detailed enough for complete justification. Their value is in ease of use, ease of understanding, and most importantly, getting managements' attention.

The technique is called the DuPont Analysis. It uses the income statement and the asset half of the balance sheet. The DuPont Analysis for ABC Manufacturing is illustrated in Figure 16A.4. It is an after tax model of ROI.

The upper half of the diagram is a flow (from right to left) of the assets which are listed in order (current assets followed by fixed assets).

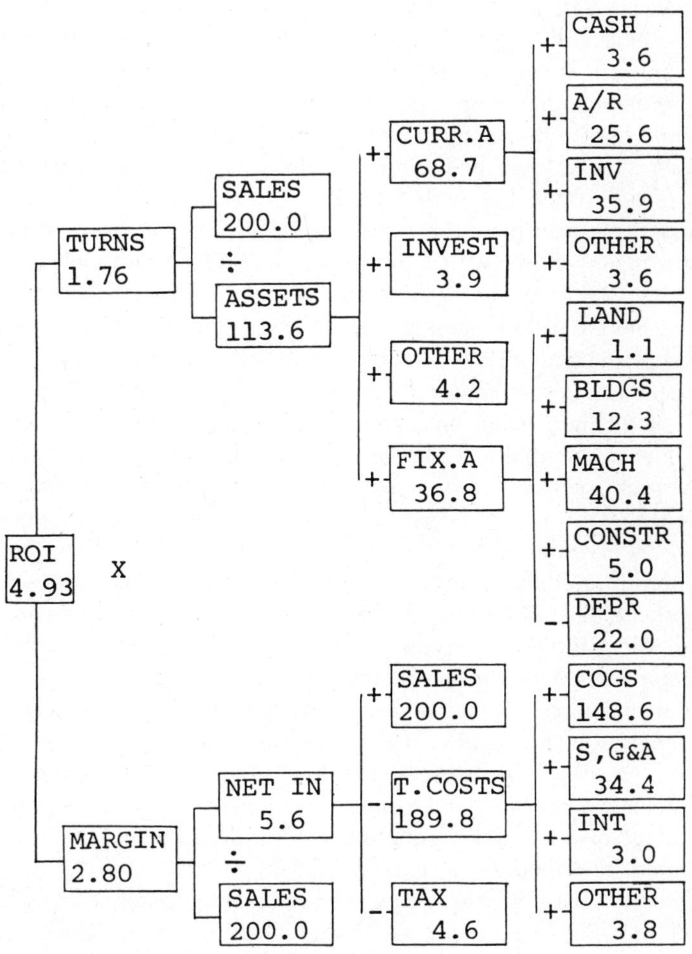

FIGURE 16A.4

Sales are divided by the total assets giving total asset turns of 1.76. The box labeled 'Assets' represents total assets of $113.6 million. The box labeled 'Turns' represents total asset turns of 1.76.

The lower portion of the diagram is the income statement. This flows from the details on the right to the net income of $5.6 million division by sales of $200.0 million for a profit margin of 2.80%.

The result of the multiplication of total asset turns by profit margin is an ROI (Return On Total Assets) of 4.93%. Return on Equity (ROE) could be presented in a box to the left of ROI. You will recall that ROE is ROI divided by (1 − Debt Ratio).

This model could be easily expanded to include more details on the right hand side. Receivables (A/R) could be aged; inventories could be split into finished, raw, and work in process; and cost of sales (COGS) could be split into material, labor and burden. Separate connecting flows could be developed for individual product lines and/or divisions.

The model illustrated can be developed from any annual report with just the income statement and asset half of the balance sheet.

The model, in a simple graphic fashion, shows a number of financial ratios and, most importantly, their relationships.

ROI is again identified as the equalizer. A supermarket with a profit margin of only 0.9% but with total asset turns of 14.4 (primarily due to inventory turns) can have the same respectable 13% after tax ROI as the computer manufacturer with a profit margin of 11.8% and total asset turns of 1.1.

The model also emphasizes the potential impact that production and inventory management has on the profitability of the company.

Manufacturing company executives, almost without exception, have ROI as one of their major measurements. In viewing the model now from left to right, it essentially defines business managers as managers of margins and managers of turns. Turns management can also be defined as asset management. The obvious largest manageable asset of the ABC Manufacturing Company is inventory.

There is another important asset that is not as easily identified on the balance sheet. That asset is (in production and inventory management terms) capacity. Clearly the capacity asset is not all of the net fixed assets, but in many companies it is a major portion of it.

If management would accurately define manufacturing capacity, it might emerge as the largest manageable asset of the company. Factory buildings, not offices and research centers, would make up the buildings asset. Production machines and tooling, not automobiles and office equipment, would be the machinery and equipment asset. Additionally, the direct labor force would be defined as a dollar value.

Depreciation is a critical element in this development of a dollar asset value of capacity. The depreciated (net fixed) assets of ABC are $36.8 million. The value before depreciation, though, is $58.8 million. What value should be used? Unfortunately depreciation (particularly older plants) tends to diminish the relative importance of these assets. The value that should be used is the replace cost. The replace cost is reported to the SEC (Securities and Exchange Commission) by public companies for its fixed assets.

The replace cost of ABC's manufacturing capacity could be significant. It is what ABC would have to pay if it had to replace that capacity today.

Inventory and capacity will now be defined as the largest manageable assets of the ABC Manufacturing Company relative to maximizing the turns portion of the DuPont model.

An examination of the income statement, particularly cost of sales (cost of goods sold—COGS) and selling, general and administrative expenses would also identify inventory and capacity as the key items in maximizing the margin portion of the model.

The simulations that follow deal with inventory and capacity management. Other simulations, particularly A/R collection period reductions, are also important, but will not be dealt with here.

All simulations apply a 46% tax rate to the increased earnings. The tax rate in the original model is 45.1%.

The inventory simulation of Figure 16A.5 demonstrates a simple use of the DuPont Analysis. Inventory has been reduced 10% assuming an inventory carrying cost of 30%. Carrying cost saving has been subtracted from cost of sales.

The changes in the income statement and balance sheet (asset side) are immediately apparent. The additional output of inventory turns would be a simple addition to the model.

[Author's Note: the computerization of such a model is a relatively simple task with the availability of easy to use financial programming languages. One of my P&IC practitioner students in the Dutchess Community College (Poughkeepsie, NY) APICS Certification Classes put this model on his personal home computer in two evenings.]

Adding the liability and stockholders' equity side of the balance sheet to the model would permit the output of all the measurements and ratios previously discussed.

Another interesting use of this particular inventory reduction model is illustrated in Figure 16A.6.

There seems to be a continuing debate about carrying costs. Are they too high? too low? One study reported shocking differences between the carrying cost used by the companies in the study to their actual carrying cost. Figure 6 summarizes the results of multiple simulations to evaluate the sensitivity of the model (the company) to the carrying cost variable. Management can then decide if it is worth determining their true inventory carry costs.

A simulation on material costs decrease is illustrated in Figure 16A.7.

The model assumes that material costs are 50% of cost of sales. This equates to 37% of the sales dollar. This has significant leverage on ROI which has been increased by over 7% assuming a 1% decrease in material

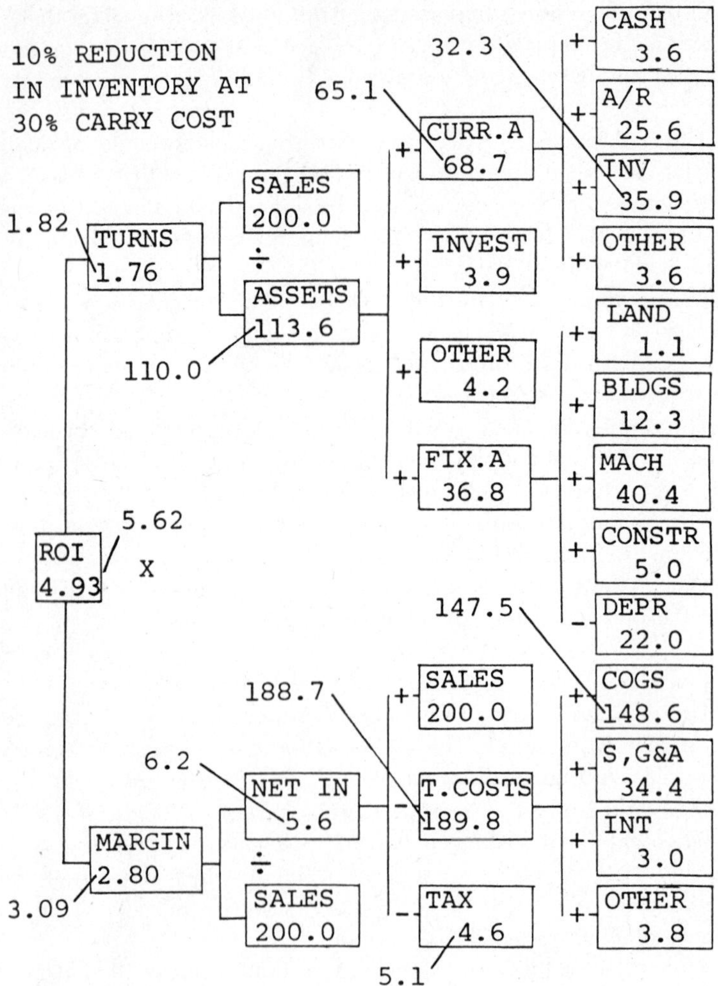

FIGURE 16A.5

Inventory Carry Cost	10% Inventory Reduction ROI (4.93%)	EPS ($1.00)
24%	5.51%	$1.08
30%	5.62%	$1.10
36%	5.72%	$1.12

FIGURE 16A.6 Effect of inventory carry cost

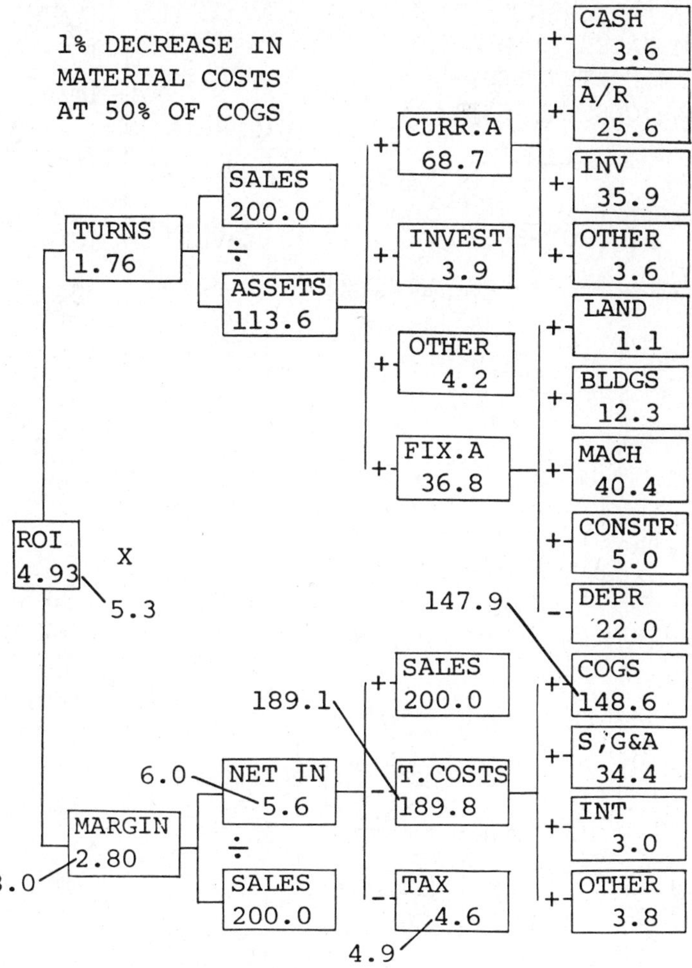

FIGURE 16A.7

costs. MRP and purchasing systems should be viewed very favorably based on these results.

The model in Figure 16A.8 could be referred to as a 'Productivity Increase' model. The simulation is evaluating a 2% increase in factory output (sales) assuming no increase in labor costs or increase in plant assets. In other words, better production and inventory control has permitted ABC Manufacturing to produce 2% more product with the same factory and work force.

Material costs and sales commissions are increased in the model by 2%. Material is assumed to be 50% of cost of sales. Sales commissions are 5% of S,G&A expenses.

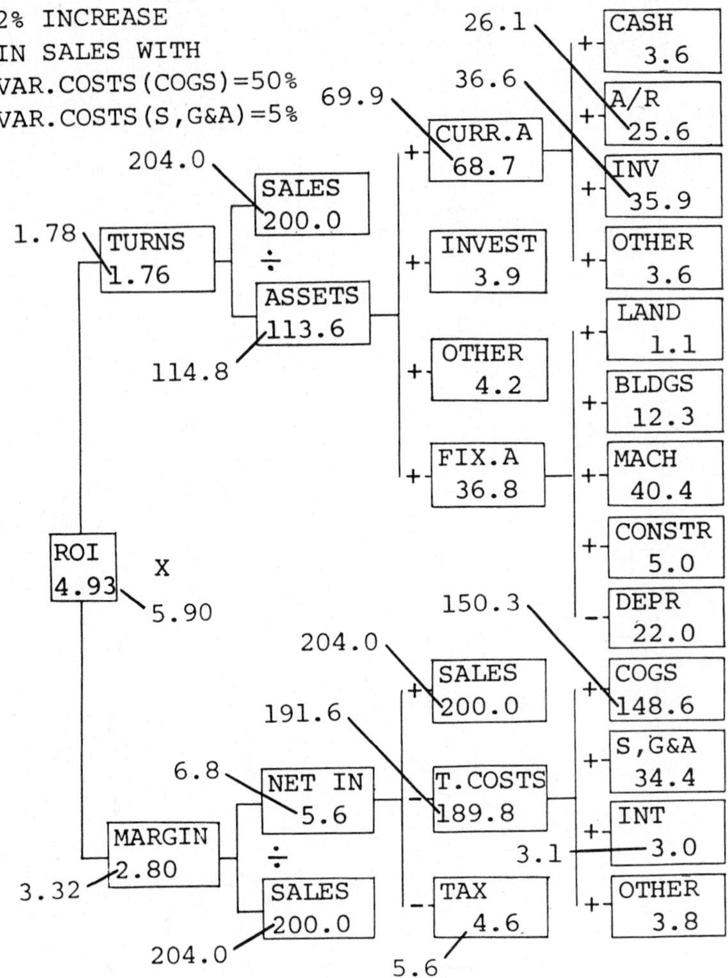

FIGURE 16A.8

Please note that S,G&A has increased (to 34.43) but it does not show in the illustration due to truncating.

A/R has been increased by 2% (collection period was held constant) and the increase is assumed to be financed at 18%. Inventory has also been increased by 2% and a 30% carrying cost has been applied.

This is a very conservative simulation. If the ABC Manufacturing Company implemented good manufacturing systems, they could conceivably produce 2% more sales and have less inventory. If there were no inventory increase, total asset turns would increase to 1.97, margins to 3.39% and ROI to 6.1%. The tax rate on the increase in before-tax earnings is 46%.

These simulations were run independently so there is no compounding from one simulation to the next. It would be a simple matter to change

	FOR AN ADDITIONAL	
	1 % ROI	20¢ EPS
Reduce Inventory (30% Carry Cost)	14.6%	20.0%
or Reduce Collection Period	14 Days	20 Days
or Reduce S,G&A Expenses	6.1%	6.0%
or Reduce Material cost (50%of COGS)	2.8%	2.9%
or Increase Productivity	2.1%	1.0%
Var. Costs (COGS) = 50%		
Var. Costs (S,G&A) = 5%		

FIGURE 16A.9

multiple items at one time. (For example: an inventory reduction, increase in output, and a material cost reduction.)

The advantage of running the simulation with changes in only one item (variable) like A/R or inventory or material cost is to allow you to judge how sensitive the model is to that variable. This helps identify the variable with the most leverage on ROI.

The results of multiple independent simulations are summarized in Figure 16A.9.

The significant profit impact of the 'Increased Productivity' simulation might be misleading. Based on the numbers, 'Increasing Productivity' would have a higher priority than 'Reduce Inventory'. The inventory system however, might be the means by which productivity is increased.

The advantage of running the simulation with multiple variables changed is to allow you to simulate what is realistically going to happen with the implementation of good production and inventory management systems. (For example: An inventory reduction accompanied by a reduction in material costs and administrative expenses).

If management has a reasonably good understanding of how production and inventory management systems effect virtually every part of their business, then they should accept proposals and justification data based on savings from many parts of the business. This also permits you to be conservative in using this model. Specifically: very small reductions in inventory and material costs accompanied by a small increase in productivity might compound to produce a yield equivalent to or even greater than a very large inventory reduction. The relative size of these improvements, of course, are easily quantified in the model.

Justification and Capital Budgeting

The justification of production and inventory management systems will be viewed by management the same as any other major expenditure. The process of planning expenditures whose returns extend into the future (beyond one year) is defined as capital budgeting.

The production and inventory control practitioner must have an appreciation for the capital budgeting process and how management will probably view proposals relative to this process. Capital budgeting is a very broad and complex subject however, and clearly beyond the scope of this paper.

Methods for evaluating and ranking proposals, as part of the capital budgeting process, will be covered here.

Three commonly used approaches are:

- Payback
- Net Present Value
- Internal Rate of Return

PAYBACK

Payback involves the calculation of the number of years to return the initial investment. Figure 16A.10 is an example of ranking two proposals using payback. Assume both projects require an investment of $150,000.

The payback on Project I is two years and on Project II it is almost three and a half years. The obvious drawback of the payback method is that it ignores the net cash flow beyond the payback period.

Managers in the business that have short horizons in their performance plans (typically yearly measurements and bonuses) will favor the payback method because the projects with faster payback produce higher profits in the short run.

Longer range production and inventory management projects (MRP is a good example) must be sold to a level of management that has longer range objectives and measurements.

Another approach is to split up large projects into smaller sub-projects and then evaluate these smaller sub-projects. Inventory accuracy or bill of material sub-projects of MRP typically provide paybacks of a year or less. It is important to insure that sub-projects can be integrated and that they are implemented in the proper sequence.

Year	Net Cash Flow	
	Project I	Project II
1	$80,000	$20,000
2	70,000	40,000
3	40,000	60,000
4	10,000	80,000
5		100,000

FIGURE 16A.10

Many companies are currently putting more emphasis on payback (regardless of its shortcomings) because of business conditions, cash flow problems, and high interest rates.

Payback is also often used as a risk measurement in combination with other methods for evaluating projects. (The shorter the payback the less the risk.)

Another disadvantage of the payback method is that it fails to consider the time value of money. In the net cash flow of the project, a dollar five years from now is worth less than a dollar today because of the interest factor. Discounted cash flow techniques accomodate the interest factor.

NET PRESENT VALUE

The net present value method calculates the present value of future returns minus the cost of the investment. Future returns are discounted at the company's cost of capital. Discounting is the opposite of compounding, as in compound interest in a savings account. $1.00 one year in the future is worth approximately $.87 today discounted at 15%. That is the reverse of investing $.87 today at 15% interest which will be worth $1.00 a year from now.

Projects I and II are evaluated in Figure 16A.11 using the net present value method.

Projects I and II are both acceptable because they have positive net present values. Project II is ranked considerably higher and would be selected over Project I (particularly if they both represented alternate solutions to the same problem).

	PROJECT I			PROJECT II		
Year	Net Cash Flow X	Discount Factor =	Present Value	Net Cash Flow X	Discount Factor =	Present Value
1	$80,000	.87	$69,600	$ 20,000	.87	$17,400
2	70,000	.76	53,200	40,000	.76	30,400
3	40,000	.66	26,400	60,000	.66	39,600
4	10,000	.57	5,700	80,000	.57	45,600
5		.50		100,000	.50	50,000
			$154,900			$183,000
		Less	150,000		Less	150,000
		NPV	$ 4,900		NPV	$ 33,000

FIGURE 16A.11 Net present value — Discounting at 15%

The Discount Factor is calculated:

$$\text{Discount Factor} = \frac{1}{(1 + C)^y}$$

C is the Cost of Capital (as a decimal) and y is the number of years in the future.

$$\text{Discount Factor For 4 Years} = \frac{1}{(1 + .15)^4} = .57$$

INTERNAL RATE OF RETURN

The internal rate of return is defined as the interest rate that causes the net present value to equal zero.

Since NPV = Present Value (discounted) − Initial Cost, the internal rate of return is the interest rate where the present value (discounted) is equal to the initial cost.

Figure 16A.12 is a table of results of trial and error calculations for Projects II's internal rate of return.

The internal rate of return for Project II is just under 22%. Similar calculations for Project I yield an internal rate of return of just under 17%.

The internal rate of return equates to the capital cost % that would make the project a break-even proposition. If the internal rate of return is higher than the cost of capital, the project is profitable.

The internal rate of return calculations, like the net present value calculations, rank Project II above Project I. A list of all projects competing for capital, in sequence of decreasing internal rate of return (or net present value) is a natural input to the capital budgeting process.

		18%		20%		22%	
Year	Net Cash Flow	Disc. Fact.	Present Value	Disc. Fact.	Present Value	Disc. Fact.	Present Value
1	$20,000	.85	$ 17,000	.83	$ 16,600	.82	$ 16,400
2	40,000	.72	28,800	.69	27,600	.67	26,800
3	60,000	.61	36,600	.58	34,800	.55	33,000
4	80,000	.52	41,600	.48	38,400	.45	36,000
5	100,000	.44	44,000	.40	40,000	.37	37,000
Present Value			$168,000		$157,400		$149,200
Less 150,000			150,000		150,000		150,000
NPV			$+18,000		$+ 7,400		$- 800

FIGURE 16A.12

Theoretically, all projects on the list that are profitable should be accepted by management. There are a number of reasons however, why management may elect not to do so. Capital rationing exists if a limit has been set on the size of the capital budget. That means that even if your project is a profitable one it may not gain approval because of a low ranking.

In proposing and selling to top management you should be aware of capital rationing and the evaluation approach and how your proposal is likely to relate to that approach. The intent here is to simply introduce the approaches and not go into the details of net present value vs. internal rate of return. It is left to the reader to gain additional knowledge if this is important.

The estimate of future cash flows, of course, is the critical input for the calculation of net present value, internal rate of return and payback.

The DuPont Model, or other models of the income statement allow for the development of estimated income statements into the future. Input to these models would include changes to costs of sales, depreciation costs, taxes, etc. Review the income statement in Figure 3 and imagine how you could project it out into the future with data from your proposal.

The DuPont Model since it includes the asset half of the balance sheet, would also permit projections of the assets, and of course inventory turns, collection period, total asset turns and ROI.

The addition of the liabilities and stockholders' equity side of the balance sheet, with future assumptions relative to the financial structure of the business, would complete the basic model of the financial reports.

At a minimum, simple manual projections of just the income statement, can prove valuable in supplying the cash flow estimates for proposal (project) evaluation.

Accuracy

Management that is being asked to make company commitments if your proposal is approved, will obviously be concerned with the accuracy and validity of the data and assumptions in the proposal.

Data representing the current view of the company should be verified by financial management. This includes the financial report data and all the additional detailed data that supports the financial reports as well as carry cost %, depreciation schedules, interest cost, etc.

If the current data is not completely accurate then the assumptions and estimates of future cash flows and savings will probably not be accepted. Even with complete accuracy of the current data, there will be challenges regarding the future.

Documented references of other companies' successes (particularly those from a similar industry) can help support your assumptions. Your own personal successful experiences as well as those of others in the business, particularly top level managers (including work experience in other companies) can also increase credibility.

If your company employs any risk analysis techniques, this should be included in your proposal.

Another excellent technique is to utilize simulations to develop the probable results of many possible courses of action. The carry cost simulation of figure 6 is a simple, but effective example.

Developing computer models of the income statement, the DuPont flow, or all the financial reports can easily permit simulation. Multiple simulations across a range of any of your assumed data, such as inventory reduction, carry cost, increase in sales, etc., can provide significant support in helping management evaluate your proposal.

Summary

Successful production and inventory management practitioners, particularly those who will be future managers and general managers, will possess skills and knowledge well beyond just the P&IC field. They will be skilled in personnel, communications, motivation, planning and finance. Financial knowledge will be essential.

This paper can be best described as a brief and very basic introduction to only a small part of the world of financial management. It was intended for readers with little or no financial background. Its purpose was to acquaint the reader with some of the financial measurements of the business as well as emphasize the impact of production and inventory management on these measurements. Additionally, it introduced a powerful simulation tool (and there are many), the DuPont analysis. Methods for evaluating and ranking proposals, as a part of the capital budgeting process, were also covered.

The overall objective was to assist the reader in selling to management through a better understanding of the goals and objectives of top management.

Another objective, which was not previously stated, was to motivate the reader to look further, to study more, and to understand better the sometimes complex and confusing, but always interesting, challenging, and absolutely essential field of financial management.

I hope it has been useful to you.

REFERENCES

'How to Read a Financial Report'
Merrill Lynch, Pierce, Fenner & Smith Inc.

'Essentials of Managerial Finance'
Third Edition
J. Fred Weston, Eugene F. Brigham
The Dryden Press, Hinsdale, Illinois

appendix 16B

OPT vs. MRP: Thoughtware vs. Software

Robert E. Fox, CPIM
Creative Output, Inc.

OPT and MRP—are they conflicting or complementary? Is one a better scheduling approach than the other? Are the differences vital to a company's survival? The real answers to these questions come through an examination of how each approach works and the results they produce. This article contrasts the software of MRP with the thoughtware of OPT and how these two approaches deal with the planning and scheduling of production. There are other dimensions to MRP and OPT (e.g., MRP can be viewed as a data base system and OPT can be used as a productivity improvement system). However, this article concentrates only on how these two approaches deal with production planning and scheduling.

This is a matter of no small importance. It is not a subject that will just be of interest to those involved in the details of scheduling. U.S. industry has spent over $10 billion installing MRP—primarily for the purpose of planning and scheduling production and materials. We have phased out the manual systems in favor of this new, better, faster computerized approach. We replaced years of hard earned experience with the supposedly better logic and capability of MRP. I believe we have done this without recognizing fully the implications of such an enormous investment. The way we schedule is one of the most important factors in determining which companies and countries will survive and thrive during the decade of the 80's. Those who fail fully to understand the concepts implicit in OPT, MRP and other approaches are unlikely to have another chance in the 90's.

Reprinted with permission, American Production and Inventory Control Society, Inc., *26th Annual International Conference Proceedings*, November 1983.

The Model

OPT and MRP will be contrasted by examining the results of a model or example—simple enough that we can apply the OPT and MRP scheduling rules manually. This will permit us to better understand the underlying approach of OPT's nine scheduling rules and the complementary conventional rules of MRP (Exhibit 1). The example, which is shown in Exhibit 2, illustrates the scheduling of a single product which is produced from two subassemblies, two manufactured parts, four purchased parts and two raw materials. The two manufactured parts, A and B, require four and three manufacturing operations respectively on four different machines (A, B, C and E).

EXHIBIT 1 Scheduling Rules

Conventional MRP	*OPT*
1. Balance capacity, then try to maintain flow.	1. Balance flow not capacity.
2. Level of utilization of any worker is determined by his own potential.	2. Level of utilization of a non-bottleneck is not determined by its own potential but by some other constraint in the system.
3. Utilization and activation of workers are the same.	3. Activation and utilization of a resource are not synonomous.
4. An hour lost at a bottleneck is just an hour lost at that resource.	4. An hour lost at a bottleneck is an hour lost for the total system.
5. An hour saved at a non-bottleneck is an hour saved at that resource.	5. An hour saved at a non-bottleneck is just a mirage.
6. Bottlenecks temporarily limit throughput but have little impact on inventories.	6. Bottlenecks govern both throughput and inventories.
7. Splitting and overlapping of batches should be discouraged.	7. The transfer batch may not and many times should not be equal to the process batch.
8. The process batch should be constant in both time and along its route.	8. The process batch should be variable not fixed.
9. Schedules should be determined by sequentially: • Predetermining the batch size. • Calculating lead time. • Assigning priorities, setting schedules according to lead time. • Adjusting the schedule according to apparent capacity constraints by repeating the above 3 steps.	9. Schedule should be established by looking at all of the constraints simultaneously. Lead times are the result of a schedule and can't be predetermined.
Motto The only way to reach a global optimum is by insuring local optimums.	Motto The sum of the local optimums is not equal to the global optimum.

EXHIBIT 2 Product-Process Structure

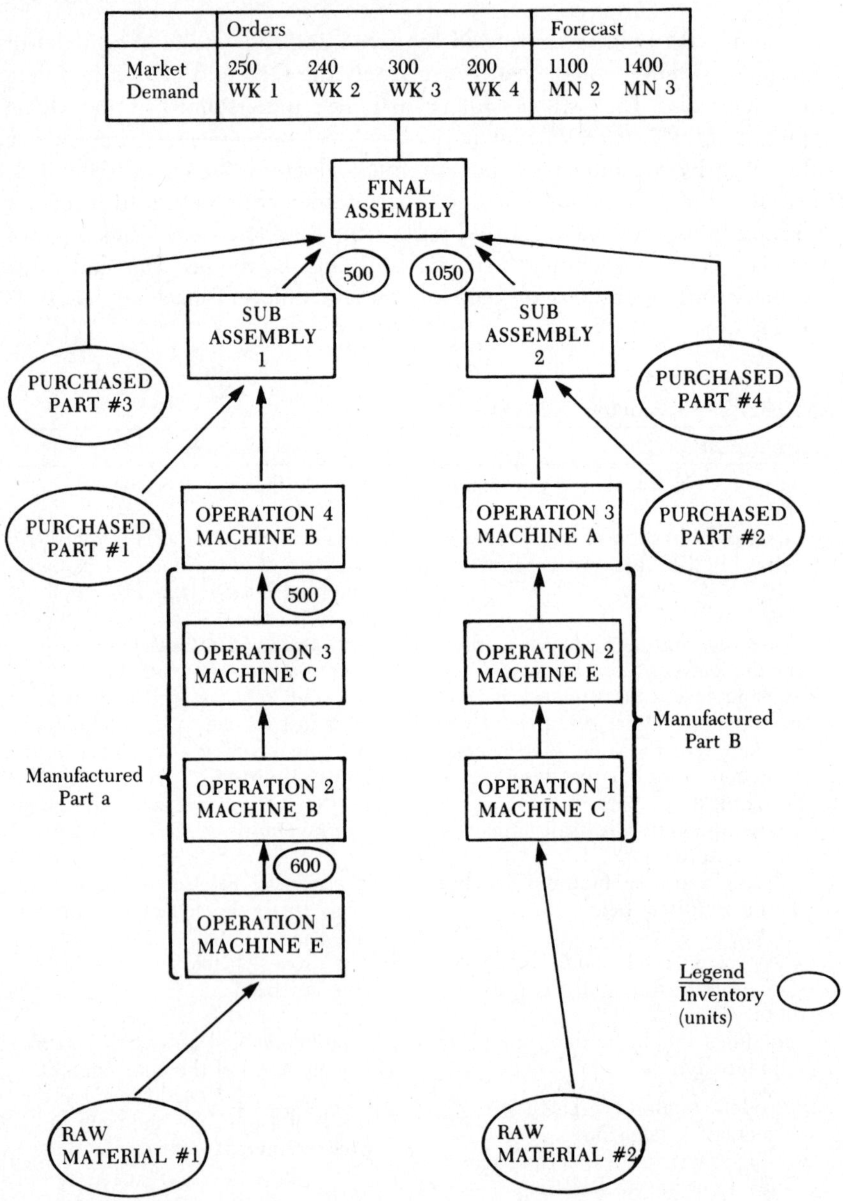

The market demand for this product is divided into four one-week increments of orders followed by two months of forecast. Also shown on Exhibit 2 is the amount and location of inventory present at the start of the first week. Additional relevent information such as the setup and processing times for the two parts and the four machines, batch sizes, raw material costs and the selling price of the end product is shown on Exhibit 3. In this example, each higher level item (e.g. assembly) requires one of each lower level item (e.g. subassembly 1 and subassembly 2).

EXHIBIT 3 Product-Process Data

• Manufacturing Times

Operation-Machine	Part	Setup (Minutes)	Time/Part (Minutes)
Final Assembly		–	6
Sub Assembly	1	–	5
Sub Assembly	2	–	5
10–E	A	60	5
20–B	A	–	10
30–C	A	60	13
40–B	A	–	16
10–C	B	60	10
20–E	B	60	2
30–A	B	60	14

• Costs

	Product	Cost
– Raw Material		
1	A	$10
2	B	10
– Purchased Parts		
1	SA–1	$10
2	SA–2	10
3	FA	10
4	FA	10

• Batch Sizes (EOQ's)

– Manufactured Part A	500
– Manufactured Part B	500
– Sub Assembly 1 and 2	Master Schedule (offset by Lead Time)
– Final Assembly	Master Schedule

• Selling Price $150

MRP—Conceptual Overview

The relevant major elements of a closed loop MRP system are shown in Exhibit 4. The first step in this process is to convert the marketing demand or "wish list" into an initial master schedule through a process of rough cut capacity planning. This process involves calculating rough cut loads on each department or work center and then manually adjusting the marketing wish list to achieve an approximate level load on each resource. Then at each level (subassembly, manufactured part, and raw material) due date

EXHIBIT 4 "Closed Loop" MRP Planning and Scheduling Process

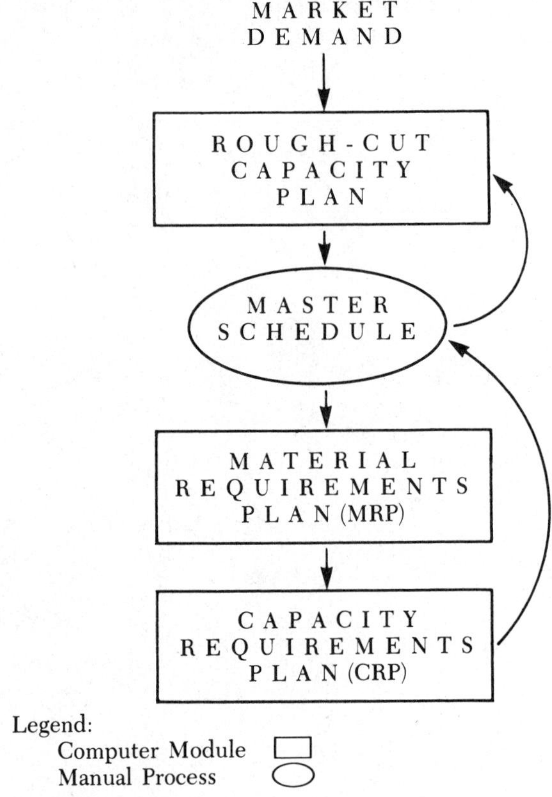

schedules are generated through the MRP scheduling logic. The results of this process are then converted into the actual workloads on the respective resources through the capacity requirements planning process (CRP).

At this stage, another manual intervention occurs. The master scheduler further adjusts the initial master schedule to compensate for any new over- or underload condition. A key facet of MRP is that these manual adjustments are made only at the master schedule and not at intermediate levels. Adjustments at intermediate levels result from master schedule changes, but are not made directly. This process of MRP scheduling, CRP load analysis and manual master schedule adjustment is repeated until the scheduler is satisfied with the results or until the time and computer resources available for scheduling are consumed. These manual interventions are necessary because the logic used to adjust the master schedule is too complex generally for programming into even the most sophisticated MRP systems.

In our example, we will focus on only the three levels of the MRP structure shown in Exhibit 5. The lead times between these levels are

EXHIBIT 5 MRP Levels

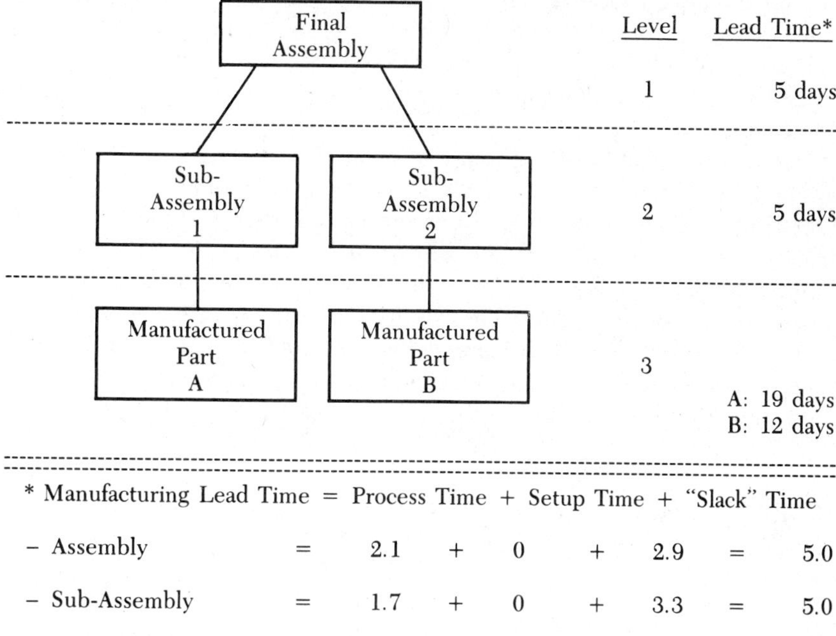

* Manufacturing Lead Time	=	Process Time	+	Setup Time	+	"Slack" Time	=	
– Assembly	=	2.1	+	0	+	2.9	=	5.0
– Sub-Assembly	=	1.7	+	0	+	3.3	=	5.0
– Manufactured Part:								
• A	=	15.3	+	0.1	+	3.6	=	19.0
• B	=	9.1	+	0.1	+	2.8	=	12.0

Assumptions:

- 3 shifts, 8 hours/shift
- Fixed manufacturing Batch Size of 500 units
- Variable Subassembly and Fixed Assembly Batch Size based on Master Schedule requirements. Example of Lead Time Calculation shown above = 500 units
- adequate supply of Raw Materials and Purchased Parts

predetermined. These lead times encompass the time required to set up various resources, process and move the parts and provide the slack to cover unexpected problems and variations in the workload. In practice the slack portion of the lead time is by far the largest portion since it is almost impossible in MRP to know the exact magnitude and timing of peak loads.

ROUGH CUT CAPACITY PLANNING (RCCP)

The first step is to convert the market demand into a doable master schedule. The generally accepted process is to net out the finished goods inventory from the market demand and then to convert the resulting finished product requirements into load profiles for the various departments or work centers. Rough cut capacity planning usually does not calculate loads for the individual resources and ignores the back scheduling that will actually occur (i.e., offsetting the demand at each level by the product lead times). Moreover, RCCP does not take into account any finished part or work-in-process inventories, and assumes no batching of the production requirements. These simplifying assumptions are made to avoid the significant computer processing time that would be required to include them. The goal is clear—to obtain a "rough cut" view of the capacity requirements.

For example, the results of this process are shown in Exhibit 6. The objective at this stage is to obtain a level load not exceeding 90%. Loading to 100% is unwise since any blip in the actual schedule would result in an "undoable" master schedule. The results show that both machines B and C are overloaded. We have ignored the assembly operations since these operations are largely manpower dependent and are not usually a production constraint. The overload in the third week is particularly troublesome. To

EXHIBIT 6 Rough Cut Capacity Planning: Market Demand Load Profiles

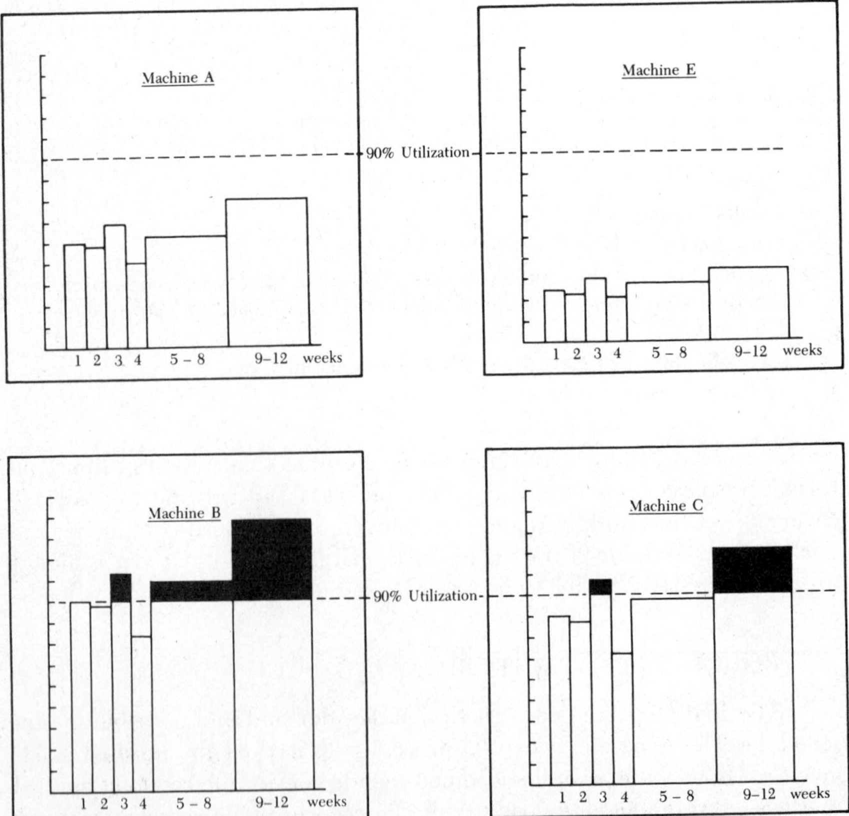

deal with this problem, the master scheduler elects to reschedule 10 units of demand from week 3 into week 2 and 30 units of demand from week 3 into week 4. In addition, he moves 10 units of demand from each of month 3 and month 4 into week 4.

The rough cut capacity planning process is repeated to determine the impact of this first master schedule. The adjustment results in a more level load on machines B and C and keeps the overload condition out in months 2 and 3 (Exhibit 7). Since these loads are based on the forecast, we are

EXHIBIT 7 Rough Cut Capacity Planning Process

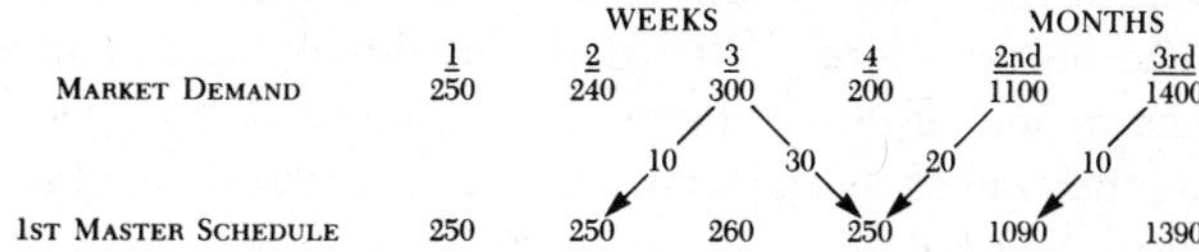

1ST MASTER SCHEDULE—LOAD PROFILES

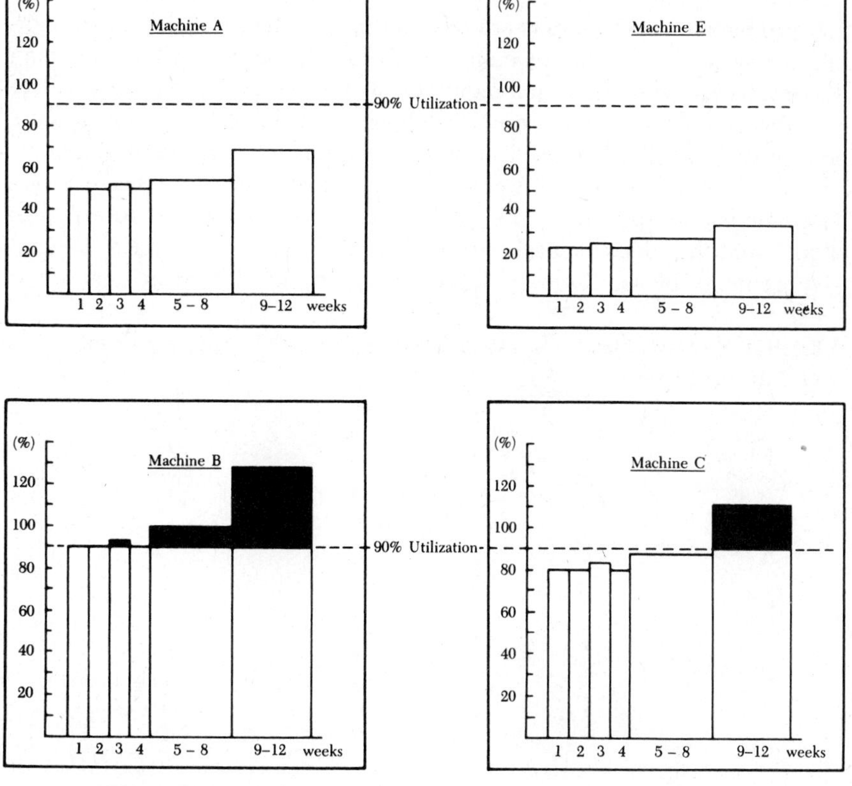

somewhat less concerned about them than we would be if the overload were to occur in close in weeks where we are dealing with firm customer orders. We have now successfully level loaded through the rough cut capacity planning approach. The next step is to submit our first master schedule to the MRP scheduling logic.

MRP SCHEDULING

The next step is to convert the master schedule into a due date schedule for the items at each level of our bill of material structure. We need to establish the quantity and time period in which the production of each item is to be completed. The MRP scheduling logic involves a level-by-level explosion and offsetting of gross requirements, aggregation of common requirements, netting of these requirements against available inventory and where appropriate a batching of requirements into economic runs.

In our example, this entails netting the requirements for finished items against any available finished goods inventory (there are none) and then exploding these net requirements into the gross requirements for various subassemblies. These gross subassembly requirements are in turn netted against any available finished subassembly inventory (500 units of subassembly 1 and 1050 units of subassembly 2). The resulting subassembly net production requirements are offset in time by the predetermined manufacturing lead times (one week) to establish the start date for producing these subassemblies. These net requirements become the production schedule for subassembly since we are not batching at this level. This same process is repeated for all other levels and items in our bill of material structure.

Exhibit 8 illustrates this process for our final assembly, subassembly 1 and manufactured part A. The basic logic of this approach is to establish a start and due date for each item to be produced. In Exhibit 8, the net requirements of subassembly 1 are phased by weeks. Each quantity is

EXHIBIT 8 MRP LOGIC—MASTER SCHEDULE #1: Explosion, Netting, and Batching Process

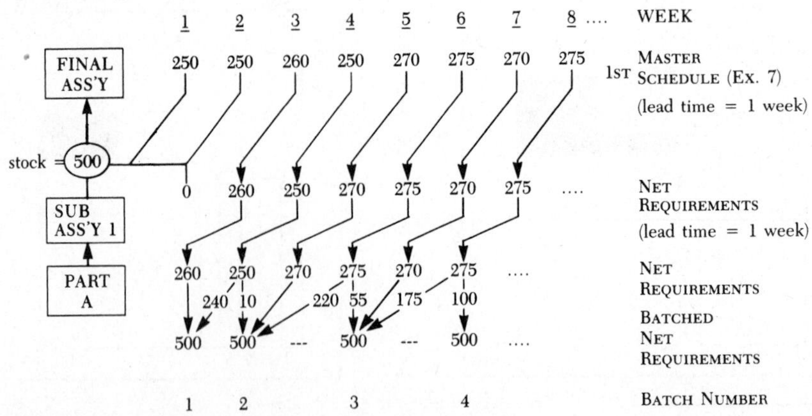

scheduled to be started in the week indicated and completed in one week (the lead time) so that they are available for use at the next higher level (final assembly). We are assuming that final assembly takes place in the week indicated and that these products can be used to meet the market demand occurring in the same week. In the case of part A, the first production requirements (batch 1) are scheduled to be started in week 1. The batch quantity of 500 will meet the needs of subassembly 1 in week 2 completely and meet those needs in week 3 partially. The remaining requirements of subassembly 1 in week 3 will be met by production batch 2 which is to be started at the beginning of week 2 and be completed by the end of the week. Essentially, the MRP scheduling process determines start and completion dates for various product requirements based on the bill of material structure and some predetermined lead times.

CAPACITY REQUIREMENTS PLANNING

The next step in our process is to convert the resulting production schedules into load profiles for each resource. Detailed schedules for the four machines in our example can be determined in a variety of ways, but the basic concepts are essentially the same. We have elected to illustrate how these detailed schedules are derived by back scheduling each item from its due date.

This approach is illustrated in Exhibit 9 for manufactured parts A and B. During the next 6 weeks, we must manufacture 4 batches of part A and 3 batches of part B if we are to meet the subassembly requirements. Batch 1 of part A is scheduled to be completed at the end of week 1. There are currently 500 pieces of work-in-process material in front of the final operation (machine B) for this part. It takes about 5½ days to process 500 pieces through this operation. As a result, we would back schedule from the end

EXHIBIT 9 MRP Master Schedule #1: Production Schedule and Machine Load Analysis

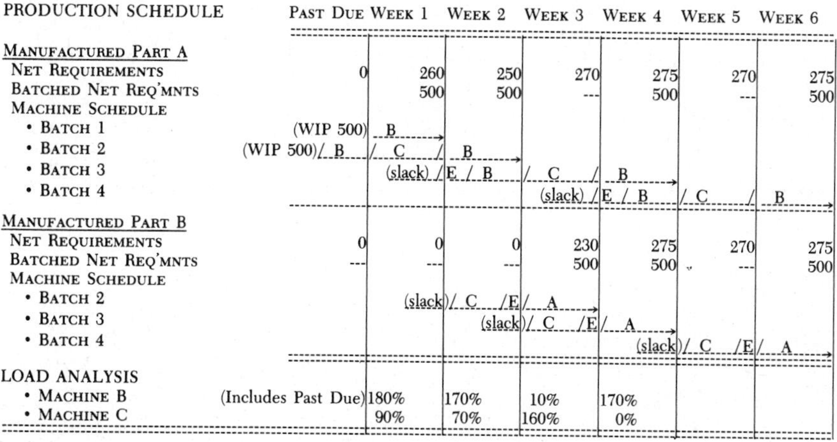

PRODUCTION SCHEDULE	PAST DUE	WEEK 1	WEEK 2	WEEK 3	WEEK 4	WEEK 5	WEEK 6
MANUFACTURED PART A							
Net Requirements	0	260	250	270	275	270	275
Batched Net Req'mnts		500	500	---	500	---	500
Machine Schedule							
• Batch 1	(WIP 500)	B →					
• Batch 2	(WIP 500)/ B	/ C /	B →				
• Batch 3		(slack) /	E / B	/ C /	B →		
• Batch 4				(slack) /	E / B	/ C /	B →
MANUFACTURED PART B							
Net Requirements	0	0	0	230	275	270	275
Batched Net Req'mnts	---	---	---	500	500	---	500
Machine Schedule							
• Batch 2		(slack)	/ C /E	/ A →			
• Batch 3			(slack)	/ C /E	/ A →		
• Batch 4					(slack)	/ C /E	/ A →
LOAD ANALYSIS							
• Machine B	(Includes Past Due)	180%	170%	10%	170%		
• Machine C		90%	70%	160%	0%		

of week 1 to arrive at a starting date for this batch on machine B. As a result of this scheduling, we find that this batch should have been started on the final day of last week if it is to be completed on time.

To illustrate the back scheduling approach further, let's look at batch 3 of part A. This batch is to be completed at the end of week 4. We schedule the final operation on machine B to complete at the end of week 4 which means it must start in the 5th day of week 3. Having the start date of the final operation, we can now schedule the preceding operation (machine C). This operation takes somewhat less than 5 days which gives us both a starting date on machine C and an ending date for the preceding operation (machine B). This process is continued for all operations involved in producing this batch. In addition we then add the slack time which has been predetermined to arrive at the date for releasing this order to the plant. The order start date is important because it establishes when the raw material is needed. It also represents the earliest date on which we should begin production on this batch. It is this type of logic, or a variation of it, that is used to determine when production should occur on our various machines. The purpose of this effort is to determine if there is sufficient capacity to meet the original master schedule.

Once these production schedules have been established we can convert them into a machine load. For the purpose of our example, we have assumed the 4 machines (A, B, C and E) can be operated 5 days a week for 3 shifts. We are assuming that this is 100% of our available capacity. The resulting load on machines B and C is shown at the bottom of Exhibit 9. There is clearly a heavy overload on machine B, plus an unbalanced load on machine C during the next 4 weeks.

EXHIBIT 10 MRP Master Schedule #1 (Manual Adjustment)

MARKET DEMAND	250	240	300	200	990	1100			
(WEEKS)	1	2	3	4	TOTAL	5	6	7	8
MASTER SCHEDULE #2	250	240	260	250	1000	275	275	275	275
		(5) (5)							
MASTER SCHEDULE #1	250	250	260	250	1010	270	275	270	275
MANUFACTURED PART A									
• NET REQUIREMENTS	260	250	270	275		270	275		
• BATCHED REQUIREMENTS	500	(500)		500			500		
• BATCH NUMBER	1	(2)		3			4		

The master scheduler needs to determine the cause of this condition so that he may adjust the master schedule and produce a doable production schedule for machines B and C. The master scheduler attempts to solve his problem by analyzing the type of information shown in Exhibit 10. Master schedule 1 calls for the production of 1010 units during the next 4 weeks. However, the market demand is for only 990 units. Currently we have 500 units of both subassemblies which can be used to meet a portion of the master schedule. However, in order to meet the remaining master schedule requirements, we must produce another 510 units of subassembly 1 which in turn requires 510 units of part A. (There is ample inventory of subassembly 2). Analyzing the information on Exhibit 10 the master scheduler realizes that if he reduced the master schedule in the first 4 weeks by just 10 units, the batched requirement for part A in week 2 would shift over to week 3. This change should move the schedule for batch 2 from week 2 to week 3 and help alleviate the overload in week 2.

By making this simple adjustment he may be able to alleviate the overload condition that currently exists in week 2. Even better he can do this without affecting at all his ability to meet the market demand. He elects to do this by shifting 5 units of the week 2 master schedule to each of weeks 5 and 7. It is interesting to note that he is essentially undoing a master schedule adjustment he made during the rough cut capacity process. In creating the first master schedule he had moved 10 units of market demand from week 3 into week 2. Now he is shifting this demand out into weeks 5 and 7. Once he has adjusted the master schedule it is necessary to make another MRP and CRP run to see the actual impact of his decision.

MRP-CRP #2

Exhibit 11 shows the changes that have occurred in the loads on machines B and C as a result of the adjustment in the master schedule. B's load has been reduced, especially in week 2, but is still significantly higher than we can tolerate. The unbalanced load on machine C has shifted but still exists. We have improved our situation but we must make yet another adjustment in the master schedule. We still have an unrealistic workload on machine B which jeopardizes the entire master schedule.

The master scheduler once again examines the source of demand on part A and the scheduling of the batch sizes of 500 (Exhibits 11 and 12). He concludes that the only way to avoid the excessive overload condition in week 1 is to shift batch 2 of part A from week 3 to week 4. To do this he must adjust the master schedule again. His only real choice is to reduce the master schedule to zero in week 5. He elects to shift 225 units of final assembly requirements to week 6 (being afraid of the effect on service if he pushed them any further out). The remaining 50 units of requirements are spread evenly over weeks 7 and 8. By making this adjustment, he ends up with master schedule #3 shown in Exhibit 12. Once he makes these

EXHIBIT 11 MRP Master Schedule #2: Production Schedule and Machine Load Analysis

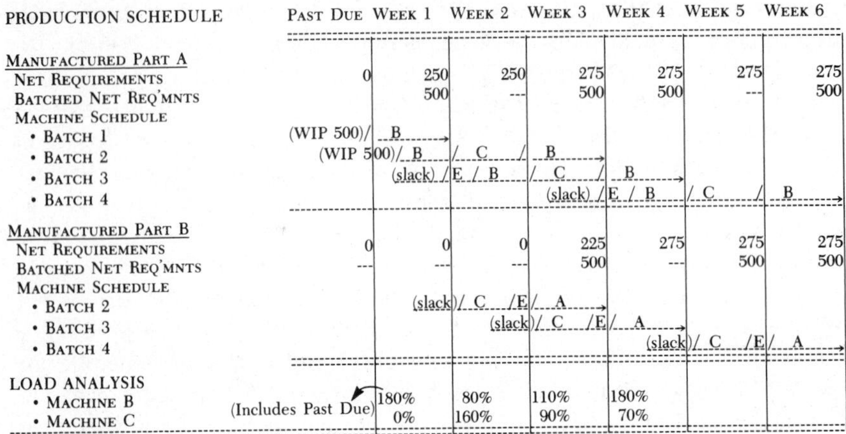

adjustments, another MRP-CRP run needs to be made to determine their impact.

MRP-CRP #3

The new master schedule is again exploded, time phased and load profiles calculated for the various resources. The machine schedules and load analysis resulting from this run are shown in Exhibit 13. The master scheduler has reduced the load in week 1 successfully and does not have

EXHIBIT 12 MRP Master Schedule #2 (Manual Adjustment)

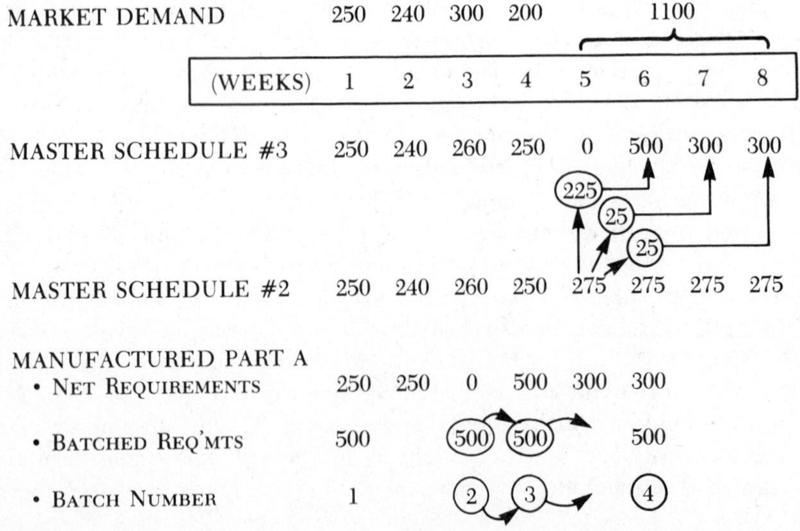

EXHIBIT 13 MRP Master Schedule #3: Production Schedule and Machine Load Analysis

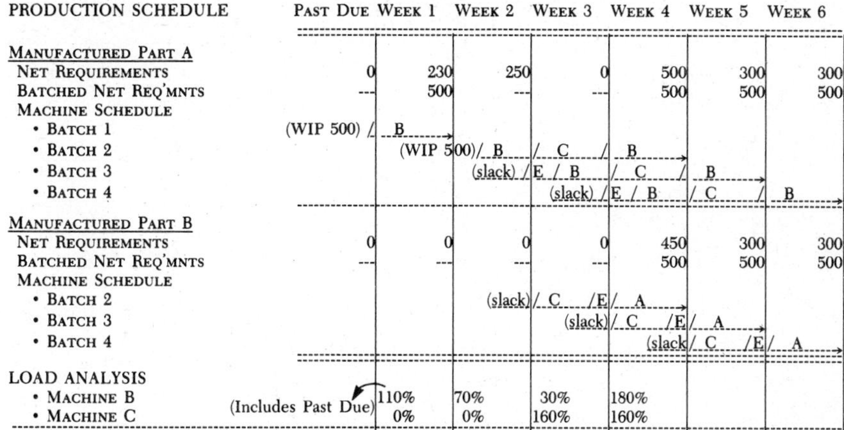

PRODUCTION SCHEDULE	Past Due	Week 1	Week 2	Week 3	Week 4	Week 5	Week 6
Manufactured Part A							
Net Requirements	0	230	250	0	500	300	300
Batched Net Req'mnts	---	500	---	---	500	500	500
Machine Schedule							
• Batch 1	(WIP 500) /	B →					
• Batch 2		(WIP 5	00)/ B	/ C /	B →		
• Batch 3			(slack) /	E / B	/ C /	B →	
• Batch 4				(slack) /	E / B	/ C /	B →
Manufactured Part B							
Net Requirements	0	0	0	0	450	300	300
Batched Net Req'mnts	---	---	---	---	500	500	500
Machine Schedule							
• Batch 2			(slack)	/ C /E	/ A →		
• Batch 3				(slack)	/ C /E	/ A →	
• Batch 4					(slack	/ C /E	/ A →
LOAD ANALYSIS							
• Machine B	(Includes Past Due)	110%	70%	30%	180%		
• Machine C		0%	0%	160%	160%		

a serious overload condition on machine B until week 4. In fact the average load is only 110% during the first four weeks—maybe he'll be ok, the load standards are probably incorrect anyway. He still has an overload condition on machine C in some weeks, but on the average has enough capacity during the next four weeks.

He concludes that this is probably the best possible schedule that he can achieve and, besides, three passes of the MRP-CRP system on the computer is the most he has ever been able to achieve. So at this stage, he accepts the master schedule along with the production schedules and machine loads that result from it. He also makes a note to himself that the production lead times need to be increased. It is clear that the reason he is overloaded and must push the master schedule out is because parts A and B were not released to production early enough. There simply isn't enough lead time to get all the work done.

RESULTS—MRP SCHEDULING LOGIC

In determining the results of our MRP schedule we must look at what actually happened and *not* on what we planned. The MRP schedule was not realistic—we planned to produce more in certain weeks 3 and 4 than we had the capacity to produce. As a result, scheduling adjustments will occur on the shop floor once the scheduling conflicts become apparent. Exhibits 14 and 15 illustrate schedule adjustments that result in a realistic schedule. These adjustments are probably the best possible ones we could make since we were able to look at the interaction of all the schedules. In reality, we are seldom afforded such a luxury and usually make scheduling adjustments that produce much poorer results. In Exhibit 16, Master Schedule #3 is met during the first five weeks, but results in lost sales of 40 units in week 3 and 225 units in week 5. We are assuming in this example that

EXHIBIT 14 MRP Master Schedule #3: Shop Floor Adjustment for Parts A and B

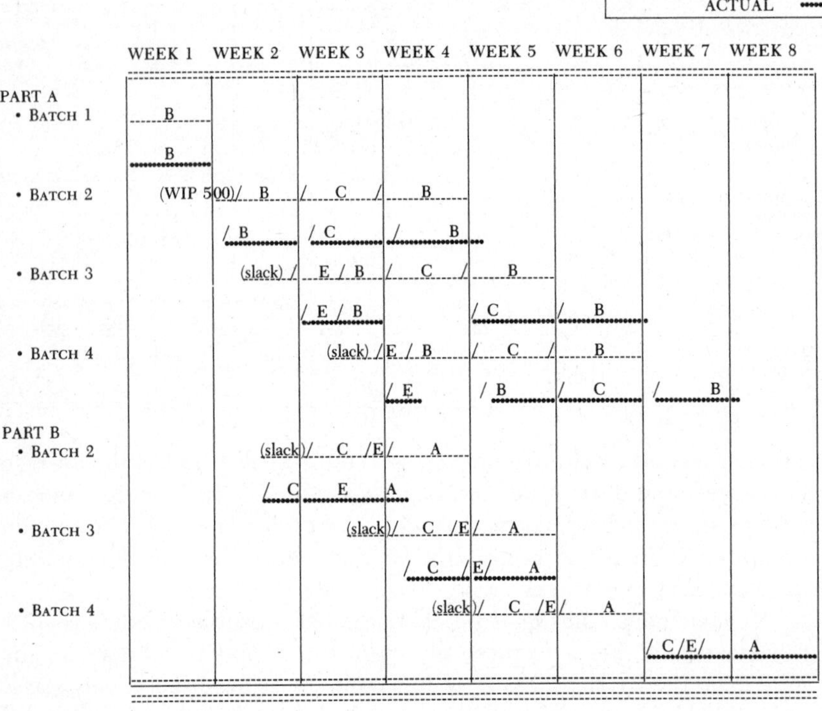

we are in a short lead time, price sensitive business and that if products are not available in the week demanded that the sales are lost. It's not a great performance, but it's probably unreasonable to think we could exactly match our manufacturing capability with Marketing's wish list.

However, we miss our master schedule badly in weeks 6, 7 and 8.

EXHIBIT 15 MRP Master Schedule #3A: Shop Floor Adjustment for Sub Assembly and Final Assembly

WEEK 1 WEEK 2 WEEK 3 WEEK 4 WEEK 5 WEEK 6 WEEK 7 WEEK 8 WEEK 9 WEEK 10

FA (250)

FA (240)

SA (260) / FA (260)

SA (250) / FA (250)

SA (500) / FA (500)

SA (300) / FA (300)

SA (300) / FA (300)

SA (200) / FA (200)

SA (300) / FA (300)

SA (240) / FA (240)

LEGEND:
PLANNED ------- (# OF UNITS SCHEDULED)
ACTUAL ••••••• (# OF UNITS PRODUCED)

EXHIBIT 16 MRP Scheduling Results

	1	2	3	4	5	6	7	8	
MARKET DEMAND	250	240	300	200	275	275	275	275	
(WEEKS)	1	2	3	4	5	6	7	8	
MASTER SCHEDULE #3 (ADJUSTED)	250	240	260	250	0	500	300	300	
ACTUAL PRODUCTION	250	240	250	250	0	300(1)	200	240(2)	
ENDING FINISHED GOODS INVENTORY	0	0	0	50	0	25	0	0	
LOST SALES									TOTAL
– UNITS	0	0	40	0	225	0	50	35	350
– DOLLARS ($000)	–	–	$6.0	–	$33.8	–	$7.5	$5.2	$52.5
CUSTOMER SERVICE	100%	100%	87%	100%	0%	100%	82%	87%	

Weeks 3–8: 78%

Weeks 1–8: 83%

(1) Assume 60% of the final assembly production originally scheduled for week 6 can be used even though this production run is not completed until week 7.

(2) Assume 30% of the final assembly production originally scheduled for week 8 can be used even though this production run is not completed until week 9.

These missed schedules are caused by the overloads on machines B and C in weeks 3 and 4 and caused the shop floor schedule adjustments shown above.

The MRP plan called for the subassembly of 500 units in week 5 and final assembly of these 500 units in week 6. Due to the overload on machines B and C Part A of batch 2 is not completed until the second day of week 5. Consequently the subassembly and final assembly schedules are delayed two days. We have assumed that 300 of the planned 300 final assemblies are available for sale in week 6. This is a very generous assumption since we are making these units available before the final assembly run is completed. Furthermore, the 300 final assemblies scheduled for week 7 are not produced until week 8 (240 units) and week 9 (60 units). Again, we are making the generous assumption that the 240 units produced in week 8 are available for sale in the same week even though the production run is not completed until the following week. The 300 final assemblies scheduled for week 8 are not produced until week 9 (60 units) and week 10 (240 units)—we are falling further and further behind. The end result is lost sales of 350 units or $52,500. Our customer for the eight week period is 83% but only 78% for the six week period affected by the MRP scheduling approach. Worse yet, it appears that performance will slip further in subsequent weeks. Maybe the master scheduler is right about the need to increase lead times.

There are other measures of our performance such as lead times (elapsed time between order release and completion) and inventories that should be analyzed. The planned and actual lead times for the manufactured parts are:

Actual Lead Time

PART	BATCH 3	BATCH 4	AVERAGE	PLANNED LEAD TIME
A	25	28	26.5	19
B	13	20	16.5	12

Not only did we underestimate our lead times, but they seem to be increasing overtime.

Inventories were measured in two ways—the average inventory on hand at the end of each week and the total amount of inventory on hand at the end of the 8th week. In both cases we have followed the OPT definition of inventory and only counted the raw material value of the material. The results of our calculations show an average weekly inventory of $70,287 and an ending inventory of $105,800.

The results of our MRP are not very encouraging. In addition our schedules were not realistic. Several ad hoc scheduling decisions had to be made on the shop floor. In calculating the results we assumed that these were sound decisions. Unfortunately, this is not always the case. While the results are not good, maybe that's the best that can be done. Now let's look at the OPT approach.

OPT—Conceptual Overview

The OPT scheduling concepts and process have been illustrated in previous articles of *Inventories and Production Magazine*. An overview of the process is shown in Exhibit 17. The bottleneck operations are first identified and used to determine where the network should be divided. The portion containing the bottlenecks and associated orders is called the critical resources portion. The remainder of the network is referred to as the non-critical resource portion. The critical resource portion of the network is scheduled forward in time (finite scheduling). This schedule becomes the true master schedule for the product since being based on the bottleneck, it controls the output of the system. The non-critical resources are then scheduled backward in time by looking simultaneously on all the constraints of the system (resources and marketing).

OPT RULE #9—ALL CONSTRAINTS SIMULTANEOUSLY

The OPT approach also begins with a rough cut capacity plan. The goal of this effort is not to massage the market demand but to identify the choke points or bottlenecks in the system. Once the capacity constraints have been identified, we are now in the position to begin applying the 9th rule of OPT—schedules should be established by looking at all the constraints

EXHIBIT 17 OPT Scheduling Conceptual Overview

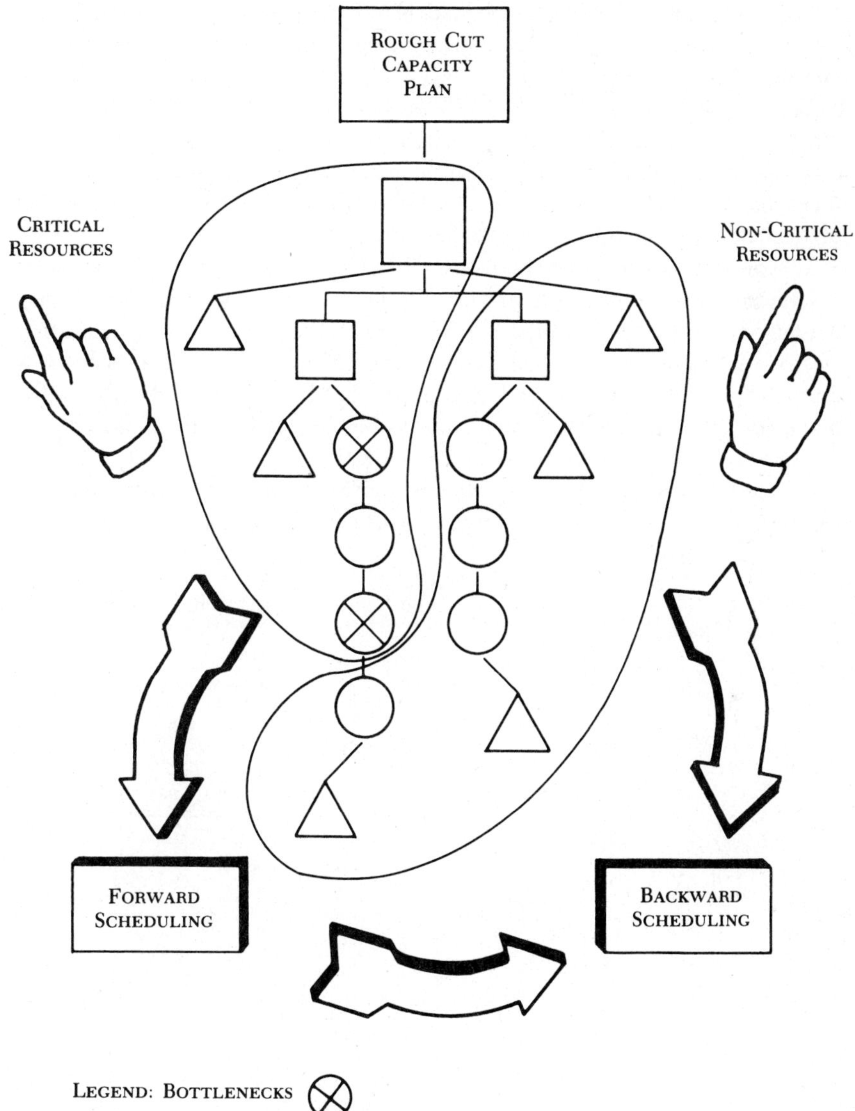

of the system simultaneously—lead times are a result of a schedule and cannot be predetermined.

The bottleneck or capacity constraint in the system was identified previously as machine B. The first step is to schedule the batches of production that must pass through machine B. Part A is the only part which passes through the bottleneck machine B. It is necessary for this part to pass through this machine for two operations before it is completed. Exhibit 18 shows a schedule for the first three batches of production of part A. Part A passes through the bottleneck machine B twice in batches 2 and 3, but only once in batch 1. In batch 1 we have an order of 500 pieces partially completed and sitting in front of the second operation performed on machine B. The schedule shown in Exhibit 18 has been developed for the bottleneck machine B by scheduling the production of the 3 batches forward in time. This schedule has been devised so it does not violate the capacity constraint of machine B. Since machine B is scheduled finitely forward in time, we never schedule more than the available capacity.

Now that we have a schedule for the bottleneck machine B, we need to schedule the remaining operations in the critical resource network (subassembly 1 and final assembly) to be certain that none of the marketing constraints are violated (i.e., all the due dates are met). These two operations are scheduled forward in time based on the bottleneck schedules. We have disregarded the planned slack time at subassembly and assembly in developing our schedules. The real purpose of this slack time is because MRP is unable to generate a schedule that realistically considers capacity constraints. We add the slack to compensate for any overload conditions that may occur.

EXHIBIT 18 OPT Schedule and Machine Load Analysis: Rule #9—All Constraints Simultaneously

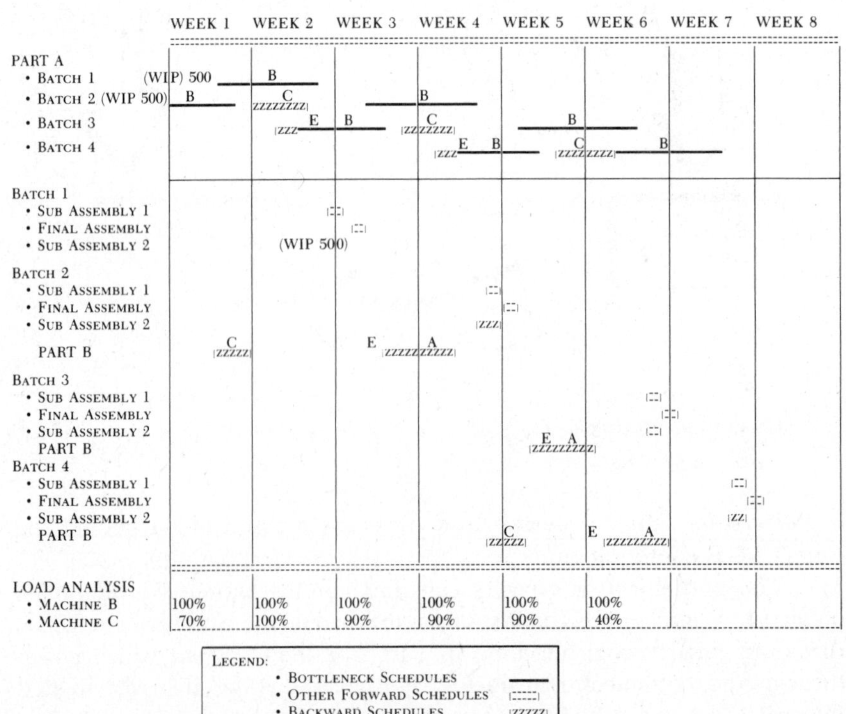

In the OPT approach we have taken the capacity constraints into account and can consequently drop this slack time in our schedule. The OPT manufacturing schedule does contain some slack to buffer against unexpected events (Murphy) but not to buffer against peak loads. Once we derive the final assembly schedule, we check to be certain it meets the market demand. In this case it does.

Now we need to schedule the remaining operations (subassembly 2, and machines A, C and E). These operations are scheduled backward in time like in MRP. However, unlike MRP, we now know that there is sufficient capacity for the required production since these are non-bottleneck resources. In addition, we don't blindly back schedule like MRP does without any regard to the resulting schedule conflicts. We check each back schedule to be certain that a conflict doesn't exist (e.g., overloading an operation). If it does, the machine schedule is adjusted until this interference is eliminated. Remember, in the 9th rule of OPT we must look on all the constraints of the system.

As can be seen in Exhibit 18, we have been able to develop a valid schedule based on rule 9. All three final assemblies are completed prior to their due dates, and we have not overloaded any of our resources. Machine B, the bottleneck, has been scheduled to its full capacity. Machine C is 100% loaded in period 2, but has excess capacity in periods 1, 3 and 4. The resulting schedule is a viable schedule that can be followed. This schedule results from looking simultaneously at all the constraints of the system. It should also be noted that the lead times are not constant. They vary based on how we scheduled our production. They have been derived, not predetermined.

OPT RULE #7—OVERLAPPING OF BATCHES

The seventh rule of OPT indicates that there should be two batch sizes—a transfer batch and a process batch. Furthermore, in many cases, the transfer batch is not and should not be equal to the process batch. This rule of OPT is one that manual schedulers know well. Essentially, it involves the overlapping of production at various operations. Let's examine the impact of applying this rule of OPT. Let us assume that we can alter the paperwork system for shop orders so that our process batches of 500 pieces can be split into batches as small as 100 pieces. This is still quite a large batch since it represents two shifts of production. While this change will involve some additional material handling, the actual cost is probably very low.

Exhibit 19 shows a schedule that uses overlapping (transfer batch not equal to process batch). In this schedule, the 3 batches are processed sequentially across the bottleneck machine B. The fourth operation (machine B) in batch 1 is the first scheduled. Then the second operation (machine B) of batch 2 is scheduled. However, in this case, we do not wait until the entire batch is completed at operation 2 to start operation 3 (machine

EXHIBIT 19 OPT Schedule and Machine Load Analysis: Rule #9 and #7—Transfer Batch & Process Batch

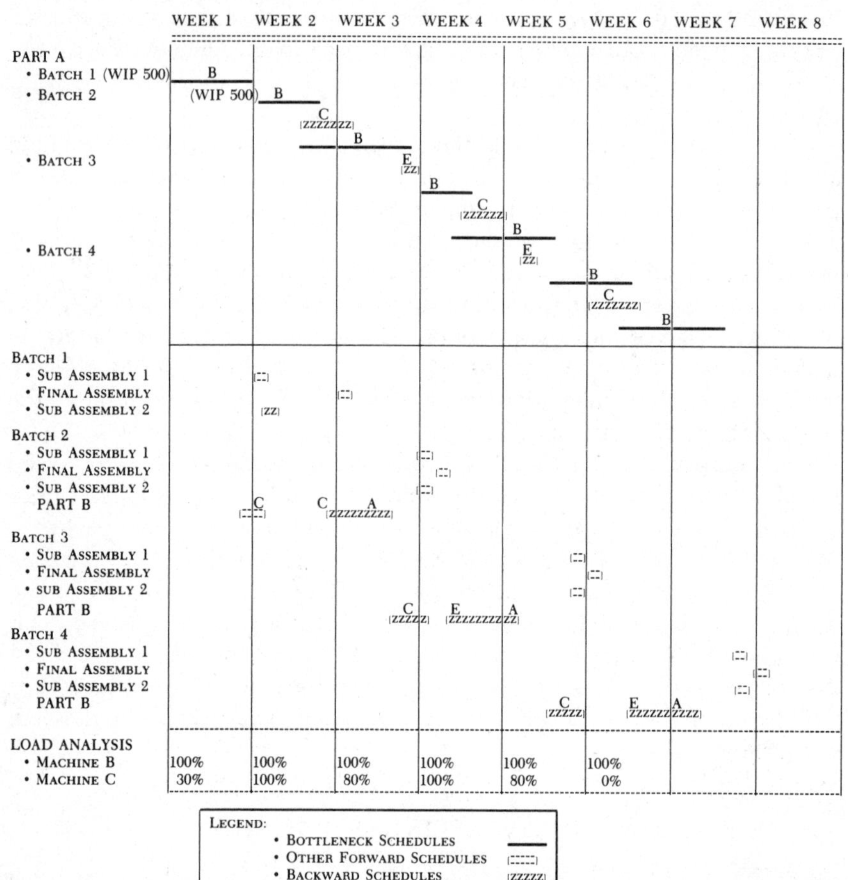

C). Each time a portion of the production (100 units) is completed, it is moved to machine C for processing at that operation. This allows us to have product available for the fourth and final operation (machine B) of batch 2 once the second operation has been completed. We are able to reuse machine B immediately for the final operation of batch 2. The same batch is being processed concurrently on machine C and machine B.

We have created an overlapping situation by splitting our process batch of 500 pieces into smaller increments and passing these increments (transfer batches) onto the next operation. The same process is repeated for batch 3. On this batch, we further increase our overlapping by beginning to process a portion of the 500 unit process batch on machine B before the entire batch is completed on the preceding operation—machine E. Using this approach, we are able to schedule the bottleneck leg of our network forward in time. Once we have the completion date of the last bottleneck operation in a batch, we then continue to schedule forward in time for subassembly 1 and the final assembly operation associated with each of these batches.

Once the assembly start date is established, we can then schedule the production of subassembly 2 and part B backward in time for each batch. It is, of course, necessary that we continually look on the capacity constraints as we schedule backward to be sure that we do not violate any of them. The schedule shown in Exhibit 19 has been devised to meet all of the marketing (due dates) and capacity constraints. The end result is again a realistic schedule. The bottleneck (machine B) operation is once against scheduled to its full capacity—100%. Machine C is fully loaded in some weeks and underloaded in others. There is no point at which we schedule more production than there is capacity available to handle it.

RESULTS—OPT SCHEDULING LOGIC

The OPT schedules developed using rules 9 and 7 provide 100% customer service (all market demands are met) and therefore do not cause any lost sales. The actual lead times from rules 9 and 7 are Exhibit 20. These lead times can be calculated for batches 3 and 4 (the only batches started completely from raw materials) directly from Exhibits 18 and 19. Two measures of inventory performance were again calculated—average inventory and ending inventory. The results were as follows:

	Rule 9	*Rule 7*
Average Inventory	$47,010	$44,500
Ending Inventory	$72,300	$61,500

In addition, the OPT schedules do not violate any capacity constraints and are therefore realistic—they can be followed.

EXHIBIT 20 OPT Results: Manufactured Parts A and B

- RULE 9

PART	PLANNED LEAD TIME	ACTUAL LEAD TIME: BATCH 3	BATCH 4	AVERAGE
A	NONE	20	17	18.5
B	NONE	14	14	14

- RULES 9 AND 7

PART	PLANNED LEAD TIME	ACTUAL LEAD TIME: BATCH 3	BATCH 4	AVERAGE
A	NONE	10	10	10
B	NONE	10.5	10.5	10.5

OPT vs. MRP—Comparison of Results

The results of using the conventional MRP scheduling rules is contrasted against the use of only two of the OPT rules (Exhibit 21). The OPT schedules are also realistic—they are schedules that can be followed. The MRP schedules were not—they created numerous conflicts that the foreman must resolve on the shop floor. We have seen in our simple example how difficult it is for the master scheduler to determine specific scheduling decisions when using MRP logic. If the master scheduler has so many problems with all the data available to him, how can we expect the people on the floor to resolve conflicts when they have much less information to make the correct scheduling decisions.

These two OPT rules were chosen because they reflect logic generally used in manual scheduling and therefore seem reasonable and familiar. However, they represent only a portion of the results possible through implementing all nine scheduling rules. Nevertheless, the results of contrasting these two OPT rules with the full power of MRP is impressive. If this business earned a pre-tax profit of 10% under the MRP approach, then the use of these two rules of OPT would increase the net profit by 125%.

In the face of such differences, we must ask ourselves who is truly responsible for the high inventories, poor customer services and long lead times that we experience. Unfortunately, the answer is clear. As the cartoon character, Pogo, would say "*We have met the enemy, and he is us*." Why have we failed to capitalize on this huge opportunity? I think it's simple—*we didn't think*. We neglected to examine closely the real logic of MRP

EXHIBIT 21 Results: MRP vs. OPT—Software vs. Thoughtware

	MRP	OPT RULE 9	OPT RULE 7	INCREASED PROFIT
• LOST SALES				
- UNITS	350	--	--	
- DOLLARS	$ 52,500	--	--	$31,500[1]
• CUSTOMER SERVICE[2]	78%	100%	100%	?
• MANUFACTURED LEAD TIME				
- PART A	26.5	18½	10	?
- PART B	16.5	14	10½	?
• AVERAGE INVENTORY	$ 70,287	$47,010	$44,500	$ 1,074[3]
• ENDING INVENTORY	$105,800	$72,300	$61,500	--
			TOTAL	$32,574

% PROFIT INCREASE	125%

(1) SELLING PRICE ($150) LESS THE RAW MATERIAL COST ($60)
(2) CONSIDERS ONLY THE PERIOD AFFECTED BY MRP AND OPT SCHEDULING PROCESS
(3) ASSUMES 25% INVENTORY CARRYING COST FOR 2 MONTHS.

and see the glaring, gaping holes in it. Remember also that no complex algorithm was used to obtain the OPT results. No magic "brown" box was involved—only simple logic that has been in front of us all along. A good algorithm is useful, but only in getting the last 10% of the benefits. The power of OPT is in the thought process behind it—the *thoughtware*—and not in any formula buried in the software.

The example used here is a simple one. Our world is much more complex. Unplanned events (Murphy) on the shop floor cause additional schedule conflicts. We will always have these surprises. However, that's no excuse to create many more additional conflicts by how we schedule and then blame everything on Murphy. The focus of this article has been on MRP and OPT as planning and scheduling systems. The weaknesses illustrated in MRP do not mean that our efforts in building MRP systems have been wasted. Quite the contrary—we need this information to schedule our plants and perform many other activities. The data base structure and other functions of MRP are needed. The body of MRP is fine, we simply need a new brain (planning and scheduling system) to tell the body how to behave. We definitely shouldn't disregard MRP. We simply need to give it a "brain transplant" to make it effective. The companies and countries that recognize and respond to this need are likely to be the ones that survive and thrive in this decade.

If we reflect back to our early MRP experiences, many of us can recall the lonely voice of an old time scheduler saying: "Something about MRP isn't right." Maybe someone who scheduled manually for years should have been listened to more closely. Perhaps we should have listened to the voice of experience. It's unfortunate he couldn't articulate his concerns more cogently. We just ended up dismissing him as being unable or unwilling to change with the times. Maybe he wasn't wrong. Maybe we were. Maybe we didn't listen and think.

As a result, we got carried away in the great MRP crusade. Unfortunately, this crusade, like its namesake, is ending in bitter disillusionment and disappointment. It's not ending as we hoped in improved productivity and the competitive advantage of reduced lead times and inventories. The real lesson for all of us is simple—let's just think. The answers may be right in front of us and well within our power to comprehend. No one has a monopoly on thinking. Hopefully exploding the myth of MRP will allow us to come to grips with the real problems of scheduling production.

Exhibit

Re-order Points for Various Safety Stock Situations

	Order Service Level OSL	Unit Service Level USL
Stockout cost known Service level unknown	Backorder penalty specified as \$8.26 $\pi = 8.26$ $Q = 1000$ $h = 30$ $D = 10000$ $OSOR = \frac{hQ}{\pi D} = \frac{30(1000)}{8.25(10000)}$ $OSOR = 0.363$ $z_{0.363} = 0.35$ $\bar{x}_L = 200, \sigma = 40$ $R = 200 + 0.35(40) = 214$	Backorder penalty specified as \$8.26 $\pi = 8.26$ $Q = 1000$ $h = 30$ $D = 10000$ $OSOR = 0.363$ $k = 0.35$ and $g(k) = 0.248$ $R = 200 + 0.35(40) = 214$ $USL = 1 - \frac{a(k)J}{Q}$ $USL = 1 - \left[\frac{0.248(40)}{10000}\right]$ $USL = 0.99008$
Stockout cost unknown Service level known	OSL specified as 0.625 $OSOR = 0.375$ $z_{0.375} = 0.32$ $\bar{x}_L = 200, \sigma = 40$ $R = 200 + 0.32(40) = 213$ σ here is taken to be the standard deviation of lead time demand	USL specified as 0.99 $USOR = 0.01$ $Q = 1000$ $\sigma = 40$ $g(k) = \frac{Q{*}USOR}{\sigma}$ $g(k) = \frac{1000{*}0.01}{40}$ $g(k) = 0.25$ $k = 0.35$ $R = 200 + 0.35(40)$ $R = 214$

index